Muggles, Monst

KULTURELLE IDENTITÄTEN

Edited by Sonja Fielitz

Studien zur Entwicklung der europäischen Kulturen der Neuzeit

Volume 2

PETER LANG

Frankfurt am Main·Berlin·Bern·Bruxelles·New York·Oxford·Wien

Claudia Fenske

Muggles, Monsters and Magicians

A Literary Analysis
of the *Harry Potter* Series

PETER LANG
Internationaler Verlag der Wissenschaften

Bibliographic Information published by the Deutsche Nationalbibliothek
The Deutsche Nationalbibliothek lists this publication in the Deutsche Nationalbibliografie; detailed bibliographic data is available in the internet at <http://www.d-nb.de>.

Zugl.: Marburg, Univ., Diss., 2006

Cover illustration:
Leonardo da Vinci,
the Proportions of the Human Body according to Vitruv,
drawing, Venice, Galleria dell'Accademia,
Gabinetto Disegni e Stampe, 228.
© Bildarchiv Foto Marburg

D 4
ISSN 1863-219X
ISBN 978-3-631-56661-9

© Peter Lang GmbH
Internationaler Verlag der Wissenschaften
Frankfurt am Main 2008
All rights reserved.

Printed in Germany 1 2 3 4 5   7

www.peterlang.de

Acknowledgements

It is a pleasure to thank those people who contributed in various ways to the completion of this book. It began as a dissertation project at the University of Marburg, supervised by Prof. Sonja Fielitz. Not only has she been an outstanding support and inspiration, but she is also a model of how to instigate excellence while showing human warmth and empathy. I also want to extend my gratitude to the whole Institute of English and American Studies at the University of Marburg for providing a stimulating scholarly environment, in particular to Dean Prof. Isabel Zollna and Prof. Martin Kuester. There were also people outside Marburg who challenged my theses on the literary phenomenon of *Harry Potter* and helped to focus my thoughts. I want to mention Dr. Malte Rehbein, Prof. Erich Runge and Dr. Katja Radke.

Every writer values the work of those accompanying him on the way from manuscript to printed book. I especially want to thank Nils Adelheidt, Dr. Wolfram Keller, Kieran Moore, Orla Mulholland, Catherine Lejtenyi and Benjamin Kloss and his team at Peter Lang Publishing Group, Berlin. Moreover I want to express my thanks to my family, friends and colleagues for the support they gave me while I was working on this book.

I dedicate this work to my first and ultimate model of intellectual honesty and brilliance – my late father Dr. Lutz Fenske (1936-2006) who gave me the scholarly confidence to begin the journey of this book and who would have loved to see it completed.

vii

Table of Contents

I. Introduction

I.1 The Worldwide Triumph of "Harry Potter"

It was like an army preparing to go to war: "Are we ready for *Harry Potter?*" yelled the manager of the Borders at Time Warner Center, New York. The crowd of excited fans answered with an hysterical "Yeah!" It was midnight of July 20th, 2007 – *Harry Potter and the Deathly Hallows*[1] was about to be released and, thus, the end was at hand for the global hype around "the Boy Who Lived" which had been going on for about ten years.[2] British bookseller Waterstone's had installed a counselling hotline for desperate fans in case the worst came true – in case Harry, the hero, died.[3] Within the first 24 hours the book sold 2.7 million copies[4] in the UK alone, adding to the estimated 325 million copies that had been sold thus far worldwide.[5]

All in all, J.K. Rowling's *Harry Potter* series has established several records so far. Economically it is the most successful children's book ever published and at the same time it has become the most widely discussed book series for young adults ever.[6] It has become a part of global popular culture and, thus, has affected every-day life. This is not only in the Western world. *Potter* has inspired a significant revival of traditional boarding school education,[7] and even in China children are crazy for *Hali Bote*.[8] Most critics consider the novels a phenomenon of globalised pop culture instead of "serious" literature.[9] The story of the little boy wizard who is destined to become the saviour of his world has been heavily criticised by scholars, teachers and the clergy. It has been argued

---

[1] Joanne Kathleen Rowling, *Harry Potter and the Deathly Hallows*, London: Bloomsbury, 2007 (henceforth: HP 7).

[2] See Motoko Rich, "Long Lines and Wide Smiles Greet the Final Volume of 'Harry Potter'," *New York Times* 21 July 2007. <http://www.nytimes.com/2007/07/21/books/21 pott.html?pagewanted=print> 6 Aug 2007.

[3] See Claudia Bröll, "Besorgte Muggles," *F.A.Z.* 5 July 2007, 18.

[4] See Felicitas von Lovenberg, "Rekordauflage, Rekordverkauf, Rekordrezensionen," *F.A.Z.* 25 July 2007, 38.

[5] See Bröll 2007.

[6] See Suman Gupta, *Re-reading Harry Potter*, Houndmills, New York: Palgrave Macmillan, 2003, 18.

[7] See Frauke Meyer-Gosau, "Potterismus. Was der deutschen Gegenwartsliteratur fehlt und Harry hat's," *Harry Potter oder Warum wir Zauberer brauchen*, ed. Olaf Kutzmutz, Wolfenbüttel: Bundesakademie für kulturelle Bildung, 2001, 7-19; Gina Thomas, "Konkurrenz für den Weihnachtsmann," *F.A.Z.* 16 Nov 2001, 53.

[8] See Mathias Jung, *Der Zauber der Wandlung: Harry Potter oder das Abenteuer der Ichwerdung*, Lahnstein: emu, 2004, 23.

[9] See Gottfried Bachl, "Harry Potter theologisch gelesen," *"Alohomora!" Ergebnisse des Ersten Wiener Harry-Potter-Symposions*, ed. Heidi Lexe, Wien: Edition Praesens, 2002, 121.

that in spite of being "funny, imaginative, [and] passably written" they did not contribute anything to the genre of children's literature.[10] Also, the books showed no "authentic imaginative vision"[11] and with all their "junk and gismos and 'stuff'" are much more like trash movies than literature.[12] Jack Zipes even wonders "[...] why such a conventional work of fantasy has been fetishized" and states: "There is nothing exceptional about Rowling's writing in comparison with that of many other gifted writers of children's and young adult literature."[13]

If these critics are right – and for the time being, they partly are – why should we analyse *Harry Potter* again? Polish writer Andrzej Stasiuk says:

> Zu speziellen literaturwissenschaftlichen Untersuchungen sehe ich keinen Anlaß. Es geht hier mehr um eine Analyse des Marktes als um eine literarische Kritik. Unser Held erweist sich einfach als nahezu ideales Produkt, befriedigt die Bedürfnisse und trifft den Geschmack von Millionen. So ähnlich wie Nescafé.[14]

Although Stasiuk is not completely wrong in his judgement on *Harry Potter*, I strongly disagree with him. This is a text which has provoked a worldwide emotional reaction. A series of books which has polarised critics and readers alike while managing to be an all-time international bestseller deserves a thorough literary analysis.[15]

The story of the global *Potter*-victory is full of superlatives. The fifth part of the series, *Order of the Phoenix*, was published in 2003 with a circulation of 8.5 million copies in Britain alone. This was the "largest ever print run for a first edition".[16] Waterstone's estimated that the next novel, *Half-Blood Prince*, sold

---

[10] See Terence Blacker, "Why does everyone like Harry Potter? He is the perfect hero for readers looking for reassurance and a nannyish moral certainty," *Independent* 13 July 1999, 4.

[11] Harold Bloom, "Can 35 million book buyers be wrong? Yes," *Wall Street Journal* 11 July 2000, A26.

[12] Carol Iannone, "Lit critic struggles with muggles, wizards," *United Press International* 17 July 2000, n. pag.

[13] Jack Zipes, *Sticks and Stones: The Troublesome Success of Children's Literature from Slovenly Peter to Harry Potter*, New York, London: Routledge 2001, 174.

[14] "I don't see any reason why we should analyse the books any further. Instead of applying literary theories to it we should analyse the book market. Our hero proves to be the ideal product for the mass market; he satisfies the needs of millions and corresponds to their tastes. Just like Nescafé." Andrzej Stasiuk, "Nein, ich mag Harry Potter nicht," *F.A.Z.* 24 Feb 2001, 43 [my translation].

[15] See Gupta 2003, 20.

[16] See Richard Adams, "Quidditch quaintness," *Guardian* 18 June 2003 <http://books.guardian.co.uk/print/0,3858,4693385-108779,00.html> 29 Dec 2007.

about ten million books internationally on its first day.[17] The books received so many literary prizes all over the world that it proved to be a scandal when *Prisoner of Azkaban* was not awarded the Whitbread Prize in 2000.[18] The same year, J.K. Rowling was rewarded the title of "Author of the Year".[19] When all *Potter* novels published by then were occupying the top ranks of its bestseller list, the *New York Times* introduced a separate list for children's literature in October 2003.[20]

International merchandising has made the series popular beyond the reach of the actual printed texts. Its impact can be compared to Tolkien's *Lord of the Rings* fifty years ago.[21] British sociologist Andrew Blake names Harry Potter among other icons of British pop culture like Sherlock Holmes or James Bond.[22] This ignores the fact that a 2001 survey showed that Harry was even more popular than the detective or the special agent.[23] *Harry Potter* has "rebranded and reglobalised" and has helped to promote Britain among young people.[24] Moreover, critics agree on the fact that the series has changed the market for children's books. Today it seems possible for every book to achieve worldwide popularity.[25] Children's literature has come into the focus of newspaper editors and media pundits.[26] It seems to be widely acknowledged fact that the books have had an impact on children's reading skills. In a survey by the *Federation of Children's Book Groups* 84 percent of British teachers stated that their pupils were more likely to read a book today than in the pre-*Potter* days. 73 percent of

---

[17] See David Smith, "Potter's magic spell turns boys into bookworms," *Observer* 10 July 2005 <http://books.guardian.co.uk/print/0,3858,5235620-108779,00.html> 3 Jan 2008.

[18] See Andrew Blake, *The Irresistible Rise of Harry Potter*, London, New York: Verso 2002, 69.

[19] See Fiachra Gibbons, "JK Rowling is author of the year," *Guardian* 4 Feb 2000 <http://books.guardian.co.uk/print/0,3858,3958817-99819,00.html> 3 Jan 2008.

[20] See Bloom 2000; Paul Bürvenich, *Der Zauber des Harry Potter: Analyse eines literarischen Welterfolgs*, Frankfurt am Main: Peter Lang 2001, 22.

[21] See Natasha Walter, "A hero of our time," *Guardian* 16 July 2005 <http://books.guard ian. co.uk/departments/childrenandteens/story/0,6000,1529506,00.html> 3 Jan 2008.

[22] See Blake 2002, 91.

[23] According to this survey, Harry Potter is by far the most popular character of British literature. He outranks Sherlock Holmes, Winnie the Pooh and James Bond, as much as Hercule Poirot, Oliver Twist or Jane Eyre. 79 % of those surveyed knew of Harry Potter. See Gina Thomas, "Konkurrenz für den Weihnachtsmann," *F.A.Z.* 16 Nov 2001, 53.

[24] See Blake 2001, 112; "Harry Potter und das große Geld," *F.A.Z.* 7 Nov 2001, 32.

[25] See Mark Lawson, "Rowling survives the hype," *Guardian* 8 July 2000 <http://books. guardian.co.uk/print/0,3858,4038362-99943,00.html> 3 Jan 2008. In particular, fantasy literature for children has become extremely popular through *Harry Potter*, says German bestselling author Cornelia Funke (see Cornelia Funke, "Kinder finden das Böse cool," *Tagesspiegel* 2 Jan 2005, S1.)

[26] See Smith 2005.

them said they regarded *Potter* as a gateway to reading chiefly for children who previously were unlikely to read.[27]

    Potter has been merchandised like no other book before it. It was – among other things – the worldwide marketing for the movies produced by Warner Bros that turned *Harry Potter* into a strong international brand. The first movie had a production budget of 150 million dollars. On its opening weekend in 2001 2.6 million Germans went to see it and tickets totalling a value of 32 million deutschmarks were sold.[28] Critics agree that merchandising for the movies ("sturzlangweilige Umsetzung[en] der Bücher"[29]) was not in the least as successful as Warner Bros had hoped,[30] but it contributed nevertheless to *Potter's* enormous popularity. Rowling herself has often declared herself a strong critic of the way her books are commercially exploited,[31] but despite this the trademark *Harry Potter* (registered in Germany as No. 30012566)[32] is worth about 4 billion dollars.[33]

    The global *Potter*-marketing machine has to deal with about 115 different illustration concepts for the books worldwide. For example, the German Harry Potter looks very different from his American or French counterparts.[34] Right from the start, publishers identified the target group of young adults as key players and gave them an active role in the series' marketing. The German publisher, Carlsen, let its readers vote on the cover of *Goblet of Fire* and allowed school magazines to print the first chapter of the book for free.[35] All this makes the publication day of each new *Potter*-book a media sensation with front pages praising Rowling's work, T-Shirts declaring "I waited for Harry" being sold and midnight openings for bookshops.[36] Even the *British Tourist Authority* has been

---

[27] See Smith 2005.

[28] See "Harry Potter und das große Geld," 2001.

[29] "utterly boring film versions of the books". Michael Althen, "Kinder, ist mir schlecht," *F.A.Z.* 13 Nov 2002, 35 [my translation].

[30] See Peter Turi, "Probleme in Hogwart," [sic!] *Werben & Verkaufen* 14 July 2005, 24-28; Wolfgang Gehrmann, "Mein Harry! Wie ein US-Medienkonzern sein Harry-Potter-Bild gegen den Rest der Welt durchsetzen will," *ZEIT* 11/2001. <http://www.zeit.de/ar chiv/2001/11/200111_entscheiden_pott.xml> 3 Jan 2008.

[31] See David Aaronovitch,"We've been muggled," *Observer* 22 June 2003. <http://books. guardian.co.uk./print/0,3858,4696309-108779,00.html> 29 Dec 2007.

[32] See Urs Jenny, "Crashkurs für Zauberlehrlinge," *SPIEGEL* 19 Nov 2001. <http://www. spiegel.de/spiegel/0,1518,168282,00.html> 3 Jan 2008.

[33] See Stephen Brown, *Wizard!: Harry Potter's Brand Magic,* London: Cyan Books, 2005, 8.

[34] See Gehrmann 2001.

[35] See Klaus Kämpfe-Burghard, "Vertriebszauber? Einblick ins Potter-Marketing," *Harry Potter oder Warum wir Zauberer brauchen,* ed. Olaf Kutzmutz, Wolfenbüttel: Bundesakademie für kulturelle Bildung, 2001, 44-59, 50-51.

[36] See "Harry Potter is back!" *ZEIT* 29/2005. <http://www.zeit.de/2005/29/0potter_mel dung> 29 Dec 2007; Monika Osberghaus, "Keine Zeit für Muggle-Muffins," *F.A.Z.* 10 July 2000, 4.

using the books for marketing Great Britain since 2001.[37] You cannot live in the Western world without ever having heard of *Harry Potter*: "Harry is now ubiquitous and noisy."[38]

Some numbers are a proof as to the the degree of the novels' economic success. The first five volumes sold about 270 million copies in 62 languages,[39] with books one to four having sold "only" 60 million copies.[40] *Half-Blood Prince* sold about ten million copies within the first 24 hours of its release, and estimates are that in Great Britain about thirteen copies were sold each second.[41] The book was also the first ever to be published in Braille on its first day.[42] Never before had five volumes of one series been on international bestseller lists and no other book ever has sold 20 million copies for 200 million euros within five years in Germany.[43] But *Potter* has had a further-reaching impact upon culture. In 2003 the word "Muggle" was entered into the *Oxford English Dictionary*, Asteroid 43844 was named "Rowling", a dinosaur discovered in South Dakota in 2007 is called "Dracorex hogwartsia"[44] and British Royal Mail has issued a special series of stamps celebrating the seven novels.[45]

Potter has affected the whole market. Whereas book sales are decreasing generally, the market share of children's books has been increasing over the last few years.[46] Spin-offs from this bonanza include the multiplication of Bloomsbury and Scholastic shares, the revived interest in French and British boarding schools, the increase in sales of children's glasses, the dubious interest in having owls as pets and the revival of "Harry" as a name.[47] But *Potter* also is an example of how a whole market can become dependent on a single product. The last, probably most successful, part of the series is feared to earn a huge deficit for booksellers, because – despite a recommended retail price of £17.99 it is now sold at £8.87. Booksellers know that there will be no successor to parallel the

---

[37] See Thomas 2001.
[38] See Aaronovitch 2003.
[39] See "Harry Potter is back!" 2005.
[40] See Gehrmann 2001.
[41] See Felicitas von Lovenberg, Felicitas, "Seele in sieben Portionen," *F.A.Z.net*, 18 July 2005. <http://www.F.A.Z..net/s/Rub117C535CDF414415BB243B181B8B60AE/Doc~E C7360A35FFF24830876ABF4420263694~ATpl~Ecommon~Sspezial.html> 3 Jan 2008.
[42] See von Lovenberg 2005.
[43] See Turi 2005, 25.
[44] See Urs Jenny, "Muss Harry sterben?" *SPIEGEL Online* 20 July 2007. <www.spiegel.de/ kultur/literatur/0,1518,494949,00.html> 6 Aug 2007.
[45] See Bröll 2007.
[46] See Konrad Heidkamp, "Harry, der Verlegertraum. Joanne K. Rowling verändert den Markt für Kinderbücher," *ZEIT* 27/2003 <http://www.zeit.de/2003/27/L-Glosse_27> 3 Jan 2008.
[47] See Brown 2005, 106-109.

fabulous sales of *Harry Potter* and fear the ramifications. In *Potter*-free 2006 Bloomsbury sales were cut by 75 percent.[48]

The internet has become the most important medium for *Potter's* fanbase. Stephen Brown, author of an analysis of *Potter*-marketing, identified about 64,000 unauthorised texts about Harry Potter in 2005 – most of them sequels or background information written by children.[49] In summer 2007, prior to the publication of *Deathly Hallows*, there was a scandal about homoerotic *Potter* fanliterature which inspired a discussion about the protection of underage fans and the underage characters of fantasy-literature.[50] *Potter* also has become a collector's item. In 2002 a signed first edition of *Philosopher's Stone* was sold for £23,800 – prices that are usually paid for W. B. Yeats, Joseph Conrad or D. H. Lawrence.[51]

All this raises the question, what do these texts have to justify such international hysteria? Many theories have been made on this point – the most common is the one that attributes the enormous success to a clever marketing strategy:

> [...] Harry Potter is above all else a marketing phenomenon. It is marketing that has turned a strictly limited edition into an international bestseller. [...] It is marketing that has made Harry Potter what he is.[52]

This is supported by the fact that marketing and merchandising are issues in the texts themselves (see V.1.G, 303). Brown explains: "They refer to almost every element of the marketing mix, as well as aspects of buyer behaviour, corporate strategy, marketing research and much, much more."[53] He points out that the marketing for the books is like a case study for successful contemporary book marketing.[54] But the publication history proves Brown to be wrong (see I.2.A, 17):[55] the first volume was published in an edition of 500 copies; no additional marketing budget was spent. It was word-of-mouth recommendation that caused the initial success. It was only when the book had attained a certain level of popularity that

---

[48] See Bröll 2007.

[49] *The Lord of the Rings* – another fantasy novel that reached cult status – only had about 14,000 such spin-off texts (see Brown 2005, 135).

[50] See Christian Stöcker, "Blogs gesperrt wegen Potter-Sex," *SPIEGEL Online* 7 Aug 2007 <http://www.spiegel.de/netzwelt/web/0,1518,498677,00.html> 7 Aug 2007.

[51] See Brown 2005, 141.

[52] See Brown 2005, 18. "Harry Potter is a global marketing phenomenon. What else would you expect?" (See Robert McCrum, "My long, dark night with Harry," *Observer* 17 July 2005 <http://books.guardian.co.uk/print/0,3858,5241113-108779,00.html> 3 Jan 2008.

[53] See Brown 2005, 19.

[54] See Brown 2005, 55; Heidi Lexe, *Pippi, Pan und Potter: Zur Motivkonstellation in den Klassikern der Kinderliteratur*, Wien: Edition Praesens, 2003, 175-176.

[55] See Edmund M. Kern, *The Wisdom of Harry Potter: What Our Favorite Hero Teaches Us about Moral Choices*, New York: Prometheus, 2003, 140.

media coverage, internet websites and movies could turn *Potter* into a global phenomenon.[56] Meanwhile *Potter* has seen his best times, as Peter Turi of the German marketing magazine *Werben & Verkaufen* declares:

> [Die] Behauptung, dass Harry Potter eine perfekte Marketing-Maschinerie sei, [bleibt] eine Lüge. Marketing-Leute erzählen sie sich gern, um sich wichtig zu machen. Das Gegenteil ist richtig: Das Marketing rund um Harry Potter ist nur selten professionell, das Ende der kommerziellen Fahnenstange längst erreicht, und viele Geschäftsmacher fielen und fallen mit Harry auf die Nase.[57]

Attributing the novels' success to marketing alone overestimates the possibilities of a product's ability to communicate. If economic success could be so easily manipulated, any children's book could be used to generate a worldwide hype. On the contrary we must wonder why this should exclusively be the case with *Harry Potter*. Why can marketers not promote every consumer good like Rowling's books?[58] It seems clear: *Harry Potter* must have more to offer than a good marketing mix.[59] The reason for its success must be in the texts themselves.[60] Nevertheless, *Potter* has inspired a new trend in marketing: it has become the symbol of "viral marketing" and companies of all branches are trying to imitate it. The idea is that little is known about the product itself and that a small community of fans helps to spread the news further and further until the product is widely known – without the visible influence of the company. Naturally, this only works for the very few products which achieve cult status among their users – like products by Apple such as the iPod for example.[61]

Many critics have tried to find explanations for Pottermania. One is that the series uses so many well-known patterns that a majority of readers are able to relate to it:

> [The] Potter story is a fairy tale, plus a bildungsroman, plus a murder mystery, plus a cosmic war of good and evil, and there's almost no classic in any of those genres that doesn't vibrate between the lines of Harry's saga.[62]

---

[56] See Turi 2005.

[57] "Stating that Harry Potter is purely a marketing success is a lie. Marketers like to promote it nevertheless, to underline their own importance. However, the opposite is true: *Potter*-marketing only is rarely professional, the series' commercial success is about to be over." (Peter Turi, "Warum Harry Potter sterben muss," *SPIEGEL Online* 16 July 2005. <http://www.spiegel.de/kultur/literatur/0,1518,365303,00.html> 3 Jan 2008 [my translation].

[58] See Brown 2005, 54.

[59] See Peter von Becker, "Das Geheimnis des Erfolges," *Tagesspiegel* 17 July 2005, S1.

[60] See Blacker 1999.

[61] See Judith Lembke, "Das magische Virus," *F.A.Z.* 21 July 2007, 18.

[62] Joan Aocella, "Under the spell," *New Yorker* 31 July 2000, 74-78.

In doing this, Rowling successfully alters stereotypes, thus creating an attractive mix of familiar and unknown elements. "Rowling's blend of the familiar and the fantastic is one of the keys to her novels' success."[63] Jack Zipes attributes *Potter's* success to an increasingly globalised pop culture.[64] To become part of worldwide pop the work in question has to conform totally to the preferences of each nation's opinion leaders: "It is impossible to be phenomenal without conforming to conventionality." *Potter*, therefore, has to be extraordinarily conventional: "[Their] absolute conformance to popular audience expectations is what makes for their phenomenality."[65]

Another reason for Pottermania seems to be that many people find it easy to identify with the eponymous hero. Amy Billone says that Harry unites male as well as female traits in his character and is attractive to girls and boys alike.[66] German author and journalist Peter von Becker believes that the books are so appealing to children because of the topics they address like school, conflicts with teachers and parents and first love. Grown-up readers regard it as a metaphor for today's global security situation with the worldwide rise of terrorism and fanaticism. In particular, the opening chapter of *Half-Blood Prince* (in which we see Muggle-World being threatened by terrorist attacks), corresponds exactly to the situation in Great Britain after the London bombings of July 2005.[67] Felicitas von Lovenberg believes that *Potter* – just as most other fantastic texts – can satisfy people's yearning for justice.[68] Moreover, *Potter* is not bound to a specific religion or political ideology (see e.g. V.5.C, 354) – which makes him interculturally acceptable.[69]

Apart from these more intellectual explanations we must not forget the entertainment which Rowling's novels provide. Creativity and a sense of humour are always mentioned as the series' major qualities.

> A stimulating narrative, broadbrush characters with whom we can identify, invention and humour, draw us in like bright lights to a circus of literary pleasures. "Literary" is about right, because Rowling has all the skills that make popular literature popular. In particular, she has the art [...] of drawing

---

[63] Kern 2003, 189.
[64] See Zipes 2001, 173.
[65] Zipes 2001, 175-176.
[66] See Amy Christine Billone, "The Boy Who Lived: From Carroll's Alice and Barrie's Peter Pan to Rowling's Harry Potter," *Children's Literature* 32 (2004): 178-202, here 191.
[67] See von Becker 2005.
[68] See von Lovenberg 2005. Jack Zipes adds: "In a world in which we are uncertain of our roles and uncertain about our capacity to defeat evil, the Harry Potter novels arrive and inform us (as do films and TV series) that if we all pull together and trust one another and follow the lead of the chosen one, evil will be overcome." (Zipes 2001, 182)
[69] See Kern 2003, 25.

the reader on, both by making him or her live through the characters and by the management of suspense.[70]

But are Rowling's texts creative and innovative? Are they so execptional as to justify the global hysteria? Apparently, you can only love or hate the novels – judging from the reactions they have inspired. In a review for *F.A.Z.*, Salman Rushdie has argued that hating a book only means reassuring one's already existing point of view. He even claims that Rowling's impact on her readers could be compared to "Uncle Tom's Cabin" or Dicken's descriptions of child poverty in the nineteenth century. This is the extent to which she has changed attitudes towards reading amongst children and young adults.[71]

With all the heated debate about *Potter* the cool literary analysis of the actual texts has been neglected so far. Everyone has his or her opinion on *Harry Potter* and pretends to know why they are good or bad for children. But hardly anyone has analysed the construction of the texts. Only recently have scholars begun to look on *Harry Potter* as what it is in the first place: a book for children and young adults.

I.1.A. History of "Potter" Criticism

The first profound and scientific analysis of the *Potter*-books was undertaken in 2000 by historian Elizabeth D. Schafer (*Exploring Harry Potter*).[72] This study – well-based as it may be – has never been revised since then and thus covers only the first three novels. Therefore, it is outdated today. Moreover, Schafer's work treats some aspects quite superficially and overreacts to some of the series' topics. For example, she tries to interpret Harry Potter as an allegorical text on German National Socialism[73] and sees the tubes that the basilisk in *Chamber of Secrets* uses to move around Hogwarts as a metaphor for giving birth.[74] Sometimes she even makes obvious mistakes and demonstrates a certain inaccurate reading of the text.[75]

---

[70]   See Colin Manlove, *From Alice to Harry Potter: Children's Fantasy in England*, Christchurch, New Zealand: Cybereditions, 2003, 187; Christina Tilmann, "Wo der Werwolf heult," *Tagesspiegel* 3 June 2004, 25.

[71]   See Salman Rushdie, "J.K. Rowling verändert die Welt," F.A.Z.net 15 July 2005 <http://www.F.A.Z..net/s/RubEBED639C476B407798B1CE808F1F6632/Doc~EE23A2 CF8C88F4E268855B6C1CE271894~ATpl~Ecommon~Scontent.html> 6 Aug 2007.

[72]   Elizabeth D. Schafer, *Exploring Harry Potter*, London: Ebury Press, 2000.

[73]   See Schafer 2000, 177-180.

[74]   See Schafer 2000, 225.

[75]   She obviously ignores the fact that Voldemort and Tom Riddle are identical characters (see Schafer 2000, 64-65).

Three years later Suman Gupta in *Re-reading Harry Potter* (2003)[76] searches for reasons for the novels' huge success and for the fierce criticism it has earned. Her work is especially relevant for sociological questions, but just as with Schafer's work, Gupta's analysis has never been revised. In 2003 *Harry Potter's World: Multidisciplinary Critical Perspectives*,[77] edited by Elizabeth E. Heilman, investigated the series from sociological, literary and political points of view. Heilman's work can still be regarded as an important contribution to *Potter*-criticism, but she does not undertake a complete analysis of the whole series. The latest and up to now most profound collection of Potter related papers is *The Ivory Tower and Harry Potter: Perspectives on a Literary Phenomenon* edited by Lana A. Whited.[78] Here we find articles by Farah Mendlesohn,[79] Mary Pharr,[80] Pat Pinsent[81] and David K. Steege[82] that can be seen as the foundation of scholarly work on *Harry Potter*. But even these profound works cannot compensate for a complete literary analysis of narratological structures.

Apart from these attempts to look into the phenomenon from a multitude of points of view, various studies on singular aspects have been published. Andrew Blake deals with the sociological background of Pottermania in *The Irresistible Rise of Harry Potter* (2002).[83] He sees *Potter* connected with the political and social situation of post-Thatcher Great Britain. He neglects the fact that *Potter's* success is not restricted to Britain, but in fact corresponds to the spiritual needs of other cultural contexts. Blake focuses on the books' success. Although – *Potter* being such an unprecedented bestseller – this point of view seems to be relevant, Blake does not contribute to the literary criticism of the series. Finally, Edmund M. Kern has undertaken an analysis of values and ideology in the *Potter* series (*The Wisdom of Harry Potter: What Our Favorite*

---

[76] Suman Gupta, *Re-reading Harry Potter*, Houndmills, New York: Palgrave Macmillan, 2003.

[77] Elizabeth E. Heilman, ed., *Harry Potter's World: Multidisciplinary Critical Perspectives*, New York, London: RoutledgeFalmer, 2003.

[78] Lana A. Whited, ed., *The Ivory Tower and Harry Potter: Perspectives on a Literary Phenomenon*, Columbia: University of Missouri Press, 2004.

[79] Farah Mendlesohn, "Crowning the King. Harry Potter and the Construction of Authority," *The Ivory Tower and Harry Potter: Perspectives on a Literary Phenomenon*, ed. Lana A. Whited, Columbia: University of Missouri Press, 2004, 159-181.

[80] Mary Pharr, "In Medias Res. Harry Potter as Hero-in-Progress," *The Ivory Tower and Harry Potter: Perspectives on a Literary Phenomenon*, ed. Lana A. Whited, Columbia: University of Missouri Press, 2004, 53-66.

[81] Pat Pinsent, "The Education of a Wizard. Harry Potter and His Predecessors," *The Ivory Tower and Harry Potter: Perspectives on a Literary Phenomenon*, ed. Lana A. Whited, Columbia: University of Missouri Press, 2004 27-50.

[82] David K. Steege, "Harry Potter, Tom Brown, and the British School Story. Lost in Transit?" *The Ivory Tower and Harry Potter: Perspectives on a Literary Phenomenon*, ed. Lana A. Whited, Columbia: University of Missouri Press, 2004, 140-156.

[83] Andrew Blake, *The Irresistible Rise of Harry Potter*, London: Verso, 2002.

Hero Teaches Us about Moral Choices (2003)[84]), but he – as well as most of the other critics – only deals with the parts I to IV. *Potter* criticism is global and not restricted to works in English. In 2001 Isabelle Smadja published *Harry Potter: Les raisons d'un succès*[85] – a work in which she analysed the first four volumes of the series. Unfortunately, her reading of the novels is at some times inaccurate, for example, when she states that there is a goblet of fire as a trophy for winning the *Triwizard Tournament*[86] and mistakes Quirrell for Pettigrew as he severs his hand in service of Voldemort.[87] Moreover, she quite desperately tries to find historical parallels between Potter and 20th-century European history. She interprets the Durmstrang vessel as a German submarine, declares Dumbledore a personification of the "Eternal (Wandering) Jew" and sees Beauxbatons instead of Hogwarts as the representative of the democratic world.[88] Even if one may establish parallels between Voldemort's dictatorship and any fascist regime (see V.1.D, 294), it seems quite hazardous to define such a direct link.

In the case of Harry Potter there are many non-scientific sources of information that are either provided by the author herself or by the multitude of fan groups. J.K. Rowling supplies information on her own website (www.jkrowling. com) and has used this way frequently to deal with letters from her fans or rumours about the possible developments of her novels. A myriad of fan groups populates the internet and exchanges ideas about the series. Such "fanlit" or "fanzines" have become a field of investigation themselves and shall not be dealt with in this book. Apart from this, nearly every newspaper in the world has published reviews or reports on the books or the movies. Among these we find articles by renowned authors. Harold Bloom asks in the *Wall Street Journal* "Can 35 million book buyers be wrong? Yes",[89] and thinks *Potter* to be utterly trivial. Antonia S. Byatt excoriates *Potter*'s success in her 2003 *New York Times* review as an indication of the growing infantilisation of society.[90]

The first scholarly books on *Harry Potter* to be published in Germany were *Harry Potter oder Warum wir Zauberer brauchen* by Olaf Kutzmutz[91] and

---

[84] Edmund M. Kern, *The Wisdom of Harry Potter: What Our Favorite Hero Teaches Us about Moral Choices*, New York: Prometheus Books, 2003.

[85] Isabelle Smadja, *Harry Potter Les raisons d'un success*. Paris: Presses Universitaires de France, 2001.

[86] See Smadja 2001, 41.

[87] See Smadja 2001, 119.

[88] See Smadja 2001, 40-42

[89] Harold Bloom, "Can 35 million book buyers be wrong? Yes," *Wall Street Journal* 11 July 2000, n. pag.

[90] See Antonia S. Byatt, "Harry Potter and the Childish Adult," *New York Times* 11 July 2003, n. pag.

[91] Olaf Kutzmutz, ed., *Harry Potter oder Warum wir Zauberer brauchen*, Wolfenbüttel: Bundesakademie für kulturelle Bildung, 2001.

"Alohomora!" by Heidi Lexe[92] – both of them summarising papers held on the occasion of *Potter* conferences. The two collections unite contributions from very different areas of research, but neither of them, naturally, gives us a complete literary analysis. The same is true for Kaspar Spinner's *Im Bann des Zauberlehrlings? Zur Faszination von Harry Potter* which analyses the novels psychological, literary and theological points of view.[93] The first German monograph on *Potter* was published in 2001. Paul Bürvenich tried the first literary analysis with his *Der Zauber des Harry Potter: Analyse eines literarischen Welterfolgs*. This unrevised book is outdated today, because it only deals with the first four novels.[94] At that time the question of plagiarism was widely discussed. Bürvenich deals with this aspect, which today has ceased to be important, in quite an amount of detail. Other German approaches to Harry Potter include Michael Maar's *Warum Nabokov Harry Potter gemocht hätte,*[95] Sandra Bak's *Harry Potter: Auf den Spuren eines zauberhaften Bestsellers,*[96] Mathias Jung's *Der Zauber der Wandlung: Harry Potter oder das Abenteuer der Ichwerdung*[97] and Linda Jelinek's *Das Phänomen Harry Potter: Eine literaturwissenschaftliche Analyse des Welterfolgs.*[98] But none of them can be regarded as a copious analysis of the series. Jelinek's work in particular, is superficial and full of trivial interpretations.

A detailed literary analysis is still missing. Lana A. Whited complains about the mixture of commercial interests, pop culture and literary criticism that until now have prevented a serious debate on *Harry Potter:* "The point is that the serious discussion we ought to be having about the literary merits of J.K. Rowling's *Harry Potter* novels is threatened by the cloud of commercialism encircling the books."[99] There are quite a lot of conferences and events concerning the books, but hardly any of them can be considered to be interested in serious

---

[92] Heidi Lexe, ed., *"Alohomora!" Ergebnisse des Ersten Wiener Harry-Potter-Symposions*, Wien: Edition Praesens, 2002.
[93] Kaspar H. Spinner, ed. *Im Bann des Zauberlehrlings? Zur Faszination von Harry Potter*, Regensburg: Friedrich Pustet, 2001.
[94] Paul Bürvenich, *Der Zauber des Harry Potter: Analyse eines literarischen Welterfolgs*, Frankfurt am Main: Peter Lang, 2001.
[95] Michael Maar, *Warum Nabokov Harry Potter gemocht hätte*, Berlin: Berliner Taschenbuch-Verlag, 2003.
[96] Sandra Bak, *Harry Potter: Auf den Spuren eines zauberhaften Bestsellers*, Frankfurt am Main: Peter Lang, 2004.
[97] Mathias Jung, *Der Zauber der Wandlung: Harry Potter oder das Abenteuer der Ichwerdung*, Lahnstein: emu, 2004.
[98] Linda Jelinek, *Das Phänomen Harry Potter: Eine literaturwissenschaftliche Analyse des Welterfolgs*, Saarbrücken: VDM, 2006.
[99] Lana A. Whited, "Harry Potter. From Craze to Classic?" *The Ivory Tower and Harry Potter: Perspectives on a Literary Phenomenon*, ed. Lana A. Whited. Columbia: University of Missouri Press, 2004, 1-12, 12.

criticism: "Nimbus" took place in 2003 in Orlando (Florida), one year later the *Potter* community met as "Convention Alley" in Canada, in autumn 2005 "Accio!" was celebrated in Great Britain and "Sectus" was held in London in July 2007. Each of these events was attended by more than 2,000 *Potter* fans; scholarly debates mixed with pseudo-serious contributions for example, the issue of elf rights.[100]

This book seeks to close the gap concerning *Harry Potter* and literary criticism. I want to focus on the narrative structures, dealing with questions like how the texts are constructed, how the various plots are working and which narrative techniques J.K. Rowling uses. Are there any well-known patterns and literary traditions we can identify? How is *Potter* to be judged in the context of children's and fantasy literature? Is there a literary reason for the overwhelming success of the novels?

This book will be based on a scrupulous reading of the text and I will refer to the terminology of Franz Stanzel,[101] Gérard Genette,[102] Jurij Lotman,[103] Gerhard Hoffmann,[104] Manfred Pfister[105] and E. M. Forster.[106] Moreover, I will deal with the books' ideological content as well as with their relationship to the genre of fantastic and children's literature.

I.2 A Word about the Author

The relation between author, narrator, text and reader has been widely discussed within literary criticism. It is obvious that the author's personal experiences must influence his writing. On the other hand, when dealing with an author's biography, literary criticism must avoid getting anywhere close to the level of the tabloid press. In the case of *Harry Potter* the question as to how far biography and text are related is not that easily answered. J.K. Rowling has been part of the phenomenon right from the start,[107] her tours and public readings reach the scale of pop concerts.[108] Through her own presence in the media she pro-

---

[100] See David Baggett and Shawn Klein, *Harry Potter and Philosophy: If Aristotle ran Hogwarts*. Chicago, La Salle: Open Court, 2004, 1; Tanja Gold, "Spellbound," *Guardian* 2 Aug 2005 <http://books.guardian.co.uk/print/0,3858,5253251-108779,00.html> 3 Jan 2008.

[101] Franz K. Stanzel, *Theorie des Erzählens* [1979], Göttingen: Vandenhoeck & Ruprecht, 2001.

[102] Gérard Genette, *Die Erzählung*, Munich: Wilhelm Fink, 1998.

[103] Jurij M. Lotman, *Die Struktur literarischer Texte* [1972], Munich: Wilhelm Fink, 1993.

[104] Gerhard Hoffmann, *Raum, Situation, erzählte Wirklichkeit: poetologische und historische Studien zum englischen und amerikanischen Roman*, Stuttgart: Metzler, 1978.

[105] Manfred Pfister, *Das Drama: Theorie und Analyse* [1977], Munich: Wilhelm Fink, 2001.

[106] Edward Morgan Forster, *Aspects of the Novel* [1927], Orlando: Harcourt, 1985.

[107] See Gupta 2003, 36.

[108] See Bürvenich 2001, 174-176.

duces further metatexts, explains backgrounds missing in the novels and interprets the characters.

Rowling's biography has always been part of the *Potter* myth, as Olaf
Kutzmutz demonstrates by means of press photos.[109] The focus has usually been
on the fairy-tale-like story of Rowling being a poor single mother dependent on
social welfare and writing her books in an Edinburgh café to save heating
money.[110] The author herself has contradicted this myth quite clearly.[111] As
Rowling has raised nearly as much interest as her novels it seems unavoidable
but to give a brief outline of her biography. I will base the following remarks on
the biographies by Anne Connie Kirk,[112] Marc Shapiro[113] and Sean Smith.[114]

I.2.A. PR vs. Reality – A Short Biography of J.K. Rowling

Joanne Kathleen Rowling was born in a middle-class family; her mother Anne
worked as a laboratory assistant, her father Pete was an engineer in aircraft construction and worked for Rolls-Royce.[115] They got to know each other at the
start of a train journey in King's Cross Station[116] and were married on March
14th, 1965.[117] Joanne Rowling was born on July 31st, 1966 in Yate, north of Bristol.[118] She took the second name Kathleen, as a young woman to commemorate
her beloved grandmother.[119] Two years later, her younger sister Dianne Rowling
was born. Joanne began reading at a very early age and she invented stories for
her sister.[120] Among her favourite books were *The Chronicles of Narnia* by C.S.
Lewis, Tolkien's works and the fantastic novels of Edith Nesbit.[121] Later she

---

[109] See Olaf Kutzmutz, "Nachricht von Aschenputtel. Joanne K. Rowling in den Medien," *Harry Potter oder Warum wir Zauberer brauchen*, ed. Olaf Kutzmutz, Wolfenbüttel: Bundesakademie für kulturelle Bildung, 2001, 59-77.

[110] See Kutzmutz 2001, 62.

[111] See Kutzmutz 2001, 65.

[112] Ann Connie Kirk, *J.K. Rowling: A Biography*, Westport, London: Greenwood Press, 2003.

[113] Marc Shapiro, *J.K. Rowling: The Wizard behind Harry Potter*, New York: St Martin's Griffin, 2004.

[114] Sean Smith, *J.K. Rowling: A Biography*, London: Micheal O'Mara Books, 2001.

[115] See Shapiro 2004, 17; Philip Nel, *J K Rowling's "Harry Potter" Novels: A Reader's Guide*, New York, London: Continuum, 2001, 7.

[116] See Kirk 2003, 10.

[117] See Kirk 2003, 11; Smith 2001, 16.

[118] Rowling names Chipping Sodbury, the more prestigious neighbouring town of Yate, as her place of birth (see Kirk 2003, 12; Shapiro 2004, 19).

[119] See Kirk 2003, 32.

[120] See Shapiro 2004, 22.

[121] See Shapiro 2004, 25.

went on to read Ian Fleming's *James Bond*, as a young girl she discovered her love for Jane Austen, whom she still names as her favourite author today.[122]

In 1974 the Rowlings moved to Tutshill (Forest of Dean), a small village across the Severn,[123] where they chose to live in an old parsonage.[124] In winter of that year the Rowling sisters began to attend Tutshill School of England, a very conservative primary school.[125] Rowling's experiences, especially with her maths teacher Mrs Morgan (who used to seat her pupils according to the results in their maths tests), traumatised the young girl.[126] Two years later she changed to Wyedean Comprehensive Secondary School in Sedbury,[127] where she was inspired and encouraged to write stories by her teacher Lucy Shephard.[128] In the late seventies, Anne was diagnosed with an especially aggressive form of multiple sclerosis, and the girls had to watch their mother's physical decline at home.[129]

Teenage life in Tutshill was far from being exciting[130] and Joanne sometimes escaped village life together with schoolmate Sean Harris in his Ford Anglia. In her last year in school she was elected head girl[131] and passed her A-Levels in 1983 with very good results, especially in French, German and English.[132] The school advised her to take the Oxford entrance exam, but Rowling failed. Later she claimed that she had not been accepted because a girl from a renowned public school was preferred.[133] Instead of going to Oxford she began her study of classics at the University of Exeter concentrating on French, Latin and Greek,[134] but did not prove to be a very ambitious student.[135] During her studies she went to teach English in Paris for a year[136] and graduated from Exe-

---

[122] See Shapiro 2004, 31; Simon Hattenstone, "Harry, Jessie and me," *Guardian* 8 July 2000 <http://books.guardian.co.uk/print/0,3858,4037903-99943,00.html> 3 Jan 2008; Kirk 2003, 33-34; Joanne Kathleen Rowling, "Live Interview on Scholastic.com," www.scholastic.com 3 Feb 2000 <http://www.scholastic.com/harrypotter/author/transcript1.htm> 3 Jan 2008.

[123] See Kirk 2003, 21.

[124] See Smith 2001, 32.

[125] See Kirk 2003, 30-31; Smith 2001, 34.

[126] See Smith 2001, 35-36.

[127] See Kirk 2003, 33; Smith 2001, 52.

[128] See Kirk 2003, 36; Smith 2001, 57-58.

[129] See Smith 2001, 70-73.

[130] See Smith 2001, 60-61.

[131] See Kirk 2003, 41.

[132] See Nel 2001, 16; Kirk 2003, 43; Rowling 2006; Shapiro 2004, 40; Smith 2001, 73-76.

[133] See Kirk 2003, 42; Smith 2001, 75-76.

[134] See Eliza T. Dresang, "Hermione Granger and the Heritage of Gender," *The Ivory Tower and Harry Potter: Perspectives on a Literary Phenomenon*, ed. Lana A. Whited, Columbia: University of Missouri Press, 2004, 211-242, here 212; Hattenstone 2000; Smith 2001, 80-83.

[135] See Kirk 2003, 44; Smith 2001, 84-85.

[136] See Shapiro 2004, 43-45; Smith 2001, 87.

ter in 1987 with quite mediocre results.[137] She then went to work as secretary in various companies and organisations, among them Amnesty International.[138] Living in London, she finally came to work in Manchester with the Chamber of Commerce and commuted regularly between the two cities. One day her train had a breakdown and was delayed four hours. In this moment, Rowling claims, she had the initial idea for *Harry Potter* (see I.2.A, 16).[139]

In 1990 she moved from London to Manchester. On December 30th the same year her mother (aged 45) died from multiple sclerosis. The 26-year-old Rowling felt guilty for not having been present during the time of her death and became depressed.[140] The loss of her mother meant the end of childhood for her. Searching for an opportunity to give her life a meaning she went to teach English in Porto (Portugal) in September 1991. There, she fell in love with Portuguese journalist Jorge Arantes. On August 28th 1992 she accepted his proposal, the marriage was held the same year on Friday, October 16th.[141] On July 27th the following year her daughter Jessica was born. By the end of 1993 she had broken up with Arantes and returned to Great Britain on November 17th. She was divorced on June 26th, 1995.[142]

Rowling went to live with her sister in Edinburgh.[143] Back in Britain she faced social disaster. Without a professional education she couldn't find a job. To make things worse she was a single mother and had to care for her daughter which prevented her from taking up a full-time job.[144] She decided to begin a one year course to become a French teacher.[145] At that time she was already writing the first part of her *Harry Potter* series.

The genesis of *Harry Potter* has become part of the *Potter* legend. Rowling herself describes the decisive train ride between Manchester and London like this:

---

[137] See Kirk 2003, 47; Smith 2001, 89, 93; Christopher Wrigley, *The Return of the Hero*, Lewes: Book Guild, 2005, 13.

[138] See Hattenstone 2000; Kirk 2003, 50-53; Shapiro 2004, 45-47; Smith 2001, 94.

[139] See Shapiro 2004, 49.

[140] See Nel 2001, 17-20; Kirk 2003, 52; Matt Seaton, "If I could talk to my mum again I'd tell her I had a daughter – and I wrote some boks and guess what happened?" *Guardian* 18 Apr 2001. <http://books.guardian.co.uk/print/0,3858,4171517-99943,00.html> 3 Jan 2008; Shapiro 2004, 51; Smith 2001, 97-99.

[141] See Hattenstone 2000; Smith 2001, 100-111, 114; Nel 2001, 17-20.

[142] See Kirk 2003, 61; Smith 2001, 129.

[143] See Shapiro 2004, 58-60; Smith 2001, 114-115; Rebecca Sutherland Borah, "Apprentice Wizards Welcome. Fan Communities and the Culture of Harry Potter," *The Ivory Tower and Harry Potter: Perspectives on a Literary Phenomenon*, ed. Lana A. Whited, Columbia: University of Missouri Press, 2004, 343-364, here 350.

[144] See Nel 2001, 17-20.

[145] See Bak 2004, 59; Hattenstone 2000; Smith 2001, 128-129.

But in 1990, my then boyfriend and I decided to move up to Manchester together. It was [...] when I was travelling back to London on my own on a crowded train, the idea for Harry Potter simply fell into my head. [...] To my immense frustration, I didn't have a functioning pen with me, and I was too shy to ask anybody if I could borrow one. I think, now, that this was probably a good thing, because I simply sat and thought, for four (delayed train) hours, and all the details bubbled up in my brain, and this scrawny, black-haired, bespectacled boy who didn't know he was a wizard became more and more real to me. I think that perhaps if I had had to slow down the ideas so that I could capture them on paper I might have stifled some of them (although sometimes I do wonder, idly, how much of what I imagined on that journey I had forgotten by the time I actually got my hands on a pen). I began to write 'Philosopher's Stone' that very evening, although those first few pages bear no resemblance at all to anything in the finished book.[146]

With this, Rowling contradicts the legend of the poor single mother depending on social welfare that cures her depression writing *Harry Potter* in Edinburgh cafés. The idea was already in existence when she went to Portugal,[147] she began to write in Porto and merely finished *Philosopher's Stone* when she was back in Scotland. At the same time she was following her course as assistant teacher, but the burden of teaching, class preparation, child care and working on *Harry Potter* soon become to exhausting.[148] She had to decide whether to write her novel or to continue her course. Her sister Dianne encouraged her to give up teaching and to finish her book.[149] In 1994 she was awarded a £8,000 scholarship by the Scottish Arts Council and was able to finance her work on *Harry Potter*. One year later she finished *Philosopher's Stone*.[150]

The search for a publisher was very difficult. The text seemed too long for a children's book and was regarded as being unsaleable.[151] Finally, Bryony Evans and Fleur Howle, editors with Christopher Little, recognised the literary quality of the book. Because of their commitment the manuscript was

---

[146] Rowling 2006. Shapiro quotes Rowling: "I was sitting on the train, just staring out of the window at some cows. It was not the most inspiring subject. When all of a sudden the idea for Harry just appeared in my mind's eye. I can't tell you why or what triggered it. But I saw the idea of Harry and the wizard school very plainly. I suddenly had the basic idea of a boy who didn't know what he was." (Shapiro 2004, 49)

[147] "When I started writing the books, I was working, in a very happy relationship, life was fine, no one had died. Everything was okay." (Hattenstone 2000)

[148] See Hattenstone 2000; Smith 2001, 141.

[149] See Nel 2001, 21; Shapiro 2004, 66.

[150] See Nel 2001, 23-24.; Shapiro 2004, 71; Sutherland Borah 2004, 351. Shapiro sees *Philosopher's Stone* finished in 1994, which contradicts all other sources. Bürvenich says Rowling got the scholarship in February 1997 and used it to begin work *Chamber of Secrets* (see Bürvenich 2001, 15).

[151] See Eberhard Rathgeb, "Was meinst Du, Harry?" *F.A.Z.* 3 July 2000, 49.

accepted.[152] But still, the search for a publisher remained fruitless. Nine publishers had already refused the novel, when Bloomsbury, a small publishing house specialising in quality children's literature, bought the rights for £1,500 in 1996.[153] Legend has it that it was Bloomsbury's proof reader, Barry Cunningham, who decided to give the novel a chance.[154] In other sources we hear that it was the enthusiasm of the editor's eight-year-old daughter which made Bloomsbury publish *Harry Potter*.[155] But the concern was there that a novel written by a woman would not sell well to boys and Rowling was advised to neutralise her first name to "J.K. Rowling"[156]. There was also the possibility that her new title's resemblance to that of another successful writer, J.R.R. Tolkien, could go in Rowling's favour.[157] In 1997, before the novel was published in Great Britain, the international rights for *Harry Potter and the Philosopher's Stone* were auctioned at the children's book fair in Bologna. The American publisher Scholastic Press paid $100,000 – a sum unprecedented in the history of children's books. This made *Potter* an event before it was even published.[158] On June 26th 1997 *Philosopher's Stone* was finally published with a first edition of 500 copies.[159] But within the first few months of publication the book sold more than 150.000 copies.[160] Two years later Warner Bros bought the movie rights. Rowling insisted on a British cast and setting. She refused any attempt to Americanise her book. Negotiations with Steven Spielberg, who was supposed to direct the movie, were cancelled for this reason.[161]

By now, *Harry Potter* had already become a phenomenon. The plagiarism charges of Nancy Stouffer and Jane Yolen made for even more media coverage. Stouffer had published a novel (*The Legend of Rah and the Muggles*) in 1984. The protagonist is called Larry Potter, his mother is named Lily. But neither in court nor through literay criticism could the claims by Stouffer be proved.[162] The same is true for *Wizard's Hall*, a novel by Jane Yolen published in 1991 that is set in a boarding school for young wizards.[163] In 2001 Rowling published two

---

[152] See Smith 2001, 130-132. Shapiro speaks of £2,000 (Shapiro 2004, 75). See Sutherland Borah 2004, 351.
[153] See Smith 2001, 137
[154] See Bröll 2007.
[155] See Jenny 2007.
[156] See Seaton 2001; Shapiro 2004, 82.
[157] Rowling denies this: "'No, it was the publisher's idea,' she says. 'They were wary of me being a woman.' Bloomsbury thought it might put off the boys, so they made her androgynous." (Hattenstone 2000)
[158] See Shapiro 2004, 75, 79-80.
[159] Other sources speak of 1,000 copies. See Jenny 2007.
[160] See Shapiro 2004, 82; Smith 2001, 151.
[161] See Smith 2001, 174-175.
[162] Bürvenich deals extensively with these charges and dismisses them.
[163] See Kirk 2003, 100-101.

further *Potter* related books for Comic Relief: *Fantastic Beasts and Where To Find Them* under the alias of Newt Scamander and *Quidditch Through the Ages* as Kennilworthy Whisp.[164]

Literary success brought financial relief. Even before *Prisoner of Azkaban* was published in July 1999 Rowling was officially listed amongst the multi-millionaires[165] of Great Britain. The same year, Exeter University conferred upon her an honorary degree[166] and the Queen awarded her the "Order Of The British Empire".[167] By March 2001 Rowling had become the most internationally successful author ever; with sales of her books exceeding those of Stephen King, Agatha Christie and even the Bible. Up to that moment *Harry Potter* had already won 21 literary prizes. In 2000 there had been a public outcry because *Potter* had not been awarded the Whitbread Book Prize.[168]

Today Rowling's fortune is estimated to be about £820 million, a 2004 ranking showed her to be much richer than the Queen and listed Rowling as the 552nd of the world's richest people, i.e. the 150 richest people in Great Britain.[169] Rowling intends to continue writing after having finished the *Potter* series; "I will have lived with Harry for thirteen years and I know I'll probably have to take some time off to grieve. But then I'll be on with the next book."[170] Stuart Pearson Wright has painted a portrait of her which is now on display in the National Portrait Gallery in London.[171] But despite her fame Rowling has been very reserved with the media. Her public appearances are rare and still rather awkward.[172] The publication of the last *Potter* novel came as a liberation, says Rowling.[173] She has no intention of writing another sequel or of returning to Harry's magical world. We must consider *Harry Potter* – finally – completed.

---

[164] See Nel 2001, 26. I am not going to deal with these two, because they are mere "spin-offs" of the series.
[165] See Smith 2001, 181.
[166] See Smith 2001, 82.
[167] See Shapiro 2004, 118.
[168] See Smith 2001, 197.
[169] See David Teather, "Harry Potter's adventures propel JK Rowling to billionares' row," *Guardian* 27 Feb 2004. <http://books.guardian.co.uk/print/0,3858,4868111-99943, 00.html> 3 Jan 2008; Felicitas von Lovenberg, "Im Bann des Guten. Auch im fünften 'Harry Potter' macht J.K. Rowling alles richtig," *F.A.Z.* 24 June 2003, 34; Jenny 2007; Bröll 2007.
[170] See Shapiro 2004, 102.
[171] See Gina Thomas, "Unkorrumpiert vom Ruhm," *F.A.Z.* 10 Sep 2005, 37.
[172] See Felicitas von Lovenberg, "Ein regelrechtes Blutbad," *F.A.Z.* 13 July 2007, 40.
[173] See Christoph Dallach, "Verhexte Orte" *SPIEGEL* 41/2007, 220.

I.2.B. How Much Rowling is in "Potter"?
– Parallels between Novel and Biography

For a long time now, Rowling has become part of her own myth and has hinted at intended parallels between her fictional creation and her own reality. She is "as perfect a contemporary hero as her creation. [...] no author could be a more ideal role model."[174] Therefore, it seems necessary to investigate the possible relationship between the author's personal experience and her novels.

The most obvious parallels between facts and fiction can be found in specific dates Rowling uses in her books: Harry was born on July 31st which is Rowling's own birthday (1966).[175] In *Prisoner of Azkaban* "Divination" teacher Sybill Trelawney tells Lavender Brown of the event she fears is going to take place on Friday, October 16th (HP 3, pp. 115 and 162). This is the day Rowling married Jorge Arantes in 1992.[176] In these cases the author deliberately uses parts of her own biography in the books. She even refers to her home; in *Deathly Hallows* we find Harry and Hermione camping in the Forest of Dean (HP 7, 297), which is precisely where Rowling grew up.

Further connections between Harry Potter and Rowling's own experiences may be found in individual characters. For a long time the tabloid press has tried to decipher which character has been inspired by whom. Finally, former neighbours of the Rowlings in Winterbourne declared their son to be Harry Potter's prototype. Rowling immediately refused, saying that she had never had her former neighbour's boy in mind while writing *Harry Potter*.[177]

The author likes to be portrayed as Harry's mother. Actress Geraldine Agnew-Somerville who plays Lily Potter in the movies, looks strikingly like Rowling.[178] Frequently, Rowling has pointed out how similar she is to her favourite character Hermione. When interviewed, she has said "If I were a character in the book, I'd probably be Hermione. She's a lot like me when I was younger. (I wasn't that clever but I was definitely that annoying at times!)".[179] She has gone on to say: "[If] Hermione was based on anyone, she was based on me when I was younger."[180] Hermione's "Patronus" is an otter – which happens

---

[174] See Blacker 1999.
[175] See Schafer 2000, 35; Shapiro 2004, 19.
[176] See Kirk 2003, 56; Smith 2001, 114.
[177] See Rowling 2006; Shapiro 2004, 27; Smith 2001, 30.
[178] See Kirk 2003, 3.
[179] Joanne Kathleen Rowling, Live Interview on Scholastic.com, www.scholastic.com, 16 Oct 2000. <http://www.scholastic.com/harrypotter/author/transcript2.htm> 3 Jan 2008.
[180] Rowling, Live Interview, 3 Feb 2000; see Mimi R. Gladstein, "Feminism and Equal Opportunity: Hermione and the Women of Hogwarts," *Harry Potter and philosophy: If Aristotle ran Hogwarts*, eds. Baggett & Klein, Chicago, La Salle: Open Court, 2004, 49-59, here 50.

to be Rowling's favourite animal.[181] The author's grandfathers Stan Volant and Ernie Rowling seem to be the role models for the driver team on the "Knight Bus",[182] whereas her grandmother Frieda Volant, who supposedly loved her dogs more than her grandchildren, might be regarded as prototype for Marge Dursley.[183] The unfair and often sadistic "Potions" teacher Severus Snape obviously unifies character traits of Rowling's primary school teacher Mrs Morgan and her chemistry teacher John Nettleship.[184] Gilderoy Lockhart, the inveterate show-off, is Rowling's comment on bragging bestseller authors.[185] Minerva McGonagall seems to have been inspired by Lucy Shepherd, the young English teacher who encouraged Rowling to write stories,[186] and Fleur Delacour's first name probably was taken from her editor Fleur Howle.[187] Rowling herself admits to have a liking for bizarre and rare names: "I was born in a place called Chipping, so perhaps that explains my love of silly names."[188] One of her favourite inspirations for finding these names is cemeteries.[189]

But there are more parallels between Rowling's life and her novels than just the characters' names. The dominating theme of longing for parents' love can be seen as Rowling's attempt to come to terms with her mother's death. When Harry sees his family in the "Mirror of Erised" in *Philosopher's Stone* for the first time we are reminded especially of Rowling's wish to tell her mother of her literary success.[190]

Having returned to Scotland after her years in Portugal, Rowling suffered from depression. In the novel she describes this state of mind precisely in the effect the "Dementors" have on their victims.[191] Even Harry's and Ron's flight to Hogwarts in a Ford Anglia (*Chamber of Secrets*) has a parallel to Rowling's own experiences: she dedicated the novel to Séan P. F. Harris, "getaway driver and foulweather friend", the teenage friend who helped her to escape the provincial claustrophobia with his turquoise Ford Anglia.[192] For a couple of months Rowling worked for Amnesty International – and she comments upon this time

---

[181] See Smith 2001, 25.
[182] See Kirk 2003, 15.
[183] See Kirk 2003; Smith 2001, 40.
[184] See Kirk 2003, 31, 35; Smith 2001, 54-55.
[185] Rowling says: "The only character who is deliberately based on a real person is Gilderoy Lockhart." (Joanne Kathleen Rowling, Transcript of J.K. Rowling's interview at the Edinburgh International Book Festival, www.scholastic.com 15 Aug 2004. <http://www.scholastic.com/harrypotter/author/transcript4.htm> 8 Jan 2007.
[186] See Smith 2001, 57-58.
[187] See Smith 2001, 130-132.
[188] See Rowling, Live Interview, 3 Feb 2000.
[189] See Kirk 2003, 29.
[190] See Hattenstone 2000; Maar 2003, 150; Smith 2001, 99.
[191] See Smith 2001, 122-125.
[192] See Kirk 2003, 40-41; Smith 2001, 73-74.

satirically when Hemione gets involved with "SPEW".[193] Like Harry and his friends she experienced the fear of teachers.[194] Like Hermione and Ron, who become school prefects, Rowling herself was elected head girl. She therefore knows the conflict between authority and friendship she describes in the text.[195] Furthermore, we must suppose Rowling to be familiar with Portuguese history. When she names one of the villains of her books Salazar, she almost certainly has Portuguese fascist dictator António de Oliveira Salazar (1889-1970) in mind.[196] In the novels, many important events take place on Halloween (see II.4, 76). Rowling frequently has said that Halloween is her favourite time of the year.[197] When she condemns social arrogance (see V.1.G, 303), we can interpret this as part of her own experience when she was refused by Oxford University.[198]

These parallels are more or less guesswork. But in one singular case Rowling deliberately refers to a real life incident. In 1999 the family of Canadian Natalie McDonald contacted Rowling. They asked for a handwritten letter for their daughter suffering from leukaemia. Rowling responded too late and the letter arrived in Canada only after Natalie's death. In *Goblet of Fire* the name "McDonald, Natalie" is sorted in Hogwarts and she becomes a "Gryffindor" (HP 4, 199).[199]

---

[193] See Nel 2001, 17.
[194] See Shapiro 2004, 32-34; Smith 2001, 35-36.
[195] See Seaton 2001; Shapiro 2004, 39; Steege 2004, 140.
[196] See Jung 2004, 102-103.
[197] See Schafer 2000, 36; Shapiro 2004, 11.
[198] See Smith 2001, 75.
[199] Joanne Kathleen Rowling, *Harry Potter and the Goblet of Fire*, London: Bloomsbury, 2000 (henceforth: HP 4). See Nel 2001, 25; Shapiro 2004, 104-108.

II. The Narrative Structure of "Harry Potter"

Umberto Eco wrote, "A novel is a machine for creating interpretations,"[1] and concluded: "The author should meet his maker directly after finishing his text. Thus, he wouldn't interfere with its dynamics."[2] Eco says this because the main characteristic of the novel is its indirectness and its being open to interpretation. So when I am analysing the narrative structures of *Harry Potter*, I will mainly deal with two questions: who narrates the novels and what is the structure of their plots? To what extent does J.K. Rowling follow the well-known patterns of fantasy and children's literature? As the series, from a narratological point of view, is not very complex, I will mainly refer to the classics of narratology: Frank Stanzel's *Theorie des Erzählens* and E. M. Forster's *Aspects of the Novel*.

II.1 Point of View – What Does it Mean?

The analysis of the narrative situation of a text has two main aspects: the author and the (fictitious) narrator. The author being the creator of the text forms his characters, and as a deliberate consequence, the narrator, as part of his creation. E. M. Forster underlines this fact saying:

> [The] reader may be moving about in worlds unrealized, but the novelist has no misgivings. He is competent, poised above his work, throwing a beam of light here, popping on a cap of invisibility there, and (*qua* plot-maker) continually negotiating with himself *qua* character-monger as to the best effect to be produced. He plans his book beforehand: [...].[3]

The author has to decide in which way the narrator shall be part of the text. He may choose to make him an active character of the story or to let him stay in the background. Each possibility opens up different varieties of procuring information for the reader. Plato was the first to define the difference between *diegesis* and *mimesis*. The first refers to the indirect form, i.e. with a figural narrator, the

---

1 Umberto Eco, *Nachschrift zum Namen der Rose*, Munich: Carl Hanser, 1984, 10 [my translation].

2 Eco 1984, 14 [my translation]. Rowling herself gives us a very good example for what Eco means concerning the relationship between author and text: when in a New York reading she said frankly that she imagined Dumbledore to be homosexual, fansites exploded with postings and newspapers were filled with reports on the subject (see "Zauberer-Outing: Dumbledore ist schwul," *SPIEGEL Online* 20 Oct 2007 <http://www.spiegel.de/kultur/literatur/0,1518,512613,00.html> 3 Jan 2008). Although the news has thrilled fans all over the world, this is not relevant from a scientific point of view: as long as the text itself does not hint at Dumbledore's sexual orientation Rowling's revelation must be regarded as literary "yellow press gossip".

3 Forster [1927] 1985, 96.

second to the readers' pretended direct access to information. The modern terms for more or less the same distinction are "telling" and "showing".[4]

There are four ways to communicate with the reader: description, report, dialogue and comment.[5] Presumably the most direct form of communication is letting a character speak,[6] followed by a narrator's report of what a character has actually spoken. In this case, the narrator filters the information he reports and decides what to pass on to the reader and what to hide. Usually, this kind of text is written in the third person with times and places shifted from "now" to "then" and "here" to "there".[7] In case the author does not use any verbs of speech and thought (*verba dicendi* or *cogitandi*) and shifts time and place,[8] indirect speech becomes free indirect discourse, a kind of "monologue of thoughts". "Interior monologue" is a form without an apparent narrator and with the characters directly communicating their feelings and impressions to the reader.[9] If the text is written in the first person and neither uses *verba dicendi* and *cogitandi* nor punctuation, we speak of "stream of consciousness". Texts written in that style are usually not structured logically, but mostly pretend to reflect a person's thoughts.[10]

Franz Stanzel names three main components for defining the point of view of a text: *modus* (mode), *person* (person) and *perspektive* (perspective).[11] The mode of a text refers to the degree of directness in the communication between author, narrator and reader[12] and translates Plato's distinction between *diegesis* and *mimesis* as "telling" and "showing" or "simple narration" and "scenic presentation" (scene).[13]

Stanzel uses the category *person* to describe the kind of personification of the narrator and to define its *seinsbereich* (realm of existence or world). If narrator and characters act on the same level of "reality" he speaks of "identische Seinsbereiche" (identical worlds).[14] For Stanzel one of the decisive criteria to define the point of view is the position of the narrator inside or outside the action:[15] if the narrator is part of the action and acts in the same world as the

---

4 See Stanzel [1975] 2001, 93, 162.
5 See Stanzel [1975] 2001, 93. Stanzel refers to Robert Petsch and Helmut Bonheim.
6 See Sonja Fielitz, *Roman: Text & Kontext*, Berlin: Cornelsen Verlag, 2001, 92.
7 See Fielitz 2001, 92-93.
8 This criterion is decisive for Genette (Genette 1998, 122-123).
9 See Fielitz 2001, 96.
10 See Fielitz 2001, 97.
11 See Fielitz 2001, 37-38; Stanzel [1975] 2001, 70.
12 See Stanzel [1975] 2001, 190.
13 See Stanzel [1975] 2001, 191.
14 See Stanzel [1975] 2001, 191.
15 This is precisely the difference Genette makes between extra- and intra-diegetic (see 26).

characters, Stanzel speaks of a first-person narrative situation. All other cases are either authorial or figural narrative situations.[16]

The third component, *perspektive* has two sub-categories. If the figural narrator reports from his own point of view, Stanzel speaks of *innenperspektive* (internal perspective).[17] If the narrator is positioned outside the action, Stanzel speaks of *aussenperspektive* (external perspective).[18] The latter one is closely related to the authorial narrative situation whereas the first one is marked by the narrator's limited point of view.[19] Using these categories Stanzel defines three narrative situations: authorial, figural and first-person narrative situation.[20]

The first decision an author must make is if he wants to use a first- or a third-person narrator.[21] No matter which form he chooses, the narrator (and thus the author) selects the information the reader gets.[22] The authorial narrator knows the past, present and future of the plot and its characters. The author uses *verba cogitandi* or *dicendi* and sometimes comments on the events. Usually the text is written in the present tense third person singular.[23] On the contrary, the first-person narrator is part of the events and very often the protagonist of the plot. This is not to be confused with the term of "reflector", a narrator that presents the events through a kind of interior monologue.[24] He relates the events directly from his point of view and does not justify the way he selects the information he gives the reader. There are also texts with an authorial narrative situation including a reflector.[25] Practically, there are hardly any texts that are narrated from one point of view only, usually various forms can be found in one text.

Gérard Genette prefers to use the term "narrative focus" instead of "point of view" or "narrative situation". From this he deducts the word "focalisation".[26] According to him there are two kinds of narration. If the reader receives more information than he needs or than the narrator logically can have at a given moment in the plot, Genette speaks of a "paralepsis".[27] The opposite case, where the reader gets less information than is available to the narrator or is required to

---

[16] See Fielitz 2001, 37-38.
[17] See Stanzel [1975] 2001, 27.
[18] See Stanzel [1975] 2001, 76.
[19] See Stanzel [1975] 2001, 170.
[20] See Stanzel [1975] 2001, 80.
[21] See Stanzel [1975] 2001, 71.
[22] See Stanzel [1975] 2001, 201.
[23] See Fielitz 2001, 40.
[24] See Stanzel [1975] 2001, 199.
[25] See Stanzel [1975] 2001, 198.
[26] See Genette 1998, 115.
[27] See Genette 1998, 236.

understand the plot, Genette calls "paralipsis".[28] This is a technique often used in detective novels.[29]

Another important criterion for defining a text's narrative structure according to Genette is "voice". Genette defines two different types of stories: the ones where the narrator is not part of the story he tells (heterodiegetic narration) and the ones where he is present in the plot (homodiegetic narration).[30] In addition to this Genette introduces the terms "intradiegetic" and "extradiegetic narration". If the narrator belongs to the text's world, it is an intradiegetic narration. If this is not the case, it is extradiegetic. Thus, Genette defines the following matrix of four different points of view:

- Extradiegetic-heterodiegetic: The narrator tells a story in which he is not present. He does not act in the text's world.
- Extradiegetic-homodiegetic: The narrator tells a story about himself, but is not part of the text's world. This is the case, for example, when he speaks about events of the past.
- Intradiegetic-heterodiegetic: The narrator is part of the story but is not present in the action (Genette refers here to Scheherazade of *One Thousand and One Nights*)
- Intradiegetic-homodiegetic: The narrator tells his own story at the time it is happening.[31]

II.1.A. The Structure of the Plot

The plot of a novel consists of many different elements that make up its structure. We must differentiate between the structure of the plot and the organisation of the text. Manfred Pfister calls the first kind *tiefenstruktur* (deep structure) and the second *oberflächenstruktur* (surface structure).[32] Both of these types correspond or contrast with each other.[33]

Dealing with the surface structure, the first information the reader gets about a text is its title as well as the titles of the individual chapters. A novel's title raises the reader's expectations and communicates directly with the target group of the book – something that has become increasingly important for the modern book market. The title may do any of the following:[34]

- indicate the main topic (*Gulliver's Travels*).
- name parts of the main plot.

---

28   See Genette 1998, 139.
29   See Genette 1998, 139. This type of paralepsis is typical for the series (see II.4.D, 87).
30   See Genette 1998, 175.
31   See Genette 1998, 120, 178.
32   See Pfister [1977] 2001, 307-308.
33   See Pfister [1977] 2001, 307-308.
34   See Fielitz 2001, 139-140.

- name the central characters of the text (*David Copperfield, Jane Eyre*).
- name roles in society (*The Vicar of Wakefield*).
- name traits of character.
- refer to things or objects central to the plot (*Perfume*).
- use well-known expressions and quotations.
- use oppositions.
- name social conditions.
- use stylistic devices.

Among other things, the author can use titles to:
- raise the readers' expectations.
- introduce the protagonist (*Hamlet*).
- comment on a character and his behaviour (*Le malade imaginaire*).
- indicate the time the story takes place (*Twelfth Night*).

This information can be deliberately wrong to confuse the reader and to play with his expectations.

In 1927 E. M. Forster stated: "We shall all agree that the fundamental aspect of the novel is its story-telling aspect."[35] He was the first author to differentiate between story and plot. The story consists of the events in their chronological order:

> [Story] is a narrative of events arranged in their time sequence – dinner coming after breakfast, Tuesday after Monday, decay after death, and so on. Qua story, it can only have one merit: that of making the audience want to know what happens next. And conversely it can only have one fault: that of making the audience not want to know what happens next. These are the only two criticisms that can be made on the story that is a story.[36]

The story is the heart of the novel, as Forster points out to his students[37] and he asks them to respect it as such:

> I must ask you to join me in repeating in exactly the right tone of voice the words with which this lecture opened. Do not say them vaguely and good-temperedly like a busman: you have not the right. Do not say them briskly and aggressively like a golfer: you know better. Say them a little sadly, and you will be correct. Yes – oh, dear, yes – the novel tells a story.[38]

---

35 Forster [1927] 1985, 25.
36 Forster [1927] 1985, 27.
37 "[The story] runs like a backbone [...]." (Forster [1927] 1985, 26); "[The] basis of a novel is a story, and a story is a narrative of events arranged in their time sequence." (Forster [1927] 1985, 30)
38 Forster [1927] 1985, 42.

The story is the backbone of the novel – the plot consists of its logical and causal order. In the aesthetic order of the novel the plot is of much higher value than the story.[39] Forster explains the difference between story and plot with the following legendary words:

> Let us define a plot. We have defined a story as a narrative of events arranged in their time-sequence. A plot is also a narrative of events, the emphasis falling on causality. "The king died and then the queen died" is a story. "The king died, and then the queen died of grief" is a plot. The time sequence is preserved, but the sense of causality overshadows it.[40]

Usually a novel has more than one (main) plot, and adds various sub-plots to it. Normally, those have a special function in reference to the main plot. Manfred Pfister names the following possible functions among others:[41]
- aesthetic function (providing diversion)
- raising attention (interruption of the main plot)
- integrative function (referring to the main plot)
- emphatic function (repeating elements of the main plot)

Pfister goes on to explain how the sub-plots can be connected to the main plot:[42]
- Additive connection: There is no relation between the narrative levels, which leads to very detailed narration.
- Correlative connection: The narrative levels contrast with each other, the sub-plot is often an allegorical version of the main-plot.
- Consecutive connection: The result of one plot sets another plot in motion.
- Interfering connection: the event of one plot leads to the next event of the other plot.

Basically, there are two different types of plots: the closed and the open plot.[43] The first has a clearly defined beginning (point of attack) and an ending, where all plots and sub-plots come to a conclusion. All mysteries are explained.[44] Poetic justice rewards the "good" characters with riches, honour or happiness and strikes the "bad" characters with loss of influence or social prestige and personal or financial losses. All conflicts are solved and the author's intention is obvious.[45] The open plot does not have a hierarchic structure in its

---

[39] See Forster [1927] 1985, 85.
[40] See Forster [1927] 1985, 86-87.
[41] See Pfister [1977] 2001, 291-294.
[42] See Fielitz 2001, 108-109.
[43] See Fielitz 2001, 110-112.
[44] See Fielitz 2001, 110-112.
[45] See Pfister [1977] 2001, 138-139.

characters, their intentions remain unclear, and their communication is unsatisfying. The action consists of more or less arbitrarily connected scenes in anachronistic order. Usually, there are various autonomous sub-plots. The text ends without a solution.[46]

Whether he chooses the open or the closed form, the author has to elaborate the way he raises and maintains the readers' attention carefully. Tension arises when the reader believes he lacks information. In this case he tries to guess in what way the plot or its characters will develop. The more the reader identifies with the protagonist the more tension he will feel.[47] The author can raise tension by introducing dream sequences, prophecies or intrigues.[48] One characteristic of narration is that the chronological order of events may be changed deliberately. Eco sees this as the true art of the novelist:

> A great novel is a novel where the author knows precisely when to accelerate and when to slow down and how he has to use his pedals while keeping up the basic rhythm of his narration.[49]

The basic elements of analysing a text's temporal structure according to Gérard Genette are:[50]

- order
- duration
- frequency

If the author changes the chronological order of events, Genette speaks of "anachrony" and defines "analepsis" (flashback; see figure 1) and "prolepsis" (anticipation; see figure 2). The author can use an analepsis to give the reader additional information. The "external analepsis" refers to events that happened before the point of attack.[51] "Internal analepsis" deals with what happened after the point of attack but before the moment they are narrated within the text.

On the contrary, a prolepsis is used to narrate things that will happen in the future.[52] Again, Genette differentiates the internal and external prolepsis.[53] A special variation of the prolepsis is the clue, a seemingly unimportant incident which only becomes relevant in retrospect. It is a clue which hints at the solution of a riddle or, in the case of a detective novel, at the murderer. If the author

---

[46] See Pfister [1977] 2001, 140.
[47] See Pfister [1977] 2001, 142-143.
[48] See Pfister [1977] 2001, 144-146.
[49] Eco 1984, 50 [my translation].
[50] See Fielitz 2001, 30-31.
[51] See Fielitz 2001, 33.
[52] See Fielitz 2001, 25.
[53] See Fielitz 2001, 46.

writes for experienced readers he can pervert this pattern and give them "false clues" or (*leurres*) or even "false false clues" (*faux leurres*).[54]

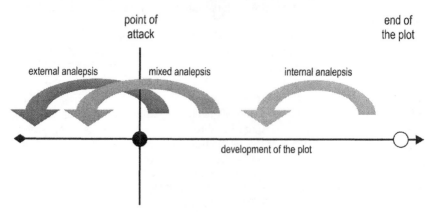

Figure 1: Analepsis according to Genette

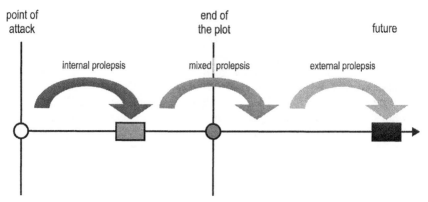

Figure 2: Prolepsis according to Genette

The duration of a narration is determined by two aspects. "Discourse time" describes the time it takes the narrator to present the events, and "narrative" or "story time" refers to the length of time that the plot actually takes. The relation between the two is one of the most important features of a text.[55] Genette defines three possible variations: "scene", "pause" and "ellipsis". Be-

---

[54] See Fielitz 2001, 52-53. I will show that J.K. Rowling uses this technique very often. Genette's *leurres* shall be called "red herrings" in English.

[55] Eco 1984, 57.

cause of the high percentage of dialogue, time of narration and narrated time are nearly equal in the scene. The pause serves to introduce detailed descriptions,[56] whereas the ellipsis is a narrative gap which gives no information and in which time does not proceed.

In addition, Genette mentions the summary, which sums up minor events and serves to connect two scenes.[57] The third category of analysing the time structure of a text is narrative frequency, i.e. the relationship between the time an event actually occurs in the text and the time in which it is narrated.[58]

In analysing the time structure of *Harry Potter* I will concentrate on the chronologial order and the speed of the narration.

II.1.B. The Narrative Structure of Detective Stories

The narrative structure of the detective novel has been analysed by Ellen Schwarz[59] and Beatrix Finke.[60] These studies shall provide the theoretical basis for analysing the time structure of *Harry Potter*.

The point of view is the decisive element of the detective novel. The author, gradually providing bits of information, gives the reader the chance to solve the mystery on his own.[61] He may give him false clues[62] (see 30) and play with his expectations and illusions.[63] To allow the reader to be a participant in the ideas of the detective, authors mostly use free indirect discourse (see 24).[64]

Beatrix Finke makes out three possible narrative focuses for the detective novel: (a) the omniscient narrator, (b) the detective as first-person narrator and (c) the victim's point of view. The two latter techniques are typical for the genre. If the detective is the first-person narrator (b) he is usually the protagonist. The reader has free indirect discourse,[65] which is a supposedly direct access to the detective's thoughts and feelings[66] and is misled each time the detective makes a mistake.[67] The reader relies on the detective's interpretations of the events and

---

[56] See Genette 1998, 71, 213-214.
[57] See Genette 1998, 69.
[58] See Genette 1998, 82-83.
[59] Ellen Schwarz, *Der phantastische Kriminalroman: Untersuchungen zu Parallelen zwischen "roman policier", "conte fantastique" und "Gothic Novel"*, Marburg: Tectum, 2001.
[60] Beatrix Finke, *Erzählsituationen und Figurenperspektiven im Detektivroman*, Amsterdam: Grüner, 1983.
[61] See Schwarz 2001, 284.
[62] See Schwarz 2001, 134.
[63] See Schwarz 2001, 207.
[64] See Finke 1983, 93; Schwarz 2001, 286.
[65] See Schwarz 2001, 188.
[66] See Finke 1983, 143.
[67] See Finke 1983, 195.

trusts him completely.[68] This corresponds with Stanzel's figural narrative situation.[69] If the text is written from the victim's point of view, the reader takes the side of the persecuted, threatened character.[70] He suffers the same fear and tension as the crime victim.[71] The dominant narrative technique is free indirect discourse or interior monologue.[72]

The detective novel does not intend to represent reality and therefore very often relies on unrealistic plots, in which chance or luck are key elements.[73] The plot is characterised by a lack of information and it focuses on events that happened before the point of attack. Usually, two plots are interwoven: the one of the detective trying to solve the "whodunnit" (detective plot) and the plot that explains why and how the crime was committed (story of the crime).

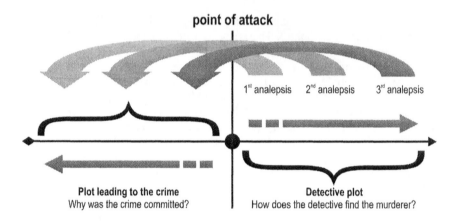

Figure 3: Narrative Structure of the Detective Novel

The development of the plot normally follows a simple pattern: at the beginning, all of a sudden, the everyday life of the protagonist is shaken by the crime,[74] and investigations begin. In one thing the detective novel differs from nearly all other narrations: it is told *à rebours*, i.e. it begins at the end of the story of the crime, when the deed is done. The point of attack is precisely at the end of one of the two stories. In the detecting part of the plot, the detective tries

---

68 See Finke 1983, 275.
69 See Finke 1983, 185.
70 See Schwarz 2001, 135.
71 See Schwarz 2001, 259.
72 See Finke 1983, 207.
73 See Schwarz 2001, 129.
74 See Schwarz 2001, 131.

to find out why the crime was committed and reconstructs the events before the point of attack. At the end of the text the mystery is solved by explaining why, how and by whom the crime was committed.[75] The detective plot is frequently interrupted by flashbacks, discoveries and figural narration. This results in anachronisms, mostly analepsis.[76]

Beatrix Finke defines a special plot pattern for the novel written from the victim's point of view: again, the text begins with the crime, but this time, the protagonist has a personal relation to the suspect or to the room in which the crime was committed. There is no detective and the authorities are not able to protect the protagonist, who must fear to be the criminal's next victim. Only in the last moment he is saved from danger.[77] I will show that these exact structural characteristics of the detective novel can be found in *Harry Potter*.

II.2 The Narrative Structures of the "Harry Potter" Novels

The relation between author and reader features quite prominently throughout the whole series. More than once characters must realise that the "real" author of a book is in no way the person they imagined. Questions of authorship and the narrator's reliability provide the background for the episodes about Gilderoy Lockhart, Riddle's diary[78] and finally the "Potions" book in *Half-Blood Prince*. Lockhart pretends to be the hero of his stories – in fact he has stolen the memories of others and constructs a non-existing self. Tom Riddle turns the relation between author and reader upside down when he communicates with his reader through his diary. The "unreliability of the constructed authors of books, who exist in the readers' imagination is the *leitmotif* of *Chamber*."[79] Only at the end of *Half-Blood Prince* Harry finds out that the author of his "Potions" book is none other than his archenemy Severus Snape. Moreover, we see books in the *Harry Potter* novels leading a life of their own as for example the "Monster Book of Monsters" (HP 3[80], 19-20).[81] So, books and the way they are written are important elements of the *Harry Potter* series.

---

[75] See Schwarz 2001, 132.
[76] See Schwarz 2001, 133.
[77] See Finke 1983, 206.
[78] See Gupta 2003, 36-37; Friedhelm Munzel, "Harry Potter und die lebendigen Bücher. Aspekte zur Faszination des Lesens aus bibliotherapeutischer Sicht," *Faszination 'Harry Potter': Was steckt dahinter?* eds. Detlev Dormeyer, Friedhelm Munzel, Münster: LIT, 2005, 83-94.
[79] See Gupta 2003, 37.
[80] Joanne Kathleen Rowling, *Harry Potter and the Prisoner of Azkaban*, London: Blooms-bury, 1999 (henceforth: HP 3).
[81] See Gupta 2003, 38.

II.2.A. Point of View – Harry as Focaliser

The *Harry Potter* novels are narrated in an extradiegetic-heterodiegetic narrative situation (see 26), i.e. the narrator is not part of the story and does not belong to the text's world, referring to Stanzel's terminology (see 24). Harry's perspective is the dominant point of view and according to Genette he is the focaliser. Emer O'Sullivan believes the texts to be chronological and presented by an omniscient narrator who often comments on or even interferes with the action.[82] Thus, she misunderstands the point of view, for in the *Harry Potter* novels there is no figural narrator. Only in very rare cases the reader is addressed directly:

> When Mr and Mrs Dursley woke up on the dull, grey Tuesday our story starts, there was nothing about the cloudy sky outside to suggest that strange and mysterious things would soon be happening all over the country. (HP 1, 8)[83]

"Our story" forms a community of perception between reader and narrator. Harry's point of view is dominant throughout the series. This is obvious on the first pages of *Philosopher's Stone*. At the beginning, the Dursleys are referred to as: "Mr and Mrs Dursley of number four, Privet Drive, were proud to say that they were perfectly normal, thank you very much." (HP 1, 7) This changes continously, and the reader is obliged to take Harry's point of view. Only a few pages later Mrs Dursley becomes "his Aunt Petunia" (HP 1, 25) and "his aunt" (HP 1, 26) and finally "Aunt Petunia" (HP 1, 28). Accepting the word "aunt" makes the reader share Harry's relation with his family. This effect is enhanced by the author / narrator using words from the magical world without further explaining them: when parts of the "Quidditch" pitch are described as resembling "the little plastic sticks Muggle children blew bubbles through" (HP 1, 182), the reader has to accept that from now on non-magical people will be "Muggles". The reader shares the magical community's point of view. The distance between "Muggles" and the reader widens, when non-magicians prove to be uninformed and stupid as for example the prime minister who thinks about "Kwidditch" (HP 6[84], 14) – a misspelling, which in this case signifies a misunderstanding of the supposedly real word.[85] Harry's sufferings at the hands of his

---

[82] Emer O'Sullivan, "Der Zauberlehrling im Internat. Harry Potter im Kontext der britischen Literaturtradition," *"Alohomora!" Ergebnisse des Ersten Wiener Harry-Potter-Symposions*, ed. Heidi Lexe, Wien: Edition Praesens, 2002, 15-39, here 33.

[83] Joanne Kathleen Rowling, *Harry Potter and the Philosopher's Stone* [1997], London: Bloomsbury, 2000 (henceforth: HP 1).

[84] Joanne Kathleen Rowling, *Harry Potter and the Half-Blood Prince*, London: Bloomsbury, 2005 (henceforth HP 6).

[85] Reinhard Ehgartner and Sandra Bak call this technique "zooming in" (see Bak 2004, 105-106; Reinhard Ehgartner, "J.K. Rowlings Harry-Potter-Romane in literarischen

family play an important role in the process of making the reader feel empathy for the hero. Mary Pharr points out that this is a "gateway into empathy".[86]

Throughout the text we find countless examples for the intense relation between the reader and Harry himself: his descriptions of rooms, character, feelings as well as judgements and comments are directly communicated to the reader. The degree of insight we get from Harry has no parallel in any other character. For example, the reader experiences a trip to the Ministry of Magic through Harry's eyes. The telephone box he and Mr Weasley have entered slowly sinks into the ground and Harry describes what he sees when they reach the entrance hall:

> After about a minute, though it felt much longer to Harry, a chink of golden light illuminated his feet and, widening, rose up his body until it hit him in the face and he had to blink to stop his eyes watering. (HP 5[87], 144)

The reader is just as nervous as Harry and feels time advancing slowly ("it felt much longer"). Like the protagonist the reader is blinded by the light. When Harry arrives in Hogsmeade a little later, again the reader experiences Harry's impressions – this time the smell of pine trees (HP 5, 219).[88] And when Mr Weasley has been badly wounded by Voldemort's snake the reader relives Harry's fear for his friend: "If Harry had ever sat through a longer night than this one, he could not remember it." (HP 5, 257) The reader has direct unfiltered access to Harry's thoughts and emotions as the following quotations show:

> Harry felt the fear drain out of him. He knew the snake wouldn't attack anyone now, though how he knew it, he couldn't have explained. (HP 2[89], 211) Harry's feeling of barely controlled panic was with him wherever he went, [...]. (HP 4[90], 349)

Koordinaten," *"Alohomora!" Ergebnisse des Ersten Wiener Harry-Potter-Symposions*, ed. Heidi Lexe, Wien: Edition Praesens, 2002, 61-81 here 62-63).

[86] Mary Pharr regards the Dursleys as a major source of funny or even grotesque situations: "Never really frightening but always nasty and absurd – [the Dursleys] are a way for the author to preserve both real sympathy for Harry and an easily accessible humor for narrative. Those who are supposed to be normal are so preposterous that we are immediately prompted to like not only their victim but also the metanormal world he is entering." (Pharr 2004, 57)

[87] Joanne Kathleen Rowling, *Harry Potter and the Order of the Phoenix*, London: Bloomsbury, 2003 (henceforth: HP 5).

[88] The same could be expressed by saying, "The smell of pine trees was in the air."

[89] Joanne Kathleen Rowling, *Harry Potter and the Chamber of Secrets* [1998], London: Bloomsbury, 2000 (henceforth: HP 2).

[90] Joanne Kathleen Rowling, *Harry Potter and the Goblet of Fire*, London: Bloomsbury, 2000 (henceforth: HP 4).

This is especially evident when Harry kisses Cho for the first time:[91]

> He could not think. A tingling sensation was spreading through him, paralysing his arms, legs and brain. She was much too close. He could see every tear clinging to her eyelashes ...
>
> *
>
> He returned to the common room half an hour later to find Hermione and Ron in the best seats by the fire; [...]. (HP 5, 503)

Even the perception of time depends on Harry's point of view as one of the first scenes in *Philosopher's Stone* shows:[92]

> The lighted dial of Dudley's watch [...] told Harry he'd be eleven in ten minutes' time. [...] Five minutes to go. Harry heard something creak outside. [...] Three minutes to go. Was that the sea, slapping hard on the rock like that? And (two minutes to go) what was that funny crunching noise? Was the rock crumbling into the sea? One minute to go and he'd be eleven. Thirty seconds ... twenty ... ten – nine – maybe he'd wake Dudley up, just to annoy him – three – two – one – BOOM. (HP 1, 54)

Rowling's style is marked by the use of free indirect discourse. Usually, she uses two variants of it: the interior monologue written in the third person, and questions Harry asks himself. The following quotation is an example of the first form:

> If he was already expelled (his heart was now thumping painfully fast), a bit more magic couldn't hurt. He had the Invisibility Cloak he had inherited from his father – what if he bewitched the trunk to make it feather-light, tied it to his broomstick, covered himself in the Cloak and flew to London? Then he could get the rest of his money out of his vault and ... begin his life as an outcast. (HP 3, 40)

Transcribed into direct speech the text could read:

> "But if I'm going to be expelled anyway, a bit more magic can't hurt. I have the Invisibility Cloak I have inherited from my father – what if I bewitch the trunk to make it feather-light, tie it to my broomstick, cover myself in the

---

[91] Reinhard Ehgartner quotes another scene to explain the same phenomenon. At the end of *Philosopher's Stone* Harry falls unconscious and only awakes in the hospital wing – as does the reader (see Ehgartner 2002, 63).

[92] Another example is Harry realising the first task of the school tournament is getting closer: "There was a week to go before February the twenty-fourth (there was still time) ... there were five days to go (he was bound to find something soon) ... three days to go (please let me find something ... please ...)." (HP 4, 526)

> Cloak and fly to London? Then I could get the rest of my money ot of my
> vault ... and begin my life as an outcast."

Three dots stand for reflection and Rowling uses them to indicate thoughts she does not make explicit (see II.2.D, 44).[93]

There are numerous examples of Harry wondering in the form of questions about things. Among these are, to name a few:

> A wizard? Him? How could he possibly be? [...] if he was really a wizard,
> why hadn't [the Dursleys] been turned into warty toads every time they'd
> tried to lock him in his cupboard? (HP 1, 67)
> [...] what if Ron and Hermione started going out together, then split up?
> Could their friendship survive it? (HP 6, 265)

These questions are also used to explain possible complications or problems to the reader. The following paragraph does not only sum up Harry's thoughts on having been selected school champion but also names the consequences:

> [Someone] else had wanted him in the Tournament, and had made sure he
> was entered. Why? To give him a treat? He didn't think so, somehow ... To
> see him make a fool of himself? Well, they were likely to get their wish ...
> But to get him *killed*? Was Moody just being his usual paranoid self?
> Couldn't someone have put Harry's name in the Goblet as a trick, a practi-
> cal joke? Did anyone really want him dead? (HP 4, 311)

On the contrary, the cases in which reported speech using *verba cogitandi* or *dicendi* is used are quite rare. One of the few examples is when Cho refuses to go to the ball with Harry, because she is already dating Cedric Diggory: "Now he suddenly realised that Cedric was in fact a useless pretty-boy who didn't have enough brains to fill an eggcup." (HP 4, 435.)

We also find some very rare examples for stream of consciousness. Rowling uses this technique chiefly to prepare the reader for sudden events or ideas of Harry's. In *Philosopher's Stone* the train of thought makes Harry realise that it must have been Hagrid who betrayed the secret of the stone to a stranger:

---

[93] The following sentences are very similar. Harry sees the first task in the school tournament approaching, "He waited, every fibre of him hoping, praying ... if it hadn't worked
... if it wasn't coming ... he seemed to be looking at everything around him through some
sort of shimmering, transparent barrier, like a heat haze, which made the enclosure and
the hundreds of faces around him swim strangely [... He] had left not only the ground behind, but also his fear ... he was back where he belonged... This was just another Quidditch match, that was all ... just another Quidditch match, and that Horntail was just another ugly opposing team ..." (HP 4, 388-389)

He watched an owl flutter toward the school across the bright blue sky, a note clamped in its mouth. Hagrid was the only one who ever sent him letters. Hagrid would never betray Dumbledore. Hagrid would never tell anyone how to get past Fluffy ... never ... but – Harry suddenly jumped to his feet. (HP 1, 285)

In *Order of the Phoenix* Harry is bored by a school book he has to read and falls asleep. Dozing off he tries to concentrate on the text, with italics marking the sentences Harry is reading.

> ...Hermione said Sirius was becoming reckless cooped up in Grimmauld Place ...
> ... *moste efficacious in the inflaming of the braine, and are therefore much used* ...
> ... the *Daily Prophet* would think his brain was inflamed if they found out that he knew what Voldemort was feeling ...
> ... *therefore much used in Confusing and Befuddlement Draughts...*
> ... confusing was the word, all right; *why* did he know what Voldemort was feeling? What was this weird connection between them, which Dumbledore had never been able to explain satisfactorily?
> ... *where the wizard is desirous* ...
> ... how Harry would like to sleep ...
> ... *of producing hot-headedness* ...
> ... it was warm and comfortable in his armchair before the fire, with the rain still beating heavily on the windowpanes, Crookshanks purring, and the crackling of the flames ...
> (HP 5, 423-424)

There are hardly any examples where the reader has access to other characters' thoughts. In *Chamber of Secrets* people wonder about the attack on the ghost Nearly Headless Nick: "What could possibly do that to a ghost, people asked each other; what terrible power could harm someone who was already dead?" (HP 2, 227) The use of the word "asked" marks the sentence as reported speech.[94]

In *Order of the Phoenix* the point of view changes. Harry is no longer the uncontradicted hero, his thoughts are now set apart from the rest of the text using italics:

> If I'm not expelled from Hogwarts, I'll put in ten Galleons, Harry found himself thinking desperately. (HP 5, 145)
> Don't be stupid, you haven't got fangs, he told himself [...], you were lying in bed, you weren't attacking anyone...

---

[94] Tom Morris comes to the same conclusion (see Tom Morris, "The Courageous Harry Potter," *Harry Potter and philosophy: If Aristotle ran Hogwarts,* eds. Baggett & Klein, Chicago, La Salle: Open Court, 2004, 9-21, here 11); Pinsent 2004, 40.

> But then, what just happened in Dumbledore's office? he asked himself. I
> felt like I wanted to attack Dumbledore, too. (HP 5, 526)

Typographically, Harry's counter-argument ("But then [...]") is marked by a break. Sometimes Harry's thoughts are now treated like direct speech, with italics replacing the quotation marks:

> And then, with a terrible stab of panic, he thought, but this is insane – if
> Voldemort's possessing me, I'm giving him a clear view into the Headquarters of the Order of the Phoenix right now! (HP 5, 544)

When the hero speaks with himself, his partner very often is a "small voice inside his head", that usually appears when Harry is envious or jealous:

> Well, Ron and Hermione were with me most of the time, said a voice inside
> Harry's head. Not all the time, though, Harry argued with himself. [...] But
> maybe, said the small voice fairly, maybe Dumbledore doesn't choose prefects because they've got themselves into a load of dangerous situations ...
> (HP 5, 187)

This change in narrative style stands for the distance the point of view takes regarding Harry's pubertal behaviour in *Order of the Phoenix*. In the following volume, *Half-Blood Prince*, this technique is used to express Harry's mixed emotions towards his growing love for Ginny:

> *She's Ron's sister*, Harry told himself firmly. *Ron's sister. She's out of
> bounds.* He would not risk his friendship with Ron for anything. (HP 6, 271)

In this conflict the arguments of reason are written in italics:

> Neither of them seemed to have noticed that a fierce battle was raging inside
> Harry's brain:
> *She's Ron's sister.*
> But she's ditched Dean!
> *She's still Ron's sister.*
> I'm his best mate!
> *That'll make it worse.*
> If I talked to him first –
> *He'd hit you.*
> What if I don't care?
> *He's your best mate!*
> (HP 6, 482)

Passages like these give the reader a clear insight into Harry's feelings. Therefore, Roland Ernould's opinion is proved to be wrong: "[Il] est inutile d'essayer de dresser un portrait un peu fouillé de Harry, et le lecteur ne participe guère à sa vie intérieure."[95] Just as incomprehensible is Maria Nikolajeva's idea that Harry is an extremely superficial character. She interprets any expressions of Harry's feelings as "narrator's statements, not representations of mental states [...]."[96]

Sometimes the author shifts the point of view completely and, thus, adds information that Harry cannot possibly have. The first chapter of *Goblet of Fire* for example, "The Riddle House"[97] (HP 4, 7-22), is narrated from gardener Frank Bryce's point of view. Through his narration the reader learns that Voldemort and Pettigrew have returned to Voldemort's hometown and that he plans to recover in his family's house. The opening lines of this chapter are written from the point of view of an omniscient narrator ("The villagers of Little Hangleton still called it 'The Riddle House' [...]."; HP 4, 7) and narrate the bizarre circumstances of the Riddle family's death fifty years ago. Frank Bryce is introduced as reflector. When he is killed by Voldemort, the point of view again changes and an omniscient narrator leads over to Harry's point of view in the second chapter: "two hundred miles away, the boy called Harry Potter awoke with a start" (HP 4, 22). Michael Maar sees this opening of the fourth book as "ein Meteorit in [der] Potter-Landschaft [...]."[98] The first chapter is the basis "mit der Frage nach dem Maulwurf in Hogwarts [...] den Spannungspunkt für den ganzen Band [...]."[99]

The author uses the same technique in the first two chapters of *Half-Blood Prince*. In "The Other Prime Minister" the reader witnesses Voldemort's return from the "Muggle" Prime Minister's point of view:

> The Prime Minister's pulse quickened at the very thought of [the] accusations, for they were neither fair nor true. How on earth was his government supposed to have stopped that bridge collapsing? [...] And how dared anyone suggest that it was lack of policemen that had resulted in those two very nasty and well-publicised murders? (HP 6, 7)

Whereas the Prime Minister is the reflector of this particular passage, the following chapter ("Spinner's End") is narrated from an omniscient narrator's

---

[95] "[It] is useless to try to draw a detailed portrait of Harry, and the reader hardly ever participates in Harry's emotional life." Roland Ernould, *Quatre approches de la magie: Du Rond des sorciers à Harry Potter*, Paris: Harmattan, 2003, 211 [my translation].

[96] Maria Nikolajeva, "Harry Potter – A Return to the Romantic Hero," *Harry Potter's World: Multidisciplinary Critical Perspectives*, ed. Elizabeth E. Heilman, New York, London: RoutledgeFalmer, 2003, 125-140, 134.

[97] This title is just another example of how Rowling uses ambiguity (see 65): it can name the house of the Riddle family or call the mansion a "house of riddles".

[98] "a meteor in the *Potter* landscape", Maar 2003, 95 [my translation].

[99] "the question as to who the spy in Hogwarts is maintains the suspense of the volume", Maar 2003, 99 [my translation].

point of view. Only in the third chapter, "Will and Won't", Harry returns as dominant point of view. This technique of changing the point of view in the first chapters is repeated in the last novels: the first chapter of *Deathly Hallows* ("The Dark Lord Ascending"), is set in Malfoy Manor and, again, Harry is absent.

Maria Nikolajeva thinks Rowling does not use any "more sophisticated narrative techniques [like] free indirect discourse, interior monologue, or psychonarration."[100] But I have proved her wrong. Although Rowling is not in the least an innovative writer it is not justified to accuse her of utter simplicity.

II.2.B. "Horrible", "nasty", "stupid" – Authorial Manipulation

The author interferes in numerous ways in the reader's perception of events. First of all this is achieved by making Harry's point of view dominant. The reader experiences the events through his eyes – Harry's enemies are his, Harry's friends can be trusted. Moreover, Rowling uses other stylistic devices to guide the reader's sympathy. For example, the names of people or places often allude to their qualities (see IV.2.A, 149). Also, Rowling often makes comments on events or characters using special adjectives or similes as in the context with Harry's family:

> [...] Harry often said that Dudley looked like a pig in a wig. (HP 1, 28)
> Harry suppressed a snort with difficulty. The Dursleys really were astonishingly stupid about their son, Dudley. (HP 5, 9)

Harry's point of view being accepted by the reader, the attributes "pig" and "stupid" are regarded as truthful descriptions of the Dursleys. Sometimes, other characters comment on people or events and affirm Harry's opinion. Such pseudo-neutral statements can be considered authorial guidance. A very good example for this seems to be the "Sorting Hat" that sings about the founders of Hogwarts:

> "Bold Gryffindor, from wild moor,
> Fair Ravenclaw, from glen,
> Sweet Hufflepuff, from valley broad,
> Shrewd Slytherin, from fen."
> (HP 4, 196)

The Sorting Hat – supposingly neutral – supports Harry's opinion on the four founders. Harry's point of view thus seems credible.

Another technique the author uses to comment on characters and events is the use of either positive or negative adjectives within the narration and from the omniscient point of view.

---

[100] Nikolajeva 2003, 134.

> Gone were the days when [Harry] had been forced to take every single one
> of the Dursleys' stupid rules. (HP 4, 42)
> "I won't give up hope then, [that they sentence you]," said Uncle Vernon
> nastily. (HP 5, 42)
> [Umbridge had] a horribly honeyed voice (HP 5, 271)

These sentences are only a few of the numerous examples where the author uses seemingly neutral descriptions to express a strong opinion. Even Harry himself is sometimes commented upon. When he fights against the troll in the bathroom, the narrator explains: "Harry then did something that was both very brave and very stupid: [...]" (HP 1, 191).

Moreover, there are a few examples of the author commenting directly in the text and introducing general remarks:

> A horrible thought struck Harry, as horrible thoughts always do when
> you're very nervous. (HP 1, 132)
> There are some things you can't share without ending up liking each other,
> and knocking out a twelve-foot mountain troll is one of them. (HP 1, 195)
> [Time] will not slow down when something unpleasant lies ahead, [...].
> (HP 4, 794)

Much more important than these rare authorial comments is the question of poetic justice. Who is successful and why? This being a question of the values taught by *Harry Potter* I will return to it later when analyising the novels' ideology (see V, 278).

II.2.C. Stylistic Devices

The importance of language has two main aspects: what is the role of oral communication within the plot, and how much does the author use language for narrative purposes?

Language is the decisive medium in the world of Harry Potter: spells must be pronounced correctly[101], one's destination must be shouted clearly while travelling by "Floo Powder" (HP 2, 57-59). Each house in Hogwarts is protected by an individual password and the Chamber of Secrets can only be opened if one speaks "Parsletongue" (the language of snakes) with an enchanted tap (HP 2, 323). As these examples show, oral communication is vitally important to produce magic and to protect you from your enemies.

---

[101] When Neville's mouth has been hurt in the last scenes of *Order of the Phoenix* he is no longer able to pronounce "Stupefy" correctly and fails at performing the spell (HP 5, 878-880). When Cho Chang is nervous because Harry stands close to her, she inflames her friend Marietta, because she confuses "Expelliarmus" and "Expelliarmious" and "Expellimellius" (HP 5, 435-436).

Rowling's stylistic capabilities have been harshly criticised by many critics. *ZEIT*-reviewer Susanne Mayer writes, the reader "ertapp[e] sich bei dem Wunsch, die Autorin möge ihre Schreibpause für einige Creative-Writing-Übungen nutzen."[102] And Robert McCrum writes in the *Observer*:

> [Rowling's] prose is as flat (and as English) as old beer [...]. When the good fairy of fiction lays her magic wand on a new writer, she must bestow three blessings: in character, in story and in language. In Rowling's case, her good fairy was lavish in the first two benefactions, but meagre in the last.[103]

But apart from critique there are a few favourable opinions on Rowling's original, creative style. Paul Bürvenich regards the dialogues of the *Harry Potter* novels as especially authentic, because they are adapted to the their readers' linguistic and intellectual level.[104] Elizabeth D. Schafer thinks Rowling develops a special "Potter-Code" using a specific system of allusions and linguistic inventions. The novels are written, Schafer continues, with a subtle note of uncertainty "in which readers are unsure of their own comprehension or fluctuating action."[105] Deborah O'Keefe believes the simple style to be an advantage,[106] and Susanne Gaschke praises Rowling's narrative technique as demanding and complex and her characters as ambivalent and difficult.[107]

Rowling frequently uses Latin and words of other foreign languages. This technique often gives meaning to characters, places and objects and provides a special appeal to adult readers. "Older readers especially try to discern the

---

[102]   "finds himself wishing the author would use the intervals between two volumes to participate in creative writing courses." (Susanne Mayer, "In den Klauen der Pubertät," *ZEIT* 27/2003. <http://www.zeit.de/2003/27/SM-Potter> 3 Jan 2008 [my translation].

[103]   See Robert McCrum, "Plot, plot, plot that's worth the weight," *Observer* 9 July 2000. <http://books.guardian.co.uk/news/articles/0,6109,341394,00.html> 3 Jan 2008.

[104]   See Bürvenich 2001, 93. But there are other opinions, as well: John Mullan says in *The Observer*: "The dialogue is peculiarly unlifelike. [...] There is no agespecific slang or teen idiom.", John Mullan, "Into the gloom," *Observer* 23 July 2005. <http://books .guardian.co.uk/print/0,3858,5244454-108779,00.html> 3 Jan 2008.

[105]   Schafer 2000, 212, 217, 219.

[106]   "J.K. Rowling's books, written in a clear, accessible, though not elegant, style, are very inviting and unintimidating to the reader, and also very complex in their intertwining of different worlds and moods." See Deborah O'Keefe, *Readers in Wonderland: The Liberating Worlds of Fantasy Fiction, from Dorothy to Harry Potter*, New York, London: Continuum, 2003, 176.

[107]   Susanne Gaschke, "Die Welt liest. Das Phänomen 'Harry Potter': Globalisierung kann angenehm und sehr anspruchsvoll sein," *ZEIT*, 30/2007. <www.zeit.de/themen/kul tur/feuilleton/harry-potter> 19 July 2007.

meanings of the names and spells," says Jann Lacoss.[108] The spells usually are derived from Latin or Romance words.[109] "I enjoy feeling that wizards would continue to use this dead language in their everyday life", explains Rowling in an interview for her American publisher Scholastic.[110] The so-called "Unforgiveable Curses" are especially interesting in this context, because they can be translated quite accurately from their Latin origins. The curse for torturing, "Crucio!", is a derivation from "crucificāre" and means "I crucify (you)!" This, of course, is an allusion to the passion of Christ.[111] "Imperio!" can be translated as "I command (you)". The curse "Avada Kedavra!" can be taken from various words. John Granger believes it to come from "I have a cadaver"[112] – an opinion I do not share. Rowling herself explains the curse quite differently: "[*Avada kedavra*] is an ancient spell in Aramaic, and it is the original of *abracadabra*, which means 'let the thing be destroyed.'"[113]

No one doubts that Rowling uses language very consciously, she even uses onomatopoeic forms.[114] I will, therefore, analyse the usage of language in the following chapter in more detail.

II.2.D. Italics and Asterisks –
Typography as Part of the Narration

Rowling makes very conscious use of the typography of her text. Writing words in capital letters or in italics always refers to either their phonetics, their emphasis or a change of speaker. Capital letters usually indicate speaking very loudly:

---

[108] Jann Lacoss, "Of Magicals and Muggles. Reversals and Revulsions at Hogwarts," *The Ivory Tower and Harry Potter: Perspectives on a Literary Phenomenon*, ed. Lana A. Whited, Columbia: University of Missouri Press, 2004, 67-88, 71.

[109] See Pinsent 2004, 31.

[110] Rowling, Live Interview, 16 Oct 2000. In another interview she reveals her poor Latin: "My Latin is patchy, to say the least, but that doesn't really matter because old spells are often in cod Latin – a funny mixture of weird languages creeps into spells. That is how I use it. Occasionally – you will stumble across something in my Latin that is, almost accidentically, grammatically correct, but that is a rarity.", Rowling 2004.

[111] See Katharine M. Grimes, "Harry Potter. Fairy Tale Prince, Real Boy and Archtypal Hero," *The Ivory Tower and Harry Potter: Perspectives on a Literary Phenomenon*, ed. Lana A. Whited, Columbia: University of Missouri Press, 2004, 89-122, here 113.

[112] See John Granger, *Looking for God in Harry Potter*, Wheaton, Illinois: Saltriver Tyndale House Publishers, 2004, 166-167.

[113] Rowling 2004. I will not discuss if she is right in her etymology of "abrakadabra".

[114] Roni Natov thinks every sound has a meaning with Rowling: "There are sneaky-sounding s's: Slytherins, Snape, Severus, Sirius and Scabbers. The h's are kind of heroic: Hogwarts, Hedwig, Hermione and Hagrid. The f's are often unpleasant types: Filch and Flitwick ... The names that sound French are usually difficult people: Madam Pince, Madam Pomfrey, and Malfoy.", Roni Natov, "Harry Potter and the Extraordinariness of the Ordinary," *The Lion and the Unicorn* 25 (2001): 310-327, here 310.

"MIND THAT TREE!" Harry bellowed, lunging for the steering wheel, but too late – "CRUNCH."(HP 2, 83)
"... ABSOLUTELY DISGUSTED, YOUR FATHER'S FACING AN IN-QUIRY AT WORK, IT'S ENTIRELY YOUR FAULT AND IF YOU PUT ANOTHER TOE OUT OF LINE WE'LL BRING YOU STRAIGHT BACK HOME." (HP 2, 98)

Sometimes she uses italics likewise:

"Tonks!" cried Mrs Weasley in exasperation [...]. (HP 5, 90)
"Filth! Scum! By-products of dirt and vileness! Half-breeds, mutants, freaks, begone from this place! How dare you befoul the house of my fathers –" (HP 5, 91)

Beginning a word with a capital letter often means it has – in additional to its lexical meaning – a special function within the magical world. "The Sight" for example means clairvoyance (HP 3, 114), "to Apparate" or "to Disapparate" (HP 3, 178; HP 4, 53) is the sudden appearance or disappearance of people or objects. And a non-traceable place is called "Unplottable" (HP 4, 185). This technique is used very frequently as for example in the following sentences:

She Banished a cushion [...]. (HP 4, 523)
"[To] See as I See, to Know as I Know ... of course, we Seers have always been feared, [...]." (HP 5, 405)

As we have already seen, it is typography that separates the different levels of discourse (see II.2.A, 38) and marks the author's increasing distance from Harry (see II.2.A, 39).

Rowling also makes the writing of her words part of the narration, when she reproduces the typography of a threatening letter or a supposedly medieval book:

You are a WickEd giRL. HaRRy PottEr desErves BetteR. gO Back wherE you cAME from mUggle. (HP 4, 588)
These plantes are moste efficacious in the inflaming of the braine, and are therefore much used in Confusing and Befuddlement Draughts, where the wizard is desirous of producing hot-headedness and recklessness ... (HP 5, 423)

Punctuation and special characters are used to mark extraordinary situations or states of mind, as we can see in the kissing scene between Harry and Cho. The three dots and the asterik represent the actual kissing that is not described in the text (see II.2.A, 35). For Joachim Kronsbein this kind of omission indicates a lack of creativeness on Rowling's behalf:

Zwar schildert [Rowling] Harrys ersten Kuss mit dem erotischen Feingefühl einer Äbtissin und den erzählerischen Techniken eines Taschenspielers, aber die Szene funktioniert: [...].[115]

The author uses the same technique to demonstrate Harry's agitation and his wish for being left alone (HP 5, 940-943).

Rowling also uses stylistic devices to express time or movement – for example when she repeats individual words:

> [Harry] knew all was lost, and fell into blackness, down ... down ... down ... (HP 1, 318)
> [They] looked at each other [...] waiting ... waiting ... (HP 5, 527)
> At last, Norbert was going ... going ... *gone*. (HP 1, 261).

"Gone" being printed in italics indicates that the action is completed and the dragon is out of sight.

In a comical way language can increase the opposition between the word and its meaning: when Rowling writes "Crabbe and Goyle guffawed sycophantically, [...]" (HP 4, 322), she uses very elaborate words to express a simple fact: "Crabbe and Goyle laughed hysterically". But it is especially funny to use such words in connection with two idiots like Crabbe and Goyle.

II.2.E. CRASH! WHOOSH! BOOM! –
Comic Style instead of Epic Narration

It is characteristic for the *Potter* novels that sentences are short and epic descriptions or contemplations are very rare. Linguistically, the texts are not very demanding and can easily be read by children (see VII.1.A, 419).

The representation of noises reminds one of comic strips. Instead of describing the quality of the noise the author uses onomatopoetic expressions:

> [They] broke into a run – CRASH. (HP 2, 77)
> "ATTAAAACK!" Crash-crash-crash: door after door flew open [...]. (HP 2, 220)
> WHOOSH. One of the Bludgers came streaking past [...]. WHOOSH. The second Bludger had grazed Harry's elbow. (HP 3, 333)
> "AAAAAARRRGH!" (HP 3, 336)
> "there came a great '*wheeeeeeeeee!*'" (HP 7, 518)

---

[115] "Although Rowling describes Harry's first kiss with as much eroticism as an abbess would do and with the narrative style of a conjuror, the scene certainly has an effect: [...]". Joachim Kronsbein, "Der Kuss des Magiers," *SPIEGEL* 30 June 2003. <http://www.spiegel.de/spiegel/0,1518,255899,00.html> 3 Jan 2008 [my translation].

There are hardly any descriptions of landscape to be found. And the few that appear in the text are quite poorly written:[116]

> The sky was a deep, clear blue now, and the first stars were starting to appear. (HP 4, 673)
> Twilight fell: the sky was turning to a light, dusky purple littered with tiny silver stars, and soon only the lights of Muggle towns gave them any clue of how far from the ground they were [...]. (HP 5, 842)

The first longer descriptive passages can be found in *Half-Blood Prince*. This indicates the series' development from childrens' to young adults' novel:

> Many miles away, the chilly mist that had pressed against the Prime Minister's windows drifted over a dirty river that wound between overgrown, rubbish-strewn banks. An immense chimney, relic of a disused mill, reared up, shadowy and ominous. There was no sound apart from the whisper of the black water and no sign of life apart from a scrawny fox [...]. (HP 6, 25)
> An eerie sight met their eyes: they were standing on the edge of a great black lake, so vast that Harry could not make out the distant banks, in a cavern so high that the ceiling, too, was out of sight. A misty greenish light shone far away in what looked like the middle of the lake; it was reflected in the completely still water below. The greenish glow and the light from the two wands were the only things that broke the otherwise velvety blackness, though their rays did not penetrate as far as Harry would have expected. The darkness was somehow denser than normal darkness. (HP 6, 524)

Rowling uses similes in her descriptions of landscape, as she does in other contexts (see II.2.G, 53):

> The castle grounds were gleaming in the sunlight as though freshly painted; [...]. (HP 5, 777)
> The sky outside was so brightly blue it looked as though it had been enamelled. (HP 4, 624).

When he escapes from the battle of Hogwarts into the Forbidden Forest, we find another, more or less epic description of landscape:

> He sprinted, half believing he could outdistance death itself, ignoring the jets of light flying in the darkness all around him, and the sound of the lake crashing like the sea, and the creaking of the Forbidden Forest though the night was windless; through grounds that seemed themselves to have risen in rebellion, he ran faster than he had ever moved in his life, and it was he

---

[116] Susanne Mayer agrees: "Landschaftsbeschreibungen misslingen mitunter kläglich." ("Descriptions of landscape fail miserably" [my translation]), Mayer 2003.

who saw the great tree first, the Willow that protected the secret at its roots with whip-like, slashing branches. (HP 7, 522-523)

In a satirical way she perverts the stereotypical ride into the sunset when she describes the Weasley twins' departure from Hogwarts:

[...] Fred and George wheeled about to tumultuous applause from the students below and sped out of the open front doors into the glorious sunset. (HP 5, 742-743)

This is to show that the author is familiar with literary conventions, but does not make innovative use of them. Instead, she disappoints the readers' expectations when she renounces epic where it would seem to be adequate. Again, the kissing scene between Harry and Cho is a good example for this (HP 5, 503): the reader wants to know how Harry experiences his first kiss – but must be content with the asterisk "*". This tendency not to give a detailed description where the reader expects it can also be seen in *Goblet of Fire*: when Harry sees the bodiless, crippled Voldemort for the first time, Rowling writes, "[It] revealed something ugly, slimy and blind – but worse, a hundred times worse." (HP 4, 693) Speaking positively, Rowling leaves it up to the reader what this could mean.[117]

II.2.F. Death Scenes

A particular field of narrative technique is the design of death scenes: on the one hand it is difficult for the author to avoid stereotypes and on the other find a way of expressing the innermost feelings of his characters. In the *Harry Potter* novels we find various death scenes. The first character to die is Cedric Diggory in *Goblet of Fire*:

A swishing noise and a second voice, which screeched the words to the night: '*Avada Kedavra*!' A blast of green light blazed through Harry's eyelids, and he heard something heavy fall to the ground beside him; [...] he opened his stinging eyes. Cedric was lying spread-eagled on the ground beside him. He was dead. For a second that contained an eternity, Harry stared into Cedric's face, at his open grey eyes, blank and expressionless as the windows of a deserted house, at his half-open mouth, which looked slightly surprised. (HP 4, 691)

---

[117] Jann Lacoss sees this as an advantage: "The paucity of description lets the audience actively participate in the performance. Each reader experiences the narrative a little differently, yet all share a basic understanding of the actions involved. Each visualizes the act at a level that is acceptable to his/her psyche." (Lacoss 2004, 80).

Shocking as this scene was to the *Potter* fan community (which had been speculating about who was going to die in the novel for months), it is – in the context of the whole series – rather insignificant. Cedric is neither a main character nor is the scene especially cruel. But it meant a turning point for the series, nevertheless: with the death of Cedric *Harry Potter* ceased to be a funny, entertaining children's novel with no serious harm happening to its characters. From then on, readers could no longer trust in a happy-ending. This sense of "things are getting worse" is intensified throughout the rest of the series: in every novel after the third part we experience the death of a character. In *Order of the Phoenix* we watch a main character die for the first time. Sirius Black's death is highly significant for Harry because he looses an important father figure. Nevertheless, the scene remains rather stereotypical and is reminiscent of the way death scenes are represented in traditional wild west movies:

> The second jet of light hit [Sirius] squarely on the chest. The laughter had not quite died from his face, but his eyes widened in shock. [...] It seemed to take Sirius an age to fall: his body curved in a graceful arc as he sank backwards through the ragged veil hanging from the arch. Harry saw the look of mingled fear and surprise on his godfather's wasted, once handsome face as he fell through the ancient doorway and disappeared behind the veil, which fluttered for a moment as though in a high wind, then fell back into place. (HP 5, 886)

There is no appropriate description of Harry's emotions. His point of view, although the decisive one throughout the novels, is of no relevance in this scene: he seems to be uninvolved where he should be deeply touched. When in *Half-Blood Prince* Dumbledore dies, we find another very clichéd description of the scene:

> A jet of green light shot from the end of Snape's wand and hit Dumbledore squarely in the chest. Harry's scream of horror never left him; silent and unmoving, he was forced to watch as Dumbledore was blasted into the air: for a split second he seemed to hang suspended beneath the shining skull, and then he fell slowly backwards, like a great rag doll, over the battlements and out of sight. (HP 6, 556)
> [There] was still no preparation for seeing [Dumbledore] here, spread-eagled, broken: the greatest wizard Harry had ever, or would ever, meet. Dumbledore's eyes were closed; but for the strange angle of his arms and legs, he might have been sleeping. (HP 6, 568

Although this time the reader experiences the scene from Harry's point of view, the way Dumbledore expires, again, is highly reminiscent of any average action movie.

Deathly Hallows is truly "deathly" and a real massacre. We come across many final moments in this last part of the series. The first character to die is Alastor Moody. We get this information from Bill Weasley, an eye-witness:

"Voldemort's curse hit Mad-Eye full in the face, he fell backwards off his broom and – there was nothing we could do, nothing, we had half a dozen of them on our own tail –" Bill's voice broke. (HP 7, 70)

We do not get much information about his death, and Rowling decides to narrate Moody's death from Bill's point of view, which is rather emotionless and matter-of-fact. About three-hundred pages later, we witness Peter Pettigrew being strangled by his own hand when he considers for a split second letting Harry go:

[Harry] saw the rat-like man's small, watery eyes widen with fear and surprise: he seemed just as shocked as Harry at what his hand had done. [...] Wandless, helpless, Pettigrew's pupils dilated in terror. His eyes had slid from Harry's face to something else [...]. Pettigrew was turning blue [and] dropped to his knees [...]. Wormtail's eyes rolled upwards in his purple face, he gave a last twitch and was still. (HP 7, 380-381)

Picturing what Rowling writes, it is a rather horrid scene, not really fit for a mere children's book. As with the description of the living, the eyes become the indicator of life with the dying. They mirror the characters' spirit. A couple of pages later another main character dies: Dobby, the little elf Harry first met in *Chamber of Secrets*. He dies saving Harry's life and having escorted him to safety. Once again it is the eyes that reflect his approaching death:

The elf swayed slightly, stars reflected in his wide, shining eyes. Together, he and Harry looked down at the silver hilt of the knife protruding from the elf's heaving chest. 'Dobby – no – HELP!' Harry bellowed towards the cottage, towards the people moving there. 'HELP!' He did not know or care whether they were wizards or Muggles, friends or foes; all he cared about was that a dark stain was spreading across Dobby's front, and that he had stretched out his thin arms to Harry with a look of supplication. [...] The elf's eyes found him, and his lips trembled with the effort to form words. 'Harry ... Potter.' And then with a little shudder the elf became quite still, and his eyes were nothing more than great glassy orbs sprinkled with light from the stars they could not see. (HP 7, 385)

The stars in Dobby's eyes form a kind of parenthesis around his passing from life to death. The scene's emotionality is much more intense than the scenes we have read so far. We experience the elf's death from Harry's point of view and are eye-witnesses of the event.

We hear more about Harry's reaction to Fred Weasley's death than about his feelings towards the friend he has lost. As in Dobby's death scene the fact that he has passed away is illustrated by his sightless eyes that cannot share the others' cognitions:

Then he heard a terrible cry that pulled at his insides, that expressed agony of a kind neither flame nor curse could cause, and he stood up, swaying, more frightened than he had been that day, more frightened, perhaps, than he had been in his life ... [...] "No - no - no!" someone was shouting. "No! Fred! No!" And Percy was shaking his brother, and Ron was kneeling beside them, and Fred's eyes stared without seeing, the ghost of his last laugh still etched upon his face. (HP 7, 512)

By far the most interesting death scene is narrated from Voldemort's point of view. It is important, because it represents the completion of the guesswork the reader has been entertaining ever since the first novel. Finally, we are being told how Harry's parents died. Nevertheless, their deaths are rather unspectacular:

[...] James came sprinting into the hall. It was easy, too easy, he had not even picked up his wand... [...] "Avada Kedavra!" The green light filled the cramped hallway, it lit the pram pushed against the wall, it made the banisters glare like lightning rods, and James Potter fell like a marionette whose strings were cut... (HP 7, 281)
At the sight of him, [Lily] dropped her son into the cot behind her and threw her arms wide, as if this would help, as if in shielding him from sight she hoped to be chosen instead... "Not Harry, not Harry, please not Harry!" [...] He could have forced her away from the cot, but it seemed more prudent to finish them all... [...] The green light flashed around the room and she dropped like her husband. (HP 7, 281)

It is obvious that Lily dies a martyr's death and her pose in death resembles Christ's crucification. She gives her life to save her child and her body language represents precisely this sacrifice: we can clearly compare Lily's martyrdom to mankind's salvation through the crucifying of Christ. The Potters' actual death is rather insignificant with regard to narrative techniques. Both of them simply "drop" or "fall". This is convincing, because we experience these scenes from the point of view of Voldemort, who is an unsentimental killer and does not show any feelings while murdering his victims.

The one scene in which Harry really mourns his parents' death is when he goes to visit their graves in Godric's Hollow in *Deathly Hallows*:[118]

And tears came before he could stop them, boiling hot then instantly freezing on his face, and what was the point in wiping them off, or pretending? He let them fall, his lips pressed hard together, looking down at the thick snow hiding from his eyes the place where the last of Lily and James lay, bones now, surely, or dust not knowing or caring that their living son stood

---

[118] We must wonder why it is only in the last part of the series that he returns to his birthplace? Why did he not have the idea of seeing his parents' grave earlier? Why did no-one tell him of its existence?

> so near, his heart still beating, alive because of their sacrifice and close to wishing, at this moment, that he was sleeping under the snow with them. (HP 7, 269)

This is one of the rare moments Rowling succeeds in describing emotions without lapsing into stereotype. The son's longing to be dead, his picturing of the state his parents' bodies are probably in – this is rather convincing and truthful.

The next death scene is a very decisive one: Severus Snape is killed by Voldemort and dying gives his memories to Harry. Having "read" these, Harry gets the answers to all the questions about Snape. Voldemort sets his snake Nagini on Snape, so he dies from her bite – a rather ghastly scene:

> There was a terrible scream. Harry saw Snape's face losing the little colour it had left, it whitened as his black eyes widened, as the snake's fangs pierced his neck, as he failed to push the enchanted cage off himself, as his knees gave way, and he fell to the floor. [...] (HP 7, 527)
> When the flask was full to the brim, and Snape looked as though there was no blood left in him, his grip on Harry's robes slackened. 'Look ... at ... me ...' he whispered. The green eyes found the black, but after a second something in the depths of the dark pair seemed to vanish, leaving them fixed, blank and empty. The hand holding Harry thudded to the floor, and Snape moved no more. (HP 7, 528)

After Harry's return to Hogwarts, he finds the victims laid out in the Great Hall – death is omnipresent in this scene. Among the dead he finds two of his best friends:[119]

> [...] Harry had a clear view of the bodies lying next to Fred: Remus and Tonks, pale and still and peaceful-looking, apparently asleep beneath the dark, enchanted ceiling. [... Harry] turned away and ran up the marble staircase. Lupin, Tonks ... he yearned not to feel ... he wished he could rip out his heart, his innards, everything that was screaming inside him ... (HP 7, 531)

In this scene we are not told how they died, it is just the fact that is stated. Thus Rowling comfortably disposes of the two outcasts and of the necessity to describe either their full integration into, or their life on the brink of, society. Nevertheless, the author gives us an insight into Harry's feelings that, this time, are very intense. The whole impact of what this battle is demanding suddenly comes upon him. This is why he decides to confront Voldemort and die for his friends.

---

[119] From the narrator's point of view it is an advantage to define that the killing curse obviously does not mutilate the victim. The dead in *Harry Potter* are always rather beautiful and hardly ever scarred.

His own death is extremely banal and narrated with a certain lack of interest:

> Harry looked back into [Voldemort's] red eyes, and wanted it to happen
> now, quickly, while he could still stand, before he lost control, before he be-
> trayed fear –
> He saw the mouth move and a flash of green light, and everything was gone.
> (HP 7, 564)

Just remember: this is the death of the novels' protagonist, the end of the boy whose life we have been following for about ten years and many thousand pages. This death scene is rather disappointing. Although it is, of course, diffi-cult to imagine what death might be like, giving the reader more information would have been appropriate.

In this and in all the other death scenes Rowling proves to be, to say the least, a very economical narrator. We could also state that in these highly emo-tional scenes the flaws in her capacity for epic description become most evident. Her death scenes are rather stereotypical. Death is nearly always represented by a change in the eyes or the sight ("everything was gone"), an unnatural move-ment or position ("spread-eagled") of the body. Her death scenes are in no way innovative. We hardly find any descriptions of the feelings death provokes, only a mere mention of the fact. This is just another proof of how Rowling misses out opportunities for great epic.

II.2.G. "Harry had ever seen" – Similes and Metaphors

Rowling's language is poor in stylistic devices.[120] The few metaphors and simi-les she uses are subject to repetition. She prefers similes introduced with "like" or "as (though)". Examples of similes with "like" are – among many others – the following:

> "Harry Potter shone like a beacon of hope [...]" (HP 2, 194)
> as darkness spread like a curtain (HP 4, 105)
> Rumours were flying [...] like highly contagious germs [...]. (HP 4, 260)
> crystal bubbles [...] looking like giant soapsuds (HP 5, 536)
> The guard around [Harry] was circling continously like giant birds of prey.
> (HP 5, 68)
> Ginny made a noise like an angry cat. (HP 5, 85)
> a hoarse, deep voice like a bullfrog's (HP 5, 123)
> the towering mill chimney seemed to hover like a giant admonitory finger.
> (HP 6, 27)

---

[120] See Bürvenich 2001, 94. Some critics like Kathrine M. Grimes see a water metaphor in the novels and the second task in the tournament as an allegory of birth. This does not seem very convincing to me, because there is no further reference to giving birth in the novels (see Grimes 2004, 120).

And his fury at Dumbledore broke over him now like lava, scorching him
inside, wiping out every other feeling. (HP 7, 287)
[...] Harry felt they were as insignificant as insects beneath that wide sky.
(HP 7, 295)
it was blissful oblivion, better than Firewhisky (HP 7, 99)[121]

The comparisons are drawn either from magical everyday-life (curtain,
soapsuds, Firewhisky), fauna[122] (contagious germs, birds of prey, angry cat,
bullfrog), or the rhetoric of hero-worship (beacon of hope). The *tertium com-
parationis* very often is quite particular, sometimes even wrong: information is
spreading like "contagious germs", which indicates the things said as dangerous,
infectious. The guard that is to protect Harry is compared to "giant birds of
prey", but in fact the witches and wizards are more like guardian angels for him.
And what is the "admonitory finger" of the chimney supposed to remind people of?

The similes introduced by "as (though)" are usually drawn from the wizards' everyday life, the *tertium* is much more precise than the images beginning
with "like". In particular Harry's emotional life is visualised in this way:

His head was spinning as though he'd just travelled miles by Floo Powder.
(HP 2, 346)
[He felt] as though he'd eaten something extremely wriggly for breakfast.
(HP 3, 329)
The days until the first task seemed to slip by as though someone had fixed
the clocks to work at double speed. (HP 4, 348-349)
[Harry] felt [...] as though he had missed a step going downstairs.
(HP 5, 500)
It was as though an invisible hand had twisted Harry's intestines and held
them tight. (HP 6, 71)
[They] passed straight through as though the dark metal were smoke
(HP 7, 9)

Rowling does not use complex and elaborate metaphors, but only refers to
things well known to the reader. Rare examples are speeches by Dumbledore
like "'And now, Harry, let us step out into the night and pursue that flighty
temptress, adventure.'" (HP 6, 58) or "'From this point forth, we shall be leaving the firm foundation of fact and journeying together through the murky
marshes of memory into thickets of wildest guess-work.'"[123] (HP 6, 187).

---

[121] In this case, Rowling uses the comparison form "better than".
[122] This characteristic of Rowling's writing can also be found in her character descriptions
(see IV.2.A, 149).
[123] Dumbledore uses the alliteration [m] here.

Moreover all events are set in direct relation to Harry's perspective: phrases like "Harry had ever seen", "had yet seen" or "had never seen" can be found frequently throughout the whole series.[124]

> [The] strangest sight Harry had ever seen. (HP 2, 219)
> [A] mad glint in Snape's eye that Harry had never seen before. (HP 3, 388)
> [The] most stunning he had yet seen inside the school. (HP 4, 432)
> [The] most peculiar kitchen Harry had ever seen (HP 7, 324)

Sometimes "to see" is replaced by other words of perception or words that indicate that Harry is doing something for the first time:

> It was the gloomiest, most depressing bathroom Harry had ever set foot in. (HP 2, 170)
> It was the most delicious thing he had ever tasted [...]. (HP 3, 218)
> [A] scene the like of which he could never have imagined. (HP 4, 109)
> [Aunt Petunia] was looking at Harry as she had never looked at him before. (HP 5, 47)
> [One] of the loudest silences Harry had ever heard. (HP 5, 353)

Harry is the only character things seem to be related to. This, again, indicates his position as reflector and his representing the point of view, which the author wants the reader to take (see IV.1.B, 147).

Another stylistic device Rowling uses frequently are alliterations as for example in "'Miserable, moaning, moping Myrtle!'" (HP 2, 148) or names like Dudley Dursley, Dedalus Diggle, Bathilda Bagshot, Cho Chang or Colin Creevey.[125] And by means of onomatopoeic expressions Rowling also imitates noises: "The train rattled, the rain hammered, the wind roared, but still, Professor Lupin slept." (HP 3, 91) The consonants [t] and [r] are creating a rythmic staccato that recalls a steam engine. Additionally, [w] and [oa] in "the wind roared" refer to the howling of the wind.

II.2.H. "Whozair?" – Dialects and Accents

When transcribing linguistic characteristics like dialects or accents, Rowling tries to be very accurate and simple. Often we find colloquial pronunciations that reflect the speaker's condition when he is tired or confused:

---

[124] We find countless examples of this: "[The] largest block of chocolate he had ever seen in his life." (HP 3, 418); "[The] most beautiful women Harry had ever seen" (HP 4, 116); "[A] face unlike any Harry had ever seen." (HP 4, 204); "[The] largest collection of lights he had yet seen." (HP 5, 69).

[125] See Bürvenich 2001, 106-107.

"Whassamatter?" said Harry groggily. (HP 2, 116)
"Wangoballwime?" (HP 4, 434)
"Whozair?" said Harry, [...]. (HP 5, 424)
"Gerremoffme!" (HP 6, 283)
"Wuzzgoinon?" (HP 6, 88)

The characters' pronunciation is used to inform the reader of their nationality or education.[126] The pupils from Beauxbatons are clearly speaking with a French accent, when they sonorise consonants and leave out initial fricatives:[127]

"Why should 'e complain?" burst out Fleur Delacour, stamping her foot. "E 'as ze chance to compete, 'asn't 'e? We 'ave all been 'oping to be chosen for weeks and weeks! Ze honour for our schools [...]. A thousand Galleons in prize money – zis is a chance many would die for!" (HP 4, 306)
"Eet was no trouble, [...]. I 'ave been longing to see 'im. You remember my seester, Gabrielle? She never stops talking about 'Arry Potter.'" (HP 6, 91)

The students from Durmstrang on the other hand are speaking with a supposedly East European accent, for they sonorise the initial fricative.

"Vell, ve have a castle also, not as big as this, nor as comfortable, I am thinking," he was telling Hermione. "Ve have just four floors, and the fires are lit only for magical purposes." (HP 4, 455)

Hagrid and the house-elf Dobby may serve as examples for how Rowling uses accents to place her characters socially: Hagrid (see IV.4.A, 218) speaks a lower class English (more of a rustic English accent). He does not pronounce the final consonants, sometimes letting out whole syllables. He also uses the singular form of "to be" where grammatically he should use the plural and omits the initial fricatives:

"Yeh know, she's a fine, well-dressed woman, an' knowin' where we was goin' I wondered 'ow she'd feel abou' clamberin' over boulders an' sleepin' in caves an' tha', bu' she never complained once." (HP 5, 469)

---

[126] See Bürvenich 2001, 94; Elizabeth E. Heilman, Anne E. Gregory, "Images of the Privileged Insider and Outcast Outsider," *Harry Potter's World: Multidisciplinary Critical Perspectives*, ed. Elizabeth E. Heilman, New York, London: RoutledgeFalmer, 2003, 241-259, here 252.

[127] J.K. Rowling has worked as teacher of English in Paris – she must be familiar with the French accent. Other examples of this: "'Dumbly-dorr must 'ave a mistake wiz ze line,' said Madame Maxime, shrugging." (HP 4, 304); "'Evidently, someone 'oo wished to give 'Ogwarts two bites at ze apple!'" (HP 4, 306); "'It is too 'eavy, all zis 'Ogwarts food, [...].'" (HP 4, 441).

Whereas Hagrid's accent is characterised by phonetic variations of standard English, the language of the house-elves is grammatically incorrect and represents more an ethnic than a phonological variety. For example, they mix up singular and plural forms:

> "They isn't my masters any more. [...] Oh, you is a bad elf. [...] I is looking after the Crouches all my life." (HP 4, 417)

Richard Adams is right in criticising the stereotypical characterisation of the house-elves: "In fact [the house-elves] appear to be slaves – and Rowling rams home the point by having them speak in a witless, sub-Gone With the Wind patois."[128]

II.2.I. "Oh Potter, you rotter" – Rhymes and Verses

Rowling very often introduces rhymes to mark words that are of particular importance to the plot: either the verses contain riddles or hints to solving them or they are funny and serve to entertain the reader. In *Goblet of Fire* the tasks the champions must perform are hinted at using rhymed riddles. The magic egg as well as the sphinx in the last task are speaking in verses:

> *"Come seek us where our voices sound,*
> *We cannot sing above the ground,*
> *And while you're searching, ponder this:*
> *We've taken what you'll sorely miss,*
> *An hour long you'll have to look,*
> *And to recover what we took,*
> *But past an hour – the prospect's black*
> *Too late, it's gone, it won't come back."*
> *(HP 4, 504)*
> *"First think of the person who lives in disguise,*
> *Who deals in secrets and tells naught but lies.*
> *Next, tell me what's always the last thing to mend,*
> *The middle of middle and end of end?*
> *And finally give me the sound often heard*
> *During the search for a hard-to-find-word.*
> *Now string them together, and answer me this*
> *Which creature would you be unwilling to kiss?"*
> (HP 4, 682-683)

Searching for the Philosopher's Stone in the first book, the children come across a riddle in verses as well:

---

[128]   See Adams 2003.

Danger lies before you, while safety lies behind,
Two of us will help you, whichever you would find,
One among us seven will let you move ahead,
Another will transport the drinker back instead,
Two among our number hold only nettle wine,
Three of us are killers, waiting hidden in line.
(HP 1, 306-307)

Verses serve to intensify the meaning of the message. That is why the Sorting Hat speaks in verse (see for example u. a. HP 1, 129) and why the wizard bank Gringotts communicates its security measures in verse:

Enter, stranger, but take heed
Of what awaits the sin of greed,
For those who take, but do not earn,
Must pay most dearly in their turn,
So if you seek beneath our floors
A treasure that was never yours,
Thief, you have been warned, beware
Of finding more than treasure there.
(HP 1, 83)

Apart from rhymes marking particular importance, they are often just funny and meant to entertain the reader. This is true, for example, for the verses Poltergeist Peeves composes:

"Oh Potter, you rotter, oh what have you done?
You're killing off students, you think it's good fun –"
(HP 2, 221)
"When there's strife and when there's trouble
Call on Peevsie, he'll make double!" (HP 6, 381)
"We did it, we bashed them, wee Potter's the One,
And Voldy's gone mouldy, so now let's have fun!" (HP 7, 597)

Ginny's ode to Harry on Valentine's Day, likewise, is above all ridiculous and therefore funny:

"His eyes are as green as a fresh pickled toad,
His hair is as dark as a blackboard.
I wish he was mine, he's really divine,
The hero who conquered the Dark Lord."
(HP 2, 258)

And the Hogwarts school anthem (which can be sung to just about any tune), is funny because in contrast to the usually quite solemn lyrics of real anthems, this song is down-to-earth. It represents the pupils' attitude to their school: they adore it and regard Hogwarts as their friendly helper to achievement:

> *"Hogwarts, Hogwarts, Hoggy Warty Hogwarts,*
> *Teach us something please,*
> *Whether we be old and bald*
> *Or young with scabby knees,*
> *Our heads could do with filling*
> *With some interesting stuff,*
> *For now they're bare and full of air,*
> *Dead flies and bits of fluff,*
> *So teach us things worth knowing,*
> *Bring back what we've forgot,*
> *Just do your best, we'll do the rest,*
> *And learn until our brains all rot."*
> (HP 1, 140)

II.3 Structure of Plot

Children's books highly depend on the plot. Some authors, like Philip Pullman, believe that children's literature is more appropriate for dealing with a broad range of subject matter than books for adults. In his Carnegie Medal Acceptance Speech (1996) the author of the famous *Northern Lights* trilogy says:

> There are some themes, some subjects, too large for adult fiction; they can only be dealt with adequately in a children's book. The reason for that is that in adult literary fiction, stories are there on sufferance. Other things are felt to be more important: technique, style, literary knowingness.[129]

Pullman goes on to criticise contemporary authors' abhorrence of story:

> The present-day would-be George Eliots take up their stories as if with a pair of tongs. They're embarrassed by them. If they could write novels without stories in them, they would. Sometimes they do.[130]

Rowling is the great exception in contemporary book market, which may be one reason for her overwhelming success among adults.

The English edition of the series contains about 4,132 pages, which makes it impossible to deal with all the volumes in detail. Thus, I want to use *Prisoner of Azkaban* as an example for how Rowling structures her novels. In this third

---

[129] Philip Pullman, "Carnegie Medal Acceptance Speech," Chartered Institute of Library and Information Professionals (CILIP), 1996. <http://www.carnegiegreenaway.org.uk/home/index.php> 30 Sep 2007.

[130] Pullman 2007.

part of *Harry Potter* we find all the typical components of Rowling's plot-making. Critics agree on Rowling's talent for creative plot-making.

> [...] a narrative that fuses a plethora of genres (from the boarding-school novel to the detective story to the epic quest) into a story that could be Exhibit A in a Joseph Campbell survey of mythic archetypes.[131]

Michael Maar even states that the plot is the true protagonist of the series.[132] Nearly every detail mentioned in the course of the action has a function,[133] which is why Philip Nel compares the economy of Rowling's style to Jane Austen.[134] Rowling often uses the genre's stereotypes in an unexpected way and makes her series "an eccentric blend of the comfortably predictable and the unsettlingly unexpected."[135]

It does not appear very fruitful to analyse what sources the author uses and where she gets her inspiration from – much has been written in guidebooks and fan literature on this particular matter. But what we can say is that Rowling uses mythology, fairy tales and fantasy novels like a seam to get her material for plot-building, but she hardly ever comments on her sources.[136]

The fourth novel is somehow special in the series and a turning point: Robert McCrum writes in the *Observer*, the volume was "storytelling of a high order indeed", and "the apotheosis of 'story'" as E. M. Forster defines it (see II.1.A, 27).[137] Other critics believe *Goblet of Fire* to be an over-ambitious example of plot-making: "The plot is over-complicated and unbelievable even by the standards of fantasy," writes Christopher Wrigley. "The attempt to internationalise the story [...] does not really work, as the visitors are little more than stereotypes. The climactic scenes carry the macabre to the excess."[138] This judgement is at least partly justified. The critical reader must wonder why there is a school tournament at all, if the whole purpose of it is to have Harry touch a Portkey. Would it not have been much easier for Harry's enemies to ensure that "Moody" make him touch an obviously harmless object in one of his classes? Why all the complications with the tournament only to make the boy touch the

---

[131] Michiko Kakutani, "An Epic Showdown as Harry Potter Is Initiated Into Adulthood," *New York Times*, 19 July 2007. <http://www.nytimes.com/2007/07/19/books/19potter. html> 23 Nov 2007.

[132] See Maar 2003, 37.

[133] See Ehgartner 2002, 70.

[134] "[The] greatness of both Austen and Rowling lies in the subtlety and dexterity with which they set their plots in motion. [...] apparently minor details frequently turn out to have much larger significance." (Nel 2001, 14)

[135] Peter Hunt, *Children's Literature*. Oxford: Blackwell Publishers, 2001, 123.

[136] See Gupta 2003, 97.

[137] McCrum 2000.

[138] Christopher Wrigley, *The Return of the Hero*, Lewes: Book Guild, 2005, 22.

cup? And did Rowling not explain at the beginning of *Goblet of Fire* that Port-keys were "objects that are used to transport wizards from one spot to another at a prearranged time" (HP 4, 81)? Why then can Harry travel back to Hogwarts using the same Portkey that brought him to Little Hangleton (HP 4, 725)?[139]

Anthony Holden is one of the few critics to criticise Rowling's plot-making:

> Her story-lines are predictable, the suspense minimal, the sentimentality cloying every page. (Did Harry, like so many child-heroes before him, HAVE to be yet another poignant orphan?)[140]

He does not realise that Rowling *does* play with stereotypes and sometimes breaks with them radically. Her story-lines are not as predictable as he sees them. Each part of the series surprises with sudden twists of the plot: Mad-Eye Moody not being himself in *Goblet of Fire*, Dumbledore dying at the end of *Half-Blood Prince* and Sirius Black being Harry's godfather – all of these developments are not precisely predictable.

The novels develop according to the ageing of their readers and become "increasingly more adult fashion", as Amanda Cockrell puts it and declares it to be very rare in children's literature.[141] In every part of the series, plot becomes more complex and the number of characters increases. *Half-Blood Prince* breaks with this trend and abruptly cuts out sub-plots that have been important in the previous parts as for example the story of Hermione's engagement with "SPEW". With each part of the series, perspectives darken and the death toll rises. The series develops from children's to young adult's literature. Felicitas von Lovenburg writing in *F.A.Z.*, comments *Half-Blood Prince* was "das bisher dunkelste Buch der Reihe, das psychologischste, gegen Ende auch das traurig-ste."[142] At the same time, the novel serves for the "tying up of loose ends in preparation for the final volume, the fabled HP 7" as Robert McCrum adds. *Half-Blood Prince* gives the reader the missing background information about Tom Riddle that clearly prepares *Deathly Hallows*,[143] that holds a special posi-tion within the series.

---

[139] See Maar 2003, 118.

[140] Anthony Holden, "Why Harry Potter doesn't cast a spell over me," *Guardian* 25 June 2000. <http://books.guardian.co.uk/print/0,3858,4033193-99943,00.html> 3 Jan 2008.

[141] Amanda Cockrell, "Harry Potter and the Secret Password. Finding Our Way in the Magi-cal Genre," *The Ivory Tower and Harry Potter: Perspectives on a Literary Phenomenon*, ed. Lana A. Whited, Columbia: University of Missouri Press, 2004, 15-26, 25.

[142] "the darkest of all the novels up to part five, the most psychological and in its ending the saddest part of the series." (von Lovenberg 2000 [my translation])

[143] McCrum 2005.

II.3.A. The Special Position of "Harry Potter and the Deathly Hallows"

The last part of the series differs from all the others in many respects, which is why I want to deal with it in a separate chapter. Critics agree on *Deathly Hallows* being the most action-loaded, consistent and thrilling part of the series.[144] About half of the readers voting on *SPIEGEL Online* said Rowling had written a "worthy conclusion" of the series, 36 percent said they were disappointed by *Deathly Hallows* and 14 percent thought it the best *Potter* ever.[145] In fact, the last part of the series tries to be an all-in-one text, meeting the expectations of critics, fans and literary experts all at the same time. This considered, Rowling is rather successful.

First of all, she tries to get back and finish every plot and sub-plot she has ever introduced. We find references to Norbert, the Norwegian Ridgeback (HP 7, 102 referring to HP 1, 249-261) – a dragon Hagrid had hatched in *Philosopher's Stone*. Once more, Harry flies with Hagrid on Sirius' motorbike (HP 7, 50) like when he was rescued after his parents' death. Harry remembers the accident of *Chamber of Secrets* when Lockhart made him lose all his bones in his right arm (HP 7, 286). He unpacks his school bag for the first time in years and finds the badge "Support CEDRIC DIGGORY and POTTER STINKS" which his opponents used in *Goblet of Fire* (HP 7, 20). Voldemort refers to the same novel when he says "'I shall need [...] to borrow a wand from one of you...'" thinking that he, thus, might be able to defeat the twin of his own wand (HP 7, 14). And the characters remember that they have seen the locket Voldemort has transformed into a "Horcrux" before (HP 7, 156 referring to HP 5, 117-121). It is the very same locket that Dumbledore and Harry recovered in *Half-Blood Prince* (HP 7, 20 referring to HP 6, 539). Rowling even shows Harry pondering a remark Bellatrix Lestrange has made in *Order of the Phoenix* (HP 7, 430 referring to HP 5, 891).

Concerning its structure, *Deathly Hallows* goes beyond the scope of the rest of the series: for the last time Harry departs from the Dursleys, but this time not to do his traditional school shopping in Diagon Alley or to meet his friends, but to be escorted to safety. He never enters Hogwarts to do his last year of education, but goes directly into hiding. Actually, we never know if he ever did his final exams and what kind of career he chooses. So the novel ceases to be a school story, it becomes "more of an outlaw adventure than a boarding-school

---

144 von Lovenberg, "Rekordauflagen," 2007.
145 Altogether 2323 votes. "Wie finden Sie den neuen 'Potter'?" *F.A.Z.net* 21 July 2007. http://www.F.A.Z..net/d/common/umfrage.aspx?rub={1DA1FB84-8C1E-4485-8CB8-7A 0FE6AD1B68}&doc={083DFF6D-236B-4AF3-9507-E876C0233A62}&set=true& go.x =6&go.y=11&votingbutton=%7bE46069AF-563C-4574-BC8B-B20448289E44%7d> 1 Aug 2007.

tale."[146] With Hermione and Harry roaming Britain and searching for "Horcruxes" *Deathly Hallows* also has elements of a traditional road movie. It becomes a real "quest" with the hero going onto a journey to look for something. Regarding Rowling's style and narrative technique we find significant changes in the last part of the series; there seems to be a much greater economy of narration, there are no redundant sub-plots as in previous novels and no dispensible new characters. Concerning her rhetorical devices she writes much longer sentences, more descriptive passages and uses less of her favourite expressions like "as though", "like" or "Harry had ever seen" (see II.2.G, 53). In some parts, the text is so different that one could speculate on the influence Bloomsbury has had on this last novel.

There is one decisive flaw in her plot-making which cannot be explained by narrative necessity, but must be regarded as the author's attempt to prevent others from writing sequels to her series: the last chapter, "Nineteen Years Later" (interestingly Rowling sets this in 2017) is in no way justified by the need to give the reader further information. We only learn that Harry and Ginny, Hermione and Ron are married and have a couple of children that go to Hogwarts – something that was to be expected. This is a rather disappointing, bourgeois happy-ending, celebrating once again the traditional family as the source of fulfillment in life. Here, Rowling bows to the conventional "happily ever after"[147] that does not go in line with the complexity and the aspired meaningfulness of the whole series.[148] Maybe she intended this to make parting with the novels easier, as Felicitas von Lovenberg suggests.[149] Nevertheless, I agree with David Hugendick saying "der Epilog danach, der ist wirklich grausig. Wirklich."[150]

Rowling frequently has said that she does not intend to write an eighth book: "No, there's no University for Wizards," she stated in an interview for Scholastic. "At the moment I'm only planning to write seven Harry Potter books. I won't say 'never', but I have no plans to write an eighth book."

---

[146] Kate Muir, "Explosive finale as young hero enters his darkest chapter," *Times Online* 21 July 2007. <http://entertainment.timesonline.co.uk/tol/arts_and_entertainment/books/article2112815.ece> 6 Aug 2007.

[147] Thomas Steinfeld, "Endlich wieder heile Welt," *Süddeutsche Zeitung* 23 July 2007. <http://www.sueddeutsche.de/kultur/artikel/930/124747> 6 Aug 2007.

[148] von Lovenberg, "Rekordauflagen," 2007.

[149] Felicitas von Lovenberg, "Ende gut, alles gut?" *F.A.Z.* 23 July 2007. <http://www.F.A.Z.net/s/Rub1DA1FB848C1E44858CB87A0FE6AD1B68/Doc~ED1FD142EB4934D8D87BC67BE25ED7573~ATpl~Ecommon~Sspezial.html> 6 Aug 2007.

[150] "the following epilogue is really dreadful. Really it is.", David Hugendick, "Zelten und grübeln," *Die ZEIT* 29/2007. <http://images.zeit.de/text/online/2007/30/harry-potter-rezension> 25 Aug 2007. [my translation]

II.3.B. Titles

The titles of the *Potter* novels follow an obvious pattern: they all begin with "Harry Potter and..." which is followed by a name. The possible reader, i.e. buyer, can easily see that he is dealing with a series:[151]

> ... the Philosopher's Stone
> ... the Chamber of Secrets
> ... the Prisoner of Azkaban
> ... the Goblet of Fire
> ... the Order of the Phoenix
> ... the Half-Blood Prince
> ... the Deathly Hallows

The names in the second part of the titles usually mention a mysterious place, an unknown object or an obscure person and raise the reader's expectation.[152] In the course of action this place, object or person turns out to be a vital part of the novel. In *Philosopher's Stone*, for example, it is exactly this magical stone that sets the plot in motion. And in *Chamber of Secrets* the subterranean room in the dungeons is home to the basilisk and the setting for the dramatic showdown between Harry and Voldemort. The same is true for all the other titles as well: the title always indicates the central element of the book.

The chapter titles can be divided in groups. Usually they, too, follow the pattern of the book titles. About eighty percent[153] contain the names of characters or magical objects like 2.12 "The Polyjuice Potion", 2.14 "Cornelius Fudge", 2.17 "The Heir of Slytherin", 2.18 "Dobby's Reward", 3.10 "The Marauder's Map" or 3.12 "The Patronus". 14 percent of the chapter titles include the names of places that are closely related to the locations of the following text. Among these are titles like 4.11 "Aboard the Hogwarts Express", 5.35 "Beyond the Veil", 1.16 "Through the Trapdoor", 5.7 "The Ministry of Magic", 5.23 "Christmas on the Closed Ward", 4.4 "Back to The Burrow" and 3.3 "The Knight Bus". Another 50 percent name what is going to happen in the chapter and clearly serve to raise readers' expectations: 3.15 "The Quidditch Final", 3.20 "The Dementors' Kiss", 4.26 "The Second Task", 4.29 "The Dream", 5.33 "Fight and Flight" and 5.38 "The Second War Begins". These titles obviously serve to mark segments in the plot. In this category we also find expository titles

---

[151] See Anne Hiebert Alton, "Generic Fusion and the Mosaic of *Harry Potter*," *Harry Potter's World: Multidisciplinary Critical Perspectives*, ed. Elizabeth E. Heilman, New York, London: RoutledgeFalmer, 2003, 141-162, here 143.

[152] See Hiebert Alton 2003.

[153] One title can belong to more than one group, which is why you will count more than 100 percent.

that are meant to structure the text: 1.1 "The Boy Who Lived" does not only mention the most important character of the following chapter but the protagonist of the whole series. In 1.8 "The Potions Master" we meet Severus Snape for the first time and 4.17 "The Four Champions" indicates that there are four instead of three school champions elected.

A smaller group of titles (15 percent) has a metaphorical meaning that only becomes clear having read the chapter. 5.25 "The Beetle at Bay" hints at Rita Skeeter being an "Animagus", 3.2 "Aunt Marge's Big Mistake" not only mentions Marge making a mistake, but also means that in this chapter she herself becomes enormous. 5.1 "Dudley Demented" mentions the stupidity of the Dursleys' son and alludes to his near deathly encounter with a "Dementor". 5.13 "Detention with Dolores" is painful, because she tortures Harry. *Dolores* being the Spanish word for "pains" the title means "Painful detention" as much as naming the teacher. And 3.9 "Grim Defeat" mentions the Gryffindors' defeat at "Quidditch", but also hints at Harry seeing the death omen, the Grim, again.

Rowling often uses rhetorical devices in her chapter titles: some alliterate or repeat sounds like 4.25 "The Egg and the Eye", 4.5 "Weasley's Wizard Wheezes", 4.24 "Rita Skeeter's Scoop", 5.14 "Percy and Padfoot", 5.33 "Fight and Flight", 3.6 "Talons and Tea Leaves" or 2.7 "Mudbloods and Murmurs". Others name three elements, which is a classical stylistic device: 4.32 "Flesh, Blood and Bone" and 3.17 "Cat, Rat and Dog". Some titles consist of metaphors like 5.19 "The Lion and the Serpent" that stand for Gryffindor and Slytherin or 2.9 "The Writing on the Wall" that alludes to the *Mene mene tekel* of the Old Testament (Daniel 5, 5 and 25-26).

Moreover, there are titles that raise the readers' expectation, but that remain incomprehensible until he has read the chapter. These enigmatic titles include 1.4 "The Keeper of the Keys" which introduces Hagrid. 5.17 "Educational Decree Number Twenty-Four" gets its full meaning only when the reader knows what the new law is about. And only having read the chapter, the reader understands who "The Only One He Ever Feared" (5.36) really is. Finally there are titles that simply repeat the title of the novel, like 2.16 "The Chamber of Secrets", 4.16 "The Goblet of Fire", 5.5 "The Order of the Phoenix". Summing up, it is obvious that Rowling uses the chapter titles very consciously.

Speaking about time and duration, the chapters can cover very different periods. 1.5 "Diagon Alley" tells us about what is happening within a single day. 1.6 "The Journey from Platform Nine and Three-Quarters" contains the action of about one month (even if the title only indicates the ten-hour-journey from London to Hogwarts) and 1.7 "The Sorting Hat" only tells us about the evening of the sorting. The length of the chapters varies just as much as the period they cover: whereas 3.20 "The Dementors' Kiss" has about nine pages, the following 3.21 "Hermione's Secret" amounts to 32 pages. This is proof of the variety of speed Rowling uses in her narration (see II.4.B, 83).

66

Reinhard Ehgartner thinks the chapters usually have a reading time of about twenty minutes, which makes them similar to the length of a TV soap opera episode. According to him, each chapter is artfully composed.[154] Very often (like soap operas) they have an open ending that makes the reader want to know how things will go on.[155] *Harry Potter* conforming to TV consumer habits is an interesting thesis which I will not discuss any further. But regarding the vast differences in length and the period covered I cannot consent to this being a general principle in Rowling.

II.3.C. Politics and School Story – The Two Levels of the Plot

Part of the appeal of Harry Potter's adventures consists of them being written and received on at least two different levels: either we read them as funny school and detective story with magical elements or we regard them as yet another variation of the eternal battle between good and evil.[156] Each level addresses different target groups. The school story is meant for children and young adults, the latter level is the more attractive one for adult readers.[157] Out of these two levels, the author composes artfully one consistent plot as Reinhard Ehgartner says:

> Fast jeder Faden, den sie im Lauf der Geschichte einfädelt, wird an späterer Stelle wieder aufgegriffen und konsequent weitergesponnen, und am Ende sehen wir sie mit zwölf Fäden in der Hand, die wie selbstverständlich ein klares Muster ergeben.[158]

Basically there are two different kinds of plot: first of all, each volume (apart from the last novel) tells a classic school and detective story, the mysteries of which are solved the end. Secondly, there is another plot working at a political level and comprising the whole series. The first kind of story chiefly addresses children and shall be referred to as children's level ($L_{Children\ (C)}$), the second is appealing to the adult reader ($L_{Adult\ (A)}$).

L_C begins and ends every single part of the series. The children are the protagonists that try to find out what is happening on L_A and throw light on an

---

[154] See Ehgartner 2002, 69.

[155] See Bürvenich 2001, 54; Schafer 2000, 220.

[156] Charles Elster introduces the terms "bildungsroman" and "heroic" level (see Charles Elster, "The Seeker of Secrets: Images of Learning, Knowing, and Schooling," *Harry Potter's World: Multidisciplinary Critical Perspectives*, ed. Elizabeth E. Heilman, New York, London: RoutledgeFalmer, 2003, 203-220, here 203.

[157] See George Beahm, *Fact, fiction, and folklore in Harry Potter's world: an unofficial guide*, Charlottesville, Virginia: Hampton Roads, 2005, XVII.

[158] "Nearly every detail she introduces in the course of action is referred to later on and consequently used. And in the end we see her with twelve threads in her hand that make up a logical pattern." (Ehgartner 2002, 70 [my translation])

apparent intrigue against Harry or Dumbledore. This is a classical detective story (see II.4.D, 87) blended with elements of the school story (see VII.1.D, 425). Normally, the children turn out to be more clever than the adults and it is them that save the day: the Philosopher's Stone is finally saved by Harry and his friends and it is them that find the Chamber of Secrets to save Ginny. In the third and fourth part of the series the adults fail completely: only the children can give proof of Sirius being innocent. Harry must face alone the mortal danger he is exposed to by the impostor Moody. Dumbledore appears in the very last moment to save him from Crouch jnr In *Order of the Phoenix* this relation between adults and children is reversed: the children find out that the adults are trying to hide the decisive prophecy in the Department of Mysteries from Voldemort, but the villain uses this to lure them into a trap.

The latter refers to events that have taken place before the point of attack of *Philosopher's Stone*. The main locations of L_A are the Ministry of Magic and the places Voldemort is hiding (Albania, Riddle House). The adult characters are the protagonists of this plot: apart from the villains these include the Weasleys and the Malfoys, the members of the "Order of the Phoenix" and the teachers of Hogwarts. The children play a minor role.

The two levels L_C and L_A both appear in the novels and usually fuse in the final climax. The pattern of L_C being a classical school and detective story and L_A addressing adult readers chiefly applies to the first four parts. At the end of *Goblet of Fire* and especially in the following volumes this pattern changes: the school story L_C looses its importance, the children increasingly interfere with L_A.

Both levels melt into a one-level plot in *Half-Blood Prince*: Harry's fight against Voldemort becomes the center of the plot, he is the protagonist of L_A and, being "The Chosen One", he is the last hope of the opposition. His enemies of L_C like Draco, Snape and the members of Slytherin House also enter L_A: Draco replaces his father as a "Death Eater", Snape apparently changes sides and kills Dumbledore. At the end of *Half-Blood Prince*, Harry decides to leave Hogwarts to fight Voldemort (HP 6, 606). At that point the two levels merge completely. *Deathly Hallows*, finally, concentrates on the political level, there is no L_C but only L_A.

II.3.D. Stories for Children and Adults – Story and Plot

The *Harry Potter* novels combine a multitude of different plots, sub-plots and stories. Untwining them is one of the tasks of this chapter. All those different plot lines add to the series' richness and colourfulness.

Summing up the story of the whole saga, we find the following:

N°	Action	Time
1.	Merope Gaunt, the last female descendant of Salazar Slytherin, falls in love with a wealthy "Muggle". Using a magic potion she forces him to marry her. Just before the birth of their first child, Tom Riddle snr realises who his wife really is and leaves her. Merope gives birth to her son in an orphanage and dies.	65 years before HP 2[159]
2.	Tom lives in the orphanage and is taken to Hogwarts by Dumbledore when he is ten. Already at this age, the boy is malicious.	55 years before HP 2
3.	Tom Riddle finds out that his mother and not his father was the wizard of his family. Learning what his father did to his mother, he begins to hate "Muggles" and kills the Riddle family.	
4.	In his fifth year at Hogwarts, Tom opens the Chamber of Secrets, releases the Basilisk, which kills a girl. Successfully, Tom blames Hagrid who is sent from the school.	50 years before HP 2
5.	Tom persuades his teacher Horace Slughorn to tell him about "Horcruxes" – a magical way to preserve a dead person's soul. He decides to make himself immortal.	
6.	Tom refuses his teachers' offers of a promising career in the Ministry. Instead, he starts working as art buyer with Borgin and Burkes. He uses his position to get hold of antiques he uses as "Horcruxes".	
7.	Together with friends, Tom (who has begun calling himself Voldemort by now) usurps power in the magical world.	
8.	Sybill Trelawney foresees that soon a child will be born that can end Voldemort's reign. One of the two is going to die.	1,5 years before HP 1
9.	Voldemort murders Harry's parents and tries to kill the infant. But his killing curse reflects from the child and hits himself instead. His reign is ended. Harry is brought to live with his "Muggle" family. Through the killing curse, Harry is transformed into a "Horcrux" for Voldemort.	HP 1
10.	Ten years later Harry learns that he is a wizard and is brought to Hogwarts.	HP 1

---

[159] See II.4, 76.

N°	Action	Time
11.	Voldemort tries to steal the Philosopher's Stone in order to heal himself. Harry sees through his intentions and prevents him from getting the stone.	HP 1
12.	In the following school year a diary by Tom Riddle is found in Hogwarts. It is one of Voldemort's "Horcruxes". Ginny Weasley is intrigued by Riddle's charm, opens the Chamber of Secrets and releases the monster. Harry kills the Basilisk and frees Ginny.	HP 2
13.	During the summer holidays the dangerous criminal Sirius Black (Harry's godfather) breaks out of the wizard prison Akzaban. He has been wrongly accused of treason and of the Potters' multiple murder. The true murderer is Peter Pettigrew, who lives as an "Animagus" in the form of a rat as Ron's pet. Harry helps to find the real culprit and reconciles with Black. Nevertheless, the vindication fails and Black has to flee.	HP 3
14.	Voldemort plans to use a school tournament in Hogwarts to lure Harry into a trap. He tricks Harry into the role of school champion and makes him participate in the tasks. He turns the winner's cup into a Portkey and forces Harry to meet him. With the help of Harry's blood, Voldemort returns to his former strength. Opposition groups itself around Dumbledore.	HP 4
15.	Voldemort wants to know what Trelawney's prophecy really says. He tries to enter the Department of Mysteries, where the prophecy is hidden. The "Order of the Phoenix" realises what he is after and protects it. Voldemort lures Harry into the Ministry to get hold of the prophecy. During a fight between the two parties, the prophecy is broken. Sirius dies.	HP 5
16.	Voldemort orders Draco Malfoy to kill Dumbledore. Snape swears to Narcissa Malfoy to protect her son and to commit the crime himself if necessary. Dumbledore makes sure Harry gets all the information he has about Voldemort. Then, knowing that he must die within the next months, because of an evil curse that has hit him, he asks Severus to kill him. Dumbledore pretends to be lured into a trap set by the "Death Eaters" and is killed by Snape. Harry witnesses the supposed murder and swears revenge.	HP 6

N°	Action	Time
17.	Harry and his friends go into hiding to look for the missing "Horcruxes" and are able to destroy most of them. Voldemort takes over power and installs his regime of terror. Harry sacrifices his life to kill Voldemort – and the little part of his soul surviving in himself. As he is the true owner of the "Deathly Hallows", three magical items that united make their master imortal, he can return to life. Voldemort is defeated forever.	HP 7

It is obvious that the basic conflict is set around the character of Voldemort. The only exception is *Prisoner of Azkaban* (see II.5, 89): the villain's attempts to usurp power are the main forces of the plot. In contrast to this, the individual parts of the series are stories with a clear ending.

While the story of the novels is easily described, the plot that includes motivation and reasons is much more complicated. Therefore, I will concentrate only on the beginning of the series to demonstrate, how the plot is constructed:

N°	Action
1.	The Dursleys, a middle-class family, are living an uneventful life in Little Whinging. One day, their one and a half-year old nephew Harry, is delivered to their threshold: his parents have been killed. The boy's mother being Petunia Dursley's sister, the family are his only living relatives. In front of the house a group of mysterious people meets and they talk about the boy having defeated a tyrant and and of his having liberated the world.
2.	Harry spends ten miserable years with the Dursleys who hate him. Shortly before his eleventh birthday he learns that he is a wizard. The master of the wizard boarding school Hogwarts has Harry brought to school to teach him magic.
3.	Harry's first year at Hogwarts begins. He makes friends and foes. A boy called Draco Malfoy becomes his arch-enemy. The teacher Snape prefers him to Harry. One wing of the castle is closed. Entering it by accident, Harry and his friends find themselves face to face with a monster – a three-headed dog that is obviously guarding something. From various hints the children draw the conclusion that it must be the Philosopher's Stone that guarantees eternal life to the bearer.

N°	Action
4.	Hagrid explains how to get past the monster. There seems to be the danger of Snape getting the magical stone to give it to Voldemort. Harry and his friends enter the forbidden wing and from there the Hogwarts dungeons, where they find Voldemort and Quirrell.
5.	Hoping to regain his strength, Voldemort tries to get hold of the stone. Quirrell is the villain's devout servant and has brought him to Hogwarts. In a duel, Harry saves the stone from Voldemort.

The plot is much more complex than the story. Additionally, there are many sub-plots that merely serve to entertain the reader. An example of this is the story about the dragon Norbert (HP 1, 249-261): Hagrid desperately wants to possess a dragon. Therefore, a stranger, presenting him with a dragon egg, is able to get his confidence. In return, Hagrid tells him about the three-headed dog. That is how Voldemort gets the required information to get past the guardian.

Another example for such a sub-plot is the story of Dobby that begins in part two. Tricking Mr. Malfoy, Harry frees Dobby from his slavery with the Malfoys (HP 2, 362-363). Thankfully Dobby helps Harry whenever he can, for example when he tells him how to succeed in the second task in *Goblet of Fire* (HP 4, 334-336). Nearly Headless Nick's Deathday Party in *Chamber of Secrets* (HP 2, 134-153) is just another sub-plot. The ghost celebrates his deathday (something the author writes about for twenty pages) and invites Harry and his friends. This episode is completely without any function for the main plot.[160]

There are many more examples of sub-plots without function for the main plot. This multitude of plots leads to a certain dramaturgical weakness: for example this is the case with the sub-plot about Hermione initiating "SPEW" (HP 4, 246-247). Until *Deathly Hallows*, when the house-elves join the battle of Hogwarts to support Dumbledore's Army, the episode has no importance at all for the main plot and merely adds to the length of the novel. Other examples of such sub-plots include:

- Harry and Ron miss the Hogwarts Express and fly to school using the Weasleys' bewitched car (HP 2, 74-95).
- Dudley Dursley goes on a diet (HP 4, 43).
- the Weasleys come to get Harry from the Dursleys (HP 4, 47-57).
- Hermione's teeth are bewitched by Draco Malfoy (HP 4, 328).
- Lockhart stages an embarrassing Valentine's Day (HP 2, 255-259).
- cleaning of the Black house of demons and items of black magic (HP 5, 117-121).

---

[160] Which is why it was omitted in the 2002 movie.

On the contrary, the following sub-plots are closely related to the main plot:
- Draco Malfoy is hurt by Buckbeak, the animal is sentenced to death, but is saved by Harry and Hermione (HP 3).
- Professor Lupin is a werewolf (HP 3).
- Harry joins the Weasleys to see the "Quidditch" World Cup (HP 4, 86-161).
- over-ambitious Barty Crouch destroys his family (HP 4).

The *Potter* stories are full of action. This is exactly what Gottfried Bachl[161] criticises: "Es gibt kaum ruhigere Lesestellen, keine Wüste, keine Pause, keine Zumutung der ereignislosen Zeit."[162] He completely ignores the fact that action is precisely what children love (see VII.1.A, 419). In the *Potter* series, various sub-plots with little or no relevance to the main plot are grouped around one central story. Each volume has a plot of its own. The central plot about Voldemort's rise, fall and return spans the whole series. This technique shows that Rowling addresses different groups of readers – the adult reader will probably be more interested in the representation of the eternal fight between good and evil, as Pat Pinsent writes:

> [The] adult readers are able to detect allegorical elements, or may sometimes feel that the complex structures and development of suspense resemble examples of the detective or thriller genre.[163]

The texts are "twofold addressed" to children and adults at the same time, which is one of their secrets of success. Children will miss out the many references and satirical allusions to everyday life, because they lack the experience. Adults, on the other hand, will not be interested in Harry's love life, but favour the development of his relatioship with Dumbledore.[164]

---

[161] See Michael Langner, "Unheil aus Hogwart? Streiflichter zur Harry-Potter-Rezeption in Theologie und Kirche," *Faszination "Harry Potter": Was steckt dahinter?* eds. Dormeyer, Detlev and Friedhelm Munzel, Münster: LIT, 2005, 17-29, here 25.

[162] "There is hardly any calm, any deserts, any pause; no reader's suffering because of uneventful passages." (Bachl 2002, 121 [my translation])

[163] Pinsent 2004, 49.

[164] This phenomenon has been widely discussed in the context of children's literature. The general opinion is that the classics of the genre like *Alice in Wonderland* or *Winnie the Pooh* can always be enjoyed by the child as much as by the adult reading the story aloud. This is achieved by using different narrative levels with the adult finding a comic if not satirical or even allegorical element in the text. Paul Bürvenich analysing stylistic devices proves the existence of such different levels in *Harry Potter* as well. See Bürvenich 2001, 97-98.

II.3.E. The "Daily Prophet" Reports – Combining Different Plots

Taking into account the multitude of different plots in the series we wonder how these are combined and are held together. All the plots which are situated within Hogwarts and belong to L_C are tied together by the identity of space and characters: pupils meet in class or during meals and the behaviour of a teacher or an event in Hogwarts sets off actions by the children. For example Dolores Umbridge's tyranny makes the whole school resist (HP 5, 695-698) and the attacks on pupils in *Chamber of Secrets* spur Harry and his friends into action.

The case with the plots belonging to L_A is different: the whole series being narrated mostly from Harry's point of view (situated on $L_{(C)}$) the information about L_A has to be included artfully. Rowling uses

- overheard dialogues.
- reports in the "Daily Prophet".
- visions and prophecies.
- characters' narrations.

For instance, among the overheard dialogues is the conversation between Mr and Mrs Weasley about Black's alleged plans to murder Harry (HP 3, 74-76) and the meeting of Cornelius Fudge and some of the Hogwarts teachers in the Leaky Cauldron in Hogsmeade (HP 3, 220-227). In both cases Harry gets vital information about Sirius Black. This kind of information serves to raise the readers' expectations: is Black going to kill Harry? How can his godfather have betrayed his parents?

The articles in the "Daily Prophet" appear regularly throughout the whole series and serve to inform the reader about the events of L_A that otherwise would not be noticeable on L_C; the report "Inquiry at the Ministry of Magic" (HP 2, 240-241) makes the reader understand that Lucius Malfoy is trying to disgrace Mr Weasley publicly. And later the reader gets to know through the newspaper that Black has been sighted close to Hogwarts (HP 3, 138). The "Daily Prophet" even serves as a means of communication within L_A. The photo of the Weasley family in Egypt makes Black realise that Pettigrew is hiding as Ron's pet rat Scabbers (HP 3, 391). In *Goblet of Fire* and *Order of the Phoenix* the newspaper plays an especially important role: when journalist Rita Skeeter appears on the Hogwarts stage the articles cease to be information and become manipulation. Craving for sensation, Rita takes sides against the Ministry and against the Weasleys (HP 4, 163-165 and 223-224). She tries to compromise Hagrid because of his being a half-giant (HP 4, 477-480) and reports in tabloid style for the women's magazine "Witch Weekly" on Harry's supposed lovesickness (HP 4, 556-558).

The newspaper becomes especially important for communication between L_A and L_C in *Order of the Phoenix*: among other things, the "Daily Prophet" reports on the intrigues that lead to Dumbledore's disempowerment (HP 5, 111), the mass breakout of "Death Eaters" from Azkaban (HP 5, 600-601) and Broderick Bode's bizarre death (HP 5, 602-603). All of this information is relevant to reconstruct L_A through the eyes of L_C. In *Half-Blood Prince* the newspaper serves to sum up all the events that happened between the end of HP 5 and the beginning of HP 6 – and tells us what kind of security measures have been taken to protect Hogwarts (HP 6, 44), that Fudge has been replaced by Rufus Scrimgeour (HP 6, 43), that Harry is now seen as the saviour of the wizarding world if not indeed a messiah (HP 6, 43) and it shows in various articles how the life of each citizen has changed because of Voldemort's terror (HP 6, 45).

Harry's visions and time travels play an important role for connecting the two levels of the plot. This is especially noticeable in *Order of the Phoenix* when the repeated dreams he has about Voldemort trying to get into the Department of Mysteries make clear how dangerous the situation for the protagonists of L_A is. Mr Weasley can only be rescued because Harry has witnessed the attack in one of his visions and knows where to find the dying man (HP 5, 511-515). These visionary dreams make Harry relive his parents' death: repeatedly he hears his mother cry out and his father begging her to save herself and the child (HP 3, 194 and 259). Sybill Trelawney (apart from her being a bad teacher; HP 3, 114-116) predicts at least two events that are of vital importance to the world of Harry Potter: the return of Pettigrew to Voldemort (HP 3, 349-350) and the birth of the saviour (HP 5, 924). The latter sets off the whole plot of the *Potter* series.

Throughout the whole saga Harry goes on various time travels and thus receives relevant information about the past. In Riddle's Diary in *Chamber of Secrets* he overhears a dialogue between former school headmaster Dippet and Tom: Harry realizes how similar Tom's situation is to his own (HP 2, 266-268). In *Goblet of Fire* Harry discovers Dumbledore's "Pensieve": he enters the headmaster's memories and relives some of the trials against "Death Eaters" that were held decades ago. Thus he gets to know that Karkaroff was a coward, that "Quidditch" hero Ludo Bagman could not be cleared of the charges against him and that Barty Crouch sent his own son to Azkaban (HP 4, 644-647). This information is decisive for understanding the plot. Harry undertakes another time travel in *Order of the Phoenix* when he looks into Snape's memories and sees how arrogant his father's attitude towards Severus was (HP 5, 704-714). This impression changes Harry's adoration of his parents and makes him question their roles for the first time. So this time travel not only explains why Snape hates Harry but also contributes to the hero's psychological development. In *Deathly Hallows*, Harry enters dying Snape's thoughts and finds the reason for his teacher's hatred towards himself: he loved Harry's mother. Harry also learns about Snape's loyalty to Dumbledore and the promise of secrecy he gave him. We, the readers, realise why Snape reacted so violently to Harry's entering his mind (HP 5, 704-714).

Finally, the author makes use of figural reports to combine different plots. First of all, these reports serve to describe events of the past: the giant spider Aragog tells Harry and Ron that the Chamber of Secrets has not been opened by Hagrid in fifty years and hints at the kind of monster that lives within it (HP 2, 299-301). The boys need this knowledge to solve the mystery. Lupin tells Harry in *Prisoner of Azkaban* that he was a friend of James' (HP 3, 261-262) and, thus, contributes to Harry getting to know his parents. Severus Snape adds the negative aspects about Harry's father (HP 3, 308). In the end, the reports by Lupin and Black help to solve the mystery about Pettigrew's treason (HP 3, 376-385). In *Goblet of Fire* Harry first finds out about Voldemort's activities in a dialogue betwenn Mr and Mrs Weasley, where they speak about the sudden disappearance of Bertha Jorkins (HP 4, 71-72). Later on, Sirius Black tells Harry about Crouch's cruelty and Bagman's dubious past (HP 4, 571-581). This knowledge is necessary to understand what is going on during the Triwizard Tournament. The reports by Crouch jnr and Voldemort at the end of HP 4 play a decisive role and explain all the riddles and mysteries of the novel: suddenly, through the confession of Crouch jnr, we understand the mayhem at the "Quidditch" World Cup, the bizarre behaviour of the real Moody and the death of Crouch snr (HP 4, 735-749). Voldemort's speech on the cemetery of Little Hangleton explains what has happened to him after the failed attempt to kill Harry (HP 4, 698-714) – where he has been, how he survived and how Pettigrew joined him. For the reader, who has experienced the whole saga from Harry's point of view up to this moment, the circle is closing and Voldemort explains the missing or questionable details of all the *Potter* novels before *Goblet of Fire*. The villain's strategy, his motivation and his unsuccessful pursuit of power become evident.

At the end of nearly every *Potter* part there is a report by Dumbledore. The headmaster explains to Harry what he knows about the background of what has just happened. Dumbledore is nearly omniscient (a role that he gives up at the beginning of *Half-Blood Prince* when he accepts Harry as his equal). In *Chamber of Secrets* he tells Harry about Tom's sad youth and his transformation into Voldemort. He also explains the connection between Voldemort's failed attempt to kill Harry and the mental bond that exists between the two. In *Order of the Phoenix*, Dumbledore tells Harry about the prophecy that has set the whole plot off and leaves Harry to be either murderer or victim (HP 5, 927). And finally, in *Deathly Hallows*, all remaining riddles are explained in "The Prince's Tale" (HP 7, 529-553).

Using these techniques (newspaper articles, dreams, visions, reports, time travels) all the information the reader gets is justified. The things Harry cannot possibly know (and with him the reader is ignorant of) are either transmitted in the very few passages narrated by an omniscient narrator or the point of view shifts to another character for a brief moment (see II.2.A, 39).

II.4 Seven Years in the Life of "Harry Potter" – Structure of Time

All the parts of the series narrate the events of one single year. They begin during the summer holidays, usually describe shopping in Diagon Alley, travelling to Hogwarts, the reception in the Great Hall, Halloween (in the first four books), Christmas, exams and, finally, the journey home.

The Hogwarts school year begins on September 1st and ends on June 30th of the following year.[165] Halloween and Christmas are important breaks in the first *Potter* books – usually at these dates decisive events occur. In *Philosopher's Stone* Harry saves Hermione from a troll on Halloween (HP 1, 189-192), on Christmas Day he sees his parents in the Mirror of Erised for the first time (HP 1, 225-227). In the following book, Harry hears the Basilisk for the first time on Halloween (HP 2, 142-151), at Christmas he and Ron try the "Polyjuice Potion". *Prisoner of Azkaban* follows this pattern as well. On Halloween Sirius Black breaks into Gryffindor Tower (HP 3, 165-175) and Harry gets a "Firebolt" as Christmas present (HP 3, 241-243). In *Goblet of Fire* Harry's name is drawn from the goblet at Halloween (HP 4, 281). In the following parts of the *Potter* series, these dates cease to be important and the pattern changes. In *Deathly Hallows*, Hermione and Harry spend Christmas in Godric's Hollow and are lured into Voldermort's trap (HP 7, "Godric's Hollow", "Bathilda's Secret").

The plot always begins and ends in summer, but every time it ends, the situation has changed compared to the beginning: things have become more complicated, the adventures Harry has had to go through have changed him and we have learnt something new about Voldemort's intrigues. His activities become more and more threatening, the number of his followers is growing. So the basic structure of the plot is a cycle, with its beginning being changed at each rotation.[166] Suman Gupta calls this technique "elaboration":

> The technical key, so to say, seems to me to be a method of elaboration both repeating and progressively delineating a finite number of situations and themes by adding ever greater degrees of complexity in their relationships.[167]

---

[165] See Schafer 2000, 91.

[166] John Granger regards this as Christian allegory: Harry is in mortal danger each year and very narrowly escapes being murdered. "The climax of Harry's hero journey invariably turns out to be a strong image of Christian hope: that death is followed by resurrection in Christ." (Granger 2004, 23)

[167] This – according to Suman Gupta – is the reason why the books have more and more pages and why the plot is getting ever more complicated. See Gupta 2003, 95-96.

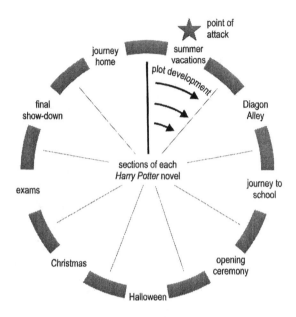

Figure 4: Circular Structure of Time

Until the publication of *Deathly Hallows*, critics had tried to find out the "real" dates and years of the *Potter* series. When and in which year are the novels set? There are two very clear dates mentioned in the novels: in the last part we read the Potters' birth and death dates on their epitaphs (HP 7, 268) – they died on Halloween 1981. Harry being fifteen months old at that time (HP 1, 65), he must have been born on July 31st, 1980[168] – the same day as the author J.K. Rowling in 1965. Neville Longbottom, the second boy the prophecy could refer to as the *Chosen One*, was born one day before Harry – as Rowling says in an interview.[169] Another hint is to be found in *Chamber of Secrets* when Nearly Headless Nick, the Gryffindor ghost, celebrates his 500th deathday. His deathday cake reads the 31st of October 1492 (HP 2, 146), which must be exactly 500

---

168 See Bürvenich 2001, 56; Schafer 2000, 45; Karin E. Westman, "Specters of Thatcherism. Contemporary British Culture in J.K. Rowling's Harry Potter Series," *The Ivory Tower and Harry Potter: Perspectives on a Literary Phenomenon*, ed. Lana A. Whited, Columbia: University of Missouri Press, 2004, 305-328, here 308; Lana A. Whited, "*Harry Potter and the Order of the Phoenix* – Epilogue," *The Ivory Tower and Harry Potter: Perspectives on a Literary Phenomenon*, ed. Lana A. Whited, Columbia: University of Missouri Press, 2004, 365-373, 369.

169 "Neville was born on the 30th of July, the day before Harry, so he too was born 'as the seventh month dies.'" (Rowling 2006)

years ago at this point. Therefore, this part of the series is set in 1992.[170] Thus, the novels are to be dated like this:[171]

1.	*Philosopher's Stone*	Halloween 1981 – June 30th, 1992
2.	*Chamber of Secrets*	July 31st, 1992 – June 30th, 1993
3.	*Prisoner of Azkaban*	July 30th, 1993 – June 30th, 1994
4.	*Goblet of Fire*	August 1994 – June 30th, 1995
5.	*Order of the Phoenix*	August 1995 – June 30th, 1996
6.	*Half-Blood Prince*	mid-July 1996 – June 30th, 1997
7.	*Deathly Hallows*	August 1997 – 30. Juni 1998 (September 1st, 2017)

But there seems to be more to these dates. In *Chamber of Secrets* (set in 1992) it is said that the chamber was opened fifty years ago, (HP 2, 242), from which one could infer that it was in 1942. Lana A. Whited points to this dating situating "the opening of the Chamber squarely during the heyday of modern human history's most notorious racial purist, Adolf Hitler."[172] This is in line with Dumbledore defeating "the dark wizard Grindelwald" (HP 1, 114) a magician who possesses an obviously Germanic name (see IV.6.H, 275). Taking into account the similarities between the racist fascist-like ideology of Voldemort and German National Socialism such identities of time cannot be a coincidence. Lana A. Whited points out that Nick's deathday, 1492, is the anagram of 1942 – yet another connection between the two years mentioned in the book. October 1492, the month of Nick's failed execution, is exactly the time when Christopher Columbus reached America. While in the US October 12th is celebrated as "Columbus Day", South America commemorates this day as "Día de la Raza" (Day of Race) and as the beginning of the destruction of their native cultures and peoples.[173] October 31st, 1922 is also the day Italian fascist Benito Mussolini came to power.

But this is not the end of interpreting Rowling's numbers and years as allusions to racism, fascism and the Second World War. The trial against Buckbeak – initiated by Lucius Malfoy – takes place on April 20th, Hitler's birthday (HP 3, 236), the failed revision and the liberation of the innocent animals happens on June 6th (HP 3, 341). This day, June 6th, seems to be the central date of *Prisoner of Azkaban*: on this day, Harry and Hermione risk entering the Shriek-

---

[170] There is yet another hint at 1992: Trelawney warns Lavender that the event she dreads will happen on Friday, 16th of October (HP 3, 115). In fact, the girl's pet rabbit dies that day (HP 3, 162). In 1992 the 16th of October was a Friday, and it happened to be Rowling's wedding day to her first husband. See Smith 2001, 114 and I.2.B, 20.

[171] There is a very precise and detailed overview of dates made by fans on the internet: <http://en.wikipedia.org/wiki/Dates_in_Harry_Potter>.

[172] Whited, "Harry Potter and the Order," 2004, 369.

[173] See Whited, "Harry Potter and the Order," 2004, 369.

ing Shack to help Ron, Pettigrew is discovered, Sirius is rehabilitated and saved. June 6th, 1944, is famous as D-Day in the real world and, thus, as the beginning of the end of World War II.[174]

Unfortunately, the dates Rowling mentions in the course of action do not match with the years the novels are set in. In *Goblet of Fire*, for example, we read about the "Sunday evening before they were due to return to Hogwarts" (HP 4, 168). This means that August 31st must be a Sunday, because the journey to Hogwarts always begins on September 1st. This day of the week and the date only match with 1980, 1986, 1997 and 2003.[175] In the same novel it is mentioned that October 31st (Halloween) is a Saturday.[176] This was the case in 1992 and 1998. The two dates Rowling gives us cannot refer to the same year and, moreover, there were no such days in 1994. This can be considered a narrative inconsistency on the author's part.[177] In *Order of the Phoenix* we find yet another "wrong" date: Monday, 2nd of September (HP 5, 251).[178] There was such a day in 1996, but not in 1995 when the novel is set. Again, this is a lack of consistency on the author's behalf.

But how does Rowling depict time in her books? On the one hand she uses her protagonist Harry to describe how time passes. When in *Philosopher's Stone* Harry sees his birthday approaching, discourse time is nearly identical with narrative time (see II.2.A, 36). When Harry feels time fly, the passing of time is dealt with on a more general level:

> Time was behaving in a more peculiar fashion than ever, rushing past in great dollops, so that one moment he seemed to be sitting down in his first lesson, History of Magic, and the next walking into lunch ... and then (where had the morning gone? The last of the dragon-free hours?) Professor McGonagall was hurrying over to him in the Great Hall. (HP 4, 381)

---

[174] Michael Maar says adequately: "Bei Mann blitzt hinter dem Faschismus das Teuflische auf, bei Rowling blitzen hinter den Teufeln Faschisten auf." ("In [Thomas Mann] we see fascism behind the demoniacal, in Rowling we find fascists behind demons." [my translation]), Maar 2003, 100; Schafer 2000, 178.

[175] See Salesianer, <http://www.salesianer.de> 3 Jan 2008.

[176] Dumbledore says: "Tomorrow night, Halloween, the Goblet will return [...]." (HP 4, 281). Later (HP 4, 284) we read, "As the next day was Saturday [...]." Halloween is celebrated on the last day of October, meaning that this must refer to a Saturday.

[177] This is what fans discuss on the internet as well: <http://en.wikipedia.org/wiki/Dates_in_Harry_Potter> 15 Oct 2007.

[178] On the first day back at school (which must be September 1st), Ron sighs during breakfast: "'That's the worst Monday I've ever seen.'" (HP 5, 21). So September 1st must be a Monday.

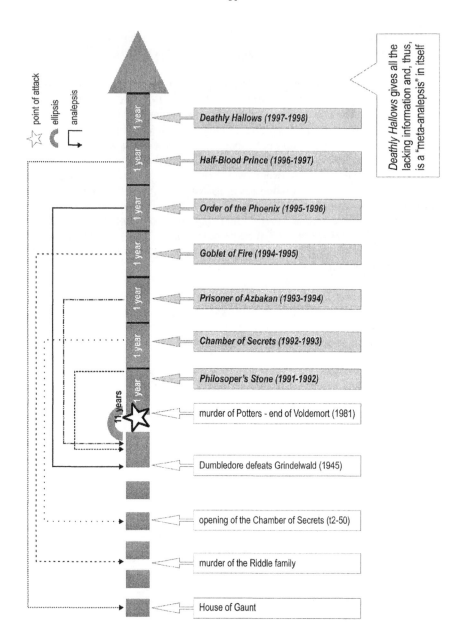

Figure 5: Timeline of all the Harry Potter *Novels*

At the end of *Order of the Phoenix* it is the sun that stands metaphorically for time going by: "late-afternoon sunshine" (HP 5, 813), "evening air" (HP 5, 825), "daylight began to fail" (HP 5, 841), "twilight fell" (HP 5, 842), "dawn was approaching" (HP 5, 901), "the sun was rising properly" (HP 5, 908), "sunlight" (HP 5, 910), "the sun was bright" (HP 5, 916) and finally: "The sun had risen fully now" (HP 5, 922). This passage ends with, "Harry could hear the sound of voices, students heading down to the Great Hall for an early breakfast, perhaps." (HP 5, 927) It is the rising of the sun and the increasing daylight that indicate time.

II.4.A. Clues, Red Herrings and Solving the Riddle – Narrative Order

Analysing the narrative order of the plot is more complicated – the author makes very conscious use of this device to raise and bind the readers' expectations. Basically, the novels are narrated in chronological order: one school year follows after the other. The whole series is narrated from an undefined future which justifies the past tense. Harry experiences the events the moment they are narrated. Further figural narrations complete the text. These reports cause so called analepses, i.e. disorders of time (see 29), that make the plot more interesting than the story. Most of these retrospectively narrate events that have happened before the point of attack in HP 1. For example, with every school year Dumbledore, Voldemort, Black or Lupin tell Harry more about the death of his parents. Only in *Deathly Hallows* he finally learns how they died entering Voldemort's thoughts (HP 7, 280-282).

On the other hand, there are many analepses that merely inform about what has happened within the same part of the series and serve to solve the riddle. In *Prisoner of Azkaban* Sirius Black adds the relevant information about his biography. In *Goblet of Fire* Barty Crouch jnr speaks about his connection with Voldemort. In *Order of the Phoenix* Dumbledore tells Harry more about the mysterious prophecy and *Half-Blood Prince* merely wholly consists of analepsis when Dumbledore and Harry go on their time travels in the headmaster's "Pensieve". In *Deathly Hallows*, finally, we learn how the Potters were murdered. The other form of anachrony is the prolepsis that anticipates information not available at that particular point in the story. This is quite rare in *Harry Potter*. Among these we can count the prophecies by Sybill Trelawney (HP 3, 349-350 and HP 5, 924).

The most important narrative technique Rowling uses are clues (see II.1.A,, 30) that hint at the further development of the plot. Rowling either hints at the right conclusion (clues) or deliberately puts the reader off the scent (red herrings or "leurres") and even makes clues look like red herrings ("faux leurres"). Examples of classical clues are:

- Ginny's unexplainable depression (HP 2, 201) – in fact, she suspects herself to be the one who unleashes the monster.
- Hagrid's report on the roosters that have been killed overnight (HP 2, 218) – later the reader realises that the Basilisk has killed them.
- the Weasleys have to go back home, because Ginny has forgotten her (Riddle-) diary (HP 2, 75).[179]
- Scabbers' mysterious illness (HP 3, 66) – at the end of *Prisoner of Azkaban* the reader learns that Scabbers is Pettigrew who is afraid of being discovered.
- Barty Crouch's appearance on the "Marauder's Map" (HP 4, 508-509) hints at the false identity of Moody – but only at the end of *Goblet of Fire* does the reader understand the full meaning.
- Kreacher's disappearance (HP 5, 554-556) and happy return (HP 5, 569) – meanwhile he has betrayed his master Black to Voldemort (HP 5, 912-914).
- Snape's hand quivers when he swears the Unbreakable Vow (HP 6, 41).[180]

The question as to why there is a "gleam of something like triumph in Dumbledore's eyes" (HP 4, 654) when he hears Harry's report on Voldemort's physical rebirth has also widely been discussed.[181] The author participated in the guesswork.[182] As *Deathly Hallows* finally showed, this was another clue: in this moment, Dumbledore knows that Voldemort has weakened himself without realising it (HP 7, 568).

Red herrings, i.e. hints that lead to wrong conclusions, are for example the following:

- Harry believes that Snape tries to kill him in a "Quidditch" accident (HP 1, 206-207) – in reality he saves him from Quirrell (HP 1, 310-311).
- overhearing a talk between the two, Harry believes Snape is blackmailing Quirrell (HP 1, 244-245) – in fact, Snape has understood that Quirrell is a servant of Voldemort's (HP 1, 312).

---

[179] Michael Maar claims that the book is mentioned in the bookstore Flourish and Blotts for the first time (HP 2, 70-72). But this is wrong. Maar probably confuses the book with the film version (see Maar 2003, 55).

[180] "'And, should it prove necessary ... if it seems Draco will fail ... [...] will you carry out the deed that the Dark Lord has ordered Draco to perform?'" (HP 6, 41). In *Deathly Hallows* we learn that Snape is Dumbledore's closest ally and, thus, shocked by having to carry out this deed.

[181] See Maar 2003, 145.

[182] "Hmmmmmm ... like all the best questions I get asked, I can't answer that one. But you are obviously reading carefully. I promise you'll find out!" (Rowling, Live Interview, 16 Oct 2000).

- Harry overhears a conversation between Fudge, Dumbledore and McGonagall in the "Three Broomsticks" and believes that Sirius has murdered his parents (HP 3, 220-227) – the opposite is true.
- Ludo Bagman tries to help Harry in the tournament and behaves suspiciously (HP 4, 487-489) – but in truth he has bet on Harry's victory and desperately needs money.

Rowling puts her readers off the scent (*faux leurres*), when she tells them about toilets being blown up in London (HP 5, 152). The reader sees this as a typical example of one of Rowling's hints at some intrigue and is surprised to find out that this episode has no meaning at all (HP 5, 539).

These examples shall suffice to demonstrate how the author makes conscious use of clues, red herrings and *faux leurres*. Without this technique *Harry Potter* would be far less exciting – only when the reader is made part of solving the riddle does he truely identify with the action.[183] He even has the chance to unravel the mystery before the protagonist does.[184]

II.4.B. Delay, Acceleration and Slow Motion – The Speed of Narration

Another category of analysing narrative time is duration, i.e. speed. How much (reading) time is required to narrate the events of a given fictive period (Genette's "duration", see II.1.A, 29)? This relation between the narrative and discourse time is not fixed, but varies very much in *Harry Potter*. Each part of the series tells us about the events of one Hogwarts school year. Usually, it begins around Harry's birthday at the end of July (HP 4, 28) and ends with the journey home at the end of June. This period, which is always the same, requires very different times to cover, and the number of pages varies enormously: whereas *Philosopher's Stone* has about 332 pages, *Goblet of Fire* and *Order of the Phoenix* have 769 and 956 pages. *Half-Blood Prince* does not follow the trend of the previous books to ever increasing lengths, but goes back to 608 pages – just the same number as *Deathly Hallows* has as the last part of the saga. As the amount of pages increases up to HP 5, so the narrative speed decreases. Only *Half-Blood Prince* returns to the level of the first *Potter* books. Wilfried von Bredow regards the changes of discourse time as one of the most important factors of Rowling's success.[185]

---

[183] This technique is characteristic of the detective novel. I shall analyse *Harry Potter* in this particular context later (II.4.D, 87).

[184] See Smadja 2001, 36.

[185] See Wilfried von Bredow, "Lord Voldemort kommt immer näher," *F.A.Z.* 12 Aug 2000, SIV.

Looking closer at the individual books, we can make out yet another pattern: in *Philosopher's Stone* it takes Rowling about 120 pages to introduce the reader to Harry and to bring him to Hogwarts. *Chamber of Secrets* already has the main focus of action shifted to Hogwarts after 90 pages. *Goblet of Fire* needs about 160 pages to cover the same period (end of July to end of August), whereas *Order of the Phoenix* has 216 pages before we see Harry at school. This shows how discourse time is extended or delayed and how speed is decreased. Having arrived in Hogwarts, speed varies enormously. Some chapters tell us about the events nearly at the same speed as things are happening, for example "The Burrow" (HP 2, 31-49), "The Deathday Party" (HP 2, 134-153), "Talons and Tea Leaves" (HP 3, 107-134), "The Triwizard Tournament" (HP 4, 190-212) or "The Hearing" (HP 5, 155-170). Others, on the contrary, gather up a couple of weeks and accelerate the narration, like, for example "The Lion and the Serpent" (HP 5, 439-463), "The Beetle at Bay" (HP 5, 599-627) or "The Madness of Mr Crouch" (HP 4, 582-612), that tells us about what happens within a period of two months. We can see that Rowling tends to be very selective and volatile in the middle part of her texts. The narration is like a line-up of individual dialogues and scenes that are connected by phrases like "a week later" (HP 2, 204), "over the next couple of weeks" (HP 4, 253) or "as they entered June" (HP 4, 60). There are hardly any pauses, summaries are very short, and the narrative focus is on the scenic representation of the events.

The author extends time consciously to describe all the events in detail. The last chapters of a *Potter* novel are usually full of action, scenic representation and narrative time corresponds to the time of action. The further the plot progresses, the slower the narration: the last chapters of each book are usually very long considering the number of pages in relation to the whole book. But concerning time they tend to deal with a very short period of a few hours. The rebirth of Voldemort within two hours on the evening of June, 24th is narrated in *Goblet of Fire* over about 100 pages, which corresponds to 13 percent of the whole book (HP 4, 657-775). In *Chamber of Secrets* the final showdown between Harry and Riddle is described on 55 pages, which is about 15 percent of the text (HP 2, 309-364) covering – again – only a few hours. And in *Order of the Phoenix* the decisive hours in the Department of Mysteries are described on 138 pages (again about 15 percent of the whole book) dealing with the events of half a day (HP 5, 790-928).

II.4.C. Developing the Plot

The *Potter* novels are texts with a closed plot; they have a clear point of attack and an ending that provides solutions to all the mysteries. All the events are explained and justified and leave no gaps open. At the end of each part the intrigue is exposed and the traitors are discovered and punished (poetic justice). Open questions are usually answered using a figural narration. This pattern is true for L_C and L_A, with L_A being completed and solved only in *Deathly Hallows*.

The whole saga is a detective story on L_A. At the point of attack in *Philosopher's Stone* we see Harry's parents being murdered and Voldemort defeated. The two things remain mysterious. Only within the following seven books can the reader unravel the background of the deed and Harry's role in it. Each part of the series, i.e. each individual L_C, is a detective story on its own: Harry and his friends are investigating and trying to find the traitor. As in a detective novel, the children find the culprit and the reason for the intrigue. On L_A the children come closer to finding out why Voldemort murdered the Potters and how he did it with every novel. In *Order of the Phoenix* we get to know the central reason for the deed: Voldemort knew that his arch-enemy was about to be born and – just like biblical king Herod (Mathew 2, 13) – he decided to kill the rival as an infant (HP 5, 924).

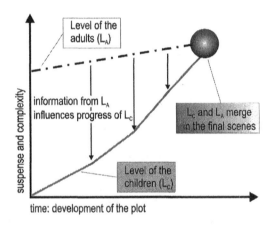

Figure 6: Plot Levels HP 1 to HP 4

Looking at the individual novels and at L_C we also find that the books are developing and we have to differentiate between two types of stories. The first three books are classical detective novels using the setting of the traditional school story (see VII.1.D, 425). The fourth part, *Goblet of Fire*, begins as a detective story, but ends with Dumbledore and Harry deciding to fight Voldemort and the political establishment. Accordingly, the last two chapters bear the titles "The Parting of the Ways" (HP 4, 750-775) and "The Beginning" (HP 4, 776-796). On these final pages of the fourth part, a significant change of pattern is performed: L_A and L_C are melted into one single level dealing with the united resistance against Voldemort.

The last three books of the series follow a completely different pattern, which is why I shall deal with them individually (see II.4.D, 87).

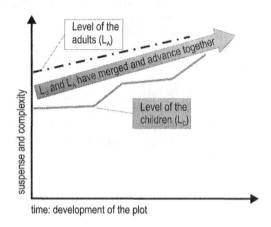

Figure 7: Plot Levels HP 5 to HP 7

But how does Rowling build up suspense? How does she maintain the readers' (and especially the child readers') interest for thousands of pages? First of all, because – just like in any detective novel – she lets her readers participate in unraveling the truth: through Harry's eyes they experience the progress of the investigation and want to know more about the classic "whodunnit". In the course of the investigation Harry has to risk his life. His being a potentially weak child against the grown-up villain of a magical world seem to make his chances for success very limited. This is exactly what makes the plot so exciting. The reader soon realises that Harry is going to survive all the attacks of the evil forces (very early on in their series' publication, Rowling announced that there were going to be seven novels – from then on it was clear that Harry could only die in the last book.) So it was less the question if Harry survived each individual novel, but more how he was going to escape. Rowling combines this kind of tension with elements of the detective novel: clues given by the author and the experience of the first novels make the reader expect a complete solution at the end of each one. Knowing this, the reader begins to work out his own hypotheses of how the plot is going to develop. The combination of the various levels and plots causes different types of tensions. With reference to the whole series we ask "Is Harry going to defeat Voldemort?" In each novel we wonder "How are the children going to unmask the traitor this time?" and "What is he planning at all?" Additionally, there are much shorter dramatic arcs that refer to the individual sub-plots, for example the events that lead to Norbert the Baby-dragon's escape (HP 1, 247-261), the story about rescuing Buckbeak (HP 3) and performing the tasks of the school tournament in *Goblet of Fire*. These relatively short sub-plots are especially appealing to children (see VII.1.A, 419).

II.4.D. "Harry Potter" as Detective Novel – Parts One to Four

It is common knowledge among *Potter* critics that the novels make manifold use of detective story elements. Anne Hiebert Alton declares the series "detective fiction", because the protagonists act as detectives. The motives of finding a murderer, brutality, crime, people disappearing, hidden identites – all of these figure in the *Potter* books. The novel best suited for finding the detective story pattern is *Chamber of Secrets*.[186] The dramatic arc is similar to "examples of the detective or thriller genre" says Pat Pinsent.[187] This is, basically, true. So let us analyse *Harry Potter* as a detective novel.

First of all, the first four parts are structured like typical detective fiction (see II.1.B, 33) with paralipses (see II.1.A, 26) and ellipses that keep back information and constitute the mystery. In *Philosopher's Stone*, for example, it is the strange and incomprehensible beginning: the reader wonders who these bizarre people who meet at night are and why they are talking about someone having been murdered. On the contrary, in *Chamber of Secrets* it is – among other elements – the story of Moaning Myrtle: although Harry and his friends get to know the ghost very early in the novel, it is only in the end that they find out that her death is related to the mystery of the hidden chamber. In *Prisoner of Azkaban* one of the ellipses concerns the mysterious illness of Ron's pet rat Scabbers and its disappearance. The explanation is given at the end: Pettigrew is afraid of Black and tries to flee. The information the reader had been deprived of is Scabber's true identity and Pettigrew's betrayal of the Potters. The main ellipsis in *Goblet of Fire* is the question as to who has put Harry's name into the goblet and is trying to plot against him.

The beginning of the classic detective novel is the crime: either it is has been, or it is about to be committed. In the *Potter* books the murder of Harry's parents is the starting point for the crime story spanning the whole series. Each of the first four books has a detective plot of its own. In *Philosopher's Stone* it is the riddle of the magic stone and its rescue. In *Chamber of Secrets* the attacks in Hogwarts, the mystery about Riddle's diary and Ginny's rescue make up the crime story. The stories are told from the detective's, i.e. Harry's, point of view, using interior monolgue as its main stylistic device. Like in a detective novel, the plot is focussed on explaining why and how someone has committed the crime. Thus, *Philosopher's Stone* explains who Harry is and how he came to

---

[186] See Hiebert Alton 2003, 145.
[187] Pinsent 2004, 49.

live with the Dursleys. *Chamber of Secrets* expands upon this information and explains the attacks on the Hogwarts students. The following part of the series begins with Black's breakout – the clarification of his true role in the Potters' death constitutes the detective story that again leads the readers back to the begining of *Philosopher's Stone*. *Goblet of Fire* begins with the question of who initiated the riots at the "Quidditch" World Cup and who put Harry's name into the goblet. Both mysteries are unravelled in the course of the plot. So with this pattern (strange events at the beginning that are explained at the end) the first four *Potter* novels conform to the basic pattern of the detective novel.

Like in the crime story there are two intertwined plots in the *Potter* novels (see II.3.C, 66). On the one hand there is the plot about the investigations: How is Harry to find out who has put his name into the goblet? How is he going to unravel the mystery about the inexplicable attacks on his fellow students? How is he going to find Sirius Black? The reader shares Harry's thoughts and accompanies him finding the explanation. On the other hand, there is the plot about the crime: Why has someone put Harry's name into the goblet? Why are Hogwarts students being attacked? Who is Black really? And what relation does he have with the Potter family? Both plots advance together. For example, the more Harry knows about Sirius' relation to his parents or about the history of the secret chamber, i.e. about things that have happened before the actual point of attack, the closer he gets to unravelling the mystery. The technique of the analepsis that is typical of the detective novel (see II.1.B, 33) is used in the *Potter* series as well. Like in the crime story, the *Potter* novels are told *à rebours*, i.e. in retrospect. As in detective fiction there is a dramatic showdown right before the end of the story. In *Philosopher's Stone* Harry has to fight against Voldemort, in *Chamber of Secrets* he descends into the hidden chamber to save Ginny from the monster. In *Prisoner of Azkaban* Sirius and he are being attacked by "Dementors" and Harry has to save his godfather from being executed, and – as has already been said before – the author very often uses clues, red herrings and *faux leurres* (see II.4, 81).

In *Goblet of Fire* this detective-novel pattern switches over to another pattern: there is no longer a detective story in which the children act as investigators with the readers sharing their experiences and being mislead by *faux leurres*. The plot's focus is on the intrigue about Harry participating in the school tournament and how he masters the difficult tasks. Although the reader suspects these things to be traps set by Voldemort, only the last chapters present the solution.[188]

---

[188] It is precisely this lack of a detective plot which makes *Goblet of Fire* quite a lengthy read.

II.5 "Harry Potter and the Prisoner of Azkaban" – A detailed Anaysis

The third part of the *Potter*-Saga is different from all the others. Apart from *Half-Blood Prince* it is the only novel without a hidden intrigue by Voldemort and it does not end with a direct showdown between the antagonists. The only focus of the plot is on Black's escape from Azkaban and his plan to murder Harry – Voldemort does not appear personally. The mystery solely lies in finding out what role Black played in the murder of the Potters. L_C is dominant and there is hardly any relevant plot on L_A. *Prisoner of Azkaban* seems plot-wise to be the best part of the series, because every detail and sub-plot serves a specific purpose within the novel's sructure. The clues are well set and make up the solution very convincingly. With about 470 pages *Prisoner of Azkaban* is one of the shorter parts of the series. At the same time it is the first novel that is no mere children's book: for the first time Harry is in mortal peril and a mass murderer seems to be planning to kill him. And it is in HP 3 that the reader realises for the first time that Magical World is not free from criminality, death and torture. The following parts of the series intensify this menacing, dark impression. *Prisoner of Azkaban* is the turning-point of the series, which is why I am going to analyse it more closely.

II.5.A. Plot, Story and Sub-Plots

The main story of *Prisoner of Azkaban* is easily told:

1. Sirius Black, is wrongly accused of murdering 13 people and sent to Azkaban. The true murderer is Peter Pettigrew. Black is able to transform into a dog and thus escapes the deadly influence of the "Dementors".
2. One day, Black sees a photo of the Weasley family in the newspaper. He recognises Pettigrew in Ron's pet rat Scabbers. To avenge his friends he breaks out of Azkaban.
3. Harry learns that Black is supposedly planning to murder him.
4. Remus Lupin, a new teacher at Hogwarts, wins Harry's confidence. Lupin is a friend of the Potters' and Black, and becomes a father figure to Harry. Lupin is a werewolf.
5. At the end of the school year Sirius Black in his canine guise kidnaps Ron to lure Harry into a trap. Thus, Harry, Sirius and Lupin meet. Harry learns the truth about Sirius' and Pettigrew's past. Pettigrew is transformed into his human shape again and taken prisoner. In this moment Lupin changes into his werewolf-form. In the resulting tumult Pettigrew is able to escape. Black is taken prisoner and is going to be executed.
6. Dumbledore sends Harry and Hermione on a time travel. Turning back time, the children succeed in saving Black.

90

Figure 8: Pot and Sub-plots in *Prisoner of Azkaban*

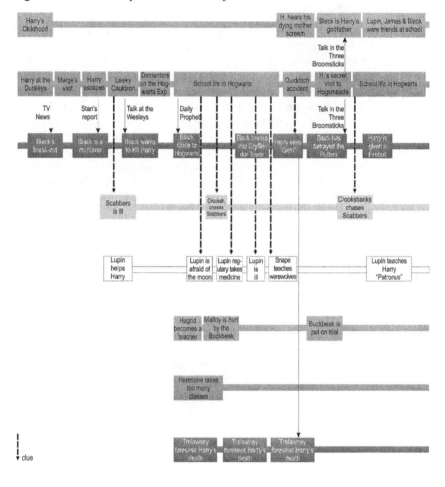

The novel consists of one main and five sub-plots (see 90): the main focus is on Black's rehabilitation, the minor plots are grouped around it.

Sub-plot 1 deals with unmasking Pettigrew and is closely related to the main plot. Its end is the unravelling of the truth about Sirius Black. Only at the end does the reader realise that this is an individual sub-plot. Scabbers' illness, its flight from Crookshanks and, finally, its disappearance can only be seen as part of a consistent plot after the rat has been found out to be an "Animagus". Until the end, the plot consists only of clues. Its protagonists are Sirius Black, Harry, the Potters, Pettigrew and Lupin.

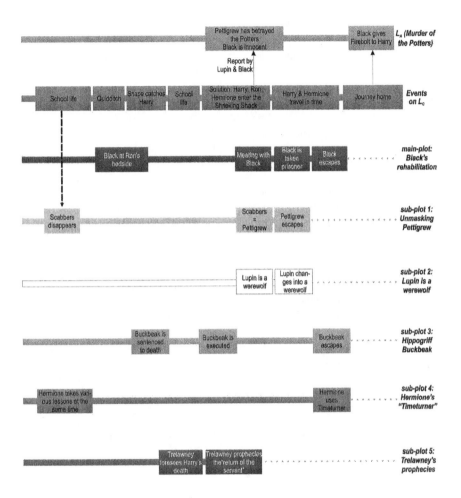

Sup-plot 2 deals with Remus Lupin and his relationship to Harry. It is a precondition for the main plot: only because Lupin teaches Harry the "Patronus Charm" can Harry save Sirius and himself from the "Dementors" at the end (HP 3, 442-444). Additionally, this sub-plot adds to the action and suspense when the only person Harry can trust turns out to be a werewolf. The characters of this plot are the same as in the main plot.

Sub-plot 3 is constructed around Hagrid's nomination as teacher for "Care of Magical Creatures" and the sentencing to death of the hippogriff Buckbeak for hurting Draco Malfoy. Rescuing the animal is important for Black's successful escape, because he can ride on its back. Nevertheless, sub-plot 3 is not very closely related to the main plot[189] and has its own protagonists: Hagrid, Harry, Ron, Hermione and Draco.

The story about Hermione's "Timeturner" is above all a recurrent theme, and not an individual plot. But only because Hermione knows how to travel in time does the main plot have a happy end, which is why I shall count it as sub-plot 4. The narrative technique Rowling uses is the same as in sub-plot 1 – there are various clues hidden in the text (HP 3, 108-109 and 265). But at first they only seem to underline Hermione's ambition and intelligence. Only in the end do we learn that she uses the "Timeturner" to follow her excessive schedule.

The sub-plot 5 about Sybill Trelawney and her seeing death omens merely adds to the novel's diversity: Sybill's bizarre behaviour gives reason to laugh, her dark visions contribute to the book's suspense. The plot is related to the main plot by the identity of characters (Trelawney, Harry, Ron, Hermione).[190]

But how are these sub-plots connected? At first, the main plot about Black's escape and rehabilitation appears as secondary narrations only: Harry and the reader first learn of Black's breakout from the "Muggle" TV news, but at this time the event's importance for the magical community is not yet clear (HP 3, 23-24). We get more information from Stan Shunpike, the conductor on the "Knight Bus". He tells Harry that Black is supposed to be guilty of murdering thirteen people (HP 3, 46-48). From the Weasleys Harry learns that he is being threatened by Black (HP 3, 74-76). Later on the "Daily Prophet" reports that Black has been sighted close to Hogwarts (HP 3, 138). Only after the first 357 pages does the character mentioned in the title appear on stage for the first time(HP 3, 364). The reader has to construct the main plot out of the various clues until the final confrontation between Harry, Sirius and Pettigrew reveals the truth. Sub-plot 3 is related to the rest of the novel by the identity of the character constellation (Harry, Ron, Hermione, Malfoy). The same is true for sub-plot 2, which is connected to the other plots by the school setting. Lessons and the interaction of teachers and students provide the background for all events of *Harry Potter*.

II.5.B. *Prisoner of Azkaban* as Detective Novel

Prisoner of Azkaban is a classic detective novel (see figure 9). At the beginning the reader learns that Harry is being threatened by Black (HP 3, 74-76), which is enhanced by Stan Shunpike's and Cornelius Fudge's information about Black's brutal-

---

[189] The flight could have been realised by any other means. Buckbeak is not obligatory for Black's escape.

[190] In the end, her prophecies are not entirely absurd: referring to Harry she repeatedly sees a great dog which she misreads as the death omen "Grim" – in fact it is Black in his animal disguise. And when she predicts Harry's death, in a way she is right as well: if Harry had not saved himself from the "Dementors" using the "Timeturner" he surely would have died.

ity. The reader constructs an image of Sirius that later turns out to be wrong. Harry's situation worsens as the authorities fail to protect him and Black is able to enter his dormitory in Hogwarts (HP 3, 175). Finally the alleged murderer kidnaps his friend Ron and thus lures him into the Shrieking Shack (HP 3, 360). Only then, on the last pages of the book, is the mystery of Harry's godfather revealed (HP 3, 364). And only then the reader is able to decipher the clues he has been given throughout the whole plot in the form of Scabbers' illness (HP 3, 66-68) or Crookshank's attacks on the rat (HP 3, 68, 159-160, 245, 359). These details only reveal their true meaning when Scabbers is found out to be Pettigrew, the traitor.

But the main plot is not the only detective plot in *Prisoner of Azkaban*: the story about Remus Lupin being a werewolf makes up another. Also in this case the author gives the reader numerous clues: the name Remus hints at him having some connection with wolves (see IV.4.D, 229), his mysterious illness (HP 3, 184-185), Snape's lesson about werewolves (HP 3, 184-188) and Lupin's Boggart (a ghost that takes the shape of whatever its opponent fears most) being a full-moon (HP 3, 151-153) – all this hints at him being a werewolf. And finally there is the mystery about Hermione's excessive schedule and her seeming to be in different places at the same time. Repeatedly we learn that she has a timetable she cannot possibly follow (HP 3, 108-109 and 272). The author uses frequent hints to allude to all of these plots and sub-plots, but only in the end do we understand their whole meaning: usually a character explains what has happened (external or internal analepsis). This makes *Prisoner of Azkaban* a classical detective novel.

Analysing narrative speed, *Prisoner of Azkaban* corresponds to the other parts of the series (see II.4, 83): whereas the plot develops quite slowly at the beginning, i.e. various chapters deal with a relatively short time, the plot accelerates in the middle part of the novel (see figure 10). Chapters 3.8 to 3.16 show quite a fast development using many ellipses. When approaching the showdown speed decreases again. This is precisely the pattern I have described for all the *Potter* novels (see II.4, 83). The next figure (see 94) shows the development of narrative speed in *Prisoner* as measured by the number of pages in relation to time covered.

There is only one weakness in the plot, as Michael Maar points out:[191] How can Snape be fooled with the "Timeturner"? Being a member of the Hogwarts staff he surely knows about Hermione using it. Would he not suspect that Black escaped by this magical device? And what about Cornelius Fudge, who as Minister for Magic had to approve Hermione's time travels: shouldn't he at least suspect that the children used the "Timeturner" to help Black and Buckbeak escape?

---

[191]   See Maar 2003, 89.

94

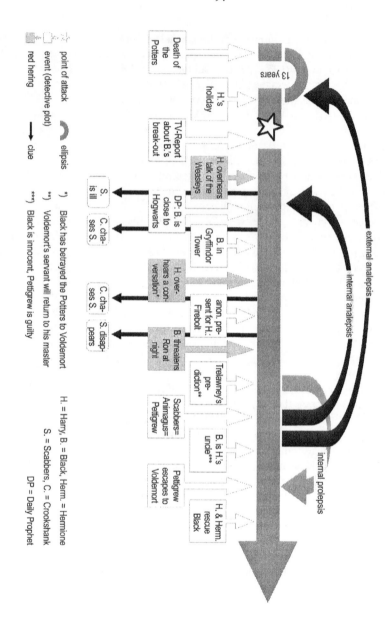

Figure 9: Prisoner of Azkaban *as Detective Novel*

II.6 Conclusion: A Very Conventional Tale

As I have shown in this chapter, the *Potter* novels are quite conventional in their narrative technique. They are narrated as a figural narration, or – in Genette's words –an extradiegetic-heterodiegetic narrative situation with Harry being focaliser (see II.2.A, 34). The author influences her readers using descriptive adjectives or (animal) similes (see II.2.B, 41 and IV.2.A, 149). Linguistically, *Potter* is not very innovative, either: Rowling writes with a simple style, enriches it with colloquial speech and elements of comic strip language. Even tragic events are described without any pathos (see II.2.E, 46 and II.2.H, 55). One of her few stylistic devices is the simile (see II.2.G, 53). Apart from that we find many stereotypically repeated descriptions. Moreover, the author uses rhymes and puns to entertain her readers (see II.2.I, 57).

The novels usually work on two plot levels – one for each individual book and one overall plot spanning the whole series. At the same time, these different levels address different target groups: while children will probably enjoy the exciting school story of the first three books, adults will be more interested in the political intrigues and the fight between good and evil (see II.3.C, 66 and II.3.D, 67). Both levels, being set at different places, are connected by newspaper articles and reports of characters (see II.3.E, 73).

The structure of time is very close to the one of the classical detective story which unravels a mystery using flashbacks (analepsis). (see II.1.A, 30) and ellipses (see II.4.D, 87). The basic pattern for organising the plot is the circle (see II.4, 77, 77) that also provides the basis for the structure of space (see III.6, 140).

Thus, *Harry Potter* is a very conventional tale. It cannot claim any special position or innovation regarding narrative techniques.

96

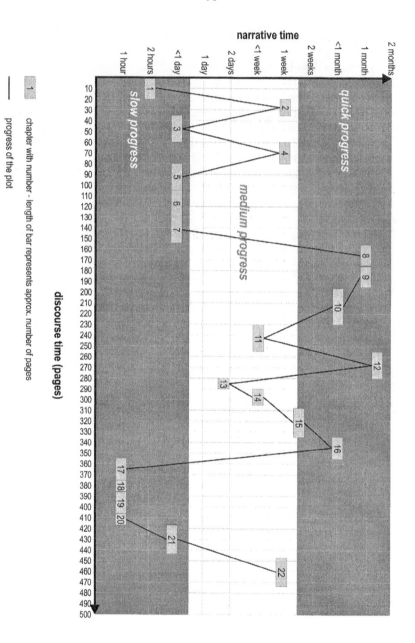

Figure 10: Narrative Speed in *Prisoner of Azkaban*

III. Narrative Space

III.1 Definition

Analysing narrative space has not been very popular in German literary criticism. Scholars have only begun to investigate narrative space properly in the second half of the twentieth century. In 1975 Alexander Ritter published *Landschaft und Raum in der Erzählkunst* and summarised the results of the discussion so far. Three years later *Raum, Situation, erzählte Wirklichkeit: poetologische und historische Studien zum englischen und amerikanischen Roman* by Gerhard Hoffmann was published and became a classic of analysing narrative space in English texts.[1]

Narrative space is not only a line-up of locations and settings, but it is an essential part of the text's basic structure. Space is "ein eigenständiges Gestaltungselement [...], das zusammen mit den verschwisterten Elementen wie Zeit, Erzählperspektive, Figur und Handlungsfolge den intendierten Gehalt bekörpert und die Struktur des Werkes bestimmt."[2] Narrative space is not an end in itself, but it is important because of its connections with the whole text.[3] Part of its relevance is due to its relationship with the individual characters, because space is always a setting for the characters' actions.[4] Characters are being described by their belonging to a certain room, landscape or object.[5]

All the narrative spaces of a text make up a pattern of contrasts and relationships: only in contrast to other locations or settings does a specific space get its meaning. This is one of the keys to interpreting the text.[6]

Descriptions of space are never arbitrarily written, they usually serve either the characterisation of a character or they add to the general interpretation of the text. The author has created his settings with a certain purpose,[7] which

---

[1] Gerhard Hoffmann, *Raum, Situation, erzählte Wirklichkeit: poetologische und historische Studien zum englischen und amerikanischen Roman*, Stuttgart: Metzler, 1978.

[2] "a stylistic device on its own [...] that together with narrative time, point of view, characters and plot makes up content and structure of the whole work." Hermann Meyer, "Raumgestaltung und Raumsymbolik in der Erzählkunst," [1963] *Landschaft und Raum in der Erzählkunst*, ed. Alexander Ritter, Darmstadt: Wissenschaftliche Buchgesellschaft, 1975, 208-231, here 231 [my translation].

[3] See Robert Petsch, "Der Raum in der Erzählung," [1942] *Landschaft und Raum in der Erzählkunst*, ed. Alexander Ritter, Darmstadt: Wissenschaftliche Buchgesellschaft, 1975, 36-44, here 36.

[4] See Pfister [1977] 2001, 338.

[5] See Pfister [1977] 2001, 339.

[6] See Pfister [1977] 2001, 339.

[7] See Daniela Berghahn, *Raumdarstellung im englischen Roman der Moderne*, Frankfurt am Main: Peter Lang, 1989, 3.

gives the reader the right to suppose a meaning behind just about any detail. He cannot even claim to understand the text if he has not deciphered the function of narrative space.[8] As Ernst Cassirer has it: "Die Sinnfunktion ist das primäre und bestimmende, die Raumstruktur das sekundäre und abhängige Moment."[9] But what precisely are the possible functions which narrative space can have in literary texts? They can serve to:

- represent cultural and geographical contrasts.
- contrast social milieus.
- pick up the characters' emotions.
- symbolise or illustrate a character's state of mind.[10]

Usually we find more detailed descriptions of narrative space in realistic or naturalistic texts where they stand for the characters' dependance upon their social milieu. On the contrary, short descriptions hint at the characters' own responsibility and the "Primat des autonomen Bewusstseins".[11] Nevertheless, descriptions of landscape or rooms have an aesthetic function as well.[12] They tend to be highly subjective and depend on the author as much as on the point of view. Author,[13] narrator and reader[14] select the information according to their own interpretation of reality. A "cosy room" can seem "untidy" to one reader and "claustrophobic" to another. This is why narrative space and its meaning can hardly be objectified,[15] especially if we deal with a figural or first person narrative situation.[16]

Various attempts have been made to classify narrative space. Basically, we can analyse it in context with psychological, philosophical, literary or communicative aspects.[17] But neither the theories of Cassirer,[18] Petsch[19] nor Maatje[20]

---

[8]   See Bruno Hillebrand, "Poetischer, philosophischer und mathematischer Raum," [1971] *Landschaft und Raum in der Erzählkunst*, ed. Alexander Ritter, Darmstadt: Wissenschaftliche Buchgesellschaft, 1975, 417-463, here 438.

[9]   "The construction of meaning is the the most important factor and the structure of narrative space depends on it." Ernst Cassirer, "Mythischer, ästhetischer und theoretischer Raum," [1930] *Landschaft und Raum in der Erzählkunst*, ed. Alexander Ritter Darmstadt: Wissenschaftliche Buchgesellschaft, 1975, 17-35, here 26 [my translation].

[10]   See Fielitz 2001, 122-123.

[11]   "primacy of the independent mind", Pfister [1977] 2001, 347-349 [my translation].

[12]   See Andrea Taubenböck, *Die binäre Raumstruktur in der Gothic novel: 18. - 20. Jahrhundert*, Munich: Wilhelm Fink, 2002, 16.

[13]   See Hillebrand 1971, 424.

[14]   See Hillebrand 1971, 419.

[15]   See Taubenböck 2002, 12.

[16]   See Daniela Berghahn, *Raumdarstellung im englischen Roman der Moderne*, Frankfurt am Main: Peter Lang, 1989, 162-163.

[17]   See Taubenböck 2002, 12-20.

[18]   See Cassirer [1930] 1975, 12-13.

seem to be suitable for analysing *Harry Potter*, because they are simply too complicated for the simple structure of the novels.

All the theories agree on one point: we must make a difference between the location described in the text and its significance for the text's meaning. Meyer distinguishes between location and narrative space:[21] location means facts about a given space like geographical details, street names and so on; narrative space is a metaphorical category and represents human emotions or states of mind.[22]

So what are narrative spaces? Basically, we can consider them regarding two aspects. Narrative space can be locations of fictitious reality and, thus, mere settings for the plot. On the other hand, it can represent a semantic field and add to the interpretation of the text.

III.1.A. Theories of Narrative Space by Hoffmann and Lotman

Gerhard Hoffmann published his analysis of narrative space in the English novel in 1978 and soon it became a classic. He defines narrative space as "situative Umsetzung von Bedeutung".[23] Basically, Hoffmann distinguishes "narrated" and "experienced room".[24] Further he defines:

- tempered space
- space of action
- conceptual space
- curious space
- fantastic / satirical space
- grotesque space
- eerie space
- visionary space
- mythic space

Tempered space is created by the narrator, the author or a character visiting it and reflects a state of mind. The space of action is marked by special objects that are exclusively available here. It has a clearly defined use for a character.[25] Conceptual space is very much alike, but focuses more in the objects re-

---

19 See Petsch [1942] 1975, 37.
20 See Frank C. Maatje, "Versuch einer Poetik des Raumes. Der lyrische, epische und dramatische Raum," [1969] *Landschaft und Raum in der Erzählkunst*, ed. Alexander Ritter, Darmstadt: Wissenschaftliche Buchgesellschaft, 1975, 392-416, here 395-403.
21 See Petsch [1942] 1975, 38.
22 Meyer [1963] 1975, 211.
23 "materialisations of meaning" [my translation]; see Hoffmann 1978, 49.
24 See Hoffmann 1978, 3-7.
25 See Hoffmann 1978, 79-81.

ferred to in the text – the character is looking for something.[26] In the curious space, things are incongruent and singular. It is fascinating, raises curiosity and usually it is described in great detail.[27] Very similar is the fantastic or satirical space where the personal experience of the character is the most important factor. It is meant as a clear contrast to the readers' reality.[28] The grotesque space might be considered an enhancement of the fantastic space: nothing makes sense, it is marked by chaos and a sense of the illogical.[29] If the character finds himself in a strange environment and cannot relate to any object in it, he has entered an eerie space. The characters are afraid and uncertain. Rooms are closed, confusing, dark and have many corridors or stairs that lead to unknown places. There are inexplicable lights and bizarre noises. Descriptions tend to be very detailed and the room embodies events of the past.[30] Visionary spaces mix the conscious with the unconscious[31] while mythic space is bound to a certain cultural context with its own religious and ideological references.[32]

Other points to be considered are: How detailed are the descriptions of spaces? Which spaces are opposed to each other? According to Hoffmann, we usually find a binary opposition.[33] Are there any patterns alongside which characters proceed through the spaces? Which characters can move from one space to another and which cannot?[34] And, finally, how are the different spaces connected to each other? Hoffmann defines three types of connections:[35]

– Connection by addition: characters cross the individual spaces one after another.
– Causal connection: the characters' journey has an aim, reaching it or not is of vital importance to the protagonist.
– Correlative connection: spaces, characters and meaning are closely related.

Classical motifs of narrative space are, according to Hoffmann, among others "fire", "rivers", "the sea", "mountains", "woods", "caverns", "gardens", "houses" and "towers".[36] Apart from these, "the city" has a special position and is ambivalent: sometimes the city represents moral decay, sometimes it stands for glamour and wealth. The city embodies the antagonism of physical prox-

---

[26] See Hoffmann 1978, 92.
[27] See Hoffmann 1978, 112-114.
[28] See Hoffmann 1978, 126.
[29] See Hoffmann 1978, 136.
[30] See Hoffmann 1978, 161-164.
[31] See Hoffmann 1978, 173.
[32] See Hoffmann 1978, 204-205.
[33] See Hoffmann 1978, 341.
[34] See Hoffmann 1978, 587-591.
[35] See Hoffmann 1978, 595-601.
[36] See Hoffmann 1978, 340-346.

imity and emotional distance of people.[37] All of these motifs can be found in the *Harry Potter* series.

By far the most suitable approach to analyse narrative space in *Harry Potter* is Jurij M. Lotman's theory. According to the Russian literary critic the structure of narrative space is divided into binary subspaces belonging to two separate semantic fields. This is the case with *Harry Potter* – as we see also in the analysis of characters (see IV.2.B., 154). Moreover, the patterns of narrative space and of good and evil characters follow the same principles, as we shall see.

For Lotman every space has its own semantic function and represents a set of values.[38] Narrative space exemplifies moral standards within an ideological context[39] and, thus, is at the very heart of the text's interpretation.[40] Plot and characters are structured by means of a "border" which separates the two binary semantic fields and cannot be overcome.[41] Characters belong to one of these two fields, i.e. narrative spaces, and must stay there. Only the protagonist is able to cross the border.[42]

III.2 Three Cheers for Chaos – Narrative Space in "Harry Potter"

Now let us turn to analyse narrative space in the *Harry Potter* series: Is there an overall pattern of space? And can narrative space be explained using the theories by Hoffmann and Lotman?[43]

III.2.A. Tidiness vs. Chaos – The Semantic Border

Analysing narrative space in *Harry Potter* according to Lotman's theory, we find an opposition that seems too logical to be ignored: the world of the "Muggles" on the one hand and Magical World on the other. But, looking closer, we find that this "border" is not the one Lotman speaks about: it only refers to the location, not to narrative space.

Some critics have tried to identify consistent metaphors in the series. Sandra Bak, for example, sees the weather as indicator for coming events. Weather conditions on arrival in Hogwarts are, as she says, hints as to what is going to

---

[37]   See Hoffmann 1978, 392-397.
[38]   See Hoffmann 1978, 313.
[39]   See Hoffmann 1978, 313.
[40]   See Hoffmann 1978, 316.
[41]   See Hoffmann 1978, 327.
[42]   See Hoffmann 1978, 328.
[43]   A complete list of locations can be found on the internet: <http://de.wikipedia.org/wiki/Handlungsorte_der_Harry-Potter-Romane> 26 Aug 2007.

happen during the following term.[44] Reinhard Ehgartner agrees with her and interprets the weather at the beginning and the end of each book as "atmospheric parenthesis" of the plot. Arriving in Hogsmeade in bad weather is a bad omen for the coming months.[45] This seems to be only partly true: if there was a continuous weather metaphor, it would have to be more dominant than it really is.

In *Philosoper's Stone* it is cold on Harry's arrival in Hogwarts ("Harry shivered in the cold night air.", HP 1, 123), but it is not mentioned what weather it is when he leaves at the end of the school year. In *Chamber of Secrets* things are the other way round: we do not know in what weather the children arrive at school, but we learn that there is "a blaze of hazy sunshine" (HP 2, 346) when they leave. In *Prisoner of Azkaban* it is very cold and raining when the Hogwarts express arrives in Hogsmeade ("It was freezing on the tiny platform; rain was driving down in icy sheets", HP 3, 97), but again we do not know what the weather is when the children return home. And in *Half-Blood Prince* we get to know that Dumbledore's funeral takes place in "bright sunlight" (HP 6, 598), but are not being told anything about the weather at the beginning or the end of the school year. Only considering *Goblet of Fire* and *Order of the Phoenix* are Bak and Ehgartner right. When the train arrives in Hogsmeade in *Goblet of Fire*, we read: "The rain was now coming down so thick and fast that it was as though buckets of ice-cold water were being emptied repeatedly over their heads" (HP 4, 189). And at the end, the weather on the day of the students' journey home is compared to the day of their arrival:

> The weather could not have been more different on the journey back to King's Cross than it had been on their way to Hogwarts the previous September. There wasn't a single cloud in the sky. (HP 4 786-787)

In *Order of the Phoenix* the weather is unsettled during the journey to school:

> The weather remained undecided [...]. Rain spattered the windows in a half-hearted way, then the sun put in a feeble appearance before clouds drifted over it once more. (HP 5, 218).

After the showdown in the ministry and Black's death the sun shines astonishingly brightly: ("The sun was rising", HP 5, 908; "sunlight", HP 5, 910; "The sun was bright", HP 5, 916). So, if the idea of a weather metaphor was right, it should be applicable to all of the *Potter* books and any arrival to or departure from Hogwarts. In this case, it should always rain when the children come to Hogwarts; each school year, Harry and his friends must survive mortal dangers at school. Although there seems to be a vague relation between weather and plot

---

[44]   See Bak 2004, 145.
[45]   See Ehgartner 2002, 73-74.

(probably chiefly inspired by creating a certain atmosphere at the beginning of the text) there is definitely no weather metaphor.

What we do find is a consistent set of characteristics that mark positive or negative spaces, i.e. a pattern of space.[46] Positive spaces are usually bright, circular, warm, slightly untidy, wide, upstairs and very often have a friendly, warm fire. Negative spaces, on the contrary, are dark, cold, very tidy, narrow and downstairs if not beneath the earth. Dumbledore's office, for example, is circular and full of secrets (HP 2, 223), the Gryffindors are living in a tower with warm, circular rooms (HP 3, 173) and McGonagall's office is warm and bright (HP 3, 100). Even in the Lovegood's kitchen most things are round. It is chaotic, and – in the first place – a positive space (HP 7, 324, 340). On the contrary, Snape's office is situated in the dungeons, which are cold and underground (HP 1, 210).[47] The only exception is the classroom of Sybill Trelawney, which is excessively positive and, therefore, negative (see III.5.A, 124). So the basic pattern of narrative space in *Harry Potter* is the following:

positive	negative
bright	dark
warm	cold
upstairs	downstairs
untidy	tidy
broad	narrow
circular	rectangular
surprising	boring
modest	snobby / pretentious[48]

According to Lotman, these are the semantic fields separated by the border. Interestingly this pattern is very similar to the structure of the Gothic Novel.[49]

Additionally, Elizabeth D. Schafer identifies a red and green opposition: Red as colour of the Gryffindors is positive, green as in the Slytherin crest is

---

[46] This does not work the other way around. Every positive space is not circular nor every negative space dark or subterranean.

[47] Sandra Bak and Reinhard Ehgartner confirm this warm-cold opposition, but see a connection with the situation the character is in. When Harry feels heat he usually is in danger or on the brink of embarrassing himself. If he is cold he is in mortal danger or in under the direct influence of Voldemort. Ehgartner compares this to the icy representation of hell in Dante's *Divina Commedia* (Canto 32) (see Bak 2004, 145; Ehgartner 2002, 73).

[48] This opposition is only barely visible in the structure of narrative space, but it is very clearly to be found in the pattern of characters (see IV.2.B, 154).

[49] It may well be that this is a notion all human beings from all cultures have.

negative.[50] In fact, negative spaces are very often somehow connected with green light. The Slytherin common room and the Chamber of Secrets are full of a greenish light (HP 2, 240; 329; HP 7, 365) and the cavern where Dumbledore and Harry are looking for Voldemort's "Horcruxes" has a "greenish glow" (HP 6, 524). Slytherin's initial on his locket is green (HP 7, 227) as is the light of the "Killing Curse" (HP 7, 503). Gryffindor's sword, on the contrary, is decorated with "deep red glittering rubies" (HP 7, 299) and the defensive "Stunning Spell" casts a "scarlet light" on the wizards (HP 7, 506). But this does not seem to be a consistent opposition: the office of Firenze is friendly and green (HP 5, 660), and Dumbledore is wearing green gowns (HP 4, 194); on the other hand, red is also the colour of Voldemort's eyes (see HP 2, 337).

According to their negative or positive quality the different locations of the *Harry Potter* series can be grouped like this:

positive	ambivalent	negative
Diagon Alley		Knockturn Alley
Hogwarts:	*Hogwarts*:	*Hogwarts*:
Great Hall	Trelawney's office	Filch's office
Gryffindor Tower		Slytherin Dun-
Dumbledore's		geon
office		Snape's office
McGonagall's		Umbridge's office
office		
Hagrid's hut		
St Mungo's		Forbidden Forest
The Burrow		Privet Drive
	Ministry:	*Ministry*:
	Department of	Courtroom No. 10
	Mysteries	

These locations also underline the qualities of the characters that belong to them.[51] Let us now turn to analyse narrative space in the *Harry Potter* novels in more detail.

---

[50] See Schafer 2000, 226f.
[51] I shall analyse the concrete meanings of these names when discussing the locations in detail.

III.3 One World, Two Realities – "Muggle" and Magical World

Narrative space in *Harry Potter* can be divided into two groups: the world of the "Muggles" and Magical World. Geographically, both are identical. The only difference between them is that "Muggles" can only see a small part of their surrounding reality, whereas wizards can see the magical dimension as well. The two worlds, thus, are "zwei Seiten der einen Wirklichkeit".[52] There are no parallel worlds, only different perceptions of the same reality.[53] Gareth B. Matthews sees this as a symbol of human perception in general: everything man considers to be true depends on his socialisation. Reality is what we choose to be.[54] The two sub-realities refer to the readers' own world, which is why Suman Gupta describes three levels of reality for *Harry Potter*: the two fictitious worlds of "Muggles" and wizards and the readers' reality.[55] Astonishingly, the magical world is much closer to the readers' world than "Muggle" reality:[56] "In political-economic terms Magic world is simply a magically enhanced version of some context of our world, probably a pre-industrial context. "[57] Magical World has a lot in common with everyday reality: the individual's descent and social network are vital to his position in society, different groups rival for influence and capitalism reigns with its competing brands and advertising.[58] "Muggles" are being manipulated by wizards and depend on their guidance.[59] Isabelle Smadja regards this opposition between magical and "Muggle" world as "la métaphore du monde de l'enfance face à l'âge adulte", because wizards tend to be as helpless in the "Muggle" world as children are in the world of their parents.[60] In my opinion, Smadja is wrong: wizards only seem to be helpless in the "Muggle" world because they are usually not allowed to use magic. If this were not the case, they would be far more powerful than any "Muggle".

Magical World is kept secret, "Muggles" are not to know that there are wizards in the country. In *Deathly Hallows* we read that this secrecy was decided upon in 1689: "'*Upon the signature of the International Statute of Secrecy*

---

52   "two sides of the same reality." Bachl 2002, 110-111 [my translation]; see Michael Silberstein, "Space, Time, and Magic," *Harry Potter and philosophy: If Aristotle ran Hogwarts*, eds. Baggett & Klein. Chicago, La Salle: Open Court, 2004, 186-199, 187.
53   See O'Keefe 2003, 178.
54   See Gareth B. Matthews, "Finding Platform 9 3/4: The Idea of a Different Reality," *Harry Potter and philosophy: If Aristotle ran Hogwarts*, eds. Baggett & Klein, Chicago, La Salle: Open Court, 2004, 175-185, here 184.
55   See Gupta 2003, 85.
56   See Gupta 2003, 91.
57   See Gupta 2003, 135-136.
58   See Gupta 2003, 92-93.
59   See Gupta 2003, 102.
60   "a metaphor of the rivalry between the worlds of children and adults", Smadja 2001, 48 [my translation].

in 1689, wizards went into hiding for good. [...] '" (HP 7, 261). In choosing
1689 Rowling hints at the English Bill of Rights that was officially declared on December 16 the very same year. The only "Muggle" that officially knows about
Magical World is the prime minister, but he is not able to tell others about it:

> The [Muggle] Prime Minister [...] would never, as long as he lived, dare
> mention this encounter to a living soul, for who in the wide world would be-
> lieve him? (HP 6, 12)

Within the "Muggle" world, there are areas that are accessible for wizards only
and invisible to non-magical people.

Magical World has its own laws, administration and rules, but it is geographically identical with the "Muggle" world nevertheless. This is why there
are no any secret passages between the two worlds. There are magical ways of
transport as well as means of protection to make some of the places invisible to
"Muggles".[61]

Both worlds seem to merge when in *Order of the Phoenix* "Dementors"
appear in Privet Drive: the fantastic suddenly comes into the non-magical world.
Harry realises the full meaning of this:

> The arrival of the Dementors in Little Whinging seemed to have breached
> the great, invisible wall that divided the relentlessly non-magical world of
> Privet Drive and the world beyond. (HP 5, 47)

The division of the two worlds is finally lifted in *Half-Blood Prince*. It becomes
evident that the destiny of both realities is interdependent, because Voldemort
terrorises the "Muggle" world: "Dementors" spread despair and depression
(HP 6, 20), the forces of evil make a bridge collapse (HP 6, 17) and, finally, it
turns out that the "Muggle" prime minister's assistent has been put under the
"Imperius Curse" (HP 6, 23). Both worlds form a unity, the fall of one brings
disaster to the other.[62]

Strangely enough, we see the fictitious wizarding world influence our
physical reality today: on a brick wall in London's King's Cross there has been
put a sign indicating "Platform 9¾" as an homage to Rowling's novels.[63]

---

[61] See Silberstein 2004, 188-190.

[62] This sudden appearance of fantastic elements in non-magical reality is not to be confused
with the reader's uncertainty as postulated by Tzvetan Todorov: The uncertainty Todorov
is speaking about refers to the reader wondering if he is to believe the things he is told or
not. This is one of the basic criteria for defining fantastic literature (see F.I.1, 469). In
this particular context there is absolutely no uncertainty on behalf of the reader: Throughout the whole series there can be no doubt that magical world exists.

[63] See Jenny 2007.

III.3.A. Broken-down and Uncomfortable – "Muggle" World

There are two ways the reader gets information about the "Muggle" world. First we share Harry's experiences with the Dursleys and second we get reports on the non-magical world through the "Daily Prophet" and by characters.[64] The world of the "Muggles" seems so unattractive that the reader automatically adopts the wizards' point of view, as Suman Gupta states:

> The Muggle world is presented within the embrace of the Magic world, and presented so as to draw the reader away from it and into the Magic world. Substantively, the Muggle world – mainly the Dursleys – is a marginal space from which the reality and pre-eminence of the Magic world is itself no more than a construction that exists (precariously) at the behest of the Magic world.[65]

The "Muggle" world appears broken-down and confronts the wizards with many problems in everday life. On their flight from the Hogwarts letters, Vernon Dursley brings his family to a "gloomy-looking hotel on the outskirts of a big city" (HP 1, 50), later to a derelict, stinking house on an island (HP 1, 53). Hagrid has his problems with using the London Tube and "complained loudly that the seats were too small and the trains too slow" (HP 1, 77), before climbing a "broken-down escalator" (HP 1, 78). Even the Ministry of Magic has its entrance in "an old red telephone box, which was missing several panes of glass and stood before a heavily graffitied wall." (HP 5, 143) And the neighbourhood of Spinner's End is bleak, lifeless and desolate:

> Many miles away, the chilly mist that had pressed against the Prime Minister's windows drifted over a dirty river that wound between overgrown, rubbish-strewn banks. An immense chimney, relic of a disused mill, reared up, shadowy and ominous. There was no sound apart from the whisper of the black water and no sign of life apart from a scrawny fox [...]. (HP 6, 25)

In the text we find real places as well as fictitious ones, but which can be traced on a map nevertheless. All of the settings are located in Great Britain and very often their names hint at their quality. The Dursleys live in Little Whinging, Surrey (HP 1, 42). The name can be derived of "to whinge" (= to complain in a mean and petty sort of way) which can be seen as a reference to the Dursleys' behaviour towards Harry.[66] The village Vernon escapes to with his family is the Railview Hotel in Cokeworth (HP 1, 51). Obviously the most nota-

---

64   See Gupta 2003, 86.
65   See Gupta 2003, 89.
66   See Rudolf Hein, *Kennen Sie Severus Snape? Auf den Spuren der sprechenden Namen bei Harry Potter*, Bamberg: Collibri und Erich Weiß, 2001, 90.

ble feature of the house is its location close to a railway line. The village's name alludes to a dirty, industrial environment and the place can only be endured by taking drugs ("coke worth"). Horace Slughorn lives in the "charming village of Budleigh Babberton" (HP 6, 61), which does not exist but incorporates perfectly the teacher's love to talk. The name also refers to the Buddleia, a flower that attracts butterflies and is typical of English cottage gardens. The village, thus, is set in "rural England". We also hear about Brockdale in West Country, where a bridge collapses, but this place does not exist either (HP 6, 10). Ottery St Catchpole, the place where the Weasleys live in "The Burrow" (HP 2, 38f) is an invention of the author's as well. The name seems to be derived from the real Ottery St Mary in the south of England. With its animal reference ("river with otters")[67] and the allusion to simple country life the place fits the poor, chaotic, but lovable Weasley family. Little Hangleton, the village where the Riddle family owns a stately villa (HP 4, 7), does not exist either. There is, nevertheless, a place called Hangleton in southern England. The word refers to the verb "to hang" (= to kill someone by hanging). The local pub is called "The Hanged Man", which underlines this meaning.[68]

We also find references to the cities of Blackpool (HP 1, 137), Bristol (HP 1, 22), Peebles (HP 2, 88) and Birmingham (HP 5, 579) as well as to the shires of Devon (HP 1, 238), Kent (HP 2, 148), Norfolk (HP 2, 88), Yorkshire (HP 5, 372), Somerset (HP 6, 19) and Wiltshire, where the Malfoys have their mansion (HP 5, 342). Moreover, we are also referred to a place called Abergavenny (HP 3, 44) – of which there are two: one in Norfolk and one in Monmouthshire – a village called Gaddley (HP 7, 356), the Welsh peninsula Anglesey (HP 3, 49), Scottish Aberdeen (HP 3, 49), the shire of Argyllshire (Grampian Mountains) (HP 3, 179), "a riverbank in Wales" (HP 7, 240) and "a tiny island in the middle of a Scottish loch" (HP 7, 258). Most of the places mentioned are located in the south of England or in Wales, some in Scotland. Remarkably, Harry and Hermione are camping in the Forest of Dean on one occasion (HP 7, 297) – which is close to the place in which Rowling grew up (I.2.B, 15). In any case, there is no pattern to be found in these references to real places.

London serves as the classic metaphor of the city (see III.3.A, 101). It has a special position within the narrative space of *Harry Potter*, because with King's Cross, the "Leaky Cauldron" in Charing Cross Road (HP 3, 49; HP 6, 106-107; HP 7, 423), Diagon Alley and the Ministry of Magic it is at the centre of the official magical world. The ministry is situated in "the very heart of London", in a "broad street lined with imposing-looking buildings and already full of traffic" (HP 5, 531). We also find a mention of Tottenham Court Road, where Harry, Ron and Hermione seek refuge in a pub (HP 7, 135). Grimmauld Place,

---

[67]   J.K. Rowling states that the otter is her favourite animal (I.2.B, 20).
[68]   See Hein 2001, 89.

the headquarters of the "Order of the Phoenix", can be reached from King's Cross by foot in only twenty minutes (HP 5, 203). And Sturgis Podmore, member of the Order, lives in Clapham, a part of London, in a street called Laburnum Gardens (HP 5, 319[69]). The hospital St Mungo's, finally, is located "in the very heart of London" in a "a broad store-lined street" (HP 5, 531), and we also hear about Elephant and Castle (HP 6, 87). But despite all these references to real London localities there are hardly any descriptions of the British capital. London is hardly ever mentioned as a location[70]

Each year, the journey to Hogwarts begins on September 1st, at eleven o'clock on platform 9¾ in King's Cross. It is not exactly described where the train passes on its way to school, but the children travel through the rural countryside of South England ("neat green fields which gave way in turn to wide, purplish moors, villages with tiny toy churches and a great city alive with cars like multi-coloured ants", HP 2, 81), pass snow-covered mountains (HP 2, 81) and enter "woods, twisting rivers and dark green hills" (HP 1, 115). So according to the pattern of narrative space described earlier (see 103) the journey leaves the very well ordered (= tidy) space of the "Muggle" world and leads to a less ordered (= untidy) space. The way back leads them the other way around: "the country-side became greener and tidier" (HP 1, 331).

There are hardly any references to places outside Great Britain. East and South East Europe are connected with evil and black magic. At the Polish border, Hagrid and Maxime meet "mad trolls", in Minsk they have to deal with vampires (HP 5, 470) and in Romania, there are not only dragons (HP 1, 211; HP 1, 250; HP 1, 256), but, again, vampires (HP 1, 147). Transylvania has its own "Quidditch" Team (HP 4, 73) and is, moreover, the location of some of Lockhart's alleged deeds (HP 2, 176). Voldemort hides in Albania (HP 2, 353; HP 4, 71; HP 4, 366), where he also kills Bertha Jorkins. Durmstrang, the infamous academy, is probably located in or close to Bulgaria (see III.5.I, 138), and – further to the east – there are Kappas in Mongolia (HP 3, 187).

Africa is a mysterious continent. The Egyptian pharaohs were wizards (HP 3, 17ff) whose magic still supplies the modern wizarding world with wealth.[71] Gilderoy Lockhart claims to have seen petrified people in Ouagadougou, the capital of Burkina Faso (HP 2, 156), and Quirrell has been given a turban by an African princess (HP 1, 147). African fans arrive to see the "Quidditch" World Cup (HP 4, 93).

America and Central Europe are hardly mentioned at all. The only reference to Germany, for example, is the mention of the Black Forest, where vam-

---

[69] There is a street named Laburnum Gardens in London, but it is located in Southgate. Clapham, on the other hand, is located south of the River Thames.

[70] There are a few comments like "a bustling road lined with shops" (HP 1, 78).

[71] Bill Weasley works for Gringotts in Egypt (HP 1, 118; HP 2, 229; HP 3, 17-19).

pires live (HP 1, 81). German "Quidditch" fans at the World Cup come from this area (HP 4, 86). We also see Voldemort search for Grindelwald in Germany. He kills a woman who pleads with him:

> "*Er wohnt hier nicht mehr!* [...] He no live here! He no live here! I know him not! [...] *Das weiß ich nicht!* He move! I know not, I know not!" (HP 7, 191).

France and Majorca and the Canary Islands are referred to as holiday destinations for "Muggles" (HP 3, 17; HP 2, 13; HP 6, 69). Bill Weasley once had a pen friend in Brazil (HP 4, 97). And Asia is mentioned as the most far away place Sirius Black can have gone to hide (HP 5, 110).

Apart from South East Europe (which has a negative connotation) the places outside Great Britain do not have a special function for the structure of narrative space in *Harry Potter*. They merely serve as decorative elements and prove that the magical world is global.

III.3.B. Square Tidiness – Privet Drive

The street the Dursleys live in is named after a poisonous plant representing small mindedness and unimaginativeness (privet). At the same time there are phonetic references to "private", which alludes to Harry's isolation when he is with his family.[72] Other streets are called Wisteria Walk (HP 5, 8) – another dangerous flower – and also Magnolia Crescent and Magnolia Road (HP 5, 15 and 19). Systematically naming streets after flowers is a characteristic of bourgeois residential areas. When water is scarce in *Order of the Phoenix* the area becomes even more boring:

> [...] a close and a drowsy silence lay over the large, square houses of Privet Drive. Cars that were usually gleaming stood dusty in their drives and lawns that were once emerald green lay parched and yellowing [...]. Deprived of their usual car-washing and lawn-mowing pursuits, the inhabitants of Privet Drive had retreated into the shade of their cool houses [...]. (HP 5, 7)

The Dursleys' home is perfectly tidy and unsurprising: "[Privet Drive was] the very last place you would expect astonishing things to happen." (HP 1, 24). Uniformity, consistency, order and cleanliness are the dominant values with Harry's family.

> [...] Privet Drive had hardly changed at all. The sun rose on the same tidy front gardens and lit up the brass number four on the Dursleys' front door; it crept into their living-room, which was almost exactly the same as it had

---

[72]   See Hein, 2001, 122.

been on the night [of Harry's arrival]. Only the photographs on the mantelpiece really showed how much time had passed. (HP 1, 25)[73]

Nymphadora Tonks remarks on the Dursleys' home:

> "Funny place," she said. "It's a bit too clean, d'you know what I mean? Bit unnatural. Oh, this is better," she added, as they entered Harry's bedroom and he turned on the light. (HP 5, 62)

Dealing with their son Dudley, the Dursleys represent consumerism and prodigality. The house (HP 1, 45) and especially Dudley's room allegorise these attitudes (see IV.4.G, 236).

Privet Drive represents narrowness and the feeling of being trapped. At first, Harry must live in a cupboard under the stairs (HP 1, 42) and his uncle does not hesitate to bar Harry's window and to pass him his meals under the door (HP 2, 28).

III.3.C. Fallen from Greatness – The Houses of Riddle and Gaunt

The house of the Riddle family is located in Little Hangleton and Voldemort stays here on his return to Great Britain. It is spacious, dark and has been uninhabited for a long time (HP 4, 12-13). The light and the fire in the room Voldemort and his servant Pettigrew are living in, are uncanny and full of negative allusions: "The fire was the only source of light in the room; it was casting long, spidery shadows upon the walls." (HP 4, 21)[74]

Close by is the house of the Gaunt family, where Tom Riddle's mother has grown up in complete neglect. Decay is to be felt in every detail of the house: it is dark, overgrown and hidden behind trees and bushes. A snake nailed to the door hints at the inhabitant's connection with Slytherin (HP 6, 190f). The house is in decay and extremely dirty:

> The Gaunts' house was now more indescribably filthy than anywhere Harry had ever seen. The ceiling was thick with cobwebs, the floor coated in grime; mouldy and rotting food lay upon the table amidst a mass of crusted pots. The only light came from a single guttering candle placed at the feet of a man with hair and beard so overgrown Harry could see neither eyes nor mouth. (HP 6, 340)

Tom Riddle unites this negative place with the splendour and greatness of his father's house. Both places represent decadence, decline and snobbishness.

---

[73] See HP 4, 25; HP 4, 55.
[74] As with the description of her characters, Rowling uses an animal comparison to characterise the place (see 236).

III.4 Moving In and Between the Worlds

In the magical world, there are various means of travelling which I am going to analyse in the following chapter. Additionally, I shall deal with the question of passage between the "Muggle" and the magical world.

III.4.A. "Tap the third brick" – Hidden Places

The magical world is protected from the "Muggles'" view; the passages from one world into the other are hidden and invisible for non-magical people. A great part of the action is set in places thus protected from the "Muggles": among these are Hogwarts, Grimmauld Place, Diagon Alley and the Ministry.

The "Leaky Cauldron" is the passage from London's Charing Cross Road to magical Diagon Alley (HP 3, 49). The pub is – as the name indicates – "dark and shabby" (HP 1, 78) and its entrance is only visible to wizards. It is situated on the "border" between the magical and the "Muggle" world and noises from both worlds are being heard in its rooms (HP 3, 62f). To enter Diagon Alley one must touch a particular brick in the wall of the pub's inconspicuous back yard with a wand ("tap the third brick from the left above the dustbin"; HP 3, 57) – and the way into Diagon Alley opens (HP 1, 80).

The Ministry is hidden from "Muggle" eyes as well – its entrance is protected by secret mechanisms and a password. You have to dial the code 62442[75] (HP 5, 844) in "an old red telephone box, which was missing several panes of glass and stood before a heavily graffitied wall" (HP 5, 143). The receptionist answers the call, the visitor explains his request and receives a name tag. Afterwards the telephone box serves as a lift and goes down into the lobby of the ministry. "Muggles" will refrain from using the box, because they think that it is out of order.

A similar mechanism protects the hospital St Mungo's. To enter the hospital one has to address a particular mannequin in the window of a closed department store. The place is so unattractive to "Muggles" that they do not pay attention (see III.5.F, 134). The people passing the store are complaining: "It's never open, that place ..." (HP 5, 532). The headquarters of the "Order of the Phoenix" are protected by another mechanism – "Grimmauld Place" is simply not visible for "Muggles" (see III.5.G, 135). And Hogwarts is protected "by more than *walls*" as Hermione explains. "There are all sorts of enchantments on it, to stop people entering by stealth. You can't just Apparate in here." (HP 3, 178).

---

[75] Much has been said about these numbers. But inspite of all the attempts to find a metaphorical meaning to them, the answer is very easy. Take a new cellphone with letters for SMS-writing added to the numbers – and type "62442": you get the word "magic".

Protecting the "Quidditch" World Cup is especially complicated. Arthur Weasley explains:

> "Muggle-Repelling Charms on every inch of [the stadium]. Every time Muggles have got anywhere near here all year, they've suddenly remembered urgent appointments and had to dash away again ..." (HP 4, 108-109)

He continues to describe how the world cup is organised:

> "[The Quidditch World Cup] is a massive organisational problem [...] and of course we just haven't got a magical site big enough to accommodate [all the visitors]. There are places Muggles can't penetrate [like] Diagon Alley or platform nine and three quarters. So we had to find a nice deserted moor, and set up as many anti-Muggle precautions as possible." (HP 4, 80-81)

Even the Hogwarts Express is invisible for "Muggles", platform 9¾ is hidden between platform nine and ten (HP 1, 104). Wizards have to walk through the wall without being seen by "Muggles" (HP 1, 331; HP 3, 81; HP 4, 181.). The train itself is a classic steam train,[76] "[...] a scarlet steam engine, puffing smoke over a platform packed with witches and wizards seeing their children onto the train." (HP 1, 105; HP 3, 81)

III.4.B. Triple Decker and Speaking Pictures – Magical Travelling and Communication

Wizards have magical ways of travelling. Adults for example Apparate in whatever place they want to:

> "Some Apparate, of course, but we have to set up safe points for them to appear, well away from Muggles. I believe there's a handy wood they're using as Apparition point." (HP 4, 80-81)

Other means of transport include "Portkeys", "Floo Powder" and the "Knight Bus" to travel longer distances:

> "They're objects that are used to transport wizards from one spot to another at a prearranged time. You can do large groups at a time if you need to. There have been two hundred Portkeys placed as strategic points around Britain [...]. Unobtrusive things, obviously, so Muggles don't go picking them up and playing with them [...] stuff they'll just think is litter ..." (HP 4, 80-81)

---

[76] Magical World makes use of steam engines – which contributes to the nostalgic character of the novels (see V.2.E, 319).

It is a "Portkey" that brings Harry and Cedric to Voldemort and back to Hogwarts at the end of *Goblet of Fire*. It is not quite clear exactly why this transport works on the way back. Travelling by "Portkey" must be planned precisely, because it only works within a given timeframe (that is why Mr Weasley has to look at his watch all the time, when they travel to the "Quidditch" World Cup; HP 4, 82 and 84). So how can the "Portkey" work, when there is no way to programme it?

Magical World also has means of public transport. With the help of "Floo Powder" wizards can travel in a network of fireplaces which is supervised by the Ministry (HP 4, 53). Nevertheless, travelling by "Floo Powder" is quite uncomfortable: the wizard enters a fireplace, throws a handful of powder into the fire and names his destination. If he does not pronounce the word correctly, he risks travelling to another place (HP 2, 57). The name "Floo Powder" can be derived from "flew" (from "to fly") and "flue", the old-fashioned word for chimney.[77] The "Knight Bus" also belongs to public transport. Its name hints at the fact that this bus is usually on duty at night. It is "'[the] emergency transport for the stranded witch or wizard. Just stick out your wand hand, step on board and we can take you anywhere you want to go [...].'" (HP 3, 41-42) The triple decker has various beds and jumps or speeds through the night (HP 3, 45).

In the course of the action the communication between paintings becomes more and more important. Portraits in the world of *Harry Potter* are alive and interact, even when the real people have died a long time ago. They even interfere with the plot or protect parts of Hogwarts by asking for passwords (HP 3, 106). As they are also able to communicate amongst each other the portraits can save Mr Weasley in *Order of the Phoenix*. Dumbledore explains: "As [the portraits] are free to move between their own portraits, they can tell us what may be happening elsewhere ...' " (HP 5, 516).[78]

III.5 Magical World

The wizarding world is global. It has the same borders, the same geography and climate as the "Muggle" world. In this world, the things "Muggles" believe to be legends or fairy tales are true.[79] The rules according to which Magical World works seem to be arbitrary and not very logical: the Weasleys, for example, do their washing up by magical means (HP 2, 42) and Dumbledore magically fills the dinner tables of Hogwarts with food (HP 3, 105). But at the same time the

---

[77] See Hein 2001, 62.
[78] It must be asked how this duplicity of people would work. But this question is too much to be asked of a playful text like *Harry Potter*.
[79] See Bürvenich 2001, 60.

house-elves must work in the kitchens (HP 4, 201-202) and Mrs Weasley does her ironing the classical, non-magical way (HP 5, 136).[80]

The most important narrative space of the whole series is Hogwarts and – close by – Hogsmeade, Hagrid's hut, the Forbidden Forest and the lake.

III.5.A. Anything Goes – The Wizarding School Hogwarts

Hogwarts is a world in itself and more of a character than a place.[81] The name derives from "hog" and "wart". "Hog" can mean pig or a barrel for beer ("hogshead"). At the same time "wart" is phonetically close to ward or warden. This connection between a closed space and caring for children seems to be quite appropriate for a boarding school.

We never learn where Hogwarts is situated, and not even Harry knows where it is (HP 1, 100). Nevertheless, there are various hints at the school being far in the north of Great Britain (HP 3, 91; HP 4, 248, 787), because the journey takes about eight hours north.[82] Locating Hogwarts in Scotland[83] corresponds with the description of landscape (HP 1, 196) and the journey: after five hours the train reaches hills (HP 3, 90) and comes from Southern England (HP 1, 112) into wild scenery:

> The countryside now flying past the window was becoming wilder. The neat fields had gone. Now there were woods, twisting rivers and dark green hills. (HP 1, 115)
> It was getting dark. He could see mountains and forests under a deep-purple sky. (HP 1, 122)
> The Hogwarts Express moved steadily north and the scenery outside the window became wilder and darker while the clouds overhead thickened. (HP 3, 89)
> The weather remained undecided as they travelled further and further north. (HP 5, 218)

Each year the journey ends in Hogsmeade (HP 1, 123; HP 3, 97; HP 4, 188). The way to school is exhausting, narrow and dark. A black lake has to be

---

[80]   See Bürvenich 2001, 62.

[81]   See Muir 2007.

[82]   The journey begins each year on September 1st at eleven o'clock in King's Cross and takes until the evening. Dusk at this time of the year is usually around seven'o clock. According to the website of British Rail (<http://www.nationalrail.co.uk> 15 Aug 2006) travelling from London to Scotland takes about that time. Starting in London at eleven takes you to Inverness by 19:35. This is only true for the Hogwarts Express if this train travels at usual train speed. If it uses magical powers to travel faster, this comparison is useless.

[83]   Critics agree on this point: "[L'école] de sorcier Poudlard [= Hogwarts] se trouve en Écosse, dans un univers parallèle au nôtre [...]." (Ernould 2003, 195); Elizabeth D. Schafer also agrees and refers to remarks by the author, see Schafer 2000, 117, 75.

crossed (HP 1, 123) or rounded on foot, because the castle is quite far from Hogsmeade station (HP 6, 151). From far away, Hogwarts with its gothic architecture is impressive and represents safety (HP 4, 190):

> Perched atop a high mountain on the other side, its windows sparkling in the starry sky, was a vast castle with many turrets and towers [...] Everyone was silent, staring up at the great castle overhead. It towered over them as they sailed nearer and nearer to the cliff on which it stood. [84]

J.K. Rowling adds:

> [I visualize] Hogwarts [as] a huge, rambling, quite scary looking castle, with a jumble of towers and battlements. Like the Weasley's [sic!] house, it isn't a building that Muggles could build, because it is supported by magic.[85]

The pattern of narrative space identified earlier (see 103) is true for Hogwarts as well. The castle is full of surprises. Even having spent various years at school, you never know the building completely:

> There were a hundred and forty-two staircases at Hogwarts: wide, sweeping ones; narrow, rickety ones; some that led somewhere different on a Friday; some with a vanishing step halfway up that you had to remember to jump. Then there were doors that wouldn't open unless you asked politely, or tickled them in exactly the right place, and doors that weren't really doors at all, but solid walls just pretending. It was also very hard to remember where anything was, because it all seemed to move around a lot. The people in the portraits kept going to visit each other and Harry was sure the coats of armour could walk. (HP 1, 144-145)
> Two years at Hogwarts hadn't taught them everything about the castle, and they had never been inside North Tower before. (HP 3, 110)

There are places that change according to the wishes of the visitor. The "Room of Requirement" or "Come and Go Room" (as the house-elves call it) only appears if it is needed. Dumbledore tells us:

> "Only this morning, [...] I took a wrong turning on the way to the bathroom and found myself in a beautifully proportioned room I have never seen before, containing a really rather magnificent collection of chamberpots. When I went back to investigate more closely, I discovered that the room had vanished. But I must keep an eye out for it. Possibly it is only accessible at five

---

[84] HP 1, 123-124. The expression "many turrets and towers" appears very frequently (HP 2, 82; HP 3, 98; HP 5, 224).
[85] Rowling Live Interview, 3 Feb 2000.

thirty in the morning. Or it may only appear at the quarter moon – or when the seeker has an exceptionally full bladder." (HP 4, 456)

The room can only be found if someone is needing it desperately, as Dobby explains Harry:[86] when he needs a place to teach his fellow students "Defence Against the Dark Arts", Harry focusses on what he is looking for: "*We need somewhere to learn to fight ... he thought. Just give us a place to practise ... somewhere they can't find us ... *"" Suddenly a door appears and Harry finds himself in the perfect classroom (HP 5, 430). The room plays a decisive role in *Half-Blood Prince*, because Draco is using it for his intrigue against Dumbledore. It has been known as hiding place for generations of Hogwarts students:

> There were alleyways and roads bordered by teetering piles of broken and damaged furniture, stowed away, perhaps, to hide the evidence of mishandled magic, or else hidden by castle-proud house-elves. There were thousands and thousands of books, no doubt banned or graffitied or stolen. There were winged catapults and Fanged Frisbees, [...]; there were chipped bottles of congealed potions, hats, jewels, cloaks; there were what looked like dragon-egg shells, corked bottles whose contents still shimmered evilly, several rusting swords and a heavy, blood-stained axe. (HP 6, 492)

In *Deathly Hallows*, the diadem of Ravenclaw – another of Voldemort's "Horcruxes" – is hidden in the room. The show-down between Draco, his gang and Harry ends in the room exploding in a magical fire (HP 7, 507-509). Another room that is constantly changing is the "Vanishing Cabinet" on the first floor: whoever enters it cannot be sure where he gets out. When Fred and George Weasley lock Montague in it, it is unclear where and when he is going to reappear: "'[It] could take weeks [before he reappears], I dunno where we sent him,' said Fred coolly." (HP 5, 690) The teachers can change the classrooms of Hogwarts according to their wishes. For example, Centaur Firenze turns "classroom eleven" into a clearing (HP 5, 660).

The castle is full of secrets and discoveries. Parts of the library are closed to the students, because they contain "dangerous books" (HP 1, 222). The entrances to the four school houses are hidden and only known to their members (HP 4, 185), and when Dumbledore tells the students about a forbidden corridor (HP 1, 139), nobody seems to be surprised. Finding one's way around the school is difficult – only the "Marauder's Map" that lists every movement in Hogwarts can help (HP 3, 212).

---

[86] "'a room that a person can only enter, [...] when they have real need of it. Sometimes it is there, and sometimes it is not, but when it appears, it is always equipped for the seeker's needs'" (HP 5, 427); "'it is always there waiting to be called into service'." (HP 5, 427)

118

Within the magical world Hogwarts is protected (HP 3, 178; HP 1, 73) and – as with most other places here – invisible for "Muggles". "'[Hogwart]'s bewitched,' said Hermione. 'If a Muggle looks at it, all they see is a mouldering old ruin with a sign over the entrance saying DANGER, DO NOT ENTER, UNSAFE.'" (HP 4, 185). Gareth B. Matthews sees similarities between Hogwarts and C.S. Lewis' magical world of Narnia.[87] But he ignores a vital difference. Whilst Narnia is only accessible from clearly defined points in the real world, Hogwarts can be reached by every wizard from just any point of Magical World.

The castle forms a pattern of narrative spaces on its own. Whereas the Gryffindors live in a tower and the Slytherins' rooms are close to the dungeons, the Hufflepuffs live next door to the kitchen[88] and the house of Ravenclaw is situated in one of the Western towers (HP 5, 437). Everything follows a high vs. low opposition.

The teachers' offices add highly to their characterisation. The obvious plurality of their chairs in the staff room ("[a] long, panelled room full of old, mismatched chairs", HP 3, 144) represents the staff's different personalities and the democratic spirit of the school.[89] Apart from the rooms within the castle walls, there are other locations on the Hogwarts grounds: Hagrid's hut, the owlery, the Forbidden Forest, the lake and the "Quidditch" pitch.

Hogwarts is ambivalent as a narrative space. It represents a cosy retreat and protection for its students, but at the same time it is a place where the children are confronted with deadly enemies.[90] It is remarkable that Hogwarts is void of modern technologies: its corridors are lit with torches, its rooms are heated with chimneys and with its old library and subterranean dungeons the school has the atmosphere of a medieval castle.[91] Modern communication technologies are not availabe. Internet, TV, mobile phones – all attributes of contemporary students' every day life are missing in Hogwarts. People communicate using post owls, travel through chimneys and talk to old oil paintings instead. Anthony Holden criticises Hogwarts in an article for the *Guardian*:

> Why on earth couldn't Hogwarts (the name is indicative of the reach of her imagination) have been a comprehensive, or an embattled secondary modern or a solid old-fashioned grammar – a school of the kind with which most of those millions of young readers can identify?[92]

---

[87] See Matthews 2004, 180.
[88] Proximity to the kitchen hints at cosiness, homeliness and warmth. Hufflepuff being the house of the upright and reliable students this association seems appropriate.
[89] See Schafer 2000, 78.
[90] See Schafer 2000, 6.
[91] See Schafer 2000, 79.
[92] See Holden 2000.

This critique is completely unjustified: it is precisely this pre-industrial setting that makes up most of the school's appeal. The *Potter* plot, set at an ordinary modern English school would be much less attractive. Apparently "millions of young readers" can identify much better with a boarding school like Hogwarts.

Magnificent, warm and upstairs – Positive spaces of the Castle

Whoever comes to Hogwarts has to enter the magnificent Entrance Hall with its "giant oak front doors" and the "flight of stone steps".[93] The wide room is in obvious opposition to the narrow house of the Dursleys:

> The Entrance Hall was so big you could have fitted the whole of the Dursleys' house in it. The stone walls were lit with flaming torches like the ones at Gringotts, the ceiling was too high to make out, and a magnificent marble staircase facing them led to the upper floors. (HP 1, 125)

The breath-taking Great Hall represents Hogwarts' splendour and tradition. It is the centre of school life and all the official ceremonies take place in here. The hall is curious, warm and well-lit (HP 4, 192; HP 4, 261):

> Harry had never even imagined such a strange and splendid place. It was lit by thousands and thousands of candles which were floating in mid-air over four long tables, where the rest of the students were sitting. These tables were laid with glittering golden plates and goblets. At the top of the Hall was another long table where the teachers were sitting. (HP 1, 128)[94]

The magical ceiling changes according to weather conditions outside (HP 1, 129; HP 3, 99; HP 4, 195; HP 2, 205). At Christmas and at Halloween the hall is magnificiently decorated and radiates splendour and prosperity:

> The Hall looked spectacular. Festoons of holly and mistletoe hung around the walls and no fewer than twelve towering Christmas trees stood around the room, some sparkling with tiny icicles, some glittering with hundreds of candles. (HP 1, 212-213)[95]
> [The Great Hall] had been decorated with hundreds and hundreds of candle-filled pumpkins, a cloud of fluttering live bats and many flaming orange streamers, which were swimming lazily across the stormy ceiling like brilliant watersnakes. (HP 3, 173)[96]

---

[93] This description appears frequently (HP 1, 124; HP 3, 99; HP 4, 190; 209).
[94] Identical descriptions of the Great Hall are frequent (HP 2, 85; 144; 205; HP 3, 101; HP 4, 192; HP 5, 225).
[95] Nearly identical descriptions are to be found in HP 2, 231; HP 3, 240-241; HP 4, 453.
[96] For further descriptions of the Halloween decorations see HP 2, 143; HP 4, 287.

Hagrid had already single-handedly delivered the usual twelve Christmas trees for the Great Hall; garlands of holly and tinsel had been twisted around the banisters of the stairs; everlasting candles glowed from inside the helmets of suits of armour and great bunches of mistletoe had been hung at intervals along the corridors. (HP 6, 284)

The rooms of Gryffindor house are warm, bright, circular and situated in a tower of the castle which spreads a friendly atmosphere: "A crackling fire was warming the circular common room, which was full of squashy armchairs and tables." Flames are dancing "merrily" (HP 4, 211). The contrast to Snape's classroom is made explicit (HP 1, 210). The dormitory and the common room are circular (HP 2, 95; HP 3, 106; HP 1, 142), the furniture is old-fashioned and shabby, but inviting:

> The Gryffindor common room looked as welcoming as ever, a cosy circular tower room full of dilapidated squashy armchairs and rickety old tables. A fire was crackling merrily in the grate [...]. (HP 5, 240)

The entrance of the tower (HP 2, 93; HP 3, 131) is being guarded by a portrait that has to be given the password:

> [They walked ...] up more and more stairs, to the hidden entrance to Gryffindor Tower. A large portrait of a fat lady in a pink dress asked them, "Password?" (HP 3, 106)

Ravenclaw, the other highly positive house of Hogwarts, is also accommodated in a tower, as we learn in *Deathly Hallows*, when Harry and Hermione go to seek Rowena's diadem: "They climbed in tight, dizzying circles" (HP 7, 472) – again, we find something round connected with a positive space: the stairs. There is no password to the tower, but anyone seeking admittance has to answer a question. The common room corresponds perfectly well with the general pattern of space:

> "The deserted Ravenclaw common room was a wide, circular room, airier than any Harry had ever seen at Hogwarts. [...] by day, the Ravenclaws would have a spectacular view of the surrounding mountains." (HP 7, 472)

Dumbledore's office also conforms to this model of space. It is splendid (HP 2, 222) and guarded by a particularly ugly gargoyle (HP 2, 221). The room is circular and full of oddities:

> [Dumbledore's office] was by far the most interesting. [...] It was a large and beautiful circular room, full of funny little noises. A number of curious

121

silver instruments stood on spindle-legged tables, whirring and emitting little puffs of smoke. (HP 2, 223)[97]

Reinhard Ehgartner points out that the idea of the adored headmaster having his office high up in a tower can already be found in Erich Kästner's *Das fliegende Klassenzimmer* (*Flying Classroom*).[98] Comparing Rowling to Kästner in this respect is obviously paying tribute to the school story as a genre.

McGonagall's office is described only once as "a small room with a large, welcoming fire" (HP 3, 100). This correlates with the positive features of "warm" and "bright" of the pattern.

The room occupied by Alastor Moody poses some difficulties, because throughout *Goblet of Fire* Barty Crouch jnr pretends to be Moody and with the help of a magical potion has taken his shape. Therefore, Moody's classroom is not his. The place is described only superficially in one single sentence as being full of "a number of exceptionally odd objects" (HP 4, 376). "Odd" is something positive in the context of *Harry Potter*.

The humble hut Hagrid is living in also corresponds with the positive features of the space pattern: it is small, slightly untidy (HP 1, 153) and only consists of one single warm and friendly room (HP 4, 290). Again, there is a fireplace and its flames are dancing "merrily" (HP 2, 125). In winter the house looks as if it was made out of gingerbread (HP 4, 440f). Being located at the edge of the Forbidden Forest the hut is the last safe place before the secrets and dangers of the woods.

Cold, tidy and subterranean – Negative Spaces of the Castle

In contrast to the Gryffindors, the Slytherins live in a subterranean room close to the dungeons (HP 2, 237; HP 3, 131; HP 2, 240; HP 7, 365). Their common room is rectangular and appears greenish, because it is situated under the Lake (HP 7, 365).

[…] rough stone walls and ceiling, from which round, greenish lamps were hanging on chains. A fire was crackling under an elaborately carved mantelpiece [...]. (HP 2, 240.)

---

[97] At night time the room appears slightly different: "The room was in half-darkness; the strange silver instruments standing on tables were silent and still rather than whirring and emitting puffs of smoke as they usually did; the portraits of old headmasters and headmistresses covering the walls were all snoozing in their frames. Behind the door, a magnificent red and gold bird the size of a swan dozed on its perch with its head under its wing." (HP 5, 514)

[98] See Ehgartner 2002, 75.

Chains evoke associations of medieval prisons. Walls and ceiling are damp (HP 2, 239). The room is "full of skulls and stuff" (HP 7, 365), unfriendly, and cold. The dungeons close-by are situated very deep under the school (HP 2, 238), they are cold (HP 1, 149; HP 2, 144) and dark, (HP 2, 144). The climaxes of *Philosopher's Stone* and *Chamber of Secrets* are set here. The room where the stone is hidden is barely described. It can be found "miles under the school" (HP 1, 298) and is reached crossing various other underground rooms. The Chamber of Secrets is situated "miles under the school" (HP 2, 324) as well.[99] To enter it, you have to slip down a nauseating, dark slide (HP 2, 324), just to find a dark, damp tunnel at its end (HP 2, 325). The chamber itself is magnificent, but dark and lit by a greenish light (HP 2, 329).

Snape's office is cold, dark and close to the dungeons as well (HP 1, 210; HP 2, 87f). Students are initmidated by its atmosphere. Dead, disgusting things are being stored in here.

> They walked down the stairs to the dungeons and then into Snape's office. [...] Snape had acquired a few more horrible slimy things in jars since last time, all standing on shelves behind his desk, glinting in the firelight and adding to the threatening atmosphere. (HP 3, 306)[100]

The room is opposed to the warm and friendly Great Hall:

> A delicious smell of food was wafting from the Great Hall, but Snape led them away from the warmth and the light, down a narrow stone staircase that led into the dungeons. [...] They entered Snape's office, shivering. (HP 2, 87-88)

The office never changes and always remains uncomfortable (HP 6, 497). When Snape becomes teacher for "Defense Against the Dark Arts", his new classroom changes immediately according to his character. It reflects sadism and cruelty:

> Snape had imposed his personality upon the room already; it was gloomier than usual as curtains had been drawn over the windows, and was lit by candlelight. New pictures adorned the walls, many of them showing people who appeared to be in pain, sporting grisly injuries or strangely contorted body parts. Nobody spoke as they settled down, looking around at the shadowy, gruesome pictures. (HP 6, 168)

---

[99] As Elizabeth D. Schafer remarks, sizes are very often exaggerated in *Harry Potter*. They serve mostly to characterise a place, not to describe it in detail (Schafer 2000, 230).

[100] There is a similar description in *Order of the Phoenix*: "The shadowy room was lined with shelves bearing hundreds of glass jars in which slimy bits of animals and plants were suspended in variously coloured potions. In one corner stood the cupboard full of ingredients that Snape had once accused Harry – not without reason – of robbing." (HP 5, 583)

Although the third room associated with Snape – his flat in Spinner's End – is not part of the school building, it shall be dealt with here: there are dark and heavy old books on his shelves, everything is in a certain state of neglect.

> They had stepped directly into a tiny sitting room, which had the feeling of a dark padded cell. The walls were completely covered in books, most of them bound in old black or brown leather; a threadbare sofa, an old armchair and a rickety table stood grouped together in a pool of dim light cast by a candle-filled lamp hung from the ceiling. The place had an air of neglect, as though it were not usually inhabited. (HP 6, 28)

Argus Filch is the Hogwarts caretaker and has an office of his own. It is windowless, narrow and smells badly (HP 2, 138). In a very methodical fashion he collects all the data of all the students he has ever punished. He puts the files in an orderly archive (HP 2, 138). Altogether his office is "a place most students avoided" (HP 2, 138).

Moaning Myrtle's bathroom is dark, gloomy, damp and depressing (HP 2, 170). Everything in here is broken or in decay:

> Under a large, cracked and spotted mirror were a row of chipped stone sinks. [...] the wooden doors to the cubicles were flaking and scratched and one of them was dangling off its hinges. (HP 2, 170)

This fits the girl's destiny: fifty years ago she became the Basilisk's first victim and has been living in the girls' bathroom bemoaning her fate ever since.

The Forbidden Forest is a no-go-area for the students (HP 1, 139). It is full of secret dangers and the habitat of powerful magical creatures (HP 1, 269). It is in here Harry and Ron meet the giant spiders (HP 2, 297) and the centaurs (HP 1, 274; HP 5, 827). The wood is dark and unsafe (HP 1, 160, 271), its paths are narrow and wind through nearly impenetrable bushes (HP 1, 271, 276).

> The path was becoming increasingly overgrown and the trees grew so closely together as they walked further and further into the Forest that it was as dark as dusk. [...] The breaking of a twig echoed loudly and the tiniest rustle of movement, even though it might have been made by an innocent sparrow, caused Harry to peer through the gloom for a culprit. (HP 5, 756-757)

The way into the wood leads "sloping downwards" (HP 2, 294). So the forest unites good and bad characteristics: it is narrow, situated on lower grounds than Hogwarts and is dark and at the same time full of surprises and magical wonders. In many parts of the series the wood serves as one of the main settings for turning points of the plot:[101] in *Philosopher's Stone* Harry meets

---

[101] See Schafer 2000, 81.

Voldemort drinking unicorn blood in the forest (HP 1, 277), in *Chamber of Secrets* he and Ron learn from the spiders about Hagrid's being innocent (HP 2, 299-301), and in *Order of the Phoenix* it is the centaurs of the woods that defeat Umbridge (HP 5, 827-829). The Forbidden Forest figures as an important place throughout the series: characters that enter it, return with new information or are somewhat transformed.

An Overload of Plush – Bizarre Spaces

There are three rooms within the space pattern that take up a special position, because they are either ambivalent or cannot be placed according to the set of values I have identified earlier (see 103). One is Sybill Trelawney's classroom, the others are Umbridge's and Slughorn's offices.

Trelawney's room is warm, circular and full of surprises, which makes it appear a positive setting in the first place. But herself being a highly dubious character we must doubt her integrity (see IV.4.I, 246). And looking closer it is obvious that all the room's characteristics are exaggerations of the positive pattern and, thus, negative. The room is so extraordinary that Harry doubts being in a classroom at all:

> [Harry] emerged into the strangest-looking classroom he had ever seen. In fact, it didn't look like a classroom at all; more like a cross between someone's attic and an old-fashioned teashop. (HP 3, 112-113)

It is too warm, too "crammed" (HP 3, 113-114) with bizarre items and is situated at an absurd distance from the rest of the school.[102] Like a being removed from reality, Trelawney resides on the top, i.e. the seventh floor[103] (HP 3, 346) of the North Tower. Everything in her room is circular: the trapdoor through which you enter the room, the tables where the students take their seats, the teapots on the shelves and the crystal balls (HP 3, 112-113; HP 4, 219). Although there is light in the room, the lamps are veiled and with their red light add to the gloomy atmosphere (HP 3, 112-113; HP 4, 219). It is insufferably hot ("gloom": HP 3, 116; 348)[104], and a sticky perfume obscures one's senses (HP 4, 219). The room in which the children are supposed to learn "The Sight" is unstructured, covered in smoke and perfume and has an entrancing atmosphere. Clear sight is not possible in this class. This judges the class's subject as much as its teacher.

---

[102] Trelawney's room is within ten minutes' walking distance from the rest of the school (HP 3, 109).

[103] "Seven" has always been a magical number. So it is quite appropriate that she resides on the seventh floor.

[104] We also read: "[...] the light cast by the lamps covered by scarves and the low-burning, sickly-scented fire was so dim [...]." (HP 5, 262)

Much the same is true for Dolores Umbridge's office: there are too many seemingly cosy things in it not to raise the reader's mistrust. Things usually representing life and vivacity are dead and dry or even artificial:

> The surfaces had all been draped in lacy covers and cloths. There were several vases full of dried flowers, each one residing on its own doily, and on one of the walls was a collection of ornamental plates, each decorated with a large technicolour kitten wearing a different bow around its neck. These were so foul that Harry stared at them [...]. (HP 5, 294)[105]

The description of her office completes Umbridge's characterisation, because just as she decorates her room in a faux-cosy style, she likes to pretend friendliness, but in fact she is emotionally dead, sadistic and even tortures the students (see IV.5.G; 260). The second space connected with her – the office we see her working in in *Deathly Hallows* – is remarkably like her Hogwarts office (HP 7, 206).

Slughorn's office is just a bit too splendid not to stir mistrust: it is much too big and on the occasion of a party lavishly decorated:[106]

> [...] Slughorn's office was much larger than the usual teacher's study. The ceiling and walls had been draped with emerald, crimson and gold hangings, so that it looked as though they were all inside a vast tent. The room was crowded and stuffy and bathed in the red light cast by an ornate golden lamp dangling from the centre of the ceiling in which real fairies were fluttering, each a brilliant speck of light. (HP 6, 295)

Slughorn himself gives just as much reason for distrust as does his office – again, the room is an indicator of his personality (see IV.5.H, 267).

Neutral Territory

There are various rooms in Hogwarts that do not fit into the pattern of narrative space. This is because most of the rooms are not described in so much detail that they can be placed on the one or the other side of the value set that seems to be most appropriate.

One of these rooms is Lockhart's office which demonstrates very well the way, in which Rowling makes the character's settings a mirror of their personality: the room is bright and decorated all over with "countless framed photographs" (HP 2, 131) of himself, some of them even signed (HP 2, 155). This is exactly the vanity Lockhart is characterised by most (see IV.4.B, 222).

---

[105] This corresponds with the character associated with this room: Dolores Umbridge (see IV.5.G, 260) is just as foul. Though she pretends to be nice and friendly she is cruel and scheming. The office with the make-believe cute animals mirrors this character trait.

[106] This is quite the atmosphere Slughorn prefers in his apartment as well (HP 6, 68).

Neutral in the sense that they do not belong to either one or the other side of our pattern are the luxurious prefect's bathroom (HP 4, 500-501), and the kitchens. Hidden behind a painting in which you have to tickle a pear to enter (HP 4, 402), the kitchens are, although subterranean, bright, spacious, warm and friendly (HP 4, 410-411). Close by are the rooms of Hufflepuff House ("in the basement near the kitchens"; HP 6, 434). These students represent benevolence and reliability and it is very fitting that their house is close to as cosy and home-like a place as a kitchen with its fire and warmth. Just as neutral are the owlery that is located in a circular room on top of West Tower (HP 4, 252) and the "Quidditch" pitch – a spectacular place with high stands on an airy field (HP 1, 181-182).

The big lake in front of Hogwarts castle, on the other hand, is an ambivalent place that must either be crossed or at least surrounded when approaching the school. It is dark, icy (HP 4, 526) and obscure (HP 4, 539-540) – fitting the negative aspects of our pattern. But at the same time the lake is full of secrets and home to many fantastic magical creatures like a giant squid, "Grindylows" and Merpeople (HP 4, 542f). So the lake cannot be regarded as an utterly negative place.

III.5.B. Wizards Among Themselves – Hogsmeade

Hogsmeade is situated on the foot of a mountain close to Hogwarts (HP 4, 565-566) and can only be entered by wizards (HP 3, 21, 87; HP 4, 350). The name could be derived from "hogshead" and "mead". The local pub is called "Hog's Head" (HP 1, 286) which makes this interpretation quite plausible. It is a bit off the main street, and, as Hermione puts it "a bit ... you know ... *dodgy* ... " (HP 5, 371). There is a sign above the entrance showing a bloody boar's head.

> A battered wooden sign hung from a rusty bracket over the door, with a picture on it of a wild boar's severed head, leaking blood on to the white cloth around it. The sign creaked in the wind as they approached. (HP 5, 371)[107]

The pub is filthy and repellent, especially on the inside (HP 5, 372). In *Deathly Hallows*, the pub becomes the decisive gateway to Hogwarts, when all the other entrances are barred to Dumbledore supporters: Aberforth Dumbledore sends the fighters of the resistance movement via a picture of his sister Ariana through to Hogwarts (HP 7, 460, 469).

Whatever is happening in Hogsmeade influences events in Hogwarts directly:[108] here Hagrid is tricked into betraying the secret about the three-headed dog (HP 1, 286), Harry listens to the decisive talk about Sirius Black (HP 3,

---

[107] Creaky signs, doors or planks are characteristic of scary settings.
[108] See Schafer 2000, 82.

220-228), and – also in Hogsmeade – Ludo Bagman tries to manipulate the Tri-wizard Tournament (HP 4, 487-488). In *Half-Blood Prince* Rosmerta, the land-lady of the "Three Broomsticks", has been put under the "Imperius Curse" and betrays Dumbledore (HP 6, 550-551). So Hogsmeade is an important place for the development of the *Potter* plot.

In Hogsmeade there is no necessity to protect the magical world from the "Muggles" – wizards are among themselves. This is why there are – like in Di-agon Alley – a couple of shops for magical items. Ron lists the following:

> "[We went into] Dervish and Banges,[109] the wizarding equipment shop, Zonko's[110] Joke Shop, into the Three Broomsticks for foaming mugs of hot Butterbeer and many places besides." (HP 3, 172)

Honeydukes is a shop for magical sweets,[111] in Scrivenshaft's Quill Shop you can buy things like "pheasant feather quills" (HP 5, 385) and Madam Puddi-foot's is the place Cho leads Harry to on Valentine's Day:

> [...] a small teashop that Harry had never noticed before. It was a cramped, steamy little place where everything seemed to have been decorated with frills or bows. Harry was reminded unpleasantly of Umbridge's office. [...] a number of golden cherubs that were hovering over each of the small, circular tables, oc-casionally throwing pink confetti over the occupants. (HP 5, 616)

Within the magical world, Hogsmeade is a historically important place: "'In Sites of Historical Sorcery it says the inn was the headquarters for the 1612[112] goblin rebellion, [...]'" (HP 3, 87). The village is full of surprises, of the unexpected, but at the same time it is a peaceful place: the thatched houses with their enchanted candles and decorated trees in winter look "like a Christmas card" (HP 3, 217).

The only house in Hogsmeade that seems rather uninviting is the "Shriek-ing Shack, the most severely haunted building in Britain" (HP 3, 87), situated outside the village (HP 3, 302; 363-364). But at the end of *Prisoner of Azkaban* the mystery about the place is explained: Lupin used the house to hide in when transformed into a werewolf, the screams that gave the building its name were his (HP 3, 379f).

---

[109] Combining a dervish with an onomatopoetic "bang" is quite appropriate for a shop sell-ing magical equipment.

[110] "Zonked" also means drunk or "stoned". The shop is described on various occasions (HP 3, 302).

[111] HP 3, 214. The name hints at "noble" sweets combining "duke" and "honey".

[112] This is the year of one of Britain's most famous witch trials: see "Pendle witch trials," *Wikipedia, The Free Encyclopedia.* 17 Oct 2007. <http://en.wikipedia.org/w/in dex.php?title=Pendle_witch_trials&oldid=165151189> 30 Oct 2007.

III.5.C. Shopping with Surprises – Diagon Alley

The name of Diagon Alley indicates its bizarre character – it contains the adverb "diagonally"[113] and describes the shape of the street ("a cobbled street which twisted and turned out of sight", HP 1, 81). Diagon Alley is the economic center of London's magical world:

> There were shops selling robes, shops selling telescopes and strange silver instruments Harry had never seen before, windows stacked with barrels of bat spleens and eels' eyes, tottering piles of spell books, quills and rolls of parchment, potion bottles, globes of the moon [...]. (HP 1, 82)

Here, the wizard can find anything he needs. Shopping marks the beginning of a new school year, because the students buy the things they need for school before leaving for Hogwarts. The following shops are mentioned:

Name	Kind of Shop	Reference
Flourish and Blotts	book shop	HP 1, 90-91
Ollivanders	shop for wands	HP 1, 92-93[114]
Eeylops Owl Emporium	shop for owls	HP 1, 92
Florean Fortescue's Ice-Cream Parlour	café	HP 3, 57-58
Madam Malkin's Robes for every Occasion	clothes shop	HP 1, 92
Magical Menagerie	shop for magical animals	HP 3, 66
Quality *Quidditch* Supplies	shop for *Quidditch* equipment	HP 1, 82
N. N.	pharmacy	HP 1, 91
Weasley's Wizard Wheezes (Nr. 93)	joke articles	HP 5, 742[115]

---

[113] See Hein 2001, 46-47.
[114] Ollivander's name could be derived from "olive" or be a paraphrase of "all-wand-er": see Hein 2001, 110.
[115] The Weasley twins open up this shop in *Order of the Phoenix*.

Diagon Alley is the place of the unexpected. The individual shops are described in detail (HP 1, 91-92). The wizard bank Gringotts (the name probably comes from "ingot", i.e. piece of gold) has its headquarters in Diagon Alley as well: the white building with silver doors and long tables where the employees are weighing treasures is the epitomy of an exclusive private bank. Goblins are running the business and attend to the clients. The safe vaults, where Harry keeps his parents' money, are situated "hundreds of miles under London, [...] deep under the Underground" (HP 1, 74). Apart from Hogwarts, Gringotts is "the safest place in the world fer anything yeah want ter keep safe" (HP 1, 73). In *Deathly Hallows* Harry and his friends must break into one of the vaults at Gringotts and we learn more about the safety installations of the bank (HP 7, "Gringotts").

When Voldemort returns and the magical world finally realises the danger, Diagon Alley changes its character completely. Fear is to be felt everywhere, happiness has gone:

> Diagon Alley had changed, the colourful, glittering window displays of spellbooks, potion ingredients and cauldrons were lost to view, hidden behind the large Ministry of Magic posters that had been pasted over them. Most of these sombre purple posters carried blown-up versions of the security advice on the Ministry pamphlets that had been sent out over the summer, but others bore moving black-and-white photographs of Death Eaters known to be on the loose. (HP 6, 108)
>
> [...] nobody was stopping to talk any more; the shoppers stayed together in their own tightly knit groups, moving intently about their business. (HP 6, 109)

Some of the shop owners have disappeared, as for example Florean Fortescue and Ollivander (HP 6, 104). Diagon Alley has changed; happiness has given way to fear. This impression deepens in *Deathly Hallows* when the street is deserted: "More shops than ever were boarded-up, though several new establishments dedicated to the Dark Arts had been created since his last visit." (HP 7, 424)

III.5.D. Shopping on the Dark Side – Knockturn Alley

Knockturn Alley is the dark counterpart of Diagon Alley. The name is a phonetic version of the adverb "nocturnally". Here, the wizard finds anything he needs for performing black magic. Harry accidentally gets to Knockturn Alley when he makes a mistake on his first travel by Floo Powder. Where Diagon Alley is colourful and exciting, Knockturn Alley is dark, evil and full of decay and death:

> [...] a dingy alleyway that seemed to be made up entirely of shops devoted to the Dark Arts. [...] Borgin and Burkes, looked like the largest [shop], but

opposite was a nasty window display of shrunken heads, and two doors down, a large cage was alive with gigantic black spiders. [...] An old wooden street sign hanging over a shop selling poisonous candles told him he was in Knockturn Alley. (HP 2, 62)

In the leading shop for black magic, Borgin and Burkes (HP 2, 57-58), Harry overhears Lucius Malfoy and his son speaking of compromising issues with the shop owner. Thus, the Malfoys are connected with death, decay and danger.

III.5.E. Chaos and Curiosities – The Ministry of Magic

The Ministry of Magic is the place of government and administration of the magical world. Its head is the Minister for Magic – Cornelius Fudge (see IV.5.A, 250) and later on Rufus Scrimgeour (see IV.5.B, 252). In *Order of the Phoenix* the Ministry becomes relevant as narrative space – the decisive last chapters of the book are set here.

The building is situated in a broad street in the middle of London (HP 5, 143). The entrance is to be found in an old, vandalised telephone box (HP 5, 843). The subterranean hall impresses the visitor with its splendour and represents the power of the institution:

> They were standing at one end of a very long and splendid hall with a highly polished, dark wood floor. The peacock blue ceiling was inlaid with gleaming golden symbols that kept moving and changing like some enormous heavenly noticeboard. The walls on each side were panelled in shiny dark wood and had many gilded fireplaces set into them. Every few seconds a witch or wizard would emerge from one of the left-hand fireplaces with a soft whoosh. On the righthand side, short queues were forming before each fireplace, waiting to depart. (HP 5, 144)

In the centre of the hall is the Fountain of Magical Brethren – a presumptuous monument to the official magical world. The statue glorifies the human race and shows its supposed ethnic supremacy:

> A group of golden statues, larger than life-size, stood in the middle of a circular pool. Tallest of them all was a noble-looking wizard with his wand pointing straight up in the air. Grouped around him were a beautiful witch, a centaur, a goblin and a house-elf. The last three were all looking adoringly up at the witch and wizard. (HP 5, 145)[116]

---

[116] Another passage describes the atrium at night, when Harry and his friends enter the ministry to save Sirius: "The only sound in the Atrium was the steady rush of water from the golden fountain, where jets from the wands of the witch and wizard, the point of the centaur's arrow, the tip of the goblin's hat and the house-elf's ears continued to gush into the surrounding pool." (HP 5, 845)

The Entrance Hall is redesigned after Voldemort's followers have over-taken power in Magical World:

> Now a gigantic statue of black stone dominated the scene. It was rather frightening, this vast sculpture of a witch and a wizard sitting on ornately carved thrones, [...]. Engraved in foot-high letters at the base of the statue were the words: MAGIC IS MIGHT. [...] Harry looked more closely and realised that what he had thought were decoratively carved thrones were actually mounds of carved humans: hundreds and hundreds of naked bodies, men, women and children, all with rather stupid, ugly faces, twisted and pressed together to support the weight of the handsomely robed wizards. (HP 7, 198-199)

Now the fountain represents the new government's attitude towards racial issues: "Muggles" exist to serve wizards. "Magic is might" is reminiscent of the simplistic slogans that characterise totalitarian regimes.

Having crossed the entrance area, the visitor reaches a smaller hall with elevators to the individual offices (HP 5, 146). Although the whole ministry is under ground you can see the sky through the windows: "'[Enchanted] windows. Magical Maintenance decide what weather we'll get every day.'" (HP 5, 149) Passing the offices of the "Aurors", the military elite of the magical world (HP 5, 149), one enters a windowless, shabby corridor where Arthur Weasley has his office:

> [...] through a second set of oak doors, into another passage, turned left, marched along another corridor, turned right into a dimly lit and distinctly shabby corridor, and finally reached a dead end, where a door on the left stood ajar, revealing a broom cupboard, and a door on the right bore a tarnished brass plaque reading: Misuse of Muggle Artefacts. Mr Weasley's dingy office seemed to be slightly smaller than the broom cupboard. (HP 5, 150-151)[117]

Long before Harry finally enters the Ministry in *Order of the Phoenix* a courtroom figures prominently in *Goblet of Fire*: when Harry enters the past in Dumbledore's "Pensieve" he finds himself in the "dimly lit" courtroom (HP 4, 634) that has "no windows, merely torches in brackets" (HP 4, 634) and is narrow like a "dungeon" (HP 4, 636). The room is "almost certainly underground" (HP 4, 636).[118] It is clearly negative, the atmosphere is "bleak and forbidding" (HP 4, 636) and the trials Harry witnesses make the reader doubt the justice of Magical World's legal system (see V.1.H, 305). In *Order of the Phoenix* Harry's own trial

---

[117] This shabby office represents the importance Magical World attributes to the "Muggles" and at the same time characterises Arthur Weasley: prestige is irrelevant for him.

[118] A similar description is to be found in *Order of the Phoenix*: "The walls were made of dark stone, dimly lit by torches. Empty benches rose on either side of him, but ahead, in the highest benches of all, were many shadowy figures." (HP 5, 155)

takes place in here, to Mr Weasley's great astonishment, because the room has not been used for years (HP 5, 153). In former times it has been the location of criminal proceedings and as such seems hardly suitable for the trial of a Hogwarts student. The room is so deeply underground that it cannot be reached by elevator, and going to courtroom no. 10 is like entering medieval dungeons:

> [...] yet another corridor, which bore a great resemblance to the one that led to Snape's dungeon at Hogwarts, with rough stone walls and torches in brackets. The doors they passed here were heavy wooden ones with iron bolts and keyholes. (HP 5, 154)

The Department of Mysteries is situated underground and lit by torches. It comprises various rooms. Even before Harry enters it he sees its entrance in his visions. Finally, he even knows where he has to look for a certain object. He sees an empty corridor, rough stone walls and a simple black door.[119] Behind this door there are a couple of connected, mysterious rooms that cannot be clearly placed within the pattern of narrative space. They combine positive (they are circular) and negative features (darkness, being underground). This unclear character meets their highly undefined status: Harry and his friends do not know if the things they see down here are dangerous or not. Whilst they are wondering about this, they cross the individual halls.

The first room is circular, dark and has a couple of doors that keep changing constantly (HP 5, 846-847). Afterwards they cross a bright rectangular room where brains are floating in an enourmous glass tank (HP 5, 848). In the centre of this mysterious room there is an old archway covered with a black veil:

> This room was larger than the last, dimly lit and rectangular, and the centre of it was sunken, forming a great stone pit some twenty feet deep. [...] Unsupported by any surrounding wall, the archway was hung with a tattered black curtain or veil which, despite the complete stillness of the cold surrounding air, was fluttering very slightly as though it had just been touched. [...] He had the strangest feeling that there was someone standing right behind the veil on the other side of the archway. (HP 5, 849)

The room is called the "Death Chamber" (HP 5, 898) and the archway seems to be the gate to the world of the dead: when Sirius falls behind the curtain it is clear to everyone that he will never return. Luna explains to Harry later on that

---

[119] There are many descriptions of the corridor leading to the "Department of Mysteries". For example: "[Harry] was walking down a deserted corridor towards a plain black door, past rough stone walls, torches, and an open doorway on to a flight of stone steps leading downstairs on the left..." (HP 5, 547); "[...] a corridor that was quite different from those above. The walls were bare; there were no windows and no doors apart from a plain black one set at the very end of the corridor." (HP 5, 154).

the dead can be heard moving and whispering behind the black cloth: "They were just lurking out of sight, that's all. You heard them." (HP 5, 948). Physical and emotional coldness are the dominant features of this room, the colour black is everywhere, there is a "complete stillness", and a sense of loneliness ("footsteps echoed loudly"). The place inspires awe and fear at the same time – Hermione is obviously afraid (HP 5, 849-850).

The next room is bright, friendly and full of a mysterious light. It stands for time and man's mortality, represented by clocks of all kind, the ticking of which can be heard ceaselessly:

> [Harry] saw clocks gleaming from every surface, large and small, grandfather and carriage, hanging in spaces between the bookcases or standing on desks ranging the length of the room, so that a busy, relentless ticking filled the place like thousands of minuscule, marching footsteps. (HP 5, 853)

The last and most important room in the Department of Mysteries is the one where prophecies are kept. Harry is supposed to steal the decisive prophecy concerning his own destiny from here to let Voldemort hear it. Filled with a blue light the room is high-ceilinged and full of shelves with crystal orbs. The prophecy Harry and Voldemort are looking for is to be found on shelf 97 (HP 5, 854). Considering the individual rooms of the department as one narrative space this part of the ministry seems to represent the basic ideological principles of Magical World. It seems to explain death and life,[120] time, future and destiny. Dumbledore adds that it also stands for warmth and humanity:

> "There is a room in the Department of Mysteries," interrupted Dumbledore, "that is kept locked at all times. It contains a force that is at once more wonderful and more terrible than death, than human intelligence, than the forces of nature. It is also, perhaps, the most mysterious of the many subjects for study that reside there. It is the power held within that room that you possess in such quantities and which Voldemort has not at all. [...] It was your heart that saved you." (HP 5, 927)

The Ministry, thus, is the main setting of the Voldemort plot: here we find the key to his fall, and it is here that he meets allies to help his rise to power again. When Hogwarts is the centre of the (children's) school plot, the ministry is the decisive space of the (adult's) political plot.

---

[120] Gryffindor ghost Nearly Headless Nick explains to Harry: "'I know nothing of the secrets of death, [...]. I believe learned wizards study the matter in the Department of Mysteries –'." (HP 5, 946).

III.5.F. The Art of Healing – St Mungo's

The name is taken from a catlike tropical animal – there is no saint of that name. The first time the reader hears of St Mungo's is in *Goblet of Fire*, when Dumbledore tells Harry about the fate of the Longbottoms (HP 4, 654). But we do not enter the hospital before *Order of the Phoenix*, when Harry goes to see Mr Weasley (HP 5, 531-533).

For reasons of space St Mungo's Hospital for Magical Maladies and Injuries is not situated in Diagon Alley, but in the heart of London in a "broad store-lined street" (HP 5, 531). Its entrance is hidden in the shop window of an apparently closed department store:

> They had arrived outside a large, old-fashioned, red-brick department store called Purge & Drowse Ltd. The place had a shabby, miserable air; the window displays consisted of a few chipped dummies with their wings askew, standing at random and modelling fashions at least ten years out of date. Large signs on all the dusty doors read: "Closed for Refurbishment". [...] a window displaying nothing but a particularly ugly female dummy. Its false eyelashes were hanging off and it was modelling a green nylon pinafore dress. (HP 5, 532)

The dummy guards the entrance of the hospital that mirrors a modern clinic – only that the diseases and treatments are very different from everything in the "Muggle" world. The entrance hall is very much like what we know of modern hospitals:

> They were in what seemed to be a crowded reception area where rows of witches and wizards sat upon rickety wooden chairs, some looking perfectly normal and perusing out-of-date copies of Witch Weekly [...]. Witches and wizards in lime-green robes were walking up and down the rows, asking questions and making notes [...]. Harry noticed the emblem embroidered on their chests: a wand and bone, crossed. "Are they doctors?" he asked Ron quietly. "Doctors?" said Ron startled. "Those Muggle nutters that cut people up? Nah, they're Healers." (HP 5, 533)

At Christmas, the hospital is nicely decorated.[121] On the five storeys the visitor finds departments for "Artefact Accidents, Creature-Induced Injuries, Magical Bugs, Potion and Plant Poisoning, Spell Damage, Visitors' Tearoom, Hospital Shop" (HP 5, 535) – all utterly unheard of medical disciplines. The

---

[121] "The reception area looked pleasantly festive: the crystal orbs that illuminated St Mungo's had been coloured red and gold to become gigantic, glowing Christmas bubbles; holly hung around every doorway; and shining white Christmas trees covered in magical snow and icicles glittered in every corner, each one topped with a gleaming gold star." (HP 5, 557)

magical world does not deal with infections, surgery or internal medicine. On the way to "'Dangerous' Dai Llewellyn Ward – Serious Bites", on the ward where Mr Weasley is hospitalised after Nagini's bite, the visitor passes portraits of renowned healers (HP 5, 536-537).

St Mungo's is a neutral place within the pattern of narrative space. It serves more as a possibility to describe yet another aspect of magical life and to add to the series' colourfulness than as means of characterisation or setting. Using Hoffmann's terminology, St Mungo's is a fantastical and satirical space (see 99) that caricatures a real hospital.

III.5.G. Grim Old House – No 12, Grimmauld Place

The house of the Black family is just what it appears to be according to its name: a "grim old place". The spelling "auld" is inspired by French, i.e. historical phonetics[122] and means "old". "Grimauld" on the other hand means "owl" in French. The name represents the house perfectly well: it breathes the past splendour of the family's "black" wizards. It is dark, shabby, full of reminiscences of death, and the evil symbol of the snake can be found everywhere.[123] Everything is cold, closed and somehow crooked. Noises sound metallic and leave a sensation of loneliness and isolation.

> [The door's] black paint was shabby and scratched. The silver doorknocker was in the form of a twisted serpent. [...] The door creaked open. [... There was] almost total darkness [in] the hall. [Harry] could smell damp, dust and a sweetish, rotting smell; the place had the feeling of a derelict building. [...] Harry had an odd feeling of foreboding; it was as though they had just entered the house of a dying person.[124] (HP 5, 72-73)

Rough stone walls, flickering light, strange items – the description of the place is full of negative words like "gloomy", "menacing", "dirty" und "dark".[125] The house is marked by decay and death. Its curtains are "moth-

---

122 "-auld" is French and pronounced [ou:ld]. It is a historical writing for modern English "old".

123 Even the door handles are made to look like a snake: "bedroom doorknob, which was shaped like a serpent's head" (HP 5, 74).

124 In fact, Sirius suffers from being jailed in Grimmauld Place so much that he is easily tempted by Voldemort to leave the safe house. This finally costs his life. So the house truly is the house of a "dying person".

125 Numerous passages prove this, for example the following: "It was scarcely less gloomy than the hall above, a cavernous room with rough stone walls. Most of the light was coming from a large fire at the far end of the room. A haze of pipe smoke hung in the air like battle fumes, through which loomed the menacing shapes of heay iron pots and pans hanging from the dark ceiling." (HP 5, 93); "The bedroom looked, if anything, even darker and gloomier than it had on first sight." (HP 5, 113); "[Harry and Ron] entered the

eaten", an umbrella stand looks "as though it had been made from a severed troll's leg", and in the corridor there is "a row of shrunken heads mounted on plaques on the wall. A closer look showed Harry that the heads belonged to house elves" (HP 5, 74). The house is dirty, infested with items of black magic and little demons which have to be cleared away before the place is inhabitable (HP 5, 113-123).

Grimmauld Place cannot be seen by "Muggles". It is situated in the heart of London and the whole area stands for decay (HP 5, 59):

> The grimy fronts of the surrounding houses were not welcoming; some of them had broken windows, glimmering dully in the light from the street-lamps, paint was peeling from many of the doors and heaps of rubbish lay outside several sets of front steps. [...] A pungent smell of rotting rubbish came from the pile of bulging binbags just inside the broken gate. (HP 5, 69-70)

The derelict building only appears when one reads a sign with the address while approaching the house. Then it suddenly can be seen between houses no. 11 and 13 (HP 5, 71).[126] Its entrance is "heavily chained and bolted" (HP 5, 577). It makes the inhabitants feel like prisoners – especially Sirius who is not allowed to leave it. Grimmauld Place has a demoralising influence on the people living here and seems to act like a human being when it defends itself against being cleaned in *Order of the Phoenix*: "[In] Harry's opinion they were really waging war on the house, which was putting up a very good fight, [...]." (HP 5, 134)

The Blacks, the original owners of the house, are omnipresent in Grimmauld Place; items of black magic, portraits and the Blacks' crest are to be found everywhere. The last remaining house-elf, Kreacher,[127] keeps reminding everyone how close the family was to Voldemort.[128] Kreacher's place, a cupboard, shows how much he has fallen prey to decay: everything in here is filthy and the elf piles stolen items out of the Blacks' posession in his cupboard. This

---

drawing room, a long, high-ceilinged room on the first floor with olive green walls covered in dirty tapestries. The carpet exhaled little clouds of dust every time someone put their foot on it and the long, moss green velvet curtains were buzzing as though swarming with invisible bees." (HP 5, 117); "[...] gloomy basement kitchen of number twelve, Grimmauld Place. The only sources of light were the fire and one guttering candle, which illuminated the remains of a solitary supper." (HP 5, 523)

[126] Leaving the house works likewise: The chains at the entrance are opened, the building vanishes after the visitor has left it: "Number twelve was shrinking rapidly as those [houses] on either side of it stretched sideways, squeezing it out of sight. One blink later, it had gone." (HP 5, 577)

[127] The name is a phonetic version of the word "creature" and refers to the elf's dubious, unclear character.

[128] "Finest fifteenth-century goblin-wrought silver, embossed with the Black family crest.", HP 5, 97.

hints at the fact that Kreacher himself is morally corrupt and is going to betray his master Sirius to Voldemort (HP 5, 555). Grimmauld Place is a negative place. Harry wonders: "What on earth were they doing in a house that looked as though it belonged to the Darkest of wizards?" (HP 5, 74).

III.5.H. Horror Without a Face – The Wizard Prison of Azkaban

The prison of the wizarding world alludes to complete isolation ("ban") and, by repeating the vowel [a] and the consonant [k], to the notorious American prison island of Alcatraz.[129] Once released, the ex-prisoners continue to suffer from the unimaginable horrors they experienced in Azkaban for the rest of their lives.[130] Like Alcatraz, Azkaban is an island, "in the Middle of the North Sea" (HP 6, 13). There is no description of Azkaban, but we do know that the true horror of the place is in the emotional torture performed by its guards, the "Dementors".

> The fortress is set on a tiny island, way out to sea, but they don't need walls and water to keep the prisoners in, not when they're all trapped inside their own heads, incapable of a single cheerful thought. Most of them go mad within weeks. (HP 3, 204)

Whereas George Beahm sees the Château d'If off the coast of Marseille as a possible model for Azkaban,[131] J.K. Rowling explains: "[Azkaban] is in the north of the North Sea. A very cold sea."[132]

The place is a nightmare, not because of the circumstances under which the prisoners are being kept, but because they go mad, losing any hope and the will to live: "Most of the prisoners go mad in there", (HP 3, 108) and "[...] most of the prisoners in [Azkaban] sit muttering to themselves in the dark, there's no sense in them." (HP 3, 227). Hagrid remembers:

> "Never bin anywhere like it. Thought I was goin' mad. Kep' goin' over horrible stuff in me mind ... the day I got expelled from Hogwarts ... day me Dad died ... day I had ter let Norbert go ... [...]. Yeh can' really remember who yeh are after a while. An' yeh can' see the point o' livin' at all." (HP 3, 239).

Finally the prisoners die of losing "the will to live." (HP 4, 575). Azkaban, therefore, represents nameless fear, madness and loss of sense.

---

[129] See Hein 2001, 21.
[130] (HP 3, 49) Hagrid, who has only been in the prison for a short time, and Sirius (HP 4, 364) shiver when Azkaban is mentioned. Even Arthur Weasley says Azkaban was "the worst place he'd ever been". On his return he is "all weak and shaking" (HP 3, 108).
[131] See Beahm 2005, 211.
[132] Rowling, Live Interview, 3 Feb 2000.

III.5.I. Magical Exchange Programme – Beauxbatons and Durmstrang

Hogwarts is not the only school of wizardry in Europe – apart from it there are Beauxbatons and Durmstrang, which are quite different from the British academy.

The French name "Beauxbatons" (= nice wands)[133] betrays its nationality. Although we are never explicitly told that it is situated in France, we realise very soon that its students and teachers are speaking English with a French accent. Beauxbatons cares for superficiality and looks, the school uniform is made of silk (HP 4, 269), winged golden horses that only drink Single Malt Whisky (HP 4, 270) are drawing the light blue carriage with which the delegation is travelling (HP 4, 267), and the school crest shows two crossing golden wands (HP 4, 267). The students are much more disciplined than the Hogwarts pupils (HP 4, 275) and behave in quite an arrogant and affected manner (HP 4, 184). Beauxbatons represents alleged high class, arrogance and expensiveness.

Durmstrang academy is – right from the beginning – a negative place. Hermione explains: "'[...] it's got a horrible reputation. [...] it puts a lot of emphasis on the Dark Arts.'" (HP 4, 184) Apparently, the school is located in Bulgaria or at least in the Balkans, because Viktor Krum, a Durmstrang student, is playing for the Bulgarian "Quidditch" national team (HP 4, 119). On the other hand, we are told that the school uniform of Durmstrang is very warm, so Hermione guesses that it must be located "'somewhere in the far north, [...]. Somewhere very cold'" (HP 4, 185). The name Durmstrang has no direct meaning, but its harsh sound is onomatopoeic: the fricatives and plosives [r], [s] and [t] hint at the rough country the students come from and give the place a Germanic touch. The syllables "durm" and "strang" remind us of the German words "Turm" (tower), "Strang" (string) or "streng" (hard). Even a phonetic inversion of "Sturm und Drang" – an age of German literature – is possible.[134] Durmstrang is associated with cold and dark "'[...] the fires are lit only for magical purposes [...] in vinter ve have very little daylight, [...].'" (HP 4, 455) Something evil, dark and menacing lies over Durmstrang and its delegation. The black school ship (HP 4, 403) evokes memories of death, decay and danger when it appears in the Hogwarts lake for the first time (HP 4, 271).

The students wear "robes of a deep, blood red" (HP 4, 276) and remind us of Crabbe and Goyle (HP 4, 271). Durmstrang stands for the racist, dark regime of Voldemort; its education is fundamentally different from Hogwarts' ideals. Teaching the Dark Arts is important, "Muggles" and children from mixed couples are not

---

[133] See Hein 2001, 21.

[134] Amanda Cockrell interprets this as a spooneristic construction of "Sturm und Drang" (see Cockrell 2004, 23). Although Durmstrang has nothing in common with the age of German literature of the same name, it may well be an allusion to Germanic culture.

admitted. Draco Malfoy says that's why his father wanted him to go to Durmstrang instead of Hogwarts (HP 4, 184). Durmstrang, thus, belongs to the same narrative space as Knockturn Alley (see III.5.D, 129). The exact locations of Beauxbatons and Durmstrang are kept secret – they are rivals (HP 4, 184; 455).

III.5.J. Charming Chaos – The Weasleys' The Burrow

The home of the Weasley family is the explicit contrast to the Dursley house in Privet Drive: "The Dursleys liked everything neat and ordered; the Weasleys' house burst with the strange and unexpected." (HP 2, 50) Like Diagon Alley, The Burrow is exciting, surprising and disorderly. This characteristic features prominently in the house's description:

> They landed next to a tumbledown garage in a small yard [...]. It looked as though it had once been a large stone pigsty, but extra rooms had been added here and there until it was several storeys high and so crooked it looked as though it was held up by magic (which [...] it probably was). Four or five chimneys were perched on top of the red roof. A lop-sided sign stuck in the ground near the entrance read "The Burrow". Round the front door lay a jumble of wellington boots and a very rusty cauldron. (HP 2, 39)
> The garden was large and, in Harry's eyes exactly what a garden sould be. The Dursleys wouldn't have liked it – there were plenty of weeds, and the grass needed cutting [...]. (HP 2, 44)

The name of the house hints at its warmth and at the Weasleys' large number of children, but at the same time alludes to the family's unconventionality. It mirrors its inhabitants' characters (see IV.3.J, 182). The Burrow represents "all that Harry craves, especially because everyone who resides there wants him to stay and enjoy life, unlike the punitive and exclusive Dursleys".[135]

III.5.K. The House of the Enemy – Malfoy Manor

The house of the Malfoys becomes a decisive setting in *Deathly Hallows*. And like all the places mentioned in the series, it corresponds very well with the character of its inhabitants. It has a "high, neatly manicured hedge", "impressive wrought-iron gates" and a garden with albino peacocks (HP 7, 9 and 369). The house represents the Malfoys' wealth and their wish to show off:

> A handsome manor house grew out of the darkness at the end of the straight drive, lights glinting in the diamond-paned downstairs windows. [...] The hallway was large, dimly lit and sumptuously decorated, with a magnificent carpet covering most of the stone floor. (HP 7, 10)

---

[135] Schafer 2000, 87.

In this house, Harry and his friends are held prisoners and Voldemort sets up his headquarters.

III.5.L. Home at Last – Godric's Hollow

Within Magical World, Godric's Hollow is a very special, well-known place, because it is the birthplace of Gryffindor (HP 7, 260) and subsequently became a popular place of residence for wizards. Being situated "in the West Country" it is close to the region Rowling herself comes from (I.2.B, 15).

> Most celebrated of these half-magical dwelling places is, perhaps, Godric's Hollow, the West Country village where the great wizard Godric Gryffindor was born, and where Bowman Wright, wizarding smith, forged the first Golden Snitch. The grave-yard is full of the names of ancient magical families, and this accounts, no doubt, for the stories of hauntings that have dogged the little church for many centuries. (HP 7, 261)

In recent times, Bathilda Bagshot, the Dumbledores and the Potters have been living there (HP 7, 132). In 1981, the Potters were assassinated by Voldemort in their home in Godric's Hollow, as a sign set up in front of their derelict house notes (HP 7, 272). The house itself is in ruins:

> The hedge had grown wild in the sixteen years [...]. Most of the cottage was still standing, [...] but the right side of the top floor had been blown apart; that, Harry was sure, was where the curse had backfired. He and Hermione stood at the gate, gazing up at the wreck of what must once have been a cottage just like those that flanked it. (HP 7, 271)

It is surprising that Rowling only brings Harry to his parents' graves in *Deathly Hallows*, the final part of the series. Would it not be more convincing to have Dumbledore leading him to the remains of his home in his first years at Hogwarts? Would it not be normal for a child to long to see the place where he and his parents lived? Introducing Godric's Hollow so late in the series is rather unsatisfying and comes as a "just in time" reference.

III.6 Conclusion: Narrative Space in "Harry Potter"

Narrative space in the *Potter* series has two aspects: location (made up by the different settings) and narrative space as described by Jurij Lotman (see III.1.A, 101). Location can be divided into two part-realities – the world of the "Muggles" and Magical World. Sharing the same geography, they differ in the selection of what magicians and non-wizards interpret as reality. Nearly all settings refer to individual characters and symbolise their personalities. On the other hand, narrative space in the semantic sense follows a clearly defined pattern, which serves mainly to represent different sets of values and does not allude to the emotional state the characters are in. We can discern a binary opposition in the sense of Jurij Lotman.

There is hardly any ambivalence to be found in the structure of narrative space. Rowling uses the same stereotypical elements that already make up the concept of space in the Gothic Novel. Dealing with the ideological content of the novels I will show that the structure of space corresponds with the opposition of antagonistic political concepts.

The story is set nearly exclusively in Great Britain, i.e. Hogwarts. Other countries are only very superficially referred to. The author hardly describes any details of space and lets the reader visualise the individual settings just as he likes. Rowling limits her descriptions – like she does with her characters (see IV.2.A, 149) – to stereotypical catch phrases she keeps repeating. Hogwarts for example is frequently referred to as having "many turrets and towers" (see footnote 84). Among the places Rowling describes more in detail are the Department of Mysteries, St Mungo's and the Ministry of Magic. One possible reason for her doing so is that these places serve as a caricature of the readers' world. There are no epic descriptions of nature, hardly any passages referring to open nature at all (see II.2.E, 46).

Applying Hoffmann's definitions of space (see III.1.A, 99) we can state: nearly all locations are mere spaces of action and as such have a clearly defined function for the plot and the characters. As explained earlier there are hardly any detailed descriptions of places, or they are of minor importance. A good example for this would be the Chamber of Secrets and the Hogwarts dungeons that are both central locations for *Chamber of Secrets* and *Philsopher's Stone*, but are only superficially described.

Nearly all of the settings have a particular use for the characters. Only Snape's dungeon and Sybill Trelawney's office can be regarded as "tempered space" (see III.1.A, 99), i.e. spaces that have an individual meaning for a specific character: Snape's room stands for the fear Harry and his friends feel toward their teacher; Trelawney's classroom obscures one's senses and represents, thus, the teacher's dubious qualifications and the ill-fame of her subject. St Mungo's and the Ministry of Magic are fantastic / satirical spaces: here, the author obviously caricatures real institutions. Eerie spaces, i.e. rooms where the characters cannot relate to anything, are frequently to be found in *Harry Potter*. The Department of Mysteries, the Forbidden Forest and the dungeons of Hogwarts are good examples of this. There are no conceptual, visionary, grotesque or mythic spaces in *Harry Potter*. The focus is clearly on the space of action.

The concept of each particular space changes in the course of action. Usually, all of the spaces appear to be very strange when they are described for the very first time (for example The Burrow, Diagon Alley or Hogwarts castle). Things are astonishing and bizarre. But as the plot progresses these spaces become gradually accepted as part of the readers' reality. Diagon Alley, Hogwarts and the ways of the Weasley family become facts and, thus, mere spaces of action.

Considering Hoffmann's question of to what extent the individual spaces are described, there are basically two things to be observed: the length of description changes and not all of the spaces are described to the same extent. In the course of the series, the descriptions of space become more elaborate. While the first novels have very few descriptions, descriptive passages increase beginning with *Goblet of Fire*. Some spaces like the Hogwarts Great Hall are repeatedly described in great detail, others like the house of the Dursley family or the Hogwarts staff room are referred to very superficially.

The different narrative spaces are simply connected by addition or cause: Harry and his friends follow the given Hogwarts curriculum of mealtimes, lessons, sports, leisure time. Things happen to them during their normal everyday school life. Only rarely do they visit specific rooms on purpose seeking to solve mysteries or find hidden objects like the dungeons in *Philosopher's Stone*, the Chamber of Secrets or the Department of Mysteries. There even is a given pattern of in which order the spaces are presented in the text:

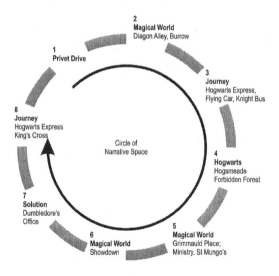

Figure 11: Harry Potter's Circular Journey

This is what Hoffmann calls a connection by cause. The other spaces are connected by addition. There is no case where the spaces are connected correlatively.

IV. Characters

IV.1 Definition of Character

"Der Charakter einer Figur ist die Summe aller im Text gegebenen binären Oppositionen zu anderen Figuren (anderen Gruppen), [...] d. h. ein Satz von Differentialmerkmalen. Der Charakter ist also ein Paradigma."[1] Thus does Jurij Lotman sum up the basics of defining a character: no more than a set of characteristics and not to be confused with a living being. A character is, above all, defined by its opposition to other characters in a text.[2] Gero von Wilpert defines character as:

> Allgemein jede in der Dichtung, besonders Epik und Drama, auftretende fiktive Person, auch Charakter genannt [...].[3]

I shall use this concept of character in the following analysis. Manfred Pfister extends the author's intention to von Wilpert's definition and defines character as "etwas intentional Gemachtes, Konstrukthaftes, Artifizielles".[4]

Characters are representatives of values in human shape. They are different from living people in their being reduced to the things the author chooses to mention about them, as for example character traits, thoughts or biographical details. Edward Morgan Forster in *Aspects of the Novel* (1927), has presented a theory of character still in use today.[5] For him it is decisive if the character can convince the reader of its existence: "The barrier of art divides them from us. They are real not because they are like ourselves (though they may be like us) but because they are convincing."[6] Therefore, Forster defines "flat" and "round characters". Flat characters are defined by very few, homogeneous features, sometimes only one single characteristic. Very often, these characters are allegorical types meant to represent a certain aspect of human behaviour. All other characters judge them likewise, and they are uncontroversial.[7]

---

[1] "A character's disposition is the sum of all the things it differs in from the other characters of the text, i.e. a set of differences. The character, thus, is a paradigm.", Lotman [1972] 1993, 356 [my translation].

[2] See Pfister [1977] 2001, 221-224.

[3] "Any fictitious person in epic or drama, also called 'character'", von Wilpert [1955] 1989, 298.

[4] "something intentionally made up, constructed, artificial", Pfister [1977] 2001, 221-224.

[5] See Forster [1927] 1985, 43-47.

[6] See Forster [1927] 1985, 62.

[7] See Fielitz 2001, 69-70; Pfister [1977] 2001, 243.

In their purest form, they are constructed round a single idea or quality: when there is more than one factor in them, we get the beginning of the curve towards the round.[8]

Their characteristics can be summed up in one single sentence and be identified by the reader whenever they appear:

[...] they never need reintroducing, never run away, have not to be watched for development, and provide their own atmosphere – little luminous disks of pre-arranged size, pushed hither and thither like counters across the void or between the stars; most satisfactory.[9]

Flat characters are in no way of an inferior literary quality: using the example of Charles Dickens, Forster explains that nearly all of his characters are, by his definition, flat. Nevertheless, they create "this wonderful feeling of human depth", and Forster concludes that "[Dickens] ought to be bad. He is actually one of our big writers, and his immense success with types suggests that there may be more in flatness than the severer critics admit."[10] Round characters, on the other hand, are more complex and usually have a biographical background. Their actions are psychologically motivated. Other characters cannot agree on them. They are ambivalent:[11] "The test of a round character is whether it is capable of surprising in a convincing way. If it never surprises, it is flat. If it does not convince, it is a flat pretending to be round."[12] Analysing *Harry Potter* I will use Forster's terminology combined with Pfister's concept of characters. Pfister defines open (or enigmatic character) and closed (or fully explained character) characters. In the first, the reader lacks important information; the character is ambivalent and mysterious. Conversely, in the second instance, the character is satisfactorily explained.[13] Apart from this, Pfister uses the categories of "static" and "dynamic" characters. "Static" means that the characters remain unchanged throughout the whole text. "Dynamic" means that they continue to learn and develop in the course of the plot.[14]

In this chapter I want to analyse how far the characters of the *Potter* novels are (a) flat or round, (b) opened or closed, (c) dynamic or static characters.

---

[8]   Forster [1927] 1985, 67.
[9]   Forster [1927] 1985, 71.
[10] Forster [1927] 1985, 72.
[11] Fielitz 2001, 70; see Pfister [1977] 2001, 244.
[12] See Forster [1927] 1985, 78.
[13] See Pfister [1977] 2001, 246-247.
[14] See Fielitz 2001, 68; Pfister [1977] 2001, 241-242.

IV.1.A. Character Constellation According to Propp and Pfister

Characters are defined by their opinions and behaviour towards other characters or ideas. Out of these positive, negative or neutral attitudes we can form groups of characters that make up a so called character constellation.[15] Criteria for grouping characters can be sex, age or religion[16] as much as opinions and their ideology.[17] All this makes up the character constellation.[18] Within this constellation, each character has a certain function. In *Morphology of the Fairy Tale*, Vladimir Propp defines specific sequences of the plot and calls them functions. Although Propp refers to the traditional Russian fairy tale, these functions can easily be applied to other texts. Propp found out that the individual functions always appear in the same order in the fairy tale.[19] He defines seven functions:[20] villain, donor, helper, princess and her father, hero, false hero and dispatcher. Not all of these functions appear in *Harry Potter*, but we do find the villain (Voldemort),[21] the hero (Harry Potter) and their respective helpers. Additionally to Propp's functions I am going to introduce a further category: the opponent. This is a character which tries to prevent the hero from fulfilling his mission, but is never really a source of danger for him.

Lotman in his *The Structure of the Artistic Text* (first English translation 1977) introduces yet another concept of evaluating characters: the ability to cross the frontier between the semantic fields of a text (see III.1.A, 101). Characters that can cross it are 'mobile'; the ones that remain in their field are "immobile".[22] Very often, only the hero is able to leave his semantic field. He enters the opposite field and returns, thus changed, in the end. Frequently, he achieves power, honour or wealth. The opponents try to prevent him from crossing the frontier.[23] Each character belongs to a narrative space,[24] and it is the author that

---

15   See Pfister [1977] 2001, 233.
16   See Pfister [1977] 2001, 228-229.
17   See Pfister [1977] 2001, 231.
18   See Pfister [1977] 2001, 232. Pfister also defines a configuration of characters. This being above all relevant for drama, I will not refer to this concept.
19 See Vladimir Propp, *Morphology of the Folktale* [1928], Austin: University of Texas Press, 2003, 19-65, 119-127.
20   See Propp [1928] 2003, 79-80; Lotman [1972] 1993, 341; Pfister [1977] 2001, 234. Further refinements of Propp have been made among others by Souriau. I will, nevertheless, stick to Propp's original pattern.
21   In fact, Voldemort corresponds to the "villain-hero" typical of the Gothic Novel (see IV.3.E, 174).
22   See Lotman [1972] 1993, 338. Lotman basically says that each text is made up of three elements: a semantic field with two opposing parts, a normally insuperable frontier and a protagonist. See Lotman [1972] 1993, 341.
23   See Lotman [1972] 1993, 342-343. Pfister calls this "blocking characters", Pfister [1977] 2001, 228.
24   See Lotman [1972] 1993, 328.

defines which space that is. One space can have different characters associated with it; on the other hand, one character can be assigned to various spaces.

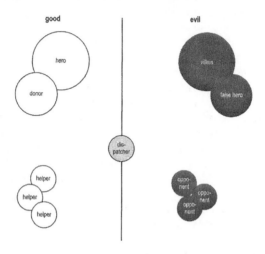

Figure 12: Functions of Characters according to Propp

Apart from grouping characters according to their function in a text, groups can be formed according to mere textual criteria like the quantity of text a character occupies, or their quality. I am going to divide the characters of *Harry Potter* into various classes according to these criteria:

class of character	criteria
protagonists	quantity: biggest part of the text
	quality: feature in the main plot
	(dynamic round characters)
minor characters 1st order	quantity: smaller part of the text
	quality: protagonists of a sub-plot
minor characters 2nd order	quantity: very small part of the text
	quality: minor character of a sub-plot
marginal character	neither relevant in quantity nor in quality

IV.1.B. What's the Message? – What the Author Wants to Tell Us

Looking at the constellation of character we usually wonder: Which character embodies the author's opinion? What is the "truth" the author wants to make us see? How does he try to manipulate us? Combining the individual points of view of the character, we get the structure of perspectives. Using Pfister's terminology *Harry Potter* has a "closed structure": there are no easy solutions, the reader has to judge for himself but receives hints from the author – either explicitly in the text or implicitly by using techniques of manipulation. In *Harry Potter* we can easily make out what Rowling wants us to believe to be true and just.

But how can an author influence the readers' perception? First of all, he can structure his characters accordingly; Pfister names – among others – the contrastive structure where a positive constrasts with a negative set of characters. The reader must be able to identify one of them as 'right'. As I am going to show, in the *Harry Potter* novels we can easily find out what Rowling wants us to believe and how she wants us to think about characters or actions. There are two clearly opposing perspectives: Harry's and Voldemort's. All characters have to choose sides with either one of them.

The author can manipulate the readers' sympathy by selecting the information he gives. Describing a character's appearance, his voice, her biography or behaviour immediately evokes either sympathy or antipathy in the reader. He may also use telling names (a technique Rowling uses in nearly all her characters, see IV.2.A, 149) and poetic justice that punishes "wrong" and rewards "good" behaviour.[25] The author also decides how much attention each character receives in the text and how elaborate their descriptions are rhetorically.[26] And finally choosing the whole text's point of view he influences the reader's perception of the plot (see IV.1.B, 147).

IV.2 The Characters in "Harry Potter"

"The fascination of the latest unfolding of J.K. Rowling's work lies in the layers of grey that she reveals between dark and light. Characters are deeply probed and eviscerated, [...]" says Kate Muir[27] in a review for *Times Online* and touches one of the most controversial points about Rowling; the quality of characterisation in her works has divided literary criticism ever since the first *Potter* book was published. Some critics claim that characterisation is one of her main strengths as a novelist and that her characters were "almost without exception, extremely realistic and convincing, due to her economic yet effective descrip-

---

25   See Lotman [1972] 1993, 94-95.
26   See Lotman [1972] 1993, 96-97.
27   Muir 2007

148

tion".[28] They say she combined "psychological realism, caricature, and melo-drama".[29] Other critics believe her characters to be superficial and unconvincing in their development.[30]

As a matter of fact, most characters have reason to act as they do. According to Forster many of them are flat characters that cannot surprise, but they are in Pfister's terms dynamic (see 144). Neville for example is traumatised by his parents' sad lot and reacts with being extremley shy. Tom Riddle hates non-magical people, because his "Muggle" father has left his mother.[31] "Jede einzel-ne der von [Rowling] eingeführten Figuren ist unverwechselbar."[32] Flat charac-ters can become round characters in the course of action as for example Filch, the Hogwarts house-keeper (see IV.6.D, 272). Roland Ernould states that Rowl-ing's characters are a bizarre mixture between exact psychological portrait and superficiality. Thus, the author never overstrains her young readers' intellect.[33]

But how are characters in the novels represented? What do we get to know about them? And what remains unsaid? According to E. M. Forster's cri-teria, most of the first novels' characters are flat, but gain complexity in the later parts of the series. Unfailing Dumbledore seems to make mistakes and doubts himself (see IV.3.L, 211). Barbarous Draco Malfoy suddenly raises our sympa-thy and becomes humane (see IV.3.L, 196). Even the protagonist has positive and negative character traits; he is compassionate, but at the same time does not stop at playing cruel tricks on his cousin Dudley or at inventing fictive tortures for other characters (see IV.3.A, 156). Severus Snape is highly ambivalent (see IV.4.C, 225), but, turns out to be a martyr in the end.

Analysing the characters in the *Harry Potter* series we face a basic prob-lem of definition: what is a character? There are numerous ghosts, zombies, ap-paritions, magically transformed people, 'wise' aninmals able to speak in human tongues, etc. So, again, what is a character?[34] I will principally treat the major and minor human characters. All non-humans will be treated as mere "decora-tive elements" and marginal characters and will, thus, not be dealt with.[35] In the

---

[28] Hiebert Alton 2003, 147.
[29] Nel 2001, 34.
[30] I will deal with this in the context of the character pattern (see IV.2.B, 152 and Mullan 2005.
[31] See Smadja 2001, 37.
[32] "Each of [Rowling's] characters is distinctive" [my translation]. See von Bredow 2000.
[33] Ernould 2003, 211.
[34] See Jason T. Eberls, "Why Voldemort Won't Just Die Already: What Wizards Can Teach Us About Personal Identity," *Harry Potter and Philosophy: If Aristotle ran Hog-warts*, eds. Baggett & Klein, Chicago, La Salle: Open Court 2004, 200-212, here 201-206.
[35] The characters of the *Potter* novels being very numerous I cannot deal with all of them. Meanwhile, there are various complete lists of characters for example in the German Wikipedia: <http://de.wikipedia.org/wiki/Figuren_der_Harry-Potter-Romane> 26 Aug 2007. There is also a complete *Harry Potter* lexicon to be found under www.hp-lexicon.org. Under

following chapter I am going to apply the theories by Forster, Pfister, Lotman and Propp to the *Potter* novels. I will deal with some of the characters in detail and show which values they represent. Therefore, I will – according to the criteria mentioned before (see IV.1.A, 146) – divide them into main characters, minor characters of 1st and 2nd order and marginal characters.

IV.2.A. Telling Names and Open Judgement –
Rowling's Characterisation Techniques

In a poll conducted by English bookseller Waterstone's, 41 percent of the children declared they preferred Hermione to all other characters. Only 19 percent voted for Harry. Ron was liked best by 13 percent.[36] Hagrid was voted favourite teacher and, quite surprisingly, was more popular than Dumbledore.[37] Such opinion polls show two things: first, there is a public discussion (heated up by Waterstone's PR) of the *Potter* characters that gives them the status of living people;[38] second it demonstrates that readers' sympathies are not that easily influenced – otherwise, Harry should have been liked best and Dumbledore as the series' *spiritus rector* should have been voted favourite teacher.

J.K. Rowling influences her readers' judgement very clearly. They experience the whole plot from Harry's point of view (see II.2.A, 34). Moreover, Rowling makes her characters comment on each other. In particular, the positive characters are constantly commenting on the "bad guys". The reader's sympathies being with Harry and his friends, he tends to believe them. In some cases Rowling makes the characters comment on themselves. Lockhart the impostor, in his constant praising of his own 'heroic' deeds, unmasks himself as unworthy of trust (see IV.4.B, 222).

The name of each character usually has a special meaning with Rowling who says of herself "I was born in a place called Chipping, so perhaps that explains my love of silly names."[39] She has always been collecting extraordinary names and makes long lists of them, she explains. Her sources include:

"Who's who in the Wizarding World" you can find a complete list of characters (<http://www.hp-lexicon.org/wizards/wizards_list.html> 26 Aug 2007). There is also a very interesting list with the translations of the names in various languages: http://en.wikipedia. org/wiki/List_of_characters_in_translations_of_Harry_Potter 30 Nov 2007.

[36] See "Harry Potter knocked off top spot," *Guardian* 8 July 2005. <http://blogs.guardian. co.uk/culturevulture/archives/2005/07/08/harry_potter-knocked_ off> 28 Sept 2007.

[37] See Smith 2005.

[38] This also became clear when Rowling came out with the news that she imagined Dumbledore to be gay.

[39] Rowling, Live Interview, 3 Feb 2000.

"War memorials, telephone directories, shop fronts, saints, villains, baby-naming books – you name it, I've got names from it! I also make up names, the most popular one being 'quidditch', of course."[40]

Nearly all of Rowling's characters have interpretative names which I will commen upon when dealing with the individual characters. These names either hint at the characters' qualities, name an object that corresponds with the characters (for example "Poppy", the nickname of Hogwarts nurse Madam Pomfrey, refers to the healing potential of the plant)[41] or they allude to things that are quite the opposite of the characters. This latter technique results in comical effects.[42] Rowling also uses the phonetical quality of the names; "Severus Snape" is very close to the word "snake" and using all the consonants [s] imitates the noise this particular animal makes. John Granger identifies the sentence "sword in hat" in "Sorting Hat" which would hint at the events of Chamber of Secrets.[43] I believe that this is only true for American English, where the [t] is pronounced [d]. Because Rowling is English I doubt this interpretation. Granger points out the non-English references the author uses: "Godric Gryffindor" consists of "god", "griffin" and the French "d'or". This makes the name translate as "divine eagle of gold".[44] Emer O'Sullivan explains how "Dumbledore" and "Gryffindor" are phonetically related, both ending with "d'or" and, thus, being associated with gold.[45] "Quidditch" seems to have derived its name from Latin "quid" and "quiddity", which is the "nature of things".[46] "Cho Chang" is Japanese and means "butterfly".[47] Sometimes the author uses anagrams like "Mirror of Erised" which becomes a "Mirror of Desire" when read backwards. This name explains its function: it shows the viewer the fulfillment of his or her greatest wish. And finally, Rowling alludes to British literature, when she names Filch's cat after a Jane Austen character from Mansfield Park (Mrs. Norris) or uses phrases from the fairy tale Three Little Pigs in the name of Hufflepuff.[48] Sometimes the author brings to life real historical people like Nicholas Flamel in Phi-

---

[40] Rowling 2006.
[41] See Nel 2001, 33.
[42] See Schafer 2000, 217.
[43] See Granger 2004, 13.
[44] See Granger 2004, 16.
[45] See O'Sullivan 2002, 23.
[46] See John Killinger, God, the Devil, and Harry Potter: A Christian Minister's Defense of the Beloved Novels, New York: Thomas Dunne, 2004, 63.
[47] See Jung 2004, 76.
[48] In this fairy tale a wolf menaces the three little pigs hidden in their house: "I'll huff and I'll puff and I'll blow your house down." The word also sounds like hard physical work, which also fits the Hufflepuffs' reputation for being hard working students. See O'Sullivan 2002, 23.

losopher's Stone. Flamel was a French alchemist from the early 15th century (1330-1418) and allegedly had produced the stone in question.[49]

Another technique to guide her readers' sympathies is Rowling's use of evaluating adjectives. Snape for example is referred to as having an "icy voice", "sallow skin", "hooked nose", "greasy hair" and spreading a "cold breeze" (HP 2, 87). His smile is "nasty" (HP 2, 158), "thin-lipped" (HP 2, 288), "unpleasant" (HP 3, 136) or even "horrible" (HP 3, 308). Of course this is a judgement of character; Snape is meant to be scary and sneaky. With giving the readers' such definite guidelines, Rowling makes sure that there can be no mistake right from the start.[50]

Analysing the individual characters, we find some techniques which Rowling uses frequently. Nearly every character has a fixed set of catchphrases applied to it. Like a trademark we find the same words over and over again. Harry, for example is constantly being described as having "jet-black hair", being "small", and "skinny" (see IV.3.A, 156). Hermione has "bushy brown hair" (see IV.3.E, Seite 174), Dumbledore has "silver hair", a "silver beard", "half-moon spectacles", "long fingers" and "a crooked nose" (see IV.3.L, 191) and Minerva McGonagall seems always to wear her hair "in a tight bun" (see IV.4.E, 231).

Apart from this technique we find that Rowling emphasises a character's eyes; they are the mirror of the character's true nature. Harry has "brilliant" or "bright green eyes" (see IV.3.A, 156), Tom Riddle has an "odd red gleam in his hungry eyes" (see IV.3.E, 179), whereas Dumbledore has "twinkling light-blue" eyes that can also become a "penetrating, light-blue stare" or "blue eyes full of fire" (seeIV.3.N, 208). Rufus Scrimgeour's eyes are "yellowish" (HP 6, 21-22) and make him resemble a wildcat. These eyes are different from the cold, pale and grey eyes of the Malfoy family (see IV.3.L, 192).

Not only are the eyes an indication of a character's essence – it is also important how someone smiles or laughs. While Tom Riddle laughs in an unnaturally high and malicious way (see IV.3.E), the Malfoys grimace (see IV.3.L, 192), Snape shows a thin-lipped, ugly smile (see IV.4.C), Dolores Umbridge smiles while sadistically punishing students (see IV.5.G), and Dumbledore laughs merrily (see IV.3.L, 209).

Rowling likes to compare her characters to animals or at least to allude to them: Tom Riddle alias Voldemort is compared with a cat, a spider or a snake (see IV.3.E), Dudley Dursley and his father resemble pigs, gorillas or whales, Petunia looks like a horse (see IV.4.G, 237), and dubious Sybill Trelawney is

---

[49] See Beahm 2005, 94.

[50] With the exception of the characters whose true identity is part of the detective plot like the impostor Moody, Sirius Black or Peter Pettigrew.

frequently compared to an insect, i.e. a "dragon fly" (see IV.4.I, 247). These comparisons serve to explain the characters.

Just as important for characterisation are the animals the wizards produce during the "Patronus Charm" or the ones they can transform into.[51] Harry's "Patronus" is a stag – which is precisely the animal his father could transform into (see IV.4.H, 244). Cho Chang – whose main feature is being beautiful – has a swan and Hermione an otter (which happens to be the author's own favourite animal; see I.2.B, 20).

IV.2.B. Hero versus "Villain Hero" – The Constellation of Characters

Harry Potter has a contrastive constellation of characters: Harry's friends and helpers nearly all have counterparts on the negative side of the pattern. The emotional warmth of the Weasleys contrasts with the coldness of the Malfoys. Petunia Dursley's abuse is in direct contrast to Molly's motherly feelings towards Harry. Sentimental Hagrid has his counterpart in the unemotional Snape, whereas Vernon Dursley as malicious, narrow-minded stepfather is the contrast to Harry's biological father.[52] Harry himself is contrasted by Draco Malfoy. The altruistic love of his parents Lily and James represent opposite values to those of the egoistic Dursley family. Dumbledore and Voldemort are just another opposition of values and their function for Harry.[53]

Because the constellation is thus clear critics have complained that the characters were "all black-and-white"[54] and "zu offensichtlich nach festen Schemata",[55] especially the teachers were too stereotypical[56]. This is wrong. It is true, nevertheless, that the author does not describe her characters in complete psychological depth (which would be inappropriate for a children's book anyway). But one must make a difference between quantity and quality of characterisation; even the minor characters are often ambivalent and "an amalgam of good and bad".[57] As Michael Maar correctly states, nearly all of Rowling's characters had "eine kleine Wunde zu verstecken, eine Schwäche zu camouflieren." With Ron it is his poverty, Neville is ashamed of his lack of magical abilities

---

[51] See Granger 2004, 38-39.
[52] See Grimes 2004, 94.
[53] See Grimes 2004, 91-92.
[54] Holden 2000.
[55] "follow too evidently a clear pattern": Andreas Platthaus, "Endstation Hogwarts," *F.A.Z.* 20 July 2002, 44 [my translation].
[56] See Schafer 2000, 56.
[57] See Schafer 2000, 42.

and Filch has to hide that he is a "Squib".[58] Wilfried von Bredow writes in his critique for *F.A.Z.*:

> Die Trennlinie zwischen den Guten und den Bösen ist aber nicht, wie einige Rowling-Kritiker gönnerhaft geschrieben haben, in simpler Klarheit festgelegt. Im Gegenteil – neben ein paar eindeutigen positiven oder negativen Identifikationsfiguren, Albus Dumbledore contra Lord Voldemort, sind es gerade die Zwiespältigkeiten und Knäuel von bewußten und unbewußten, von großherzigen und egoistischen Motiven der Personen, von Moral und Interessen, die den Romanen ihre geistige Glaubwürdigkeit geben.[59]

The constellation of the *Harry Potter* novels can be described through Propp's functions of hero, villain, helper and the additionally defined opponent.[60] Harry is the hero persecuting evil. He does this because he has to. It is not his free will or wish. Harry is a very passive hero reacting more than acting deliberately.[61] Voldemort is the villain actively seeking to destroy his enemies. He sets the plot in motion and constantly provokes the events of which it consists. This is why he resembles the "villain-hero" typical of the Gothic Novel of the 18th and 19th century. He is Propp's villain and hero at the same time. The vast majority of characters belong to the category of helpers. They enable the true hero to defeat his enemy, saving him from persecution, solving difficult tasks and transforming him. I count Hermione (solving all the riddles), the Weasleys, Dumbledore, Hagrid, Lupin and Harry's parents (whose ghosts make sure he can return to Hogwarts at the end of *Goblet of Fire*) among these helpers. The adversaries of the helpers are the opponents. The Malfoys and Snape can be included in this category. Characters like Gilderoy Lockhart, Peter Pettigrew, Quirrell and the Crouches are opponents, but they also embody elements of the false hero: they all seem to be someone else when we first meet them. Ginny

---

[58] "hide a wound or weakness", Maar 2003, 49 [my translation].

[59] "The borderline between good and bad is not – as some of Rowling's critics would patronisingly say – simple and clear. On the contrary – apart from some very definite positive or negative characters to identify with i.e. Albus Dumbledore against Lord Voldemort, it is the ambivalence and the conflicts between the conscious and the unconscious, between the generous and egoistic motivations of people, between moral and personal interests that give the novels their intellectual truth.", von Bredow 2000 [my translation].

[60] Isabelle Smadja uses Propp's categories as well: see Smadja 2001, 7.

[61] This is evident in all parts of the series. In *Philosopher's Stone* Voldemort wants to get the stone promising eternal life and kill Harry; Harry must defend himself. In *Chamber of Secrets* students are being attacked and Ginny is lured into a trap; Again, Harry is forced to fight. *Prisoner of Azkaban* differs from the others in the fact that it is not Voldemort who initiates the plot, but Sirius Black. There is no final showdown between Harry and his arch-enemy either. But again Harry reacts to being menaced. In *Goblet of Fire* Harry is forced to participate in the tournament. It is only in the last part of the series, that Harry takes action against Voldemort.

Weasley might be the princess – being abducted by the evil Tom Riddle into the dragon's lair (*Chamber of Secrets*). Harry has to save her, and later she becomes his girlfriend, wife and then mother of his children.

Katherine M. Grimes points out further similarities between the characters of fairy tales and the ones featuring in *Harry Potter*, where she sees Hagrid as "the fairy tale hunter, the savior in such tales as 'Little Red Riding Hood' and 'Snow White'", Sirius Black as a form of beast from *Beauty and the Beast* and Molly Weasley as Mother Holle from the German fairy tale *Frau Holle*. For Grimes, Voldemort is the wolf from the woods and Petunia Dursley the evil stepmother featuring in most European fairy tales.[62] So *Harry Potter* refers to basic elements of the fairy tale.

According to Lotman's theory that each character belongs to one of two semantic spaces, we do find corresponding elements in *Harry Potter*. In analysing the structure of narrative space I am going to show that there is a very definite pattern of good and bad spaces (see III.2.A, 101). This is also true for the characters. Both patterns are identical in that they see chaos and disorder as something positive. Conforming to norms and obeying rules, on the contrary, is negative:

positive	**negative**
chaos	order
non-conformity	conformity
modesty	greed
being well-educated	no education
no ambition	ambition
braveness	cowardice
respect for nature	no respect for nature
(rationality)	emotions
(justice)	arbitrariness
(compassion)	pitilessness
(aggression)	aggression
(gentleness)	brutality

In addition, Elizabeth D. Schafer identifes a cold-warm opposition (see III, 103).[63] The pattern is ambivalent concerning the opposition of the following emotions: arbitrariness, pitilessness, aggression and brutality. Harry himself is shown to be aggressive, cruel and ready to use physical violence. But, nevertheless, being peaceful and renouncing violence is not a negative value; Dumbledore is a forgiving man and – of course – a positive character. This leads us to conclude that it is more important *who* is violent and aggressive (see V,

---

[62]   See Grimes 2004, 94-96
[63]   Evil has a cold voice, friends speak in warm tones: see Schafer 2000, 222.

278). But analysing the ideological content of *Harry Potter* we will see that it is of great relevance *why* someone is aggressive or cruel and how serious he is in this. There is a certain contradiction in that being well educated is good, but working hard to achieve knowledge is bad: when Hermione voluntarily does additional work for school she is regarded as being something of a careerist. But when she is – because of her extra work – able to help them out of difficult situations, she is admired by all.

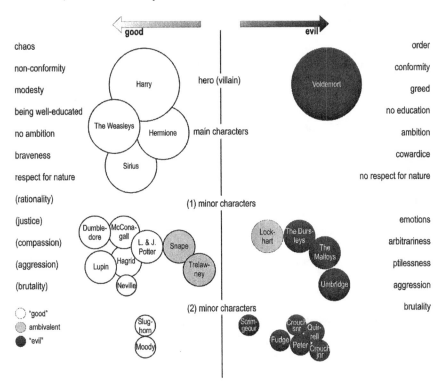

Figure 13: Constellation of Characters in Harry Potter

As I have said before (see IV.1.A, 145) Lotman makes a difference between mobile and immobile characters. In *Harry Potter* none of the characters is able to cross the frontier between the two semantic spaces: Voldemort and Harry act in the same part of reality but they both remain in their own separate spheres. When Harry witnesses Voldemort rallying his supporters in *Goblet of Fire*, the setting of the scene is the cemetery of Little Hangleton. The semantic spaces corresponding to the patterns of space and characters stay unchanged. Harry is not tempted to join Voldemort's supporters, nor does the villain try to meet the boy in his own ideological world. They meet at the frontier, so to speak, but never cross it. Considering the frontier a mere line between good and evil (which is not Lotman's intention) then Harry and Voldemort are indeed the only characters able to cross it: Harry is the first to meet the arch-enemy personally, and Voldemort is repeatedly able to enter Hogwarts.

IV.3 Main Characters

According to the definition (see IV.1.A, 146) I shall call characters that receive the greatest attention within the text (quantity) and play major roles in the main plot main characters. The main characters are, therefore: Harry himself, Hermione, Ron (together with his family)[64] and Albus Dumbledore. Sirius Black, the Malfoys and Tom Riddle alias Voldemort (who could also be counted as the true hero of the novels; see IV.3.E) are also main characters.

IV.3.A. "I don't go looking for trouble, [...]. Trouble usually finds me."[65] – Harry James Potter

Harry and James are both names of British kings (see IV.4.H, 244). 'Harry' is a French form of the English name 'Henry', 'Henry' being Germanic and meaning 'home rule'.[66] Phonetically, 'Harry' hints at 'to harass' and 'heir'.[67] 'To harry' also means to bother or even 'to devastate'. The phrase 'Tom, Dick or Harry' is used to refer to the average everyman. His last name, Potter, can be interpreted as an allusion to the Christian representations of God: in Genesis, God is said to have created man out of clay, which is why the Orthodox church calls god a potter.[68]

So the boy is royal, a chosen one, a troublemaker and an heir. His name embraces the everyday with alongside of the qualities of Germanic nobility. This seems quite appropriate for a 'normal' boy who is to become the world's saviour.[69] In its simplicity the name is a contrast to the names which have foreign origins like Malfoy, McGonagall or the Old English Dumbledore.[70] Common as his name is, Harry is a controversial character and ambivalent to the values for

---

[64] Even Percy returns to his parents' values in *Deathly Hallows*.
[65] See HP 3, 85.
[66] See "Henry", *Dictionary of First Names* [1990] 2000, 114.
[67] See Granger 2004, 111-112.
[68] See Granger 2004, 113-114. Granger finds a phonetic similarity with Latin *pater* – but this only is true for American English.
[69] It is also the name of Beatrix Potter (1866-1943), one of the most popular authors of English children's literature.
[70] See Nikolajeva 2003, 131.

which he stands. Being the protagonist, he does not show a lot of initiative, and most of the time he is forced to react to the actions of his enemies. In the course of the series, Harry grows from a poor orphan into a self-conscious young man accepting his role in saving his world from terror and oppression. But, nevertheless, he is not the classic epic hero.[71] In the last part of the series we learn that he is a descendant of Ignotus Peverell (HP 7, 349) and thus, from a very old family. Born on the 31st of July 1980 (see II.4, 78 and IV.5.C, 253) in Godric's Hollow (see III.5.L, 140), he survives Voldemort's attack on his family on 31st of October 1981 (Halloween), because his mother's sacrificing love makes the villain's killing curse fire back and destroys the attacker. This gives him protection until his seventeenth birthday (HP 7, 33) as Dumbledore explains: "She gave you a lingering protection he never expected, a protection that flows in your veins to this day" (HP 5, 918). Harry only receives a scar – a mark of Cain,[72] which marks him as the chosen one from now on. After the murder of his parents the orphan boy goes to live with his mother's family, the Dursleys who lead a bourgeois life in suburban Little Whinging. The Dursleys hate anything magical and maltreat both physcially and emotionally the boy whenever they can (see IV.4.G, 236). Harry, being ignorant of his special, magical descent believes his parents have died in a car accident. He wishes for "some unknown relation coming to take him away" (HP 1, 37), because he feels his relatives' hate. His wish for parents or at least for grown-ups he can trust remains even when he has come to Hogwarts:

> What he really wanted [...] was someone like – someone like a *parent*: An adult wizard whose advice he could ask without feeling stupid, someone who cared about him, who had had experience of Dark Magic... (HP 4, 30)

Shortly after his eleventh birthday on 31st of July 1991 Harry learns the truth about his family and is taken to the wizard boarding school Hogwarts, where he starts his magical education. But Voldemort has not yet been finally defeated – Harry's time at school is marked by ever new intrigues of the villain trying to regain his power.

Harry is an unimpressive, small and skinny boy, when we meet him for he first time in *Philosopher's Stone*. Apart from his magically growing untidy hair (HP 1, 27-28) and his scar there is nothing special about him:

---

[71] *Harry Potter* can be considered an "Entwicklungsroman" where the protagonist has to grow up and develop his own set of values. Nevertheless, *Potter* is much more children's novel and a fantasy text. The fantastic aspect is dominant. This is why I am not going to analyse *Potter* in the context of the genre of "Entwicklungsroman".

[72] See Natov 2001, 127.

[...] Harry had always been small and skinny for his age. He looked even
smaller and skinnier than he really was because all he had to wear were old
clothes of Dudley's and Dudley was about four times bigger than he was.
Harry had a thin face, knobbly knees, black hair and bright-green eyes. He
wore round glasses held together with a lot of Sellotape because of all the
times Dudley had punched him on the nose. The only thing Harry liked
about his own appearance was a very thin scar on his forehead which was
shaped like a bolt of lightning. He had had it as long as he could remember
[...]. (HP 1, 27)

This physical inferiority continues like a leitmotif through all the descriptions. In
Chamber of Secrets we read: "Harry [...] was small and skinny, with brilliant
green eyes and jet-black hair that was always untidy. He wore round glasses,
and on his foreheard was a thin, lightning-shaped scar." (HP 2, 10). It is not
quite plausible how this boy can be a good sportsman, as Roland Ernould points
out. His being a "Quidditch" hero seems quite far-fetched.[73] Harry plays as
"seeker" in this dangerous and action packed flying game. This can be read on a
metaphorical level; the whole plot is based on Harry looking for solutions, items
and seeking to understand his own role in the world.[74]

In *Prisoner of Azkaban* he has grown, but still seems quite weak:

Harry, though still rather small and skinny for his age, had grown a few
inches over the last year. His jet-black hair, however, was just as it always
had been: stubbornly untidy, whatever he did to it. The eyes behind his
glasses were bright green, and on his forehead, clearly visible through his
hair, was a thin scar, shaped like a bolt of lightning. (HP 3, 12)

He always remains the green-eyed, skinny boy with untidy black hair (HP 4, 23).[75]
The people who meet him for the first time keep repeating that he looks like his
father and has his mother's eyes.[76] The similarities with his family are so obvious that Harry recognises his relatives at once when seeing them for the first
time in the Mirror of Erised:

[Harry saw] other people in the mirror and saw other pairs of green eyes like
his, other noses like his, even a little old man who looked as though he had
Harry's knobbly knees – Harry was looking at his family, for the first time
in his life. (HP 1, 226).

---

[73] See Ernould 2003, 212.
[74] See Schafer 2000, 48.
[75] Also see HP 5, 7.
[76] Dumbledore: "'[...] but you do look extraordinarily like James. Except for your eyes ...
you have your mother's eyes.'" (HP 3, 460); Hagrid: "'Yeh look a lot like yer dad, but
yeh've got yer mum's eyes.'" (HP 1, 56); "'[He] looks exactly like James.' 'Except the
eyes, [...]. Lily's eyes.'" (HP 5, 58). Finally, these remarks get on Harry's nerves (HP 6, 70).

Dumbledore explains how unusual it is that Harry sees his family instead of worldly riches:

> "[You] remain pure of heart, just as pure as you were at the age of eleven, when you stared into a mirror that reflected your heart's desire, and it showed you only the way to thwart Lord Voldemort, and not immortality or riches. Harry, have you any idea how few wizards could have seen what you saw in that mirror?" (HP 6, 478)

Harry finds a father figure in Albus Dumbledore, even if this relationship is characterised by their difference in hierarchy and their mutual respect. When in *Half-Blood Prince* Harry is alone with Dumbledore outside the school for the first time, he feels strange: "Harry felt distinctly awkward [...]. He had never had a proper conversation with his headmaster outside Hogwarts before; there was usually a desk between them." (HP 6, 59). Harry never wavers in his loyality to Dumbledore. When Scrimgeour tries to persuade him to support his party he declares himself solidly united with Dumbledore: "'Dumbledore's man through and through, aren't you, Potter?' 'Yeah, I am,' said Harry. 'Glad we straightened that out.'" (HP 6, 326). The headmaster makes him feel safe; "[...] I do not think you need worry about being attacked tonight. [...]. You are with me, [...]. This will do, Harry.'" (HP 6, 59). He guarantees stability – wherever Dumbledore is, Harry can feel safe. This relation is reversed at the end of *Half-Blood Prince* when the old wizard, weakened by the poison he has drunk, says to Harry: "'I am not worried, Harry, [...] I am with you'" (HP 6, 540). It is all the more surprising for the reader to find out that Dumbledore obviously used Harry as a means to destroy Voldemort and Harry's rather cool reaction to this discovery is also worthy of note (HP 7, 555). Harry is much more disappointed to find out that his surrogate father did not tell him about his own ambivalent past and his friendship with Gellert Grindelwald (HP 7, 287, 295). Dumbledore's death – which, after James Potter and Sirius Black represents the loss of a third father for Harry – means the final end of Harry's childhood:

> [Harry] must abandon for ever the illusion he ought to have lost at the age of one: that the shelter of a parent's arms meant that nothing could hurt him. (HP 6, 601)

Kneeling at Dumbledore's lifeless body Harry realises what his death means:

> Harry reached out, straightened the half-moon spectacles upon the crooked nose and wiped a trickle of blood from the mouth with his own sleeve. Then he gazed down at the wise old face and tried to absorb the enormous and incomprehensible truth: that never again would Dumbledore speak to him, never again could he help... (HP 6, 568)

In *Deathly Hallows* we learn that Harry is the seventh of Voldemort's "Horcruxes", accidentally created by the villain when he killed Harry's parents (HP 7, 568). This fact explains the similarities between Voldemort and Harry (HP 7, 550). Therefore, he must die if he wants to defeat his enemy. So he surrenders himself to Voldemort and is killed: "He saw the mouth move and a flash of green light, and everything was gone." (HP 7, 564), but being master of the "Deathly Hallows" he survives his own death. Again, choice is the decisive factor in the plot: in a rather bizarre twilight zone between life and death (set in King's Cross – another place of parting, and with platform 9¾ a border between two worlds) he meets Dumbledore and learns that he can either go back to fight Voldemort or "board a train", probably to the realm of death (HP 7, 578). Harry decides to go back and only because of this decision can Voldemort be defeated. When everything is over we hear Harry say "'I've had enough trouble for a lifetime.'" (HP 7, 600) and having followed his adventures for seven novels we heartily agree with him.

IV.3.B. "Difficult. Very difficult" – Harry's Nature

Harry is extraordinarily brave, somehow ambitious and feels under pressure to prove himself. This mixture makes the Sorting Hat doubt into which house to sort him. Hesitating between Slytherin and Gryffindor, it takes him a long time to make Harry join the latter. It is Harry's own plea that leads to this decision:[77]

> "Difficult. Very difficult. Plenty of courage, I see. Not a bad mind, either. There's talent, oh my goodness, yes – and a nice thirst to prove yourself, now that's interesting ... So where shall I put you?" Harry gripped the edges of the stool and thought "Not Slytherin, not Slytherin." "Not Slytherin, eh?" said the small voice. "Are you sure? You could be great, you know, it's all here in your head, and Slytherin will help you on the way to greatness, no doubt about that – no? Well, if you're sure – better be GRYFFINDOR!" (HP 1, 133)[78]

With this ambiguity Harry is not a mere flat character. The other characters' opinions about him are very diverse.

Soon Harry becomes the leader of his friends. For example when he guides them to the midnight duel with Malfoy in *Philosopher's Stone*[79] he tells

---

[77] Considering the importance the house has for each student, this is Harry's first decisive choice. He chooses not to be a Slytherin, although we do not know why he does this. This proves that it is a person's own choice that decides his destiny (see V.6.A, 367).

[78] The "Sorting Hat" underlines its decision in *Chamber of Secrets*: "'But I stand by what I said before – [...] you would have done well in Slytherin.'" (HP 2, 224).

[79] "Harry hissed at [Hermione] to be quiet and beckoned them all forward. [...]'This way!' Harry shouted to the others [...]." (HP 1, 173).

them going through the trap door: "If you want to go back, I won't blame you'...'You can take the Cloak, I won't need it now.'" (HP 1, 296). And as "Quidditch" captain he is able to assert his authority against show-off McLaggen ("[Harry] was forced to remind him who was Captain.", HP 6, 383). When hiding as outlaws together with Hermione he clearly is the boss: "'You get back in the warm.' She hesitated, but recognised the dismissal." (HP 7, 295).

His braveness sometimes comes close to foolhardiness, for example when he attacks the troll in *Philosopher's Stone* (HP 1, 191). Nonchalantly he tells Hermione and Ron "'Well – I was lucky once, wasn't I?' said Harry, pointing at his scar. 'I might get lucky again.'" (HP 1, 308).

Realising in *Prisoner of Azkaban* that the alleged murderer Black plans to kill him he takes it easy and is only annoyed about his being prevented from visiting Hogsmeade (HP 3, 77).[80] In *Chamber of Secrets*, confronted with hundreds of man-eating giant spiders and expecting to die he is "ready to die fighting" (HP 2, 301). And facing Voldemort in *Goblet of Fire* he remains upright:

> Harry did not bow. He was not going to let Voldemort play with him before killing him ... he was not going to give him that satisfaction ... (HP 4, 715)
> [He] was not going to die crouching here like a child playing hide-and-seek; he was not going to die kneeling at Voldemort's feet ... he was going to die upright like his father, and he was going to die trying to defend himself, even if no defence was possible ... (HP 4, 718)

When all seems lost, he goes on: "'[...] I'm going to keep fighting even if you've given up.'" (HP 7, 458). Dumbledore frequently[81] praises his braveness and Lupin thinks "'what you fear most of all is – fear. Very wise, Harry.'" (HP 3, 170). But as soon as he is dealing with the lives of his friends he becomes careful. When Sirius proposes in *Order of the Phoenix* to visit him more often in Hogwarts, he refuses because he fears for his godfather's life. Hurt by this declination, he reproaches Harry for not being as brave as his father: "'You're less like your father than I thought,' he said finally, a definite coolness in his voice. 'The risk would've made it fun for James.'" (HP 5, 339).[82]

The conflict with Dolores Umbridge in *Order of the Phoenix* becomes a test of both their willpowers: "[This] was between himself and Umbridge, a private battle of wills." (HP 5, 299). Bravely he endures her torture so as not to be-

---

[80] Harry is a daredevil playing "Quidditch": "[Harry] went into a perfectly controlled dive, brushing the grassy pitch with his toes before rising thirty, forty, fifty feet into the air again [...]." (HP 3, 277).

[81] Dumbledore tells Harry about his fight with Voldemort in *Philosopher's Stone*: "'[...] you were doing very well on your own, I must say.'" (HP 1, 319). And he rewards him extra points for "pure nerve and outstanding courage" (HP 1, 328).

[82] Harry learns later that his father was always willing to take a risk and often acted without considering the consequences: see IV.4.H, 242.

tray himself: "He knew [Umbridge] was watching him for signs of weakness and he was not going to show any." (HP 5, 297). Again he is praised for his braveness (HP 5, 315). Harry is satisfied with his role in organising the resistance against the new headmistress: 'Knowing they were doing something to resist Umbridge and the Ministry, and that he was a key part of the rebellion, gave Harry a feeling of immense satisfaction.' (HP 5, 388). And seeing how his fellow students excel in "Dumbledore's Army" he feels proud of himself.[83]

Harry is an independent and strong person and the only one of his class to be able to resist the impostor Moody's "Imperius Curse" (HP 4, 255). And he realises instantly that Scrimgeour wants to abuse him for his own interests:

> "You don't care whether I live or die, but you do care that I help you convince everyone you're winning the war against Voldemort. I haven't forgotten, Minister ..." He raised his right fist. There [...] were the scars which Dolores Umbridge had forced him to carve into his own flesh: *I must not tell lies.* "I don't remember you rushing to my defence when I was trying to tell everyone Voldemort was back. The Ministry wasn't so keen to be pals last year." (HP 6, 325)

Harry has firm principles and to stick by them he breaks rules. Never does he meet with serious consequences; usually his behaviour is justified. He knows when higher interests are at stake. His behaviour combines frankness, impertinence and unscrupulousness.[84] When his uncle Vernon accuses him of watching the news daily Harry replies snappishly: "'Well, it changes every day, you see' [...]." (HP 5, 12). Shortly afterwards Vernon defends himself "'We're not stupid, you know'", and Harry replies: "'Well, *that's* news to me,' [...]." (HP 5, 13). He can hardly keep himself from provoking Dudley:[85] "... he'd love to vent some of his frustration on the boys who had once made his life hell" (HP 5, 18). Insulting his cousin satisfies him:

---

[83] "Harry felt himself positively swelling with pride as he watched them all." (HP 5, 501); "[...] swelling with pride as he looked aroand at his fellow DA members and saw how far they had come." (HP 5, 667).

[84] Harry can be quite cheeky. He answers Petunia who bleaches an old school uniform of Dudley's for him: "'I didn't realise it had to be so wet.'" (HP 1, 41). Although Harry is treated quite unfairly by his family this remark is not likely to improve on the situation. Having finished his first year in Hogwarts he looks forward to the time with his family: "[...] the grin that was spreading over his face. 'They don't know we're not allowed to use magic at home. I'm going to have a lot of fun with Dudley this summer ...'" (HP 1, 332). And travelling on the "Knight Bus" he unscrupulously pretends to be Neville Longbottom (HP 3, 43).

[85] "Harry was pointing the wand directly at Dudley's heart. Harry could feel fourteen years' hatred of Dudley pounding in his veins – what wouldn't he give to strike now, to jinx Dudley so thoroughly he'd have to crawl home like an insect, struck dumb, sprouting feelers ..." (HP 5, 22-23); Harry even menaces his family: "'So I can do whatever I like. You've got three seconds. One – two –.'" (HP 5, 36).

"Did he say you look like a pig that's been taught to walk on its hind legs?" [...] It gave Harry enormous satisfaction to know how furious he was making Dudley; he felt as though he was siphoning off his own frustration into his cousin, the only outlet he had. (HP 5, 20).[86]

Harry is not afraid of authorities like Dolores Umbridge. When she deliberately minimises the danger of Voldemort's possible return, he makes fun of her speaking in "a mock thoughtful voice" (HP 5, 271). As a leader he does not tolerate contradiction.[87]

So of all Hogwarts students Harry is probably the one to break rules most often.[88] He ignores the strictures placed on visiting Hogsmeade as much as nightly curfews. When a whole part of the castle is closed in *Philosopher's Stone* he is very much tempted to visit it. Ignoring rules very often saves his and his friends' lives and is, thus, positive in the context of poetic justice. Whenever Harry breaks a rule this is regarded as moral courage. When he and Hermione travel through time in *Prisoner of Azkaban* he breaks the basic law of such travelling, i.e. "You must not be seen". He believes he has seen his father in the woods and now reliving the scene wants to wait for him. But James does not appear, and Harry has to act. Coming from the future he changes the past and so saves Sirius and himself from the "Dementors". (HP 3, 441-443) Had he stuck to the rule not to interfere with the past he would have died.[89] This kind of rule-breaking shows Harry's "sense of civic responsibility";[90] if some higher good is at stake, then clinging to rules is secondary. This is what marks the difference between Harry and characters like the Crouches (see IV.4.J, 248), or egoistic Voldemort (see IV.3.E, 179). Nevertheless, his attitude towards rules is uncomfortably close to Gellert Grindelwald's "For the Higher Good". With the only difference being that Harry's idea of "good" is different from Grindewald's.

---

[86] Harry tells Dudley: "'Not as stupid as you look, are you, Dud? But I s'pose, if you were, you wouldn't be able to walk and talk at the same time.'" (HP 5, 21).

[87] Being criticised for his teaching he says: "'But if you think it's beneath you, you can leave,' [...]." (HP 5, 433). Even Hermione is careful when criticising Harry: "'You ... this isn't a criticism, Harry! But you do ... sort of ... I mean – don't you think you've got a bit of a – a saving people thing?'" (HP 5, 806).

[88] Snape is somehow right when he tells Karkaroff: "'Don't go blaming Dumbledore for Potter's determination to break rules. He has been crossing lines ever since he arrived here'", HP 4, 303; see Pharr 2004, 62.

[89] Harry does not care for rules set by the Dursleys: "Gone were the days when he had been forced to take every single one of the Dursleys' stupid rules." (HP 4, 42).

[90] See Schafer 2000, 237.

Harry is proud[91] and conscious of his role as being "different"[92]. In *Half-Blood Prince* he is publicly named "the chosen one" and in the "Daily Prophet" it is reported that "*Some are going so far as to call Potter the 'Chosen One', believing that the prophecy names him as the only one who will be able to rid us of He Who Must Not Be Named.*" (HP 6, 43). Although Harry claims he "did not enjoy the sensation of standing in a very bright spotlight" (HP 6, 130), and likes to think of himself as modest,[93] he is offended when ignored by others.[94] Accordingly the "Sorting Hat" sees a "thirst to prove yourself" in him (see p. 160). Dumbledore's high opinion of Harry seems to be one reason for Harry's excessive self-esteem, only he does not realise it:

> "You were not a pampered little prince, but as normal a boy as I could have hoped under the circumstances. [...] You rose magnificently to the challenge that faced you and sooner – much sooner – than I had anticipated, you found yourself face to face with Voldemort. [...] You fought a man's fight. I was ... prouder of you than I can say." (HP 5, 919-920)

This feature of Harry's personality becomes most evident in *Order of the Phoenix* when Harry feels self-pity most of the time, whether because his friends do not write to him,[95] Dumbledore is quite cool towards him,[96] Ron and Hermione have been made prefects instead of him,[97] other students avoid him

---

[91] When the Dursleys have ordered him to paint a garden bank Harry's pride is hurt. "'Wish they could see famous Harry Potter now,' he thought savagely, [...]." (HP 2, 16).

[92] The author / narrator supports this status: "[...] Harry wasn't a normal boy. As a matter of fact, he was as not normal as it is possible to be." (HP 2, 9).

[93] When people at the "Quidditch" World Cup are staring at him, we read: "Harry was used to people looking curiously at him [...], but it always made him feel uncomfortable." (HP 4, 83).

[94] Leaving the hospital wing after a "Quidditch" accident he is "[...] feeling slightly hurt that [Ron and Hermione] weren't interested in whether he had his bones back or not." (HP 2, 198).

[95] „The injustice of it all welled up inside [Harry] so that he wanted to yell with fury." (HP 5, 17); "'I'VE BEEN STUCK AT THE DURSLEYS' FOR A MONTH! AND I'VE HANDLED MORE THAN YOU TWO'VE EVER MANAGED AND DUMBLEDORE KNOWS IT – WHO SAVED THE PHILOSOPHER'S STONE? WHO GOT RID OF RIDDLE? WHO SAVED BOTH YOUR SKINS FROM THE DEMENTORS?'" (HP 5, 78).

[96] "The thought that Dumbledore had been in the house on the eve of his hearing and not asked to see him made him feel, if it were possible, even worse." (HP 5, 137); Phineas Nigellus tells Harry: "'Has it not occurred to you, my poor puffed-up popinjay, that there might be an excellent reason why the headmaster of Hogwarts is not confiding every tiny detail of his plans to you? Have you never paused, while feeling hard-done-by, to note that following Dumbledore's orders has never yet led you into harm? [...] I have better things to do than listen to adolescent agonising ... good-day to you.'" (HP 5, 546).

[97] "'[...] if he had known the prefect badge was on its way, he would have expected it to come to him, not Ron. Did this make him as arrogant as Draco Malfoy? Did he think

(HP 5, 240) or because his friends are quarrelling.[98] With this mixture of self-pity and self-esteem Harry meets other people's resentment.[99] At the same time he minimises his own merits in the fight against Voldemort:

> "[But] all of that stuff was luck – I didn't know what I was doing half the time, I didn't plan any of it, I just did whatever I could think of, and I nearly always had help – [...]. I just blundered through it all, I didn't have a clue what I was doing – STOP LAUGHING! [...] *You don't know what it's like!* You – neither of you – you've never had to face him, have you?" (HP 5, 363)

Harry is torn between being "chosen" and fears that he is guilty of Sirius' death:

> It was his fault Sirius had died; it was all his fault. If he, Harry, had not been stupid enough to fall for Voldemort's trick, if he had not been so convinced that what he had seen in his dream was real, if he had only opened his mind to the possibility that Voldemort was, as Hermione had said, banking on Harry's *love of playing the hero* ... (HP 5, 901-902)

Thoughtlessly, he and Ron fly to school in *Chamber of Secrets*, but learning that he has not only severly damaged the "Whomping Willow" but has also landed the Weasleys in trouble, he feels ashamed.[100] Harry frequently feels ashamed or guilty (HP 3, 266; 296). This is one of the reasons why he is unable to respond to his critics and clings stubbornly to his opinions.[101]

Apart from this, truthfulness and fairness are the most important features of Harry's personality.[102] This is why he refuses Ludo Bagman's help in performing the tournament tasks (HP 4, 488). Harry shows "humility, loyalty, de-

---

[98] himself superior to everyone else? Did he really believe he was better than Ron? No, said the small voice. [...] I'm better at Quidditch, said the voice. But I'm not better at anything else.'" (HP 5, 187); "feeling of ill-usage" (HP 5, 187).

[98] "Serve them right, he thought, why can't they give it a rest ... bickering all the time ... it's enough to drive anyone up the wall." (HP 5, 262).

[99] "'Oh, stop feeling all misunderstood,' said Hermione sharply." (HP 5, 550); Snape: "'[...] Potter is very like his father [...]. he's so arrogant that criticism simply bounces off him,' [...].'" (HP 5, 573); Lucius Malfoy: "'[Potter] has a great weakness for heroics;' [...]." (HP 5, 860).

[100] When Mr Weasley gets into trouble because of Harry using his flying car, "[Harry's] insides were burning with guilt. [...] After all Mr and Mrs Weasley had done for him over the summer ..." (HP 2, 99). Having hurt the "Whomping Willow" makes him feel "another twinge of guilt" (HP 2, 99). In *Goblet of Fire* "[...] Harry still got a sick, burning feeling of shame in his stomach" (HP 4, 345) because Rita Skeeter writes more about him than about the other school champions.

[101] "Harry thought [Hermione] was probably right, but he wasn't going to tell her that." (HP 1, 173). He can be quite fussy: "[He was just] liking to get Quidditch terms correct" (HP 4, 348).

[102] See Killinger 2004, 76.

termination, and perseverance" and embodies "the power of faith and friendship to make anything possible".[103] Dumbledore calls him "'a remarkably selfless person'" (HP 7, 573), and the goblin Griphook says: "'If there was a wizard of whom I would believe that they did not seek personal gain, [...] it would be you, Harry Potter.'" (HP 7, 394).

Harry mostly feels sympathy for those who deserve it – and these deserving candidates are determined by Harry. Without any emotion, he enjoys bothering his cousin if feeling bored. Eventually, he even tires of this (HP 2, 14). In this Harry is no different from Dudley or Draco: "[...] Harry had enjoyed muttering nonsense words under his breath and watching Dudley tearing out of the room as fast as his fat legs would carry him." (HP 2, 14).[104] He is satisfied at seeing how shocked Vernon is when hearing that Harry's godfather is an alleged murderer ("grinning broadly at the look of horror on Uncle Vernon's face"; HP 3, 468).[105] In other situations we see Harry showing pity, even when it is difficult for him not to have Pettigrew executed by Lupin and Black immediately (HP 3, 404). Even the "Death Eaters" recognise him, because he never aims to kill but only stuns or disarms his opponents. When Remus tells him to kill instead of only defend himself, he says

> "I won't blast people out of my way just because they're there," said Harry.
> "That's Voldemort's job." (HP 7, 64).

Harry is emotional and capable of love. Dumbledore declares this to be his most significant attribute: "'[The] fact that you can feel pain like this is your greatest strength. [...] You care so much you feel as though you will bleed to death with the pain of it.'" (HP 5, 905). This ability to feel for others finally even makes him feel sorry for Draco:

> [Harry] had not forgotten the fear in Malfoy's voice [...]. Harry did not believe that Malfoy would have killed Dumbledore. He despised Malfoy still for his infatuation with the Dark Arts, but now the tiniest drop of pity mingled with his dislike. Where, Harry wondered, was Malfoy now, and what was Voldemort making him do under threat of killing him and his parents. (HP 6, 596)

---

[103] See Schafer 2000, 48-49.
[104] "'I'm trying to decide what would be the best spell to set it on fire,' said Harry." (HP 2, 15)
[105] Later he threatens Vernon that his uncle Sirius will take revenge on the Dursleys and enjoys the effect: "[Harry] stopped there to enjoy the effect of these words." (HP 4, 42).

But being emotional also means being cruel and aggressive. Very often Harry becomes angry, feels hatred and rage.[106] This is very obvious when he first meets Sirius:

> He had forgotten about magic – he had forgotten that he was short and skinny and thirteen, whereas Black was a tall, fullgrown man. All Harry knew was that he wanted to hurt Black as badly as he could and that he didn't care how much he got hurt in return ... (HP 3, 366)
> Now was the moment to avenge his mother and father. He was going to kill Black. He had to kill Black. This was his chance ... (HP 3, 369)

These emotions immediately turn into understanding and admiration when he learns that Pettigrew is the true murderer of his parents. Now he fervently defends Sirius against Snape: "'YOU'RE PATHETIC! [...] JUST BECAUSE THEY MADE A FOOL OF YOU AT SCHOOL YOU WON'T EVEN LISTEN –'" (HP 3, 389). Harry is even able to imagine torture,[107] but trying to use the "Cruciatus Curse" against Bellatrix Lestrange he fails, because his hatred is not strong enough: "'You need to really want to cause pain – to enjoy it – righteous anger won't hurt me for long –'" (HP 5, 890-891)[108] Harry's hatred is a flash in the pan compared to the malicious intentions of Voldemort's followers. But it leads him to use an unknown curse against Draco – "Sectumsempra" which causes Draco to be hit by invisible axes (HP 6, 489). Also, he can hate enough to wish for Snape's death (HP 6, 159).[109]

---

[106] Harry's hatred is mentioned quite frequently: "glaring back at Malfoy in hatred" (HP 2, 187); being confused with Slytherin's heir, "he was in such a fury" (HP 2, 218); meeting Riddle in *Chamber of Secrets* he speaks with a "quiet voice full of hatred" (HP 2, 337); seeing Sirius for the first time he feels "boiling hate" and the wish to kill (HP 3, 365); not even Ron is save from Harry's hatred: "[...] at this moment he hated everything about Ron" (HP 4, 368). "Harry found he was so full of rage and hatred he was shaking" (HP 5, 817); "[He] hated [Umbridge] more than Snape. [...]. She's evil, he thought, as he climbed a staircase to the seventh floor, she's an evil, twisted, mad old –"(HP 5, 301); "Hatred rose in Harry such as he had never known before; he flung himself out from behind the fountain and bellowed 'Crucio!'" (HP 5, 890-891).

[107] When Draco insults his mother: "He had completely forgotten that all the teachers were watching. All he wanted to do was cause Malfoy as much pain as possible [...]." (HP 5, 456); "[Harry] was so angry with Umbridge he could not think of a punishment bad enough for her, though Ron's suggestion of having her fed to a box of starving Blast-Ended Skrewts had its merits." (HP 5, 797); witnessing Snape humiliating Hermione he longs to torture his teacher: "[...] if only he knew how to do the Cruciatus curse ... he'd have Snape flat on his back like that spider, jerking and twitching ..." (HP 4, 330).

[108] This is why he cannot torture Snape after his alleged murder of Dumbledore: "'No Unforgiveable Curses from you, Potter! [...] You haven't got the nerve or the ability –'" (HP 6, 562).

[109] Ironically, Harry is right: since Riddle has been denied the job, it is jinxed (HP 6, 418). At the end of the year, Snape really has disappeared.

The boy is a very gifted wizard. The Sorting Hat (HP 1, 133), Mr Ollivander (HP 1, 96) and Dumbledore (HP 5, 922) tell him so. Nevertheless he is not very ambitious – only in "Defence Against the Dark Arts" is he able to exceed Hermione (HP 5, 362).[110] He gets his "OWLs" in seven subjects (HP 6, 100) – even in "Potions" – which makes him belong to the school's top set.

Harry is rich. His parents have left him quite a considerable fortune which is kept in Gringotts (HP 1, 85). He uses this money very carefully and tries not to waste it (HP 3, 58). Being kept poor by the Dursleys, Harry is used to modesty. This sets him apart from the Malfoys or the Blacks who are "rolling in wizard gold" (HP 2, 36-37). Strikingly, Harry is shown receiving presents from the Weasleys, Sirius and other friends but hardly ever do we hear of *him* giving someone a present.[111]

The adventures of Harry Potter show him in his personal development. He grows from being a hot-tempered child into a responsible, morally conscious young adult.[112] Most of all he learns to accept his role as "chosen".[113] To grow up he has to get to know his abilities and his destiny.[114] Step by step, he has to learn that the basic difference between good and evil lies in being able to choose. Striving for power means moral corruption and the realisation of this is Harry's true education.[115] Thus, Harry combines good and bad character traits[116] and each decision he makes brings him closer to both sides. This underlines one of the basic messages of the novels: man cannot run away from openly confessing his will and he must use the freedom of choice given to him (HP 4, 784) (see V.6.A, 367).

IV.3.C. Hermione, Cho and Ginny – Harry Reaches Puberty

There is only one thing Harry is afraid of: girls. When forced to ask a girl to dance with im at the "Yule Ball" he panics – "But now that he [...] was facing the prospect of asking a girl to the ball, he thought he'd rather have another round with the Horntail." (HP 4, 424). When asking adored Cho Chang he can only stammer "'Wangoballwime?'" (HP 4, 434), and because he has hesitated to ask her for such a long time she has already promised to dance with Cedric Dig-

---

[110] McGonagall says of Harry, "'He has achieved high marks in all Defence Against the Dark Arts tests set by a competent teacher.'" (HP 5, 731).

[111] See Corinna Cornelius, *Harry Potter – geretteter Retter im Kampf gegen dunkle Mächte? Religionspädagogischer Blick auf religiöse Implikationen, archaisch-mythologische Motive and supranaturale Elemente*, Münster: LIT, 2003, 24-25; Mendlesohn 2004, 173.

[112] See Granger 2004, 77.

[113] See Elster 2003, 217; von Lovenberg 2003.

[114] See Pharr 2004, 55.

[115] See Pharr 2004, 63.

[116] See Schafer 2000, 47.

gory.[117] In the next part of the series Harry and Cho become a short-term couple. First, he tries to impress her on the way to school,[118] but then is too reserved to get closer.[119] Only the shared experience with "Dumbledore's Army" leads to the first love scene of the series and to his first kiss (HP 5, 502-503). After this he is "in a state of shock." (HP 5, 503) And when asked "How was it?", he says truthfully, and very unromantically, "'Wet'" (HP 5, 504). The prospect of having to meet with Cho's expectations makes him feel awkward:

> Hermione's words opened up a whole new vista of frightening possibilities. He tried to imagine going somewhere with Cho – Hogsmeade, perhaps – and being alone with her for hours at a time. Of course, she would have been expecting him to ask her out after what just happened ... the thought made his stomach clench painfully. (HP 5, 506)

In the beginning this first date develops much better than he had thought: "Harry could hardly believe how easy it was to talk to her – no more difficult, in fact, than talking to Ron and Hermione –" (HP 5, 614). But when Cho leads him to the over-romantic Café Madam Puddifoot's he gets nervous:

> [The couple at the next table] were holding hands. The sight made Harry feel uncomfortable, particularly when, looking around the teashop, he saw that it was full of nothing but couples, all of them holding hands. Perhaps Cho would expect him to hold her hand. (HP 5, 616)

Thus, under pressure and completely inexperienced, Harry blunders and finally forces a furious Cho to leave the café. He feels misunderstood, but Hermione explains: "'Well, I'm sorry, but you were a bit tactless.'" (HP 5, 630). After this short experience with Cho he realises that it is Ginny he loves. And consequently he is torn between fear of Ron's reproaches and his feelings:

> But unbidden into his mind came an image of that same deserted corridor with himself kissing Ginny instead ... the monster in his chest purred ... but then he saw Ron ripping open the tapestry curtain and drawing his wand on Harry, shouting things like "betrayal of trust" ... "supposed to be my friend"... (HP 6, 270)

In his wildest dreams he experiences tragic-heroic love scenes that help solving his dilemma:

---

[117] The presence of Cho Chang makes him feel "a slight jolt in the region of his stomach that he didn't think had anything to do with nerves." (HP 3, 281).

[118] "He would have liked Cho to discover him sitting with a group of very cool people laughing their heads off at a joke he had just told; [...]." (HP 5, 210).

[119] "Harry's stomach did a back-flip" (HP 5, 374).

> "Ginny came in to visit while you were unconscious," [said Ron], after a long pause, and Harry's imagination zoomed into overdrive, rapidly constructing a scene in which Ginny, weeping over his lifeless form, confessed her feelings of deep attraction to him while Ron gave them his blessing ... (HP 6, 391)

In these passages we find the first erotic allusions of the *Potter* series – Harry has hit puberty:

> [Harry] was still trying not to think about Ginny any more than he could help, despite the fact that she kept cropping up in his dreams in ways that made him devoutly thankful that Ron could not perform Legilimency. (HP 6, 286-287)

He experiences his awakening sexuality as something alien, something he cannot relate to – like an animal leading an independent life inside his body. When he has reason to hope that Ginny will respond in the desired way to his feelings, this animal stirs: "The drowsing creature in Harry's chest suddenly raised its head, sniffing the air hopefully." (HP 6, 396) And later, when he can be sure of her attraction, it celebrates: "[Harry's] insides were suddenly dancing the conga." (HP 6, 481). After a "Quidditch" match the two finally come together and kiss:

> Harry looked around; there was Ginny running towards him; she had a hard, blazing look in her face as she threw her arms around him. And without thinking, without planning it, without worrying about the fact that fifty people were watching, Harry kissed her. (HP 6, 499)

But – like all epic heroes – Harry must leave his love to continue his mission. At the end of *Half-Blood Prince* he renounces Ginny in order not to make her a target of Voldemort's. But, as in all traditional fairy tales, the hero gets his princess in the end. When Voldemort is finally defeated, Harry and Ginny come together, marry and have three children whom they name in remembrance of the people that gave their lives for the liberation of Magical World: James is the eldest and Lily the youngest (HP 7, 603-607). The third child is called Albus Severus and Harry explains why: "'Albus Severus, [...] you were named for two headmasters of Hogwarts. One of them was a Slytherin and he was probably the bravest man I ever knew.'" (HP 7, 607)

IV.3.D. Stuck in the Middle

Harry is a polarising figure. The other characters' opinions of him are very diverse, just as diverse as the judgements by literary critics. One side – consisting of Dumbledore, Harry's friends and helpers – glorifies him as the chosen messiah. They are only too ready to forgive his faults. They stress his greatness, his goodness and his bravery.[120] Dumbledore underlines his achievement and his maturity when he says at the end of *Goblet of Fire*: "'You have shouldered a grown wizard's burden and found yourself equal to it – '" (HP 4, 757). Ginny adores him and dedicates an embarrassing poem to him:

> "His eyes are green as a fresh pickled toad,
> His hair is as dark as a blackboard.
> I wish he was mine, he's really divine,
> The hero who conquered the Dark Lord."
> (HP 2, 258).

Harry's opponents criticise his zeal to outdo others and his continued rule-breaking as much as his openmindedness towards "Muggles" and "half-bloods". His most prominent critics are the Malfoy family and Snape.[121] For Cornelius Fudge, Harry is a self-loving weirdo as he tells Dumbledore:

> "[The] boy was full of some crackpot story at the end of last year, too – his tales are getting taller, and you're still swallowing them – the boy can talk to snakes, Dumbledore, and you still think he's trustworthy?" (HP 4, 766)

For Harry's enemies "Moody" (= Crouch jnr) and Prof. Quirrell it is Harry's independent judgement that is in their way. The impostor Moody says: "'[....] you have a streak of pride and independence that might have ruined all.'" (HP 4, 733) and Quirrell explains: "'You're too nosy to live, Potter.'" (HP 1, 311) Others think that Harry's survival of Voldemort's killing curse might be a

---

[120] Hermione: "'Harry – you're a great wizard, you know.'" (HP 1, 308). The house-elf Dobby is one of Harry's biggest fans: "'Dobby has heard of your greatness, sir, but of your goodness, Dobby never knew ... [...] Harry Potter is humble and modest [...]. Harry Potter is valiant and bold! [... Harry Potter] is too great, too good, to lose.'" (HP 2, 21-22). Harry presents Dobby with the sweater knitted by Mrs Weasley: "'Dobby knew sir must be a great wizard, for he is Harry Potter's greatest friend, but Dobby did not know that he was also as generous of spirit, as noble, as selfless –'" (HP 4, 447). Dobby also praises Harry's readiness to make sacrifices: "'Harry Potter risks his own life for his friends! [...] So noble! So valiant!'" (HP 2, 195). Another fan of Harry's is Colin Creevey who continuously takes photos of him and asks for his autograph (HP 2, 106-107). Both Dobby and Colin are among the victims in *Deathly Hallows*.

[121] Draco tells Harry: "'You never miss a chance to show off, do you?'" (HP 4, 187); Snape "'To me, Potter, you are nothing but a nasty little boy who considers rules to be beneath him.'" (HP 4, 561); Draco: "'Saint Potter, the Mudbloods' friend [...]. He's another one with no proper wizard feeling, or he wouldn't go aroand with that jumped-up Granger Mudblood.'" (HP 2, 242). This opposition is underlined by the narrator calling Draco "[Harry's] arch-enemy" (HP 2, 15); Malfoy: "'[...] and as for Potter ... my father says it's a matter of time before the Ministry has him carted off to St Mungo's ... apparently they've got a special ward for people whose brains have been addled by magic.'" (HP 5, 399).

sign of his own dark magic forces: "'Only a really powerful Dark Wizard could have survived a curse like that.'" (HP 2, 216). Again and again Rowling hints at Harry being closer to Voldemort than he knows. He speaks "parseltongue", the language of snakes (HP 2, 211). He is aggressive, sometimes full of hatred and believes in his own importance – just as Tom Riddle did as a young man. One reason for this is that Voldemort's attack has transmitted some of his powers onto Harry (HP 6, 477). Their destinies are intertwined, as Harry gets to know in *Half-Blood Prince*. One has to kill the other: "he must be either murderer or victim" (HP 5, 934).

Both of their biographies are remarkably similar (see IV.3.E, 174).

> "[There] are strange likenesses between us [...]. Both halfbloods, orphans, raised by Muggles. Probably the only two Parselmouths to come to Hogwarts since the great Slytherin himself. We even *look* alike ..." (HP 2, 340)

Tom and Harry hate their "Muggle" relations – Tom not only accused the innocent Hagrid of killing Myrtle to avoid the school's closure but he also killed his own family. Harry realises that he has a certain sympathy for Tom.[122] They both lie to their headmasters about the Basilisk (HP 2, 264). And in *Order of the Phoenix* they have a spiritual connection: Harry shares Voldemort's emotions (HP 5, 420-421),[123] and experiences events from the point of view of Voldemort's snake (HP 5, 529). He even seems possessed by Voldemort, as Moody says:

> "[There's] something funny about the Potter kid, we all know that. [...] The boy's seeing things from inside You-Know-Who's snake. Obviously, Potter doesn't realise what that means, but if You-Know-Who's possessing him –" (HP 5, 541)

Harry is desperate when he overhears this and decides to leave Grimmauld Place: "He felt dirty, contaminated, as though he were carrying some deadly germ [...]." (HP 5, 542-544)

Apart from sharing similar personalities Harry and Voldemort have related wands; they both have a feather from Dumbledore's phoenix Fawkes inside (HP 1, 96). However, whereas Voldemort's wand is made from poisonous yew, Harry's consists of holly. This becomes extremely important for Harry. It saves his life in *Goblet of Fire*, because the two related wands cannot defeat each other (HP 4, 718 and 755). In Magical World, the wand chooses the wizard and its allegiance must be won as we learn in *Deathly Hallows* (HP 7, 419, 595).

---

[122] "Tom Riddle had turned Hagrid in because he was faced with the prospect of a Muggle orphanage if the school closed. Harry now knew exactly how he had felt." (HP 2, 279).

[123] Snape: "'[...] you are sharing the Dark Lord's thoughts and emotions.'" (HP 5, 585).

In literary criticism the quality of the protagonist's character has controversially been discussed. The character's appeal is believed to be in his being a normal boy and not a super hero.[124] Unlike the forces of evil Harry does not act out of egoistic intentions.[125] Only because he is altruistic can he find the Philosopher's Stone.[126] Because Harry has "respect for elders, peers and younger children" and behaves himself "using titles to address adults, including Lord Voldemort" Elizabeth D. Schafer regards him as a "model for good etiquette, and his life story serves as a parable for children coming of age in the next millenium".[127] His role as "male Cinderella",[128] i.e. an "orphelin classique maltraité par une famille d'adoption cruelle"[129] makes the reader identify with him. As Schafer puts it: "Harry is appealing because he represents someone entirely powerless becoming empowered beyond most people's expectations."[130] A hero against his wishes, struggling with the deficiencies of his personality and with the tragic circumstances of his life, Harry is an authentic character.[131] He seems to suffer for his unvoluntarily achieved victories.[132] And unlike the heroes of other works of fantasy literature (like in the *Chronicles of Narnia* or *Lord of the Rings*) Harry is not a personification of the author's ideological principles.[133]

The character's critics underline Harry's negative character traits – "But if we identify with Harry we are supporting a hero who lies, cheats, and breaks school rules as and when he feels like it; his friends do likewise."[134] They claim the character is flat, too superficial and "not a boy of depth or subtlety".[135] He is an average boy and not a splendorous hero. He represents braveness and straightforwardness, but has moments of occasional aggressiveness, and is often led by his emotions to cruelty. It is precisely these contradictions which make the reader identify with Harry.

---

[124] See Bürvenich 2001, 115; Grimes 2004, 90.
[125] See Bürvenich 2001, 115.
[126] See Bürvenich 2001, 124.
[127] Schafer 2000, 237-238.
[128] Jung 2004, 29.
[129] "the classic orphan maltreated by his cruel surrogate family", Ernould 2003, 211, [my translation].
[130] Schafer 2000, 50.
[131] See von Bredow 2000; von Lovenberg 2003.
[132] See Linus Hauser, "Harry Potter – einer der tausendgestaltigen Helden," *Faszination 'Harry Potter': Was steckt dahinter?*, eds. Detlev Dormeyer, Friedhelm Munzel, Münster: LIT, 2005, 7-15, here 14.
[133] See Hywel Williams, "A whole new narrative," *Guardian* 7 Nov 2001. <http://books.guardian.co.uk/print/0,3858,4293510-99943,00.html> 3 Jan 2008.
[134] Blake 2002, 97.
[135] McCrum 2000.

174

IV.3.E. Villain Without a Name – *You-Know-Who*

Tom Riddle has various names. He names himself after his grandfather Marvolo which recalls *mal* (bad) and *volo* (to want, I want). This means "malicious" or even "I want evil". Thomas (Doubting Thomas) is an apostle, and the name means twin.[136] Fearfully he is called "He-Who-Must-Not-Be-Named" or "You-Know-Who" – as if not referring to him by his proper name can reduce the danger.[137] His followers respectfully call him "The Dark Lord". The name Voldemort alludes to Latin or Romance sources: *vol-* can be the first syllable of the first person singluar of Latin *velle* (*volō*, I want to) as much as of *volare* (to fly). The word "de" signalises possession in French or Spanish. And "mort" alludes to French *la mort* or Latin *mors, mortis* – both meaning death. All together the name means something like "will to death" or "flight of death".[138] John Granger interprets it as "flight from death", but this ignores French grammar.[139] But as this version alludes to Voldemort's fear of his own death and his striving for immortality it does, nevertheless, feel justified. Richard Adams even reads the name as a form of "theft of corpses".[140]

In the character of the villain we find all the negative elements of the pattern; Voldemort demands absolute obedience and conformity. He is greedy, cruel, acts arbitrarily, strives for power and is, still, a coward.

IV.3.F. From Rags to Riches – The Way of Evil

Only in *Half-Blood Prince* does the reader get to know more details about Tom. He comes from the Gaunt family which descends directly from Salazar Slytherin (HP 6, 196). This alludes to John of Gaunt, Duke of Lancaster (1340-1399). The family is very old. Marvolo claims to have the ring of the Peverells (HP 7, 347) which hints at William Peverel (c.1050-c.1115), a Norman knight who fought in the Battle of Hastings and who was probably an illegitimate son of William I.[141]

---

[136] See "Thomas," *Dictionary of First Names* [1990] 2000, 222.
[137] The idea of name taboos is quite common. In Judaism the name of god (Jahwe) is not to be pronounced. Reading the name is substituted by *Adonaj* ("Lord") or *Adonaj Elohim* ("Lord God"). And in Christian popular belief there is the idea that naming the devil calls him. This is why there are many (German) synonyms for him, i.e. "Daus" ("Ei, der Daus"), "Leibhaftiger" or "Herr / Fürst der Finsternis". The idea that naming a person calls him is, therefore, quite old and no invention of J.K. Rowling's. In *Deathly Hallows* there is a real taboo put on the name: whoever says it, is arrested immediately (HP 7, 316).
[138] Hein sees this as the basic meaning of the name (see Hein 2001, 148).
[139] See Granger 2004, 108.
[140] See Adams 2003.
[141] See "The House of Gaunt," *Wikipedia, The Free Encyclopedia.* <http://en.wikipedia.org/w/index.php?title=The_House_of_Gaunt&oldid=154008448> 27 Aug 2007. 28 Aug 2007.

The name, of course, also includes the adjective "gaunt" which fits a family which has degenerated through incest and prodigality:

> Marvolo, his son Morfin and his daughter Merope were the last of the Gaunts, a very ancient wizarding family noted for a vein of instability and violence that flourished through the generations due to their habit of marrying their own cousins. Lack of sense coupled with a great liking for grandeur meant that the family gold was squandered several generations before Marvolo was born. (HP 6, 201)[142]

All members of the family are physically deformed and neglected:

> [Morfin Gaunt was standing in rags] before them [and] had thick hair so matted with dirt it could have been any colour. Several of his teeth were missing. His eyes were small and dark and stared in opposite directions. He might have looked comical, but he did not; the effect was frightening [...]. (HP 6, 191)
>
> [Marvolo Gaunt] was shorter than [Morfin], and oddly proportioned; his shoulders were very broad and his arms overlong, which, with his bright brown eyes, short scrubby hair and wrinkled face, gave him the look of a powerful, aged monkey. (HP 6, 192)
>
> [Merope Gaunt was a] girl whose ragged dress was the exact colour of the dirty stone wall behind her. [...] Her hair was lank and dull and she had a plain, pale, rather heavy face. Her eyes, like her brother's, stared in opposite directions. [Harry] had never seen a more defeated-looking person. (HP 6, 194)

Tom's mother Merope falls in love with the "Muggle" squire's son on whose grounds the family dwell in a miserable cottage. Using a love potion she makes him marry her. When the effect of the potion is weakening, Tom sees the true character of his wife and leaves her – although she is pregnant. Mourning the loss of her beloved husband Merope renounces her magical powers (HP 6, 245), runs helplessly through the streets of London and sells her last items from Slytherin's possession to Burke, the dealer in antiques.[143] In labour she seeks asylum in an orphanage, gives birth to her son and shortly afterwards dies.[144]

---

[142] Again, these are telling names: Merope alludes to "myope", which hints at her bad sight; Marvolo means "wishing ill" (see IV.3.E, 174), and Morfin is the phonetical equivalent of "morphine".

[143] Burke tells us a locket had been "'brought in by a young witch just before Christmas, oh, many years ago now. She said she needed the gold badly, well, that much was obvious. Covered in rags and pretty far along ... going to have a baby, see.'" He took advantage of her situation and paid her very little money (HP 6, 245).

[144] The director of the orphanage, Mrs Cole, remembers: "'New Year's Eve and bitter cold, snowing, you know. Nasty night. And this girl, not much older than I was myself at the time, came staggering up the front steps. Well, she wasn't the first. We took her in and she had the baby within the hour. And she was dead in another hour. [... She] told me he

176

Even in his childhood, Tom is a bully: he tortures other children, steals and uses his magical abilities to oppress others.[145] When he is eleven, he is taken to Hogwarts. At that time he is the spitting image of his good-looking father.

> There was no trace of the Gaunts in Tom Riddle's face. Merope had got her dying wish: he was his handsome father in miniature, tall for eleven years old, dark-haired and pale. (HP 6, 252)

Already, at this early stage of his life, Tom is convinced of his being different and better than others: "I knew I was special. Always, I knew there was something." (HP 6, 254). Dumbledore characterises Tom's personal deficits correctly:

> "In fact, his ability to speak to serpents did not make me nearly as uneasy as his obvious instincts for cruelty, secrecy and domination. [...] There he showed his contempt for anything that tied him to other people, anything that made him ordinary. Even then, he wished to be different, separate, notorious. He shed his name, as you know, within a few short years of that conversation and created the mask of 'Lord Voldemort' behind which he has been hidden for so long." (HP 6, 259)

Tom becomes a top student and a favourite with the teachers:

> He showed no sign of outward arrogance or aggression at all. As an unusually talented and very good-looking orphan, he naturally drew attention and sympathy from the staff almost from the moment of his arrival. He seemed polite, quiet and thirsty for knowledge. Nearly all were favourably impressed by him." (HP 6, 337)

He begins to investigate into his ancestry. He realises that the wizard in the family was not his father, but his mother. Disappointedly he realises that "his father had never set foot in Hogwarts." This is the moment he changes his name. (HP 6, 339).

---

was to be named Tom, for his father, and Marvolo for her father [...] and she said the boy's surname was to be Riddle. And she died soon after that without another word.'" (HP 6, 249).

[145] Mrs Cole tells Dumbledore about strange occurences: "'Billy Stubb's rabbit ... well, Tom said he didn't do it and I don't see how he could have done, but even so, it didn't hang itself from the rafters, did it? [...] Amy Benson and Dennis Bishop were never quite right afterwards, and all we ever got out of them was that they'd gone into a cave with Tom Riddle. He swore they'd just gone exploring, but something happened in there, I'm sure of it. And well, there have been a lot of things, funny things ...'" (HP 6, 250-251).

"[Voldemort] was a name I was already using at Hogwarts, [...]. You think I was going to use my filthy Muggle father's name for ever? I, in whose veins runs the blood of Salazar Slytherin himself, through my mother's side? I, keep the name of a foul, common Muggle, who abandoned me even before I was born, just because he found out his wife was a witch?" (HP 2, 337)[146]

He is the top student in his fifth year and he finds out how to open the secret chamber and sets its monster loose (HP 2, 335). Later, wrongly accusing Hagrid of the deed, he becomes the school's hero: Hagrid stands no chance against Tom. "Poor but brilliant, parentless but so *brave*, school Prefect, model student" (HP 2, 335), he seems to be more trustworthy than Hagrid, an outsider. (see IV.4.A, 218). He is expelled; Tom is rewarded a school trophy and becomes head boy (HP 2, 253; 264). About the same time Tom takes revenge on his father's family, killing all his relatives, and manipulates his uncle Morfin's memory so that he accuses himself of the crime. Morfin is sentenced to imprionment in Azkaban and dies in prison (HP 6, 343-344). Horace Slughorn is himself tricked into explaining to Tom how he can preserve parts of his soul in "Horcruxes" – and achieve immortality, something Tom is aiming at (HP 6, 469-471).

Tom does not use his genius for a conventional career:

"[He] was probably the most brilliant student Hogwarts has ever seen. [...] I taught him myself [...]. He disappeared after leaving the school ... travelled far and wide ... sank so deeply into the Dark Arts, consorted with the very worst of our kind, underwent so many dangerous, magical transformations, that when he resurfaced as Lord Voldemort, he was barely recognisable. Hardly anyone connected Lord Voldemort with the clever, handsome boy who was once Head Boy here." (HP 2, 353)
"[Tom] reached the seventh year of his schooling with, [...] top grades in every examination he had taken. [...] Nearly everybody expected spectacular things from Tom Riddle, Prefect, Head Boy, winner of the Special Award for Service to the School. I know that several teachers, Professor Slughorn amongst them, suggested that he join the Ministry of Magic, offered to set appointments, put him in touch with useful contacts. He refused all offers. The next thing the staff knew, Voldemort was working at Borgin and Burkes." (HP 6, 403-404)[147]

---

[146] At the end of *Goblet of Fire* Voldemort tells Harry: "'You stand, Harry Potter, upon the remains of my late father,' he hissed softly. 'A Muggle and a fool ... very like your dear mother. [...] My father lived there. My mother, a witch who lived here in this village, fell in love with him. But he abandoned her when she told him what she was ... he didn't like magic, my father ... He left her and returned to his Muggle parents before I was even born, Potter, and she died giving birth to me, leaving me to be raised in a Muggle orphanage ... but I vowed to find him ... I revenged myself upon him, that fool who gave me his name ... Tom Riddle ...'" (HP 4, 700).

[147] This is important: Riddle actively decides against a civil career (see V.6.A, 367).

After finishing school Tom applies for a job at Hogwarts teaching "Defence Against the Dark Arts". Dumbledore suspects non-altruistic motives:

> "Hogwarts was where he had been happiest; the first and only place he had felt at home. [...] Secondly, the castle is a stronghold of ancient magic. [...] And thirdly, as a teacher, he would have had great power and influence over young witches and wizards." (HP 6, 403-404)

Tom's first job is a position with antiques dealer Borgin & Burkes of Diagon Alley (see III.5.C, 128). He works as buying agent and is able get hold of some very elaborate artifacts belonging to the four founders of Hogwarts. He uses these as "Horcruxes" to preserve parts of his soul. But each time he portions his soul into preservable parts he has to commit a murder. Nevertheless, he creates seven "Horcruxes" that must be destroyed to defeat him: the diary Harry has destroyed in *Chamber of Secrets*, a ring and a locket of Slytherin's, a cup of Helga Hufflepuff's, his snake Nagini (HP 6, 471-473), Ravenclaw's diadem and Harry Potter himself. The side effects on himself are disastrous: "'[...] his soul was mutilated beyond the realms of what we might call usual evil ...'" (HP 6, 469). It is only now that Tom becomes the personification of evil. It is his fear of death and his arrogance that deforms and mutilates him personally. His fear that his life might end one day makes him lose any respect for life itself. Importantly, it is his own free will that makes him act like this.

Once he has transformed himself in this fashion he has finally achieved the ability to become a dictator. When his follower, Severus Snape, brings him news of Trelawney's prophecy (HP 6, 509) he decides to kill the child in question at once. The failure of this attack is the temporary end of his reign and the beginning of *Philosopher's Stone*.

IV.3.G. Beauty and the Beast – Voldemort's Appearance

Tom Riddle's appearance changes; the once handsome young man becomes a mutilated villain and until *Goblet of Fire* he is no more than a bodiless spirit. In *Chamber of Secrets* he is a sixteen-year-old boy with "jet-black hair" (HP 2, 263)[148] and a "soft voice" (HP 2, 330). He claims to look very much like Harry (HP 2, 340). When working for Borgin & Burkes he is a very good-looking young man (HP 6, 406). But the magical mutilations he inflicts upon himself to achieve immortality mark him:

> It was as though his features had been burned and blurred; they were waxy and oddly distorted, and the whites of the eyes now had a permanently

---

[148] Something we frequently find in reference to Harry (see IV.3.A, 156).

bloody look, though the pupils were not yet the slits that Harry knew they would become. (HP 6, 413)

At the end of his dictatorship he is physically destroyed. In *Philosopher's Stone* we see him weakened and depending on Quirrell (HP 1, 316). He only consists of a nearly lifeless, reptile-like face: "[He] was chalk white with glaring red eyes and slits for nostrils, like a snake."; (HP 1, 315). Again we find eyes, smile and a comparison with animals (cat, spider, snake) to be the main features of the characterisation. His eyes are "gleaming red" (HP 4, 693-694) and reflect his cruelty ("red gleam in his hungry eyes", HP 2, 337), as much as surprise or fear.[149] His voice is cold ("strangely high-pitched, and cold as a sudden blast of icy wind", HP 4, 13)[150] and menacing ("menace in the cold voice", HP 4, 15), and he laughs a "high, cold, mirthless laugh" (HP 4, 698; also 18). His smile is "terrible" (HP 4, 711) and "awful" (HP 2, 340). He hisses like a snake (HP 1, 316; HP 4, 16; HP 4, 702-705). His long fingers underline the spider-like appearance ("unnaturally long-fingered hands"; "hands were like large, pale spiders"; "long, white forefinger", HP 4, 698-699; "a long-fingered hand", "Voldemort's long forefinger", HP 6, 408). The white colour of his skin makes him appear zombie-like. He appears like a skeleton, like a decaying body ("slimy" HP 4, 693-694) with a face like a skull without a nasal bone: "Whiter than a skull, with wide, livid scarlet eyes, and a nose that was as flat as a snake's with slits for nostrils [...]." (HP 4, 697). Voldemort perceives his surroundings by sniffing like an animal ("He put back his terrible face and sniffed, his slit-like nostrils widening.", HP 4, 701).[151]

IV.3.H. Magically Mutilated – Profile of a Mass Murderer

Already in his childhood Tom is cruel and sadistic. In the orphanage he enjoys torturing the other children (see footnote 145, 176). Being convinced of his being special he despises his bourgeois name – "'You dislike the name "Tom"?' 'There are a lot of Toms,' muttered Riddle" (HP 6, 257). Emotionally crippled, he is able to rally a lot of supporters around him but cannot enjoy their company. Dumbledore explains: "'Lord Voldemort has never had a friend, nor do I believe

---

149 Very frequently, we read that his eyes are red: "wide, livid scarlet eyes" (HP 4, 697); "the red eyes, whose pupils were slits, like a cat's, gleamed still more brightly through the darkness" (HP 4, 698); "his red eyes" (HP 4, 700); "pitiless red eyes" (HP 4, 716); "red eyes wide with astonishment" (HP 4, 719); "his wide, red eyes were still shocked" (HP 4, 721); "Voldemort's red eyes widened with shock" (HP 4, 721); "the momentary red gleam in Voldemort's eyes" (HP 6, 410)

150 "a high, cold voice empty of any human kindness ..." (HP 5, 801).

151 In *Order of the Phoenix* these characteristics are summarised as follows: "'Can't I, Potter?' said a high, cold voice. [...] Tall, thin and black-hooded, his terrible snakelike face white and gaunt, his scarlet, slit-pupilled eyes staring ..." (HP 5, 892-893)

that he has ever wanted one.'" (HP 6, 260)[152] It is the absence of any positive sentiment that marks the difference between Harry and him (HP 6, 476). Voldemort wants to eliminate everything humane in his person to appear supernatural.[153] Human lives do not count for him – he is completely morally corrupt.[154]

Tom is "pitiless" (HP 4, 711), cruel and acts arbitrarily. Murder is for him a legitimate means to get to power ('"I killed Bertha because I had to.'", HP 4, 18). Nevertheless, he is a "great wizard" (HP 1, 96; HP 1, 312). He enjoys cruelty ("cruel amusement", HP 4, 17), and does not care for Magical World's taboos as for example the sanctity of unicorns (HP 1, 279). In *Goblet of Fire* we see Voldemort with his followers and understand what his evil consists of: the devoted Pettigrew who has cut his own hand off to help his master is deliberately tortured. And the "Death Eaters" present are more apprehensive than happy about the return of their leader (HP 4, 693-713).

It is rather unconvincing to see Voldemort admit to mistakes in *Deathly Hallows*. In a meeting with his followers he says: '"That Potter lives is due more to my errors, than to his triumphs.'" and '"I have been careless [...]. But I know better now.'" (HP 7, 13). This is, in my opinion, a break in the character's consistency – Voldemort as he is represented in the first six novels would never reflect upon his acts critically and speak of his "mistakes". Like all evil characters Voldemort is greedy – for immortality, riches and power. This greed is reason enough to kill Hepzibah Smith, just to get her antiques ('"This time [...] he killed not for revenge, but for gain.'", HP 6, 411). Voldemort's true strength is his falseness, his secrecy, and his ability to raise discord, as Sirius explains: '"Voldemort doesn't march up to people's houses and bang on their front doors, [...]. He tricks, jinxes and blackmails them. He's well-practised at operating in secret.'" (HP 5, 111). He has the "gift for spreading discord and enmity" (HP 5, 248) and is able to weaken his enemies.

The villain has two aims: unlimited power and immortality ('"You know my goal – to conquer death.'", HP 4, 708). He appreciates courage in his inferior enemies and in his followers ('"I always value bravery [...]'.", HP 1, 316). He himself is frequently afraid; for example when he realises that Harry might be able to defeat him ("Voldemort [...] looked astonished, and almost fearful [...]", HP 4, 720). At other occasions, when there is no real danger, he is fearless:

---

[152] Later we find: "[...] Riddle undoubtedly felt no affection for any of [his dedicated friends]." (HP 6, 338).

[153] See David and Catherine Deavel, "A Skewed Reflection: The Nature of Evil," *Harry Potter and Philosophy: If Aristotle ran Hogwarts.* eds. Baggett & Klein, Chicago, La Salle: Open Court, 2004, 132-147,here 141.

[154] See Jennifer Hart Weed, "Voldemort, Boethius, and the Destructive Effects of Evil," *Harry Potter and Philosophy: If Aristotle ran Hogwarts*, eds. Baggett & Klein, Chicago, La Salle: Open Court, 2004, 148-157, here 153.

Harry could not help but feel a resentful admiration for Voldemort's complete lack of fear. His face merely expressed disgust and, perhaps, disappointment. (HP 6, 341)

IV.3.I. Villain-hero and True Protagonist

Voldemort is the archetype of evil: the fallen angel Lucifer turning from grace. (Gundel Mattenklott identifies all attributes of the dark lord – from the title to the snake whose milk he drinks.) All of this marks him as a satanic character of Jewish-Christian tradition.[155] A personification of death, he is probably the most miserable and tragic character of the series.[156]

You-Know-Who embodies the racism against non-magical or people of mixed descent; those he wants to extinguish. Ironically, Voldemort himself is a "mud-blood". Literary criticism often has compared Voldemort's racism to Adolf Hitler and his ideology, i.e. any inhumane dictatorship.[157] The name of his legendary ancestor, Salazar Slytherin, alludes not only to the Portuguese dictator António de Oliveira Salazar, who ruled Portugal from 1932 to 1968, but it abbreviates "SS" – just like the paramilitary "Schutzstaffel" of the German Nazis.[158] Voldemort's regime has quite a lot of parallels with the racism of German National Socialism,[159] and he himself has certain similarities with Hitler, as Isabelle Smadja indicates:

> [Sa] haine raciale envers les [Muggles] évoque l'antisémitisme du dictateur allemand. De même, le caractère paradoxal de la haine de Hitler envers les non-aryens, lui dont le physique était l'opposé exact de celui de l'aryen, trouve son pendant dans l'étrange haine de Voldemort envers les [Muggles], alors qu'il a lui-même du sang [de Muggles] dans les veines.[160]

These comparisons are absolutely justified: Voldemort is the personification of totalitarianism and racism. It is important that Voldemort deliberately chooses his own way, although – brilliant as he is – he has many other options.

---

[155] See Gundel Mattenklott, "Text aus Texten. Phantastische Traditionen bei Harry Potter," *Harry Potter oder Warum wir Zauberer brauchen*, ed. Olaf Kutzmutz, Wolfenbüttel: Bandesakademie für kulturelle Bildung, 2001, 33-43, here 41.
[156] See Mattenklott 2001, 41.
[157] See Cornelius 2003, 70; Schafer 2000, 65.
[158] See Ernould 2003, 199.
[159] See Bürvenich 2001, 69.
[160] "His racial hatred of "Muggles" is reminiscent of the German dictator's antisemitism. At the same time, Hitler's hatred of all non-aryans which is contradicted by his non-aryan physical appearance, finds its correspondance in Voldemort's strange hatred of Muggles: he himself has Muggle-blood in his veins.", Smadja 2001, 40, [my translation].

Harry and his enemy are linked by the prophecy, and Harry, being an accidentally created "Horcrux", shares many character traits with Voldemort as well as abilities (see IV.3.A, 160). When Voldemort set out to kill baby-Harry and the killing curse backfired, he transmitted a part of his soul to the boy. Therefore, Harry serves as his "Horcrux" (HP 7, 568). The prophecy claiming that they must kill each other or evil cannot be defeated refers to this soul-preserving quality of Harry's. But Voldemort, not realising this fatal connection between them, becomes vulnerable when choosing Harry's blood for his resurrection in *Goblet of Fire*. This is why Dumbledore shows "something like triumph" (HP 4, 604) when Harry tells him of the Black Mass in the cemetery. He knows that from now on Voldemort cannot do serious harm to Harry (HP 7, 568). In *Order of the Phoenix* Harry and his nemesis begin to share a spiritual link that proves to be vital in defeating Voldemort in the end. The villain is "Harry's shadow side, his dark twin, and Harry must meet and defeat him."[161] And finally, after many tricks and turnings of the plot, he is able to destroy Voldemort (HP 7, 596). Voldemort is reduced to being the"small, soft thumpings of something that flapped, flailed and struggled. It was a pitiful noise, yet also slightly indecent." (HP 7, 565)

The character of Voldemort is in no way dynamic and does not develop in the least. Nevertheless, he is the driving force behind the whole plot. In fact, speaking in terms of Lotman he is the only one to cross the semantic frontier between good and evil. He spurs the other characters into action and forces Harry to confront him many times before their final duel. In *Chamber of Secrects* he opens the hidden chamber and kidnaps Ginny Weasley – Harry must react to save his friend. In *Goblet of Fire* he has to survive another of one Voldemort's intrigues.[162] So Voldemort is the true hero of the series just as much as the villain-hero of the Gothic Novel.

IV.3.J. Heroic Civil Servants – The Weasley Family

The Weasleys unite all the positive qualities of the novels: they are chaotic, free-spirited, live on a rather small family income, enjoy a pleasant life as long as possible and fight against evil. They represent compassion and innate goodness, justice and tolerance.[163] The Weasleys become a surrogate family for Harry.

Father Arthur is the most important representative of the values embodied by the Weasleys. His name clearly refers to legendary King Arthur. At the beginning we see him as a rather superficial weirdo who has a bizarre fondness for "Mug-

---

[161] Cockrell 2004, 20.

[162] *Prisoner of Azkaban* is an exception, because it is Sirius Black that starts the plot escaping from Azkaban.

[163] Percy Weasley temporarily breaks off from family and returns in *Deathly Hallows*.

gles"[164] and is not even able to cope with the gnomes in his garden ("'Dad's too soft with them, he thinks they're funny ...'", HP 2, 45). In the course of the series, the character becomes more complex. This balding, shabby man[165] works for the Misuse of Muggle Artefacts department at the Ministry of Magic (HP 2, 31) which allows him to explore his interest in non-magical humans. He does not care that his work is being laughed at by many of his colleagues. He changes jobs in *Half-Blood Prince* and heads the "Office for the Detection and Confiscation of Counterfeit Defensive Spells and Protective Objects" (HP 6, 84). Arthur Weasley is one of the few wizards taking a caring interest in "Muggles"[166] and dedicates his life to improving "Muggle"-Wizard relations.[167] Nevertheless he and his family do not accept their own non-magical relations, and rather hush up a distant cousin working as an accountant (HP 1, 110). His interest in "Muggles" is quite abstract and has a rather racist attitude: "Muggles" are interesting for ethnical studies, but they are certainly not equal.

Mr Weasley likes to experiment with non-magical technology, which is illegal (HP 2, 46)[168] and secretly sympathises with his creative, troublesome sons (HP 2, 46; HP 4, 62). Fascinated by "Muggle" technology[169] his greatest wish is to know "'how aeroplanes stay up'" (HP 6, 85). When he collects Harry from the Dursleys in *Goblet of Fire* part of the comical effects result from the misunderstandings between Harry's family and Mr Weasley:

---

[164] Fred on his father: "'Dad's mad about everything to do with Muggles, our shed's full of Muggle stuff. He takes it apart, puts spells on it and puts it back together again.'" (HP 2, 38).

[165] "[Mr Weasley] was a thin man, going bald, but the little hair he had was as red as any of his children's. He was wearing long green robes which were dusty and travel-worn." (HP 2, 45). We find a very similar description in *Goblet of Fire* ("tall, thin and balding"; HP 4, 53) and *Half-Blood Prince* ("a thin, balding, red-haired wizard wearing horn-rimmed spectacles and a long and dusty travelling cloak", HP 6, 86).

[166] He uses the accidental meeting with Hermione's parents in Diagon Alley to question them about "Muggle" way of life (HP 2, 65-66 and 73). These scenes add to the comical side of the novels. The reader laughs about the scientific interest the wizards take in "Muggles".

[167] He is outraged when George and Fred tease Dudley with magical toffees: "'That sort of behaviour seriously undermines wizard-Muggle relations! I spend half my life campaigning against the mistreatment of Muggles, and my own sons –'." (HP 4, 62).

[168] Christian commentator Richard Abanes criticises Mr Weasley's behaviour: "Mr Weasley himself seems to be the source of his children's tendency toward rule-breaking and lying.", see Richard Abanes, *Harry Potter, Narnia, and The Lord of the Rings*, Eugene, Oregon: Harvest House, 2005,148.

[169] After his promotion he misses his old job as his wife says: "'[...] So you see, it's a very important job, and I tell him, it's just silly to miss dealing with spark-plugs and toasters and all the rest of that Muggle rubbish.'" (HP 6, 84).

[Mr Weasley] loved everything to do with Muggles. Harry could see him itching to go and examine the television and the video recorder. "They run off ecletricity [sic!] – [...]. I collect plugs." (HP 4, 54).

And although Vernon Dursley throws a vase at him, Arthur feels rather sorry for Harry's uncle instead of being angry (HP 4, 55). Only when he realises how badly Harry is treated by his relatives does Mr Weasley become outraged (HP 4, 57). This caring understanding for others sets him appart from Voldemort's followers and the Malfoy family. In *Chamber of Secrets* when Lucius Malfoy publicly insults Arthur he loses his temper and attacks him. (HP 2, 71). Arthur Weasley is not a naive pacifist, as a "fully qualified wizard" (HP 4, 29) he is ready to use violence if necessary and can rejoice in his enemy's bad luck.[170]

Mother Molly is the decisive factor in the family's daily life. She is a "short, plump, kind-faced woman" (HP 2, 40)[171] and can turn into "a sabretoothed tiger" (HP 2, 40) when aroused to anger. She is the classic housewife wearing a flowered apron and carrying a wooden spoon instead of a wand (HP 2, 40). She is the stereotype of the caring mother.[172] As in other cases, Rowling uses Molly's name to characterise her. Her name alludes to the words "moll", "to mollify" and "mollycoddle". Her husband calls her "Mollywobbles" (HP 6, 86) – a conglomerate pun consisting of "collywobbles" and "to mollify". In *Order of the Phoenix* Molly is tortured by nightmares about the death of her family and sobs:

"I see them d-d-dead all the time! [...] All the t-t-time! I d-d-dream about it ... [...]. D-d-don't tell Arthur [...]. I d-d-don't want him to know ... being silly ..." (HP 5, 198).

Although she herself is an active member of the resistance against Voldemort she does not want her children to take any risks (HP 5, 410; HP 7, 486). When it is time to say goodbye she usually becomes very emotional: "Mrs Weasley dissolved into tears at the moment of parting. Admittedly, it took very little to set her off lately [...]." (HP 6, 327)[173] In *Deathly Hallows* she experiences the death of her son Fred. So when Bellatrix Lestrange is about to attack

---

[170] "'So he's worried,' said Mr Weasley with grim satisfaction. 'Oh, I'd love to get Lucius Malfoy for something ...'" (HP 2, 65).

[171] Also: "a short, plump woman with a very kind face, though her eyes were presently narrowed with suspicion." (HP 4, 62).

[172] "Molly Weasley is very much the archetypal mother, having given birth to the magical number of seven children and helping the good Harry by giving him what he needs on his mission: a surrogate family [...].", Grimes 2004, 96.

[173] Rowling in an interview says of Molly Weasley: "Before her marriage Mrs Weasley was Molly Prewett. As you will note from chapter one, Philosopher's Stone, she has lost close family members to Voldemort." (Rowling 2006).

Ginny, she lunges at her screaming "'You - will - never - touch - our - children - again!'" and kills her (HP 7, 589-590). This must be considered a part of poetic justice; it is the motherly domesticated housewife defeating the independent, strong, but evil and fanatical woman.

The Weasley family consists of: the eldest son, Bill, who is working as a "curse breaker" (HP 3, 15)[174] for the wizard bank Gringotts in Africa, Charlie the dragon tamer in Romania, careerist Percy, the fun-loving twins Fred and George, Harry's best friend Ron and their youngest sister Ginny. They all have red hair ("all with flaming red hair", HP 1, 103).[175] So the family's name can refer to the colour of the fox but also to the weasel.[176]

Harry's friend Ron[177] is the sixth child of his parents. This sets him under pressure given the popularity and talents of his brothers:[178]

> "I'm the sixth in our family to go to Hogwarts. You can say I've got a lot to live up to. Bill and Charlie have already left – Bill was Head Boy and Charlie was captain of Quidditch. Now Percy's a Prefect. Fred and George mess around a lot, but they still get really good marks and everyone thinks they're really funny. Everyone expects me to do as well as the others, but if I do, it's no big deal, because they did it first. You never get anything new, either, with five brothers. I've got Bill's old robes, Charlie's old wand and Percy's old rat." (HP 1, 110-111)

His second name, Bilius, could be derived from "bile" (= inclination to anger),[179] because he is much more emotional than he seems at first. The "freckle-faced, red-haired, long-nosed" (HP 2, 30) boy is an excellent chess player (HP 1, 303). Although continuously being second in line after Harry and his brothers Ron only rarely becomes jealous.[180] Only in *Goblet of Fire* when he believes Harry has smuggled his name into the goblet to compete in the tournament, is he

---

[174] This clearly alludes to the broker at the stock exchange.

[175] Their father lovingly calls them "redheads" (HP 4, 83).

[176] See Hein 2001, 150-151. Rowling says she took the name from "weasel": "In Britain and Ireland the weasel has a bad reputation as an unfortunate, even malevolent, animal. However, since childhood I have had a great fondness for the family mustelidae; not so much malignant as maligned, in my opinion." See Rowling 2006.

[177] The name is derived from Latin *Reginaldus* (= power, authority), English "Reginald" (see "Reginald", *Dictionary of First Names* [1990] 2000, 195). Others indicate Germanic sources like "Reinhold" (= resolutions, to preside over): see "Reinhold", *Lexion der Vornamen* 1974, 175.

[178] Sadly he wonders: "'Why is everything I own rubbish?'" (HP 4, 175).

[179] See Beahm 2005, 138.

[180] In *Order of the Phoenix* he has suddenly grown: "[Ron] seemed to have grown several more inches during their month apart, making him taller and more gangly looking than ever, though the long nose, bright red hair and freckles were the same." (HP 5, 75)

envious (HP 4, 317).[181] He enjoys sudden fame when he is the first one to come face to face with Sirius Black at night in *Prisoner of Azkaban*: "For the first time in his life, people were paying more attention to him than to Harry, and it was clear that Ron was rather enjoying the experience." (HP 3, 293) When he becomes prefect in *Order of the Phoenix* his self-confidence increases as his appointment comes as a surprise.[182] Proudly he wears his badge (HP 5, 188) and is happy to have finally gained some power ("'[...] and we can give out punishments if people are misbehaving. I can't wait to get Crabbe and Goyle for something ...'"; HP 5, 212). In the end he becomes confident enough to apply for keeper on the Gryffindor "Quidditch" team. Although he gains acceptance his first matches are disastrous:[183] "His greatest weakness was a tendency to lose confidence after he'd made a blunder" (HP 5, 442). Demoralised by the Slytherins' singing[184] he loses all his confidence ("'I'm rubbish,' croaked Ron. 'I'm lousy. I can't play to save my life.'", HP 5, 445) and has to struggle to participate in the next match ("[Ron was] clutching his stomach and starting straight ahead again, his jaw set and his complexion pale grey.", HP 5, 448). Only when he plays a crucial role in winning the decisive match against Ravenclaw does the situation change. The song turns into a eulogy,[185] he himself becomes the hero and for the first time in his life he is worshipped by his fellow students (HP 5, 774 and 775).

This gives him the self-confidence he needs for helping Harry to defeat Voldemort in *Deathly Hallows*. Having left his family to support Harry he gets frustrated with the obviously hopeless situation and leaves his friends (HP 7, 253), only to return later on (HP 7, 308). There is no real point to this episode but Rowling seems rather keen to add depth to her character – without succeeding. Later, Voldemort tries to set Ron against Harry when he is about to destroy the "Horcrux": suddenly there is a voice speaking to Ron about his innermost wishes and fears, trying to trick him into not destroying the locket (HP 7, 306).

---

[181] Hermione explains to Harry why Ron feels offended: "'[...] Ron's got all those brothers to compete against at home, and you're his best friend, and you're really famous – he's always shunted to one side whenever people see you, and he puts up with it, and he never mentions it, but I suppose this is just one time too many ...'" (HP 4, 318); see Bürvenich 2001, 76.

[182] His brother comments: "'No one in their right mind would make Ron a prefect.'" (HP 5, 181).

[183] Draco after the match: "'I've never seen a worse Keeper. ..'" (HP 5, 455).

[184] Draco Malfoy has composed the following stanzas: "Weasley cannot save a thing / He cannot block a single ring / That's why Slytherins all sing: / Weasley is our King. / Weasley was born in a bin / He always lets the Quaffle in / Weasley will make sure we win / Weasley is our King." (HP 5, 450).

[185] "Weasley is our King / Weasley is our King / He didn't let the Quaffle in / Weasley is our King ... / [...] Weasley can save anything / He never leaves a single ring, / That's why Gryffindors all sing: / Weasley is our King." (HP 5, 772).

Having resisted evil's temptation Ron develops leadership qualities (HP 7, 354) and plays a vital part in the last battle of Hogwarts. In *Order of the Phoenix* it is frequently hinted at Ron being in love with Hermione; jealously he follows her writing letters to "Quidditch" star Viktor Krum ("suspiciously", HP 5, 367; "accusingly", HP 5, 368). When Hermione kisses him just before his first match he is completely aghast: "He touched the spot on his face where Hermione had kissed him, looking puzzled, [...]." (HP 5, 446). But he is not yet able to deal with these emotions, which is why Hermione accuses him of being "'the most insensitive wart I have ever had the misfortune to meet'" (HP 5, 505) and having "the emotional range of a teaspoon" (HP 5, 506). In *Half-Blood Prince* Ron proves his sexual potency with a very demonstrative relation with Lavender Brown (see 336). Only in *Deathly Hallows* do Ron and Hermione come together (HP 7, 502-503), get married and have two children – Rose and Hugo (HP 7, 603-607). Like most of the other characters, Ron is very superficial and flat in the first parts of the series, a boy standing in Harry's and his brothers' shadow. He lacks Harry's mythical status and his brothers' various talents. Only in the last three novels of the series does Ron find his place in society and emancipates himself from his family and friends.

Ron's little sister Ginevra "Ginny"[186] is "a small, red-headed figure" (HP 2, 42) and in love with Harry right from the start ("Ginny seemed very prone to knocking things over whenever Harry entered a room." HP 2, 51).[187] In *Order of the Phoenix* she starts going out with another boy (HP 5, 385-386; 951), but ends up going out with Harry in *Half-Blood Prince* (HP 6, 499). Although Harry splits up with her to protect her from Voldemort's revenge in *Half-Blood Prince*, they finally become a couple in *Deathly Hallows* and end up being married and having three children (HP 7, 603-605). Lucius Malfoy tricks her into reading Riddle's diary which makes her unleash the Basilisk at her fellow-students in *Chamber of Secrets*. Like most of her brothers she breaks rules and even lies to her mother (HP 5, 88). She joins "Dumbledore's Army" and is among those who enter the "Department of Mysteries" to save Sirius. Ginny is brave, independent and a good "Quidditch" player. Her name is derived from Ginevra or Guinevere (King Arthur's wife) and an abbrevation of Virginia (= virgin).[188]

The twins Fred and George are, above all, representatives of rule-breaking in just about any form. Fittingly, their birthday is the first of April; April Fool's

---

[186] Her name is a form of Geneviève, the patron saint of Paris (ca. 422-512) who played an important role in defending the city against Attila and the Huns; see "Genevieve", *Dictionary of First Names* [1990] 2000, 103.

[187] See also: "very taken with Harry" (HP 4, 63); she brings him a self-made get-well-card (HP 3, 199) and has an embarrassing song sung to him on Valentine's Day (HP 2, 258).

[188] Rowling explains in an interview: "Ginny (full name Ginevra, not Virginia), is the first girl to be born into the Weasley clan for several generations." (See Rowling 2006).

Day.[189] They like the idea that people think Harry to be the heir of Slytherin in *Chamber of Secrets* (HP 2, 228), tease their brother Percy because of his arrogance as Head Boy of Hogwarts (HP 3, 72-76) and do not hesitate to lock him up in an Egyptian pyramid (HP 3, 72). In *Goblet of Fire* they try to enter the tournament, because "'The champions'll get to do all sorts of stuff you'd never be allowed to do normally.'" (HP 4, 209) The two are very popular with their fellow-students and enjoy being "in the thick of things, and the noisy centre of attention" (HP 4, 244). When Harry secretly hands them his prize money from the "Triwizard Tournament" they invest in magical joke articles and test them unscrupulously on younger students (HP 5, 280-281; 407-408; 595). They leave Hogwarts without finishing their education, setting loose enormous fireworks and transforming parts of the building into a huge swamp just to make fun of hedamistress Umbridge[190] (HP 5, 741). In *Half-Blood Prince* they have opened a shop in Diagon Alley called "Weasley's Wizard Wheezes".[191] Apart from all the funny aspects about them, they are among the victims of the final confrontation with evil. George looses an ear in fighting the "Death Eaters" in *Deathly Hallows* (HP 7, 67)[192] and Fred is killed during the battle of Hogwarts (HP 7, 512).

The oldest Weasley boy, Bill (= abbrevation of William and, thus, a royal name) is the star of the family and a favourite with his mother. A mixture between yuppie and popstar as Harry realises admiringly:

> Bill came as something of a surprise. Harry knew that he worked for the wizarding bank, Gringotts, that he had been Head Boy of Hogwarts, [...]. However, Bill was – there was no other word for it – *cool*. He was tall, with long hair that he had tied back in a ponytail. He was wearing an earring with what looked like a fang dangling from it. His clothes would not have looked out of place at a rock concert, except that Harry recognised his boots to be made, not of leather, but of dragon hide. (HP 4, 61)

In *Deathly Hallows* he marries Fleur Delacour (HP 7, 603-607), whom he got to know when she was doing an internship at Gringotts. Like his brothers, Bill suffers at the hands of Voldemort's followers when werewolf Fenrir Greyback bites him and mutilates his face forever "Harry] saw an unrecognisable face laying on Bill's pillow, so badly slashed and ripped that he looked grotesque." (HP 6, 572).

---

[189] Rowling says in an interview: "Fred and George were born – when else? – on April Fool's Day." (See Rowling 2006).

[190] "'We don't care about staying any more. We'd walk out right now if we weren't determined to do our bit for Dumbledore first.'" (HP 5, 690).

[191] In *Half-Blood Prince* we find a detailed description of their shop – and even their mother must admit: "'I must say, I didn't approve of [their joke shop] at first, but they do seem to have a bit of a flair for business!'" (HP 6, 87).

[192] It turns out at the end that he was accidently hit by Snape trying to protect him from the "Death Eaters'" killing curses (HP 7, 552).

The fifth Weasley brother, Charlie, has managed to make a profession out of his love for dragons. He is "working with dragons in Romania" – although it is never really explained what this means.

> [The] large hand, which Harry shook, [had] calluses and blisters [...]. This had to be Charlie, who worked with dragons in Romania. Charlie was built like the twins, shorter and stockier than Percy and Ron, who were both long and lanky. He had a broad, good-natured face, which was weatherbeaten and so freckly that he looked almost tanned; his arms were muscly, and one of them had a large, shiny burn on it. (HP 4, 61)

While the Weasleys are antagonists to the "Death Eaters" and their families they are role models for others. Neville's grandmother calls them "'fine, fine people'" (HP 5, 565). The Weasleys are among the oldest magical families of England (HP 2, 360) but live in rather poor conditions, because Arthur does not earn a lot of money.[193] Their main opponents are the Malfoys (see IV.3.L, 231) (HP 1, 120). The Weasleys are Harry's most important helpers, providing him not only with a home[194] but also hiding and defending him against Voldemort. This is why their magical clock that indicates each family member's state of danger constantly declares all of them to be in "mortal peril" (HP 6, 85). At the same time Harry makes up for this by saving many of the family members from certain death in the course of the series:

> "You saved Ginny ... you saved Arthur ... now you've saved Ron ... [...] Well, all I can say is that it was a lucky day for the Weasleys when Ron decided to sit in your compartment on the Hogwarts Express, Harry." (HP 6, 378)

Andrew Blake declares the Weasleys and the Dursleys to be representatives of opposing concepts of family:

> If the Dursleys caricature 1990s suburbia, the Weasleys are a caricature of the 1950s family – the lunch-preparing mother at home, several children at work or school, and the father a middle-rank, underpaid, hard-working civil servant.[195]

Here again we see the nostalgic view on supposedly "good old times" which the novels propose (see V.2.E, 317).

---

[193] He is not interested in a prestigious position. Ron says: "'Dad could've got promotion any time [...] he just likes it where he is [...].'" (HP 4, 188). And his wife adds: "'It's Arthur's fondness for Muggles that has held him back at the Ministry all these years. Fudge thinks he lacks proper wizarding pride.'" (HP 4, 770).
[194] See Bürvenich 2001, 73; Lacoss 2004, 78.
[195] Blake 2002, 65.

IV.3.K. A Good Careerist – Percy Weasley

Percy is the only Weasley to leave the family's set of values and take an active part against his parents. His name is taken from Percival, the youngest of King Arthur's knights and he differs from his brothers in his unhealthy ambition[196] and his predeliction for showing-off.[197] Ron assumes he plans to become Minister for Magic (HP 2, 67). He frequently is referred to as being or behaving "pompously", and when he does finally manage to become Head Boy of Hogwarts he is utterly spoiled by the experience.[198] His arrogance, self-love and a slavish trust in hierarchies becomes married to an unmerciful correctness. After Sirius' escape he declares boastfully: "'If I manage to get into the Ministry, I'll have a lot of proposals to make about Magical Law Enforcement!'" (HP 3, 461) When he ends up working for the Ministry he begins bossing his friends and relatives around (HP 4, 61).[199] He hero-worships his pedantic boss Bartemius Crouch[200] (HP 4, 67) and glorifies Crouch's cruel action against his own son as unwavering application of wizard law (HP 4, 581).

In *Order of the Phoenix* he and his father quarrel about the policy of the Ministry, which results in Percy renouncing his family and taking sides with Minister Fudge (HP 5, 83). When Harry has to come to the Ministry for a hearing he meets Percy, who pretends not to know him (HP 5, 156). On another occasion Percy proves to be a true bootlicking careerist who unconditionally worships authority: "Percy Weasley let out a hearty laugh. 'Oh, very good, Minister, very good!'" (HP 5, 676) Percy writes a letter to his brother Ron on the occasion of him being made prefect and chooses an arrogant, presumptuous style to praise him for "following in my footsteps". He goes on to warn him of further contact with Harry, because this "could be damaging your future prospects." According to his brother, Ron is supposed to trust "Dolores Umbridge, a truly delightful woman who I know will be only too happy to advise you". Percy is as cruel as to send back his mother's Christmas gift – the traditional handmade jumper (HP 5, 553).

---

[196] In Flourish and Blotts he reads respective guidebooks: "deeply immersed in a small and deeply boring book called 'Prefects Who Gained Power. A study of Hogwarts prefects and their later careers,'" (HP 2, 67); Ron accuses him: "'You're just worried I'm going to mess up your chances of being head boy.'" (HP 2, 172).

[197] "Percy [...] disapproved of what he termed their childish behaviour [...]. He had already told them pompously that he was only staying over Christmas because it was his duty as a prefect to support the teachers during this troubled time." (HP 2, 229).

[198] "It was rather like being introduced to the mayor. [... Percy was] swelling with pride." (HP 3, 71).

[199] Ron says of Percy: "[...] Percy loves rules. He'd just say Crouch was refusing to break them for his own son." (HP 4, 581).

[200] Crouch does not even know Percy's name and does not like his behaviour, either: "'I've left young Weatherby in charge ... very enthusiastic ... a little over-enthusiastic, if truth be told ...'" (HP 4, 309) (see IV.4.J, 248).

This attitude of Percy's being quite a given fact throughout the novels it comes as a suprise when he changes sides in *Deathly Hallows* and admits:

> "I was a fool! [...] I was an idiot, I was a pompous prat, I was a - a –" "Ministry-loving, family-disowning, power-hungry moron," said Fred. Percy swallowed. "Yes, I was!" "Well, you can't say fairer than that," said Fred, holding out his hand to Percy. (HP 7, 487)

Percy Weasley is – no matter what makes him return to his family in the end – a ruthless careerist/opportunist. At the same time he serves to illustrate Rowling's point of free choice: being from a positive background Percy may choose to join his parents' enemies and to collaborate with evil. It is not the set of values he grows up with that ensures his position in life. (see IV.3.L, 191 und V.6.A, 367).

IV.3.L. Snakes, Devils and Poisonous Plants – The Malfoys

The Malfoys are the most prominent opponents of good – in the school plot as much as on the broader political scale. All their malice is embodied by their name. The syllable "mal" is taken from Latin and means "bad, evil". "Foy" can derive from Latin *fides* (= belief, loyalty), i.e. French *la foi*, and allude to English "foe" at the same time. In this combination it is the opposite of "bona fide" meaning "without fraud or deception".[201] Both interpretations seem to fit the "Death Eater" family.

Their first names are just as negative: Draco referrs to Latin *draco, draconis* (snake or dragon)[202] and the historical character of Draco of Athens who gave his name to an especially severe punishment in 621 (draconian punishment).[203] His father's name Lucius is also taken from Latin: *lucidus* means "bright" or "shining". Lucifer also stands for the morning star in Latin. But in Christian tradition the name is notorious. The angel Lucifer having fallen from grace, became the devil.[204] And Narcissa's name refers to Greek mythology, where Narcissus stands for ruin by self-love and vanity.[205] George Beahm mentions that Narcissus also was an athlete of the 2nd century who murdered a Roman em-

---

[201] See "bona fide," *Oxford English Dictionary online*. Oxford: Oxford University Press, 2006. <http://erf.sbb.spk-berlin.de/han/356448509/dictionary.oed.com/cgi/entry/500 24829?single=1&query_type=word&queryword=bona+fide&first=1&max_to_show= 10> 5 Jan 2008.

[202] See "draco", *Der kleine Stowasser: Lateinisch-Deutsches Schulwörterbuch*, Munich: G. Freytag, 1980, 148.

[203] See Hein 2001, 95.

[204] See Cockrell 2004, 23.

[205] His Greek name is "Narkissos" and because he rejects Eos he is punished by being transformed into a flower, see Lurker 1979, 517.

peror.[206] The relation between the Malfoy family and the murderer of kings is obvious: Draco sets out to kill Dumbledore in *Half-Blood Prince* and his father tries to bring Voldemort back to power. On the other hand the narcissus is a poisonous flower that represents – among other things – death in Greek mythology. Phonetically with its [s] and [ts] the name alludes to the hissing of a snake.[207]

The Malfoys are rich, belong to the wizard nobility (HP 2, 36-37) and live in a "Wiltshire mansion" (HP 5, 342; see III.5.K, 139). After Voldemort's first fall they quickly renounce their allegiance to the Dark Lord.[208]

> "I've heard of his family," said Ron darkly. "They were some of the first to come back to our side after You-Know-Who disappeared. Said they'd been bewitched. My dad doesn't believe it. He says Malfoy's father didn't need an excuse to go over to the Dark Side." (HP 1, 121-122)

Hagrid goes even further: "'Rotten ter the core, the whole family, everyone knows that. No Malfoy's worth listenin' ter. Bad blood, that's what it is.'"[209] (HP 2, 72). In fact, Lucius has never given up his sympathies for his old master, but Voldemort suspects him to be an opportunist:

> "Lucius, my slippery friend, [...]. I am told that you have not renounced the old ways, though to the world you present a respectable face. You are still ready to take the lead in a spot of Muggle-torture, I believe? Yet you never tried to find me, Lucius [...]." (HP 4, 704)

All of the Malfoys have been in Slytherin House ("'I know I'll be in Slytherin, all our family have been [...].'", HP 1, 88; HP 2, 173) and they all look alike, with their pale, pointed faces and nearly white hair:

> A pale boy with a pointed face and white-blond hair, Draco greatly resembled his father. His mother [Narcissa] was blond, too; tall and slim, she would have been nice looking if she hadn't been wearing a look that suggested there was a nasty smell under her nose. (HP 4, 114)

Again their eyes and their smile betray their true characters ("malevolent grin", HP 3, 303; "a cold and satisfied smile", HP 2, 282). Their eyes are "cold" (HP 2,

---

[206] See George Beahm, *Fact, fiction, and folklore in Harry Potter's world: an unofficial guide*, Charlottesville, Virginia: Hampton Roads, 2005, 110.

[207] See Granger 2004, 109.

[208] George / Fred Weasley on Lucius Malfoy: "'He was a big supporter of You-Know-Who. [...] Dad reckons he was right in You-KnowWho's inner circle.'" (HP 2, 36).

[209] This mentioning of "bad blood" is just as racist as Voldemort's idea of "pure blood".

153), "pale" (HP 3, 91)[210] and "glinting maliciously" (HP 3, 98).[211] They clearly contrast with Dumbledore's blue eyes: "Dumbledore had not taken his bright blue eyes off Lucius Malfoy's cold grey ones." (HP 2, 284)[212]

The Malfoys are plotters. When Harry first meets Draco the eleven-year old declares he is willing to smuggle a broomstick into school (HP 1, 88), and his father Lucius apparently hides forbidden artefacts in his house (HP 2, 59-61; HP 2, 243). When appointed prefect Draco takes advantage of his position to bully other students ("'Malfoy was being absolutely foul to a first-year back there.'", HP 5, 220; HP 5, 688-689).

All of the Malfoys are arrogant ("'Father says it's a crime if I'm not picked to play for my house, and I must say, I agree.'", HP 1, 88) and openly show dislike for people of other beliefs or with less money. That is why the Weasleys are "riff-raff" (HP 1, 120) to them.[213]

> "My father told me all the Weasleys have red hair, freckles and more chil-
> dren than they can afford." He turned back to Harry. "You'll soon find out
> some wizarding families are much better than others, Potter. You don't want
> to go making friends with the wrong sort. I can help you there." He held out
> his hand to shake Harry's, but Harry didn't take it. (HP 1, 120)

But first of all the Malfoys are racists. Upon their first casual meeting Draco asks Harry:

> "But [your parents] were OUR kind, weren't they? [...] I really don't think
> they should let the other sort in, do you? [...] I think they should keep it in
> the old wizarding families." (HP 1, 89)[214]

Everyone cooperating with "Muggles" is violating wizard pride – just another point against the Weasleys:

---

[210] We read about Lucius Malfoy: "The man who followed [Draco] could only be his father. He had the same pale, pointed face and identical cold grey eyes." (HP 2, 58).

[211] Also: "Malfoy's eyes were shining malevolently" (HP 3, 139); "his eyes were sparkling maliciously." (HP 3, 335). And learning of Dumbledore's reinstatement as headmaster his eyes become "slits of fury" (HP 2, 359).

[212] "those cold grey eyes" (HP 5, 173); "Lucius Malfoy's grey eyes were gleaming." (HP 5, 864); "[...] his cold grey eyes narrowed and fixed upon Harry's face. 'Well, well, well ... Patronus Potter,' said Lucius Malfoy coolly." (HP 5, 173).

[213] Draco Malfoy about the Gryffindor "Quidditch" Team: "'[...] Potter, who's got no par-
ents, then there's the Weasleys, who've got no money – you should be on the team, Longbottom, you've got no brains.'" (HP 1, 241).

[214] Following Draco's definition, Harry's parents were not "our kind": Lily was "Muggle"-
born. The Malfoys' opinion on Hogwarts is clear: "'Father says [...] the school needs rid-
ding of all the Mudblood filth [...].'" (HP 2, 243).

"Arthur Weasley loves Muggles so much he should snap his wand in half and go and join them [...]. You'd never know the Weasleys were pure-bloods, the way they behave." (HP 2, 241).[215]

To damage Arthur Weasley's reputation Lucius Malfoy makes his daughter Ginny open the secret chamber in *Chamber of Secrets*. Malfoy's true aim is to prevent the enactment of a "Muggle"-friendly law which Weasley is working at.[216] His son Draco composes a song to make fun of the Weasleys (see note 184, 186):

> "We wanted to write another couple of verses! [...] But we couldn't find rhymes for fat and ugly – we wanted to sing about his mother, see –. [...] we couldn't fit in *useless loser* either – for his rather, you know –." (HP 5, 455-456)

41-year old Lucius (HP 5, 342) is powerful and scheming.[217] In his schooldays he was prefect of Slytherin house (HP 7, 540). He says of himself: "'The name Malfoy still commands a certain respect [...].'" (HP 2, 59)[218] And even when he has to resign as governor of Hogwarts in *Chamber of Secrets* (HP 2, 365), his political influence remains enormous. He carefully seeks to improve his family's image by contributing funds to St Mungo's Hospital for Magical Maladies and Injuries (HP 4, 115). Minister for Magic Cornelius Fudge has been financially dependent upon him for many years. In this way, Malfoy has ensured himself quite an influential position without holding any official office (HP 5, 174). George Beahm calls him a "Machiavellian schemer with an evil nature".[219]

His son does not make any effort to hide his family's connections and their making use of it. When the Slytherin "Quidditch" team is admitted to training again he boasts about his father's influence: "'Well, it was pretty much automatic, I mean, [Umbridge] knows my father really well, he's always pop-

---

[215] Harry is being attacked by Draco, as well: "'Saint Potter, the Mudbloods' friend [...]. He's another one with no proper wizard feeling, or he wouldn't go around with that jumped-up Granger Mudblood.'" (HP 2, 242). The ideological opposition between the two families becomes clear when Lucius Malfoy and Arthur Weasley quarrel: "'Dear me, what's the use of being a disgrace to the name of wizard if they don't even pay you well for it?' 'We have a very different idea of what disgraces the name of wizard, Malfoy,' [Mr Weasley] said, [...]." And when he sees Hermione's family with the Weasleys Malfoy says: "'The company you keep, Weasley ... and I thought your family could sink no lower.'" (HP 2, 71).

[216] See Westman 2004, 315.

[217] He smuggles the fateful diary into Ginny's basket in *Chamber of Secrets* to make her unleash the Basilisk and thereby to discredit her father (HP 2, 361).

[218] Draco says of his father: "'Father's always associated with the top people at the Ministry [...].'" (HP 4, 188). Mrs Weasley warns her husband: "'That family's trouble, don't go biting off more than you can chew.'" (HP 2, 65).

[219] Beahm 2005, 110.

ping in and out of the Ministry ..."' (HP 5, 399) And facing the oncoming "OWL"-exams he believes himself very well protected from failing by his family connections (HP 6, 778). When, in *Order of the Phoenix* Lucius Malfoy is discovered to be a *"Death Eater"* and sent to Azkaban, Draco swears to revenge his father's fall on Harry (HP 5, 935).

Magical World knows capitalism, conspicuous consumption and brand hype. The Malfoys are very rich and like to outdo others when it comes to demonstrating their wealth.[220] Just like Dudley Dursley in the "Muggle" world Draco is spoilt by his parents with food ("his usual supply of sweets and cakes from home", HP 4, 214) and expensive gifts that ensure his social status. The Slytherin "Quidditch" team only accepts him because his father has supplied all the players with brandnew Nimbus 2001 broomsticks (HP 2, 122). He sneers at poorer students (Lucius Malfoy says to Ginny Weasley: "'Here, girl – take your book – it's the best your father can give you [...].'", HP 2, 72).[221]

The Malfoys are cruel, aggressive and do not show any compassion for either humans or animals. Draco regards the hippogriff Buckbeak with disdain and insults him as an "ugly great brute" (HP 3, 130). Hagrid's dog Fang starts to snarl when it sees Lucius Malfoy (HP 2, 282).[222] Draco does not hesitate to kick defeated Harry in the face, thus breaking his nose (HP 6, 147). In *Half-Blood Prince* Draco has replaced his father as a "Death Eater" (HP 6, 125) and joins Voldemort's followers. Being quite a coward himself, he lets others do the dirty work for him. For this purpose Draco always has two ruffians, Crabbe and Goyle, around him – his only friends (HP 1, 120). These two are greedy and stupid (HP 2, 233):[223]

> Crabbe and Goyle seemed to exist to do Malfoy's bidding. They were both wide and muscly; Crabbe was the taller, with a pudding-basin haircut and a very thick neck; Goyle had short, bristly hair and long, gorilla arms. (HP 3, 90)

In *Deathly Hallows*, when the Malfoys' star is sinking, the two turn against their former leader and refuse to take orders from him any longer (HP 7, 506). Draco Malfoy is easily scared[224] and tends to flee when confronted with danger (HP 4, 404) – he even seems afraid of Harry: "[Harry] saw [Malfoy's]

---

[220] Malfoy says of the Weasleys' old brooms: "'You could raffle off those Cleansweep Fives, I expect a museum would bid for them.'" (HP 2, 123)

[221] Draco to Hagrid about his house: "'[...] you call this a house?'" (HP 2, 283).

[222] "One person, however, seemed to be thoroughly enjoying the atmosphere of terror and suspicion." (HP 2, 287).

[223] "Crabbe and Goyle, his enormous, thuggish cronies, both of whom appeared to have grown at least a foot during the summer." (HP 4, 186); "Goyle, who was almost as stupid as he was mean" (HP 1, 330).

[224] See Bürvenich 2001, 81.

eyes widen with fear: Malfoy thought Harry was attacking him." (HP 2, 187) Apart from this he is quite a mediocre student and his father fears he might turn out "a thief or a plunderer" (HP 2, 60). With all these character traits, Draco seems to be a "magical Dudley Dursley". A propensity to consume, greediness, meaness, cowardice, cruelty and a lack of education characterise him as much as Dudley, as Harry realises: "Draco Malfoy made Dudley Dursley look like a kind, thoughtful and sensitive boy." (HP 2, 36).

This situation changes in *Half-Blood Prince* when Draco sets out on a mission which Voldemort intends to be his death: he is to kill Albus Dumbledore, and if he fails, his family is going to be extinguished. His mother Narcissa is desperate and demonstrates true motherly love for her son pleading with Snape to help Draco complete his task (HP 6, 41). When it comes to really killing his headmaster, Draco shows positive feelings for the first time and Harry nearly sympathises with him (HP 6, 301, 443-444). Desperate because of the mission he is not meant to complete, the boy goes to see Moaning Myrtle to cry in her bathroom:

> "I mean he's sensitive, people bully him, too, and he feels lonely and hasn't got anybody to talk to, and he's not afraid to show his feelings and cry!" (HP 6, 433)
> "No one can help me," said Malfoy. His whole body was shaking. "I can't do it ... I can't ... it won't work ... and unless I do it soon ... he says he'll kill me ..." [...] Malfoy was crying – actually crying – tears streaming down his pale face into the grimy basin. (HP 6, 488)

Suddenly Draco is a victim and no longer an offender. But his trying to use the "Cruciatus Curse" on Harry directly after this demonstration of emotions again shows his cruelty. However, when Harry does not hesitate to nearly kill Draco by trying "Sectumsempra" on him, both boys seem morally equal to each other. Having nearly completed his mission and on the verge of being able to kill Dumbledore, Draco is unable to perform the deed. He cannot commit murder and his situation is desperate:[225]

> "I've got to do it! He'll kill me! He'll kill my whole family! [...] He told me to do it or he'll kill me. I've got no choice." [...] Malfoy was showing less resolution than ever. (HP 6, 552-555)

Harry feels sympathy for him – even after Dumbledore's death (HP 6, 596). Our sympathies grow when we witness the family's suffering at Volde-

---

[225] Ideologically it is important that it is lack of choice that makes Draco despair. The elimination of options leads to Draco's (evil) deeds. I will investigate further into this connection between free choice and goodness when dealing with the novels' ideological content (see V.6.A, 367). In fact, Draco has a choice: he could change sides and trust Dumbledore.

mort's hands in *Deathly Hallows*. Narcissa and Lucius cling to each other and are obviously afraid of falling out of favour with their master (HP 7, 14). When they become fearful for their son's life in the last battle of Hogwarts, they no longer care about Voldemort's victory. Narcissa lies to him in order to be able to enter the castle and look for her son (HP 7, 581-582) and Lucius, severely beaten, pleads for his son's life (HP 7, 515). Between Harry and Draco there seems to be a silent understanding suddenly: Draco refuses to tell Voldemort that, of course, he has recognised Harry when he is caught by the "Snatchers" (HP 7, 371-372). Harry even saves his life in the exploding "Room of Requirement". Finally, during the victory celebration, the Malfoys stand aside – once again they have become outsiders (HP 7, 597). In the last chapter we see Draco:

> with his wife and son, a dark coat buttoned up to his throat. His hair was receding somewhat, which emphasised the pointed chin. The new boy resembled Draco as much as Albus resembled Harry. Draco caught sight of Harry [...], nodded curtly and turned away again. "So that's little Scorpius," said Ron. (HP 7, 605)

So although the Malfoys are rather flat characters in the beginning, they acquire a certain complexity in the course of the series. In the end, continuity is ensured by Harry, Ron and Draco sending their children to Hogwarts in the same year. Fittingly, Draco has called his son "Scorpio" – yet another poisonous animal – to continue the family tradition.

IV.3.M. "Such a bossy know-it-all" – Hermione Jean[226] Granger

> "Nobody in my family's magic at all, it was such a surprise when I got my letter, but I was ever so pleased, of course, I mean, it's the very best school of witchcraft there is, I've heard, of course, I just hope it will be enough – I'm Hermione Granger, by the way, who are you?" (HP 1, 117)

Hermione is not a very appealing character when we first meet her. She is the stereotype of an eager student and know-it-all included in every school story. But from this beginning she develops into an important member of Harry's peer group and a decisive contributor to Voldemort's downfall. Because she is such a talented witch, she is – right from the beginning – able to get Harry and his friends out of just about any dangerous situation and solves nearly every riddle.[227] Regarding the character pattern, Hermione appears to be too ambitious at first (negative) but acquires astonishing knowledge (positive).

---

[226] We hear of her middle name in *Deathly Hallows* (HP 7, 106).

[227] Hermione is the only one who knows how to manage the Cornish Pixies set loose by Lockhart: she uses a "Freezing Charm" (HP 2, 114). Likewise she is the first to under-

Her name is quite complex. Her surname Granger refers to the tenant of a farm and, thus, indicates her simple "Muggle" background. Her first name is the female form of Hermes, the messenger between mortal men and and the gods of Greek mythology.[228] In this capacity he is also a representative of wisdom and science.[229] Hermione is also the name of Helena of Troy's daughter.[230] Other possible references include a character from Shakespeare's *A Winter's Tale*: unjustly accused of adultery, this Hermione pretends to be dead and awaits her rehabilitation – disguised as a statue. Nevertheless, the similarities between Shakespeare's and Rowling's characters are limited to their temporarily turning to stone.[231] So all things considered Hermione's name hints at a talented girl from a humble background.

With her "bushy brown hair" (among others HP 1, 116; HP 2, 64) she is described as "stunningly pretty" (HP 4, 346), but we lack a detailed description of her looks. Her only physical deficit seems to be her "rather long front teeth" (HP 1, 116). To overcome this she applies a special reducement charm to them (HP 4, 442). In *Goblet of Fire* she has her coming out at the Yule Ball:

> She had done something with her hair; it was no longer bushy, but sleek and shiny, and twisted up into an elegant knot at the back of her head. She was wearing robes made of a floaty, periwinkle-blue material, and she was holding herself differently, somehow – or maybe it was merely the absence of the twenty or so books she usually had slung over her back. (HP 4, 452)

Hermione is "muggle-born", i.e. from non-magical descent.[232] Her parents are dentists (HP 1, 215). She is a rather resolute girl ("She had a bossy sort of voice", HP 1, 116), who is very sure of herself and not in the least shy. When we first meet her on the Hogwarts Express we notice her commitment to her fellow students searching the train for Neville's toad (HP 1, 116). She has quite a high opinion of her own qualities and knows herself to be an excellent student: even before arriving at Hogwarts she is sure she will be sorted into Gryffindor or Ravenclaw – the houses that stand for bravery and intelligence (HP 1, 117). She also believes herself to be more mature than the other students as she complains about the others "'behaving very childishly, racing up and down the corridors, [...].'" (HP 1, 122). Her "Patronus" is a "shining silver otter" (HP 5, 668).[233]

---

stand that Lupin is a werewolf (HP 3, 372). Hermione teaches Ron "Wingardium Leviosa", with which he can defeat the troll (HP 1, 187).

[228] See "Hermióne," *Lexikon der Vornamen* 1974, 110; and "Hermione," *Dictionary of First Names* [1990] 2000, 115.

[229] See von Wilpert [1955] 1989, 370-371.

[230] See Dresang 2004, 213.

[231] Rowling does not see this parallel (see Beahm 2005, 98).

[232] Her birthday is September 19th:see Rowling 2006.

[233] The otter is Rowling's favourite animal, as well (see I.2.B, 20).

Hermione excels at all subjects and applies herself diligently to her studies (among others HP 3, 18)[234] she never looks down on less able students, but helps them to do their schoolwork (HP 5, 332).[235] Nevertheless, she feels jealous when Harry is able to achieve highest marks with the help of the comments in his "Potions" book in *Half-Blood Prince* ("Hermione's expression could not have been any smugger; she had loathed being out-performed in every Potions class.", HP 6, 353). In typically female fashion, she tends to minimise her own achievement "'I got a few extra books for background reading, [...].'" – the reader knows that this must mean long hours of extra studying (HP 1, 117). Usually, we see her hidden behind piles of books deep in study ("behind her tottering pile of Ancient Rune books", "bent over her Runes translation", HP 5, 632-633). Naturally she is the first to have finished her homework ("who of course was up to date with all her work", HP 5, 388). Hermione clearly is the best student of her year (HP 2, 178).[236] She gets ten "O"s (= outstanding) at her "OWL"s (HP 6, 101). Appropriately her pet cat Crookshanks is the most intelligent of cats (HP 3, 392).[237] Because of her extraordinary talent the "Sorting Hat" had first intended to sort her into Ravenclaw as Hermione admits in *Order of the Phoenix*.[238] It is not only her hard work which makes her successful but most of all her analytic intelligence.[239] In the end, Harry and Ron must repeatedly admit that she is brilliant (HP 7, 288; 344; 392).

At first Hermione is despised by all the students ("she was such a bossy know-it-all", HP 1, 179; "'It's no wonder no one can stand her,' [Ron] said to Harry [...] 'She's a nightmare, honestly.'", HP 1, 187).[240] She is very law-abiding[241] and likes to be correct. Her story is – as Farah Mendlesohn remarks –

---

[235] "Hermione, as was her custom, had spent a large part of the day drawing up revision timetables for the three of them." (HP 5, 716).

[236] Her skills are frequently commented upon by other characters. Hagrid says about her: "'An' they haven't invented a spell our Hermione can't do [...].'" (HP 2, 127); "Moody" calls her "'the cleverest witch of your age I've ever met, [...].'" (HP 3, 372) and advises her to consider a career as an "auror", because: "'Mind works the right way, Granger.'" (HP 4, 619); Ron says of her excessive timetable: "'I know you're good, Hermione, but no one's that good.'" (HP 3, 109); Harry finally tells her: "'I'm not as good as you, [...].'" (HP 1, 308).

[237] The name could be taken from cartoonist George Cruikshank (1792-1878), who illustrated Dicken's novels and is famous for his political satire: see Dresang 2004, 227.

[238] Being told her knowledge already has reached NEWT-level she says: "'Oh ... well ... yes, I suppose it is. [...] Well, the Sorting Hat did seriously considered putting me in Ravenclaw [...].'" (HP 5, 440-441).

[239] See Gladstein 2004, 52-53.

[240] Even Snape hates her and declares her an "insufferable know-it-all" (HP 3, 187).

[241] Hermione asks Harry to hand in the "Marauder's Map" (HP 3, 215) and does not want him to go to Hogsmeade without proper permission from his family (HP 3, 216).

one "of learning conformity to a new social milieu."[242] Such people tend to adjust with extreme correctness to their new environment. Only in the course of time does Hermione begin to question rules and to act more according to their intention than to their wording. It is only when she learns to lie in order to protect others that she is accepted into Harry's peer group (HP 1, 193-195). Later she does not refrain from stealing the ingredients for "Polyjuice Potion" from Snape's office (HP 2, 202).[243] In *Prisoner of Azkaban* she attacks Snape because he threatens to kill Sirius Black (HP 3, 390). All of this confers upon her the respect of Harry and Ron ("Hermione had become a bit more relaxed about breaking rules [...] and she was much nicer for it.", HP 1, 197).

Hermione stands for democracy and clinging to basic human-rights principles. When Harry founds "Dumbledore's Army" she insists on his formal election as their leader (HP 5, 432). Finally she differentiates between school rules and official law, when she tells George and Fred, who are planning to blackmail someone that: "'This isn't some silly school rule [...]'" (HP 4, 618).[244] In *Order of the Phoenix* she admits to the fun of breaking rules ("'I think I'm feeling a bit ... rebellious.'" HP 5, 698). At this stage, she has learnt to look to the "greater good" which lies above the rules.("It was a mark of the seriousness of the situation that Hermione made no objection to the smashing up of the Transfiguration department", HP 5, 810).

Apart from this, Hermione is very responsible and usually cares more for the common good than for herself. She tries to make Harry and Ron chicken out of the duel with Malfoy, because she fears a loss of reputation and house points for Gryffindor: "'[...] think of the points you'll lose Gryffindor if you're caught, and you're bound to be. It's really very selfish of you." (HP 1, 169) Given this strong notion of justice, Hermione is the only character actively to take action for the house-elves' rights. She founds a society for their protection (HP 4, 409-411), which is later re-named "SPEW" ("Society for the Promotion of Elfish Welfare", HP 5, 89). Naively she completely ignores the elves' bizarre love for their enslavement. When she begins to hide clothes that would free the finder in Gryffindor common room, the elves refuse to clean it (HP 5, 283).

The importance she puts in fairness becomes even more evident when she and Ron are appointed prefects in *Order of the Phoenix*. Whereas Ron delights in the idea of being able to punish others from now on, Hermione recalls him to his duty: "'You're not supposed to abuse your position, Ron!'" (HP 5, 212) When he wants to try Firewhisky in Hogsmeade's "Hog's Head" she prevents

---

[242] See Mendlesohn 2004, 168.

[243] In fact, she initiates the forbidden brewing of the potion. Ron remarks: "'I never thought I'd see the day when you'd be persuading us to break rules,' [...]". (HP 2, 181).

[244] Ron accuses her of putting her homework above anything else: "'I didn't think there was anything in the universe more important than homework!' said Ron. 'Don't be silly, of course there is,' said Hermione." (HP 5, 361).

him from doing so: "'You – are – a – *prefect*', snarled Hermione." (HP 5, 374) In her zeal for justice she is not always very astute, as Ron says: "'You're so naive,' said Ron, 'you think just because you're all honourable and trustworthy [...].'" (HP 5, 392)

Hermione stands for rationality and knowledge. At the end of *Philosopher's Stone*, Dumbledore rewards her "for the use of cool logic in the face of fire" (HP 1, 328). Thus, she is the clear antagonist to the "Divination" teacher Sybill Trelawney (see IV.4.I, 246) who regards her as "hopelessly Mundane" (HP 3, 322). Hermione sticks to knowledge based in science and trusts in established authorities. At the beginning of *Goblet of Fire* Harry imagines how she would react if confronted with his strange fears: she would "[...] go straight to the headmaster of Hogwarts, and in the meantime, consult a book." (HP 4, 28). And, if the school library does not give her the answers to her questions, she is shocked:

> Meanwhile, the Hogwarts library had failed Hermione for the first time in living memory. She was so shocked, she even forgot that she was annoyed at Harry for his trick with the bezoar. (HP 6, 357)

But even she is not without prejudices; her remarks about Luna Lovegood whose father is the editor of the yellow press magazine "Quibbler" show this clearly: "'Well, I wouldn't expect anything else from someone whose father runs *The Quibbler*'" (HP 5, 291). The contrast between the two girls is obvious: Luna is a fan of bizarre and esoteric phenomena, Hermione sticks to reliable science.[245]

Being a Gryffindor, Hermione is courageous. She bravely defends unpopular opinions about her friends and authorities. When Harry is anonymously given a brandnew "Firebolt" broomstick she betrays his secret to McGonagall because she (correctly, as we learn at the end of this volume) assumes that it has come from Sirius Black (HP 3, 244 and 252). She fearlessly stands up to Rita Skeeter (whom she calls a "'horrible woman'", HP 4, 492), Sybill Trelawney ("'That lesson was absolute rubbish [...].'", HP 3, 123 and HP 3, 322) and even to Dolores Umbridge. Arguing rationally and acting in a legally correct manner, she first corners her new "Defence Against the Dark Arts" teacher (HP 5, 268-270) and calls her

---

[245] Luna accuses her of being "narrow-minded" (HP 5, 382). With the introduction of Luna we have an interesting development in narrative space: within the "real" phantastic world of the wizards suddenly there is another, unreal space where we find strange creatures only a few wizards believe in. In fact, "Heliopaths" are just as unreal as the "Hogwarts Express" leaving from platform 9 ¾.

"[...] that stupid puffed-up, power-crazy old – [...]" (HP 5, 688)
"That evil woman!" gasped Hermione [...]. (HP 5, 796).

Hermione is the one to lure Umbridge to the centaurs where she is abducted and finally defeated (HP 5, 821-824). But she is also able to admit to her own mistakes and apologise if necessary (HP 3, 316). She deletes herself from her parents' minds to protect them in case she is arrested (HP 7, 84). Furthermore, when tortured by Bellatrix Lestrange with the "Cruciatus Curse" she does not betray her friends but comes up with a surprising lie (HP 7, 376-377)

As rational as Hermione is, she is not emotionless. She is able to control herself and keep her feelings hidden.[246] She keeps her cool in the face of accusations after Skeeter's reports on her alleged love-affair with Harry (HP 4, 347). When Harry has managed to complete his first task it is only the marks of her fingernails in her face that betray her concern for him (HP 4, 393). She is loyal to her friends. When Harry and Ron have completely forgotten their promise to help Hagrid in his defence of Buckbeak, it is Hermione who takes the time to see him, right in the middle of exams. "'She's got her heart in the right place,'" declares Hagrid leaving the two boys more than embarassed (HP 3, 297). In *Goblet of Fire*, Hermione is among the few who believe Harry when he says that he has not entered his name into the goblet himself (HP 4, 317). Beginning in *Half-Blood Prince* we suppose her to be in love with Ron, helping him to enter the "Quidditch" team (HP 6, 214) and calling him a "filthy hypocrite" (HP 6, 281) when he sees his short-time girlfriend Lavender Brown. She decides to go out with Ron's arch-enemy McLaggen to provoke him (HP 6, 297). At the same time she denies her feelings: "'He's at perfect liberty to kiss whomever he likes, [...]. I really couldn't care less.'" (HP 6, 285) Finally, they end up as a couple, right before entering the final battle (HP 7, 502-503). In the last chapter we see them with their two children Rose and Hugo (HP 7, 603-607).

In the course of the series Hermione develops a good sense of perception for the feelings of others. She is able to analyse Sirius' bad mood at their leaving Grimmauld Place (HP 5, 178). She understands at once that Harry is in love with Cho (HP 5, 387), and realises the change in him after their first kiss (HP 5, 504). Hermione is also the one who understands Cho's emotional chaos and analyses it correctly (HP 5, 505-506).

Nevertheless, there are some inconsistencies in the character: Hermione's analytical intelligence fails her completely in the case of Gilderoy Lockhart (amongst others HP 2, 111 and 190). Here she is the naive adoring school girl and defends the object of her admiration against any critics. This seems just as unconvincing as her tearing a page from a school book (HP 2, 312). Harry and

---

[246] Nevertheless, she cries when she realises that her fellow-students do not like her (HP 1, 187) and she hits Malfoy when he laughs about Hagrid feeling sorry for Buckbeak (HP 3, 317).

Ron find this page still in her hand when she lies petrified in the hospital wing and they are able to get the decisive hint from it – even when not able to actively participate in the adventure, Hermione still helps her friends.

However, it is not really imaginable that Hermione would mistake a cat's hair for a human one which changes her into an animal instead of a Slytherin girl (HP 2, 237).[247] Considering her intellectual excellence it is also unconvincing that she should be bad at playing chess (HP 1, 235). Farah Mendlesohn calls this an inconsistency of the author's that serves to provide Harry with an appropriate peer group.[248] At these points, Rowling sticks to well-known stereotypes (see V.4.D, 346):[249]

> Repeatedly Rowling has Hermione *shriek, squeak, wail, squeal,* and *whimper,* verbs never applied to the male characters in the book. [...] Adverbial phrases are often no better – Hermione acts *in alarm, hysterically* [... and] often bursts into tears [...].[250]

Hermione possesses emotional intelligence – a quality usually seen in women.[251] It is astonishing that the girl does not seem to have a "best friend" and belongs to a peer group of boys.[252] Her feminity is not of relevance – neither to her, nor to her friends.[253] Only at the Yule Ball in *Goblet of Fire* does she appear as a beautiful young lady for the first time (HP 4, 452).[254]

The character of Hermione has been controversially discussed by critics. Peter Appelbaum claims she was much less "cool" than the boy characters and represented as a mere "nerd".[255] But this is only partly true: although Hermione represents effort and ambition more than any other character, she also stands for bravery, rationality and the ability to break rules if she chooses to do so. Her role is not limited to the "highly intelligent, overachieving, somewhat annoying

---

[247] See Elizabeth E. Heilman, "Blue Wizards and Pink Witches: Representations of Gender, Identity and Power," *Harry Potter's World: Multidisciplinary Critical Perspectives*, ed. Elizabeth E. Heilman, New York, London: RoutledgeFalmer, 2003, 221-239, here 224; Mendlesohn 2004, 168.

[248] See Mendlesohn 2004, 172.

[249] See Schafer 2000, 54.

[250] Dresang 2004, 223.

[251] See Angelika Walser, "Potter'sche Moralpädagogik," *Leben, Tod and Zauberstab: Auf theologischer Spurensuche in 'Harry Potter'*, eds. Christoph Drexler, Nikolaus Wandinger, Münster: LIT, 2004, 79-102, here 84.

[252] See Dresang 2004, 231.

[253] See Ernould 2003, 213.

[254] See Dresang 2004, 233.

[255] See Peter Appelbaum, "Harry Potter's World: Magic, Technoculture, and Becoming Human" *Harry Potter's World: Multidisciplinary Critical Perspectives*, ed. Elizabeth E. Heilman, New York, London: RoutledgeFalmer, 2003, 25-51, here 39.

student".[256] She plays an important role in solving many riddles and she rescues the boys from many dangerous situations. Without her Voldemort would have got the Philosopher's Stone, the Basilisk would have killed the students of Hogwarts, and were it not for her ability to travel through time, Buckbeak and Black would have been killed. It is Hermione that literally puts an end to Umbridge's rule at Hogwarts. She withstands Bellatrix' "Cruciatus Curse" in *Deathly Hallows* (HP 7, 376-377) and – especially in this last part of the series – she is just as vital to bringing about Voldemort's downfall as Harry.

Elizabeth E. Heilman believes her to be mere nothing more than an "enabler" for the boys,[257] but this, given the role she plays in *Deathly Hallows*, is definitely not the case. Even her seemingly absurd action for "SPEW" and the house-elves pays off in the end – it is Dobby (set free by Harry in *Chamber of Secrets* and encouraged by Hermione's ideas of elven-rights) that saves them from Malfoy Manor (HP 7, 378-358), sacrificing himself. And, in the final battle of Hogwarts the house-elves participate actively on the side of Harry and "Dumbledore's Army". So Eliza T. Dresang is right in saying:

> Rowling's Hermione is a strong, intelligent, thoughtful, compassionate female who is not only assisting the males with whom she has an interdependent relationship but also working to become her own agent as well as a catalyst for social change.[258]

Hermione refers to the stereotype character of the "girl supergenius" (see VI, 386) frequently to be found in fantasy literature. She knows the answer to nearly every question but has to justify her being clever. J.K. Rowling has admitted to identifying with her.[259]

IV.3.N. Gazing Wisely through Half-moon Spectacles – Albus Dumbledore

Dumbledore has a long name: Albus Percival Wulfric Brian Dumbledore. And each of these brings positive allusions to the character. "Dumbledore" is, as the author says, supposed to be Old English for "bee" which is a symbol of sociability, effort, virginity, sweetness[260] and Christ[261] or for May beetle (symbol of

---

[256] See Dresang 2004, 221.
[257] See Heilman "Blue Wizards and Pink Witches" 2003. 224.
[258] Dresang 2004, 242.
[259] "I have often said that Hermione is a bit like me when I was younger. I think I was seen by other people as a right little know-it-all, but I hope that it is clear that underneath Hermione's swottiness there is a lot of insecurity and a great fear of failure (as shown by her Boggart in Prisoner of Azkaban)." (Rowling 2006)
[260] See Beahm 2005, 90-92; Cockrell 2004, 23; Dresang 2004, 212; and Granger 2004, 108.
[261] See Lurker 1991, 91-92; Granger 2004, 108.

spring).[262] Albus is Latin and means "white" – the classic symbol of light, chasteness, peace and innocence[263] – just as his hair is.[264] Percival refers to Arthur's knight and Wulfric is a saint and a healer from the 12th century. Brian, finally, is Celtic and means hill.[265] So Dumbledore unites Christian beliefs and Celtic myths.[266]

We do not learn much about him at first. He is "the greatest wizard of the age", "a great man" (HP 1, 114; HP 2, 23; HP 3, 102; HP 3, 106), but we do not learn why. The first reference to Dumbledore is a "Chocolate Frog" card:

> Albus Dumbledore, currently Headmaster of Hogwarts. Considered by many the greatest wizard of modern times, Professor Dumbledore is particularly famous for his defeat of the dark wizard Grindelwald in 1945,[267] for the discovery of the twelve uses of dragon's blood and his work on alchemy with his partner, Nicolas Flamel. Professor Dumbledore enjoys chamber music and tenpin bowling. (HP 1, 114)

Until the very end of the series no one would ever have questioned the moral status of Albus Dumbledore, the wise old headmaster of Hogwarts. But in *Deathly Hallows* we learn of his own difficult childhood and youth and, moreover, of his fascination with the Dark Arts.

Dumbledore has a brother called Aberforth (three years his junior, HP 7, 22) who has been on trial for casting "inappropriate charms on a goat" (HP 4, 495). He is the innkeeper of the "Hog's Head" in Hogsmeade and we meet him in *Deathly Hallows* when he saves Harry, Ron and Hermione from the "Death Eaters" (HP 7, 450-452). Aberforth looks remarkably like his brother Albus (HP 7, 451; 454). He advises Harry to give up and go into hiding (HP 7, 452).

Their sister Ariana was beaten up by "Muggle" boys when she was six years old and consequently refused to use magic, which drove her mad (HP 7, 454-455). Percival, their father, went after the boys, killed them and was sent to Azkaban where he died (HP 7, 21). The family kept Ariana's condition secret for fear that she might be taken away to the closed ward in St Mungo's (HP 7, 455). When she was fourteen, she accidentally killed her mother Kendra in one of her fits (HP 7, 455-456). A year later she died in another accident, killed

---

[262] See Lurker 1991, 365.
[263] See Lurker 1991, 824. The name also refers to Saint Alban, one of the first British martyrs: see "Alban," *Dictionary of First Names* [1990] 2000, 17.
[264] See Hein 2001, 51.
[265] See "Brian," *Dictionary of First Names* [1990] 2000, 42. Beahm translates it as Celtic word for "strong": Beahm 2005, 90-92.
[266] Rowling declares, Dumbledore was "a hundred and fifty" years old: Rowling, Live Interview, 16 Oct 2000.
[267] There is, of course, a striking similarity with the end of World War II. The name "Grindelwald" also alludes to Germany (see II.4, 78).

probably by Albus' friend Grindelwald (HP 7, 23; 457). On Ariana's and Kendra's grave in Godric's Hollow we read *"Where your treasure is, there will your heart be also."* (HP 7, 266)

Albus Dumbledore is a highly gifted wizard. Mrs Marchbanks, with whom he did his "NEWTs" says that he "'did things with a wand I'd never seen before.'" (HP 5, 782-783) He always supported "Muggle" rights and was "the most brilliant student ever seen at the school", furthermore, he "won every prize of note that the school offered " and indeed "was soon in regular correspondence with the most notable magical names of the day" (HP 7, 22). Thus qualified he is the only wizard Voldemort is afraid of (HP 1, 18; HP 2, 23).

Having finished his education he goes home to care for his sister Ariana, but when he becomes friends with Gellert Grindelwald he neglects her (HP 7, 456). When she is killed in an accident, Dumbledore feels guilty and ashamed. This feeling never leaves him (HP 7, 457-458).

In a New York lecture in October 2007, Rowling said she imagined Dumbledore to be gay and in love with Grindelwald.[268] This revelation caused worldwide discussion amongst fans. Dumbledore's sexual orientation became a topic of considerable debate on the internet. In the text, there is no hint at all from which one could infer his homosexuality. The only hint at possible, but then homoerotic and at the same time paedophilic elements in Dumbledore's relation with Harry is when wizarding world's scandal-mongering journalist Rita Skeeter writes in her biography of his "unnatural interest" in Harry and calls their relation "unhealthy, even sinister" (HP 7, 28-29). But this is the only sentence that might be interpreted as an allusion to a supposed sexual interest in Harry, and, again, this refers more to paedophilia than to homosexuality. As the text does not give any further convincing hint at Dumbledore's being homosexual I do not want to comment on this additional information which the author supplied posthumously in an interview. Dumbledore is not married, does not have children and has never been seen to be interested in a female – so far, so good. But this is consistent with fantastic literature in general: the "Merlin"-type wizard master like Tolkien's Gandalf is never married. I therefore want to remind the reader of Eco's statement that the author should never comment on his own text (see II, 23).

Being friends with Grindelwald, he discusses the question of wizard superiority with him. In a letter to his friend he writes:

> "Your point about wizard dominance being FOR THE MUGGLES' OWN GOOD – this, I think, is the crucial point. Yes, we have been given power and, yes, that power gives us the right to rule, but it also gives us responsibilities over the ruled. We must stress this point; it will be the foundation

---

[268] See "Zauberer-Outing: Dumbledore ist schwul," *SPIEGEL Online* 20 Oct 2007 <http://www.spiegel.de/kultur/literatur/0,1518,512613,00.html> 3 Jan 2008.

stone upon which we build. Where we are opposed, as we surely will be, this must be the basis of all our counter-arguments. We seize control FOR THE GREATER GOOD. And from this it follows that where we meet resistance, we must use only the force that is necessary and no more." (HP 7, 291)

This is highly reminiscent of Carlyle's strong just man (see V.1.B, 289) and Rousseau's general will (V.1.B, 292). Together with Grindelwald he develops the idea of becoming master of the "Deathly Hallows" which grant immortality to the person rightfully uniting the three items. In this desire to be immortal he resembles Voldemort (HP 7, 571). When he gets a hold of the ring with the "Resurrection Stone", the last missing item, he is tempted into putting the ring on. As the ring is cursed, he is severely injured and condemned to die (HP 7, 546). Snape tells him:

"The ring carried a curse of extraordinary power, to contain it is all we can hope for; I have trapped the curse in one hand for the time being – [… How long you have] I cannot tell. Maybe a year. There is no halting such a spell forever. It will spread, eventually, it is the sort of curse that strengthens over time." (HP 7, 546)[269]

Frequently, Dumbledore has been offered the job as Minister for Magic, but has rejected the offer on the grounds of his duties at Hogwarts as headmaster (HP 1, 74-75; HP 5, 109; HP 7, 22).[270] The true reason why he never wanted to gain power is his frustration with himself (HP 7, 575). Nevertheless, Cornelius Fudge distrusts him and suspects him of conspiracy.[271]

When the reader first meets him, these events are forgotten by most wizards. We see him evacuating baby Harry to live with his "Muggle" family. In this first description we find all the elements we are going to meet again and again throughout the series in reference to Albus Dumbledore:

Nothing like this man had ever been seen in Privet Drive. He was tall, thin and very old, judging by the silver of his hair and beard, which were both long enough to tuck into his belt. He was wearing long robes, a purple cloak which swept the ground and high-heeled, buckled boots. His blue eyes were light, bright and sparkling behind half-moon spectacles and his nose was

---

[269] This is highly reminiscent of cancer.

[270] Voldemort wonders why Dumbledore has never accepted the job: "'I merely wondered why you – who is so often asked for advice by the Ministry, and who has twice, I think, been offered the post of Minister' – 'Three times at the last count, actually,' said Dumbledore. 'But the Ministry never attracted me as a career.'" (HP 6, 414).

[271] See Bürvenich 2001, 91. Katherine M. Grimes sees Dumbledore as magical world's *spiritus rector*: "Albus Dumbledore is [...] almost godlike in that he controls the entire school, which is in many ways the center of the wizarding world because the government is ineffective and almost ridiculous." (Grimes 2004, 95)

very long and crooked, as though it had been broken at least twice. This man's name was Albus Dumbledore. (HP 1, 15)

His "silver hair" (HP 1, 113)[272], his "silver beard" (HP 2, 86)[273], "half-moon spectacles" (HP 1, 113)[274], "long fingers" (HP 2, 155)[275] and "crooked nose" (HP 1, 113)[276] are his most important features.[277] His robes tend to be representative ("magnificent deep-green robes embroidered with many stars and moons", HP 4, 194-195),[278] but he is able to make fun of himself and dresses up to meet every occasion ("Dumbledore had swapped his pointed wizard's hat for a flowered bonnet", HP 1, 220).

Again, it is his eyes that characterise him ("twinkling light-blue gaze", HP 2, 158; "his eyes twinkling", HP 3, 247; "penetrating, light-blue stare", HP 2, 226). Usually they look in a friendly way upon others, but facing his enemies Dumbledore can appear fiery ("His blue eyes were full of a fire Harry had never seen before.", HP 2, 282; "fire was still blazing in his blue eyes", HP 2, 283). These eyes are in obvious contrast to Malfoy's eyes ("Dumbledore had not taken his bright blue eyes off Lucius Malfoy's cold grey ones", HP 2, 284). Dumbledore's true power can be felt in dramatic moments:

> At that moment, Harry fully understood for the first time why people said Dumbledore was the only wizard Voldemort had ever feared. The look upon Dumbledore's face as he stared down at the unconscious form of Mad-Eye Moody was more terrible than Harry could ever have imagined. There was no benign smile upon Dumbledore's face, no twinkle in the eyes behind the spectacles. There was cold fury in every line of the ancient face; a sense of power radiated from Dumbledore as though he was giving off burning heat. (HP 4, 736)

---

[272] HP 1, 134; HP 4, 194-195.
[273] HP 3, 355; HP 4, 29; HP 5, 157.
[274] HP 2, 86; HP 2, 155; HP 3, 102; HP 4, 194-195; HP 5, 157.
[275] HP 4, 194-195; HP 5, 917.
[276] HP 2, 155; HP 3, 102; HP 4, 29; HP 5, 157.
[277] Isabelle Smadja absurdly interprets Dumbledore as representative of the "Eternal (Wandering) Jew". She draws the conclusion that the Potter series is about antisemitism and fascism with Durmstrang being the fascist stronghold and Dumbledore representing Jewish resistance. I believe this too far fetched and consider this a misinterpreation. There is no nothing whatsoever to prove this thesis; see Smadja 2001, 40-41.
[278] "[...] Professor Dumbledore, sitting in his high-backed golden chair at the centre of the long staff table, wearing deep purple robes scattered with silvery stars and a matching hat." (HP 5, 226) Even when being woken in the middle of the night, Dumbledore is adequately dressed: "He was wearing a magnificently embroidered purple and gold dressing gown over a snowy white nightshirt, but seemed wide-awake, his penetrating light blue eyes fixed intently upon Professor Mc Gonagall." (HP 5, 514).

We also read about his appearance: "[...] once again he seemed to radiate that indefinable sense of power" (HP 4, 765) and "[There] was something impressive about the sight of [Dumbledore] framed in the doorway against an oddly misty night." (HP 5, 656) His "thunderous voice" (HP 5, 898) addresses his enemy.[279] He is brave – one example of this being his wish to be Lily and James Potter's "Secret Keeper"[280] (HP 3, 223).

But one of his most important features is his humility[281] which is not to be confused with false modesty. He knows exactly how extremely talented he is ("'My brain surprises even me sometimes ...'", HP 1, 323). His ability to laugh about himself makes him a very approachable wise man. He is no saint. Rowling also shows him in everyday situations like a visit to the hospital wing where he wears a "long woolly dressing gown and a nightcap" (HP 2, 195). And Harry imagines Dumbledore at the seaside where he would seem rather out of place; "with his long silver beard, full-length wizard's robes and pointed hat, stretched out on a beach somewhere, rubbing suntan lotion into his long crooked nose" (HP 4, 29). At meal times he puts his long beard above his shoulder "so as to keep it out of the way of his plate [...]" (HP 5, 232). The wise old wizard likes to relate anecdotes about himself (claiming he would see a pair of wollen socks in the "Mirror of Erised"; HP 1, 232) and speaks about himself visiting the toilet at night (HP 4, 456). He is unpretentious ("chuckling merrily at a joke Professor Flitwick had just read him.", HP 1, 220) and likes to choose rather stupid passwords for his office like "Sherbet Lemon" (HP 2, 222) or "Cockroach cluster" (HP 4, 629). Dumbledore likes telling jokes (HP 4, 206) and makes fun of his being deprived of his official titles: "'But Dumbledore says he doesn't care what they do as long as they don't take him off the Chocolate Frog Cards,' [...]." (HP 5, 111)[282]

There is a certain friendliness and serenity about him. He is benevolent ("smile benignly", HP 5, 657) and compassionate. Harry, vandalising Dumbledore's office when he is outraged by his uncle Sirius' death, is told in a mild voice: "'By all means continue destroying my possessions, [...] I daresay I have too many.'" (HP 5, 906) Dumbledore is a good and caring teacher.[283]

This is his strength, but also his greatest weakness, for he makes quite disputable decisions. He lets Hagrid return to Hogwarts (HP 1, 69), accepts werewolf Lupin as a pupil (HP 3, 383) and employs the liberated house-elves Dobby and Winky (HP 4, 415). He finds caring words for half-giant Maxime

---

[279] Philip Nel compares this powerful eloquence with Churchill: see Nel 2001, 44.
[280] This is a sort of password in human shape: only the "Secret Keeper" knows where the person in question is.
[281] See Lisa Cherrett, *The Triumph of Goodness: Biblical Themes in the Harry Potter Stories*, Oxford: The Bible Reading Fellowship, 2003, 127.
[282] In this *Harry Potter* differs from other great fantasy epics. Tolkien's Gandalf in *Lord of the Rings* would never speak about going to the toilet.
[283] See Bürvenich 2001, 89.

(HP 4, 630) and is one of the few to believe Harry that he is not behind the attacks on students (HP 2, 226). Dumbledore is also among the few wizards to be interested in the "Muggle" world (HP 4, 653). He is even merciful with Kreacher: "'Kreacher is what he has been made by wizards, Harry,' said Dumbledore. 'Yes, he is to be pitied'" (HP 5, 914).[284] Against public opinion he has taken sides with the nearly extinct giants of Great Britain (HP 5, 474). But sometimes even he fails; why does he employ Gilderoy Lockhart? With all his wisdom, Dumbledore should have known him for what he is.[285]

Right until the end of the whole series Harry (and the reader) wonders why Dumbledore trusts Severus Snape. This is especially so when we are led to believe that Snape murders his master in *Half-Blood Prince* and we cannot help but feel it to be an inconsistency in the author's characterisation. There are hints that Snape has saved his life (HP 6, 470-471) and we see that Dumbledore is not in the least ready to discuss the reason for his actions with Harry. He says "'I have been tolerant enough to answer that question already,' said Dumbledore, but he did not sound very tolerant any more. 'My answer has not changed'" (HP 6, 336). When Dumbledore, lying helpless on the floor pleads with Severus who ends up killing him anyway, we cannot but suspect a hidden plan:

> "Severus ..." The sound frightened Harry beyond anything he had experienced all evening. For the first time, Dumbledore was pleading. [...]
> "Severus ... please ..." Snape raised his wand and pointed it directly at Dumbledore. "*Avada Kedavra!*" (HP 6, 556)

The explanation is simple: being condemned to die from the curse hidden in the "Resurrection Stone", Dumbledore asks Snape to kill him to prove himself a reliable follower of Voldemort's and to protect Draco (HP 7, 548-550).

Dumbledore trusts others (HP 4, 497; HP 4, 514) which is why people trust him in return: "You couldn't help trusting Albus Dumbledore, [...]." (HP 3, 102).[286] He makes them feel safe. When forced to temporarily resign his job as headmaster fear spreads through Hogwarts (HP 2, 286). He believes in love as the biggest of all magical powers. Voldemort contradicts him ("'But nothing I have seen in the world has supported your famous pronouncements that love is more powerful than my kind of magic, Dumbledore.'", HP 6, 415). He is forgiving and gentle. When they express his own beliefs, his students may occasionally be allowed to swear ("'I have gone temporarily deaf and haven't any idea what you said, Harry'", HP 4, 494). Criticising him is possible (HP 1, 324-325),

---

[284] Letting Kreacher live and showing him care and affection plays a vital role in finding the locket, one of the "Horcruxes", in *Deathly Hallows* (HP 7, 158).

[285] See Mendlesohn 2004, 175.

[286] Mary Pharr says correctly: "Dumbledore operates by trust as much as by skill [...].", Pharr 2004, 60.

he even encourages the house-elves to call him "a barmy old codger" (HP 4, 416). With such humane attitudes Dumbledore is a natural enemy to Voldemort and his followers, as Draco says openly: "'Father's always said Dumbledore's the worst thing that's ever happened to this place.'" (HP 2, 241-242). Voldemort spitefully calls him a "champion of commoners, of Mudbloods and *Muggles*" (HP 4, 702).

The headmaster is strongly opposed to using physical violence. While he can accept a physical threat upon himself he does not permit any force to be brought to bear upon his students. When Marietta is questioned by Umbridge about "Dumbledore's Army" he intervenes when she threatens the girl:

> A split second later Dumbledore was on his feet, his wand raised [...]. "I cannot allow you to manhandle my students, Dolores," said Dumbledore and, for the first time, he looked angry. (HP 5, 679)

The well-being of his students is most vital to him – he loves and enjoys being a teacher: "'[To] a wizard such as myself, there can be nothing more important than passing on ancient skills, helping hone young minds.'" (HP 6, 414)

Dumbledore is not afraid of death – which sets him apart from Voldemort as he tells the villain frankly: "'Indeed, your failure to understand that there are things much worse than death has always been your greatest weakness – [...].'" (HP 5, 895) He can even speak about his own death with a certain lightness:

> "[...] death is coming for me as surely as the Chudley Cannons will finish bottom of this year's league. I confess I should prefer a quick, painless exit to the protracted and messy affair it will be if, for instance, Greyback is involved [...]." (HP 7, 548)

Dumbledore proves to be rather prophetic, when he foresees what is going to happen. He orders Snape to show that he knows how Harry is going to confront Voldemort:

> "If there comes a time when Lord Voldemort stops sending that snake forth to do his bidding, but keeps it safe beside him, under magical protection, then, I think, it will be safe to tell Harry." (HP 7, 550)

In *Order of the Phoenix* we see Dumbledore emotional and desperate for the first time. He blames himself for Sirius' death and cries (HP 5, 928). He also accuses himself of having paid more attention to Harry's safety than to the well-being of the community on the whole.

> "I cared about you too much, [...]. I cared more for your happiness than your knowing the truth, more for your peace of mind than my plan, more for your life than the lives that might be lost if the plan failed. [...] What did I care if

numbers of nameless and faceless people and creatures were slaughtered in the vague future, if in the here and now you were alive, and well, and happy?" (HP 5, 921)[287]

This understandable behaviour seems a weakness to him, "an old man's mistakes" and "the failings of age" (HP 5, 908). He seems to be old and tired ("The light fell upon Dumbledore, upon the silver of his eyebrows and beard, upon the lines gouged deeply into his face." (HP 5, 908)[288]

Dumbledore's relation with Harry is quite questionable: Harry loves and trusts his headmaster like he would a father. Dumbledore is moved when he hears how Harry has openly insulted Minister for Magic Rufus Scrimgeour and declared himself "Dumbledore's man" (HP 6, 335). First it is Dumbledore that makes Harry feel safe ("'[...] I do not think you need worry about being attacked tonight. [...]. You are with me, [...]. This will do, Harry.'", HP 6, 59). But this changes as Dumbledore weakens. Harry becomes his partner in the search for the "Horcruxes". When they visit the cave where the locket is hidden, Harry becomes Dumbledore's helper and finally his saviour. It is when Harry leads Dumbledore back to Hogwarts that their relationship changes. Dumbledore now feels protected by Harry: "'I am not worried, Harry, [...]. I am with you.'" (HP 6, 540) Now Harry has taken the lead. Nevertheless, this relation temporarily becomes quite questionable in *Deathly Hallows*: when we witness Dumbledore, in Snape's memories, speaking about having kept Harry alive to "die at the right moment" (HP 7, 550) we must regard this (opportunism?) as a betrayal.

Dumbledore's main aim in life is to reconcile "Muggles" and wizards and to prevent Voldemort from returning to power. Therefore, he publicly criticises the ministry and its administration (HP 4, 639) which finally leads to open opposition with Cornelius Fudge:

> "You are blinded," said Dumbledore, his voice rising now, the aura of power around him palpable, his eyes blazing once more, "by the love of the office you hold, Cornelius! You place too much importance, and you always have done, on the so called purity of blood! You fail to recognise that it matters not what someone is born, but what they grow to be! Your Dementor has just destroyed the last remaining member of a pure-blood family as old as any – and see what that man chose to make of his life! I tell you now – take the steps I have suggested, and you will be remembered, in office or out, as one of the bravest and greatest Ministers for Magic we have ever

---

[287] This passage is rather open to interpretation. Nevertheless, I believe that – although we find the Hogwarts headmaster rather fervent in expressing his feelings here – these words could still be tolerable without interpreting them as a declaration of paedophilic love.

[288] "Dumbledore closed his eyes and buried his face in his longfingered hands. Harry watched him, but this uncharacteristic sign of exhaustion, or sadness, or whatever it was from Dumbledore, did not soften him." (HP 5, 917).

known. Fail to act – and history will remember you as the man who stepped aside, and allowed Voldemort a second chance to destroy the world we have tried to rebuild!" (HP 4, 767-768)

Dumbledore believes "it matters not what someone is born, but what they grow to be" and proclaims an ideology of individual responsibility where everyone must choose what to make of his life. It is not his descent but his choices that form a human being. He is not perfect himself, but is able to accept his mistakes. Because he is fallible, he is able to forgive others.[289] Isabelle Smadja calls him a true "humanist".[290] He is the preserver of a positive but realistic attitude to life. Rules are only relevant as long as they are not in conflict with higher, more important principles.[291] For *Harry Potter* Albus Dumbledore is the fixed star of the novels' moral universe, just like the lion Aslan in Lewis' *Chronicles of Narnia* or Gandalf in Tolkien's Middle-Earth.[292] He is more than Harry's mentor – as Gandalf is for Frodo, Dumbledore is the hidden force behind Harry's actions.[293] In the course of the plot he becomes more and more charismatic, his role as grey eminence in the background ever more important.[294] In particular, it is when Dumbledore's actions appear rather questionable in *Deathly Hallows* that his character loses much of its flatness.

Dumbledore's death scene in no way mirrors the character's importance for the series. Again, Rowling misses the chance to write in a grand epic style (II.2.E, 46).

> A jet of green light shot from the end of Snape's wand and hit Dumbledore squarely in the chest. Harry's scream of horror never left him; silent and unmoving, he was forced to watch as Dumbledore was blasted into the air: for a split second he seemed to hang suspended beneath the shining skull, and then he fell slowly backwards, like a great rag doll, over the battlements and out of sight. (HP 6, 556)

Just as short and stereotypical as this scene is Harry's reaction to the death of yet another father figure (see IV.3.A, 156):

> [There] was still no preparation for seeing [Dumbledore] here, spread-eagled, broken: the greatest wizard Harry had ever, or would ever, meet.

---

[289] See Drexler, Wandinger 2004, 33.
[290] Smadja 2001, 3-4.
[291] See Ernould 2003, 200.
[292] See Nicholas Lezard, "Under her spell," *Guardian* 28 June 2003. <http://books.guardian. co.uk/print/0,3858,4700210-99943,00.html> 3 Jan 2008; Mendlesohn 2004, 176.
[293] See Pharr 2004, 61.
[294] See Hiebert Alton 2003, 149.

Dumbledore's eyes were closed; but for the strange angle of his arms and legs, he might have been sleeping. (HP 6, 568)

IV.3.O. Black Dog Star – Sirius Black

Sirius first appears as criminal on the run in *Prisoner of Azkaban*. Only later we get to know that he is the victim of intrigue and, in actual fact, Harry's godfather. This mixture between threat and sympathy is hinted at in his name: Sirius is phonetically identical with "serious"[295] and at the same time a bright star and centre of constellation Canis Major. This is combined with black, which is his surname. The character, thus, unites light and dark.[296]

His outward appearance is rather scary. He is "sunken-faced" (HP 3, 45), and "gaunt" (HP 3, 24; HP 3, 402). His "matted, elbow-length tangle" (HP 3, 24)[297] makes him look shabby. In the context of this character we frequently read phrases referring to death and decay:

> If eyes hadn't been shining out of the deep, dark sockets, he might have been a corpse. The waxy skin was stretched so tigtly over the bones of his face, it looked like a skull. His yellow teeth were bared in a grin. (HP 3, 365)

With "his waxy white skin" he seems "just like [a vampire]." (HP 3, 46)[298] The description which Ron gives after he has seen Black at his bedside at night could embody any sleeper's nightmare:

> [He looked] like a skeleton, with loads of filthy hair [...] holding this great long knife, must've been twelve inches [...] and he looked at me, and I looked at him, and then I yelled, and he scarpered. (HP 3, 293).

His laughter is, like Voldemort's, a "horrible, mirthless" sound, (HP 3, 396) and like a villain he has something snake-like about him when he "hissed so venomously that Pettigrew took a step backwards." (HP 3, 398)

Given this thoroughly negative appearance his transformation into Harry's trustworthy friend is rather astonishing. When he first sees his parents' wedding photos, Sirius appears to be quite friendly to him: "His face wasn't sunken and waxy, but handsome, full of laughter." (HP 3, 230). And when Harry sees him smile for the first time, Sirius becomes a completely different person: "The dif-

---

[295] In *Half-Blood Prince* the "Muggle" Prime Minister reads the name as "Serious" (HP 6, 13).

[296] This also refers to the fact that Sirius is able to transform into a black dog: see Hein 2001, 27.

[297] See also: "long, matted hair" (HP 3, 45); "mass of filthy, matted hair" (HP 3, 365); "long dark hair falling aroand his grinning face" (HP 5, 334).

[298] There are other references to him being corpse-like: "bony hand" (HP 3, 392); "face more skull-like than ever" (HP 3, 396); "that deadened, haunted look." (HP 4, 364).

ference it made was startling, as though a person ten years younger was shining through the starved mask [...]." (HP 3, 408). A few months later the traces of his time in Azkaban are gone:

> [...] the hair was short and clean now, Sirius' face was fuller, and he looked younger, much more like the only photograph Harry had of him, which had been taken at the Potters' wedding. (HP 4, 364).[299]

Only in *Order of the Phoenix* does the reader get to know Sirius' family background. The Blacks are an ancient pure-blood family of wizards quite attached to Voldemort (HP 5, 90). The motto of the "Noble and Most Ancient House of Black" is "Toujours pur" (HP 5, 127) – "always pure" – and expresses their racist attitude. Sirius is Narcissa Malfoy's (see IV.3.L, 231) and Bellatrix Lestrange's cousin (HP 5, 131). Full of hatred for his parents and their ideology, he leaves home at the age of sixteen: "'Because I hated the whole lot of them: my parents, with their pure-blood mania, convinced that to be a Black made you practically royal ... my idiot brother, soft enough to believe them ...'". Sirius goes to live with Harry's grandparents, the Potters. One year later he has his own flat.

His brother Regulus Black[300] at first lives up to his parents' expectations and goes to join the "Death Eaters", but turns against Voldemort the moment he personally experiences his master's sadistic cruelty. He and his house-elf Kreacher get the "Horcrux" locket from the cave and Regulus sacrifices his life drinking the poison in which it is hidden (HP 7, "Kreacher's Tale"). For his family he simply disappears and it is commonly believed that he was killed by Voldemort's followers for treason (HP 5, 127-128).

Sirius is the last surviving heir and full of hatred for his family. He says about his mother: "'My mother didn't have a heart [...]. She kept herself alive out of pure spite.'" (HP 5, 125) Cleaning up his parent's house is, most of all, a means of taking revenge on his family, especially when members of the order throw away the possessions of its former inhabitants. (HP 5, 133)

Sirius stands on the positive side of the character pattern. He is intelligent,[301] and does not stick to rules. Cornelius Fudge relates how an apparently

---

[299] This quick recovery is not quite convincing considering the horrors of Azkaban (see III.5.H, 137) and the fact that Sirius has been in prison for more than twelve years.

[300] The name hints at his being very law-abiding.

[301] McGonagall says of Sirius and his friend James Potter: "'Ringleaders of their little gang. Both very bright, of course – exceptionally bright, in fact – but I don't think we've ever had such a pair of troublemakers [...].'"(HP 3, 211). Remus Lupin goes even further and says: "'Your father and Sirius here were the cleverest students in the school, [...].'" (HP 3, 381).

unaltered Sirius endures his emprisonment in Azkaban.[302] Black is one of the few characters who dares to pronounce Voldemort's full name (HP 4, 367). He represents bravery and audacity. When Fred and George fear for their father's life he explains: "'[There] are things worth dying for!'" (HP 5, 525) He even supports the secret students' society "Dumbledore's Army", because: "'Well, better expelled and able to defend yourselves than sitting safely in school without a clue'", (HP 5, 410-411).

Rowling's dealing with Sirius is yet another example of how she artfully gives the readers false clues to raise wrong expectations.[303] We get to know the character via comments by other characters and all seem to agree that he is a dangerous criminal. A worried mother says: "'I won't let any of the children out alone until he's back in Azkaban.'" (HP 3, 8) On the radio he is said to be "armed and extremely dangerous" (HP 3, 23), the "Daily Prophet" calls him *"possibly the most infamous prisoner ever to be held in Azkaban fortress"* (HP 3, 46) and Fudge makes a statement that Black is mentally disturbed and *"'a danger to anyone who crosses him, magic or Muggle.'"* (HP 3, 46) Stan Shunpike, working on the "Knight Bus" tells Harry (and the reader) that "'Black woz a big supporter of You-Know-'Oo'" (HP 3, 47) and Arthur Weasley tells his wife he firmly believes Black is intending to kill Harry (HP 3, 75). But this very clear image is destroyed *peu à peu*. In Hogsmeade, Harry listens to a talk in the "Three Broomsticks" (HP 3, 220-223): Black was very unlikely to work for Voldemort. He was the Potters' best man, godfather to their son and their "Secret Keeper". When Hagrid tells the group that he met Black crying in the ruins of the Potters' house after their death (HP 3, 224), the reader begins to suspect that their is more to Black and tension is raised. How are these different views of the same character going to be explained? Finally, it is Remus Lupin who tells Harry Sirius' true story. (HP 3, 382-384).

In *Order of the Phoenix* we learn that Sirius has his bad character traits. In his "Occlumency" lessons Harry witnesses him and his father tormenting Snape (HP 5, 708-711). Lupin confirms: "'[Your] father and Sirius were the best in the school at whatever they did – everyone thought they were the height of cool – if they sometimes got a bit carried away – [...]'" (HP 5, 737).[304] And Sirius' treatment of Kreacher, his dead mother's house-elf, is just as bad and makes him appear a rather heartless person. When Kreacher is missed he cynically says: "'Of

---

[302] "'I was shocked at how normal Black seemed. He spoke quite rationally to me. [...] asked if I'd finished with my newspaper, cool as you please, said he missed doing the crosswords. Yes, I was astounded at how little effect the Dementors seemed to be having on him [...].'" (HP 3, 227). Later we learn that this "being normal" is due to Sirius' ability to turn into a dog that cannot be affected by the "Dementors".

[303] These false clues are typical for detective stories (see II.1.B, 31).

[304] Sirius confirms this: "'No one would have made me a prefect, I spent too much time in detention with James. Lupin was the good boy, he got the badge.'" (HP 5, 191).

course, he might have crawled into the airing cupboard and died ... but I mustn't get hopes up.'" (HP 5, 556)[305]

Sirius tends to be hot-tempered and thoughtless. Mrs Weasley tells him "'Meaning you have been known to act rashly, [...]'" (HP 5, 104). And he becomes even more so when he has to stay in his parents' house for safety reasons instead of fighting Voldemort.[306] He turns bitter and there are many references to his bad, i.e. depressed, mood to be found in the text. His voice sounds "hard and bitter" (HP 5, 91), he "smiled sadly" (HP 5, 132) and is speaking "gloomily" (HP 5, 132) with a "definite note of bitterness in [his] voice" (HP 5, 337). He becomes sarcastic (HP 5, 99). He even admits to appreciating a "Dementor's" attack to end his apparently useless existence ("'Personally, I'd have welcomed a Dementor attack. A deadly struggle for my soul would have broken the monotony nicely.'", HP 5, 96). Hermione is the only one to be able to explain his feelings:

> "[He] probably felt a bit guilty himself, because I think a part of him was really hoping you'd be expelled. Then you'd both be outcasts together. [...] Sirius gets confused about whether you're you or your father, Harry." (HP 5, 178)

And it is also Hermione who suspects Sirius' true ideas about "Dumbledore's Army":

> "You don't think he has become ... sort of ... reckless ... since he's been cooped up in Grimmauld Place? You don't think he's ... kind of ... living through us? [...] I think he's really frustrated at how little he can do where he is ... so I think he's keen to kind of ... egg us on." (HP 5, 417)

It is important for the interpretation of the whole series that Sirius dies because he is proud, inhumane and treats his inferiors badly. His pride not being satisfied, he tries to provoke pointlessly dangerous situations like accompanying Harry to King's Cross – this is where Lucius Malfoy recognises him (HP 5, 574). His inability to be polite with Kreacher makes the elf betray him. Only because of this treason is Voldemort able to lure Harry into the "Department of Mysteries". But even this does not lead automatically to Sirius' death. Again it

---

[305] Dumbledore explains to Harry: "'Sirius was not a cruel man, he was kind to house-elves in general. He had no love for Kreacher, because Kreacher was a living reminder of the home Sirius had hated.'" (HP 5, 916).

[306] He is especially unhappy that his arch-enemy Severus Snape is allowed to work for the order: "'There's not much I can do for the Order of the Phoenix ... or so Dumbledore feels. [...] Listening to Snape's reports, having to take all his snide hints that he's out there risking his life while I'm sat on my backside here having a nice comfortable time ... asking me how he cleaning's going –'" (HP 5, 97). Snape provokes him: "'[...] I know you like to feel ... involved.'" (HP 5, 571).

is his misplaced belief in his own invulnerability which makes him an easy target in the duel with his cousin Bellatrix:[307]

> Harry saw Sirius duck Bellatrix's jet of red light; he was laughing at her. "Come on, you can do better than that!" he yelled, his voice echoing around the cavernous room. The second jet of light hit him squarely on the chest. The laughter had not quite died from his face, but his eyes widened in shock. [...] It seemed to take Sirius an age to fall: his body curved in a graceful arc as he sank backwards through the ragged veil hanging from the arch. (HP 5, 886)

IV.4 First-order Minor Characters

Among the First-order Minor Characters are (a) the characters that have less text dedicated to them than the main characters and that (b) are protagonists of a sub-plot (see IV.1.A, 146). Among these I count Rubeus Hagrid, Gilderoy Lockhart, Remus Lupin, Sybill Trelawney, Harry's parents and Neville Longbottom. Likewise I am going to include the Dursleys whom I will describe in the context of "Muggles" in general. These characters differ from the Second-Order Minor Characters in that they do play an important role in one of the sub-plots.

IV.4.A. The Trouble With … – Rubeus Hagrid

Hagrid is – above all else – one thing: big. Only in *Goblet of Fire* do we learn that he is a half-giant and, thus, part of an ethnic minority which is discriminated against. His mother was the giant Fridwulfa[308] (HP 4, 479):

> "It was my mother [...]. She was one o' the las' ones in Britain. 'Course, I can' remember her too well ... she left, see. When I was abou' three. She wasn' really the maternal sort. [...] Me dad was broken-hearted when she wen'. Tiny little bloke, my dad was. By the time I was six I could lift him up an' put him on top o' the dresser if he annoyed me. Used ter make him laugh ... [...] Dad raised me ... but he died, o' course, jus' after I started school. Sorta had ter make me own way after that. Dumbledore was a real help, mind. Very kind ter me, he was ..." (HP 4, 467)

For Voldemort's supporters Hagrid is a "mudblood" because of his non-wizard descent.[309] The "Keeper of Keys and Grounds" of Hogwarts (HP 1, 57) (we do not learn what this really means)[310] is intimidatingly big and looks wild:

---

[307] Dumbledore defends Sirius and blames himself for risking his life: "'Sirius was a brave, clever and energetic man, and such men are not usually content to sit at home in hiding while they believe others to be in danger.'" (HP 5, 907). In fact, the character dies because of its bad character traits.

[308] The name is Germanic and means something like "friendly she-wolf": see Hein 2001, 74.

He was almost twice as tall as a normal man and at least five times as wide. He looked simply too big to be allowed, and so WILD – long tangles of bush black hair and beard hid most of his face, he had hands the size of dustbin lids and his feet in their leather boots were like baby dolphins. (HP 1, 21)[311]

Characteristics of his looks are his height,[312] black hair and beard[313] and his "beetle-black eyes" (HP 2, 63).[314] Even when Hagrid tries to improve his rather shabby looks he fails; he simply does not have any taste.[315]

As with all the other characters, Hagrid's name is part of his characterisation. "Hag-rid" literally means bewitched or tormented by nightmares. Rowling says the word is taken from Old English without indicating the direct source.[316] *Rubeus* is Latin and either a form of *rubēre* (being red), *ruber* (red) or directly takgen from *rubeus* (coming from a bramble bush).[317] George Beahm sees the name derived from "rube", which is applied to a rather uneducated and unpolished person.[318]

In his third year at Hogwarts, Hagrid was wrongly accused of opening the secret chamber and unleashing the Basilisk. Tom Riddle saw to his being expelled. In later years, Dumbledore admitted him back to Hogwarts as gamekeeper (HP 1, 69). Nevertheless, Hagrid is not allowed to do magic – however, he does it anyway and carries his wand with him disguised as a pink umbrella (HP 2, 129).

Rowling makes his language an important means of characterisation. She reproduces a sociolect which omits the final consonants[319] (see II.2.H, 55). This makes Hagrid appear uneducated and seems to meet the prejudices against giants and his person in particular, as Farah Mendlesohn criticises:

---

[309] Draco calls Hagrid "riff-raff" (HP 1, 120).
[310] See Bürvenich 2001, 83.
[311] Also HP 1, 55.
[312] Also HP 1, 325.
[313] "shaggy mane of hair and a wild, tangled beard" (HP 1, 55); "his great bristling beard" (HP 2, 63); "shaggy black hair" (HP 2, 226).
[314] We also find "beetleblack eyes" (HP 3, 133) and "like black beetles" (HP 1, 55).
[315] When dressing up to impress Mme Maxime the result is not very satisfying: "Hagrid was wearing his best (and very horrible) hairy brown suit, plus a checked yellow-and-orange tie. [...] he had evidently tried to tame his hair using large quantities of what appeared to be axle grease. It was now slicked down into two bunches [...]." (HP 4, 290).
[316] See Dresang 2004, 212.
[317] See "*rubēre, ruber*" and "*rubeus*", Stowasser 1980, 402.
[318] See Beahm 2005, 101.
[319] See also "'Shoulda known!'" (HP 5, 465).

[... His] lack of intelligence and self-control actually *fulfill* the stereotypes associated with his ethnicity, thus permitting Harry and his friends to demonstrate their 'tolerance' and to show that Harry is a 'good chap'.[320]

It seems quite unlikely that having been and lived in Hogwarts for such a long time he should not have adapted linguistically to the well-educated majority. "Whatever his social origins, association with the school would have changed that to some degree." Again, Farah Mendlesohn is absolutely right.[321] Hagrid lacks true intelligence and influence. As soon as he tries to act on his own account, he makes things worse. Harry and his friends usually have to come to his rescue, as for example in the episode regarding the dragon Norbert in *Philosopher's Stone*. He is like a child – a sharp contrast to the apparently grown up and rational children from middle-class backgrounds.[322] Hagrid is emotional and very sensitive, a sentimental child.[323] His simplicity is reflected in *Deathly Hallows* when he is on the run for celebrating a "Support Harry Potter" party in Hogwarts (HP 7, 358) and when he tries to protect the giant spiders in the last battle (HP 7, 519-520). Moreover, he is very loyal to Dumbledore[324] and becomes aggressive when he faces Voldemort's supporters.[325] Bravely he fights for his friends.[326] But his naïveté and talkativeness make him a security problem. First he tells the children that Nicolas Flamel is part of the secrecy surrounding the closed corridor in *Philosopher's Stone* (HP 1, 286), then he explains to a complete stranger how to get around the three-headed dog (HP 1, 209). He likes being flattered (HP 1, 251) and believes in authorities.[327] Hagrid is compassionate with all living beings[328] and just loves magical creatures.[329] The biggest at-

---

[320] Mendlesohn 2004, 166.

[321] Mendlesohn 2004, 166.

[322] Mendlesohn 2004, 166.

[323] See Bürvenich 2001, 86.

[324] Hagrid says to Mr Dursley: "'Never-' he thundered, '-insult-Albus-Dumbledore-in-front-of-me!'" (HP 1, 68).

[325] "'If I'd got ter Black before little Pettigrew did, I wouldn't've messed around with wands – I'd've ripped him limb – from – limb.'" (HP 3, 226).

[326] Hagrid would testify for Harry (HP 2, 226). And Harry says "Hagrid was one of the bravest people Harry knew." (HP 3, 49). Dumbledore trusts him blind: "I would trust Hagrid with my life,' said Dumbledore." (HP 1, 21).

[327] "It was most unlike Hagrid to criticise a Hogwarts teacher [...]." (HP 2, 126).

[328] Even the giant spider Aragog says of Hagrid "'Hagrid is my good friend, and a good man.'" (HP 2, 299). Lovingly he calls Buckbeak "Beaky" – which seems a bit out of place for such a dangerous animal (HP 3, 315). In *Deathly Hallows* we see him trying to rescue the giant spiders (HP 7, 519-520).

[329] "Hagrid had an unfortunate liking for large and monstrous creatures. [...] And if, as a boy, Hagrid had heard that a monster was hidden somewhere in the castle, Harry was sure he'd have gone to any lengths for a glimpse of it." (HP 2, 269). At school he used to

tention Hagrid can pay a person is only to be compared with the care he shows for his favourite animals: Harry sees him looking at Mme Maxime "with a rapt, misty-eyed expression Harry had only ever seen him wear once before – when he had been looking at the baby dragon, Norbert." (HP 4, 293) From this journey he takes back his half-brother Grawp and hides him in the Forbidden Forest. Against the odds, the giant proves to be intelligible and saves Harry and Hermione from the centaurs (HP 5, 832-834). Without Grawp's interference both would have suffered the same fate as Dolores Umbridge. So the plot, i.e. poetic justice, rewards Hagrid's compassionate attitude.

Yet, Hagrid's qualifcations as a teacher remain doubtful. Whereas Luna Lovegood believes him to be a rather bad teacher (HP 5, 223), his substitute Grubbly-Plank tells inspector Umbridge that his class has been very well instructed (HP 5, 358-359). His own love for magical creatures makes him forget the dangers which some of his study objects provide for students[330] – some of them even get hurt, like Draco Malfoy in *Prisoner of Azkaban*. Students he does not like are criticised harshly: "'Now, if yeh've finished askin' stupid questions, follow me!'" (HP 5, 489) His influence on the children is rather bad, because he tends to get them into extremely dangerous situations, for example confronting them with self-bred magical creatures (Blast-Ended Skrewts) in *Order of the Phoenix*.[331] Dolores Umbridge puts him "on probation" because of her own prejudices against half-giants (HP 5, 605).

Hagrid is quite a simple, unsurprising character. He does not develop but remains static and flat. Even in *Order of the Phoenix* when Hagrid and Mme Maxime try to win the giants' support he remains rather flat and is limited to some rather superficial features: big, coarse, emotional, just. He is an important helper of Harry's. Michael Maar identifies quite a plausible parallel to Christian mythology: the giant Christopher carries Christ through a river. He is the patron saint of pilots, drivers and captains, and usually carries a stick with him. The giant Hagrid saves Harry using a flying motorbike and later he evacuates him from an island. He frequently carries a pink umbrella – his hidden wand.[332] This may make Hagrid just another Christopher.

---

get into trouble for this "'[He was] in trouble every other week, trying to raise werewolf cubs under his bed, sneaking off to the Forbidden Forest to wrestle trolls.'" (HP 2, 335).

[330] Ron complains: "'[Hagrid] always thinks monsters aren't as bad as they're made out, [...].'" (HP 2, 302). He finds the biting school books he has chosen for his class amusing – even if some of his students are hurt by them (HP 3, 125).

[331] See Bürvenich 2001, 86.

[332] See Maar 2003, 60.

222

IV.4.B. Impostor and Popstar – Gilderoy Lockhart

Nomen est omen – pretension and imposture are already to be found in the character's name. It unites French *roi* (= king) and German *gülden* (= golden) and makes its bearer a "golden king". Gilderoy also is the name of a Scottish robber who was famous for his good looks and who was eventually hanged because of his crimes.[333] Lockhart is a city in Australia close to Wagga Wagga where Lockhart claims to have wrestled with a werewolf.[334] The phonetical parallels with "to lock" and "heart" make him appear heartless, which in fact he is. Lockhart is a flat character, but highly amusing. Michael Maar compares him to the stereotypes of Dickens or Thackeray.[335]

The best-selling author (one of his works is a biography with the title "Magical Me", HP 2, 67) has written a whole series of more or less useful household books ("Gilderoy Lockhart's Guide to household Pests", HP 2, 43) and is "a very good-looking wizard with wavy blond hair and bright blue eyes [...]" (HP 2, 43) who even manages to charm Mrs Weasley.[336] He loves fashionable clothes and prefers bright colours,[337] especially lilac (HP 2, 111).

> The real Lockhart was wearing robes of forget-me-not blue which exactly matched his eyes; his pointed wizard's hat was set at a jaunty angle on his wavy hair. (HP 2, 68).[338]

One of his vanities is his "enormous loopy signature" (HP 2, 178) and his decorating his classroom with many of his portraits that are constantly combing and looking into mirrors (HP 2, 155-156). Lockhart usually has a bunch of photos bearing his signature on him.[339]

But he is not only vain in his appearance – he is also presumptuous in his behaviour, trying to instruct Mme Sprout (HP 2, 100) and Hagrid (HP 2, 125). Snape reacts appropriately and tells him: "'Excuse me,' said Snape icily, 'but I

---

[333] See Hein 2001, 90.
[334] See Hein 2001, 90.
[335] See Maar 2003, 44.
[336] "'Oh, he is marvellous,' she said." (HP 2, 43).
[337] Here we find one of the rare authorial comments: "It was remarkable how he could show every one of those brilliant teeth even when he wasn't talking." (HP 2, 101). The constantly glittering teeth work as *pars pro toto* when Harry recognises Lockhart by his "glitter of teeth" (HP 2, 188).
[338] This ridiculous vanity is a running gag in *Chamber of Secrets*. It is reported that Lockhart frequently changes his robes: "sweeping robes of turquoise, his golden hair shining under a perfectly positioned turquoise hat with gold trimming" (HP 2, 100); "robes of aquamarine" (HP 2, 86); "robes of deep plum" (HP 2, 205); "lurid pink robes to match the [Valentine] decorations" (HP 2, 255); "robes of palest mauve" (HP 2, 125).
[339] "Shining brightly on the walls [...] were countless framed photographs of Lockhart. He had even signed a few of them. Another large pile lay on his desk." (HP 2, 131).

believe I am the Potions master at this school.'" (HP 2, 158) Lockhart can be assured of his colleagues' opprobrium.[340]

He is a master of self-promotion and Harry is merely an instrument from which to gain even more popularity: "'Together, you and I are worth the front page.'" (HP 2, 69) He loses any tact when reminding Harry that he, Lockhart, is already an internationally famous wizard whereas Harry (who has defeated Voldemort) is less popular.[341]

> "[...] I know what you're thinking! 'It's all right for him, he's an internationally famous wizard already!' [...] a few people have heard of you, haven't they? [...] it's not quite as good as winning *"Witch Weekly"'s* Most-Charming-Smile Award five times in a row, as I have – but it's a *start*, Harry, it's a *start*." (HP 2, 101-102)

His self-importance is at its height when he makes himself a subject of his lessons,[342] asks his own students fifty-four questions about his person in an exam (HP 2, 111), or rewards the top student with a signed edition of his autobiography (HP 2, 177). Lockhart uses just about any pretext to speak about his heroic deeds[343] and loves to exaggerate.

At the same time, he is an impostor – he only became a teacher at Hogwarts as a result of Quirrell's death the year before and the job is supposed to be jinxed, so no one else dares to accept it (HP 2, 126). Despite his obvious incompetence[344] he is able, for a long time, to bluff his way through the Hogwarts

---

[340] Full of hatred his colleagues make use of this opportunity to unmask him: "[...] the other teachers were looking at him with something remarkably like hatred." (HP 2, 316); despite Lockhart's laments they remain "stony-faced" (HP 2, 317).

[341] Yet another proof of his presumptuousness is the most embarrassing Valentine's Day he initiates (HP 2, 255-258).

[342] "[He] read passages from his books to them, and sometimes re-enacted some of the more dramatic bits. He usually picked Harry to help him with these reconstructions; [...]." (HP 2, 176).

[343] "'[...] another village will remember me forever as the hero who delivered them from the monthly terror of werewolf attacks.'" (HP 2, 177). "'[...] to defend yourselves as I myself have done on countless occasions – for full details, see my published works.'" (HP 2, 206). Writing a get-well card to Hermione he mentions all his honours (HP 2, 247). He even pretends to be an excellent "Quidditch" player and tries to instruct Harry: "'I was asked to try for the National Squad, but preferred to dedicate my life to the eradication of the Dark Forces. [...] Always happy to pass on my expertise to less able players ...'" (HP 2, 178).

[344] He unleashes completely harmless Cornish Pixies and proves to be unable to get rid of them. The little creatures wreck the classroom (HP 2, 113). Seeing Filch's petrified cat he speculates absurdly about the reasons (HP 2, 155). And instead of helping Harry after his "Quidditch" accident, he uses the wrong charm and makes all his bones disappear (HP 2, 188-190). Another good example for Lockhart's incompetence is his duel with

community, especially so with the female students. Ron and Harry realise long before Hermione does that Lockhart is a fraud.[345] And even Lockhart himself seems to realise, in a way, that he is utterly incompetent: when his "Memory Charm" backfires on him he is "humming placidly to himself" (HP 2, 348) and wondering: "'Am I a Professor? [...] I expect I was hopeless, was I?'" (HP 2, 355)

This mixture between incompetence, arrogance and imposture not only makes him an amusing eccentric, but also a serious threat to his pupils when he is willing to sacrifice their lives for his stardom (HP 2, 321; 326). In fact, he has not done any of his heroic deeds himself, but has stolen all the stories, using "Memory Charms" on the true heroes. Lockhart is a lying coward. Making use of the structures of the book market he has stylised himself a hero. He has realised that society does not appreciate true achievement, but image and public relations:[346]

> "Books can be misleading, [...]. My books wouldn't have sold half as well if people didn't think *I'd* done all those things. No one wants to read about some ugly old Armenian warlock, even if he did save a village from werewolves. He'd look dreadful on the front cover. No dress sense at all. And the witch who banished the Bandon Banshee had a hare lip. [...] If there's one thing I pride myself on, it's my Memory Charms." (HP 2, 320)

In *Order of the Phoenix* Rowling lets Lockhart reappear – which is not a very happy narrative move.[347] When Harry, Ron and Hermione meet him on the closed ward of St Mungo's he seems completely unchanged: "He had wavy blond hair, bright blue eyes and a broad vacant smile that revealed dazzlingly white teeth." (HP 5, 560) He still loves to give autographs ("'Now, how many autographs would you like? I can do joined-up writing now, you know!'", HP 5, 561) and reacts quite boastfully when told of his teaching life at Hogwarts: "'Taught you everything you know, I expect, did I?'" (HP 5, 561) He still

---

Snape where he first is disarmed by Snape (HP 2, 207), loses his wand (HP 2, 210) and later throws the snake conjured by Draco into the students' crowd (HP 2, 211).

[345] After the disaster with the Cornish Pixies Harry explains to Hermione: "'Hermione, he didn't have a clue what he was doing.' 'Rubbish,' said Hermione. 'You've read his books – look at all those amazing things he's done ...' 'He says he's done,' Ron muttered. " (HP 2, 114). Ron: "'[...] he's a brainless git, [...]'"; Hermione: "'He is not a brainless git, [...].'" (HP 2, 178). Ron: "'I haven't learned anything from him except not to set pixies loose.'" (HP 2, 271). Hagrid: "'If one word of it was true, I'll eat my kettle.'" (HP 2, 126).

[346] Rowling has frequently said Lockhart represents a living person: "I assure you that the person on whom Gilderoy was modelled was even more objectionable than his fictional counterpart. He used to tell whopping great fibs about his past life, all of them designed to demonstrate what a wonderful, brave and brilliant person he was." (Rowling 2006).

[347] This is very likely not due to narrative necessity but to the character's enormous success. Principally, it was Kenneth Branagh's interpretation of Lockhart in the 2002 film version which has contributed to the character's popularity.

receives fan mail, but does not know why: "'I am not forgotten, you know, no, I still receive a very great deal of fan mail ... Gladys Gudgeon writes *weekly* ... I just wish I knew *why* ... [...] I suspect it is simply my good looks ...'" (HP 5, 563). The healers hope for him to get better: "'He was rather well known a few years ago; we very much hope that this liking for giving autographs is a sign that his memory might be starting to come back.'" (HP 5 562) Lockhart loses his memory forever. This is his poetic justice. His self-love, cruelty and unscrupulousness make him lose his mind.

IV.4.C. Hostile Martyr – Severus Snape

Severus Snape remains a highly ambivalent character right up until the end of *Deathly Hallows*. Dying a martyr's death, he finally reveals his innermost memories and feelings to Harry, and makes us understand his actions (HP 7, "The Prince's Tale"). For a long time, Rowling keeps us in the dark about Snape: a former "Death Eater", alleged murderer of Dumbledore and arch-enemy of Harry's, at the same time he is a member of the "Order of the Phoenix" and Harry's saviour in *Philosopher's Stone* and *Half-Blood Prince* (HP 6, 563) – we simply do not know what to make of Snape.

Severus is Latin and means "severe", which seems an appropriate name for him. Combined with the verb "to snap" the name fits him very well.[348] Phonetically the name also alludes to "snake", the symbol of evil. His nickname "Snivellus" (HP 5, 573) might come from "to snivel" and mark him a coward. Rowling herself has explained the name was taken from a town in Great Britain.[349]

Snape is a cool, unkempt and apparently evil character. His voice is "very cold" (HP 2, 87) or even "icy" (HP 4, 559), his black hair is greasy, his nose hooked: "[His] black robes [were] rippling in a cold breeze [...]. He was a thin man with sallow skin, a hooked nose and greasy, shoulderlength black hair [...]." (HP 2, 87)[350] Again it is his glittering black eyes that tell us all about Snape's

---

[348] See Hein 2001, 136.

[349] See Dresang 2004, 212. 25 miles north of Ipswich there is a village called Snape. On its website (<http://www.snapevillage.org.uk> 31 Jan 2006) the municipality explicity says it does not provide any information on Rowling's character Severus Snape. Instead, they offer a link to Rowling's website.

[350] See also: "[...] a teacher with greasy black hair, a hooked nose and swallow skin" (HP 1, 138); "dark, greasy-haired head and prominent nose" (HP 5, 89). Philip Nel criticises Rowling for making Snape corresponding to classical representation of Jews (see Nel 2001, 34). I do not see any point in this criticism. If Snape was meant to resemble antisemitic stereotypes, there would have to be more elements than just his features: The classical anti-Semitic stereotype includes avarice, enterprise and cunning.

character, they are frequently mentioned (for example HP 2, 157 and HP 5, 584).[351] This glittering can be poisonous[352] or even mad (HP 3, 388).

Snape's smile – so characteristic of every character – is "nasty" (HP 2, 158), "thin-lipped" (HP 2, 288), "unpleasant" (HP 3, 136) and at times "horrible" (HP 3, 308; HP 5, 259). Smiling, he shows his "uneven, yellowish teeth" (HP 3, 309). Frequently we find terms like "ugly flush" (HP 5, 571) or "low, dangerous voice" (HP 5, 650) applied to him. When in rage he is completely out of control: "Snape's lips were shaking, his face was white, his teeth were bared." (HP 5, 714-715)

Being led to believe that he is an evil character, we only realise in *Deathly Hallows* what a tragic character he is: the son of Eileen Prince and "Muggle" Tobias Snape (HP 6, 594). The marriage of his parents not being a very happy one, he experienced domestic violence in his childhood and remains an outsider:

> [A] hook-nosed man was shouting at a cowering woman, while a small dark-haired boy cried in the corner ... a greasy haired teenager sat alone in a dark bedroom, pointing his wand at the ceiling, shooting down flies ... a girl was laughing as a scrawny boy tried to mount a bucking broomstick –
> (HP 5, 651)

Already as a boy, Severus is a rather unkempt and neglected person:

> Snape-the-teenager had a stringy, pallid look about him, like a plant kept in the dark. His hair was lank and greasy and was flopping on to the table, his hooked nose barely half an inch from the surface of the parchment as he scribbled. [...] Round-shouldered, yet angular, he walked in a twitchy manner that recalled a spider, and his oily hair was jumping about his face. (HP 5, 705-707)

In *Deathly Hallows* we learn that he grew up in the neighbourhood of the Evans family and fell in love with one of their daughters – Lily, Harry's mother. He recognised her as a witch and revealed to her that she was about to be invited to attend Hogwarts. Lily did not want to disappoint her sister Petunia in the first place and was offended by his revelation (HP 7, 534-536). Later, when the two children went to Hogwarts together, Severus was sorted into Slytherin, Lily into Gryffindor. The Gryffindors around James Potter and his friends used to bully Snape as we learn from Harry's "Occlumency" experiences with Snape in *Order of the Phoenix* (HP 5, 711-713). Feeling ashamed of his status as a non-pure-

---

[351] See also HP 3, 140; HP 3, 185; HP 3, 307; HP 5, 651 and "cold black eyes fixed unblinkingly upon Harry, dislike etched in every line of his face." (HP 5, 584).

[352] "a look of pure venom" (HP 2, 91); "Snape was looking murderous." (HP 2, 207); "His black eyes were alight with malice." (HP 4, 303); "[The] black eyes [were] flashing dangerously." (HP 3, 308).

blood wizard he begins to call himself "Half-Blood Prince" – using his mother's maiden name "Prince" (HP 6, 594).

Over the years, Severus became fascinated with the "Dark Arts" and associated with people subscribing to racist ideas. One day, Severus calls Lily a "Mudblood" which causes the breaking of their friendship (HP 7, 540-542). Nevertheless, Snape is going to love Lily for all of his life – he has the same "Patronus" as Lily Evans, a silver-white doe (HP 7, 551-552; 593). Even when she marries James Potter and has a child, he never stops loving her. Having finished his education at Hogwarts he becomes a follower of Voldemort and, thus, a "Death Eater". He is the one to eavesdrop on Dumbledore and to betray Trelawney's prophecy to Voldemort (HP 6, 511-513). But then he is shocked to find that his master interprets it as referring to Lily Evans and her baby boy and intends to kill the whole family. Severus pleads with him to spare Lily while killing the boy, but Voldemort refuses. Fearing for his love he resorts to Dumbledore who seizes the opportunity to turn Severus against Voldemort. Dumbledore promises to hide the family – if Snape is willing to change sides (HP 7, 543-544). Astonishingly, Snape asks him for secrecy (HP 7, 544-545) and stays in Hogwarts as "Potions" teacher – in *Order of the Phoenix* we hear that he has been teaching there for fourteen years (HP 5, 402). A year later he becomes teacher for "Defence Against the Dark Arts" (HP 6, 158-159) and finally, after Dumbledore's death, headmaster (HP 7, 186).

To get into the inner circle of Voldemort's followers he must come up with a lie about his career as double agent, and promises Narcissa Malfoy to help Draco to murder Dumbledore (HP 6, 41). In fact, *he* is the one to kill the headmaster (HP 6, 556) and Harry, i.e. the reader, is led to believe that Snape has gone over to the side of evil. Only in one of the last chapters of *Deathly Hallows* ("The Prince's Tale") do we get to know what really happened.

Dumbledore had been fatally wounded putting on Slytherin's cursed ring, so he decided to use his own death to install Snape as a trustworthy follower of Voldemort's and to secure the school's future. When the time comes, Dumbledore asks Snape to kill him, thus to save his intended murderer Draco's soul, and to help him "avoid pain and humiliation" when he is condemned to die a painful death from the curse (HP 7, 547-548) He also asks Snape to "'do all in your power to protect the students of Hogwarts'" (HP 7, 547), which is why Snape becomes headmaster. Being part of Voldemort's death squads, Snape has always tried to help the members of the "Order of the Phoenix" (HP 7, 552-553), Harry's friends and Harry himself: he does not betray Harry's and Hermione's whereabouts to Voldemort (HP 7, 553) and leads Harry, on Dumbledore's orders (HP 7, 553), to Gryffindor's sword (HP 7, 298). He even tells Phineas Nigellus off for calling Hermione a "Mudblood" (HP 7, 553). He does all of this out of love for Lily Potter, whose signature he carries with him like a talisman (HP 7, 552-553).

This makes him more furious when he learns that Dumbledore's plan for destroying Voldemort includes Harry's death. In the following dialogue, Snape apparently cares much more for the boy than Dumbledore does:

> "I thought ... all these years ... that we were protecting him for her. For Lily." "We have protected him because it has been essential to teach him, to raise him, to let him try his strength, [...]." [...] "You have kept him alive so that he can die at the right moment?" "Don't be shocked Severus. How many men and women have you watched die?" [...] "Everything was supposed to be to keep Lily Potter's son safe. Now you tell me you have been raising him like a pig for slaughter –" "But this is touching, Severus," said Dumbledore seriously. "Have you grown to care for the boy, after all?" (HP 7, 550)

Nevertheless, everything comes as planned by Dumbledore and Snape is able to penetrate Voldemort's inner circle. With Snape's having apparently killed Dumbledore, the villain holds him for the true owner of the "Elder Wand". He believes this to be the reason why he cannot master the wand himself and plans to kill Snape. The flaw in Voldemort's plan is that Harry is the true owner of the wand, because he defeated Draco (HP 7, 595). So Voldemort kills Snape:

> "There was a terrible scream. Harry saw Snape's face losing the little colour it had left, it whitened as his black eyes widened, as the snake's fangs pierced his neck, as he failed to push the enchanted cage off himself, as his knees gave way, and he fell to the floor." (HP 7, 527)

Dying he gives his memories, i.e. the answers to all questions, to Harry (HP 7, 528).

> When the flask was full to the brim, and Snape looked as though there was no blood left in him, his grip on Harry's robes slackened. "Look ... at ... me ..." he whispered. The green eyes found the black, but after a second something in the depths of the dark pair seemed to vanish, leaving them fixed, blank and empty. The hand holding Harry thudded to the floor, and Snape moved no more. (HP 7, 528)

In his last moments, Snape sees Lily Potter in Harry's eyes. Only then does Harry realise the heroic aspect to Snape's character. Nineteen years later he tells his son, whom he named after Severus: "'you were named for two headmasters of Hogwarts. One of them was a Slytherin and he was probably the bravest man I ever knew.'" (HP 7, 607)

Snape unites all of the negative values: as "Potions" teacher he is coldly accurate and unjust. He acts arbitrarily[353] and irrationally. He is aggressive,

---

[353] There are numerous examples for this: Snape prefers Draco right from the start and is clearly biased against Harry, Ron and Hermione (HP 1, 150-152). He even blames Harry

cruel, sneaky and malicious. He plots against Lupin (HP 3, 386) and tries to make his class understand that he is a werewolf (HP 3, 186-188). On the other hand Snape represents bravery when he enters the "Shrieking Shack" in *Prisoner of Azkaban* to save his pupils (HP 3, 389), or in *Philosopher's Stone* protects Harry from Quirrell's attempted murder (HP 1, 311). Despite this ambivalence, Snape is working for the "Order of the Phoenix" – although only Dumbledore and Hermione trust him (HP 5, 82). It is Snape that tries to teach Harry "Occlumency" to strengthen his resistance against Voldemort (HP 5, 572) and he is the one to give Dolores Umbridge false and, later on, no "Veritaserum" at all to prevent her from questioning Harry (HP 5, 818-819). Throughout the series we are led to doubt Snape's loyalty to Dumbledore: Ron believes Snape might teach Harry "Occlumency" to give Voldemort easier access to him (HP 5, 611), and Umbridge mentions that Lucius Malfoy holds Snape in high esteem (HP 5, 819). With all of this we ultimately know that Snape is a positive character, and even Dumbledore admits in the end, that he should have been a Gryffindor: "'You are a braver man by far than Igor Karkaroff. You know, I sometimes think we Sort too soon...'" (HP 7, 545).

Snape may be considered the only real round character of the novels. At first Snape is a stereotypical, flat character that only becomes interesting when we realise in *Philosopher's Stone* that his surface does not reflect his inside – something in which Rowling differs quite significantly from other writers of fantasy literature for children.[354] As "stereotypically unpleasant teacher" he belongs to the novels' fixed set of characters and his actions are closely followed by the readers.[355] Nevertheless, his love story with Lily Potter and his secretly benevolent attitude do not really convince the reader: Why should he insist on secrecy in the first place? Why does he hate Harry so much and then is not able – after his parents' death – to overcome his hatred for James? Should he not he care at least a bit for the son of his true love?

IV.4.D. No Werewolves, Please! – Remus John Lupin

This name arouses suspicion – there are too many allusions to wolves to be overseen. Remus is one of the founding twins of Rome that – as legend has it – were fed and raised by a she-wolf. "Lupin" contains references to *lupus*, the Latin word for wolf. Remus' nickname is Moony (HP 3, 373) – a hint at his very special relationship with the moon. As a child he was bitten by a werewolf

---

for Neville's bad performance at "Potions" (HP 1, 153) and deliberately spoils Harry's potion just to give him bad marks: "maliciously, emptying Harry's cauldron" (HP 5, 403).
[354] See Maar 2003, 46.
[355] See Pinsent 2004, 37.

(HP 3, 379) and has been suffering from the monthly transformations into a monster ever since. Dumbledore takes him to Hogwarts despite his condition:[356]

> "Dumbledore's trust has meant everything to me. He let me into Hogwarts as a boy, and he gave me a job, when I have been shunned all my adult life, unable to find paid work because of what I am." (HP 3, 383)

At the end of *Prisoner of Azkaban* he is discovered to be a werewolf (HP 3, 372). Remus Lupin was a good friend of Harry's father[357] and one of the authors of the "Marauder's Map" (HP 3, 373). He was even made prefect (HP 5, 191).

When Harry first meets him on the "Hogwarts Express" Lupin is quite a shabby character:

> [He wore a] shabby set of wizard's robes which had been darned in several places. He looked ill and exhausted. Though he seemed quite young, his light-brown hair was flecked with grey. (HP 3, 84)[358]

He defends Harry, Ron and Hermione against the "Dementors" searching the train (HP 3, 93). His being tired and sick is the outward mark of his continously changing condition as a werewolf:

> Though still quite young, Lupin looked tired and rather ill; he had more grey hairs than when Harry had last said goodbye to him and his robes were more patched and shabbier than ever. (HP 5, 57)[359]

Lupin is a positive character, very sensitive and becomes a surrogate father not only to Harry: even Neville gains self-confidence in Lupin's lessons (HP 3, 145). Remus represents bravery (he is among the few to pronounce Voldemort's name: HP 3, 169), defends Harry against Snape (HP 3, 312-315) and confronts Draco Malfoy (HP 3, 99). He is against physical violence and prevents Harry from killing Sirius in *Prisoner of Azkaban* (HP 3, 370). I cannot confirm Roland Ernould's opinion that Lupin is "coquet, narcissique et fan-

---

[356] See Wrigley 2005, 20.

[357] When Harry tells him that he hears his parents' last seconds every time a "Dementor" approaches him, Lupin is deeply touched: "Harry suddenly realised that there were tears on his face mingling with the sweat. [...] 'You heard James?' said Lupin, in a strange voice. [...] 'We were friends at Hogwarts.'" (HP 3, 261).

[358] "Lupin looked particularly shabby next to all the other teachers in their best robes." (HP 3, 104); "Lupin smiled vaguely and placed his tatty old briefcase on the teacher's desk. He was as shabby as ever but looked healthier than he had on the train, [...]." (HP 3, 142); "[...] there were dark shadows beneath his eyes" (HP 3, 201); "grey hairs and the lines on his young face" (HP 3, 203).

[359] There are many hints. In Snape's memories he is "rather pale and peaky" (HP 5, 707).

taisiste".[360] Christopher Wrigley interprets him as a metaphor for homosexuality, which in my opinion is utterly absurd. Lupin represents the condition of being "different", of "the other", as one set apart from social mainstream by illness, status and prejudice. In *Half-Blood Prince* Lupin and Tonks fall in love, in *Deathly Hallows* they have got married and have a baby boy named Teddy (HP 7, 415). Lupin berates himself for having married Tonks and thus, of having made her a social outcast (HP 7, 175). He tries to join Harry in his fight against Voldemort, but Harry refuses and reminds him of his duty to his family. In the final battle of Hogwarts Lupin and Tonks die (HP 7, 531), but their son Teddy Remus grows up as a sort of family relation with the Weasleys and finally falls in love with Victoire Weasley, Fleur's and Bill's daughter (HP 7, 605).

The deaths of Remus and Tonks are – from a plot-centred point of view – rather unnecessary. We must wonder if this was not the most convenient way for Rowling to dispose of characters disturbing her picture of the happy bourgeois middle class. If the couple had remained alive they would have posed many questions concerning the integration of minorities and social marginalisation. In letting them die, Rowling avoids giving answers.

IV.4.E. Bun and Eagle Eye – Minerva McGonagall

A woman called Minerva must be wise, as she shares her name with the ancient Roman goddess of wisdom and science, and the daughter of Juno and Jupiter.[361] Her big round glasses could be an allusion to Minerva's heraldic animal – the owl. McGonagall is the name of a quite untalented Scottish poet (1852-1902),[362] but also stands for Scottish severity and tradition.[363] The combination of wisdom and severity characterises her very well although the possible allusion to a lack of talent is not very convincing.

Minerva McGonagall is the Victorian teacher of "Transfiguration" – the science of physically transforming things or beings.[364] She is "a sprightly seventy"[365] and has been teaching in Hogwarts for 39 years (HP 5, 357). She is an "Animagus" and as such she can transform into an animal – usually a cat with

---

[360] Ernould 2003, 207.
[361] See Beahm 2005, 113.
[362] Hein refers to an interview where Rowling says she took the name from this poet (see Hein 2001, 96).
[363] See Schafer 2000, 58.
[364] See also: "a rather severe-looking woman" (HP 1, 16); "[Professor McGonagall] wasn't a teacher to cross. Strict and clever, she gave them a talking-to the moment they had sat down in her first class." (HP 1, 147); "[She] was still extremely strict." (HP 2, 89).
[365] Rowling, Live Interview, 16 Oct 2000.

eyes that resemble McGonagall's glasses.[366] The stereotypical elements of her characterisation include her "square glasses" (HP 1, 16),[367] her "beady eye" (HP 2, 311) and her hair, always worn in "a tight bun" (HP 1, 16; HP 2, 86; HP 3, 99). This strict hairstyle represents her correctness and moral incorruptibility. Her gaze is "positively hawklike" (HP 5, 236) – she sees and understands everything. This outward sternness is misleading: Minerva McGonagall has a good sense of humour[368] and can be very emotional, especially when the well-being of her students[369] is at stake or a game of "Quidditch"[370] is concerned. She completely looses her coolness when fighting Voldemort (HP 4, 761). The only time she appears to lose confidence and seems worried is when Dolores Umbridge appears in Hogwarts. Minerva realises that she has been sent to gain control over the school. Harry remarks "Her tone of voice [...] was not brisk, crisp and stern; it was low and anxious and somehow much more human than usual." (HP 5, 275).

But even McGonagall is not without fault: she willingly allows Harry and Ron to convince her that taking house points from Gryffindor is not really necessary in *Chamber of Secrets* (HP 2, 92). She can be very bitchy with "Divination" teacher Sybill Trelawney,[371] and sometimes even malicious as when she explains to Peeves how to make the chandelier fall on Dolores Umbridge: "[...] Harry witnessed Professor McGonagall [...] tell the poltergeist out of the corner of her mouth, '[The crystal chandelier] unscrews the other way.'" (HP 5, 746) She very openly shows her opposition to the new regime. McGonagall tells Harry, sure in the knowledge that Umbridge – who wants to prevent the boy from becoming an "Auror"– is listening: "'I will assist you to become an Auror if it is the last thing I do! If I have to coach you nightly, I will make sure you

---

[366] See also: "square glasses exactly the shape of the markings the cat had had around its eyes" (HP 1, 16); "a tabby cat with spectacle markings aroand her eyes." (HP 3, 120).

[367] She is also said to be "a bespectacled witch" (HP 2, 86) with "square spectacles" (HP 3, 99).

[368] In high spirits she lets Hagrid kiss her: "Hagrid [...] finally kissing Professor McGonagall on the cheek, who, to Harry's amazement, giggled and blushed, her top hat lop-sided." (HP 1, 220).

[369] Speaking about the attack on Hermione in *Chamber of Secrets* she has a "surprisingly gentle voice" (HP 2, 277). When Harry says he wants to visit Hermione in hospital he sees "a tear glistening in her beady eye" (HP 2, 311).

[370] When Draco fouls Harry "[she] was actually shaking her fist in Malfoy's direction; her hat had fallen off, and she, too, was shouting furiously." (HP 3, 336). When Gryffindor wins the house cup she is "sobbing harder even than Wood, wiping her eyes with an enormous Gryffindor flag" (HP 3, 338). She is even partial when it comes to "Quidditch" (HP 5, 442).

[371] She becomes quite bitchy when Trelawney seems to be surprised by Lupin's absence at dinner: "'But surely you already knew that, Sybill' said Professor McGonagall, her eyebrows raised. [...] 'Certainly I knew, Minerva,' she said quietly. 'But one does not parade the fact that one is All-Knowing. I frequently act as though I am not possessed of the Inner Eye, so as not to make others nervous.' 'That explains a great deal,' said Professor McGonagall tartly." (HP 3, 248).

achieve the required results!'" (HP 5, 732) She is even more openly defiant when she communicates to the students an order from her new headmistress:

> "Our new – Headmistress –" Professor McGonagall pronounced the word with the same look on her face that Aunt Petunia had whenever she was contemplating a particularly stubborn bit of dirt "– has asked the Heads of House to tell their students that cheating will be punished most severely – because, of course, your examination results will reflect upon the Headmistress's new regime at the school –" Professor McGonagall gave a tiny sigh; [...]. – "however, that is no reason not to do your very best. You have your own futures to think about." (HP 5, 780)

Facing Umbridge, McGonagall is very outspoken: "'You see, I do not generally permit people to talk when I'm talking.'" (HP 5, 356) And when Hagrid is arrested by Umbridge's helpers, McGonagall fights for him, is badly injured and taken to St Mungo's. Her absence causes fear among her students (HP 5, 803), however at the end of the school year she returns.

McGonagall is a strong, independent woman and the antithesis of Severus Snape.[372] She is a "wise woman", standing for comfort and authority at the same time.[373] Within the adult plot she represents the same female type as Hermione within the children's plot. McGonagall is highly talented but usually plays second fiddle to the men.

> Like Hermione, she is book smart, but not wise, powerful, or brave. [Her] secondary status is also evident in the nature of her interactions with students. Unlike Headmaster Dumbledore, students can trick her. [...] She is sentimental and lacks discernment.[374]

Minerva McGonagall is a positive character, a member of the "Order of the Phoenix" and an important helper for Harry. In *Deathly Hallows* she is the one to decide to fight Voldemort (HP 7, 479). Although we believe her to be morally faultless she does not act impartially all the time. Even though she is a non-conformist, we are never led to doubt her qualities. At the same time her character does not develop. All of this makes her a flat and static creation.

IV.4.F. "Na, we're best left alone." – "Muggles"

"Muggle" is a made-up word, the origins of which are not very obvious. According to Hein, Joanne K. Rowling has said that the word came from "mug". In the world of Harry Potter the word stands for people without magical skills, but

---

[372] See Dresang 2004, 234-235.
[373] See Grimes 2004, 96.
[374] Heilman "Blue Wizards and Pink Witches" 2003, 225; see Mendlesohn 2004, 175.

is frequently used as an insult: "'A Muggle,' said Hagrid. 'It's what we call non-magic folk like [the Dursleys].'" (HP 1, 62) There is a clear distinction between "us" and "them" as Hagrid says: "'About OUR world, I mean. YOUR world. MY world. YER PARENTS' WORLD." (HP 1, 59) He later explains that wizards usually come from families of wizards, but there are exceptions. "'[Some] o' the best [witches and wizards] I ever saw were the only ones with magic in 'em in a long line o' Muggles [...].'" (HP 1, 90). One's magical skills don't depend on one's parentage[375] (Hermione's parents, for example, are "Muggle" dentists[376]).

The "Muggle" world is of no relevance to the wizards, their knowledge is utterly useless in Magical World.[377] In fact, it is wizards that determine the "Muggles'" fate and all the great philosophers and scientists were in truth wizards.[378] "Muggles" are not supposed to know about the existence of wizards. This construction of parallel worlds is one of the fundamental weak points in the narrative structure of *Harry Potter*. Rowling cannot fully convince her readers how such gigantic camouflage is supposed to work. This becomes particularly obvious when wizards are born in "Muggle" families and are sent to Hogwarts at the age of elven. Revealing to her that she is a witch, Severus Snape explains to Lily Evans that "someone from the school" will come to see her parents and explain to them about Hogwarts (HP 7, 535).

Only in "The Other Minister" (HP 6, 7-24) do we learn why the "Muggle" Prime Ministers, who usually know about Magical World, do not publicise their knowledge:

> The Prime Minister [...] realised that he would never, as long as he lived, dare mention this encounter [with Cornelius Fudge] to a living soul, for who in the wide world would believe him? (HP 6, 12)

But why is secrecy so important? We hardly get any convincing reason for it. Hagrid explains right at the beginning of the series:

---

[375] Ron explains to Harry: "'There's loads of people who come from Muggle families and they learn quick enough.'" (HP 1, 112).

[376] "'Nobody in my family's magic at all, it was such a surprise when I got my letter, [...].'" (HP 1, 117).

[377] When Harry tries to show off with his knowledge about stalagmites Hagrid is utterly unimpressed: "'[What's] the difference between a stalagmite and a stactite?' 'Stalagmite's got an 'm' in it,' said Hagrid." (HP 1, 85). And looking for matches Hermione even forgets that she is a witch (HP 1, 299).

[378] In *Prisoner of Azkaban* we frequently find allusions to the Egyptian Pharaohs being wizards (HP 3, 15-16), and Ron says in reference to the chocolate frog pictures of "Famous Witches and Wizards": "'I've got about five hundred, but I haven't got Agrippa or Ptolemy.'" (HP 1, 113).

"[The Ministry's] main job is to keep it from the Muggles that there's still witches an' wizards up an' down the country." "Why?" "WHY? Blimey, Harry, everyone'd be wantin' magic solutions to their problems. Nah, we're best left alone." (HP 1, 75)

This seems to be quite a trivial rationale and is unconvincing. In *Deathly Hallows* we learn more about the history of "Muggle"-Wizard relations (HP 7, 261). Even close relatives are left in the dark about the magic in their families: "'I'm half and half,' said Seamus. 'Me dad's a Muggle. Mam didn't tell him she was a witch 'til after they were married. Bit of a nasty shock for him.'" (HP 1, 137). Still, there must be quite a few "Muggles" who know about the magical community and send their magically gifted children to Hogwarts. Hermione even takes her parents to Diagon Alley (HP 2, 65 und 71).

But what would happen if "Muggles" learnt of the existence of Magical World? We are told of the magical community's fear of being discovered,[379] but never get to know the possible consequences of such a discovery. One access to Magical World is hidden in the Leaky Cauldron – a pub on Charing Cross Road (HP 1, 78). Nevertheless, Magical World is accessible from many points in "Muggle" world. It is not a hidden universe set apart from "reality", but another dimension to what non-magical people believe to be real.

How to treat "Muggles" is one of the crucial questions of Magical World. Some advocate treating them fairly and are interested in their way of life.[380] Others, especially Voldemort and his followers, regard "Muggles" as utterly worthless – and undeserving of basic rights. They outlaw "Muggles" and their descendants – even if they have magical talent. Wizards of non-magical descent are insulted as "mudbloods". Both attitudes towards non-wizards share a certain level of racism.[381] To be a "Muggle" is a shame, anyhow.[382]

---

[379] McGonagall: "'A fine thing it would be if, on the very day You-Know-Who seems to have disappeared at last, the Muggles found out about us all.'" (HP 1, 17). Ron on dragons in Great Britain: "'Our lot have to keep putting spells on Muggles who've spotted them, to make them forget.'" (HP 1, 250). About returning from platform 9 ¾ to "Muggle" King's Cross: "[...] letting them go through the gate in twos and threes so they didn't attract attention by all busting out of a solid wall at once and alarming the Muggles." (HP 1, 331).

[380] Like Mr Weasley, who is fascinated by "Muggle" technology (see IV.3.J, 182).

[381] This kind of racism is evident when the celebrating wizards call out to the "Muggles": "'Even Muggles like yourself should be celebrating, this happy, happy day!'" (HP 1, 11). McGonagall says: "'Well, they're not completely stupid. They were bound to notice something.'" (HP 1, 16) and the Potters being dead, Hagrid fears the worst for their son "'But I c-c-can't stand it – Lily an' James dead – an' poor little Harry off ter live with Muggles –'" (HP 1, 23).

[382] Even the Weasleys are ashamed of their "Muggle" relations. Ron says: "'I think Mum's got a second cousin who's an accountant, but we never talk about him.'" (HP 1, 110). Hagrid wants to punish himself by being "'made ter live as a Muggle!'" (HP 1, 326).

The relation between the two communities is marked by a complete lack of understanding. Things from the "Muggle" world appear exotic to the wizards: "[Hagrid] kept pointing at perfectly ordinary things like parking meters and saying loudly, 'See that, Harry? Things these Muggles dream up, eh?'" (HP 1, 75). "Muggles", on the other hand, close their eyes to magic and try to find rational explanations for supernatural phenomenons. When, on the day of Voldemort's fall (31st of October 1981), the "Muggle" news reports on an extraordinary amount of day-time activity by owls (the postal services in Magical World), the presenter finds this very entertaining: "'Experts are unable to explain why the owls have suddenly changed their sleeping pattern.' The news reader allowed himself a grin. 'Most mysterious.'" (HP 1, 12)[383]

IV.4.G. Pigs, Horses and Fanatics – The Dursleys

The Dursleys – Petunia, Vernon and their son Dudley – represent the negative values. As Elizabeth D. Schafer puts it: "[The Dursleys] are repulsive, ignorant, arrogant, narcisstic, greedy, mean-spirited, humorless people who seem to have no souls."[384] Frequently, Rowling compares them with animals to make the reader see their grotesqueness. "Dursley" is a common English name of families and of places.[385] "Vernon" occurs just as frequently. Petunia is named after a poisonous plant; "Dudley" is probably taken from "dud" or from the name of a city in the West Midlands.[386] At the same time, "Dudley" is a modern English name.

All the Dursleys are ugly.[387] The men are fat and brawny:[388] "[Mr Dursley] was a big, beefy man with hardly any neck, although he did have a very large moustache." (HP 1, 7). His fingers are "sausage-like" (HP 5, 11). He has "small, sharp eyes" (HP 2, 9) and sometimes he has "a mad gleam dancing in his eyes" (HP 2, 28). Vernon Dursley is the "director of a firm called Grunnings, which made drills" (HP 1, 7). There he deals with drilling holes – a mere office worker – and sits with "his back to the window in his office on the ninth floor." (HP 1, 9) He eyes remain closed to the outer world. The name of the firm seems to be an onomatopoetic word which imitates the sound of drills

---

[383] The author plays on this misunderstanding and a great part of the novels' satire results from it – as for example in the following dialogue between Harry and Ron: "'But in, you know, the Muggle world, people just stay put in photos.' 'Do they? What, they don't move at all?' Ron sounded amazed. 'WEIRD!'" (HP 1, 114).

[384] Schafer 2000, 55.

[385] Sean Smith names an "innocuous Gloucestershire town" as the source. As Rowling comes from this part of Britain this can very well be true (see Smith 2001, 29).

[386] See Smith 2001, 30.

[387] Again, the character's appearance corresponds with its moral qualities.

[388] Also: "Vernon, a large beefy man with very little neck and a lot of moustache." (HP 3, 23). Frequently, he is compared to animlas like a rhino (HP 2, 9) or "an angry bull" (HP 2, 34).

combined with the prefix "gru-" that usually stands for displeasure. Vernon is a coward ("A braver man than Vernon Dursley [...].", HP 1, 59) and aggressive. He does not even dare to speak out the word "wizard" (HP 5, 45). The narrator, i.e. the author, uses very negative adjectives in reference to Vernon, as for example his "grin[ning] in a horrible, manic way" (HP 5, 11). In accordance with the value pattern (see V.2.E, 319) he cannot stand the presence of owls (against nature) and cries out: "'I WILL NOT HAVE ANY MORE *OWLS* IN MY HOUSE!'" (HP 5, 35). Alastor Moody declares Vernon an idiot: "'I expect what you're not aware of would fill several books, Dursley,' [...]." (HP 5, 954) He is narrow-minded and false, a "consummate prig and hypocrite, disgusted at the thought of something unconventional in his family."[389]

His son Dudley is just as disagreeable as Vernon:

> Dudley looked a lot like Uncle Vernon. He had a large, pink face, not much neck, small, watery blue eyes and thick, blond hair that lay smoothly on his thick, fat head. Aunt Petunia often said that Dudley looked like a baby angel – Harry often said that Dudley looked like a pig in a wig. (HP 1, 28)[390]

Dudley is the true boss of the family, a tyrant[391] who is "grotesque, greedy, sneaky and stupid".[392] He possesses very few positive character traits.[393] He is compared to a pig,[394] a gorilla (HP 1, 33) and a whale (HP 4, 35). Finally, in *Goblet of Fire* he is so fat,[395] that no school uniform fits him any longer and he is put on an unsuccessful diet (HP 4, 34-35). Already as a toddler he is choleric (HP 1, 8) and has learnt to emotionally blackmail his parents (HP 1, 30). Cruel ("Dudley and Piers wanted to see huge, poisonous cobras and thick, man-crushing pythons.", HP 1, 34) and cowardly as he is ("Piers Polkiss [...] was usually the one who held people's arms behind their backs while Dudley hit them.", HP 1, 31) he enjoys tantalising everyone else, especially his cousin Harry (HP 1, 38-39). His parents see him as beyond reproach and adore him ("The Dursleys had a small son called Dudley and in their opinion there was no finer boy anywhere.", HP 1, 7). This "fine boy" becomes the terror of the neighbourhood ("Neighbourhood children all around were terrified of [Dudley ...].", HP 5, 18), more so when he becomes Junior Heavyweight Inter-School Boxing Champion of the Southeast (HP 5, 17). Sadistically he delights in the screams of

---

389 Pharr 2004, 56.
390 Also: "Dudley was very fat and hated exercise – [...]" (HP 1, 27).
391 Bürvenich 2001, 71.
392 Pharr 2004, 56.
393 See Smith 2001, 30.
394 This comparison with a pig runs through the whole series. See also: "porky shoulder" (HP 3, 27); "piggy little eyes" (HP 4, 37; HP 6, 53); "porky hands" (HP 4, 49).
395 "[...] Dudley had finally achieved what he'd been threatening to do since the age of three, and become wider than he was tall." (HP 4, 41).

a ten-year-old (HP 5, 19). Vandalising "Big D" – as he likes to call himself – (HP 5, 19) and his gang patrol the neighbourhood ("[... Harry] sank on to the only [swings] that Dudley and his friends had not yet managed to break, [...].", HP 5, 16), with his parents believing him to be taking tea with other children. The Dursleys are happy with what they believe to be their son's popularity: "'He's got so many little friends, he's so popular ...'" (HP 5, 9). Only Harry knows why Dudley keeps away from home for such a long time:

> Harry knew perfectly well that [...] he and his gang spent every evening vandalising the play park, smoking on street corners and throwing stones at passing cars and children. (HP 5, 9)

When Harry wants to watch the news, Vernon gets angry: "'As if a normal boy cares what's on the news – Dudley hasn't got a clue what's going on; doubt he knows who the Prime Minister is!'" (HP 5, 8). What Vernon regards as normal is in truth a devastating statement about his son. Dudley is the victim of his over-caring parents who have neglected him emotionally and have made him a repugnant person. Nevertheless, when Harry has saved his life in *Order of the Phoenix* Dudley begins to treat his cousin in a more friendly way. Parting for good in *Deathly Hallows*, we even see him thanking Harry, wishing him well and telling him that he is "no waste of space" (HP 7, 38-39).

Aunt Petunia, neé Evans, is meagre, blond,[396] has a shrill voice (HP 1, 25) and a false laugh (HP 2, 19) – in which she resembles Dolores Umbridge (see IV.5.G). She is socially ambitious, pretending to belong to the upper classes when she is "sipping her coffee with her little finger sticking out" (HP 3, 35). Nosily and maliciously, she oberves what is going on the neighbourhood ("She was the nosiest woman in the world and spent most of her life spying on her boring, law-abiding neighbours.", HP 3, 24)[397] and follows the yellow press.[398] Petunia is "horse-faced" (HP 3, 31)[399] but hates animals (HP 3, 31). Her story is one of misunderstood feelings and jealousy of her witch-sister Lily:

> "[My dratted sister] came home every holiday with her pockets full of frogspawn, turning teacups into rats. I was the only one who saw her for what

---

[396] "Mrs Dursley was thin and blonde and had nearly twice the usual amount of neck, which came in very useful as she spent so much of her time craning over garden fences, spying on the neighbours." (HP 1, 7). Thus, she is the opposite of motherly Molly Weasley (see IV.3.J, 184).

[397] Interestingly the author puts "boring" on a level with "law-abiding".

[398] She comments on a TV report on a actor's divorce: "'As if we're interested in their sordid affairs,' sniffed Aunt Petunia, who had followed the case obsessively in every magazine she could lay her bony hands on." (HP 5, 10).

[399] "Aunt Petunia's thin, horsy face now appeared beside Uncle Vernon's wide, purple one." (HP 5, 12)

she was – a freak! But for my mother and father, oh no, it was Lily this and Lily that, they were proud of having a witch in the family!" (HP 1, 62)[400]

In *Deathly Hallows* we learn more about the relation between the two Evans sisters (see IV.4.H, 243). Petunia obviously envied Lily[401] and wrote to Dumbledore to ask him to admit her to Hogwarts as well (HP 7, 536-537). Being rejected, she began to hate her sister. She negates the existence of Magical World and, thus, the magical part of her own personality.[402] In *Order of the Phoenix* Petunia all of a sudden admits to knowing more about wizards, and she explains to Vernon what "Howlers" and "Dementors" are, and who Lord Voldemort is (HP 5, 40). Only at this point, when she begins to tell the truth, Harry can see his mother's sister in her:

> The furious pretence that Aunt Petunia had maintained all Harry's life – that there was no magic and no world other than the world she inhabited with Uncle Vernon – seemed to have fallen away. (HP 5, 47)

From Dumbledore Harry learns that it is because of Petunia admitting him to her house that he has been protected from Voldemort all those years: "'She knows that allowing you houseroom may well have kept you alive for the past fifteen years.'" (HP 5, 919) In *Half-Blood Prince* Dumbledore reproaches them for the way they have mistreated Harry for all his childhood years. At the same time he criticises their education and compares modest, compassionate Harry to spoilt Dudley:

> "You have never treated Harry as a son. He has known nothing but neglect and often cruelty at your hands. The best that can be said is that he has at least escaped the appalling damage you have inflicted upon the unfortunate boy sitting between you." (HP 6, 57)

In the final parting scene in *Deathly Hallows*, Aunt Petunia obviously wants to say something to Harry, but in the end decides to stay silent (HP 7, 41). Another, minor family member is Vernon's sister Marge. She looks quite like her brother (HP 3, 29-30), excessively loves and breeds bulldogs and pampers a

---

[400] This means that Lily Potter, nee Evans, did not follow the rules, either. She would not have been allowed to use magic at home.

[401] See Pharr 2004, 56.

[402] Jung 2004, 30; see Diana Mertz Hsieh, "Dursley Duplicity. The Morality and Psychology of Self-Deception," *Harry Potter and Philosophy: If Aristotle ran Hogwarts,* eds. Baggett & Klein, Chicago, La Salle: Open Court, 2004, 22-37, 33.

dog called "Ripper" (HP 3, 29-30).[403] As self-indulgent as her love for dogs is her drinking (HP 3, 35).

The Dursleys represent excess, greed and consumption. They judge others superficially according to their cars (HP 4, 49) and their looks. Above all else it is materialistic excess that marks their way of life. They lavish presents on their son: "The table was almost hidden beneath all Dudley's birthday presents." (HP 1, 26-30). Among these "the new computer he wanted, not to mention the second television and the racing bike" and "the racing bike, a cine-camera, a remote-control aeroplane, sixteen new computer games and a video recorder. [Dudley] was ripping the paper off a gold wristwatch [...]." (HP 1, 29-30) But this is not enough: "Dudley, meanwhile, was counting his [birthday] presents. His face fell. 'Thirty-six,' he said, looking up at his mother and father. 'That's two less than last year.'" Instead of sanctioning his son's greed, Mr Dursley praises him: "'Little tyke wants his money's worth, just like his father. Atta boy, Dudley!'"

Things are dealt with carelessly; Dudley is only interested in possessing, and not in using his presents. The description of his devastated room with all his broken toys illustrates the boy's character. Dudley does not read (uneducated), runs the neighbours' dog over with his toy tank (cruel), exchanges a living animal for a weapon (no respect for nature) and in rage destroys his own TV set (irrational).

> Nearly everything in [Dudley's room] was broken. The month old cine-camera was lying on top of a small, working tank Dudley had once driven over next door's dog; in the corner was Dudley's first-ever television set, which he'd put his foot through when his favourite programme had been cancelled; there was a large bird-cage which had once held a parrot that Dudley had swapped at school for a real air-rifle, which was up on a shelf with the end all bent because Dudley had sat on it. Other shelves were full of books. They were the only things in the room that looked as though they'd never been touched. (HP 1, 45-46)[404]

Dudley stands for all the bad habits which modern youth is accused of: an addiction to television, excessive playing of computer games ("He was hungry, he'd missed five television programmes he'd wanted to see and he'd never gone so long without blowing up an alien on his computer.", HP 1, 50) and a preference for junk food ("fizzy drinks and cakes, chocolate bars and burgers", HP 4, 35).[405]

---

[403] This follows the same pattern as narrative space (see 103): exaggerated positive features are bad.

[404] Also: "[...] Dudley had already broken his new cine-camera, crashed his remote-control aeroplane and, first time on his racing bike, knocked down old Mrs Figg as she crossed Privet Drive on her crutches." (HP 1, 39).

[405] Also: "[he] had been complaining loudly about the long walk between the fridge and the television in the living room. Dudley had spent most of the summer in the kitchen, his

The Dursleys spoil their own child and deprive their nephew of the most basic things: Harry never gets new clothes but has to wear Dudley's (HP 1, 27), has not been given pocket money in six years, (HP 2, 78) and only receives "presents" like toothpicks, a letter telling him to stay at school during holidays (HP 2, 230), paper handkerchiefs (HP 4, 447) and old socks (HP 1, 52). Harry is imprisoned in his room and gets his food through the cat flap (HP 2, 28). Harry even suspects his family of secretly hoping for him to drown when they don't let him participate in swimming lessons (HP 4, 506). Their relationship is highly ambivalent – the Dursleys fear and hate their nephew: "The Dursleys [had] the general wish of keeping Harry as miserable as possible, coupled with their fear of his powers, [...]." (HP 4, 31)

Conforming to rules and keeping order – these are the most important things in the life of the Dursleys. The legendary first sentence of the series makes this clear right from the beginning, playing with different notions of "normal":

> Mr and Mrs Dursley, of number four, Privet Drive, were proud to say that they were perfectly normal, thank you very much. They were the last people you'd expect to be involved in anything strange or mysterious, because they just didn't hold with such nonsense. (HP 1, 7)

Normality means being just like everyone else. Differences are to be prevented; the Potter side of the family has to be kept secret.[406] Creativity and fantasy are – disguised as concern for the sensitive youth – *per se* bad: "Mr Dursley couldn't bear people who dressed in funny clothes – the get-ups you saw on young people!" (HP 1, 9).[407] Harry's talent for magic to them is an "abnormality" (HP 2, 8), an "unnaturalness" (HP 4, 41), something to be ashamed of ("[...] having a wizard in the family was a matter of deepest shame.", HP 2, 10) and to be got rid of (HP 1, 331).[408] This negative attitude towards strangers or magic also extends to non-magical, non-British people and their way of life. Petunia, for example,

---

piggy little eyes fixed on the screen and his five chins wobbling as he ate continually." (HP 3, 23).

[406] "The Dursleys had everything they wanted, but they also had a secret, and their greatest fear was that somebody would discover it. They didn't think they could bear it if anyone found out about the Potters." (HP 1, 7); "Their worst fear was that anyone would find out that they were connected (however distantly) with people like Mrs Weasley." (HP 4, 39). "Mrs Dursley pretended she didn't have a sister, because her sister and her good-for-nothing husband were as undursleyish as it was possible to be. The Dursleys shuddered to think what the neighbours would say if the Potters arrived in the street." (HP 1, 7-8). Anything suspect is hidden from the neighbours (HP 5, 11).

[407] "[Mr Dursley] didn't approve of imagination." (HP 1, 11).

[408] We can also feel sympathy with the Dursleys when we read: "The imminent arrival at their house of an assortment of wizards was making the Dursleys uptight and irritable." (HP 4, 47). Who wouldn't?

suspects poisoning from foreign food when her son falls ill ("'Did Mrs Polkiss give you something foreign for tea?'", HP 5, 33). Even the Dursleys' dream of a "holiday home in Majorca" (HP 2, 13) fits into their xenophobia, because Majorca is famous for its infrastructure for British tourists. There is probably nothing "foreign" left to be afraid of. To Harry his relatives do not even appear human. When Dobby tells him about his sufferings at the Malfoys, Harry says: "'This makes the Dursleys sound almost human.'" (HP 2, 21); – but only "almost".

The characters of the Dursleys are extremely flat. Even when Petunia and Dudley appear to have more depth than Vernon, it does not make them psychologically convincing. The Dursleys are caricatures of a certain bourgeois way of life instead of round characters. From the narrative point of view they serve as a contrast to the Weasley family (see IV.3.J, 182): whereas Ron's relatives stand for motherly love, emotionality, warmth and homeliness, Harry's family embodies coldness, cruelty and narrow-mindedness. They are representatives of a certain social milieu of the 1990s[409] as Richard Adams points out in the *Guardian*:

> The Dursleys are Rowling's epitome of the modern middle class: crass, mean-spirited and grasping, living in a detached house in the suburb of Little Whinging. Vernon works in middle management while Petunia is a curtain-twitching housewife. The Dursleys [...] not Voldemort, are the real villains.[410]

They are like Dickensian child-haters[411] and would be accused of child abuse in the real world.[412] The Dursleys represent the typical stepfamily of children's literature expressing the opposition between young people and their parents: "[They] echo readers' parents, disapproving of adolescent friends, music, or clothes."[413]

IV.4.H. Without Glorification – Lily and James Potter

The Potters' surname is in no way extraordinary, but in fact, very common indeed (see IV.3.A, 156). Harry's mother Lily is named after a flower, whose white blossom is often a symbol of the Virgin Mary[414] and – at the same time – of death.[415] Her maiden name, Evans, is a reference to the biblical Eve – the first of

---

[409] See Blake 2002, 65.
[410] See Adams 2003.
[411] See Pharr 2004, 57.
[412] See Lacoss 2004, 78.
[413] See Cockrell 2004, 21.
[414] See Lurker 1991, 435-436.
[415] See Granger 2004, 110; Maar 2003, 60; "Lily," *Dictionary of First Names* [1990], 2000,152.

all women. James is a variety of Jacob,[416] who in the Old Testament was one of the twelve fathers of the tribes of Israel.[417] It also alludes to Scottish-English royalty.[418]

The story of Harry's parents is part of the novels' detective plot and is only revealed in the last parts of the series – until then they remain rather flat and unimportant. In *Deathly Hallows* we learn of Lily Evans' childhood and her early friendship with Severus Snape. The two Evans sisters liked each other very much when they were little girls (HP 7, 532-534). When Severus Snape, a boy of the neighbourhood, revealed to Lily, the younger of the two, that she was a witch and about to leave for Hogwarts, their relation began to deteriorate. When she first took the Hogwarts Express Lily met Harry's father and Sirius (HP 7, 538), but it would take a couple of years for the two to come together. Both of Harry's parents were born in 1960, their epitaph in Godric's Hollow reads:

> *James Potter, born 27 March 1960, died 31 October 1981*
> *Lily Potter, born 30 January 1960, died 31 October 1981*
> *The last enemy that shall be destroyed is death.*
> (HP 7, 268)

There are only very vague and superficial descriptions of Harry's parents:

> [Harry's mother] was a very pretty woman. She had dark red hair and her eyes – her eyes are just like mine, Harry thought, edging a little closer to the glass. Bright green – exactly the same shape, but then he noticed that she was crying; smiling, but crying at the same time. The tall, thin, black-haired man standing next to her put his arm around her. He wore glasses, and his hair was very untidy. It stuck up at the back, just like Harry's did. (HP 1, 226)

Lily Potter (Evans) is – above anything else – "pretty" and looks like her son.[419] Her wedding photo shows her "alight with happiness, arm in arm with his Dad." (HP 3, 230) Wandmaker Ollivander remembers that she bought a wand made of willow: "'Nice wand for charm work'" (HP 1, 93). Lily is equipped for "charms" not for "curses" – this makes her sympathetic. Obviously she did not obey the rules either (HP 1, 62) as her sister Petunia reports.[420] In *Half-Blood Prince* we learn from Horace Slughorn that Lily was highly talented and charming:

---

[416] See Hein 2001, 120; "James," *Dictionary of First Names* [1990], 2000, 128.
[417] See Maar 2003, 60.
[418] See Granger 2004, 110.
[419] Some examples include when Ollivander says to Harry: "'You have your mother's eyes.'" (HP 1, 93); Dumbledore: "'[You] have your mother's eyes.'" (HP 3, 460).
[420] Both sisters are named after flowers: whereas the lily represents purity and virginity, the petunia is a poisonous plant without metaphoric meaning.

"You shouldn't have favourites as a teacher, of course, but [Lily Evans] was one of mine. [...] One of the brightest I ever taught. Vivacious, you know. Charming girl. [...] Very cheeky answers I used to get back, too." (HP 6, 70-71)

Slughorn characterises her as everybody's darling: "'I don't imagine anyone who met her wouldn't have liked her ... very brave ... very funny ... it was the most horrible thing ...'" (HP 6, 458). For the Dursleys, the Potters are "'weirdos, [...] the world's better off without them'" (HP 1, 66). Nevertheless, Lily Potter remains rather flat as a character. There is hardly anything apart from Harry's mysterious survival that makes us interested in her.

James Potter, on the contrary, is rather ambivalent. His son has inherited his "untidy black hair" (e.g. HP 1, 226; HP 3, 230). Dumbledore says: "'[You] do look *extraordinarily* like James'" (HP 3, 460). James was an excellent "Quidditch player" (HP 1, 166), a good flyer (HP 3, 401) and "would have been highly disappointed if his son had never found any of the secret passages out of the castle'" (HP 3, 457). Snape accuses Harry and his father of arrogance (HP 3, 389) and Harry realises in *Order of the Phoenix* that this is true: "[...] his father had been every bit as arrogant as Snape had always told him" (HP 5, 715 and 718). Having glorified his father until then, at that moment Harry develops a more realistic view of him (HP 5, 734). James' wand was made of mahogany and "excellent for transfiguration" (HP 1, 93). This alludes to James having been an "Animagus" and his ability to transform into a stag. This is where he got his alias "Prongs" from. It surely is no coincidence that Harry's "Patronus" is a stag (HP 3, 443). Both Harry's parents were top students at Hogwarts,[421] became head boy and girl and were very loyal to Dumbledore (HP 1, 64).

Harry meets apparitions of his parents quite often. Quite bizarre is his meeting them in *Goblet of Fire* when they emerge as smoky shadows from Voldemort's wand and protect their son:

> The smoky shadow of a young woman with long hair fell to the ground [...]. "You're father's coming ..." she said quitely. "He wants to see you ... it will be all right ... hold on ..." And he came ... first his head, then his body ... tall and untidy-haired like Harry, the smoky, shadowy form of James Potter blossomed from the end of Voldemort's wand [...]. (HP 4, 723)[422]

---

[421] Lupin: "'Your father and Sirius here were the cleverest students in the school, [...].'" (HP 3, 381); and: "'[Your] father and Sirius were the best in the schol at whatever they did – everyone thought they were the height of cool – if they sometimes got a bit carried away –'" (HP 5, 737).

[422] We must wonder what being dead in Magical World really means. Unfortunately, the text does not explain this any further.

Later on in *Order of the Phoenix* Harry enters Snape's childhood memories in one of their "Occlumency" lessons. He first realises how very much alike he and his father look:

> [A] boy with untidy black hair ... very untidy black hair ... [...] his fifteen-year-old father [...] James's hair stuck up at the back exactly as Harry's did, his hands could have been Harry's and Harry could tell that, when James stood up, they would be within an inch of each other in height. (HP 5, 706)

Harry experiences his father's arrogance and presumptuousness when he bullies Snape – who is much weaker than he is – just to impress Lily (HP 5, 708-711). She tries to stop him:

> "Messing up your hair because you think it looks cool or looks like you've just got off your broomstick, showing off with that stupid Snitch, walking down corridors and hexing anyone who annoys you just because you can – I'm surprised your broomstick can get off the ground with that fat head on it. You make me SICK." (HP 5, 714)

James does not care for rules[423] – like his son he decides when to obey and when not. McGonagall says about him and Sirius: "'I don't think we've ever had such a pair of troublemakers – [...]'" (HP 3, 221). Taking risks, being daring and showing off – this is what matters to James. Sirius accuses Harry that he is "'less like your father than I thought, [...]. The risk would've made it fun for James'" (HP 5, 339). Only in his last year at Hogwarts does James change ("'Once James had deflated his head a bit,' said Sirius. 'And stopped hexing people just for the fun of it,' said Lupin.", HP 5, 738) and falls in love with Lily Evans.

Their death is a mystery to their son and in each part of the series we learn a bit more about it. The Potters knew they were being hunted by Voldemort (HP 3, 222) and protected their whereabouts using Peter Pettigrew as their "Secret Keeper". Pettigrew betrayed them to Voldemort. In *Prisoner of Azkaban* Harry relives the killing scene (HP 3, 261). Voldemort tells him: "'Yes boy, your parents were brave ... I killed your father first and he put up a courageous fight ... but your mother needn't have died ... she was trying to protect you'" (HP 1, 316). According to him James died "straight-backed and proud" (HP 4, 715). In *Deathly Hallows* Harry relives the death of his parents inside Voldemort's mind (HP 7, 280-282).

There are two memorials to the Potters: on the graveyard in Godric's Hollow there is a bewitched war memorial that turns into the shape of Harry's par-

---

[423] Sirius says of himself and James: "'No one would have made me a prefect, I spent too much time in detention with James.'" (HP 5, 191).

ents, when a witch or wizard passes it (HP 7, 265), and in front of their derelict house there is a sign:

> On this spot, on the night of 31 October 1981,
> Lily and James Potter lost their lives.
> Their son, Harry, remains the only wizard ever
> to have survived the Killing Curse.
> This house, invisible to Muggles, has been left
> in its ruined state as a monument to the Potters
> and as a reminder of the violence
> that tore apart their family.
> (HP 7, 272)

IV.4.I. "Glittering, oversize dragonfly" – Sybill Trelawney

Sybill is the name of a seeress: in ancient Greece Sybill was the word and name of a fortune-telling woman. In Christian mythology there are twelve such seeresses frequently portrayed in paintings and sculputres (the most famous being in Michelangelo's Sistine Chapel ceiling).[424] Her surname is not as easily to interpret. There is a Cornish folksong about a supposed bishop Jonathan Trelawney imprisoned in the Tower of London in 1687.[425]

The character of Trelawney is rather ambivalent, but not round according to Forster's criteria; she represents irrationality and treats her students rather cruelly. Her first appearance is already quite melodramatic – she loves self-dramatisation:

> A voice came suddenly out of the shadows, a soft, misty sort of voice. "Welcome," it said. "How nice to see you in the physical world at last." Harry's immediate impression was of a large, glittering insect. [She] was very thin; her large glasses magnified her eyes to several times their natural size, and she was draped in a gauzy spangled shawl. Innumerable chains and beads hung around her spindly neck, and her arms and hands were encrusted with bangles and rings. (HP 3, 113)

Her appearance is marked by her huge glasses, her magnified eyes[426] (which are the physical signs of her metaphysical sight) and her resemblance to

---

[424] See Lurker 1991, 678-679; "Sybil," *Dictionary of First Names* [1990], 2000. 216.
[425] See Hein 2001, 144.
[426] See also: "enormous eyes" (HP 3, 247); "with her glasses hugely magnifying her eyes" (HP 5, 262); "great beacon-like eyes" (HP 6, 156).

an insect, ie. a dragon-fly[427]. With her "misty voice" she usually appears "out of the shadows" (HP 3, 320),[428] her smile is "dewy" (HP 3, 323).

Sybill's talents are highly debated among her fellow teachers; her prophecies usually tend to be wrong or trivial. She can be quite cruel, when she publicly announces that Harry is going to die soon (HP 3, 118;[429] HP 3, 155), hints to Neville at his grandmother's grave illness or warns the Patil twins of a red-haired boy and Friday, 16th of October (HP 3, 114-115). Moreover, she tells her students that around "'Easter, one of our number will leave us for ever'" (HP 3, 115), and predicts that Neville is going to smash his teacup[430] (HP 3, 116). These prophecies she mixes with superstition.[431] Nevertheless, all of her prophecies come – usually in a very trivial way – true, which shows that she is not utterly talentless. In the course of her career she makes at least two authentic predictions changing her voice and behaviour:

> [...] a loud harsh voice spoke behind [Harry]. "It will happen tonight."
> Harry wheeled around. Professor Trelawney had gone rigid in her armchair; her eyes were unfocused and her mouth sagging. (HP 3, 349-350)

It is Sybill's prophecy that sets off the whole plot of Voldemort and Harry: when she applied for a job in Hogwarts she told Dumbledore that only one of the two wizards could survive (HP 6, 400).

For Ron and Hermione she is "a right old fraud" (HP 3, 347),[432] and her colleagues do not accept her, as McGonagall hints to her students:

> "Tell me, which of you will be dying this year? [...] Sybill Trelawney has predicted the death of one student a year since she arrived at this school. None of them has died yet. Seeing death omens is her favourite way of greeting a new class." (HP 3, 120-121)

Trelawney has been teaching at Hogwarts for about 16 years (HP 5, 923). The way she speaks about herself ("'I find that descending too often into the hustle

---

[427] Also: "making her look more than ever like a glittering, oversize dragonfly" (HP 3, 247); "A thin woman, heavily draped in shawls and glittering with strings of beads, she always reminded Harry of some kind of insect, with her glasses hugely magnifying her eyes." (HP 5, 262).

[428] See also: "misty, dreamy voice" (HP 5, 263).

[429] Maybe she confuses Sirius in his dog-shape with the death omen "Grim".

[430] He probably breaks it because Trelawney makes him feel even more insecure than usual?

[431] When there are twelve people at a table she does not want to join: the one first leaving the table is supposed to die (HP 3, 247). She is even interested in card tricks that remind us of "Muggle" magic: "[Professor Trelawney] muttering to herself as she shuffled a pack of dirty-looking playing cards, reading them as she walked." (HP 6, 185).

[432] "'I don't hate her, [...]. I just think she's an absolutely apalling teacher and a real old fraud.'" (HP 5, 404).

and bustle of the main school clouds my Inner Eye'" HP 3, 114),[433] the manner in which she divides her students into adepts (whom she usually finds amongst the girls) and "untalented" and her inability to cope with critique (HP 3, 322) make her guru-like. She stands for irrationality and arbitrariness. Hermione hates her and leaves her class (HP 3, 322-323), which ironically makes Trelawney's prophecy about someone leaving the class come true. Nevertheless, Sybill is "great-great-granddaughter of the celebrated Seer Cassandra Trelawney" (HP 5, 348-349).[434] Dumbledore grants her asylum in Hogwarts and protects her from Voldemort's wrath. In *Order of the Phoenix* Sybill is the first victim of Dolores Umbridge and sacked. Sybill reacts hysterically hearing about her probation:

> [Somewhat] hysterical [she said.] "You know what to do! Or am I such a sub-standard teacher that you have never learned how to open a book?" [...] her magnified eyes [were] full of tears [...]. (HP 5, 404)

She takes to drinking and neglects herself:

> Professor Trelawney was standing in the middle of the Entrance Hall with her wand in one hand and an empty sherry bottle in the other, looking utterly mad. Her hair was sticking up on end, her glasses were lop-sided so that one eye was magnified more than the other; her innumerable shawls and scarves were trailing haphazardly from her shoulders, giving the impression that she was falling apart at the seams. (HP 5, 654)[435]

In *Deathly Hallows* we see her play her part in the battle of Hogwarts, sacrificing her orbs to throw them at the attackers (HP 7, 519) – something we would not have believed her to be capable of. Sybill Trelawney is a flat character, but figures quite prominently in *Prisoner of Azkaban* and *Order of the Phoenix*. As she is the one to make the decisive prophecy, I count her as a first-order minor character.

IV.4.J. Merciless till Death – Barty Crouch, Father and Son

Once again Rowling chooses her names well. "Crouching" is just what Barty Crouch snr and jnr do in front of authorities. Their first name is an abbrevation

---

[433] She pretends to be suffering from her talent: "'[The] Inner Eye can be a burden, you know....'" (HP 3, 323).

[434] Dumbledore: "'The applicant, however, was the great-great-granddaughter of a very famous, very gifted Seer [...].'" (HP 5, 923).

[435] In *Half-Blood Prince* she frequently appears to be drunk: "Harry could smell cooking sherry again." (HP 6, 297); "[Harry] saw Professor Trelawney sprawled upon the floor, her head covered in one of her many shawls, several sherry bottles lying beside her, one broken." (HP 6, 505).

of Bartimaeus, a blind beggar healed by Jesus (Mark 10, 46-52). Creeping blindly – this is what the Crouches do. Crouch snr is Head of the Department of International Magical Co-operation (HP 4, 279) in the Ministry and infamous for his rigidness:

> Barty Crouch was a stiff, upright, elderly man, dressed in an impeccably crisp suit and tie. The parting in his short grey hair was almost unnaturally straight and his narrow toothbrush moustache looked as though he trimmed it using a slide-rule. His shoes were very highly polished. (HP 4, 102)[436]

Only when half-dead does he lose this fastidious attitude (HP 4, 601-602). But even before this occurs he has something "dead" about him, "an almost skull-like appearance" (HP 4, 304) and seems to be ill. ("There were dark shadows beneath his eyes, and a thin papery look about his wrinkled skin [...].", HP 4, 308). He has mercilessly prosecuted Voldemort's followers when he was Head of the Department of Magical Law Enforcement (HP 4, 572) and has never hesitated to apply radical measures (HP 4, 573). He does not even spare his own son, when he was convicted as a "Death Eater". Fearing for his political career he sent the 19-year-old boy to Azkaban (HP 4, 575).[437] He is believed to have died in prison, but in truth Crouch jnr was secretly replaced by his terminally ill mother who died in Azkaban. His father – despite his rigidness – hid the son in his house (HP 4, 575). But all of this has not helped to save his career; instead of him it was Cornelius Fudge who was appointed Minister for Magic (HP 4, 576) and he "was shunted sideways into the Department of International Magical Co-operation." (HP 4, 576) Crouch snr is a powerful wizard. Sirius describes him: "'He's a great wizard, Barty Crouch, powerfully magical – and powerhungry. [... He] was always very outspoken against the Dark side." (HP 4, 572).[438] He reveals his pitilessness in the treatment of his house-elf Winky when he sacks her (an irredeemable shame for an elf) (HP 4, 148).

Barty Crouch jnr is just like his father. This "pale-skinned, slightly freckled" man, "with a mop of fair hair" (HP 4, 739) uses "Polyjuice Potion" so as to impersonate Alastor Moody in *Goblet of Fire*. Only on the last pages of the novel do we learn of his true identity. Crouch jnr believes his fate very similar to Voldemort's:[439]

---

[436] See also: "great believer in rigidly following rules" (HP 4, 102); "His toothbrush moustache and severe parting looked very odd [...]." (HP 4, 279).

[437] Sirius: "Crouch's fatherly affection stretched just far enough to give his son a trial and, by all accounts, it wasn't much more than an excuse for Crouch to show how much he hated the boy [...] then he sent him straight to Azkaban." (HP 4, 574).

[438] Comparing Crouch to Alastor Moody we find: "'[They] say old Mad-Eye's obsessed with catching Dark wizards [...] but Mad-Eye's nothing – nothing – compared to Barty Crouch.'" (HP 4, 518).

[439] "'It was my dream, my greatest ambition, to serve him, to prove myself to him.'" (HP 4, 745).

"Both of us, for instance, had very disappointing fathers ... very disappointing indeed. Both of us suffered the indignity, Harry, of being named after those fathers. And both of us had the pleasure ... the very great pleasure ... of killing our fathers, to ensure the continued rise of the Dark Order!" (HP 4, 735)

Just like his father he is merciless, cruel and a murderer: he not only kills his father (HP 4, 748), but participates in the torturing of the Longbottoms. His adoration of evil ensures him Voldemort's high esteem; he calls him: "'my most faithful servant [...] who has already re-entered my service.'" (HP 4, 706) Neither of the Crouches are ambivalent or dynamic – both are rather flat characters focused on the bad characteristics of the value pattern. They only differ in the degree of ther malignance and the side they choose to be on.

IV.5 Second-order Minor Characters

These are the characters that are of lesser relevance for the text, but are, nevertheless, dealt with in detail. They differ from the marginal characters in the quantity and quality of their descriptions.

IV.5.A. Stately Fop – Prime Minister Cornelius Fudge

Someone whose name refers to sticky sweets or has the verbal meaning "to do something clumsily or inadequately or misrepresent or falsify"[440] must stand for weakness and incompetence. His first name derives from the Roman patrician Cornelia. Fudge is a weak, one-dimensional character. Power-hungry but inactive and harmless, he represents the establishment of Magical World. In his appearance we find signs of untidiness and a whiff of nonchalance which he compensates for with his authority as Minister for Magic:

> [He was a] very odd-looking man. The stranger was a short, portly man with rumpled grey hair and an anxious expression. He was wearing a strange mixture of clothes: a pin-striped suit, a scarlet tie, a long black cloak and pointed purple boots. Under his arm he carried a lime-green bowler. (HP 2, 281)

---

[440] "to patch or 'fake' *up*; to 'cook' accounts. Often in schoolboy language: To make (a problem) look as if it had been correctly worked, by altering figures; to conceal the defects of (a map or other drawing) by adjustment of the parts, so that no glaring disproportion is observed; and in other like uses". "to fudge," *Oxford English Dictionary online*. Oxford: University Press, 2006. 5 Jan 2008 <http://erf.sbb.spk-berlin.de /han/356448509/ dictionary.oed.com/cgi/entry/50090591?query_type=word&queryword=fudge&first=1& max_to_show=10&sort_type=alpha&result_place=1&search_id=mHwR-ClRQyY-3116&hi lite=50090591> 5 Jan 2008. Also see Beahm 2005, 96.

The features frequently applied to Fudge are "portly man", who wears a "pinstriped cloak", with a fondness for the colour green.[441] Fudge is the Prime Minister of Magical World and as such cooperates with the "Muggle" government (which we learn on the occasion of Sirius' outbreak from Azkaban, HP 3, 46), but does not accept them as fully equal, either. This is why he does not promote Arthur Weasley (HP 4, 770). Fudge only became Minister for Magic when Dumbledore had already refused (HP 1, 75) (see IV.3.L, 191).[442] Therefore, Fudge distrusts him and believes him eager to "seize power" (HP 5, 337):

> "Fudge thinks Dumbledore's plotting to overthrow him. He thinks Dumbledore wants to be Minister for Magic. [... He's] never quite forgotten how much popular support Dumbledore had, even though Dumbledore never applied for the job." (HP 5, 108-109)

There are rumours that Fudge unscrupulously tries to get the goblins' fortune (HP 5, 215) and supports a private army of fire spirits (HP 5, 382) – all of which turns out to be nonsense.
He is emotional, sometimes choleric[443] and, at the same time, easy-going, stupid[444] and out of touch with reality. The idea of Voldemort returning is completely out of the question for him, because this would threaten his cosy way of life.[445] Stability is the highest value for him – even when it is a make-believe peace enabling Voldemort to return. Dumbledore accuses him of racism and argues with him:

> "You are blinded," said Dumbledore, his voice rising now, the aura of power around him palpable, his eyes blazing once more, "by the love of the office you hold, Cornelius! You place too much importance, and you always have done,

---

[441] The spelling of "pin(-)striped" varies. Green is also a dubious colour (III.2.A, 103). Also: "a portly little man in a long, pinstriped cloak, looked cold and exhausted." (HP 3, 50); "Fudge took off his pinstriped cloak and tossed it aside, then hitched up the trousers of his bottle-green suit and sat down opposite Harry." (HP 3, 51-52); "a portly man in a lime-green bowler hat and a pinstriped cloak: Cornelius Fudge, Minister for Magic." (HP 3, 218); "Fudge was a portly man who often sported a lime-green bowler hat [...]." (HP 5, 156); "[...] his long pinstriped cloak, a lime-green bowler hat in his hand." (HP 6, 9).

[442] We do not get any explanation as to how the Minister for Magic is chosen (see V.1.C, 290).

[443] In this he equals Vernon Dursley: "[...] a shade of magenta of which Uncle Vernon would have been proud." (HP 5, 166).

[444] "Fudge stared at Dumbledore with a very silly expression on his face, [...]." (HP 5, 682).

[445] "a short, angry wizard stood before [Harry], refusing, point-blank, to accept the prospect of disruption in his comfortable and ordered world." (HP 4, 766). Angrily he says to Dumbledore: "'It seems to me that you are all determined to start a panic that will destabilise everything we have worked for these last thirteen years!'" (HP 4, 766); "'Fudge just can't bring himself to face it. It's so much more comfortable to convince himself Dumbledore's trying to destabilise him.'" (HP 5, 109).

on the so called purity of blood! You fail to recognise that it matters not what someone is born, but what they grow to be!" (HP 4, 767-768)

Short-sightedly (HP 4, 771) he closes his eyes on Harry's report on Voldemort's return (HP 4, 765). Cornelius Fudge is, thus, an increasingly negative character. He acts irrationally and out of cowardice.[446] He refuses to face reality and is consequently replaced with Rufus Scrimgeour in *Order of the Phoenix* (HP 6, 20).

IV.5.B. Dynamism and Marketing – Rufus Scrimgeour

Fudge's successor is Rufus Scrimgeour, a man that radiates energy and is, like nearly all of Rowling's characters, compared to an animal – a limping lion:

> [Rufus Scrimgeour] looked rather like an old lion. There were streaks of grey in his mane of tawny hair and his bushy eyebrows; he had keen yellowish eyes behind a pair of wire-rimmed spectacles and a certain rangy, loping grace even though he walked with a slight limp. There was an immediate impression of shrewdness and toughness; the Prime Minister thought he understood why the wizarding community preferred Scrimgeour to Fudge as a leader in these dangerous times.(HP 6, 21-22)[447]

Until being appointed Minister for Magic Scrimgeour was head of the "Aurors", the special forces in the fight against dark magic. Quite early there are rumours that he has fallen out with Dumbledore (HP 6, 44) who believes that Scrimgeour is keeping him under surveillance (HP 6, 335). As a talented, energetic man he is much more suited to being Minister for Magic than his predecessor. Dumbledore says of him:

> "He is able, certainly. A more decisive and forceful personality than Cornelius. [...] Rufus is a man of action and, having fought Dark wizards most of his working life, does not underestimate Lord Voldemort." (HP 6, 62)

His name combines "scrim" (a rough cotton material or a theatre drop) and Rufus, the name of Roman emperors, as whom he is just as energetic and strong-minded. *Rufus* is Latin and means red-haired.[448] Moreover, there is a species of wolves called *canis rufus* – red wolf.

---

[446] He does not even dare to name Voldemort in an interview for the "Daily Prophet" and refers to him as "'the wizard styling himself Lord – well, you know who I mean –'" (HP 5, 929).

[447] Later, this is underlined again: "[...] a large black-and-white picture of a man with a lion-like mane of thick hair and a rather ravaged face." (HP 6, 43). His hair is his trademark: "mane of greying hair and his black cloak flecked with snow" (HP 6, 320).

[448] See "Rufus," *Dictionary of First Names* [1990], 2000, 201.

Scrimgeour is an experienced politician and knows that it is public relations and image that count – not talent or achievement. Media coverage is more
important than facts. When Harry spends Christmas with the Weasleys, Scrimgeour comes to see him at The Burrow and tries to persuade him to collaborate
with him (HP 6, 322-326). He intends to demonstrate to the public that the
"Chosen One" supports him and his policy.

> "It would give everyone a lift to think you were more involved [...]. The
> 'Chosen One', you know … it's all about giving people hope, the feeling
> that exciting things are happening." (HP 6, 324)

But Harry refuses – he understands that Scrimgeour is only trying to spruce up
his image.

Rufus is the prototype of a powerful politician playing with public opinion
and the media. When Voldemort attacks the Ministry, Scrimgeour proves his
quality: although the "Death Eaters" torture him, he does not tell them of
Harry's whereabouts (HP 7, 170) and is finally killed by them (HP 7, 133). Despite being quite a dubious character at the beginning, he turns out to be brave
and fights on the side of the "Order of the Phoenix". Nevertheless, he is a flat
and static character.

IV.5.C. Clumsy but Brave – Neville Longbottom

Longbottom is not a very flattering name, but fitting for a boy who, at first,
seems quite slow and dim-witted. At the same time the name could be an hom-
mage to J.R.R. Tolkien. In *The Lord of the Rings* a part of the idyllic Shire is
called Longbottom and produces one of the best tobaccos on Middle Earth.[449]
Neville's first name combines negation ("ne") and the French word *ville* (town),
which makes it something like "nowhere" or "nothing".[450] Christopher Wrigley
explains that his name, his looks and the mentioning of the family's favourite
holiday place, Blackpool, marks the Longbottoms as "Lancashire working or
lower-middle class".[451]

The Longbottoms' story is tragic: Neville's parents where tortured by four
"Death Eaters" – among them Bellatrix Lestrange and Crouch jnr (HP 4, 646) –
leaving them insane for the rest of their lives.

> "[Neville's] father, Frank, was an Auror [...]. He and his wife were tortured
> for information about Voldemort's whereabouts after he lost his powers, as
> you heard. [...] they are insane. They are both in St Mungo's Hospital for

---

[449] See Beahm 2005, 107.
[450] See Granger 2004, 107.
[451] Wrigley 2005, 11.

Magical Maladies and Injuries. I believe Neville visits them [...]. They do not recognise him." (HP 4, 655)[452]

In *Order of the Phoenix* Harry, Ron and Hermione meet Neville and his grandmother at Christmas in St Mungo's. The coincidental meeting embarrasses Neville (HP 5, 565-566). His parents' case is hopeless, his mother Alice ("Her face was thin and worn now, her eyes seemed overlarge and her hair, which had turned white, was wispy and dead-looking.", HP 5, 567) gives her son chewing-gum paper as a gift. Neville takes and keeps it.

Although he is quite a misfit in the first parts of the series, Neville turns out to be suprisingly important for the plot. Trelawney's prophecy may refer to either Harry or Neville, because the latter is born on the 30th of July, one day before Harry (HP 5, 925) and, thus, also "as the seventh month dies".[453] And really, Neville plays an important role in the final defeat of Voldemort in *Deathly Hallows*.

Neville is brave, but at first not a very competent wizard. He is "round-faced" (HP 1, 105; HP 2, 96; HP 4, 186) and an "accident-prone boy with the worst memory of anyone Harry had ever met" (HP 2, 96). The first time we meet him in *Philosopher's Stone* he is looking for his pet toad Trevor.[454] Even his grandmother, with whom he is living, is not very confident in his talent.[455] The boy has an extremely bad memory[456] and causes one catastrophe after the other: he melts his fellow students' cauldron by accident (HP 1, 152), has an accident in his first flying lesson ever (HP 1, 161)[457] and loses a note with the Gryffindor password giving Black access to Harry's dormitory (HP 3, 291). Severus Snape harasses him and Neville is so afraid of him that his "Boggart" (a ghost taking the shape of whatever his adversary fears most) appears as Snape. The teacher's judgement on Neville is devastating: "'Longbottom causes devastation with the simplest spells'" (HP 2, 209) he says, and warns Remus: "'Possi-

---

[452] Grandma Longbottom explains to Harry, Ron and Hermione: "'My son and his wife [...] were tortured into insanity by You-Know-Who's followers. [...] They were Aurors, [...] and very well respected within the wizarding community.'" (HP 5, 566).

[453] Rowling 2006.

[454] At the "Hogwarts Express" Harry sees "a round-faced boy who was saying 'Gran, I've lost my toad again.' 'Oh, NEVILLE,' he heard the old woman sigh." (HP 1, 105).

[455] She sends her permission for Neville to go to Hogsmeade directly to McGonagall: "Your grandmother sent yours to me directly [...]. She seemed to think it was safer." (HP 3, 163).

[456] He locks himself out of the dormitory, because "'I couldn't remember the new password to get in to bed.'" (HP 1, 171). See also "extremely forgetful boy" (HP 4, 186); "Neville's memory was notoriously poor." (HP 4, 211); "[...] Neville almost always forgot to pack something." (HP 4, 214).

[457] His grandma was right not to permit him to fly: "Neville had never been on a broomstick in his life, because his grandmother had never let him near one. [...] Neville managed to have an extraordinary number of accidents even with both feet on the ground." (HP 1, 158).

bly no one's warned you, Lupin, but this class contains Neville Longbottom.'"[458] (HP 3, 144) His grandmother speaks badly about him: "'[He] hasn't got his father's talent [...]'" (HP 5, 566). Therefore, Neville has a very low self-esteem ("'[...] everyone knows I'm almost a Squib.'"[459], HP 2, 201), presenting himself to Luna Lovegood saying: "'I'm nobody'" (HP 5, 208). McGonagall understands when she says: "'There's nothing wrong with your work, except lack of confidence'" (HP 5, 286). The only subject Neville is good in is herbology (HP 4, 242; HP 5, 209). As a Gryffindor he is brave. Already in his first year, Dumbledore praises his attempts to prevent Harry and Ron from their nightly expeditions: "'It takes a great deal of bravery to stand up to our enemies, but just as much to stand up to our friends'" (HP 1, 329). And Neville himself provokes Malfoy saying: "'I'm worth twelve of you ...'" (HP 1, 241).

In *Order of the Phoenix* Neville begins an astonishing development: with the aid of Harry's special classes in "Dumbledore's Army" he improves "beyond recognition" (HP 5, 500) and gains self-esteem. After a while "only Hermione mastered the [Shield Charm] faster than Neville" (HP 5, 610). Bravely he fights for Ginny (HP 5, 816) and is determined to participate in saving Sirius from the Ministry:

> "'We were all in the DA together [...]. It was all supposed to be about fighting You-Know-Who, wasn't it? And this is the first chance we've had to do something real – or was that all just a game or something?'" (HP 5, 836)

Finally, in *Deathly Hallows*, Neville does play a decisive part in killing Voldemort: Neville has begun to organise resistance in Hogwarts and commands "Dumbledore's Army" (HP 7, 460), his long hair being the symbol of the outlaw (HP 7, 459). Suddenly, everyone is praising him – his grandmother tells him she is proud of him (HP 7, 464) and his fellow-students look up to him (HP 7, 465). Neville is the one to destroy the last remaining "Horcrux" when Harry has already died (HP 7, 586-587). In another act of bravery he manages to pull Gryffindor's sword from the burning Sorting Hat and kills the snake Nagini with it.

---

[458] The verb "contain" usually refers to possibly toxic chemical ingredients.

[459] A "Squib" is a child from a wizard family but who does not have any magical skills himself. Argus Filch is a "Squib" as we learn in *Goblet of Fire* (IV.6.D, 272). Neville's family was happy to find out that he had at least some magic in him: "'[...] the family thought I was all Muggle for ages. My great-uncle Algie kept trying to catch me off my guard and force some magic out of me – he pushed me off the end of Blackpool pier once, I nearly drowned – but nothing happened until I was eight. Great-uncle Algie came round for tea and he was hanging me out of an upstairs window by the ankles when my great auntie Enid offered him a meringue and he accidentally let go. But I bounced – all the way down the garden and into the road. They were all really pleased. Gran was crying, she was so happy.'" (HP 1, 137).

In the very last chapter "Nineteen Years Later" we hear that Neville has returned to Hogwarts and teaches Herbology (HP 7, 606).

Despite his development, Neville is yet another flat, but rather dynamic character. He has nothing ambivalent about him.

IV.5.D. Battle-Scarred Dark Wizard Catcher – Alastor Moody

It is quite difficult to evaluate the character of Alastor Moody, because when we first meet him in *Goblet of Fire* he is not himself but replaced with the help of "Polyjuice Potion" by Barty Crouch jnr The real Moody is the impostor's prisoner and liberated only at the end of the novel.

Moody is, indeed, quite freakish – so his surname, again, fits him very well. Alastor is a character of Greek mythology and an avenger embodying family feuds and original sin. In Roman mythology Alastor is a troublesome character instigating people to murder and sin.

His first entrance on the *Potter* stage is quite impressive:

> [There] was a deafening rumble of thunder, and the doors of the Great Hall banged open. A man stood in the doorway, leaning upon a long staff, shrouded in a black travelling cloak. Every head in the Great Hall swivelled towards the stranger, suddenly brightly illuminated by a fork of lightning that flashed across the ceiling. He lowered his hood, shook out a long mane of grizzled, dark grey hair [...]. A *clunk* echoed through the Hall on his every step. [...] The lightning had thrown the man's face into sharp relief, and it was a face unlike any Harry had ever seen. It looked as though it had been carved out of weathered wood by someone who had only the vaguest idea of what human faces were supposed to look like, and was none too skilled with a chisel. Every inch of skin seemed to be scarred. The mouth looked like a diagonal gash, and a large chunk of the nose was missing. But it was the man's eyes that made him frightening. One of them was small, dark and beady. The other was large, round as a coin, and a vivid, electric blue. The blue eye was moving ceaselessly, without blinking, and was rolling up, down and from side to side, quite independently of the normal eye – and then it rolled right over, pointing into the back of the man's head, so that all they could see was whiteness. [...] He stretched out a hand that was as badly scarred as his face [...]. (HP 4, 204-205)

Although this scene seems to be very dramatic, again, it shows the typical elements of Rowling's characterisation techniques. We experience the scene from Harry's point of view ("Harry had ever seen": see II.2.G, 53). It is Moody's eyes that characterise him most. His magical eye rotates in his injured face and gazes through his scarred skull. The characteristics "strange", "frightening" and "chaotic" – even "ruined" – are dominant features. Alastor Moody was the "Auror" that caught "Death Eater" Igor Karkaroff and followed his trial

(HP 4, 638). In order to keep an eye on the ex-collaborator with Voldemort, Dumbledore has asked him to teach in Hogwarts (HP 4, 232).

The character of Alastor Moody is yet another example of how Rowling uses false clues to raise her readers' expectations. In this case she does it the other way around as with Sirius Black[460] (see IV.3.O, 216). The former "Auror" is a character to be trusted under any circumstance, because most of the positive characters have a very good opinion of him: the Weasleys hold him in high-esteem,[461] he takes Harry's side against Draco Malfoy (HP 4, 226-227) and strengthens Neville's self-confidence (HP 4, 242). He becomes Harry's mentor just as much as Remus Lupin (HP 4, 242-243). Later we realise that it is Crouch alias Moody trying to take revenge on the Malfoys and to gain as much influence on Harry as possible to lead him to Voldemort. Moody represents non-violence and compassion.[462] When working as an "Auror" he tried to use as little violence as possible.[463] But his cruel treatment of Draco (whom he transfigures into a ferret) (HP 4, 226-227) and his live-demonstration of the "Unforgiveable Curses" in front of his class do not quite fit this image of him. This is a first hint that there is something wrong with Moody in *Goblet of Fire*. But with him being described as bizarre and a bit mad,[464] this information does not appear too disturbing. When he takes all his meals in his own room (HP 4, 353) we believe this is due to his paranoia. We do not suspect that Barty Crouch has to take his "Polyjuice Potion" in private. This is a completely surprising twist of the plot.[465]

When we meet him again in *Order of the Phoenix* he has turned into a key figure of the resistance against Voldemort, but does not figure very prominently in the action. At the beginning of *Deathly Hallows* he dies trying to escort Harry from Privet Drive to The Burrow (HP 7, 69-70).

---

[460] Also: "looking as strange and frightening as ever" (HP 4, 231); "carved wooden leg, ending in a clawed foot" (HP 4, 206); "grizzled grey hair out of his twisted and scarred face" (HP 4, 232); "mutilated face" (HP 4, 284); "Mad-Eye Moody, who had long grizzled grey hair and a large chunk missing from his nose [...]. One eye was small, dark and beady, the other large, roand and electric blue – [...]." (HP 5, 58); "looking quite as sinister" (HP 5, 952).

[461] Bill Weasley: "'Moody was a great wizard in his time.'"; Mrs Weasley to George: "'Your father thinks very highly of Mad-Eye Moody [...].'"; Charlie says: "'He's an old friend of Dumbledore's.'" (HP 4, 179).

[462] Although he shows malicious joy when threatening Vernon Dursley: "'Are you threatening me, sir?'[...] 'Yes, I am,' said Mad-Eye, who seemed rather pleased [...]." (HP 5, 955).

[463] Sirius says of him: "[Moody] never killed if he could help it. Always brought people in alive where possible. He was tough, but he never descended to the level of the Death Eaters [sic!]. Crouch, though ... he's a different matter ... [...]." (HP 4, 579).

[464] According to Sirius Moody was "'the best Auror the Ministry ever had'" (HP 4, 366), but has a lot of criminal records (HP 4, 178), and generally is considered a "nutter" (HP 4, 179; 224).

[465] Why does Moody teach Harry to resist the "Imperius Curse"? (HP 4, 256)

Alastor Moody is a positive character: untidy, rational and brave. The few negative features about him are due to him being replaced by Crouch in *Goblet of Fire*. Nevertheless, the character is flat and static.

IV.5.E. Wormtail and Rat – Peter Pettigrew

Wormtail is a very characteristic nickname for a two-faced double agent and magical loser, especially when it has been conferred upon him by his friends (HP 3, 382). Even his real name is not much more flattering; referring to him being "petty"[466] or even a "pet" (which as Ron's rat Scabbers he really is). The second part of his name [gru] can either be interpreted as the past tense of "to grow" or as an allusion to "grue" (from "gruesome").[467] His first name Peter is the name of the apostle Simon Peter who denies Jesus three times (Matthew 6, 40-43). Peter is an ambivalent character – loyal and disloyal at the same time, thus, quite a becoming patron for the Potters' false friend and traitor Pettigrew.[468]

His appearance is quite neglected: he is fat, small and weak. In his Hogwarts times he desperately tried to be part of the peer group around James and Sirius, but was never fully accepted by them (HP 3, 225.). Snape remembers him as "a small, mousy-haired[469] boy with a pointed nose. Wormtail looked anxious; he was chewing his fingernails, staring down at his paper [...]." (HP 5, 707) When finally regaining his human form in *Prisoner of Azkaban* he is unkempt, nearly bald and somehow still rat-like:

> He was a very short man, hardly taller than Harry and Hermione. His thin, colourless hair was unkempt and there was a large bald patch on top. He had the shrunken appearance of a plump man who had lost a lot of weight in a short time. His skin looked grubby, almost like Scabbers's fur, and something of the rat lingered around his pointed nose and his very small, watery eyes. (HP 3, 395)

He is faceless and characterless, not only when he betrays the Potters to Voldemort, but also when dealing with Harry: "Pettigrew burst into tears. It was horrible to watch: he looked like an oversized, balding baby, cowering on the floor." (HP 3, 403) He inspires pity and disgust at the same time, pleading for his life (HP 3, 405) and suffering his master's contempt (HP 4, 13).

Again, Pettigrew is an example of Rowling's way of playing with her readers' expectations. At first he appears as a tragic hero, a martyr for his friends

---

[466] See Bürvenich 2001, 105.
[467] John Granger considers this as a version of "pet who grew": Granger 2004, 105.
[468] See Granger 2004, 105.
[469] This is a hint at the rat-shape Pettigrew is going to live in for many years.

who tries to avenge their death by duelling Sirius Black (HP 3, 225).[470] In truth he only tries to conceal his own treason. The plan works: Black is regarded as a mad killer and taken to Azkaban; Pettigrew is awarded the "Order of Merlin, First Class" (HP 3, 226). Only at the end of *Prisoner of Azkaban* do we learn the truth: the real traitor is Pettigrew who was the Potters' "Secret Keeper" (HP 3, 393). He feigned being killed by Black to go into hiding transformed into a rat (HP 3, 393). Doing this he blows up a street and kills thirteen people.

Pettigrew is shrewd but untalented and, therefore, the meanest of Voldemort's followers. Even his master realises: "'Your devotion is nothing more than cowardice. You would not be here if you had anywhere else to go'" (HP 4, 16). Mercilessly Voldemort lets him suffer, although he has been depending on him to keep him alive: "'I need somebody with brains [and] loyalty [...] and you, unfortunately, fulfil neither requirement'" (HP 4, 17). Nevertheless, Pettigrew is devoted to him, unscrupulous and cruel. His devotion extends to sacrificing his own hand to contribute to Voldemort's physical resurrection (HP 4, 695). But even this gesture does not improve his rank within Voldemort's hierarchy. In *Half-Blood Prince* we see him a servant to Severus Snape in Spinner's End:

> The man crept hunchbacked down the last few steps and moved into the room. He had small, watery eyes, a pointed nose and wore an unpleasant simper. His left hand was caressing his right, which looked as though it were encased in a bright silver glove. (HP 6, 29)

Pettigrew finally dies in *Deathly Hallows*, because he shows a trace of mercy when Harry and his friends are being held in the Malfoy Mansion. At that moment the magical silver hand which Voldemort gave him to replace the one he sacrificed turns against him and strangles him (HP 7, 380-381). The character of Wormtail is yet another flat and static character. There is no development whatsoever.

IV.5.F. Stinking Assassin – Prof. Quirrell

Professor Quirrell seems to be a harmless, senile teacher in the beginning; however, this changes in the course of action. His name may refer to "squirrell" or to "quarrel". In any case, his name marks him as bizarre.[471] At the end of *Prisoner of Azkaban* he is unmasked as a traitor and supporter of Voldemort's. Quirrell is pale, with "one of his eyes [...] twitching" (HP 1, 80), he wears a strange "large purple turban" (HP 1, 134) and continuously smells of garlic (HP 1, 147) – a

---

[470] Harry overhears Fudge saying: "'Pettigrew died a hero's death. [...] Pettigrew cornered Black. [...] he was sobbing. 'Lily and James, Sirius! How could you!' And then he went for his wand. [...] Black was quicker. Blew Pettigrew to smithereens ...'" (HP 3, 225).

[471] See Beahm 2005, 122; Hein 2001, 126.

grotesque figure. Underneath his turban he hides the deformed Voldemort and keeps him alive (HP 1, 277). At a "Quidditch" match he tries to kill Harry[472] and uses Snape's ill fame to make everyone believe that the "Potions" master makes Harry's broomstick twist: "'[...] Severus does seem the type, [...]. So useful to have him swooping around like an overgrown bat'" (HP 1, 310).[473] Voldemort kills him after he fails to bring him Harry Potter.

IV.5.G. Painful Detention – Dolores Jane Umbridge

Dolores is Spanish and means "pains" – a becoming name for the school dictator Umbridge. Usually the name refers to the pain of the Virgin Mary, but with Umbridge it alludes to her cruel torture of the students.[474] Her surname is the phonetic equivalent of "umbrage" which in the phrase "to give or take umbrage" can mean insulting someone or feeling insulted.[475]

When we first meet her in *Order of the Phoenix* (HP 5, 156), she is Senior Undersecretary to the Minister (HP 5, 480) – quite a ridiculous title combining the opposite ideas of "senior" and "under". At the same time, the title hints at the bureaucracy within the Ministry. In the description of the character we find a lot of judgmental elements; she even is compared to Vernon Dursley:

> She was rather squat with a broad, flabby face, as little neck as Uncle Vernon and a very wide, slack mouth. Her eyes were large, round and slightly bulging. Even the little black velvet bow perched on top of her short curly hair put him in mind of a large fly she was about to catch on a long sticky tongue. (HP 5, 165)

She has "thick, stubby fingers on which she wore a number of ugly old rings." (HP 5, 297)[476] – her jewellery hints especially at an old-fashioned, greedy and self-indulgent person. In *Deathly Hallows* we see her completely unchanged by the events of *Order of the Phoenix*. She remains the "squat, toad-

---

[472] "'I tried to kill you. [...] if Snape hadn't been muttering a countercurse, trying to save you.'" (HP 1, 311).

[473] Again an allusion to an animal – this time it is a character commenting on another character.

[474] A possible anagram reads "Go, Sir Dumbledore": see <http://www.anagramgenius.com/archive/dolores-umbridge.html> 26 Nov 2007.

[475] "to umbrage = to shade or shadow; also *fig.*, to overshadow, put in the shade; to colour over, disguise; to give a pretext or ground for; to offend, displease; to be, or to stand, in (...) umbrage = to be in disfavour." See "to umbrage," *Oxford English Dictionary online*. Oxford: University Press, 2006. <http://erf.sbb.spk-berlin.de/han/ 356448509/dictionary. oed.com/cgi/entry/50261688?query_type=word& queryword=umbrage&first=1&max_ to_show=10&sort_type=alpha&result_place=2& search_id=mHwR-bdiC5u-3128&hilite= 50261688> 5 Jan 2008. Also see Beahm 2005, 132.

[476] Also: "a stubby, short-fingered hand covered in ugly old-fashioned rings." (HP 5, 412).

like witch wearing a velvet bow in her short hair and clutching a clipboard to her chest" (HP 7, 202). Her short height represents a lack of inner qualities[477]and her eyes are "bulging" (HP 5, 439). With her old-fashioned dresses[478] she seems like a spinster:[479]

> She looked, Harry thought, like somebody's maiden aunt: squat, with short, curly, mouse-brown hair in which she had placed a horrible pink Alice band that matched the fluffy pink cardigan she wore over her robes. Then she turned her face slightly to take a sip from her goblet and he saw, with a shock of recognition, a pallid, toadlike face and a pair of prominent, pouchy eyes. (HP 5, 226)

Again, it is the voice that marks her and frequently appears. Her "high, girlish voice" (HP 5, 654) represents her falseness: "[Her] fluttery, girlish, high-pitched voice [and] silvery laugh […] made the hairs on the back of Harry's neck stand up" (HP 5, 165-166). Her voice unites exactly the features that characterise Umbridge: a mixture between friendliness and beastliness.[480] Her "Patronus" is a cat (HP 7, 214) – an animal which supposedly possesses seven lives.

Umbridge is devious and scheming. She hides her true feelings behind her superficial amiability, as Harry soon realises. When she gives him detention and sends him with a note to McGonagall she speaks "triumphantly" but at the same time calls him "'Mr Potter, dear'" (HP 5, 272-273). Pretending to be reserved she constantly puts herself in the spotlight whenever possible. Her slight cough[481] serves to interrupt nearly everyone and is, in truth, a demonstration of power. She lies and pretends not to say what she explicitly says afterwards. When she remarks, "'I do not wish to criticise how things have been run in this school'" (HP 5, 269), she does exactly this. In her friendliness she is bitchy. Questioning Hagrid about his absence from Hogwarts she comments on his having been "on holiday": "'Yes, as gamekeeper fresh air must be so difficult to come by, […]'" (HP 5, 483). She is extremely biased and she evaluates Hagrid's

---

[477] "Professor Umbridge stood up. She was so short that this did not make a great deal of difference, but her fussy, simpering demeanour had given place to a hard fury that made her broad, flabby face look oddly sinister." (HP 5, 732).

[478] "a luridly flowered set of robes that blended only too well with the table-cloth on the desk behind her." (HP 5, 294).

[479] This corresponds with the referring narrative structure where Umbridge is linked to "dead" and "lifeless" (see 125).

[480] See also: "deadly voice" (HP 5, 655); "her softest, most sweetly girlish voice" (HP 5, 273); "sugary voice" (HP 5, 294).

[481] "'Hem, hem,' said Professor Umbridge, employing the same silly little cough she had used to interrupt Dumbledore on the first night of term. […] 'Hem, hem,' […]." (HP 5, 355).

lessons and arbitrarily interprets his students' opinion (HP 5, 493-495). She frequently plots against her adversaries in the background.[482]

From the very beginning Umbridge is frequently compared to a toad: "[Harry] thought she looked just like a large, pale toad" (HP 5, 165). Everything about her seems to be sticky, moist and sycophantic: "Even the little black velvet bow perched on top of her short curly hair put him in mind of a large fly she was about to catch on a long sticky tongue." (HP 5, 165)[483] This comparison underlines her actual powerlessness which she – just like a toad – hides behind a loud croaking. Like a toad hunting down its prey without having to get close to it, Umbridge is at first a phantom menace: only with help from the Ministry and her intrigues is she able finally to achieve her goal.

Her main characteristics are cruelty and perversion. Smiling, giggling and apparently friendly, she tortures students and colleagues alike. Phrases like "nasty litle laugh" (HP 5, 270) and "horribly honeyed voice" (HP 5, 271) are dominant in her characterisation. She turns out to be sadistic when she tortures Harry in his detention: instead of writing with ink he has to use a quill that scratches "I must not tell lies" into the skin of his own hand. On the first evening of his detention she rejoices in Harry's upcoming pains: "'Oh, you won't need ink,' said Professor Umbridge with the merest suggestion of a laugh in her voice" (HP 5, 296). And when later on she sees Harry's inflamed hand she openly shows her pleasure "smiling [...] widely" (HP 5, 301). Torturing the boy she smiles "sweetly" (HP 5, 304) and comments in a pseudo-compassionate way upon his pains: "'Yes, it hurts, doesn't it?' she said softly" (HP 5, 305). She uses physical violence on Marietta who has been magically silenced by Kingsley Shacklebolt (HP 5, 679).

Not only is it Harry and his friends who suffer under Umbridge: Sybill Trelawney is maltreated by her as well (HP 5, 347–350),[484] and finally sent away. Umbridge delights in Sybill sobbing and pleading:

---

482   She says to McGonagall: "'[You] remember how you overrode me, when I was unwilling to allow the Gryffindor Quidditch team to re-form? How you took the case to Dumbledore, who insisted that the team be allowed to play? Well, now, I couldn't have that. I contacted the Minister at once, and he quite agreed with me that the High Inquisitor has to have the power to strip pupils of privileges, or she – that is to say, I – would have less authority than common teachers.'" (HP 5, 459-460).

483   See also: "The toadlike witch on his right, however, merely gazed at Dumbledore, her face quite expressionless." (HP 5, 169); "the toadlike witch" (HP 5, 171 and 172); "a pallid, toadlike face and a pair of prominent, pouchy eyes." (HP 5, 226); "pouchy toad's eyes" (HP 5, 267); "toadlike smile" (HP 5, 349); "a green tweed cloak that greatly enhanced her resemblance to a giant toad" (HP 5, 458); "her wide toad's mouth" (HP 5, 635); "her toadlike face" (HP 5, 655).

484   "She lurked by the fire [...] interrupting Professor Trelawney's increasingly hysterical talks with difficult questions about ornithomancy and heptomology, insisting that she

263

[...] Harry was revolted to see the enjoyment stretching her toadlike face as she watched Professor Trelawney sink, sobbing uncontrollably, on to one of her trunks, [...]. [Umbridge showed] an expression of gloating enjoyment, as Professor Trelawney shuddered and moaned, rocking backwards and forwards on her trunk in paroxysms of grief. (HP 5, 655)

Brutality and sadism – that is what Umbridge hides behind the smiling facade. She takes pleasure in the suffering of others,[485] which sometimes seems to border on eroticism.[486]

Like all the negative characters, Umbridge is a coward – she is even afraid of the Weasleys' magical fireworks. "[...] Umbridge and Filch [...] both yelled with fright [...]" (HP 5, 696). The centaurs make her panic ("Umbridge uttering odd little whimpers of terror", HP 5, 828). She even lets her students – children and her wards – walk in front of her into the Forbidden Forest: "'The Ministry places a rather higher value on my life than yours, I'm afraid'" (HP 5, 826). This is a moral perversion, because in most cultures, the lives of children are highly valued.

Umbridge's lessons are dictatorial. Manners are important – studying is not.[487] The students are supposed to put up their hands to speak, but are not allowed to speak when she supposes them to criticise her (HP 5, 268-271). Her didactics are highly insufficient and consist of reading a book. Each lesson starts with her saying "'Wands away, please. There will be no need to talk.'" (e.g. HP 5, 406) Umbridge calls this "'a carefully structured, theory-centred, Ministry-approved course of defensive magic'" (HP 5, 266). Everything the Ministry announces is right and students are not allowed their own opinion. When Hermione wonders about the aim of her lessons, Umbridge simply refuses to answer:

"Are you a Ministry-trained educational expert, Miss Granger?" asked Professor Umbridge, in her falsely sweet voice. "No, but –" "Well then, I'm afraid you are not qualified to decide what the 'whole point' of any class is." (HP 5, 269)

---

[485] predict students' answers before they gave them and demanding that she demonstrate her skill at the crystal ball, the tea leaves and the rune stones in turn." (HP 5, 608). She obviously enjoys announcing the life-long "Quidditch" ban on Harry and the Weasleys "smiling still more broadly [...and] with a look of the utmost satisfaction, Umbridge left the room, leaving a horrified silence in her wake." (HP 5, 459-461).

[486] After arresting the members of "Dumbledore's Army" we read: "There was an indecent excitement in her voice, [...] a callous pleasure [...]." (HP 5, 672).

[487] Discipline and obedience to the rules are the most important. The way the students have to address their teacher is clearly defined: "'I should like you, please, to reply 'Good afternoon, Professor Umbridge.' One more time, please. Good afternoon, class!'" (HP 5, 265); "'When I ask you a question, I should like you to reply, 'Yes, Professor Umbridge', or 'No, Professor Umbridge.'" (HP 5, 266).

There is a certain irony in Umbridge becoming "High Inquisitor" of Hogwarts. This office was originally instituted in the Late Middle Ages and refers to special powers granted by the Vatican to torture prisoners, i.e. heretics, who were usually accused of practising magic. So Umbridge holds an office which deals with torturing wizards and witches. Having become headmistress of Hogwarts, Umbridge controls the whole school with a mixture of censorship, brutality and absolute control – just like any totalitarian regime does:[488] "[... It was] her furious desire to bring every aspect of life at Hogwarts under her personal control" (HP 5, 608).

She has the post opened; the school becomes a prison which no one can escape.[489] Umbridge even forms her own students' police. Nevertheless, she is so narcissistic that she does not realise how much everybody hates her.[490] On her first evening at Hogwarts she makes the students her enemies by addressing them in the wrong manner at the wrong time:

> [This] woman obviously did not know how things were done at Hogwarts. [...] She gave another little throat-clearing cough (*'hem, hem'*) and continued. [... All the pupils] looked rather taken-aback at being addressed as [happy little faces] as though they were five years old. [...] 'I'm sure we'll be very good friends!' [...]. (HP 5, 236)[491]

Hermione is the first to realise that "'she's here to spy on us all, that's obvious'" (HP 5, 280). She fervently hates Umbridge,[492] Ron regards her as an "'old hag'" and "sick" (HP 5, 302-303) and Harry says: "'She's evil, [...]. Twisted.'" (HP 5, 308) Even Cho Chang, who is not a very rebellious character, criticises her, saying "'That Umbridge woman's foul, [...]'" (HP 5, 315). Only the negative characters favour Umbridge. Percy, writing to his brother Ron, describes her as a "'truly delightful woman'" (HP 5, 331). Argus Filch believes that with Umbridge as headmistress his chance of physically punishing the students has come:

> "But when Educational Decree Number Twenty-nine comes in, Potter, I'll be allowed to [whip you raw and string you up by the ankles in my office ...]

---

[488] von Lovenberg 2003.
[489] "My Inquisitorial Squad is opening and reading all owl post entering and leaving the castle. And Mr Filch is observing all secret passages in and out of the castle." (HP 5, 695).
[490] "Professor Umbridge did not seem to notice the restlessness of her audience." (HP 5, 237).
[491] This is just another example of how Rowling guides her readers: after this introduction we know that Umbridge is a negative character.
[492] See also: "'She's an awful woman,' said Hermione in a small voice. 'Awful.'" (HP 5, 360); "'That foul, lying, twisting old gargoyle!'" stormed Hermione half an hour later, [...]. (HP 5, 495); "'that stupid puffed-up, power-crazy old –'" (HP 5, 688).

... oh, things are going to be very different around here with *her* in charge ..." (HP 5, 692)

Umbridge is not a very talented witch – she does not even succeed in healing Marietta from Hermione's charm (HP 5, 675). And she cannot cope with the swamp produced by the Weasley twins inside the castle.[493] The symbol of her incapacity is her "unusually short [wand]" (HP 5, 265). Like the other negative characters, Umbridge does not like animals. She tries to drive away Hagrid's friendly dog Fang in a ridiculous fashion using her handbag: "'Get away,' she snapped, waving her handbag at Fang, who had bounded up to her and was attempting to lick her face" (HP 5, 480). In particular, Umbridge denies magical creatures equal rights: werewolves, giants and centaurs are her favourite enemies. Sirius tells Harry:

"[She] drafted a bit of anti-werewolf legislation two years ago that makes it almost impossible for [Lupin] to get a job. [...] she loathes part-humans; she campaigned to have merpeople rounded up and tagged last year, too." (HP 5, 336)

Her excessive hunger for power leads to her losing control. Instead of reigning supreme she causes the school's community to rebel. Her colleagues delight in her helplessness in the face of the Weasley brothers' jokes: "Though [the fireworks] caused plenty of disruption, particularly the firecrackers, the other teachers didn't seem to mind them very much" (HP 5, 697).[494] This practically non-violent resistance also includes poltergeist Peeves: "Peeves [...] spent hours at a time floating along after Umbridge and blowing loud raspberries every time she spoke" (HP 5, 746). The students add to the chaos by using the Weasley twins' magical snackbox (HP 5, 746). The only true delinquent in all of this is Dolores Umbridge herself. She breaks the law and betrays Cornelius Fudge as she herself admits:

"The Cruciatus Curse ought to loosen [Potter's] tongue [...]. What Cornelius doesn't know won't hurt him, [...]. He never knew I ordered Dementors to go after Potter last summer, but he was delighted to be given a chance to expel him, all the same. [...] *Somebody* had to act." (HP 5, 820-821)

---

[493] "Harry was certain that teachers like McGonagall or Flitwick could have removed the swamp in an instant but, just as in the case of Fred and George's Wildfire Whiz-bangs, they seemed to prefer to watch Umbridge struggle." (HP 5, 744).

[494] Pretending to be incompetent they ask Umbridge for help: "Harry saw, with immense satisfaction, a dishevelled and soot-blackened Umbridge tottering sweaty-faced from Professor Flitwick's classroom." (HP 5, 697).

She not only intends to use an "Unforgiveable Curse" on a child but also acts against the interests of the Ministry. This is high treason and an example of administration making its own laws and running wildly out of control. Her end is quite inglorious. Dumbledore frees her from the centaurs and she recovers in the hospital wing not saying anything: "Since she had returned to the castle she had not, as far as any of them knew, uttered a single word" (HP 5, 933). Trying to leave the castle unseen, Peeves makes her look extremely silly:

> [Umbridge] had crept out of the hospital wing during dinnertime, evidently hoping to depart undetected, but unfortunately for her, she met Peeves on the way, who seized his last chance to do as Fred had instructed, and chased her gleefully from the premises whacking her alternately with a walking stick and a sock full of chalk. (HP 5, 941)

Dolores Umbridge obviously is one of the most negative characters of the whole series, but is more subtle than the Malfoys or the Dursleys. It is important for the interpretation of the series that her dictatorship fails because of the non-violent resistance of her colleagues and students. This holds a clear message: the more you control and mistrust your fellow human beings, the less power you have in the long run. Oppression and dictatorship cannot cut off freedom and democracy for ever. Human rights will have to be granted in the end.

Astonishingly, Dolores Umbridge is not suspended after her misconduct at Hogwarts: she continues to work for the ministry. In *Deathly Hallows* we meet her again as Head of the Muggle-born Registration Commission (HP 7, 206) where she plays an infamous role in persecuting non-pure-blood wizards. She has written a pamphlet entitled *"MUDBLOODS and the Dangers They Pose to a Peaceful Pure-Blood Society."* The cover is decorated with a highly agitational illustration: "Beneath the title was a picture of a red rose, with a simpering face in the middle of its petals, being strangled by a green weed with fangs and a scowl" (HP 7, 205). During the hearings she presides over, she again proves to be sadistic (HP 7, 212-220). "Umbridge, the persecutor-in-pink"[495] has black-mailed Mundungus Fletcher to give her Slytherin's locket (HP 7, 182) with which she now pretends to be from an ancient family (HP 7, 215). Obviously, she is in touch with the people assaulting Harry and his escort in the second chapter of *Deathly Hallows*, because she has seized dead Mad-Eye's magical eye, put it into her office door and uses it to spy on her employees (HP 7, 206).

Although not physically violent or dangerous in herself, Umbridge represents a nameless, institutionalised horror. She belongs to an environment where the individual gets into the mills of anonymous bodies of bureaucracy. The hearings she presides over are reminiscent of Kafka's *The Trial*. Critics have cor-

---

[495] See Muir 2007.

rectly called her "the most memorably flesh-creeping [monster]" of the novels and "far more terrifying [...] than demon king Voldemort".[496]

IV.5.H. *Networking* par Excellence – Horace Slughorn

His name refers to slime (slug) and loud noises (horn, trumpet), and this quite suits Horace E. F. Slughorn (HP 6, 135).[497] He likes to praise himself and tends to "name-drop", letting everybody know how very much he is associated with celebrities and high society: "'I remember dear Gwenog telling me – Gwenog Jones, I mean, of course, Captain of the Holyhead Harpies –'" (HP 6, 140). Like a spider he weaves a net of connections[498] as Dumbledore points out:

> "He also likes the company of the famous, the successful and the powerful. He enjoys the feeling that he influences these people. He has never wanted to occupy the throne himself; he prefers the back seat – more room to spread out, you see. He used to handpick favourites at Hogwarts, sometimes for their ambition or their brains, sometimes for their charm or their talent, and he had an uncanny knack for choosing those who would go on to become outstanding in their various fields." (HP 6, 75)

Nevertheless, Slughorn is no impostor like Gilderoy Lockhart (see IV.4.B, 222) – he is highly talented. His first name refers to Roman poet Quintus Horatius Flaccus – one of the most important poets of the Augustan Age. His sentence *Carpe diem quam minimum credula postero* ("Use the day, don't trust the next day") could be Slughorn's motto. He enjoys the present and tries to live as pleasantly as possible as Harry remarks when looking around Slughorn's room:

> It was stuffy and cluttered, yet nobody could say it was uncomfortable; there were soft chairs and footstools, drinks and books, boxes of chocolates and plump cushions. If Harry had not known who lived there, he would have guessed at a rich, fussy old lady. (HP 6, 68)[499]

---

[496] See Kemp 2003.
[497] See "Horace Slughorn." *Wikipedia, The Free Encyclopedia.* 22 Aug 2007. <http://en.wikipedia.org/w/index.php?title=Horace_Slughorn&oldid=152871522> 22 Aug 2007.
[498] On his first visit Slughorn already takes the opportunity to point out his collection of autographs to Harry: "[...] smiling in a self-satisfied way, and pointed at the many glittering photograph frames on the dresser, each peopled with tiny moving occupants. 'All ex-students, all signed.'" (HP 6, 72). See also: "Harry had a sudden and vivid mental image of a great swollen spider, spinning a web around him, twitching a thread here and there to bring its large and juicy flies a little closer." (HP 6, 75). Mrs Weasley laments: "'The Ministry's littered with Slughorn's old favourites, he was always good at giving leg-ups, but he never had much time for Arthur – didn't seem to think he was enough of a high-flier.'" (HP 6, 83).
[499] Dumbledore says of him: "'Horace [...] likes his comfort.'" (HP 6, 75).

His appearance reflects this attitude to life as well:

> [...] an enormously fat, bald old man who was massaging his lower belly and squinting up at Dumbledore with an aggrieved and watery eye [...]. The wand-light sparkled on his shiny pate, his prominent eyes, his enormous, silver walrus-like moustache, and the highly polished buttons on the maroon velvet jacket he was wearing over a pair of lilac silk pyjamas. The top of his head barely reached Dumbledore's chin. (HP 6, 65)

And just like all the other characters, Slughorn is frequently compared to an animal – in this case a walrus (HP 6, 89), with watery eyes (HP 6, 70). Astonishingly, he was head of Slytherin house in the times of Tom Riddle (HP 6, 71).[500]

When we meet him in *Order of the Phoenix* he shows traces of cowardice, racism and cruelty (see IV.3.L, 191). Harry's mother Lily was one of his favourites, although he seems to be prejudiced against "Muggle"-borns: "'Your mother was Muggle-born, of course. Couldn't believe it when I found out. Thought she must have been pure-blood, she was so good'" (HP 6, 71). At the same time he fervently declares himself not to be racist: "'You mustn't think I'm prejudiced! [...] No, no, no!'" (HP 6, 71). In *Order of the Phoenix* he has been "'on the move for a year'" (HP 6, 69). And although he admits to the Order's bravery he does not want to join himself: "'I don't personally fancy the mortality rate'" (HP 6, 73). Afraid of his own disreputable memories, he has manipulated his brain and does not remember that he was the one to show Riddle how to creat "Horcruxes" (HP 6, 348). He vigorously denies having helped Tom (HP 6, 356). And out of cowardice and cruelty he lets "'a house-elf taste every bottle after what happened to your poor friend Rupert'"[501] (HP 6, 454).

In fact, Slughorn should be a negative character. But he also is an – at first reluctant –helper to Harry. Surprisingly, we find him actively fighting against Voldemort in *Deathly Hallows*. When all of his house has been evacuated from Hogwarts he returns and urges the others on to fight. Together with McGonagall he takes on Voldemort before Harry does (HP 7, 479). So, Slughorn is the example of a positive Slytherin: cunning and clever, but brave and upright when necessary. Nevertheless, he is not very likeable.

IV.5.I. Wit beyond measure – Luna Lovegood

Luna is the Latin word for "moon". The girl being "dreamy" and "misty", her name fits her quite well. It also alludes to "lunatic" or "loony", the latter word being her nickname. Her surname consists of "love" and "good" which may

---

[500] It is important to note that not all Slytherin characters are bad, Slughorn is not very likeable but he is a good character.

[501] Ron is not important enough for Slughorn to remember his name correctly.

mean "good to love", i.e. lovable or complaisant. Her strange appearance and her bizarre esoteric behaviour make her an outsider:

> She had straggly, waist-length, dirty blonde hair, very pale eye-brows and protuberant eyes that gave her a permanently surprised look. [...] The girl gave off an aura of distinct dottiness. Perhaps it was the fact that she had stuck her wand behind her left ear for safekeeping, or that she had chosen to wear a necklace of Butterbeer corks, or that she was reading a magazine upside-down. [...] She did not seem to need to blink as much as normal humans. (HP 5, 207-208)

Luna is a highly talented witch and as such belongs to Ravenclaw. Her father, Xenophilius[502] Lovegood, is the chief editor of "The Quibbler", a magazine dealing with highly dubious subjects. She first enters the *Potter* stage in *Order of the Phoenix* and is looked down upon by Harry, Ron and Hermione. But in the course of the plot she turns out to be a decisive helper. In an interview with her father's magazine "The Quibbler", Harry can make public what the ministry wants to hide: Voldemort's return. Luna is also the one to explain to Harry why he can see the magical skeleton-like horses ("Thestrals"): just like herself he has seen people die.[503] Luna is brave and brilliant. She joins "Dumbledore's Army", fights in the "Department of Mysteries" and helps Harry to enter Ravenclaw Tower in *Deathly Hallows*. Voldemort has her taken hostage to force her father to support him.

Luna usually appears to be "on her own and looking so dreamy she might have walked in by accident" (HP 5, 374).[504] Her fellow-students laugh about her strange looks[505] and her bizarre statements.[506] Just for fun they steal or hide her things and each year she must search for them before leaving Hogwarts for the holidays. Patiently, she endures such jokes and Harry finally sees her as soulmate.[507] Luna is a flat and static character.

---

[502] The name means "friend of the strange".

[503] Luna has seen her mother die (HP 5, 948). Riding the terrible looking skeleton-horses does not frighten her: "Luna was already in place, sitting side-saddle and adjusting her robes as though she did this every day." (HP 5, 840).

[504] "[Luna] simply watched [Ron] for a while as though he were a mildly interesting television programme." (HP 5, 223).

[505] "Luna Lovegood gazing dreamily into space." (HP 5, 376).

[506] "'Wit beyond measure is man's greatest treasure,' said Luna in a sing-song voice." (HP 5, 208)

[507] "[Harry] was feeling sorry for Luna. [...] 'I think they think me a bit odd, you know. Some people call me 'Loony' Lovegood, actually.' Harry looked at her and the new feeling of pity intensified rather painfully." (HP 5, 947).

IV.6 Marginal Characters

These are the characters without any decisive influence on the main or sub-plots of the novels. Nevertheless I shall deal with them briefly.

IV.6.A. Cedric Diggory

Cedric Diggory[508] is "Seeker" of Hufflepuff "Quidditch" Team: "tall, good-looking", "strong and silent" (HP 3, 183) – in other words a heart-throb, who is taller and older than Harry (HP 3, 189), and a very good student and prefect in *Goblet of Fire* (HP 4, 259.[509] In *Prisoner of Azkaban* when Harry has suffered a severe accident in a "Quidditch" match between Gryffindor and Hufflepuff Cedric wants to annul the game (HP 3, 196). His father Amos works at the Department for the Regulation and Control of Magical Creatures, and is very proud of his son (HP 4, 83-84). Cedric competes as school champion in *Goblet of Fire*. He is forcibly taken to Little Hangleton with Harry. Voldemort kills him right away (HP 4, 691). Cedric is the first character of the series that dies. He is a one-dimensional flat character.

IV.6.B. Viktor Krum

Eighteen-year-old "Quidditch" hero Krum is Harry's opponent, Hermione's first love and, at first, quite a dubious character. He is a *victor* (i.e. Latin for "winner") in "Quidditch" where he plays as "Seeker" for the Bulgarian national team. Krum is neither likeable with his "surly face with heavy black eyebrows" (HP 4, 95) nor handsome:

> Viktor Krum was thin, dark and sallow-skinned, with a large curved nose and thick black eyebrows. He looked like an overgrown bird of prey. It was hard to believe he was only eighteen. (HP 4, 119)[510]

Without his broomstick he seems "slightly duck-footed and distinctly round-shouldered" (HP 4, 131). His English has a very hard accent (which the text reflects phonetically). His surname is derived from a Bulgarian Khan, a fa-

---

[508] Hein sees Beatrix Potter's mole Diggory Diggory Delvet of *Appley Dapply's Nursery Rhymes* as relevant: see Hein 2001, 47.

[509] The name was invented by Sir Walter Scott for his novel *Ivanhoe*. Ivanhoe's father is an Anglo-Saxon nobleman fighting against Norman invaders. See "Cedric," *Dictionary of First Names* [1990], 2000. 53.

[510] Krum is limited to just a few characteristics like "a prominent, curved nose and thick black eyebrows." (HP 4, 272). He is compared to an animal as well.

mous military leader (803-814).[511] Everything about him seems aggressive, which is why it is astonishing to see him falling in love with Hermione (HP 4, 600) whom he asks out to the Yule Ball. Finally he criticises head master Igor Karkaroff. The development from adversary to friend, from Durmstrang representative to Hermione's friend and Dumbledore follower is not very convincing. Krum is quite a one-dimensional and flat character.

IV.6.C. Mundungus Fletcher

Mundungus Fletcher is a member of the "Order of the Phoenix", but not a very reliable one. He drinks, lets himself go and is continuously involved in dubious business:

> There was a loud *crack* and a strong smell of drink mingled with stale tobacco filled the air as a squat, unshaven man in a tattered overcoat materialised right in front of them. He had short, bandy legs, long straggly ginger hair and bloodshot, baggy eyes that gave him the doleful look of a basset hound. He was also clutching a silvery bundle that Harry recognised at once as an Inivisibility Cloak. (HP 5, 30-31)

The first part of his name "mund-" is taken from "mundane", "-dungus" is derived from "dung", which is also his nickname (HP 5, 95). His surname, Fletcher, is the name of a profession: someone who makes arrows. So, again, this name is quite fitting for a person working in the underground and preferring not to be involved in battle. In fact, he is a "stinking arrow-maker"[512] or even a "world filth arrow-maker".[513] Fletcher is lazy and unreliable, skipping meetings (HP 5, 95), showing off his cheating on others (HP 5, 100) and trying to hide stolen cauldrons in Grimmauld Place (HP 5, 122). He even steals artefacts, among them Voldemort's "Horcrux" locket, from the Blacks' house and handles them (HP 7, 164). Sirius says of him: "'He's useful, [...]. Knows all the crooks – well, he would, seeing as he's one himself. But he's also very loyal to Dumbledore, who helped him out of a tight spot once'" (HP 5, 101). He helps to protect Harry when disguised as a witch. He is present at his first meeting with "Dumbledore's Army" in the "Hogs's Head" (HP 5, 409). His unreliability causes Mad-Eye Moody's death in *Deathly Hallows* (HP 7, 69-70).

---

[511] See Hein 2001, 87 and Beahm 2005, 104 who gives us 808 to 814 as the years of his reign.
[512] See Beahm 2005, 95.
[513] See Granger 2004, 108.

IV.6.D. Argus Filch

Argus is the Hogwarts caretaker and sees just about everything. His first name is, therefore, taken from the hundred-eye giant servant to the Greek goddess Hera.[514] His surname phonetically resembles "filth"[515] and at the same time means "to steal something". His cat, Mrs Norris, is named after a scheming character in Jane Austen's *Mansfield Park*[516] and is just as disagreeable:

> Filch owned a cat called Mrs Norris, a scrawny, dustcoloured creature with bulging, lamp-like eyes just like Filch's. [...] Filch knew the secret passage-ways of the school better than anyone [...] and could pop up as suddenly as any of the ghosts. The students all hated him and it was the dearest ambition of many to give Mrs Norris a good kick. (HP 1, 145-146)

Filch is a totally negative character, "a bad-tempered, failed wizard who waged a constant war against the students [...]" (HP 3, 143), and his description is limited to just a few characteristics. He is cruel and sadistic[517] and a "Squib" (HP 2, 156). To improve his standing with the Hogwarts students (whom he calls "filthy little beasts", HP 5, 692) he follows a distance course in magic (HP 2, 139-140; HP 2, 160). Filch might be an example of a more complex character, if he figured more prominently in the novels: in fact, he is a tragic character filled with self-hate which causes his brutally open hatred towards the students.[518]

His office is over-tidy and orderly. Filch persecutes any rule-breaking. When Umbridge is headmistress for a couple of months, Filch looks forward to being able to use physical punishment on the students (HP 5, 692):

> "Approval for whipping ... Approval for Whipping ... I can do it at last ... they've had it coming to them for years ..." He pulled out a piece of parch-ment, kissed it [...]. (HP 5, 740)

From then on he patrols the corridors "with a horsewhip ready in his hands, des-perate to catch miscreants, but the problem was that there were now so many of them he never knew which way to turn" (HP 5, 745).

---

[514] See Beahm 2005, 92-94.
[515] See Granger 2004, 106.
[516] See Beahm 2005, 16. Jane Austen is Rowling's favourite author (see I.2.A, 14) so the name probably is an homage to Austen.
[517] See also: "Harry wondered what their punishment was going to be. It must be something really horrible, or Filch wouldn't be sounding so delighted." (HP 1, 269).
[518] See Bürvenich 2001, 83-84.

IV.6.E. Ludo Bagman

Ludo Bagman is Head of the "Department of Magical Games and Sports" (HP 4, 279), former player on the English national "Quidditch" team (HP 4, 89), and probably bears the most interesting of all the telling names Rowling invents: *lūdō, lūsī, lūsus* is Latin for "to play", but also for "to mock" or "to deceive". Phonetically "Ludo" is very close to "lewd".[519] A character with such a name has to be untrustworthy. "To bag", moreover, means taking something without permission, while not intending to steal, which hints at his incorrect behaviour. He tries to pay his gambling debts with money he gains from betting on Harry winning the school tournament. And, finally, a bagman is a messenger for bribes.[520] His surname also alludes to "bagatelle". So with all the fuss he causes, Ludo Bagman is quite unimportant and at the same time careless: he neither takes Bertha Jorkins' disappearance seriously (HP 4, 71) nor cares sufficiently about security at the "Quidditch" World Cup.[521] Convicted of being a "Death Eater", he was found not guilty because of his enormous popularity as a "Quidditch" player (HP 4, 642-644) – a good example for the deficiency of magical world's legal system (see V.1.H, 305). He is a "powerfully built man gone slightly to seed" has a "large belly" and his "nose was squashed". He is like a school boy with his "round blue eyes, short blond hair and rosy complexion" (HP 4, 99).

Like Sirius Black, Bagman is meant to be misinterpreted by the reader: Crouch's house-elf Winky says about him: "'Mr Bagman is a bad wizard! A very bad wizard! My master isn't liking him, oh no, not at all!'" (HP 4, 418). The reader tends to believe Crouch more than the dubious Bagman. And when he offers to help Harry to cheat in the tournament (HP 4, 488), he becomes even more suspect. In the end it turns out that he is a harmless gambler trying to make money with Harry's possible win of the cup (HP 4, 793).

IV.6.F. Rita Skeeter

Rita's Christian name and surname almost rhyme (['riːˌtə ˈskiːˌtə]) and they play with the Latin word for "pearl".[522] This is very fitting for a woman who likes to dress flamboyantly and is convinced of her own importance.[523] Sometimes she dresses in pink (HP 4, 331), sometimes in bilious green (HP 4, 397)

---

[519] See Hein 2001, 22.
[520] See Hein 2001, 22.
[521] "'And Ludo Bagman's not helping. [...] not a worry about anti-Muggle security." (HP 4, 89).
[522] Rita is derived from Margaret. See "Margaret," *Dictionary of First Names* [1990] 2000. 161.
[523] John Granger interprets this as "read-a-(mo-)squito". This is only true for American English. See Granger 2004, 53.

and then again in banana yellow (HP 4, 490). With these colours and her three gold teeth (HP 4, 333) she is a very gaudy person:

> Her hair was set in elaborate and curiously rigid curls that contrasted oddly with her heavy-jawed face. She wore jewelled spectacles. The thick fingers clutching her crocodile-skin handbag ended in two-inch nails, painted crimson. (HP 4, 332)

Rita is a journalist for magical world's yellow press, delights in gossip and works for the "Daily Prophet" and "Witch Weekly". She loves scandal and uses the freedom of the press as a pretext to manipulate public opinion. Percy says of her: "'That woman's got it in for the Ministry of Magic! [...] Last week she was saying we're wasting our time quibbling about cauldron thickness [...].'" (HP 4, 164); Bill thinks "'[She] never makes anyone look good, called me 'a long-haired pillock'.'" (HP 4, 170); and even Dumbledore describes her work as "'Enchantingly nasty, [...] I particularly enjoyed your description of me as an obsolete dingbat'" (HP 4, 336). In her reports she sometimes makes a tragic hero out of Harry, and sometimes she makes him appear a dangerous lunatic, while Hermione becomes a man-eating vamp. Like all the negative characters, Rita is a coward and horrified when Voldemort's name is pronounced: "[...] at the sound of Voldemort's name, Rita had jumped so badly she had slopped half her glass of Firewhisky down herself" (HP 5, 625).

Rita is an unregistered "Animagus" (HP 4, 792; HP 5, 627) and can transform into a beetle. This is how she gains access to many secret meetings. Hermione finds her out and locks her into a glass. In *Order of the Phoenix* she can blackmail Rita into writing a long interview with Harry for "The Quibbler" which makes his version of Voldemort's return public. And in *Deathly Hallows* she publishes a best-selling biography about Albus Dumbledore (HP 7, 26-29). Rita is an utterly negative character. She is egoistic and pitiless and promotes Voldemort's interests without noticing: her reports help to destabilise Magical World when she turns public opinion against Dumbledore or Harry. Rita represents the dangers of mass media in Western societies.

IV.6.G. Salazar Slytherin

Slytherin is one of Hogwarts' founders and the source of all the racist evil ("'[Slytherin] started all this pure-blood stuff.'", HP 2, 167) in Magical World. Long dead, we only learn about him in stories posthumously related about him. For the positive characters he is "'a twisted old loony'" (HP 2, 166). His name alludes to "slither" or "slithery" – both referring to the movements of a snake. The word also connotes danger and menace. Slytherin was able to speak with snakes (HP 2, 213) and has chosen them as his heraldic animal.

His first name is somehow oriental and reminds us of "Sala"-din or "Sara"-cen – names that are reminiscent of the Crusades. Moreover, the name resembles the name of António Oliveira de Salazar, the fascist dictator of Portugal (1932-1968). With Rowling having lived in Portugal for quite a long time and her being familiar with Portuguese politics this name marks Slytherin as a fascist.

IV.6.H. Gellert Grindelwald

Grindelwald is, together with Voldemort and Slytherin the third racist villain of the novels. We first hear of him in *Philosopher's Stone* when Harry eats his first "Chocolate Frog" on the Hogwarts Express (HP 1, 114) but he does not appear personally before *Deathly Hallows*. Grindelwald, whose name is taken from a municipality in the district of Interlaken (Bern, Switzerland), is Bathilda Bagshot's nephew (HP 7, 290) and is "gleeful" and "wild" (HP 7, 208). He is just as brilliant as Dumbledore, but a ruthless wizard. He attends Durmstrang but is expelled for "twisted experiments" at the age of sixteen (HP 7, 290). Visiting his aunt in Godric's Hollow, he becomes friends with the Dumbledores' son Albus. Even then he ponders wizards' superiority over "Muggles" and discusses his racist ideas with Albus Dumbledore. In one of their debates Dumbledore uses the phrase "for the greater good" which becomes Grindelwald's slogan (HP 7, 294). During a scuffle with his friend, he kills Dumbledore's sister Ariana and flees from Godric's Hollow.

We never learn much about his deeds, but we must assume that on the Continent he is what Voldemort is for Great Britain. His name having a certain Germanic touch the character strongly alludes to Hitler's Nazi regime. Grindelwald imprisons his opponents in a prison called "Nurmengard" (HP 7, 294) – again, the name refers to Scandinavian, i.e. Germanic, mythology. When his reign is over, Grindelwald is detained in Nurmengard himself and is said to have shown "remorse in later years" (HP 7, 576). Searching for the "Elder Wand", Voldemort tortures and finally kills him (HP 7, 382).

IV.6.I. Igor Karkaroff

Karkaroff was one of Voldemort's followers and a "Death Eater". The suffix "-aroff" reminds us of Russian names – and, thus, of the West's arch-enemy during the Cold War. His first name Igor is just as typically Russian, although it originally comes from Scandinavia (Ingvar).[524] In the descriptions of this character we find many words referring to iciness, ugliness and lack of emotion:

---

[524]   See "Igor," *Lexikon der Vornamen*, 1974, 115.

[...] tall and thin like Dumbledore, but his white hair was short, and his goatee (finishing in a small curl) did not entirely hide his rather weak chin. [...] his teeth were rather yellow, and Harry noticed that his smile did not extend to his eyes, which remained cold and shrewd. (HP 4, 272)[525]

His voice is "fruity, unctuous" and he usually wears furs (HP 4, 272). He treats his students badly and pitilessly, calling one of them, in public a "disgusting boy" (HP 4, 283). Moreover, he is a coward[526] and disloyal even to Voldemort himself. Harry learns from Sirius how weak-minded Karkaroff is – a political chameleon changing colour whenever it seems suitable:

"He was caught, he was in Azkaban with me, but he got released. [...] He did a deal with the Ministry of Magic [...]. He said he'd seen the error of his ways, and then he named names ... he put a load of other people into Azkaban in his place ... he's not very popular in there, I can tell you. [...] he's been teaching the Dark Arts to every student who passes through that school of his." (HP 4, 365)

Viktor Krum tells Harry that Karkaroff did not participate in the work on board the Durmstrang school ship (HP 4, 786). When he hears about Voldemort's return, Karkaroff tries to escape (HP 4, 731) but he is found dead a couple of months later (HP 6, 103).

IV.7 Conclusion: Black and White – and Grey

The characters in the series may be divided into "goodies" and "baddies" quite easily. There is hardly any ambivalence, but psychologically, the characters are very well explained. The protagonist has his dark sides (see IV.3.A, 160), the villain is an orphan lacking motherly love (see IV.3.E, 174), the Weasleys have racisct tendencies (see IV.3.J, 182) and the Malfoys are being ill-treated by Voldemort which makes us feel sympathy for them (see IV.3.L, 191). Omniscient Dumbledore must admit to mistakes and is revealed to have entertained racist concepts in his youth (see IV.3.N, 204). Aunt Petunia is to be pitied because of her being neglected (see IV.4.G, 236), and Argus Filch is a tragic character (see IV.6.D, 272). The government fails, and even Harry's beloved parents are not as spotless as they appear at first (see IV.4.H, 242). So, we find a micro-

---

[525] Rowling uses "yellow teeth" for negative characters (see IV.4.C, 225) and is referring to Karkaroff mentioned again (HP 4, 455).

[526] There are various hints at his fear. Meeting Moody there is "A terrible look of mingled fury and fear came over his face." (HP 4, 284). Sirius says of him: "'[...] Karkaroff doesn't strike me as the type who'd go back to Voldemort unless he knew Voldemort was powerful enough to protect him.'" (HP 4, 367). And Severus Snape says: "'Karkaroff fears the Dark Lord's vengeance.'" (HP 4, 769).

cosm of characters that seem very plausible in their behaviour, but none of them develops psychologically or intellectually in the course of the plot. Most of the characters are, thus, static and flat, although they may turn out to be different from what the reader first expected.

There is a very clear pattern of what marks a good or a bad character (see IV.2.B, 154), which is true for all of the characters. Rowling uses language, names and fixed phrases for each character to describe him. Very often she compares her characters to animals or plants. Their smile and their eyes serve to make clear if a character is good or bad.

We may conclude that Rowling's characters are, indeed, all black and white, but that we do find them very convincing in their psychological construction. Thus, apart from the black and white we can make out *some* grey in her characters.

V. The Ideology of "Harry Potter"

The following chapter tries to meet many requirements. On the one hand it is meant to analyse the values presented by the *Harry Potter* series. On the other hand it will have to deal with highly complex philosophical concepts that are usually dealt with in philosophy, political science or theology. This work does not pretend to be able to compete with these.

Some of the most important questions are: What are values? Which values are to be discussed? These can already inspire endless philosophical debates. I will follow the idea that the Western world has two basic sets of values: the human rights charter of the UN based on the declaration of human rights (1789) and the Ten Commandments. I will analyse the *Potter* series against the background of these two sets of values.

Speaking of values, another important factor is the way the author influences us (see II.2.B, 41). What kind of truth is presented to the reader? What is right and what is wrong in the context of the novels? Which character benefits from its actions and who is punished in the end? So we must once again look into the structure of the text as well.

V.1 Democracy and Human Rights

Harry Potter is living in two different systems of government: the non-magical "Muggle" world and the state of the wizards. Whereas "Muggle" society basically corresponds to the reality of contemporary Great Britain, Magical World is not as easily characterised. In fact, it is not an ideal state; wizards must defend it against Voldemort. Although it is supposed to stand for tolerance, equality and justice it is, in truth, based on slavery, and not legitimised by elections.

V.1.A. Equality and Racism

The world of *Harry Potter* is a world of prejudice, inequality and racism. This is expressed in Voldemort's ideology as much as – very subtly – in the official magical world.

Voldemort divides people into "pure-bloods", "mudbloods" and "Muggle-borns", i.e. wizards from all-magical families and those that have one or more non-magical parents. According to him, only "pure-bloods" deserve to be full members of society, all other people are – just like "Muggles" – despicable and outlaws. When in *Deathly Hallows* Voldemort gains complete control over the Ministry he introduces a legislation stripping all non-"pure-bloods" of their civil rights (HP 7, 172-173).

This idea is not only in breach of basic human rights but is inherently wrong as Ron explains:

> "[It] doesn't make any difference at all. Look at Neville Longbottom – he's pure-blood and he can hardly stand a cauldron the right way up. [...] Dirty blood, see. [...] It's mad. Most wizards these days are halfblood anyway. If we hadn't married Muggles we'd've died out." (HP 2, 128)

Even Snape has to admit when asked: "'Does it make a difference, being Muggle-born?' Snape hesitated. [...] 'No,' he said. 'It doesn't make any difference.'" (HP 7, 535) The Malfoys embody this thinking. Lucius reproaches his son for his bad results at school: "'I would have thought you'd be ashamed that a girl of no wizard family beat you in every exam.'" (HP 2, 60) Later he openly comes out with his opinion: "'Wizard blood is counting for less everywhere –' 'Not with me,' said Mr Malfoy, [...].'" (HP 2, 61) Draco continuously insults Hermione because of her heritage as a "filthy little Mudblood" (HP 2, 123) and defames her as "impure" and "dirty", and goes so far as to say "'But don't touch my hand, now. I've just washed it you see, don't want Mudblood sliming it up'" (HP 4, 327). He menaces his fellow-students and after the first attack of the Basilisk he says: "'You'll be next, Mudbloods!'" (HP 2, 152-153). He sets his hopes into the return of Voldemort "'They'll be the first to go, now the Dark Lord's back! Mudbloods and Muggle-lovers first!'" (HP 4, 790). In *Deathly Hallows* we see that he is quite deceived in this and that he and his family are among the ones to suffer from Voldemort's new order.

The main source of this ideology is Salazar Slytherin one of the Hogwarts founders (see IV.6.G, 274):

> "Slytherin wished to be more selective about the students admitted to Hogwarts. He believed that magical learning should be kept within all-magic families. He disliked taking students of Muggle parentage, believing them to be untrustworthy." (HP 2, 164-165)

Being the last descendant of Slytherin, Voldemort feels called to revive his ideas.

The positive characters like Harry and Dumbledore are against all racism. If they speak inattentively about other beings they are usually corrected by their friends.[1] Facing death, Dumbledore still insists on the equality of all beings. Malfoy is surprised and asks: "'You care about me saying 'Mudblood' when I'm

---

[1]   See Nils Kulik, *Das Gute und das Böse in der phantastischen Kinder- und Jugendliteratur: Eine Untersuchung bezogen auf Werke von Joanne K. Rowling, J.R.R. Tolkien, Michael Ende, Astrid Lindgren, Wolfgang und Heike Hohlbein, Otfried Preußler und Frederik Hertmann*, Oldenburg: Universitätsverlag, 2005, 316.

about to kill you?' 'Yes, I do,' said Dumbledore [...]" (HP 6, 551-552). And Hagrid wishes for Harry to win the tournament – just to demonstrate that a "mudblood" like him is able to outdo all other wizards:

> "I'd love yeh ter win, I really would. It'd show 'em all ... yeh don' have ter be pure-blood ter do it. Yeh don' have ter be ashamed of what yeh are. It'd show 'em Dumbledore's the one who's righ', lettin' anyone in as long as they can do magic." (HP 4, 497-498)

According to this idea of purity of the magical race, non-magical "Muggles" are worthless beings, fair game and subject to cruel treatment by wizards (HP 4, 138-140). Arthur Weasley stands for the opposite attitude towards "Muggles" – with a kind of "patronizing curiosity"[2] he studies the non-magic community and initiates "Muggle"-friendly legislation. Lucius Malfoy says: "'his ridiculous Muggle Protection Act should be scrapped immediately'" (HP 2, 241), and his son Draco adds: "'Arthur Weasley loves Muggles so much he should snap his wand in half and go and join them, [...]. You'd never know the Weasleys were pure-bloods, the way they behave.'" (HP 2, 241) But even Weasley hushes up his "Muggle" relative (see IV.3.J, 183).[3] His sympathising with "Muggles" makes Arthur Weasley an outsider in the heavily biased establishment of Magical World. "'It's Arthur's fondness for Muggles that has held him back at the Ministry all these years. Fudge thinks he lacks proper wizarding pride.'" (HP 4, 770) In fact, Minister for Magic Cornelius Fudge is racist (see IV.5.A, 250), as Hermione points out: "'Look at Fudge, jumping to conclusions about [Hagrid's mother], just because she's part giant. Who needs that sort of prejudice?'" (HP 4, 658) Dumbeldore accuses him:

> "You place too much importance, and you always have done, on the so called purity of blood! You fail to recognise that it matters not what someone is born, but what they grow to be! Your Dementor has just destroyed the last remaing member of a pure-blood family as old as any – and see what that man chose to make of his life!" (HP 4, 767-768)

This shows that the representatives of the offical magical community are racist – they do not treat "Muggles" as truly equal, but even if they pretend to protect them, they do so in a very patronising way. "Mudbloods" may be accepted by their friends (who, of course, would not include Voldemort's followers), but their families are frequently made fun of.[4] The wizards are ruling

---

[2]   All of those hostile to non-magical people fail to realise that "Muggles" have to be much cleverer than wizards, because they cannot use magic to ease their daily life; see Mendlesohn 2004, 177.

[3]   Mendlesohn 2004, 177.

[4]   See Steege 2004, 155.

the "Muggles" without them knowing.[5] They are being kept in ignorance, which is supposed to be "better" for them *and* the wizards. Everyone accepts the fact that non-magical people are racially inferior. The only question being disputed among wizards is how to deal with them. Suman Gupta has described this attitude as typical of British imperialism in the 19th century, which can also be found in the writings of Rudyard Kipling.[6] The message of *Harry Potter* is:

> There are superior and inferior races, and the latter are necessarily at the mercy of the former. It behoves the superior races to *choose* to be benign to the inferior races, to leave the inferior races free and in control of their spaces (however defined), as a moral obligation.[7]

The way "Muggles" are being represented throughout the novels betrays the racist undertone; the most prominent "Muggles" – the Dursleys – are grotesque, incompetent and cruel. They are somehow crippled by their birth on the wrong side of life[8] and cannot participate in the fun of wizarding life. Through no fault of their own they are condemned to live a life of mediocrity. Christian children's book author John Houghton explains: "This select elect approach is the crassest form of elitism and mere mortals don't even get a look in. A Hindu caste system could not be more cruel."[9] A character's physiognomy betrays his true character. So, all of the Dursleys are ugly; the males are fat and the women are grotesque. For Reinhard Ehgartner this is yet another proof that Rowling represents her "Muggle" characters with a kind of chauvinism that borders on discrimination.[10] The most obvious proof for the wizards' racism is at the "Quidditch" World Cup: the majority of wizards tolerate or even acclaim "Muggles" being tortured by "Death Eaters" – the classic behaviour of followers in any totalitarian regime. Racism is tolerated in Magical World.[11]

In fact, the *Harry Potter* novels do emphasise the importance of heritage and blood. One's ancestry determines one's social status. This "blood ideology" (as Corinna Cornelius calls it)[12] must be very carefully analysed taking into account the role of racism in 20th-century history. Although the good characters reject the idea of someone being "pure" and "mud-blood" racism is right at the centre of the novels' plot. It reflects, thus, the importance our societies place in

---

5   See Gupta 2003, 102; Ernould 2003, 224.
6   Gupta 2003, 105; 108f; Mendlesohn 2004, 177.
7   Gupta 2003, 109.
8   See Blake 2002, 105-106.
9   See John Houghton, *A Closer Look at Harry Potter: Bending and Shaping the Minds of Our Children*, Eastbourne: Kingsway Communications, 2001, 66.
10 See Ehgartner 2002, 77-78.
11 See Westman 2004, 322. Mendlessohn sees this as reminiscent of *Men in Black*: Mendlesohn 2004, 177.
12 See Cornelius 2003, 70.

racial affiliation.[13] Reinhard Ehgartner is right saying that there is a general contradiction in the novels: racism is officially rejected, but through the plot and the constellation of characters it is indirectly acknowledged.[14]

Magical World is an elitist society of the privileged setting themselves apart by dress, education and language.[15] It is a form of apartheid where only the class of wizards is allowed to use magic and the vast majority is denied political participation. Some of the magical creatures are treated like vermin although they can think and speak (like the garden gnomes of the Weasleys: HP 2, 43-45).[16]

Racial prejudice also strikes half-breeds like Hagrid. When it becomes public that he is half-giant, he is no longer trusted and permitted to teach (HP 4, 477-479). Nevertheless, Hagrid decides to stand up against discrimination and wants to "'stand up an' say – I am what I am, an' I'm not ashamed.'" (HP 4, 497) Together with Mme Maxime, headmistress of Beauxbatons and half-giant like Hagrid, he tries to make the giants join in the fight against Voldemort (HP 5, 464-485). Other groups are suffering just the same fate: elves are being held as slaves to serve rich wizarding families; Lupin is marginalised because of his being a werewolf. His condition resembles an infectious disease and makes him into a pariah.[17] When he marries Tonks, he makes her an outcast: "'Even her own family is disgusted by our marriage, [...].'" (HP 7, 175-176) When she is pregnant (HP 7, 174), Voldemort's followers refer to the child as a "cub" instead of a "baby" (HP 7, 17). Even the wise centaurs are considered "filthy half-breeds" (HP 5, 829) by some,[18] and Sibyll Trelwaney laments: "'we Seers have always been feared, always persecuted ... it is – alas – our fate.'" (HP 5, 405) Nevertheless, treating elves, seers and giants as equals is decisive for the victory of good: only the house-elf Dobby can save Harry and his friends in *Deathly Hallows*, Trelawney throws her orbs at the attackers and when Grawp arrives at the scene of battle, Voldemort's followers are so surprised that they do not see Neville taking Gryffindor's sword and Harry putting on the Invisibility Cloak (HP 7, 587).

By law non-humans are not allowed to carry wands – an important handicap in a world based on the use of magic:

> "[Clause] three of the Code of Wand Use [says:] *No non-human creature is permitted to carry or use a wand.*" (HP 4, 148)

---

[13]   See Gupta 2003, 103.
[14]   See Ehgartner 2002, 78.
[15]   See Lacoss 2004, 69.
[16]   See Mendlesohn 2004, 178.
[17]   His condition is generally regarded as a metaphor of stigmatisation because of illness, i.e. HIV (see Nel 2001, 15; Westman 2004, 323; Whited "From Craze to Classic" 2004, 8).
[18]   This makes Umbridge a racist.

Griphook the goblin laments that "'Wizards refuse to share the secrets of wand-lore with other magical beings, they deny us the possibility of extending our powers!'" (HP 7, 395) Letting him complain thus Rowling confirms implicitly that races are not equal: because human beings do not share their knowledge of magic with other races, these are handicapped. But why can goblins not develop their own wands? Obviously their intellectual capacity is insufficient and inferior to humans'. And, although the relations between goblin and wizard have apparently been rather bad throughout history ("'There has been fault on both sides [...].'", HP 7, 417), this seems to be somewhat attributable to the basic disgust goblins inspire – even Harry does not like them (HP 7, 412).

Another group on the brink of society are the "Squibs": "someone who was born into a wizarding family but hasn't got any magic powers." (HP 2, 159) The way they have been treated in former times is reminiscent of the situation of handicapped people in the 60s and 70s: "'Squibs were usually shipped off to Muggle schools and encouraged to integrate into the Muggle community ... much kinder than trying to find them a place in the wizarding world, where they must always be second class; [...].'" (HP 7, 130) Argus Filch is just such a non-magical magician and has to lead a wretched life as Hogwarts caretaker. Even in the society of ghosts we see discrimination: Nearly Headless Nick is denied memebership in the "Headless Hunt" because he is not really headless:

> "But you would think, wouldn't you," he erupted suddenly, [...] "that getting hit forty-five times in the neck with a blunt axe would qualify you to join the Headless Hunt? *We can only accept huntsmen whose heads have parted company with their bodies.*'" (HP 2, 135-136)

Racism is not limited to the magical world. The "Muggles" are just as prejudiced. Vernon's sister Marge compares Harry's lineage to that of her dogs:

> "If there's something rotten on the *inside*, there's nothing anyone can do about it. [...] It's one of the basic rules of breeding. [...] If there's something wrong with the bitch, there'll be something wrong with the pup – (HP 3, 33)

For her, the breeding of dogs follows the same rules as human socialisation. Determined to eliminate weakness in her breed she has "inferior" puppies killed (although she does not dare to do the actual killing herself). "'It all comes down to blood, [...]. Bad blood will out.'" (HP 3, 35) This is directed primarily at Harry and his parents. The Dursleys agree with her – and, thus, admit to their racist attitude against Magical World. Vernon regards Harry's talent as abnormal and the boy himself as delinquent (see IV.4.G). So, the Dursleys are just as racist as the Malfoys.

Apart from the racial difference between "Muggles", magical beasts and wizards there is a strong division of social classes in magical world. This is never even questioned:[19] ancient families like the Malfoys or the Blacks are the magical nobility. They are rich, have great houses and legions of house-elves to serve them.[20] Their children are sorted into Gryffindor or Slytherin. Characters like Cedric Diggory of Hufflepuff with their directness and loyalty represent a kind of "working-class masculinity".[21]

Harry's peer group consists of outsiders: Ron who is from a poor family, Hermione who is "Muggle"-born and of course Harry himself is the suspicious "chosen one". [22] There are many reasons to discriminate against someone: sex, social class, friends, family background, race, culture or nationality are determinant of one's status. Heilman and Gregory correctly draw the conclusion: "As such, the *Harry Potter* books legitimize numerous forms of social inequality and their related cultural norms, rituals, and traditions."[23]

Critics have frequently pointed out that this is a specific British element within the texts. Richard Adams says that "the themes of specifically British class prejudice and social commentary [...] run through the books".[24] And Karin E. Westman says Rowling shows the "institutionalized snobbery of British boarding school and university life".[25] This includes that good education must be paid for:[26] even the Dursleys send their son Dudley to Smeltings, a public school. Its main defect is not its costs or its quality, but its pretence: Smeltings is a cheap imitation of the famous English public schools and its name hints at the children being smelted to conform to one single model.

> It is a "minor" public school, aspiring to compete with the likes of Eton and Harrow in the construction of "traditions" such as the Smeltings' Stick, but it makes itself ludicrous in its self-consious competiton. In the eyes of Tory England, it commits the unforgivable sin of vulgarity.[27]

---

[19]   See Kern 2003, 153.

[20]   The Weasleys, who are just as ancient and "pure-blood", are atypical for this social class.

[21]   See Heilman, "Blue Wizards and Pink Witches", 2003, 232.

[22]   See Heilman "Blue Wizards and Pink Witches" 2003, 220-221.

[23]   Heilman, Gregory 2003, 242.

[24]   Adams 2003.

[25]   Karin E. Westman, "Spectres of Thatcherism. Contemporary British Culture in J.K. Rowling's Harry Potter Series," *The Ivory Tower and Harry Potter: Perspectives on a Literary Phenomenon,* ed. Lana A. Whited, Columbia: University of Missouri Press, 2004, 305-328, here 325.

[26]   We do not know if the families have to pay fees in Hogwarts. On the one hand, we see the Weasleys complaining about how much money the education of their children costs them (HP 2, 52), on the other hand, the author stresses that every child in Britain can attend Hogwarts: "Everyone who shows magical ability before their eleventh birthday will automatically gain a place at Hogwarts; there is no question of not being 'magical enough'; you are either magical or you are not. There is no obligation to take up the place, however; a family might not want their child to attend Hogwarts." (Rowling 2006).

[27]   Mendlesohn 2004, 168.

It is not the class system as such that is criticised but the resulting arrogance and pretence.[28] The novels deal with a very British topic: what role do the privileges of the nobility play today? What is it that makes them the object of public interest?[29] Therefore, Farah Mendlesohn sees Rowling's novels as

> rooted in a distinctively English liberalism that is marked [...] by its insistence that it is not ideological but only 'fair'. Its ideology is its very claim to a nebulous and nonexistent impartiality.[30]

In fact, the criteria of fairness, justice and reason *do* play important roles in the value system of *Harry Potter* (see IV.2.B, 154). Rowling follows, thus, the ideology of J.R.R. Tolkien and C.S. Lewis, both writing their novels "as a lament for old England, for the values of the shires and for a 'greener' and simpler world."[31] The suburban world of the Dursleys represents a belief in the consequences of progress which sits very well with the views of Tolkien and Lewis. Both authors make their worlds the conservative contrast of modernity.[32] Rowling's novels show a world of "hegemonic, hierarchical middle-class social and cultural values"[33] with two rivalling concepts of aristocracy: the good characters like Dumbledore and the Weasleys belong to a social elite as much as the negative characters. But in contrast to these they use their superiority to promote the interests of others and the whole community. This is how they legitimise their nobility:

> But finally, this linkage creates a vision of fantasy in which aristocracy is allied with the country gentry in the care of the inferior; a High Toryism or modern liberalism where everyone is nice, and tolerant; where women are in the home and use their magic to speed the cooking and cleaning [...] and where differences are accepted but we all know who is inferior to whom and treat them nicely because they *are* inferior [...].[34]

The positive characters represent "true England", just as Bilbo Baggins and the Shire did with Tolkien.[35] Although Rowling criticises "bad aristocracy" embodied by the Malfoys, Blacks and Gaunts, the "true" nobility is described in a very favourable way: "[The] *Harry Potter* novels not only appeal to the desire

---

28   See Joachim Kalka, "Abfahrt am Gleis Neundreiviertel im Bahnhof King's Cross," *F.A.Z.* 6 July 2000, 56.
29   See Westman 2004, 306.
30   Mendlesohn 2004, 159.
31   Mendlesohn 2004, 166.
32   Mendlesohn 2004, 167.
33   Tammy Turner-Vorbeck, "Pottermania: Good, Clean Fun or Cultural Hegemony?" *Harry Potter's World: Multidisciplinary Critical Perspectives*, ed. Elizabeth E. Heilman, New York, London: RoutledgeFalmer, 2003. 13-24, here 20.
34   Mendlesohn 2004, 170.
35   Mendlesohn 2004, 169.

to be among the elect but also mollify dissent against a system that depends upon birthright instead of merit."[36] Only the negative characters like the Malfoys (see IV.3.L, 195), or Tom Riddle (see IV.3.F, 174) celebrate their class conceit.[37] The true villains are aristocrats who take advantage of their position. The Dursleys' mistake is that they try to belong to a social class they are not entitled to.[38]

Magical World does not respect the basic human right of equality of all people. The first article of the French declaration of human rights (1789) is clearly violated:

> Les hommes naissent et demeurent libres et égaux en droits. Les distinctions sociales ne peuvent être fondées que sur l'utilité commune.

The first article of the Universal Declaration of Human Rights (commonly known as the "UN Human Rights Charter" of 1948) is directly taken from the French model:

> All human beings are born free and equal in dignity and rights.

The second article specifies:

> Everyone is entitled to all the rights and freedoms set forth in this Declaration, without distinction of any kind, such as race, colour, sex, language, religion, political or other opinion, national or social origin, property, birth or other status.

This exact distinction is made in magical world. Even positive characters like Dumbledore or the Weasleys are not promoting elf rights nor accept "Muggles" as complete equals. Nevertheless, the self-perception of the magical establishment is quite different as the "Fountain of Magical Brethren" in the Ministry shows:

> A group of golden statues, larger than life-size, stood in the middle of a circular pool. Tallest of them all was a noble-looking wizard with his wand pointing straight up in the air. Grouped around him were a beautiful witch, a centaur, a goblin and a house-elf. The last three were all looking adoringly up at the witch and wizard. Glittering jets of water were flying from the ends of their wands, the point of the centaur's arrow, the tip of the goblin's hat and each of the house-elf's ears [...]. (HP 5, 145)

---

36 Nel 2001, 43.
37 See Natov 2001, 133.
38 See Mendlesohn 2004, 167.

This is reminiscent of the self-glorifying monuments of totalitarian regimes. The unity of magical races portrayed in the statue is an illusion. Harry quickly realises this:

> He looked up into the handsome wizard's face, but close-to Harry thought he looked rather weak and foolish. The witch was wearing a vapid smile like a beauty contestant, and from what Harry knew of goblins and centaurs, they were most unlikely to be caught staring so soppily at humans of any description. Only the house-elf's attitude of creeping servility looked convincing. (HP 5, 175)

During the duel between Dumbledore and Voldemort the fountain is smashed – a symbol of its falseness: the proclaimed unity has never existed and now, after Voldemort's return, even this superficial harmony is destroyed. All peoples, races and individuals must chose sides. Dumbledore tells Harry:

> "Indifference and neglect often do much more damage than outright dislike ... the fountain we destroyed tonight told a lie. We wizards have mistreated and abused our fellows for too long, and we are now reaping our reward." (HP 5, 916)

But what is Rowling's message with all this? What does she want the reader to accept as truth? Primarily it is the bad characters that are racist. The characters the reader sympathises with pretend to promote "Muggle" rights and equality of all beings. Nevertheless we do not see Dumbledore actively demanding elf freedom, although he gives Dobby and Winky a home in Hogwarts and offers them payment. The only character to promote elf rights is Hermione (see V.1.F) and she is being made fun of. Even the Weasleys are prejudiced against their own "Muggle" relatives (HP 1, 110).

The plot demonstrates how absurd Voldemort's racism is: Hermione as "Muggle"-born is, by far, the best student of Hogwarts. Harry, who is a "mudblood" is able to defeat Voldemort. The good characters' belief in racial equality is, thus, based on facts and not on ideology.[39] We also see the absurdness of Voldemort's racial prejudice in his own character: he himself is a "mudblood" – his mother Merope was married to a "Muggle". And Severus Snape, who also believes in racial differences, had a "Muggle" father as well (HP 6, 594). In fact, Voldemort's supporters contradict their own requirements for racial purity.

Despite the fact that that one of the basic ideas behind the novels is one of of tolerance and pluralism, a very subtle form of uncontradicted prejudice is still found at the core of the setting. Magical World is in no way an ideal world, its basis is characterised by "the same mentality that produces the evils of racism,

---

[39] See Kulik 2005, 306.

classism and sexism."[40] On the surface the texts do preach tolerance but at the same time non-humans or people from non-magical families are denied basic rights. "In this they embody inherently conservative and hierarchical notions of authority clothed in evangelistic mythopoetic fantasy."[41] But sugarcoating reality is not the role of literature:[42] Magical World reflects the reader's reality with all its social, political and ideological deficits. We may consider the novels' many-layered avoidance of a black-and-white attitude to reality their main achievement. Although magical world is not an ideal society, it is better and more humane than Voldemort's reign of terror. Kingsley Shacklebolt representing the "free wizard society" says "'We're all human, aren't we? Every human life is worth the same, and worth saving.'" (HP 7, 357)

V.1.B. Political Systems

One of the most important topics of the *Harry Potter* series is the moral legitimisation of power.[43] We find about four different ways to deal with power. Voldemort wants to defeat death and seeks eternal power. Fearing death he becomes a tyrant. Barty Crouch snr represents institutionalised power blindly sticking to rules – he becomes a merciless tyrant as well. Cornelius Fudge is power-addicted and selfishly does everything to stay in office. Only Dumbledore, who might be considered the most powerful of the four, is able to deal with his power in a responsible way. He only demonstrates his true capacity when facing his enemies.[44] In contrast to all the other representatives of power he does not use his position for personal enrichment. His authority is not based on official positions – which he even refuses – but on moral integrity.[45] Out of the four kinds of power represented in the novels, his management of his superiority is the strictly positive and benign. It is important that he is nothing more than a headmaster: Dumbledore does not hold any office, or official position in Magical World's hierarchy whatsoever.[46] Philip Nel, therefore, is right in stating that all official power structures of Magical World are deficient and inadequate:[47] its administration is full of selfish and corrupt people. Either they are

---

[40] Houghton 2001, 86.
[41] Mendlesohn 2004, 181.
[42] See Gupta 2003, 106.
[43] See Nel 2001, 40. John Houghton calls the novels "sombre books about the exercise of power" (Houghton 2001, 44).
[44] See Cherrett 2003, 121-124.
[45] See Catherine Deavel, "Character, Choice, and Harry Potter," *Logos: A Journal of Catholic Thought and Culture*, 4 (Autumn 2002): 49-64, here 54; Kulik 2005, 307.
[46] We read that he is "Chief Warlock on the Wizengamot – that's the Wizard High Court" (HP 5, 111). But we are not being told what this involves.
[47] See Nel 2001, 39.

lazy like Ludo Bagman, dubious like Rufus Scrimgeour, incompetent like Cornelius Fudge or merciless like Barty Crouch. So in the texts we find a basic distrust of officials and government. In contrast, hierarchies based on personal authority, competence and moral integrity (like Dumbledore or McGonagall) are acceptable. The unofficial underground association "Order of the Phoenix" is more trustworthy than the ministry.[48] Again, it is important to see that the character with the highest moral standards is a headmaster – Rowling expresses her belief that the education of future citizens is of paramount importance.[49] Characters like Barty Crouch snr or Cornelius Fudge demonstrate that striving for power leads to associating with the forces of evil.[50]

The core conflict of the novels is the antagonism between two political systems. Both of them are conservative, the official magical world, with its aristocratic structures, granting more rights to a privileged nobility than to the average citizen, as much as Voldemort's totalitarian regime does. Farah Mendlesohn goes even further, describing a conflict between the suburban conservatism[51] of the Dursleys[52] and the nobility's claim to power represented by the Malfoys and the Blacks. According to her, Rowling distances herself from such inequality by birth, but in truth justifies the aristocracy's privileges by introducing liberal, open-minded aristocrats like the Weasleys and Sirius Black. Making a non-aristocrat like Harry the protagonist of her novels, she softens her fantasy world's social defects without criticising the existing hierarchy itself.[53]

Different as the political systems of Voldemort and Dumbledore may appear, they have one thing in common: neither of them is democratic. They only differ in their set of values. Both can be described referring to the ideas of Thomas Carlyle (1795-1881). In his political essays, Carlyle has expressed the idea of the "strong just man". For him it is not democracy that guarantees freedom and justice, but the choice of the right leader who will rule his people in the ideal way:

> Find in any country the Ablest Man that exists there; raise *him* to the supreme place, and loyally reverence him: you have a perfect government for that country; no ballot-box, parliamentary eloquence, voting, constitution-building, or other machinery whatsoever can improve it a whit. It is in the perfect state; an ideal country. The Ablest Man; he means also the truest-

---

48 Christopher Wrigley correctly states that there is no clear political message in Rowling's work: Wrigley 2005, 13.
49 See Grimes 2004, 114.
50 See Kulik 2005, 322
51 Confronted with such interpretations the author reacts with utter incomprehension: see Hattenstone 2000.
52 John Granger sees in Marge's behaviour a "rather transparent caricature of Margaret Thatcher and her uncharitable opinions about dole recipients": Granger 2004, 77.
53 See Mendlesohn 2004, 167.

hearted, justest, the Noblest Man: what he *tells us to do* must be precisely the wisest, fittest, that we could anywhere or anyhow learn; – the thing which it will in all ways behove us, with right loyal thankfulness, and nothing doubting, to do! Our *doing* and life were then, so far as government could regulate it, well regulated; that were the ideal of constitutions.[54]

This "strong just man" has no need of a democratic legitimisation. His power is based on natural innate moral strength and wisdom. He will never abuse his power, because he will know the limits of his might wisely. It is, naturally, of course, highly questionable as to who is declaring an individual "the" leader. Who empowers the "Ablest Man"? Carlyle believes that everyone will happily serve such a leader:

> The Commander over Men; he to whose will our wills are to be subordinated, and loyalley surrender themselves, and find their welfare in doing so, may be reckoned the most important of Great Men.[55]

Carlyle sees the choice of the wrong man as the main reason for public malcontent, revolutions and upheavals.[56] I am going to show that not only Voldemort's regime is based on this concept of Carlyle's, but that the official government of Magical World works on the same basis.

Dumbledore as *spiritus rector* of the whole series tells us, what his idea of leadership is:

> "[Those] who are best suited to power are those who have never sought it. Those who, like you [Harry], have leadership thrust upon them, and take up the mantle because they must, and find to their own surprise that they wear it well." (HP 7, 575)

So what is it that Rowling wants to tell us? How is a society supposed to work on this basis? This remains the author's secret.

V.1.C. The Official State of Wizards

Let us first have a look at the official workings of Magical World. J.K. Rowling gives us a very detailed description of the Ministry of Magic. In *Order of the*

---

54 Thomas Carlyle, "The Hero as King. Cromwell, Napoleon: Modern Revolutionism [Lecture VI, Friday, 22nd May, 1840]," *On Heroes, Hero-Worship, & the Heroic in History*, ed. Michael Goldberg, Berkeley, Los Angeles, Oxford: University of California Press, 1993, 169-170.
55 Carlyle, [1840] 1993, 169.
56 Carlyle, [1840] 1993, 170.

Phoenix the Ministry becomes a major location of her plot (see III.5.E, 130).[57] The administration's activities and intrigues are part of the political plot underlying the whole series (see II.3.C, 66). The Ministry's "'main job is to keep it from the Muggles that there's still witches an' wizards up an' down the country.'" (HP Bd. 1, 74-75) But we are neither told how this powerful institution is being organised nor do we learn how Magical World is governed.

The Ministry is more than a mere accumulation of departments. It is the centre of power, the seat of government and to some extent it can even be considered the government itself. There are various sub-divisions, as for example:

- Accidental Magic Reversal Squad (HP 4, 78; 98) – this is where the "Obliviators" work
- Committee for the Disposal of Dangerous Creatures (HP 3, 236)
- Committee on Experimental Charms (HP 4, 98)
- Dark Force Defence League (HP 4, 665)
- Department for the Regulation and Control of Magical Creatures (HP 4, 83; 150)
- Department of International Magical Co-operation (HP 4, 45; 65; 279)
- Department of Magical Catastrophes (HP 3, 226)
- Department of Magical Games and Sports (HP 4, 38; 279)
- Department of Magical Transportation (HP 4, 77)
- Department of Mysteries (HP 4, 98) – the Department of the "Unspeakables"
- Floo Regulation Panel (HP 4, 53)
- Goblin Liason Office (HP 4, 98)
- Improper Use of Magic Office (HP 2, 27)
- International Confederation of Wizards (HP 4, 306)[58]
- Magical Law Enforcement Squad (HP 3, 226)[59]
- Misuse of Muggle Artefacts Office (HP 2, 38)

All of these individual departments are being led by a head that seems to be reporting directly to the Minister for Magic. The Minister is a kind of Prime Minister to the magical community. But in contrast to the real Prime Minister, he is not elected by the people but "appointed" (HP 6, 43). It remains completely unclear who is in charge of these appointments and on what basis a person can be appointed to become Minister for Magic. Obviously, Magical World has no parliament and no elections: within the seven years which the series covers there

---

[57] Marina Warner even calls the "Ministry of Magic" "protofascist" (Marina Warner, "Did Harry have to grow up?" *Observer* 29 June 2003. <http://books.guardian.co.uk/print/0,3 858,4701095-99943,00.html> 3 Jan 2008.

[58] The main body is the *International Confederation of Wizards' Conference* (HP 4, 336).

[59] The "Hit Wizards" seem to be the fighting troop of this department.

is no hint whatsoever at possible elections. If Magical World was a democracy there should have been elections within this period of time. Dumbledore has been "offered" the job of Minister at various times but refused it:

> "I merely wondered why you – who is so often asked for advice by the Ministry, and who has twice, I think, been offered the post of Minister–" "Three times at the last count, actually," said Dumbledore. "But the Ministry never attracted me as a career." (HP 6, 414)

Who "offers" the job? And who decides on the candidates? How is the Minister legitimised? These questions remain unanswered throughout the whole series. Magical World seems to be governed by a kind of general will in the sense of Jean-Jacques Rousseau, represented by a single institution that does not need any further legitimisation. The Minister has the power to appoint the Hogwarts headmaster[60] without consulting anyone else. The "Daily Prophet" reports:

> "This is not the first time in recent weeks that the Minister, Cornelius Fudge, has used new laws to effect improvements at the wizarding school." (HP 5, 341)

The Minister can be unseated (Cornelius Fudge suffers this fate after what happens in *Order of the Phoenix*), but it is never explained who is actually responsible for the impeachment or even the end of his term. In office, his power seems to be limited only by his own instincts and values. Obviously, there are no institutions whatsoever to control him. The Minister is also able to decide if laws are to be passed or not: in *Prisoner of Azkaban* when Harry uses magic in the "Muggle" world he must be punished according to wizard law. But Fudge refrains from doing so saying "'Circumstances change, Harry ...'" (HP 3, 54). And Dumbledore is just as arbitrary: he stands fast against all accusations, knows the answer to almost any question and is usually right. Not only is he the absolute ruler of Hogwarts, he also has the power to overrule law. When Harry reminds him that underage wizards are not allowed to use magic outside school Dumbledore says:

> "If there is an attack", said Dumbledore, "I give you permission to use any counter-jinx or -curse that might occur to you." (HP 6, 59)

Why is he allowed to do so? This idea of leadership, again, corresponds with Carlyle's principle of the "strong just man". On the one hand he obviously is able to overrule the decisions of the Bureau for Improper Use of Magic, on the other hand he personally has to testify in court to save Harry from being ex-

---

[60] It is not clear how the headmaster shares power with the twelve governors.

pelled from Hogwarts. Neither is he able to annul the wrongful conviction of Buckbeak (HP 3, 354).[61] Here, Dumbledore is subject to the law just like any other wizard and admits: "'I have no power to make other men see the truth, or to overrule the Minister for Magic ...'" (HP 3, 423). In fact, there are laws in Magical World (see V.1.H, 305) – but it remains uncertain who initiates or passes them and who sees to them being followed.

So, Magical World is neither democratic nor does it conform to ideas of basic human rights. Thus, it does not correspond to the Western idea of democracy.[62] There is no hint at a constitution, separation of powers or civil participation. This violates arcticle 3 of the French declaration of human rights (1789):

> Le principe de toute souveraineté réside essentiellement dans la nation, nul corps, nul individu ne peut exercer d'autorité qui n'en émane expressément.

According to article 16, we could state that Magical World is not a legitimate state at all:

> Toute société dans laquelle la garantie des droits n'est pas assurée, ni la séparation des pouvoirs déterminée, n'a pas de Constitution.

The system's representatives are all more or less inefficient "hero kings" – neither Fudge nor Scrimgeour fulfil Carlyle's expectations as "strong just men" and are weak in their moral integrity and their leadership qualities. The novels demonstrate the problems of exercising power. It is obvious that a parliament could play an important role in correcting Fudge's incompetence and Scrimgeour's hunger for publicity. There is obviously no one to prevent Fudge's ally, Dolores Umbridge, from turning Hogwarts into a totalitarian state, and to stop her "spiritual fascism"[63] when she abolishes basic civil rights.[64] It is no official institution that ends her reign, but the non-violent resistance of the Hogwarts community (see IV.5.G, 260). In contrast, Cornelius Fudge (David and Catherine Deavel call him "the archetypal ineffectual administrator"[65]; see IV.5.A, 250) does not interfere in Hogwarts and, again, proves his incompetence. Harry is outraged about the politicians shouting at Scrimgeour:

> "You never get it right, you people, do you? Either we've got Fudge, pretending everything's lovely while people get murdered right under his nose, or we've got you, chucking the wrong people into jail and trying to pretend you've got the Chosen One working for you!" (HP 6, 325)

---

61   Dumbledore frees Buckbeak in the end. This proves that he can indeed overrule Fudge.
62   See Bürvenich 2001, 58.
63   See Jung 2004, 18.
64   See Maar 2003, 160.
65   Deavel 2004, 143.

The officials of Magical World are over-bureaucratic cowards,[66] who are both corrupt and inefficient.[67] The Ministry is poorly organised (HP 5, 144-154) and works chiefly to maintain itself, and not because of a "deep commitment to moral order in the universe."[68]

But it is not only the politicians of magical world who are deficient – the "Muggle" prime minister is just as corrupt. At the beginning of *Half-Blood Prince* the nameless politician learns that Voldemort's followers are causing the catastrophes and accidents his country is suffering from. But instead of trying to find solutions he only thinks about his chances of being re-elected:

> It was infuriating to discover the reason for all these terrible disasters and not to be able to tell the public; almost worse than it being the government's fault after all. (HP 6, 18)
> The idea of invisible creatures swooping through the towns and countryside, spreading despair and hopelessness in his voters, made him feel quite faint. (HP 6, 20)

In the world of the *Harry Potter* novels power seems to have much to do with shallow words and appearances. Harry realises "that bangs and smoke were more often the marks of ineptitude than expertise." (HP 6, 522).

V.1.D. Reigns of Terror

There are two reigns of terror in the novels: the villains Voldemort and Grindelwald both set up their own terroristic regimes. While we do not learn much about Grindelwald, we experience Voldemort's regime rather directly. Sirius describes to Harry what life was like when Voldemort was in power:

> "You're scared for yourself, and your family, and your friends. Every week, news comes of more deaths, more disappearances, more torturing ... the Ministry of Magic's in disarray, they don't know what to do, they're trying to keep everything hidden from the Muggles, but meanwhile, Muggles are dying too. Terror every where ... panic ... confusion ... that's how it used to be." (HP 4, 572-573)

There are no laws except the rule of unconditional obedience and devotion. The leader's word is the law, his wish commandment. His rule is one of arbitrariness; his subordinates are at his mercy. Draco explains the principles of Voldemort's reign to his friends:

66　See Robert Misik, "Liebling der Muggel," *Taz* 1/2/3 Oct 2005, 21.
67　See Nel 2001, 39.
68　See Killinger 2004, 167.

295

"[...] when the Dark Lord takes over, is he going to care how many O.W.L.s or N.E.W.T.s anyone's got? Of course he isn't ... it'll be all about the kind of service he received, the level of devotion he has shown." (HP 6, 145)

His rule is founded on faith, devotion and obedience – not knowledge or rationality. The shared belief in the mighty "führer"[69] makes up the community. Snape explains that the "loss of faith" is the worst crime to be found guilty of in Voldemort's world. Mercy is only shown when convenient for the leader: "'[If] he had not forgiven we who lost faith at that time, he would have very few followers left.'" (HP 6, 32) Devotion has to be demonstrated in behaviour and in the willingness to commit masochistic self-mutilation. At Voldemort's resurrection the "Death Eaters" must humiliate themselves and kiss his cloak. They do not show any sign of joy at the return of their master – only fear (HP 4, 701–704). Disloyalty is severely punished. Voldemort accuses Pettigrew of having failed and of being hesitant and demands him to suffer physical pain. He has to cut off one of his hands and admit that the pain he is enduring is a just punishment for his incompetence. Finally he is forced to thank Voldemort for a new, magical hand (HP 4, 703). "'May your loyalty never waver again, Wormtail,' said Voldemort. 'No, my Lord ... never, my Lord ...'" (HP 4, 704) Nevertheless, his master does not trust him and this new hand actually spies on Pettigrew's thoughts. In *Deathly Hallows*, when Pettigrew, for a split second considers helping Harry to escape (HP 7, 381), the hand turns against him and strangles him to death. Lucius Malfoy who has arranged himself with the new regime after Voldemort's fall is likewise criticised: "'I expect more faithful service in future.' 'Of course, my Lord, of course ... you are merciful, thank you ...'" (HP 4, 705). Malfoy has proven himself lacking in faith and devotion, the "mercy" he is forced to thank for is a perverted form of the compassion Dumbledore proves to his son Draco in *Half-Blood Prince* (see V.5.D, 357). The outer symbol of admittance to Voldemort's inner circle is a mark which each "Death Eater" has burned into his arm (HP 4, 769) and which Voldemort can also use to summon his followers.[70]

As soon as Voldemort is resurrected terror spreads. Public life becomes marked by fear, disloyal former "Death Eaters" like Karkaroff are being murdered, and others like ice-café owner Florean Fortescue or wandmaker Ollivander disappear[71] (HP 6, 104). Diagon Alley, which used to be such a friendly, merry place, has changed completely:

---

[69] It is appropriate to use this specific German word.
[70] In totalitarian regimes, such permanent signs mark victims and persecutors alike. In Nazi Germany for example, the SS had their blood group written onto their arms, just as the concentration camp prisoners had a tattoo with their number.
[71] In *Deathly Hallows* we learn that Voldemort needs him to work on his wand.

[Nobody] was stopping to talk any more; the shoppers stayed together in their own tightly knit groups, moving intently about their business. (HP 6, 109)

Fear is what Voldemort wants to base his new reign on. He plans to form an army of "Dementors" and giants:

"The Dementors will join us ... they are our natural allies ... we will recall the banished giants ... I shall have all my devoted servants returned to me, and an army of creatures whom all fear ..." (HP 4, 705)

People are being threatened with biblical punishments (2 Moses 12): Anyone opposing Voldemort risks a werewolf attack on his children ("'Voldemort has threatened to unleash [Fenrir Greyback] upon people's sons and daughters; it is a threat that usually produces good results.'", HP 6, 314). Once in power, Voldemort has children kidnapped to "'force their relatives to behave'" and uses force on the parents to gain control over the children (HP 7, 463).[72] The Malfoys are being punished as their son has to accomplish an impossible mission for their master which becomes a "'Slow torture for Draco's parents, while they watch him fail and pay the price.'" (HP 7, 547) This is collective punishment or "kin liability" as it has been practised in Nazi Germany, Stalin's Soviet Union or Mao's China.

Critics have never ceased to point out the resemblance Voldemort's reign bears to German National Socialism (see IV.3.H, 179). As I have shown the novels' timeline also hints at such references (see II.4, 78). Voldemort's racism, Salazar Slytherin's initials,[73] the German sounding name of Gellert Grindelwald[74] and the skull the "Death Eaters" identify by[75] all allude to this specific background. Suman Gupta calls Voldemort the "Death Eaters'" "führer".[76]

When Voldemort comes to power, the most obvious change is in the government's attitude towards "Muggles". Using simplistic metaphors worthy of any demagogue, Voldemort explains:

"Many of our oldest family trees become a little diseased over time, […]. You must prune yours, must you not, to keep it healthy? Cut away those

---

[72] Dumbledore's brother Aberforth suggests using the same practice – but Harry refuses: "'And it never occurred to any of you to keep a few Slytherins hostage? There are kids of Death Eaters you've just sent to safety. Wouldn't it have been a bit smarter to keep 'em there?' 'It wouldn't stop Voldemort,' said Harry, 'and your brother would never have done it.'" (HP 7, 500).
[73] See Smadja 2001, 15.
[74] See Nel 2001, 44.
[75] See Maar 2003, 101.
[76] See Gupta 2003, 114.

parts that threaten the health of the rest. [...] we shall cut away the canker that infects us until only those of the true blood remain..." (HP 7, 16-17)

"Muggle"-borns must register, pseudo-scientific research is undertaken (HP 7, 205) to show that "'magic can only be passed from person to person when wizards reproduce. Where no proven wizarding ancestry exists, therefore, the so-called Muggle-born is likely to have obtained magical power by theft or force.'" (HP 7, 172) Everyone has to "'prove that that you have at least one close wizarding relative'" (HP 7, 172-173). This is, of course, highly reminiscent of Hitler's Nuremberg Laws (1935). "Muggle"-borns become outcasts of society – Harry and Hermione meet them in Diagon Alley (HP 7, 424), where some of them are begging for money and pity. Voldemort and his followers do not even consider them human beings:

> "How did it offend you? [...] Some of these Wandless can be troublesome [...]. While they do nothing but beg I have no objection, but one of them actually asked me to plead her case at the Ministry last week. 'I'm a witch, sir, I'm a witch, let me prove it to you!' [...]. As if I was going to give her my wand – [...]." (HP 7, 425-426)

Killing "Muggles" has become "little more than a recreational sport" (HP 7, 356). Nevertheless, there is resistance. "Potterwatch" is an independent underground radio station informing its listeners about what really goes on in wizarding world, and some have the courage to protect the "Muggles" in their neighbourhood (HP 7, 357). All this, of course, is highly reminiscent of the Holocaust as Kate Muir points out:

> Shadows of the Holocaust hang over Voldemort's compulsory Register of Muggle-Borns, the subsequent (Kafkaesque) trial and punishment of those with "contaminated" blood, and his decoration of the Ministry of Magic with a black statue of a pure-blood witch and wizard, atop a stone pile of the dead, naked bodies of Muggles.[77]

Voldemort uses a system of collaborators to imprison alleged opposition members. These "'[Snatchers are] everywhere, gangs trying to earn gold by rounding up Muggle-borns and blood traitors, there's a reward from the Ministry for everyone captured.'" (HP 7, 311) Like all totalitarian systems, Voldemort controls the youth by synchronising their socialisation. Attendance at Hogwarts becomes compulsory, and a means of monitoring the racial descent of the students (HP 7, 173). All this is part of Voldemort's "Gleichschaltung" – a policy used to gain control over every aspect of everyday life with the goal of eliminat-

---

[77]   Muir 2007.

ing individualism. Likewise, "'all radio programmes are following You-Know-Who's line'" (HP 7, 355). At school, children are being indoctrinated against "Muggles" (HP 7, 462) and are taught to use the "Cruciatus Curse" against offenders (HP 7, 462).

While some of the situations in the last novel are attempts to mimic Nazi Germany in an almost unbearaby flat way, there is absolutely no reason to read the novels as a metaphor for the Third Reich. Elizabeth D. Schafer reads "Ravenclaw" as a reference to the concentration camp Ravensbrück and interprets the Chamber of Secrets as an allusion to the death chambers of the concentration camps – which in my opinion is extremeley far-fetched.[78] Isabelle Smadja goes even further. She absurdly regards Beauxbatons and Durmstrang as representatives of the Western Allies fighting the Soviet Union and Germany during World War II. To her the ship carrying the Durmstrang delegation to Hogwarts is a metaphor for German submarine warfare, and Karkaroff's flight from Voldemort resembles the German retreat in 1941. All this culminates in her interpreting Harry's scar as the infamous SS-sign.[79] This is utter nonsense and cannot in the least be justified by the text. This is an attempt to make the novels more important and symbolic than they can possibly be. There are definitely relations between Voldemort's ideology and German National Socialism – but this is true for many other totalitarian regimes. Voldemort is no German Nazi, but a power-hungry racist trying to wipe out "inferior" ethnic groups. This is true for the American Klu Klux Klan, the Serbian fascists during the Balkan Wars of the 1990s and Mao's Red Brigades. Rowling does not refer to one racist regime in particular.

Fear causes fear – Voldemort knows that his reign is fragile, because it is founded on terror. The more he oppresses the people the less certain is his power in the long run. Dumbledore explains this:

> "Voldemort himself created his worst enemy, just as tyrants everywhere do! Have you any idea how much tyrants fear the people they oppress? All of them realise that, one day, amongst their many victims, there is sure to be one who rises against them and strikes back! Voldemort is no different!" (HP 6, 477)

Freedom, justice and the wish for personal safety cannot forever be oppressed. Tyrants will be overthrown in the end, because their power is illegitimate. So neither Voldemort's regime, nor the official state of the wizards is democratic, but they differ in their core values. Whereas the official magical world proclaims – at least on the surface – equality and freedom for everyone, Voldemort's ideology is based on unconditional devotion, bondage and terror.

---

[78] See Schafer 2000, 178.
[79] See Smadja 2001, 41-42.

There is yet another regime of terror – Grindelwald's reign. We learn little about it: "*As Grindelwald never extended his campaign of terror to Britain, however, the details of his rise to power are not widely known here.*", writes Rita Skeeter (HP 7, 290). This, again, can be seen as a possible reference to Nazi Germany. Not only does he have a German name, but also he is said to have been in Germany (HP 7, 191). Is Grindelwald the German version of Voldemort, or possibly a representative of fascism? He even uses – like the German Nazis did with the swastika – the ancient symbol of the "Deathly Hallows" which, thus, becomes a symbol of evil (HP 7, 329). Nevertheless, we learn how he got his ideas and his motto "For the Greater Good" – it was Dumbledore, who inspired him:

> "Your point about wizard dominance being FOR THE MUGGLES' OWN GOOD - this, I think, is the crucial point. Yes, we have been given power and, yes, that power gives us the right to rule, but it also gives us responsibilities over the ruled. We must stress this point, it will be the foundation stone upon which we build. Where we are opposed, as we surely will be, this must be the basis of all our counter-arguments. We seize control FOR THE GREATER GOOD. And from this it follows that where we meet resistance, we must use only the force that is necessary and no more." (HP 7, 291)

Here, Rowling relates to Carlyle and his idea of a "strong just man". Anything, according to Dumbledore's letter, can be justified if it is in the alleged possible interest of the community, the "greater good". Interestingly, Grindelwald uses this motto and becomes a dictator. Even more interestingly, Harry's rule-breaking is very often justified by the idea that his disobedience serves a "greater good". So what is the difference between Dumbledore's, Grindelwald's and Harry's understanding of "the greater good"? Dumbledore aims at fulfilling Carlyle's ideal of the "benign dictator". To protect the weak, wizards must "seize control". "Muggles" are unable to live without the guidance of the magical community. Grindelwald believes that "Muggles" are worthless beings and therefore should be ruled, i.e. enslaved by wizards. Harry, being a schoolboy, wants to cling to higher principles of justice, equality and freedom. He sees "the greater good" fulfilled in what we would call human rights. Wherever they are violated or at stake, he feels free to take any measures he considers necessary, even if they are illegal. The differences only lie in the aims characters are pursuing and in what they define as "the greater good". When Harry plans tricking Griphook into helping him, he wonders for a short moment if he should feel ashamed of himself: "He remembered the words that had been engraved over the gateway to Nurmengard: For the Greater Good. He pushed the idea away. What choice did they have?" (HP 7, 411)

V.1.E. Religious and Freedom of Opinion

Basically, every citizen of Magical World is allowed to express his opinion. This pluralism is commonly believed to be one of the core values of the wizard society. Dumbledore encourages Dobby and Winky (see IV.3.N, 211), just like Harry, to make use of the freedom of opinion. He explains:

> "Ah, Harry, how often this happens, even between the best of friends! Each of us believes that what he has to say is much more important than anything the other might have to contribute!" (HP 6, 336)

But this open-mindedness soon ends: speaking about public security or his friend Severus Snape, Dumbledore becomes very intolerant and denies others their opinion (see IV.3.N, 210).

Granting freedom of opinion distinguishes the good characters – only bad characters like Voldemort or Dolores Umbridge deny free speech (see IV.5.G, 263). In the case of Umbridge this seals her fate. The total control of the Hogwarts community, censorship (HP 5, 640) and the introduction of a private secret service ("Inquisitorial Squad", HP 5, 688-689) cause the school's rebellion against her. The more she tries to control students and colleagues the more things get out of her hands. The non-violent resistance of the school finally provokes the end of her time as headmistress. Her failure is the direct consequence of her striving for control and of her oppressing freedom of opinion.

V.1.F. Freedom and Oppression

Personal freedom is the basis of all Western democracies. The UN Human Rights Charter guarantees in article 3 and 4:

> Everyone has the right to life, liberty and security of person. No one shall be held in slavery or servitude; slavery and the slave trade shall be prohibited in all their forms.

But Magical World does not fulfill these requirements. The official state and Voldemort likewise rely on slavery which is widely accepted. Voldemort enslaves his followers and threatens them with death and clan liability. In official Magical World, slavery is institutionalised: house-elves are no social class, but an independent race of human-like beings held in slavery.[80] Like many marginalised groups, their English is marked by incorrect grammar[81] (see II.2.H, 55) and resembles the tendentious characterisation of blacks in *Gone With the Wind*

---

[80]   See Gupta 2003, 123.
[81]   See Heilman, Gregory 2003, 244; Nel 2001, 46.

(1939).[82] But we never learn which language is their mother-tongue – for English must be a second language to them. Conforming to law they are enslaved – and everyone including moral authorities like Dumbledore or McGonagall seem to approve of their status. The elves themselves are represented as "simple souls who merely wish to serve their families to the best of their ability."[83]

The treatment of slaves is left to their masters; the elves do not have any rights. On the contrary, as soon as they dare to act against the interests of their masters they are obliged to commit self-mortification. Dobby is hitting himself (HP 2, 193) and Winky forces herself to limp (HP 4, 140). The obvious symbol of their enslavement is their ragged clothes:

> "Tis a mark of the house-elf's enslavement, sir. Dobby can only be freed if his masters present him with clothes, sir." (HP 2, 193)

We can only assume how hard the everday life of the elves must be when Dobby says: "'Dobby is used to death threats, sir. Dobby gets them five times a day at home.'" (HP 2, 193), or when Crouch accuses Winky (who is self-sacrificingly caring for him and his son):

> "I have no use for a house-elf who disobeys me [...]. I have no use for a servant who forgets what is due to her master, and to her master's reputation." (HP 4, 155)

Horace Slughorn admits openly that he is afraid of being poisoned and therefore has every one of his drinks tested by a house-elf before taking it himself (HP 6, 454). Thus, he accepts tacitly the possible death of one of his servants. Voldemort even enjoys the sufferings of Kreacher, whom he uses to test the defences around his "Horcrux" (HP 7, 160). It is completely legal to treat house-elves like that. Led by the author, the reader accepts this as a natural part of magical world. Slavery is generally accepted – violence against the slaves is not.[84]

Enslavement is made easy, because the elves are being held in a state of immaturity and accept their condition as constitutional. Their code of honour includes masochism and the unconditional fulfillment of their masters' wishes. Winky laments that life in freedom is dishonourable and feels ashamed about her dismissal (HP 4, 154-155): "'Winky is properly ashamed of being freed!'" (HP 4, 416) She and all the other house-elves refuse to enjoy life:

> "House-elves is not supposed to have fun [...]. House-elves does what they is told." (HP 4, 112)

---

[82] See Mendlesohn 2004, 179.
[83] See Mendlesohn 2004, 179.
[84] See Gupta 2003, 113.

"[But] house-elves has no right to be unhappy when there is work to be done and masters to be served." (HP 4, 585)
"[Winky] is not sure you did Dobby a favour, sir, when you is setting him free. [...] Freedom is going to Dobby's head, sir [...]. Ideas above his station, sir. Can't get another position, sir. [...] *He is wanting paying for his work, sir.*" (HP 4, 111)

This equating freedom and shame leads to the Hogwarts house-elves refusing to clean Gryffindor Tower: Hermione has laid out clothes in the common room hoping that some of the elves find them (being presented with clothes ensures freedom to an elf). The elves are afraid to find them and do not dare to enter the room. Dobby has to do the cleaning on his own:

"None of them will clean Gryffindor Tower any more, not with the hats and socks hidden everywhere, they finds them insulting, sir. Dobby does it all himself, sir, [...]." (HP 5, 425)

But even Dobby who is the only elf understanding that he has rights at all cannot free himself completely from slavery. He is not able to enjoy freedom and ends up as a "charity case"[85] in Hogwarts.

"Dobby likes freedom, miss, but he isn't wanting too much, miss, he likes work better." (HP 4, 415)
"[The houselves are] *happy*. They think they've got the best job in the world –" "That's because they're uneducated and brainwashed!" (HP 4, 263)

Even Dumbledore does not do anything to free the elves. The only character working actively against slavery is Hermione. She founds "SPEW", the Society for the Promotion of Elfish Welfare (HP 5, 89), and tries to make people see the unjustice of slavery.

"Our short-term aims, [...] are to secure house-elves fair wages and working conditions. Our long-term aims include changing the law about non-wand-use, and trying to get an elf into the Department for the Regulation and Control of Magical Creatures, because they're shockingly underrepresented." (HP 4, 247)

It is significant that it is a human being that frees the elves. They are not able to fight for their own rights, but need help to promote their rights. This is quite a paternalistic, incapacitating idea that justifies the elves' inferior status.[86] Farah Mendlesohn sees a connection between the situation of the elves and the

---

[85] Mendlesohn 2004, 179.
[86] See Heilman, Gregory 2003, 244.

ideas of anti-abolitionists in the American Civil War.[87] It remains unclear why Rowling introduces this sub-plot. Does she want to comment on the idealistic attitudes of young people?[88] In any case, Hermione's commitment to the elves is useless and sometimes ridiculous. Nevertheless, in *Deathly Hallows* Dobby gives his life to save Harry (HP 7, 384f) and dies "a free elf" as he proudly tells his attackers (HP 7, 384, 389). This shows the elves' power and importance – but it does not have anything to do with Hermione's society. The other characters laugh about her, and Ron jokingly suggests the founding of "SPUG" – the Society for the Protection of Ugly Goblins (HP 4, 490). Harry supports Hermione but without any real enthusiasm. Anyway, the elves' enslavement does not suit him either. At his first encounter with Dobby he feels instinctively that the elf is a person, not an object. Consequently, he does not address him with "What are you?" but "Who are you?" (HP 2, 18-19). Finally he uses a trick on Lucius Malfoy to free Dobby from his master (HP 2, 362). For Dobby and the house-elves Harry is the hero who has liberated them from Voldemort's slavery – although we never learn to what extent their situation was worse in the past:

> "If he knew what he means to us, to the lowly, the enslaved, us dregs of the magical world! Dobby remembers how it was when He Who Must Not Be Named was at the height of his powers, sir! We house-elves were treated like vermin, sir. [… Life] has improved for my kind since you triumphed over He Who Must Not Be Named. [… It] was a new dawn, sir, and Harry Potter shone like a beacon of hope for those of us who thought the dark days would never end, sir ..." (HP 2, 193-194)

It remains unclear in how far Harry has helped improve the elves' condition. Within the plot, slavery is the cause of much evil. Kreacher, the Blacks' house-elf, is mistreated by Sirius and takes revenge on him by betraying his master to Voldemort. Winky is bound to the Crouchs and does not tell anyone about their son being alive. Because of this, Sirius and Cedric die. So, widely as slavery is accepted in Magical World, it is a source of conflict, betrayal and suffering for all.

V.1.G. Ownership and Possession

If we were only to take into account the Dursley plot of the novels, the reader would read *Harry Potter* as a critique of capitalism. But looking closer we find that consumption is at the very heart of magical society. This positive counter-

---

[87] See Mendlesohn 2004, 180.

[88] See Ernould 2003, 227; Dieter Petzold, "Die Harry Potter-Bücher: Märchen, *fantasy fiction, school stories* – und was noch?" *Im Bann des Zauberlehrlings? Zur Faszination von Harry Potter*, ed. Kaspar H. Spinner, Regensburg: Friedrich Pustet, 2001, 21-41, here 33.

image of "Muggle" world is capitalist and "a community complete with its own international bank, global trade, and thriving monopolies alongside entrepreneurial ventures."[89] The difference between the two worlds is only in Harry's position. In "Muggle" World he is barred from economic participation, because he has no money. In Magical World Harry is rich and can buy whatever he wants.

It is amazing how Rowling imitates and adapts everday publicity to the needs of a society of wizards. Her fictive advertisements, slogans and campaigns are extremely well done and seem to be very professional.[90] In the wizarding world there are trademarks, new stylish products replacing outdated ones like the broomstick Nimbus 2000 which is outdone by the Nimbus 2001.[91] People yield to the temptations of the market and young adults particularly love to go shopping in Hogsmeade.[92] In Rowling's world, buying broomsticks or sweets is a way of participation and finding acceptance in one's peer group.[93] Harry himself is marketeer's dream: a boy from a wealthy family that can freely decide what he wants to buy.[94] But Harry is a modest boy and saves his money. Although he has the financial means to buy whatever he wants he does not yield to unlimited consumption.[95]

Greed is the mark of bad characters; good characters are modest (see IV.2.B, 154). In contrast to Harry, the Weasleys or Dumbledore, the Dursleys and the Malfoys are materialistic. Wealth and the ability to buy are used to show-off and demonstrate social status. The author presents this behaviour as negative. When Lucius Malfoy bribes the Slytherin "Quidditch" team with new broomsticks and makes fun of the Weasleys' shabby "Cleansweeps" (HP 2, 124) it is clear that this is completely unacceptable. The negative characters boast with their possessions – thus the reader is bound to dislike them. This is the same with the Dursleys. Their idiot son Dudley is flooded with presents – but never makes any reasonable use of them (see IV.4.G, 237). Consumption has ruined the boy's character as Dumbledore remarks:

> "The best that can be said is that [Harry] has at least escaped the appalling damage you have inflicted upon the unfortunate boy sitting between you." (HP 6, 57)

---

[89]   See Westman 2004, 310.
[90]   See Bürvenich 2001, 61; Gupta 2003, 136-138.
[91]   See Elizabeth Teare, "Harry Potter and the Technology of Magic," *The Ivory Tower and Harry Potter: Perspectives on a Literary Phenomenon*, ed. Lana A. Whited, Columbia: University of Missouri Press, 2004, 329-342, here 341.
[92]   See Teare 2004.
[93]   See Westman 2004, 311.
[94]   See Gupta 2003, 135.
[95]   See Westman 2004, 311.

The boy's physical deformity reflects his moral inferiority caused by his parents' over-indulgence and materialistic values.[96] Vernon sets an example to his son when he praises his new car "'in very loud voices, so that the rest of the street would notice it too'" (HP 3, 9).

With *Harry Potter* wealth correlates with power and racism (see IV.2.B, 154). Positive characters are poor or at least modest.[97] This relation is also expressed by the plot itself. If Ron had been able to afford a new wand in *Chamber of Secrets* Lockhart's "Memory Charm" would not have fired back but hit Ron and Harry instead. The Weasleys' poverty saves not only their son and daughter but also Magical World's messiah. So, even on this level the texts favour modesty and condemn materialism.

V.1.H. Law and Justice

"'Innocent until proven guilty, Severus, [...].'" (HP 2, 158) says Dumbledore to Snape when he wants to expel Ron and Harry in *Chamber of Secrets*. Thus, he adheres to a basic human right (Universal Declaration of Human Rights, article 11, paragraph 1):

> Everyone charged with a penal offence has the right to be presumed innocent until proved guilty according to law in a public trial at which he has had all the guarantees necessary for his defence.

The official magical world has a criminal court and trials are held in public. But apart from that its judiciary is highly defective. There is no counsel for the defence – we never see the accused with a solicitor, neither Igor Karkaroff (HP 4, 637-642) nor Barty Crouch jnr (HP 4, 644-647) or Ludo Bagman (HP 4, 642-644). They appear in court chained to their seat. They are allowed to defend themselves but without the help of a counsel, which decisively weakens their defence. This disagrees with article 8 of the Universal Declaration of Human Rights:

> Everyone has the right to an effective remedy by the competent national tribunals for acts violating the fundamental rights granted him by the constitution or by law.

Further, one must doubt if really all citizens are equal. Famous "Quidditch" star and "Death Eater" Ludo Bagman is acquitted (HP 4, 643-644). Justice is not blind but takes a careful look at who appears in court. The conditions in Azkaban where the prisoners go mad or are intellectually destroyed by "Dementors" violates article 5 of the UN Charter:

---

[96] See Blake 2002, 79.
[97] See Mendlesohn 2004, 173.

306

No one shall be subjected to torture or to cruel, inhuman or degrading treatment or punishment.

Although Rowling pretends to describe a modern legal system, it is in fact a highly dubious set-up and not in the least bit fair. Basically, Magical World believes that breaking rules must be punished – or in Hagrid's words: "'Yeh've done wrong an' now yeh've got ter pay fer it.'" (HP 1, 270) Anyone violating the law has to fear the consequences. When Fred Weasley wants to sleep during the day because he has been up all night to save Harry from the Dursleys, his mother prevents him from doing so: "'You will not, [...]. It's your own fault you've been up all night.'" (HP 2, 42) But at the same time, Harry again and again saves his own life and the lives of his friends by disregarding rules. His rule-breaking is hardly ever punished but in the end sanctified by poetic justice (see IV.3.B, 162).

There is frequent mention of "wizard law" (HP 4, 233) – but Rowling never explains what this is. Probably it is based on Anglo-Saxon case law, because Hermione, Ron and Harry are looking up cases from 1722 and 1296 to defend Buckbeak (HP 3, 240). We read about various individual acts and decrees of Magical World – among them these:

- "Decree for the Restriction of Underage Wizardry" (HP 3, 39): underage wizards are not allowed to use magic outside Hogwarts (HP 2, 14) (only in emergencies: HP 2, 78)
- "Misuse of Muggle Artefacts": it is forbidden to magically transform non-magical items (HP 2, 240)[98]
- It is forbidden to change the past during time travels[99] (HP 3, 429)
- For "Apparating", people need a licence (HP 4, 77)
- It is forbidden to use magic in "Muggle" world (HP 1, 91; HP 4, 90)
- "Code of Wand Use" (HP 4, 148)
- "Guidelines for the Treatment of Non-Wizard Part-Humans" (HP 4, 164)
- "International Ban on Duelling" (HP 4, 464)
- The use of "veritaserum" "is controlled by very strict Ministry guidelines" (HP 4, 562-563)
- "Animagi" must register (HP 1, 378)[100]

---

[98] This is why Ali Bashir is not allowed to import flying carpets: "'carpets are defined as a Muggle Artefact by the Registry of Proscribed Charmable Objects, [...]'" (HP 4, 103-104.).

[99] Hermione erklärt: "'[Awful] things have happened when wizards have meddled with time ... loads of them ended up killing their past or future selves by mistake!'" (HP 3, 429).

[100] "[The] Ministry keeps tabs on witches and wizards who can become animals; there's a register showing what animal they become, and their markings and things... [...] There have only been seven Animagi this century [...]." (HP 3, 378).

Apart from this there are the "Unforgiveable Curses" that are "'most heavily punished by wizarding law'" (HP 4, 233). Among these are the psychological curse "Imperius", the torture curse "Cruciatus" and the killing curse "Avada Kedavra". So the society of wizards punishes the removing of a person's free will, torturing or killing them. Consequentially, the use of these curses is heavily punished:

> "Now ... those three curses – Avada Kedavra, Imperius and Cruciatus – are known as the Unforgivable Curses. The use of any one of them on a fellow human being is enough to earn a life sentence in Azkaban." (HP 4, 239)

Whereas the wizard state has a legal system (imperfect as it may seem), Voldemort does not obey any legal institutions. His regime is marked by its complete lack of rights, the only punishment being death. On this point, Dursley and Voldemort agree. When the TV news report Sirius' escape from Azkaban, Vernon announces that "'hanging's the only way to deal with these people'" (HP 3, 24). Even Harry approves of the death penalty:

> "[Black] deserves it," he said suddenly. "You think so?" said Lupin lightly. "Do you really think anyone deserves that?" "Yes," said Harry defiantly. "For ... for some things ..." (HP 3, 268)

That fact that Harry is wrong in his judgement on Black and that he finally finds an important father figure in him clearly argues against the death penalty.

Apart from written law there are many unwritten rules in Magical World regulating the coexistence of the different groups in magical world. One of these is the ban on killing unicorns which leads to the perpetrator's moral corruption as Firenze, the centaur explains:

> "[...] it is a monstrous thing, to slay a unicorn, [...]. Only one who has nothing to lose, and everything to gain would commit such a crime. [...] You have slain something pure and defenceless to save yourself and you will have but a half life, a cursed life, from the moment the blood touches your lips." (HP 1, 279-280)

Children are similarly untouchable: "'the slaughter of foals is a terrible crime – we do not touch the innocent.'" (HP 5, 769) The violation of such taboos is the first sign of a society's decadence. Ronan, another centaur, explains:

> "Always the innocent are the first victims, [...]. So it has been for ages past, so it is now." (HP 1, 274)

The text's attitudes to justice are ambivalent. On the one hand they promote equality, abidance of the law and just punishment. On the other hand, Magical World has a highly deficient legal system. Laws can be adjusted to fit a specific situation and Harry – inspite of his rule-breaking – is a positive character. There seems to be a hidden message that laws must be questioned and in no case to be accepted blindly. Unquestioningly obeying laws enslaves people and makes them opportunists, just like Voldemort's followers. It is each and everyone's morality that makes him come to the right (or wrong) decision. Again, this refers to Carlyle's ideas (see V.1.B, 289). Unwritten moral standards are the true basis of society and of much more importance than official laws.

V.1.I. Violence

The use of violence is not well-regulated in the world of *Harry Potter*. Theoretically, human rights dictate the state monopoly on legitimate force. The French declaration of human rights has it in article 12:

> La garantie des droits de l'homme et du citoyen nécessite une force publique: cette force est donc instituée pour l'avantage de tous et non pour l'utilité particulière de ceux auxquels elle est confiée.

Such a monopoly needs an institution to carry it out – usually a police force or an army. In the world of *Harry Potter* the only such force seems to be the "Aurors" who defend the state against terrorism. They are an elite troop and have special rights, i.e. the right to search homes without warrant (HP 4, 514). The "Aurors" are only recruited from the top of the class – Harry dreams of joining them (HP 5, 728), but we never know if he finally makes it. Other special forces include the "Accidental Magic Reversal Squad" (HP 4, 98) and the "Obliviators" (HP 4, 98). Both see to reverse magical disasters caused by accident so as to ensure that Magical World is kept secret from the "Muggles".

Harry himself uses violence either when made to (for example in the "Triwizard Tournament")[101] or when he has to defend himself or his friends. Usually he does not aim to kill someone, but only disarms his enemies using "Expelliarmus". In *Deathly Hallows* we learn the "Death Eaters" recognise him by this non-violent behaviour and his friends ask him to kill rather to disarray (HP 7, 64).

There is no marked difference between positive and negative characters as far as violence is concerned. All the students use violence playing "Quidditch" – which is a very risky game.[102] Peace-loving Arthur Weasley assaults Lucius

---

[101] See Pinsent 2004, 36.
[102] See Konrad Heidkamp, "Zauberhafte Abziehbilder," *ZEIT* 48/2001 <http://www.zeit.de /archiv/2001/48/200148_potterfilm.xml> 3 Jan 2008.

Malfoy (HP 2, 70-71) and his wife is "walloping [her son Fred] with her broom-stick" (HP 3, 217). Hermione, usually the one to keep calm, slaps Malfoy in the face (HP 3, 317), Lupin and Black want to kill Pettigrew (HP 3, 402-404) and even Harry envisions how to torture Sirius when he first meets him:

> [He] wanted to hurt Black as badly as he could. (HP 3, 366)
> Now was the moment to avenge his mother and father. He was going to kill Black. He had to kill Black. This was his chance. (HP 3, 369)

It is much more the question *why* someone uses physical violence. If it happens in the name of some "higher good"[103] like justice or freedom, violence is accepted as a legitimate means of battle. Less astonishing is the fact that nega-tive characters like Harry's aunt Marge or Argus Filch favour the use of physical punishment for children:[104]

> "I won't have this namby-pamby, wishy-washy nonsense about not hitting people who deserve it. A good thrashing is all what's needed in ninety-nine cases out of a hundred. [...] Make it clear that you approve the use of ex-treme force in [Harry's] case." (HP 3, 32)
> "It's just a pity they let the old punishments die out ... hang you by your wrists from the ceiling for a few days, I've got the chains still in my office, keep 'em well oiled in case they're ever needed ..." (HP 1, 269)

But good and bad characters differ in the degree of pleasure they take from cruelty. Whereas the positive characters regret having to use violence, the negative ones delight in torturing others: Argus Filch is happy about being per-mitted to whip students (see IV.6.D, 272), Dudley Dursley loves playing a game with the meaningful title "Mega-Mutilation Part Three" (HP 4, 33), and Dolores Umbridge tortures Harry betraying a sadistic pleasure in his pain (see IV.5.G). At the "Quidditch" World Cup we see that the majority of wizards do not object to violence: when the "Death Eaters" torture "Muggles", most of them cheer or at least keep silent. Senseless cruelty is acceptable to the wizard society.[105]

The *Potter* novels do not proclaim non-violence as the first means of solv-ing conflicts. Just as with the question of breaking or obeying rules everyone has to decide for himself and on the background of his personal morals and priorities when and to what extent to use violence. Nevertheless, sadism and torture are clearly rejected. The basic message is that violence may be used under special circumstances and in defence of justice or freedom.[106]

---

[103] Mark that Gellert Grindelwald's slogan "For the greater good" is very similar to this atti-tude.
[104] She contradicts her own statement by spoiling her nephew Dudley.
[105] See Westman 2004, 321.
[106] See Pinsent 2004, 37.

V.2 The Society of Wizards

Human rights do not deal with all the aspects of a society. There are values and issues that have developed independently. Among these are friendship, bravery and industry, but also nationalism, ecology and media. In the following chapter I am going to analyse these values which belong to no specific canon.

V.2.A. Friendship and Loyalty

Friendship, loyalty, togetherness and a very British version of sportsmanship[107] are held in high esteem, and all of the positive characters in the series are marked by these characteristics. This is exemplified by the kind of loyalty Hermione demonstrates in *Philosopher's Stone* when she unexpectedly lies to a teacher. It is only after this that she is admitted into Hary's peer group (see IV.3.M). From then on the Hermione, Harry and Ron stick together, just like James, Peter and Sirius did in their younger days. These precursors even became "Animagi" to keep their werewolf-friend Remus company:

> "And they didn't desert me at all. Instead they did something for me that would make my transformations not only bearable, but the best times of my life. They became Animagi." (HP 3, 381)

Betraying or neglecting a friend, on the other hand, is a sign of failure and evil. When Ron and Harry promise Hagrid to help him defend Buckbeak, they simply forget. But they feel deeply ashamed when Hagrid says: "'I thought you two'd value yer friend more'n broomsticks or rats. Tha's all.'" (HP 3, 297) Pettigrew's betrayal of the Potters seals his fate as a submissive servant. Only Voldemort does not have any friends and obviously does not want to have any either. His followers are chattels dependent on him – they are not equal partners: "'Lord Voldemort has never had a friend, nor do I believe that he has ever wanted one.'" (HP 6, 260)

Rowling does not idealise friendship. Friends can quarrel but later solve their problems out. The relationship between Harry, Ron and Hermione endures many disagreements – in *Deathly Hallows* Ron abandons the company of Hermione and Harry, only to return later on. Before that we see them overcome the quarrel about Scabbers in *Prisoner of Azkaban* and Ron's short-term relationship with Lavender Brown in *Half-Blood Prince*. Dumbledore explains to Harry that there is no true friendship without disagreement:

---

[107] See Parvin Sadigh, "Harry Potter in der Schule? Of course!" *ZEIT* 29/2005. <http://www.zeit.de/2005/29/harrypotter_pro> 3 Jan 2008.

"Ah, Harry, how often this happens, even between the best of friends! Each
of us believes that what he has to say is much more important than anything
the other might have to contribute!" (HP 6, 336)

When Neville is trying to prevent Harry from leaving Gryffindor Tower at
midnight, Dumbledore awards him extra house points for "'a great deal of bravery [and standing] up to our friends'" (HP 1, 329). Harry's loyalty to Dumbledore saves him in the Chamber of Secrets, when the headmaster's phoenix
Fawkes comes to rescue him. As Dumbledore explains: "'Nothing but [real loy-
alty] could have called Fawkes to you.'" (HP 2, 356)

Harald Thorsrud claims that the novels depict various types of friendship
already described by Aristotle. The "useful" friendship which is convenient to
both sides is embodied by Voldemort and his followers. The "Death Eaters" follow him because they are afraid and they hope to improve their own status.[108]
There are no positive emotions. Malfoy and his cronies Crabbe and Goyle represent "pleasant" friendship; both sides like to have the other around. Draco
appreciates their hero worship (this changes in *Deathly Hallows*; HP 7, 506) and
they like to associate with the nobility.[109] Finally there is "true" friendship,
which is unselfish and relies on feelings. This kind of friendship unites Ron,
Hermione and Harry[110] and is vitally important for Harry. Only with the help of
his friends can he defeat Voldemort. In *Philosopher's Stone* Dumbledore rushes
to his aid. In *Chamber of Secrets* Dumbledore's phoenix brings him a weapon
and heals him from Basilisk venom. Hermione is the decisive helper in *Prisoner
of Azkaban*, whereas it is the dead that help Harry in *Goblet of Fire* and *Deathly
Hallows*. It is the positive relationship Harry has with other people which makes
him successful.[111] This kind of friendship cannot be threatened by conflicts and
controversies, which sets it apart from the negative characters' relationships
amongst each other:[112] They cannot accept being criticised.

Friendship also has a great importance when it comes to battling evil –
Cedric Diggory dies because he is loyal to Harry and a fair competitor. Voldemort accidentally lures him into the trap set for Harry and kills "the spare" before dealing with Harry (HP 4, 688). Loyalty, trust, faithfulness and reliability
are major values in the *Harry Potter* series and an important weapon in fighting
the forces of darkness:

---

[108] See Harald Thorsrud, "Voldemort's Agents, Malfoy's Cronies, and Hagrid's Chums:
Friendship in *Harry Potter*," *Harry Potter and Philosophy: If Aristotle ran Hogwarts*,
eds. Baggett & Klein. Chicago, La Salle: Open Court, 2004, 38-48, 39; Bürvenich 2001,
115.

[109] See Thorsrud 2004, 40.

[110] See Thorsrud 2004, 43-45.

[111] See Drexler, Wandinger 2004, 39; Walser 2004, 85.

[112] See von Lovenberg 2003.

"[In] the light of Lord Voldemort's return, we are only as strong as we are united, as weak as we are divided. Lord Voldemort's gift for spreading discord and enmity is very great. We can fight it only by showing an equally strong bond of friendship and trust." (HP 4, 784)

V.2.B. Concepts of Nation and Nationalism

Reaction and attitude towards strangers distinguishes good and evil. The positive characters work for international cooperation and understand that this is their major strength. Dumbledore says:

> "Differences of habit and language are nothing at all if our aims are identical and our hearts are open. [...] I say to you all, once again – in the light of Lord Voldemort's return we are only as strong as we are united, as weak as we are divided." (HP 4, 784)

Nevertheless, there is rivalry when the nations meet at the "Quidditch" World Cup (HP 4, 86-131) or in the "Triwizard Tournament". Here, the novels indulge in colourful stereotypes:[113] Africans wear "long white robes" and are "roasting what looked like a rabbit on a bright purple fire". Middle-aged witches from the US enjoy American campus romanticism "gossiping happily beneath a spangled banner stretched between their tents which read: 'The Salem Witches' Institute'" (HP 4, 93) – alluding to one of the most infamous witch trials, the Salem witch trials that were held between February 1692 and May 1693.[114] Likewise, we find rather stereotyped anglocentric descriptions of Durmstrang and Beauxbatons.[115] Durmstrang representatives are rather sinister and give cause for distrust (the school seems to be in the Balkans; see III.5.I, 138), whereas the French from Beauxbatons are arrogant and blasé (HP 4, 275-280). Fleur Delacour first appears as the typical French "bitch" complaining about food, being afraid of putting on weight and disapproving of anything English (HP 4, 441). Only when Harry saves her sister Gabrielle (HP 4, 551) does she become approachable and even decides to improve her English (HP 4, 785). During an internship with Gringotts she falls in love with Bill Weasley. But the cultural differences, again, lead to misunderstandings: Fleur's mediterranean enthusiam simply does not fit into the Weasleys' modest way of life. Finally, when she vows to stay with Bill despite his being mutilated by Fenrir Greyback she and her future mother-in-law reconcile. Even then, Fleur points out the different eating habits of France and England:

---

[113] See Whited, "From Craze to Classic", 8.
[114] "Salem witch trials." Wikipedia, The Free Encyclopedia. 12 Dec 2007. <http://en.wikipedia.org/w/index.php?title=Salem_witch_trials&oldid=177493282> 14 Dec 2007.
[115] See Ehgartner 2002, 79.

313

"... so eet ees lucky 'e is marrying me," said Fleur happily, plumping up Bill's pillows, 'because ze British overcook their meat, I 'ave always said this." (HP 6, 591)

In *Harry Potter* France is the country of hot temper and passion. Hagrid sees Olympe's nationality as reason for her uncontrolled accesses of rage: "'spect it's the French in her ...'" (HP 5, 477). Taking a look at the description of Fleur's family on the occasion of her wedding, we find all of Britain's French prejudices united: enthusiastic mediterranean temper, flattery, exaggerated manners and of course French woman seducing English husbands or boyfriends:

> Monsieur Delacour was [...] a head shorter [than his wife] and exremely plump, with a little, pointed, black beard. However, he looked good-natured. Bouncing towards Mrs Weasley on high-heeled boots, he kissed her twice on each cheek, leaving her flustered. [...] "Dear lady!" said Monsieur Delacour, still holding Mrs Weasley's hand between his own two plump ones and beaming. [...] "Enchantée," [Madame Delacour] said. "Your 'usband 'as been telling us such amusing stories!" Mr Weasley gave a maniacal laugh; Mrs Weasley threw him a look, upon which he became immediately silent and assumed an expression appropriate to the sickbed of a close friend. [...] Gabrielle [...] gave Harry a glowing look, batting her eyelashes. Ginny cleared her throat loudly. (HP 7, 92-93)

Moreover, it is striking that negative characters usually have a French or Romance sounding name, like Voldemort or Malfoy. The good characters, on the other hand, have Anglo-Saxon names.[116]

Apart from these rather entertaining and common stereotypes[117] the text leaves platitudinous nationalism bordering on xenophobia mostly to the negative characters. Petunia asks her son during a bout of indigestion: "'Did Mrs Polkiss give you something foreign for tea?'" (HP 5, 33) Even Hagrid, annoyed when Olympe ignores him, says: "'Yeh can' trust any of 'em [foreigners].'" (HP 4, 612)

In conclusion, the characters' English background is never really mentioned. Strangers are to be distrusted.[118] Countries outside Great Britain are not considered equal. It somehow seems that Rowling only mentions them to be politically correct – not to give a realistic view of a globalised world.[119] Strikingly, minor characters like the Patil twins or Cho Chang have a Commonwealth back-

---

[116] See Adams 2003; Blake 2002, 109; Mullan 2005.
[117] This opposition between England and France is a common pattern already used by Enid Blyton (see VII.2.B).
[118] See Heilman, Gregory 2003, 254.
[119] See Turner-Vorbeck 2003, 20; Heilman, Gregory 2003, 255.

ground.[120] In Great Britain, *Harry Potter* is read as a revival of traditional English values.[121] Author Richard Adams says:

> It's no coincidence that Rowling herself is an honorary member of the British Weights and Measures Association – which defends the ounce and pint, and calls the metric system 'a political philosophy'.[122]

Harry Potter can also be regarded as a comment on Britain's role in a globalised world and in particular after 9/11 – although the novels were bestsellers before the attack on the World Trade Center.[123]

V.2.C. Bravery and Cowardice

Bravery, courage and heroism are key values in the *Potter* novels (see IV.2.B, 154): they are widely acknowledged at school ("pure nerve and outstanding courage", HP 1, 328), in society (Pettigrew's mother is rewarded "the Order of Merlin, First Class, and Pettigrew's finger in a box" (HP 3, 233) for her son's "hero's death" (HP 3, 225)), and at sports ("[Krum] was very brave, wasn't he?", HP 4, 129). Above all, Harry's courage is praised:

> "You have shown bravery equal to those who died fighting Voldemort at the height of his powers." (HP 4, 757)
> "[Harry] showed, in every respect, the sort of bravery that few wizards have ever shown in facing Lord Voldemort, and for this, I honour him." (HP 4, 783)

Cowardice is publicly unmasked. "Moody" tells Draco: "'I don't like people who attack when their opponent's back's turned, [...]. Stinking, cowardly, scummy thing to do ...'" (HP 4, 226). In fact, it is mostly the negative characters that are fearful (see IV.2.B, 154). Fear is usually a sign of uncertainty, of being afraid of the unknown, as Dumbledore explains to Harry:

> "There is nothing to be feared from a body, Harry, any more than there is anything to be feared from the darkness. Lord Voldemort, who of course secretly fears both, disagrees. But once again he reveals his own lack of wisdom. It is the unknown we fear when we look upon death and darkness, nothing more." (HP 6, 529)

But bravery and courage are not limited to the good characters or the Gryffindors. Phineas Nigellus regards them as characteristics of Slytherin as

---

[120] See Heilman, Gregory 2003, 255.
[121] See "Harry Potter und das große Geld", 2001.
[122] Adams 2003.
[123] See Williams 2001.

well – only that Slytherins combine them with a sense of profit: "'We Slytherins are brave, yes, but not stupid. For instance, given the choice, we will always choose to save our own necks.'" (HP 5, 545)

The students frequently advise each other to be brave and upright. Ron asks Neville to report Draco for his unallowed use of the "Leg Locker Curse": "'I don't want more trouble,' he murmured. 'You've got to stand up to him, Neville!' said Ron." (HP 1, 236) Hermione accuses Ron and Harry of not getting their priorities right and of being afraid of brewing "Polyjuice Potion":

> "Well, if you two are going to chicken out, fine. [...] *I* don't want to break rules, you know. *I* think threatening Muggleborns is far worse than brewing up a difficult potion." (HP 2, 181)

Dumbledore also reminds Harry that bravery begins by calling things their proper names: "'Call him Voldemort, Harry. Always use the proper name for things. Fear of a name increases fear of the thing itself.'" (HP 1, 320)

Being brave also means to be disciplined and self-possessed – this is the only chance to be successful. In *Order of the Phoenix* we see how important the control of one's emotions and thoughts is. Voldemort is able to lure Harry into a trap because he uses telepathy.

V.2.D. Education and Ambition

Being well-educated is desirable – as long as you do not have to work hard for it. Basically, this is the novels' idea about education. We do find opposition to this in the constellation of characters (see IV.2.B, 154 and IV.3.M, 197). The Hogwarts hymn tells us how important education is in Magical World: "'Teach us something please ... Our heads could do with filling ... So teach us things worth knowing ...'" (HP 1, 140). "Worth knowing" is the operative point – amassing useless facts and figures is useless. On the occasion of Harry and his friends getting detention, Hagrid says: "'Writin' lines! What good's that ter anyone? Yeh'll do summat useful or yeh'll get out.'" (HP 1, 270)

Hogwarts is kept open under any circumstances to make it possible for the children to continue their education, as McGonagall explains: "'The whole point of keeping the school open at this time is for you to receive your education, [...]'" (HP 2, 306). Education is indispensible for growing up and for surviving in a hostile environment.[124]

Nevertheless, it is "uncool" to follow the lessons attentively. Ron accuses Hermione: "'D'you think we've got nothing better to do in Potions than listen to Snape?'" (HP 2, 174) and says of Tom Riddle's outstanding results at school:

---

[124] See Smadja 2001, 100-102.

"'Prefect, Head Boy – probably top of every class.' 'You say that like it's a bad thing,' said Hermione, in a slightly hurt voice.'" (HP 2, 254) When Percy Weasley becomes head boy he is very proud (see IV.3.K, 190), but at the same time he is teased by his brothers and sisters: "'If we're not careful, we'll have another Head Boy in the family. I don't think I could stand the shame.'" (HP 2, 54) The only character who is respected despite working hard for school is Hermione – although her behaviour seems quite bizarre:

> [Harry] did not usually lie in bed reading his textbooks; that sort of behaviour, as Ron rightly said, was indecent in anybody except Hermione, who was simply weird that way. (HP 6, 223)

Ron, on the contrary, represents the "normal boy" preferring sports and jokes to hard school work.[125] Over-zealous students are suspicious; ambition is one of the characteristics of Slytherins.[126] Although not every ambitious student must end up an evil criminal, Slytherin brings forth people like the Malfoys or Tom Riddle in whose career ambition clearly plays a negative role. They use their talents to subdue others.[127]

To conclude, the novels' attitude towards education and ambition is rather ambivalent: although book-learning is quite useless, personal development depends on life at school. Daily lessons are frequently regarded as tedious distractions from "the real thing", but school is highly influential in the students' future social behaviour.[128] Moreover, the knowledge acquired at school enables Harry to investigate further and eventually to defeat Voldemort.[129] "Important knowledge [is] hidden knowledge. It is the hero's role to actively seek, uncover, and use secret knowledge despite interferences."[130] Book-knowledge needs common sense to be really useful.[131] This attitude towards learning and education is consistent with the values of the classical school story (see VII.1.D, 425). Education is the key to independence and fulfilment as the counter-example of the house-elves demonstrates. They only accept their lot because they are "uneducated and brainwashed" (HP 4, 263). So knowledge and education are top-ranking values in the world of *Harry Potter*.

---

[125] See Elster 2003, 208.
[126] See Steven W. Patterson, "Is Ambition a Virtue? Why Slytherin Belongs at Hogwarts," *Harry Potter and Philosophy: If Aristotle ran Hogwarts*, eds. David Baggett & Shawn Klein, Chicago, La Salle: Open Court, 2004, 121-131, 127.
[127] See Patterson 2004, 131.
[128] See Elster 2003, 204-206.
[129] See Mendlesohn 2004, 169.
[130] See Elster 2003, 216.
[131] See Ernould 2003, 232.

V.2.E. Nature and Environment

In the world of *Harry Potter* we see that it is only the positive characters that treat fauna and flora respectfully. Harry shares the little food he gets from the Dursleys with his owl Hedwig (HP 2, 29). Hagrid wants to please Buckbeak (who has been sentenced to death) a last time: "'I owe him that ...'" (HP 3, 317) Animals in *Harry Potter* have feelings; they can be happy, hurt or proud and interact as equals with the human characters. We read about Harry's owl Hedwig:[132]

> [Hedwig] looked extremely pleased with herself. She gave Harry an affectionate nip with her beak [...]. (HP 3, 14)
> Hedwig's large amber eyes were reproachful, [...]. (HP 3, 29)
> [Hedwig was] clicking her beak in the way that meant she was annoyed. (HP 4, 43)
> [Hedwig] was evidently still furious about his lack of gratitude. (HP 4, 252)

When the owl dies in *Deathly Hallows* (HP 7, 52) it is like losing an old and intimate friend:

> The realisation crashed over him: he felt ashamed of himself as the tears stung his eyes. The owl had been his companion, his one great link with the magical world whenever he had been forced to return to the Dursleys. (HP 7, 61)

Hermione's cat Crookshanks is a very intelligent animal. For Sirius he is an important helper:

> "He's the most intelligent of his kind I've ever met. He recognised Peter for what he was straight away. And when he met me, he knew I was no dog. [...] Finally I managed to communicate to him what I was after, and [...] he stole the passwords into Gryffindor Tower [...]." (HP 3, 392)

The cat can even open the secret passage under the "Whomping Willow" (HP 3, 435). Animals recognise negative characters immediately. Hagrid's dog Fang starts barking the moment Lucius Malfoy stands right in front of him (HP 2, 282).[133]

But it is not only the good characters which have animals as their helpers. Voldemort keeps the snake Nagini[134] as a pet – and as a safe for his soul, for she is one of his "Horcruxes". Nagini even feeds him when he is not able to take human form (HP 4, 14). She is "[a] gigantic snake, at least twelve feet long" (HP 4, 19) and has a "diamond-patterned tail" (HP 4, 20).

---

[132] See Jung 2004, 153; Lacoss 2004, 78.
[133] This characteristic of animals is already found in Enid Blyton: see VII.2.B.
[134] The name clearly refers to the Asian "Naga" – a Buddhist representation of a class of beings, generally held to be a snake.

Good characters prove their moral quality in the compassionate way they treat their fellow-beings. For instance, Arthur Weasley will never get rid of the gnomes in his garden: "'They'll be back, [...]. They love it here ... Dad's too soft with them, he thinks they're funny ...'" (HP 2, 45). Likewise, Hagrid loves monsters and jeopardises everyone when he settles giant spiders in the "Forbidden Forest" (HP 2, 269). Bad characters, on the other hand, pointlessly kill animals and violate their rights. The students are asked to maltreat animals when they must prepare different kinds of potion during Snape's lesson. They use spiders (HP 2, 169), behead caterpillars (HP 3, 137), hash crocodile hearts (HP 3, 201), chop scarab beetles (HP 4, 558), and at one point, Harry is occupied by "[disembowling] a barrelful of horned toads" (HP 4, 230). Although other lessons use animals as well (in "Transfiguration" they must change birds into guinea pigs) (HP 4, 421), Snape's subject is the only onewhere the animals get hurt. McGonagall, on the other hand, asks her students to be careful: when Ron is about to injure the frog he is working on with his broken wand McGonagall is "not pleased" (HP 2, 105), and Harry is accused of maltreating his frog:

> "Harry, you're squashing your frog." Harry looked down; he was indeed squeezing his bullfrog so tightly its eyes were popping; [...]. The bullfrog on which [Hermione] was practising her Silencing Charm was struck dumb mid-croak and glared at her reproachfully. [...] The large and ugly raven in front of [Ron] let out a derisive craw. (HP 5, 414)

When the false Professor Moody shows the effects of the "Unforgiveable Curses" on a spider (HP 4, 234-237), the reader starts to doubt him. Positive characters respect nature and would never be cruel on animals. Draco Malfoy is pleased that Buckbeak has been sentenced to death (HP 3, 341), Bellatrix Lestrange kills a fox without any reason (HP 6, 25) and Viktor Krum hurts the dragon he is fighting in the "Triwizard Tournament" which leads to the jury taking marks off him:

> "Only thing is, [the dragon] went trampling around in agony and squashed half the real eggs – they took marks off for that, he wasn't supposed to do any damage to them." (HP 4, 394)

Fred and George Weasley tantalise animals out of thoughtlessness. They try to find out "what would happen if you fed a Filibuster Firework to a Salamander. Fred had 'rescued' the brilliant orange, fire-dwelling lizard from a Care of Magical Creatures class" (HP 2, 143). But in this they do not differentiate between man and beast. They test their magical sweets on younger fellow students (see IV.3.J).

Humans and animals are a part of the same community; their cohabitation is regulated by law. Animals must observe the law as much as human beings (the hippogriff Buckbeak is put to trial – not Hagrid who took him to class: HP 3, 240). Animals are much more intelligent than "Muggles" suppose them to be. But on the other hand, some wizards are able to transform into animals.[135] Knowing about flora and fauna is decisive. The students turned to stone by the Basilisk can only be revived using mandrakes, and "Devil's Snare" in *Philosopher's Stone* can only be dealt with by knowing their biology. Knowledge of plants and animals is decisive in defeating Voldemort.[136] Magical world is highly dependent on animals – the most important system of communication consisting of post owls.[137] But this is not the only ecological message of the texts. The friendly community of wizards is a direct conrast to the inhumane, technology-crazy world of the "Muggles". In contrast to them, wizards are living in an ecologically healthy environment[138] which can do without the dubious achievements of modern technology. The Dursleys represent the exaggerated use of all things high tech[139] which is contrary to the pre-industrial world of Hogwarts with all its magic and secrets. Wizards don't need technology – Isabelle Smadja reads the first scene of *Philosopher's Stone* where Dumbledore switches off the lights in Privet Drive as a metaphor for the shortcomings of human technology.[140] Hogwarts, on the other hand, is a place where conservative elements are most dominant. The timetable includes medieval subjects like alchemy and the ambience of the old castle could be taken directly from a nineteenth century Gothic Novel.[141] Magical World is a nostalgic, conservative world. The novels advocate a positive attitude towards nature. True moral greatness includes respect for the environment. Everyone maltreating his fellow-beings – human and non-human – is morally corrupt.

V.2.F. Freedom of Press and Media

J.K. Rowling has personally had very negative experiences with the press; therefore, the media of her magical world is quite dubious as well.[142] The daily press is used by all the interest groups to influence public opinion. Apart from the "Daily Prophet" there is the woman's magazine "Witch Weekly", the scandal sheet "Quibbler" and the broadcasting station "Wizarding Wireless Network" ("WWN") (HP 4, 428).[143] It is public relations and media that secure power in

---

[135] "Animagi (wizards who could transform at will into animals)." (HP 3, 120).
[136] See Smadja 2001, 29-30.
[137] See Smadja 2001, 29-30.
[138] See Smadja 2001, 32.
[139] See Smadja 2001, 32.
[140] See Smadja 2001, 32.
[141] See Steege 2004, 155.
[142] See O'Sullivan 2002, 27.
[143] The name, of course, is a variation of "BBC" or "CNN".

wizard society. Throughout the texts there are many examples of how the media influences politics and public awareness.

Quacksalver Gilderoy Lockhart can only be successful because he is perfect at playing with the media (see IV.4.B, 222). He systematically tries to use Harry for his own public relations and has himself portrayed with Harry at various times (HP 2, 69). Rufus Scrimgeour – in contrast to his predecessor Cornelius Fudge – also understands how to be present in the press. Thus, he tries to persuade Harry to appear in public with him (see IV.5.B, 252).

The influence of media coverage is especially visible in *Goblet of Fire* and *Order of the Phoenix*. After the fiasco at the "Quidditch" world cup the "Daily Prophet" agitates against the Ministry:[144]

> *SCENES OF TERROR AT THE QUIDDITCH WORLD CUP*, complete with a twinkling, black-and-white photograph of the Dark Mark over the tree-tops. (HP 4, 163)
> If the terrified wizards and witches who waited breathlessly for news at the edge of the wood expected reassurance from the Ministry of Magic, they were sadly disappointed. (HP 4, 165)

Officials try to control the damage, but without any success. The Ministry has to act (HP 4, 164). Later, during the "Triwizard Tournament" reports by scandal journalist Rita Skeeter (see IV.6.F, 273) show us the power of the media. She makes Harry look like the lonely, suffering hero of the tournament:

> "I suppose I get my strength from my parents, I know they'd be very proud of me if they could see me now ... yes, sometimes at night I still cry about them, I'm not ashamed to admit it." (HP 4, 345)

Rita never loses sight of selling the story.[145] Asked to write an objective report she says coolly: "'There's no market for a story like that [...]." (HP 5, 625) In addition to her hero's tale about Harry she writes a tragic piece on the boy's alleged love for Hermione:

> Harry has found love at Hogwarts. His close friend, Colin Creevey, says that Harry is rarely seen out of the company of one Hermione Granger, a stunningly pretty Muggle-born girl who, like Harry, is one of the top students in school. (HP 4, 346)

---

144 The newspaper's research is not very profound: they call Arthur Weasley "Arnold Weasley" (HP 4, 224). This shows how unimportant he is and how negligent the "Prophet" is.
145 Harry understands why Rita has to make up new stories about him: "'She can't keep writing about what a tragic little hero I am, it'll get boring.'" (HP 4, 427)

Harry answers back, but Rita counters "'Our readers have the right to know the truth, Harry, I am merely doing my job –'" (HP 4, 491). When Harry refuses to speak to her, she simply invents scandalous stories about him and makes him appear mentally unhinged: *"HARRY POTTER 'DISTURBED AND DANGER-OUS'"* (HP 4, 663-664). Hermione calls Rita a "horrible woman". Rita takes her revenge by writing a report on her for "Witch Weekly" in which she speculates on Hermione's love life:

> HARRY POTTER'S SECRET HEARTACHE: A boy like no other, perhaps – yet a boy suffering all the usual pangs of adolescence, writes Rita Skeeter. Deprived of love since the tragic demise of his parents, fourteen-year-old Harry Potter thought he had found solace in his steady girlfriend at Hog-warts, Muggle-born Hermione Granger.[146] [...] Miss Granger, a plain but ambitious girl,[147] seems to have a taste for famous wizards that Harry alone cannot satisfy. Since the arrival at Hogwarts of Viktor Krum [...] Miss Granger has been toying with both boys' affections. (HP 4, 556)

After this article, Hermione receives hate mail. Even Hagrid suffers from Rita's hunger for stories, when she writes a report with the title: *"DUMBLE-DORE'S GIANT MISTAKE"* (HP 4, 477-480). Hagrid is temporarily suspended. It is only when Hermione finds out that Rita is a non-registered "Animagus", i.e. that she can transform into a beetle (see IV.6.F, 273) (which is regarded as a criminal offence in Magical World) do things change: Hermione blackmails her and makes her write an objective report. In *Order of the Phoenix* a campaign initiated by the Ministry marks Harry as mad, traumatised and obsessed with being "chosen". This can only be answered by a media counterattack: Harry gives Rita an exclusive interview for the "Quibbler" (HP 5, 637) and tells her everything about Voldemort's resurrection. This interview changes public opin-ion, for now people believe Harry instead of the Ministry. In *Deathly Hallows* she has published a biography of Dumbledore and is interviewed herself for the press. She has a very lurid exclusive at-home interview written about her titled: "DUMBLEDORE – THE TRUTH AT LAST?", (HP 7, 25) pretending that eve-ryone has been desperate to know more about Dumbledore and hinting at possi-ble revelations about him. The reviews are highly biased and try to scandalise the Hogwarts headmaster. Suggestive questions lead the reader in, so that Rita can prepare him for the text:

> WHY was the man tipped to be Minister for Magic content to remain a mere headmaster? WHAT was the real purpose of the secret organisa-

---

[146] The newspaper mentioning Hermione's non-magical parents goes to show how important this information is.

[147] Before, Hermione has been described as "stunningly pretty" (HP 4, 346). So the paper always chooses the appropriate notion for its stories.

tion known as the Order of the Phoenix? HOW did Dumbledore really meet his end? (HP 7, 26)

In Magical World, the press is powerful enough to deny the truth and to affirm lies. The public is not interested in the truth as long as there is no media coverage of it. Whoever controls the press in Magical World is opinion leader.

V.3 Hogwarts – A System on its Own

"Hogwarts [...] seems to me an academy more tiresome than grotesque" said critic Harold Bloom of the wizard school.[148] Thus, he not only misconceives the school's colourfulness, but also the central meaning it has for the novels. Within Magical World, Hogwarts is an independent system with its own rules, hierarchy and groups. This is why I am going to analyse Hogwarts in detail.

The school has twelve governors that install, control and unseat the headmaster (HP 2, 359). Within Hogwarts the headmaster is rather untouchable, a *primus inter pares*. His orders must be followed. His office is a bit apart from the other school rooms and you need a password to get in (see 120). Dining in the Great Hall, the headmaster occupies the front seat of the high table (HP 1, 134). There is no mention of conferences or institutionalised participation of other teachers or even students. Dumbledore is the powerful "strong just man" of Hogwarts (see V.1.B, 289), with the school's set of values based on the headmanster's moral integrity. When Dumbledore temporarily has to leave Hogwarts in *Chamber of Secrets* (HP 2, 282-283), terror and fear are spread. His successor Dolores Umbridge briefly shows in *Order of the Phoenix* how much the free spirit depends on the morals of the school's headmaster. At the same time, this episode demonstrates how powerful non-violent resistance can be. Despite all the power Umbridge has given herself, she is not able to rule her school in opposition to students and teachers.

But what is the spirit of Hogwarts like? The school's hymn sums up the objectives and dreams of the school's community:

> "Hogwarts, Hogwarts,
> Hoggy Warty Hogwarts,
> Teach us something please,
> Whether we be old and bald
> Or young with scabby knees,
> Our heads could do with filling
> With some interesting stuff,
> For now they're bare and full of air,
> Dead flies and bits of fluff,

---

[148] Bloom 2000.

So teach us things worth knowing,
Bring back what we've forgot,
Just do your best, we'll do the rest,
And learn until our brains all rot. "
(HP 1, 140)

Apart from the satiric character of the song, there are two things worth mentioning. First, Hogwarts is open to everyone. It is not only about learning magic but also about developing one's character and growing up. Second, the students vow to work hard for their education and to continue to do so "until our brains all rot." Application is important in Hogwarts.

Hogwarts' reputation is excellent. Justin Finch-Fletchley, a "Muggle" born student was bound to go to Eton ("'My name was down for Eton, you know, [...].'"; HP 2, 105).[149] But to his great relief he got a letter from Hogwarts. This shows that even Eton is nothing compared to the wizard school. Dudley Dursley's school, Smeltings, is not only much worse than Hogwarts but also sticks ridiculously to outdated traditions.[150] Hogwarts is over a thousand years old. Its founding is shrouded in legend:

> "Hogwarts was founded over a thousand years ago – the precise date is uncertain – by the four greatest witches and wizards of the age. The four school houses are named after them: Godric Gryffindor, Helga Hufflepuff, Rowena Ravenclaw and Salazar Slytherin.[151] They built this castle together, far from prying Muggle eyes, for it was an age when magic was feared by common people, and witches and wizards suffered much persecution." (HP 2, 164)

The school seems to have about 800 students[152] and is in constant rivalry with other academies. Before the Durmstrang and Beauxbatons delegations arrive, McGonagall asks Neville:

---

[149] Justin is a Hufflepuff, which is not the house of the intellectual elite. This means that Eton is nothing compared to Hogwarts, otherwise Justin would have been a Ravenclaw.

[150] "Smeltings boys wore a maroon tailcoat, orange knickerbockers, a flat straw hat, and a knobbly stick, used for hitting each other while the teachers weren't looking. This was supposed to be good training for later life." (HP 1, 40). Smeltings is an unworthy, ridiculous institution.

[151] This enumeration of names shows how much Rowling loves to alliterate her names; see II.2.G, 55.

[152] We can figure out this number easily. Three quarters of the spectators at the "Quidditch" Finales wear the colours of Gryffindor, only 200 wear the Slytherins' green. This means that 200 students make up one quarter of the school's pupils. So Hogwarts must have about 800 students. (HP 1, 329-330).

"Longbottom, kindly do *not* reveal that you can't even perform a simple switching Spell in front of anyone from Durmstrang!" (HP 4, 260)

The names of the characters show us that Hogwarts is multi-ethnic:[153] Angelina Johnson, Parvati Patil, Cho Chang – these names belong to children of non-European descent and probably from a non-Christian background. Nevertheless, Hogwarts celebrates Christmas and Easter "but there are no feasts for Rosh Hashanah or Diwali. This is not so much multiculturalism as naive monoculturalism. "[154]

The most important elements of Hogwarts society are the four houses tracing back to the four founders, as the "Sorting Hat" explains:

"Now each of these four founders
Formed their own house, for each
Did value different virtues
In the ones they had to teach.
By Gryffindor, the bravest were
Prized far beyond the rest;
For Ravenclaw, the cleverest
Would always be the best;
For Hufflepuff, hard workers were
Most worthy of admission;
And power-hungry Slytherin
Loved those of great ambition. "
(HP 4, 196)
"Said Slytherin, 'We'll teach just those
Whose ancestry is purest.'
Said Ravenclaw, 'We'll teach those whose
Intelligence is surest.'
Said Gryffindor, 'We'll teach all those
With brave deeds to their name, '
Said Hufflepuff, 'I'll teach the lot
And treat them just the same. "
(HP 5, 229)

In Hogwarts, any talent is appreciated; the students are accepted with their individual qualifications. Their personality is as important as their intellectual brilliance.

"[...] Gryffindor,
Where dwell the brave at heart,
Their daring, nerve and chivalry
Set Gryffindors apart;

---

[153] See Kern 2003, 209.
[154] Adams 2003.

[...]
Hufflepuff,
Where they are just and loyal,
Those patient Hufflepuffs are true
And unafraid of toil;
[...]
Ravenclaw,
If you've a ready mind,
Where those of wit and learning,
Will always find their kind;
[...]
Slytherin,
[...]
Those cunning folk use any means
To achieve their ends."
(HP 1, 130)

Each year, the "Sorting Hat" divides the newcoming students into the four houses. This is of vital importance to the students, for the houses will be their place of socialisation. Its values will form the students' characters for all their life. Or as McGonagall says: "'The Sorting is a very important ceremony because, while you are here, your house will be something like your family within Hogwarts.'" (HP 1, 126) The houses provide the children with a feeling of belonging; they are the surrogate families students identify with. Each has its own coat of arms:

> Enormous silk banners hung from the walls, each of them representing a Hogwarts house – red with a gold lion for Gryffindor, blue with a bronze eagle for Ravenclaw, yellow with a black badger for Hufflepuff, and green with a silver serpent for Slytherin. [The] largest banner of all bore the Hogwarts coat of arms: lion, eagle, badger and snake united around a large letter 'H'. (HP 4, 261)

At the same time this division creates peer pressure and forces the students to conform to their house's rules. The four groups are rivals – as much in "Quidditch" as in the house point system (a highly biased way of rewarding good and punishing bad behaviour). Belonging to a house puts everyone under pressure. When Harry, Neville and Hermione are caught on a night-time excursion and lose house points for Gryffindor, they are cut by their fellow-students: "Everywhere Harry went, people pointed and didn't trouble to lower their voices as they insulted him." (HP 1, 265) The houses' rivalry becomes especially dangerous when the community considers standing united against Voldemort. The "Sorting Hat" is worried and changes his song:

"Listen closely to my song:
Though condemned I am to split you
Still I worry that it's wrong,
though I must fulfil my duty
And must quarter every year
Still I wonder whether Sorting
May not bring the end I fear. "
(HP 5, 229)

Apart from the houses that divide students according to character, there is a distinction of class being made. Every year some students are appointed special offices by the teachers: there are prefects, head boy and girl (HP 1, 107). The students chosen for these offices wear special badges to distinguish them from others: "[...] Harry noticed a shiny silver badge on [Percy's] chest with the letter on it" (HP 1, 107).[155] They enjoy several privileges; for example they have separate luxurious bathrooms (see 126).

Hogwarts' community is marked by many written and unwritten rules. One of the most important rules is the unconditional respect for and obedience to teachers. For example, Dumbledore reminds Harry to call Snape "Professor Snape" (HP 1, 322; HP 5, 909). It is forbidden to leave the dormitories at night, detentions have to be fulfilled without using magic (HP 2, 130) and there is an "anti-cheating spell" during exams (HP 1, 283). Snape also mentions that "'[...] fighting is against Hogwarts rules, [...]'" (HP 1, 212).

Whoever violates rules is punished. Either he gets detention and has to do extra work (something Snape and Umbridge seem to prefer) or points are taken from his house. Argus Filch dreams of reintroducing physical punishment ("[Filch] was always begging Dumbledore to let him suspend students by their ankles from the ceiling.", HP 2, 138); finally, Dolores Umbridge grants him the right to whip the students. But even without physical pain, punishment in Hogwarts can be cruel: when Neville accidentally betrays the password to Gryffindor Tower to Sirius Black, he is no longer told any more passwords. Painfully, he has to wait outside the door until someone lets him in or out (HP 3, 294) – a very embarrassing procedure that marks him out as a loser. The impostor "Moody" does not hesitate to transform Draco into a ferret to punish him. McGonagall is appalled at this and tells him:

> "Moody, we *never* use Transfiguration as a punishment! [...] We give detentions, Moody! Or speak to the offender's Head of house!" (HP 4, 227)

Nevertheless, the students delight in breaking rules. Harry and his friends can only survive some of their adventures because they do not obey school rules

---

[155] Later Ron and Hermione are made prefects (HP 5, 182-183).

but replace them with their own priorities. When Hermione warns Harry that one more attempt of rule breaking might make Gryffindor lose the "House Cup", he explains to her how unimportant rules are:

> "Losing points doesn't matter any more, can't you see? D'you think [Voldemort] will leave you and your family alone if Gryffindor win the house Cup?" (HP 1, 291)

In *Chamber of Secrets* Hermione has adopted this attitude completely:

> "*I* don't want to break rules, you know. *I* think threatening Mugglebors is far worse than brewing up a difficult potion." (HP 2, 181)

Rule breaking adds to a student's reputation among his fellows. When Ron and Harry fly to Hogwarts in a bewitched car and are being punished, the Gryffindors celebrate their daredevilry with enthusiasm (HP 2, 94-95). Lupin tells Harry that his father "'James would have been highly disappointed if his son had never found any of the secret passages out of the castle'" (HP 3, 457). For Fred Weasley the inventors of the "Marauder's Map" are "'Noble men, working tirelessly to help a new generation of law-breakers, [...]'" (HP 3, 210). Breaking rules is sometimes even officially rewarded. McGonagall notes that Harry and Ron break about "'a hundred school rules into pieces along the way'" (HP 2, 352) when they go into the "Chamber of Secrets", but in the end they are successful and save Hogwarts from the Basilisk. Instead of suspending them from school, Dumbledore rewards them:

> "You will both receive Special Awards for Services to the School and [...] I think two hundred points apiece for Gryffindor." (HP 2, 355)

Sticking to rules may lead to becoming a victim of evil forces. The fake Moody proclaims that "'Decent people are so easy to manipulate'" (HP 4, 733). Conformity is to be viewed critically; independent judgement leads to success. This is why the legal system of Hogwarts is rather ambivalent. Just as in Magical World in general (see V.1.H, 305), justice is not always granted. Partiality is not only especially obvious in "Quidditch" (HP 1, 205; HP 3, 267), but also in the individual behaviour of the teachers. Above all, Snape favours his own students: "Snape was the head of Slytherin house, and generally favoured his own students before all others" (HP 3, 135).

The house point system seems rather arbitrary, as well. Each house is awarded points for good marks or for the individual behaviour of its students. Likewise, points are taken off for rule breaking or bad behaviour. Nevertheless, each teacher seems to be free to give or take points as he likes. Points can also be rewarded by the prefects. Amongst others, we see points being given or taken in these situations:

- McGonagall takes off five points from Gryffindor, because Hermione wanted to fight the troll on her own (HP 1, 194)
- For saving Hermione from the troll, Harry and Ron are rewarded five points each (HP 1, 194)
- Snape takes one point from Harry because he did not help Neville with his potions (HP 1, 153)
- Hermione helps Neville in "Potions" – Snape takes five points off for that (HP 3, 141
- Snape takes one point from Gryffindor, because Harry was cheeky (HP 1, 152)
- Snape tells Hermione: "'Five more points from Gryffindor for being an insufferable know-it-all.'" (HP 3, 187)
- McGonagall takes twenty points from Malfoy, because she catches him outside Slytherin house at night (HP 1, 260)
- McGonagall takes fifty points from Neville, Harry and Hermione each, because she supposes them to hold conspirative meetings at night (HP 1, 264)
- Dumbledore rewards Harry sixty, Neville ten and Ron and Hermione fifty points each for saving the "Philosopher's Stone" (HP 1, 328-329)
- Percy as prefect takes five points from Gryffindor, because Ron does not care enough for Ginny (which has absolutely nothing to do with his education and is a private matter between the two brothers) (HP 2, 172)

This short list (there are many more examples to be found in the text) shows that there is no objective system for taking or rewarding points. In particular, Snape, Percy and later on Umbridge's "Inquisitorial Squad" (HP 5, 688) use house points in their private conflicts. The system is rather arbitrary and open to abuse.

But what do Hogwarts students learn? Magic is a proper science in the world of *Harry Potter* and needs to be studied. Only after seven years of systematic studies is the young witch or wizard fully qualified. Hogwarts education has two levels. Until they are fifteen, wizards study for their "OWLs", the "Ordinary Wizarding Levels" (HP 4, 64). After seven years in Hogwarts, they finally pass the "NEWTs" ("Nastily Exhausting Wizarding Tests", HP 1, 339). This corresponds with the English education system with its exams formerly known as "O-Levels" ("Ordinary Levels") and "A-Levels" ("Advanced Levels"). These exams consist of written as well as practical tests (HP 3, 342-344; HP 5, 781-792). We do not know if Hogwarts education is free or if parents have to pay tuition fees.

Lessons are held in the morning and in the afternoon, interrupted by lunch break. Meals are taken in the "Great Hall". The beginning of lessons is announced by a "booming bell" (HP 4, 215). Lessons consist of ex cathedra teaching and free experimentation, as for example in "Potions" and "Transfiguration". We learn about the following subjects:

- "Arithmancy" (HP 2, 272)
- "Astrology" (HP 1, 146-147)
- "Care of Magical Creatures" (HP 2, 272)
- "Charms" (HP 1, 146-147)
- "Defence Against the Dark Arts" (HP 1, 146-147)
- "Divination" (HP 3, 115)
- "Flying" (HP Bd. 1, 157)
- "Herbology" (HP 1, 146-147)
- "History of Magic" (HP 1, 146-147)
- "Muggle Studies" ("a soft option") (HP 2, 272)
- "Potions" (HP 4, 257)
- "Study of Ancient Runes" (HP 2, 272)
- "Transfiguration" (HP 1, 146-147)

Classical subjects like mathematics, writing, reading or even foreign languages, geography or politics are not mentioned at all. Lessons only deal with magic. Subject matter includes: "research antidotes" (HP 4, 257) in "Potions", "Summoning Charms" (HP 4, 257) in "Charms", the "Goblin Rebellions of the eighteenth century" (HP 4, 257) in "History of Magic", "hex-deflection" (HP 4, 594) in "Defence Against the Dark Arts" and the transformation of animals or objects[156] in "Transfiguration". During the summer break the students have to write essays at home with titles like "Witch-Burning in the Fourteenth Century Was Completely Pointless – discuss" (HP 3, 7) or "Explain why Muggles Need Electricity" (HP 3, 271).

Hogwarts, the small political "sub-system" of Magical World, is just as inadequate as the official system. It is arbitrary; justice is not always granted. Existing rules can be applied – or not. Rule breakers are considered heroes by the students. Children do not learn anything about other countries, races or social systems – knowledge that might be uselful in a globalised fight against Voldemort. The ability to question the given situation is not part of the official teaching; critical thinking is not encouraged by the curriculum. Nevertheless,

---

[156] Among other things we read about "turning a beetle into a button" (HP 2, 105); "the pair of white rabbits he was supposed to be turning into slippers" (HP 2, 306); "to turn a hedgehog into a satisfactory pincushion. I might remind you that your pincushion, Thomas, still curls up in fright if anyone aproaches it with a pin." (HP 4, 257); "the guinea-fowl they had been changing into guinea-pigs" (HP 4, 421).

Hogwarts is – unlike the rest of Magical World – a place of equality among students. Every child can study and develop according to his or her abilities and likings. So, in conclusion, Hogwarts is a good place to be for all boys and girls.

V.4 It's a Man's World? – Women Characters

The topic of female characters has been discussed *in extenso*.[157] Most critics (such as Susanne Beyer for example) complain of the superficiality with which Rowling describes women.[158] The majority of girls are represented as "anti-intellectual and most keenly interested in the low-status magic of Divination Class".[159] Even the world of magical creatures and ghosts is very stereotypical. Men are usually more adventurous than women, girls either cry or study.[160] The opposite opinion is represented by Mimi R. Gladstein. She believes women are equal in magical world[161] and female teachers and students are decisive members of the Hogwarts community.[162]

In fact, in Hogwarts there is a clear separation of the sexes – the dormitories are accordingly protected:

> [Ron] was on the sixth stair when there was a loud, wailing, klaxon-like sound and the steps melted together to make a long, smooth stone slide like a helter-skelter. [...] "Er – I don't think we're allowed in the girls' dormitories," said Harry [...]. "Hermione's allowed in our dormitory, how come we're not allowed – ?" "Well it's an old-fashioned rule," said Hermione, [...], "but it says in *Hogwarts: A History*, that the founders thought boys were less trustworthy than girls." (HP 5, 391)

Girls and boys differ in character and behaviour; women are – according to the Hogwarts founders – more reliable than men. With the novels' multitude of apparently equal female characters these stereotypes are surprising. But we must acknowledge that women in the world of *Harry Potter* play a rather subordinate role. There are fewer women than men among the characters to begin with. Secondly, women are very often tidy, modest and emotional and they tend to conform to rules. Most of them are anti-racist and compassionate (see IV.2.B,

---

[157] See Billone 2004, 197.
[158] See Susanne Beyer, Nikolaus von Festenberg, "Ein Volk von Zauberlehrlingen," *SPIEGEL*, 20 Nov 2000. <http://www.spiegel.de/spiegel/0,1518,104665,00.html> 3 Jan 2008.
[159] See Heilman, "Blue Wizards and Pink Witches", 2003, 223.
[160] See Deborah L. Thompson, "Deconstructing Harry: Casting a Critical Eye on the Witches and Wizards of Hogwarts," *Beauty, Brains, and Brawn: The Construction of Gender in Children's Literature*, ed. Susan Lehr, Portsmouth: Heinemann, 2001, 42-50, here 43.
[161] See Gladstein 2004, 49.
[162] See Gladstein 2004. 56-58.

154). However, dubious characters are often women – we see this even with minor characters like Trelawney, Rita Skeeter, Petunia or Mrs. Figg.[163] Only a few female characters influence the main plot:[164] Hermione, the female members of the Weasley clan (Ginny, Molly) and the teachers McGonagall, Trelawney and Umbridge. Lily Potter and Petunia Dursley also belong in this category. Most of them do not even have much power – they tend to be inferior to men. McGonagall is influential, but has to conform to Dumbledore's decisions. Above all else, she is competent, rational and upright. Within the Hogwarts staff she has a rather distinguished position, because she is Head of Gryffindor House. She corresponds with Blyton's "headmistress" type (see VII.2.B, 445). Despite being highly qualified she seems to be narrow-minded where Dumbledore tends to be generous. She does not possess the same grandeur as the headmaster[165] nor is she an attractive woman[166] (see IV.4.E, 231). Powerful women usually cease to appear female. McGonagall, Bellatrix Lestrange and Dolores Umbridge do not have much feminity left. Bellatrix Lestrange is as emotional and irrational as any of the other female characters, but she has become a cruel fanatic:

> She glared up at him through heavily lidded eyes, an arrogant, disdainful smile playing around her thin mouth. [...] she retained vestiges of great good looks, but something – perhaps Azkaban – had taken most of her beauty. (HP 5, 600)

In her devotedness to Voldemort we find traces of sexual dependence as the following scene shows:

> [...] Bellatrix leaned towards Voldemort, for mere words could not demonstrate her longing for closeness. [...] Her face flooded with colour; her eyes welled with tears of delight. (HP 7, 15-16)

When Harry comes face-to-face with her he sees "her mad eyes staring through the slits in her hood" (HP 5, 861). Further on we read: "Azkaban had hollowed Bellatrix Lestrange's face, making it gaunt and skull-like, but it was alive with a feverish fanatical glow" (HP 5, 861). She appears corpse-like; there is nothing womanly about her. Dolores Umbridge is different. She appears as a fake-woman, a make-believe female and tries to appear friendly, emotional and sweet. In fact, she is cruel, sadistic and heartless (see IV.5.G). In spite of the authority of her office she has no personal charisma. Hermione, on the other

---

[163] See Dresang 2004, 223.
[164] See Billone 2004, 179.
[165] See Dresang 2004, 226; Mendlesohn 2004, 175.
[166] See Heilman, "Blue Wizards and Pink Witches", 2003, 228.

hand, is highly controversial. Although she is top of class and intellectually superior to any of her fellow-students, she is no opinion leader.[167] Usually it is Harry's "stupid bravery" and his breaking of the rules that save the day.[168] Hermione is the well-educated daughter of a middle-class family, highly talented but not very adventurous[169] and – above everything else – rather unathletic.[170] Molly Weasley can be quite stern in the education of her children, but outside her family she has no power whatsoever. Without contradiction she has to accept that all of her family get involved in the highly dangerous activities of the "Order of the Phoenix" and is tormented by visions of death (HP 5, 198-200). Fleur Delacour is chosen as school champion, but in the tournament she comes out last.[171] In *Deathly Hallows* we see her as a rather competent and brave member of the resistance, but even then she corresponds to the traditional role pattern, nursing the injured and cooking for everyone (HP 7, "Shell Cottage", 414).

The inferiority of women is visible even with the Hogwarts founders: The decisive, basic conflict is between the two men – Slytherin and Gryffindor. Rowena Ravenclaw is – despite her intellectual brilliance – quite irrelevant, and Helga Hufflepuff, whose premises are adjacent to the kitchen (see 126), embodies the motherly type of woman. Neither of the two witches has any influence in the conflict between the two men. Their activities are of no relevance for the school's development.

V.4.A. Types of Women

The *Harry Potter* novels indulge in some of the most common stereotypes about women. Andrew Blake says: "The books are suffused with gender differences which are taken for granted as part of the narrative strategy [...]."[172] Basically, there are three types of women in *Harry Potter*:

- the omniscient woman
- the hysterical, over-emotional girl
- the "good friend" girl

Hermione and McGonagall represent the first type (see IV.3.M, 197).[173] The over-emotional type is embodied by Molly Weasley, Sibyll Trelawney, Cho

---

[167] See Gladstein 2004, 50-51.
[168] See Gladstein 2004, 50-51.
[169] See Adams 2003.
[170] See Thompson 2001, 45.
[171] See Heilman, "Blue Wizards and Pink Witches", 2003, 224.
[172] See Blake 2002, 39.
[173] Her being an intellectual she is not interested in "Quidditch". Intellectual and physical ability are not combined in *Harry Potter*. "'Hermione,' said Harry, shaking his head,

Chang (and her friends) and Fleur Delacour. Ginny Weasley and Nymphadora Tonks correspond with the last type, the "good friend" girl.

It is in *Deathly Hallows* that Hermione proves to be particularly brave and ingenious – the boys frequently tell her so:

> Harry: "[...] you were incredible. I'd be dead if you hadn't been there to help me." (HP 7, 288)
> "Hermione, you're a genius, a total genius, I can't believe we got out of that!"[...] "You're a genius," Ron repeated, looking awed. "Yeah, you are, Hermione," agreed Harry fervently, "I don't know what we'd do without you." (HP 7, 344)
> "You were amazing [...] coming up with that story when she was hurting you like that" (HP 7, 392)

Nevertheless, this very open and direct way of underlining Hermione's superiority in the last novel of the series appears rather flat to me. It seems like Rowling wants to state once and for all that she does not cling to role clichés.

Female characters are frequently hysterical, giggling and do not get the earnestness of the situation – at least in the opinion of the boys. Even rational Hermione is often said to be afraid, weeping or sobbing.[174] "Hermione had sunk to the floor in fright; Ron pulled out his own wand [...]"(HP 1, 192) – this is the man-as-protector stereotype. When speaking about Moody's death she "squeals" and "bursts into tears" (HP 7, 82) – although everyone is sad and mourns their friend, she is the only one to express her feelings in such a dramatic way. When telling Harry about the way she manipulated her parents' memories to protect them from Voldemort's revenge her "eyes are swiming with tears again" (HP 7, 84). At the same time, Hermione admits that her book-learning is inferior to Harry's courage and bravery.

> "Harry – you're a great wizard, you know? [...] Books! And cleverness! There are more important things – friendship and bravery and – oh Harry – be *careful*!" (HP 1, 308)

Hermione's emotionality is set in clear opposition to Harry's rationality when "her panic seem[s] to clear Harry's head" (HP 7, 139). Deliberately,she takes up a subordinate position, prepares tea for him and takes his orders: "'You get back in the warm.' She hesitated, but recognised the dismissal." (HP 7, 295) Despite her heroic deeds and her wisdom, she also knows her place in the hierarchy of things.

'you're good on feelings and stuff, but you just don't understand about Quidditch.'" (HP 5, 633).

[174] See Dresang 2004, 237; Heilman, "Blue Wizards and Pink Witches", 2003, 226-227.

Women tend to either be seduced or seduce others. The magical "Veela" are the best example of this. In truth they are ugly birds of prey but can transform into beautiful women in whose presence men go mad (HP 4, 126 and 141-142) It is no coincidence, either, that it is a girl which is abducted in *Chamber of Secrets*. In *Deathly Hallows* we find clear references to women as mere sexual objects when Fenrir Greyback, taking a look at Hermione, his prisoner, says: "'Delicious girl ... what a treat ... I do enjoy the softness of the skin...'" (HP 7, 362) This menacing male dominance alludes to an intended rape and conforms to particular male sexual desires.

Women have their own yellow press in Magical World. Like "Woman's Weekly" there is "Witch Weekly". This is a periodical combining Rita Skeeter's gossip columns and household-related topics as the cover demonstrates: "The moving picture on the front showed a curly-haired witch who was smiling toothily and pointing at a large sponge cake with her wand" (HP 4, 556). Appropriately, the magazine annually awards the *Most-Charming-Smile Award*[175] instead of a prize for magical excellence.

Rowling even refers to the stereotypical woman's fear of mice. When Lavender Brown has to hand out mice in McGonagall's class, the teacher feels obliged to remind her "'don't be silly, girl, they won't hurt you'" (HP 5, 355). Ron tells Harry they absolutely must attend Bill and Fleur's wedding – despite the general state of crisis Magical World is in – because his mother and future sister-in-law have their own "domestic" priorities:

> "They'll kill us if we miss [the wedding]." [...] "Don't they realise how important – ?" "'Course they don't,' said Ron. "They haven't got a clue."
> (HP 7, 76)

Women are intriguing and false. Some of the girls, for example Lavender Brown or Romilda Vane, are even deceitful. This is true not only for human beings – female dragons are "a lot more vicious" than male ones (HP 7, 102). Women tend to over-dramatise emotions; Ginny Weasley simply panics when she first meets Harry. This is just what many of the girls do when "Quidditch" hero Viktor Krum comes to Hogwarts. "Several sixth-year girls were frantically searching their pockets as they walked – 'Oh, I don't believe it, I haven't got a single quill on me –' 'D'you think he'd sign my hat in lipstick?'" (HP 4, 273). It is the women that fall for Lockhart's tall tales. This is amply demonstrated when he has a book-signing at Flourish and Blotts (HP 2, 67-70):

> "We can actually meet him!" Hermione squealed. "I mean, he's written almost the whole booklist!" The crowd seemed to be made up mostly of witches around Mrs Weasley's age. A harassed-looking wizard stood at the

---

[175] Lockhart has won award about five times already (HP 2, 110).

door, saying, "Calmly, please ladies ... don't push, there ... mind the books, now ..." [...] "Oh, there you are, good," said Mrs Weasley. She sounded breathless and kept patting her hair. "We'll be able to see him in a minute ..." (HP 2, 67-68)

While the women hysterically push into the shop and even the usually rational Hermione becomes excited, an unnerved male shop clerk has to keep order.[176] Women are irrational and tend to cry when disappointed: "Two of the girls who had not been selected had dissolved into tears, and were sobbing with their heads on their arms" (HP 4, 296). Sybill Trelawney draws her support chiefly from among the girls:[177]

> Parvati Patil and Lavender Brown had taken to haunting Professor Trelawney's tower room at lunchtimes, and always returned with annoyingly superior looks on their faces, as though they knew things the others didn't (HP 3, 155).

But these adepts prove to be unreliable. When Trelawney is suspended from her job and centaur Firenze takes over, the girls immediately fall in love with him: "'A *gorgeous* centaur ...' sighed Parvati" (HP 5, 659). Even competent women like Hermione are frequently crying, squealing or wailing.[178] We also see female emotionality on the occasion of the Yule Ball in *Goblet of Fire*:

> [...] it was amazing how many girls Hogwarts suddenly seemed to hold; [Harry] had never quite noticed that before. Girls giggling and whispering in the corridors, girls shrieking with laughter as boys passed them, girls excitedly comparing notes on what they were going to wear on Christmas night ... "Why do they have to move in packs?" Harry asked Ron [...]. (HP 4, 424)

When Harry finally brings himself to asking Cho Chang to the ball, it proves to be difficult to meet her on her own: "[Cho] seemed to go [to the bathroom] with an escort of four or five girls" (HP 4, 433). Brushed off, Harry is fuming: "Giggling should be made illegal, Harry thought furiously, as all the girls around Cho started doing it" (HP 4, 433). Later, when he is regarded as "The Chosen One" and has become a popular hero, he is suddenly highly attractive for the girls. A couple of them start following him everywhere and some of them try to make him fall in love with them trying to get his attention and using

---

[176] In this context we read rather ironical comments by men about women. Fred Weasley, while reading his booklist for the upcoming school year says "'You've been told to get all Lockhart's books, too! [...] The new Defence Against the Dark Arts teacher must be a fan – bet it's a witch.'" (HP 2, 52).

[177] Also HP 3, 115, 323.

[178] See Dresang 2004, 223.

love potions. On the "Hogwarts Express" girls are discussing who of them is going to address him:

> [...] a group of fourth-year girls was whispering and giggling together on the other side of the glass. "You ask him!" "No, you!", "I'll do it!" (HP 6, 132)

At Christmas, many of them try to stage a meeting with Harry underneath the mistleoe:

> Large groups of girls tended to converge underneath the mistletoe bunches every time Harry went past, which caused blockages in the corridors; [...]. (HP 6, 284)

Many girls apply for the Gryffindor "Quidditch" team when Harry becomes captain. During the try-outs it becomes clear that it is not the sport they are after:

> The second group comprised ten of the silliest girls Harry had ever encountered, who, when he blew his whistle, merely fell about giggling and clutching each other. (HP 6, 211)

This kind of behaviour is exemplified by Romilda Vane,[179] who follows Harry at every turn and Lavender Brown,[180] Ron's first girlfriend. Romilda sends Harry a box of chocolates poisoned with love potion hoping to make him fall in love with her (HP 6, 367-370). When this plan fails and Harry goes out with Ginny Weasley instead, she continues to be interested in Harry – this time in his body:

> "[...] Romilda Vane [asks] me if it's true you've got a Hippogriff tattooed across your chest." [...] "What did you tell her?" "I told her it's a Hungarian Horntail," said Ginny [...]. "Much more macho." (HP 6, 500)

Girls just love to gossip. When Hermione pretends to be in love with McLaggen she becomes the object of profound analysis:

> At once Lavender and Parvati put their heads together to discuss this new development, with everything they had ever heard about McLaggen, and all they had ever guessed about Hermione. (HP 6, 294)

Lavender Brown chums up with Ron and finally is successful – Hermione, with all her rationality is left out in the cold:

---

[179] Her family name is reminiscent of "vain" and Latin *vanitas* and, thus, hints at her meaninglessness.
[180] Lavender is an ingredient of perfume; Brown is one of the most common English names.

Hermione's remonstration was drowned by a loud giggle; Lavender Brown
had apparently found Ron's remark highly amusing. (HP 6, 164)

Ron's relation with Lavender is only meant to demonstrate his virility, whereas
she enjoys being permitted into the circle of Harry's friends. It is not the exchange of ideas or sharing common interests, it is all about showing off their
awakening sexuality:

> Firstly, Harry had to put up with the frequent presence of Lavender Brown,
> who seemed to regard any moment that she was not kissing Ron as a mo-
> ment wasted; [...]. (HP 6, 284)

Lavender plagues Ron, interferes in his friendship with Harry and interrupts
their meetings ("But at that moment there was a loud squeal of 'Won-Won!' and
Lavender Brown came hurtling out of nowhere and flung herself into Ron's
arms.", HP 6, 329).

Yet another example of pubescent female behaviour and the basic misunderstanding between the sexes is Harry's relation with Cho Chang. She is an excellent "Quidditch" player,[181] "extremely pretty" [182] (HP 3, 281) and one year
Harry's senior. First she dates Cedric Diggory, but after his death she becomes
approachable for Harry. Like any schoolgirl of her age, she becomes nervous
when Harry is close[183] and tries to provoke situations where the two are on their
own.[184] In *Order of the Phoenix* Harry experiences his first kiss – ending in Cho
beginning to cry (HP 5, 501-503). Harry is helpless. Hermione must explain the
situation to him (HP 5, 505-506). The following date on Valentine's Day takes a
disastrous turn: Cho proposes Madam Puddifoot's Café. But caught between
fulfilling her expectations, Cho's interest in Cedric's death and her being jealous
of Hermione, Harry feels very uncomfortable. Finally, they quarrel (HP 5,
616-620). The reader experiences the scene from Harry's point of view:

> He simply did not understand what had happened; half an hour ago they had
> been getting along fine. "Women!" he muttered angrily, sloshing down the

---

[181] "'She's a fourth-year, and she's pretty good [at Quidditch].'" (HP 3, 276); "undoubtedly
a very good flier" (HP 3, 282).

[182] "a very pretty girl" (HP 4, 96); "she was very pretty" (HP 4, 425); "A very pretty girl
with long, shiny black hair was standing in the doorway smiling at him: Cho Chang, the
Seeker on the Ravenclaw Quidditch team." (HP 5, 210).

[183] "'Oh no,' said Cho rather wildly as he approached. 'Expelliarmious! I mean, Expellimellius! I – oh, sorry, Marietta!'" (HP 5, 435).

[184] "Cho made rather a business of fastening the catch on her bag before leaving, her long
dark curtain of hair swinging forwards to hide her face, but her friend stood beside her,
arms folded, clicking her tongue, so that Cho had little choice but to leave with her."
(HP 5, 384-585)

rain-washed street with his hands in his pockets. "What did she want to talk about Cedric for, anyway? Why does she always want to drag up a subject that makes her act like a human hosepipe?" (HP 5, 620)

When Cho's best friend Marietta betrays "Dumbledore's Army" to Umbridge, Harry and Cho break up.[185]

Ginny Weasley embodies the type of "good friend" girl, participating in the boys' games and apparently not interested in what we must consider "typically female".[186] She is easy-going, fun to be with, quick-witted and her manner is contrasted favourably with her friends' childish behaviour. She even joins in the boys' making fun of them when she tells Romilda that Harry has a dragon tattooed on his chest (HP 6, 500). Ginny is a very good "Quidditch" player (here she exceeds Hermione who is not interested in any sport: HP 6, 503), because even as a child she ignored her brothers' ban on using their brooms:

> "She's been breaking into your broom shed in the garden since the age of six and taking each of your brooms out in turn when you weren't looking, [...]." (HP 5, 632)

When Ron, in a fit of fraternal machismo, feels obliged to remind her of her good reputation, Ginny angrily defends herself:

> "It is none of your business who I go out with or what I do with them, Ron –"
> "Yeah, it is!" said Ron, just as angrily. "D'you think I want people saying my sister's a –"
> "A what?" shoutet Ginny, drawing her wand. "A *what* exactly?"
> (HP 6, 268-269)

Finally, it is Ginny who becomes Harry's girlfriend and later his wife. Her behaviour is "normal" compared to the other girls who are either hysterical (Cho, Romilda) or over-intelligent (Hermione). But Rowling feels the necessity to let Harry declare that

> "[Ginny] was not tearful; that was one of the many wonderful things about Ginny, she was rarely weepy. He had sometimes thought that having six brothers must have toughened her up." (HP 7, 199)

There is one other woman whose behaviour is rewarded by the plot. Nymphadora Tonks, who is another "good friend" girl, ends up marrying Remus

---

[185] "'She's a lovely person, really [...]. She just made a mis-take [sic]-'" (HP 5, 701).
[186] See Heilman, "Blue Wizards and Pink Witches", 2003, 230.

Lupin (HP 6, 582) and having a baby, Ted, with him (HP 7, 415). Bravely, both fight in the last battle of Hogwarts and die (HP 7, 531).

Most of the female characters care about their looks. "Real" men (aside from the fraud Gilderoy Lockhart: see IV.4.B, 222), on the contrary, do not. Even Hermione has dressed up for the Yule Ball – and is observed to be a girl for the first time. With the help of magical plastic surgery she has managed to shrink her rather big front teeth.[187] Farah Mendlesohn is right in criticising Rowling for this short episode. Instead of propagating contentment with one's looks, the author seems to promote the idea of artificially changing one's appearance to conform to norms pre-set by the fashion industry.[188] Elizabeth E. Heilman makes this a general comment on girls in *Harry Potter*:

> The message to girls is: get a makeover. You are not okay. It is disturbing that the females that are most physically beautiful - the Veelas - are not even human. They are portrayed as male fantasy sex objects able to seduce, beguile, and confuse males.[189]

The second character that pays too much attention to her looks is Fleur Delacour.[190] She is blond, blue-eyed and of magical beauty:[191] "A long sheet of silvery blonde hair fell almost to her waist. She had large, deep blue eyes, and very white, even teeth." (HP 4, 277). Even great exertions cannot touch or change her impeccable looks (HP 4, 352). In Hogwarts she focuses on not becoming fat and constantly complains about the food: "'It is too 'eavy, all zis 'Ogwarts food,' [...]" (HP 4, 441). She fears: "'I will not fit into my dress robes!'" (HP 4, 441) Appearances are highly important for her:

> "... Bill and I 'ave almost decided on only two bridesmaids, Ginny and Gabrielle will look very sweet togezzer. I am theenking of dressing zem in pale gold – pink would of course be 'orrible with Ginny's air –" (HP 6, 126)

Arrogant and aloof like all the students from Beauxbatons[192] she only becomes likeable when Harry saves her sister Gabrielle (HP 4, 598). When her boyfriend Bill is scarred for life by the werewolf Greyback, Fleur proves to have more depth than the reader expected. Instead of giving up her plans of marriage Fleur shows emotional maturity:

---

187 See Heilman, "Blue Wizards and Pink Witches", 2003, 229.
188 See Mendlesohn 2004, 175.
189 See Heilman, "Blue Wizards and Pink Witches", 2003, 229.
190 Her name alludes to nobility: *fleur* is the "flower" and *de la cour* means "belonging to the court".
191 Her grandmother was a "Veela" (HP 4, 338).
192 Hermione says of her: "'She really thinks a lot of herself, that one, doesn't she?'" (HP 4, 441).

340

"It would take more zan a werewolf to stop Bill loving me! [...] What do I care how 'e looks? I am good-looking enough for both of us, I theenk! All these scars show is zat my husband is brave!" (HP 6, 581)

Nymphadora Tonks[193] is just as vain. Being a "Metamorphmagus" (HP 5, 63) she can change her looks into whatever form she likes. When we first meet her in *Order of the Phoenix* her hair is pink. Tonks represents a young, fashion-oriented generation of witches, but at the same time she appeals to male Lolita-fantasies:

> [She] had a pale heart-shaped face, twinkling eyes, and short spiky hair that was a violent shade of violet.(HP 5, 58).
> [...] her bright bubble-gum-pink hair gleaming in the sunlight filtering through the dirty glass of the station ceiling, wearing heavily patched jeans and a bright purple T-shirt bearing the legend The Weird Sisters. (HP 5, 952).

Her first name Nymphadora alludes to a psychological disorder: nymphomaniacs are addicted to sex. Even in highly dangerous situations[194] Tonks finds the time to consider her looks:

> Tonks paused at [Harry's] open wardrobe to look critically at her reflection in the mirror on the inside of the door. "You know, I don't think violet's really my colour," she said pensively, tugging at a lock of spiky hair. "D'you think it makes me look a bit peaky?" (HP 5, 62-63)

That looks matter for a woman's reputation in Magical World is also to be seen in the fate of Moaning Myrtle, the female ghost haunting the toilets. Because of her huge glasses she is teased by her fellow-students.[195] Cho Chang, on the other hand, corresponds with the cliché of the attractive, erotically submissive Asian woman.[196] Women frequently appear in groups. "Angelina, Alicia and Katie" are as much a clique as "Parvati Patil, Padma Patil and Lavender Brown". This reinforces the impression that women are not represented as individuals but as types of their sex.[197]

Just as stereotypical is the general representation of the family life of the Dursleys and the Weasleys. Both families have a stay-at-home mother who cares

---

[193] Her name is derived from the nymphs of Greek mythology. At the same time her name refers to a disorder of the female sexuality.
[194] When Harry is escorted to Hogwarts by the "Advance Guard" everyone agrees that they are in mortal peril (HP 5, 66-68).
[195] See Heilman, "Blue Wizards and Pink Witches", 2003, 229.
[196] See Heilman, "Blue Wizards and Pink Witches", 2003, 230
[197] See Heilman, "Blue Wizards and Pink Witches", 2003, 228.

for the children while the father provides the family's income.[198] Although Mrs Weasley has been to Hogwarts, she only uses her magical skills for doing her everyday housework,[199] Hermione – like a good housewife and mother – packs the boys' bags before departing in *Deathly Hallows* ("'I'm just waiting for the rest of your pants to come out of the wash, Ron –'": HP 7, 98) and Fleur, the former Triwizard competitor, is using magic to wash up and to cook (HP 7, 412-414). When Molly Weasley finally kills Bellatrix Lestrange, it is motherly love defeating the strong, independent and evil woman as Molly's battle cry shows: "'You – will – never – touch – our – children – again!'" (HP 7, 589). So the novels promote traditional role models without presenting exceptions. There are no single-mothers, divorced parents or homosexuals; we do not find adopted children or broken families.[200]

V.4.B. Harry's Point of View

As Harry is the focus of the author's narration (see II.2.A, 34), it is important to have a look at how he perceives the women, i.e. girls of his class. What does he think about them? We do find various comments from his point of view.

> [...] Harry was left to ponder in silence the depths to which girls would sink to get revenge. (HP 6, 294)
> That's what they should teach us here, [Harry] thought, [...] how girls' brains work ... it'd be more useful than Divination, anyway ... (HP 5, 508)

There are quite a few passages showing the lack of understanding between boys and girls:

> Girls were very strange sometimes. (HP 6, 293)
> "Quidditch!" said Hermione angrily. "Is that all boys care about? Cormac hasn't asked me one single question about myself, no, I've just been treated to A Hundred Great Saves Made by Cormac McLaggen non-stop, ever since – oh no, here he comes!" (HP 6, 298)
> "You should write a book," Ron told Hermione as he cut up his potatoes, "translating mad things girls do so boys can understand them." (HP 5, 631)

Often, these blanket judgements remain unanswered, the girls in question hardly ever reply as in the following scene:

---

[198] See Heilman, "Blue Wizards and Pink Witches", 2003, 228; John Kornfeld, Laurie Prothro, "Comedy, Conflict, and Community: Home and Family in *Harry Potter*," *Harry Potter's World: Multidisciplinary Critical Perspectives,* ed. Elizabeth E. Heilman, New York, London: RoutledgeFalmer, 2003 187-202, here 189-190.

[199] See Mendlesohn 2004, 170.

[200] See Turner-Vorbeck 2003, 20.

"[Tonks] lost her nerve. Women," [Ron] said wisely to Harry. "They're easily upset." "And yet," said Hermione, coming out of her reverie, "I doubt
you'd find a *woman* who sulked for half an hour because Madam Rosmerta
didn't laugh at their joke [...]." (HP 6, 438)

And when Harry is just about to deny women magical competence, Hermione
decidedly contradicts him:

"Listen, Hermione, I can tell it's not a girl. I can just tell." "The truth is that
you don't think a girl would have been clever enough," said Hermione
angrily. (HP 6, 503)

To Harry, women tend to be incompetent and over-emotional. His point of view
corresponds with common stereotypes about women.

V.4.C. Fine Young Criminals –
Male Adolescents in "Harry Potter"[201]

Looking at the boys and men in Harry's world, we basically find – apart from
the "good" and the "bad" characters – two different types alongside another pattern based on the degree of masculinity which the different males represent:
"succesful, strong" and "failed, weak" men. So what marks a male character as
strong? The strong male characters show charisma, leadership qualities and are
respected or even feared in their community. Most of them (like Harry, his father or the Weasleys) are good at sports, i.e. "Quidditch". They are prone to getting into trouble. Harry laments in *Prisoner of Azkaban*: "I don't go looking for
trouble – trouble usually finds me." (HP 2 85). All of these men are mediocre
students. The weak characters, on the contrary, represent opposite values. They
are ridiculous, objects of derision and mere followers of others. They do not act
on their own account, but are instructed and led by the strong men, the leaders of
their communities. They somehow seem disabled and deformed, either socially
or in their magical, physical skills.

So, combining the good-bad pattern (see IV.2.B, 154) with the strong-
weak oppostion, we can make out four types of masculinity. Heroic masculinity means that the corresponding characters are both strong and morally good.
Among them we find Harry Potter, Ron Weasley, Sirius Black, James Potter,
Rubeus Hagrid, Alastor Moody, Cedric Diggory, Viktor Krum, Arthur Weasley,
Albus Dumbledore and Remus Lupin. In all of them we find the characteristics
of good characters as well as the features which mark out strong males. Harry,

---

[201] The following chapter was presented at the 28th International Association for the Fantastic in the Arts (IAFA) conference in Fort Lauderdale, Florida on March 19th, 2006.

for example, is bound to get into trouble. He is headstrong, stubborn, a good sportsman, but not an ambitious student. Success on the "Quidditch" pitch means much more to him than excelling in his final exams. The same is true for

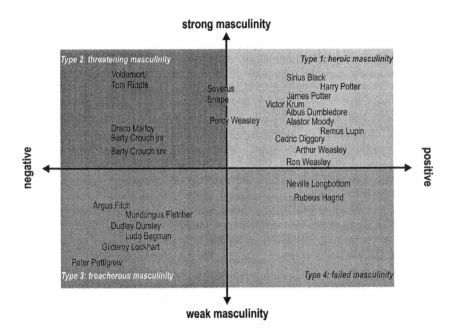

Figure 14: Types of Masculinity in Harry *Potter*

his father James, Ron Weasley or Sirius Black. None of them is top of his class. Hagrid has not even finished his Hogwarts education and was – unjustly – expelled. Viktor Krum represents the sports idol par excellence: he is one of the best players at the "Quidditch" World Cup. These men are leaders; people follow them easily. Harry himself becomes the leader of his peer group in his first year at Hogwarts, when he leads the others on into the school's dungeons, where the Philosophers' Stone is hidden. While the others hesitate to go on, he automatically tells them where to go and what to do (HP 1, 296). Dumbledore is the spiritual leader of Hogwarts and a father figure for the children. Moody is the epitome of a war veteran, hardened by his experiences. And James Potter, Harry's father, used to show off and was admired by most of his fellow students.

Most of these men are notorious troublemakers, as McGonagall points out when she says of Sirius and James: "'I don't think we've ever had such a pair of troublemakers – [...]."' (HP 3, 221). Harry, Ron and Hagrid try to outdo each other in breaking or at least bending rules. Astonishingly, they are hardly ever punished for it, and in actual fact they are usually rewarded for their slightly illegal actions which lead to their success or even survival.

Arthur Weasley and Remus Lupin are somewhat outsiders in this group: in contrast to the other heroic males, they are not held in high esteem by others, but lead a life at the brink of society. Weasley is laughed at because he is interested in "Muggles", Lupin is marginalised because of his "werewolf illness" (something we might consider a symbol of stigmatisation, either because of AIDS, because someone is disabled or deformed in physical appearance). They belong in this group nevertheless, because they are highly respected among the "insiders" – the group supporting Harry and "the good cause", i.e. the "Order of the Phoenix". It is their judgement that counts and not the opinion of the official magical world. They are the ones to set moral standards and are determined to fight bravely for their mission.

The characters grouped in the category of threatening masculinity are Harry's adversaries. They are: Voldemort (Tom Riddle), Percy Weasley, Draco Malfoy, Severus Snape and Barty Crouch snr. These men are – above anything else – characterised by their ambitions, by their belief that they are better than all others: Voldemort / Tom Riddle as the last surviving heir of Slytherin believes in his own racial superiority, Percy Weasley thinks he knows best what is right or wrong, and Barty Crouch's ambition to become Minister for Magic leads him to persecute his own family. Draco Malfoy adopts his family's views of racial purity and Severus Snape – although suffering from a feeling of his own irrelevancy and mediocricy – takes pride in being an expert on potions and dark arts.

Their ambition makes them ignore their fellow beings and their needs. These men feel that it is up to them to set the standards. Like their heroic counterparts they are leaders and believe in their mission. All of them have a strong notion of law and order – either as followers or leaders: Voldemort demands unlimited respect and devotion of his "Death Eaters", Barty Crouch – believing in his own strong interpretation of right and wrong – cruelly applies the toughest laws on his own son. On the side of those who merely follow there is a good example in Percy, who easily adopts the moral standards of the official magical world without questioning their use. Draco Malfoy follows the ways of his parents and only in the end of *Half-Blood Prince* realises that this might have led him into a trap. Lessons with Severus Snape are characterised by their non-democratic, disciplinarian approach, where students are not allowed to speak out. All of these men are more or less fanatics and believe in what they are doing. They are often sadistic and delight in torturing others. Voldemort especially enjoys the sufferings of his victims like Peter Pettigrew (who feels the pain of his cut-off hand) or Harry Potter (who is afraid when he has to confront Voldemort). But even Severus Snape or Draco Malfoy seem to like the way they frighten the weak – be it students in class or be it weaker peers. Treacherous masculinity unites Dudley Dursley, Peter Pettigrew, Mundungus Fletcher, Ludo Bagman, Gilderoy Lockhart and Argus Filch. All of them are weak and command less respect within their communities than the strong characters. Lockhart, being a bestselling author and very popular with his mostly female readers, seems to be an exception. But on a closer look we see that his strength is false. His reputation is built on treachery and lies. In fact, Lockhart is a weak opportunist. Being asked to go down into the "Chamber of Secrets" to rescue Ginny, he tries to flee. Ludo Bagman is popular as a "Quidditch" champion – but in reality he turns out to be a gambler possessed of loose morals. Pettigrew is believed to be a hero – but in fact he has betrayed the Potters to Voldemort and, thus, is their true murderer. Finally, Argus Filch is a "Squib" – a magician who is unable to perform magic – and thus an outcast of magical society. The men of this group are all more or less cowards; they do not act openly, but choose weaker opponents or work undercover. Dudley prefers torturing younger children, Pettigrew chooses to live as a rat in order not to have to face his enemies and Mundungus Fletcher is a smuggler and criminal. These men belong neither to the intellectual nor the physical elite of Magical World, but are in fact, very un-intellectual if not stupid like Dudley Dursley.

The last category I want to analyse is the group of the "failed males", incorporating Neville Longbottom, Colin Creevey and Horace Slughorn.[202] The expression "failed" goes back to Kern.[203] Neville is (at least throughout most of the text) neither strong, nor intelligent, nor treacherous. He is brave, but "accident-prone" (HP 2, p. 96). He is neither intellectually nor physically successful, is laughed at by most of the children and even the teachers. Neville depends heavily on others to help him out of trouble with his school work as well as in dangerous situations. He gets into trouble, not because he deliberately breaks rules, but because he is not able to cope with everyday life. His friends have a protective attitude towards him – no one takes Neville seriously, no one sees him as a role model. Not so drastic is Colin Creevey's situation. He hero-worships Harry, continously takes photos of him and tries to be near him all the time. Colin and his younger brother Dennis are weak and heavily depend on others.

To conclude, men are more likely to get into trouble than women. We hardly ever hear about Hermione, Lavender Brown or Parvati Patil conflicting with rules, teachers or representatives of the official magical world. In the vast

---

[202] Notice how this characterisation changes during the last battle of Hogwarts. All of the mentioned characters fight heroically for Harry and against Voldemort – Colin even dies, Neville plays a decisive role in killing Voldemort, because he destroys his snake, which is one of his "Horcruxes". After *Deathly Hallows* we do not find any weak and "failed" men.

[203] See Kern 2003, 234.

majority of cases it is the men that actively break rules or are at odds with the authorities.

Men have a tendency to be weak performers at school – Harry himself only excels at Defence Against the Dark Arts, but hardly anything else. Ron is not any better, and Hagrid even had to leave Hogwarts without having finished his education. Only Albus Dumbledore and Tom Riddle have been excellent students. Men also are the ones to set moral standards, either for the "good" or the "bad" side. It is obvious that the best type of masculinity in *Harry Potter* is the "heroic masculinity". Among them we find the role models for young readers. A successful man is charismatic, a leader, talented, respected or feared, good at sport, a bad student and – above all – highly likely to get into conflict with the law. What is troublesome about these role models is that the men belonging to this group are ambiguous in their moral values. They are rulebreakers (criminals), they are aggressive and cruel (even the good ones), they are passionate and sometimes irrational or sadistic. So what we find here is a representation of a prototype of the "adolescent male entitled to misbehave".[204] Men are likely to be criminals, to be cruel and to act irrationally – a point that is currently under discussion in Western societies. So *Harry Potter* could be interpreted as giving a couple of good examples for problematic young males.

V.4.D. Conclusion: A Great Variation of ... – Clichés

Harry Potter mainly presents dominant male characters to its readers. The novels would be completely different if they dealt with Harriet instead of Harry Potter.[205] Jack Zipes has called Magical World a "phallocentric world, and the test of a male's virtue is whether he will win contest after contest with his wand."[206] Women are either intellectually inferior or have less power than men. There are no women that combine power with competence. We must ask as to how far this must be regarded a basic weakness of the novels. But as already indicated, the world of *Harry Potter* is not meant to be perfect – which is also true for its attitude towards female emancipation. Women are just as emancipated in Magical World as in our real world, which is still dominated by males.[207] The stories about Harry Potter are just referring to this rather unsatisfying situation.[208] We may accuse Rowling of not giving enough progressive role models to her readers. Mimi R. Gladstein believes that women are completely equal in Harry's

---

[204] See Kornfeld, Prothro 2003, 190-191.
[205] See Terri Doughty, "Locating Harry Potter in the 'Boys' Book' Market," *The Ivory Tower and Harry Potter: Perspectives on a Literary Phenomenon*, ed. Lana A. Whited, Columbia: University of Missouri Press, 2004, 243-257, here 257.
[206] Zipes 2001, 183.
[207] See Thompson 2001, 42.
[208] See Dresang 2004, 237.

world and that Rowling turns common stereotypes of emotional women and rational men upside down.[209] Personally, I do not see any way to support her thesis. Women are described in a very conventional way, but this is also true for the men (see V.4.C, 342). Mathias Jung's idea that the novels challenge the traditional family is just as misinformed.[210] All the families we meet in *Harry Potter* perfectly correspond with traditional role models. No matter how different the stereotypes of women may be – Magical World is paternalistic[211] and Hogwarts dominated by males.[212]

Also, male characters very often appear as dominant, braver and more interesting than women. Elizabeth E. Heilman proves that there are as many male as female characters in the novels. Nevertheless, the main characters are – with some rare exceptions – men.[213] At the same time, boys are just as stereotypically described as girls.[214] While men break rules and take risks, women mostly obey the rules and more often show fear than men. There is even one scene which can be read as an incidence of sexual harassment. At the "Quidditch" world cup a group of "Death Eaters" tortures the campsite owner's family and makes them float upside down in mid-air (HP 4, 135). The woman's skirt falls down, her pants are exposed and the marauders hoot and leer. This scene clearly alludes to a rape scene, i.e. men revelling in their sexual dominance over women.[215]

V.5 *"Harry Potter"*: A Christian Perspective

Harry Potter has frequently been accused of satanism. Declamatory speeches have been given, the Pope has warned against reading the novels and some schools have banned the books from their libraries – Rowling's series has provoked a wide reaction from Christians. In November 2001 the British "Association of Teachers and Lecturers" (ATL) publicly warned against the dangers of young people being fascinated with witchcraft and wizardry.[216] German MP Benno Zierer (CSU) asked for the movies not to be released in Germany because he believed "so much occultism dangerous for six-year-olds."[217] Cardinal Joseph Ratzinger lamented the "Zersetzung des Christentums in der Seele, ehe

[209] See Gladstein 2004, 55.
[210] See Jung 2004, 31.
[211] See Blake 2002, 43.
[212] See Dresang 2004, 226.
[213] See Adams 2003; Heilman, "Blue Wizards and Pink Witches", 2003, 223.
[214] See Kern 2003, 149.
[215] See Gupta 2003, 102.
[216] See Jenny 2001.
[217] See Martin Wolf,. "Kassensturz im Zauberreich," *SPIEGEL-Jahreschronik 2001*. <http://www.spiegel.de/jahreschronik/0,1518,173852,00.html> 28 Aug 2007.

es überhaupt recht wachsen konnte."[218] In a published letter to the German Catholic *Potter*-slasher Gabriele Kuby, he declares the novels to be possessed of "subtile Verführung [...], die unmerklich und gerade dadurch tief wirke [...]".[219] However, none of them could stop Harry's victory over German nurseries.[220] The rather fierce reactions, especially on behalf of the American public, even contributed to the novels' popularity and placed the books in the media again and again.[221]

But what is it that faithful Christians cannot accept in *Harry Potter*? Basically, it is the content and setting of the text that are deemed satanic. Main representatives of Christian criticism are American Richard Abanes and German sociologist[222] Gabriele Kuby. Abanes reads the novels as an elevation of disobedience, violence, magic and revenge.[223] John Granger[224] and John Killinger, American clergymen and literary critics, declare *Potter* to be "profound, edifying Christian morality tales"[225] and "[a story] so basic to Christian belief".[226] Over and over again critics have compared *Harry Potter* to *Lord of the Rings*, whereas Christian critics always have pointed out the specific Christian message intended by J.R.R. Tolkien.[227] In contrast to Tolkien, J.K. Rowling is not an avowed Christian; her novels are not meant to convey any religious message whatsoever. Edmund Kern describes what Rowling seems to believe in: "We find faith in one's self, faith in one's friends, and faith in the power of love, but we find relatively little expression of faith in a higher being who secures and guarantees victory over evil."[228] At first glance, all the excitement about the

---

[218] "corruption of Christianity before having the chance of growing". See Ludger Lütkehaus, "Joseph Kardinal Ratzinger – Anti-Potter," *ZEIT* 48/2003 <http://www.zeit.de/2003/48/Lebenshilfe_2fEthikrat_48.> 3 Jan 2008

[219] "a subtle hidden and penetrating seduction", "Ratzinger mag Potter nicht," *SPIEGEL Online* 14 July 2005. <http://www.spiegel.de/kultur/literatur/0,1518,365173,00.html> 2 Jan 2007.

[220] There is a good overview of the German Christian *Potter* criticism to be found on the internet <http://www.markus-tomberg.de>.

[221] See Whited, "From Craze to Classic", 2004, 3-4.

[222] See Michael Langner, "Unheil aus Hogwart? Streiflichter zur Harry-Potter-Rezeption in Theologie und Kirche," *Faszination 'Harry Potter': Was steckt dahinter?*, eds. Detlev Dormeyer, Friedhelm Munzel, Münster: LIT, 2005, 17-29, here 23.

[223] See Richard Abanes, *Harry Potter and the Bible: The Menace behind the Magick*, Camp Hill, Pennsylvania: Horizon Books, 2001, 260-261.

[224] John Granger counts among the critics who have discovered *Harry Potter* to be a major source of income. Within the Christian criticism he represents the idea that *Potter* is a deeply Christian work. Granger even has his own website <http://www.hogwartsprofessor.com>.

[225] See Granger 2004, 115.

[226] See Killinger 2004, 39.

[227] See Abanes 2001, 239 and 169-170.

[228] Kern 2003, 218.

novels seems to be quite unjustified. The novels simply do not deal with any religious belief. The world of *Harry Potter* is non-religious and does not acknowledge any belief in a higher being.[229] But although the novels do not contain any theological statements, they do proclaim a certain set of values that can agree or disagree with Christian beliefs. Drexler and Wandinger call this the "implicit theology" of the texts.[230] Therefore, it is justified to analyse the series within the context of religion – bearing in mind that this book mainly deals with literary analysis instead of theology.

V.5.A. Charges of Satanism, Witchcraft and Wizardry

Most Christian critics accuse the *Potter* novels of satanism and claim that they provide information about occult practices, thus promoting superstition.[231] The problem with these allegations is obvious. Only someone believing in magic has the need to distinguish between good ("white") and bad ("black") magic. In other words, if you believe that there are real witches and wizards, then you must emphatically engage with Harry's world. If not, (like most people in the Western hemisphere) you can completely ignore the fact that the novels are set in a magical environment.

Of course we can understand Voldemort to be the devil; his career is quite similar to that of the angel Lucifer.[232] And it is justified to read the last chapters of *Goblet of Fire* in the context of satanic black celebrations.[233] But this does not include "Verhöhnung der Eucharistie" as Michael Maar suggests.[234] Salzburg-based theologian Gottfried Bachl answers correctly that satanism involves worshipping Satan – Voldemort, nevertheless, is being fought and finally defeated by the positive characters. Only the negative characters render him homage.[235] If the texts permitted a satanic interpretation, Voldemort would have to be glorified by the positive characters as well. At the same time, satanism includes orgiastic feasts – something we never hear about in *Harry Potter*.[236] Gottfried Wurst, analysing the novels in the context of theology, states that the church's criticism of the

---

[229] See Blake 2002, 96; Ernould 2003, 215; Houghton 2001, 58; Jenny 2001.
[230] See Drexler, Wandinger 2004, 25; auch Cherrett 2003, 10-11.
[231] See Abanes 2001, 23-25, 58-59, 12-14.
[232] See Jung 2004, 99; Connie Neal, *The Gospel According to Harry Potter: Spirituality in the Stories of the World's Most Famous Seeker*, Louisville, London: Westminster John Knox Press, 2002, 7.
[233] See Ernould 2003, 217; Granger 2004, 152.
[234] "mocking the Eucharist", Michael Maar, "Das Böse als junger Mann," *F.A.Z.net*. 1 Oct 2005. <http://www.F.A.Z..net/s/Rub117C535CDF414415BB243B181B8B60AE/Doc~EE7 E1EDCDFCBF4021A3488CD43F2DDD64~ATpl~Ecommon~Scontent.html> 3 Jan 2008.
[235] See Bachl 2002, 118.
[236] See Bachl 2002, 119.

series is mainly based on incorrect use of terms: esotericism (and the novels can be considered esoteric) is wrongfully equalled with occultism and satanism.[237]

Richard Abanes goes even further and regards any description of magical rites as disagreeing with Christianity. He interprets the use of anagrams like "Tom Marvolo Riddle" (= "I am Lord Voldemort", HP 2, 337), as proof of satanism.[238] This, in my opinion, is highly dubious. Along with Rowling's books we would have to condemn a lot of magazines with their riddle pages. Magic in Magical World is nothing more than a substitute for technology and engineering.[239] Furthermore, magic is used to introduce funny, satirical elements. Rowling herself has underlined her very sceptical view of magic and fortune-telling.[240]

A special case within the chorus of Christian critics is the German Catholic convert Gabriele Kuby, who is quite renowned in the context of missionary literature.[241] Fervently she fights against Harry Potter[242] and says: "Harry Potter ist böse. Die Wirkungen werden verheerend sein. Ich stehe bestürzt vor dem Ausmaß der Verblendung."[243] To her the novels depict a "Welt der Rassenideologie und des Blutopfers, der Gewalt und des Grauens, des Ekels und des Terrors, der ständigen Bedrohung und der Besessenheit [...]."[244] It is obvious how Kuby comes to these conclusions. She deliberately distorts and even misreads the text to find proof for her absurd ideas. In this, she makes quite a lot of mistakes and one must wonder if she has read the text at all. Hagrid becomes the thief of the "Philosopher's Stone", Neville's patient grandmother is a disgusting old hag and Sirius is regarded as an accomplice at the torture of the Longbottoms:

> Warum sich die Großmutter in der geschlossenen Anstalt befindet, erfährt der Leser nicht. Die Großmutter dürfte für die meisten Leser eine positive Gestalt sein. Diese hier hat eine klauenartige Hand und findet nichts dabei, dass man ihre Tochter und ihren Schwiegersohn bis zum Wahnsinn gefoltert hat. Es gibt keinen Hinweis, dass der Patenonkel Sirius etwas dagegen hat, dass seine Kusine [Bellatrix] so etwas tut.[245]

---

[237] See Gottfried Wurst, "Harry Potter: eine heilsame Aufregung," "Alohomora!" Ergebnisse des Ersten Wiener Harry-Potter-Symposions, ed. Heidi Lexe, Vienna: Edition Praesens, 2002, 97-108, here 99.

[238] See Abanes 2001, 30-31.

[239] See Cherrett 2003, 15.

[240] See Rowling 2006.

[241] See Jung 2004, 24.

[242] See Lütkehaus 2003.

[243] "Harry Potter is dangerous. The results will be terrifying. I'm shocked at this degree of blindness." Gabriele Kuby, Harry Potter – der globale Schub in okkultes Heidentum: Kisslegg: Fe-Medienverlag, 2002, 8 [my translation].

[244] "world of racism and blood sacrifice, of violence and horror, of disgust and terror, of continuous threats and possession", Kuby 2002, 9, [my translation].

[245] "We never learn why his grandmother is on the closed ward. A grandmother is supposed to be a good character for most readers. But this one has a claw-like hand and does not

Writing this she only shows that she hasn't read the text closely. This also is the case when she writes about Voldemort drinking Harry's blood and interprets this as a sign of cannibalism.[246] After quite a lot of distortions of the truth she then seriously proposes that *Harry Potter* was written by the devil using Rowling as his tool:

> Klar ist, dass hier eine äußerst raffinierte Intelligenz am Werk ist, die systematisch die Desorientierung über Gut und Böse betreibt, durch Langzeitgewöhnung an das Grausame und Ekelerregende, durch Faszination und Veralltäglichung von Magie. Sollte das alles ein unbeabsichtigtes Nebenprodukt [von Rowlings] Schaffen sein? Der Leser möge das selbst beurteilen.[247]

I must join Mathias Jung in asking if Kuby has read the same books as I have,[248] and if she has, if she really understood the text? Accusing Rowling of trying to make children adepts of Satan is absolutely absurd and unsustainable.

V.5.B. Christian Symbols and Issues

There are quite a lot of archaic, Christian issues in *Harry Potter*. Most of them have become part of the canon of Western literature and cannot, therefore, be interpreted as hinting at exclusively Christian values.

One of the most evident issues of the novels is the attempt to murder the god-child, i.e. the saving messiah. Voldemort has heard of a prophecy foretelling his downfall at the hands of a child and attempts to kill Harry when he is still an infant. This reminds us of the very common theme of the tyrant trying to kill a rival as a baby. Among the most prominent examples for this motif we find the Massacre of the Innocents (Matt. 2:16-18) and Pharoah's order to kill all male Hebrew children (Exod. ii 1:22). The rivals always survive. Jesus's family escapes to Egypt, Moses is saved by Pharaoh's daughter – and Harry survives staying with the Dursleys. This motif about the birth of a chosen leader or mes-

---

care about her daughter and son-in-law being tortured into madness. There is no hint at godfather Sirius being against his cousin doing something like that." Kuby 2002, 127 [my translation].

[246] Kuby 2002, 29-31.

[247] "It is obvious that there is a highly artful intelligence at work that systematically disorients us about good and evil. It tries to make us get used to terror, disgust, and fascinate us by the banality of magic. Should this be no more than the unintended by-product of Rowling's creation? The reader may come to his own conclusion." Kuby 2002, 37-38 [my translation].

[248] See Jung 2004, 107.

siah was very common in ancient literature.[249] Harry's rescue is a modern variant of this myth.[250]

Harry's delivery at the Dursleys' threshold has many parallels with the Nativity. Just as in the Gospel of Luke, it is night-time when a flying messenger (Hagrid on his motorbike) appears and tells the others about the child Redeemer. Just like the Magi, three adults worship the baby boy (Dumbledore, McGonagall und Hagrid). Clothed in linen the child is laid down and magical lights are to be seen in the nocturnal sky (HP 1, 16).[251]

On a symbolic level we find the fight between the lion (Book of Revelation 5:5) representing Jesus and the snake embodying evil. Gryffindor has a lion in its coat of arms whereas Slytherin and Voldemort are associated with a snake, the Christian symbol of evil.[252] Like C.S. Lewis in his *Chronicles of Narnia* (where the lion Aslan represents Jesus), J.K. Rowling uses the lion as symbol of good.[253] Voldemort, on the contrary, personally resembles a snake with his red eyes and his slit-like nostrils.[254] Even the names of the principal opponents begin with "G" (Gryffindor, God) and "S" (Slytherin, Satan).[255] Etymologically "Godric" is derived from "god" and the Old English "rice" (= rich). The founder of the heroic house of Gryffindor, thus, is "rich in God".[256]

Harry's career reminds us in many ways of Jesus' biography as Detlev Dormeyer points out, comparing the novel to the Gospel of Thomas.[257] The Old Testament announces the birth of a messiah more than once – for example in the Book of Micah (Mic. 5:1) we read:

> But thou, Bethlehem Ephratah, though thou be little among the thousands of Judah, yet out of thee shall he come forth unto me that is to be ruler in Israel; whose goings forth have been from of old, from everlasting.

---

[249] See Cornelius 2003, 49; Schafer 2000, 165-166.
[250] See Cornelius 2003, 49.
[251] See Cornelius 2003, 49-51; Jung 2004, 35; Neal 2002, 7.
[252] See Granger 2004, 109; Killinger 2004, 23.
[253] See Granger 2004, 17; Killinger 2004, 22.
[254] See Jung 2004, 137.
[255] See Killinger 2004, 51; Smadja 2001, 46.
[256] Edmund Kern is mistaken when he derives the name from "law" and interprets "Godric" as "god's law": Kern 2003, 219.
[257] See Dormeyer, "Das apokryphe Kindheitsevangelium des Thomas und 'Harry Potter' von J.K. Rowling," *Faszination 'Harry Potter': Was steckt dahinter?*, eds. Detlev Dormeyer, Friedhelm Munzel, Münster: LIT, 2005, 31-42.

And in Isaiah (Isa. 9:6):

> For unto us a child is born, unto us a son is given: and the government shall
> be upon his shoulder: and his name shall be called Wonderful, Counsellor,
> The mighty God, The everlasting Father, The Prince of Peace.

Harry's birth is also announced by a prophecy. It reads:

> The one with the power to vanquish the Dark Lord approaches ... born to
> those who have thrice defied him, born as the seventh month dies ... and the
> Dark Lord will mark him as equal, but he will have power the Dark Lord
> knows not ... and either must die at the hand of the other for neither can live
> while the other survives ... the one with the power to vanquish the Dark
> Lord will be born as the seventh month dies ...(HP 5, 916)

Both children – Harry and Jesus – survive their attack, escape into hiding
and return when they are about eleven or twelve years old to fulfill their mission.[258] As the Apocrypha tells us of Jesus and the miracles he performs during
his childhood, we read about magical things happening around Harry. He jumps
off a roof, his hair grows overnight (HP 1, 32) and he causes glass to vanish
(HP 1, 36).[259] Kern goes even further (in my opinion much too far) and reads the
novels as an allegory of the Gospels:

> In each book, Harry metaphorically dies and descends into hell (the Forbid-
> den Corridor, the Chamber of Secrets, the Shrieking Shack, the cemetery),
> only to be metaphorically reborn and ascend into heaven (when order is re-
> stored). And it requires little effort to see Harry as a Christ figure.[260]

Forgiveness is one of the major topics of *Harry Potter*; i.e. Dumbledore's
"giving second chances" (see IV.3.N, 210).[261] This attitude is highly Christian:
he who has suffered must be able to forgive to be healed and redeemed.[262] There
are many examples of forgiveness to be found in the series: Hagrid is forgiven
his betrayal of the secret protecting the "Philosopher's Stone"; having renounced
Voldemort, Snape is given a second chance by Dumbledore; and Ginny is *not*
accused of having herself been caught by Voldemort in *Chamber of Secrets*. All

---

[258] See Drexler, Wandinger 2004, 66.
[259] See Killinger 2004, 26-29.
[260] Kern 2003, 216.
[261] See Cherrett 2003, 64-66.
[262] See Drexler, Wandinger 2004, 30.

of them are pardoned.[263] On the contrary, Barty Crouch snr cannot forgive – and fails because he hates first his son and later himself.[264]

Harry's mother dies to save her Redeemer son. Christian critics have interpreted this as a variant of the sacrificial death of Jesus. Lily gives her life so that her son may live to save the world.[265] I do not agree with this interpretation: Lily dies because she wants to protect her son out of motherly love; it is not the idea of saving the world that makes her sacrifice herself.[266]

Apart from that, we find Christian authors connecting Harry's activities to specific scriptures. I do not want to join in this kind of discussion: a literary analysis is not the place for theological debates. Finally, I want to suggest that the values promoted in *Harry Potter* sit very well with the catalogue of Cardinal Virtues and the Seven Deadly Sins. Prudence (*prudentia*), Justice (*iustitia*), Fortitude (*fortitudo*) and Temperance (*temperantia*) are positive values (see IV.2.B, 154). Furthermore, Faith (*fides*), Charity (*caritas*) and Hope (*spes*) are at the centre of Rowling's value pattern. The so called Seven Deadly Sins are represented by the negative characters: Pride (*superbia*), Greed (*avaritia*), Envy (*invidia*) and Gluttony (*gula*) are the basic characteristics of the Malfoys, Gilderoy Lockhart and Dolores Umbridge. Only Wrath (*ira*) is to be found in good and evil characters, whereas Lust (*luxuria*) is irrelevant in the context of the novels. Sloth (*acedia*) is a deadly sin as well – but Harry and his friends are neither lazy nor dull. Although they do not always work at school they exercise for "Quidditch" or work to save Magical World. In conclusion, the novels conform very well to Christian ethics.

V.5.C. Manifestations of Religion

Although there is no mention of any particular belief in the novels, we find many references to Christianity. For example, Ollivander's shop sign reads "Makers of Fine Wands since 382 BC" (HP 1, 92). Christmas is celebrated every year: the "Great Hall" is decorated with twelve Christmas trees (HP 1, 212), candles are lit (HP 1, 213), presents are made (HP 1, 216) and a feast is held: "A hundred fat, roast turkeys, mountains of roast and boiled potatoes [...]" (HP 1, 220).

> [The] usual twelve Christmas trees in the Great Hall were bedecked with everything from luminous holly berries to real, hooting, golden owls, and the suits of armour had all been bewitched to sing carols whenever anyone passed them. It was quite something to hear 'Oh Come, All Ye Faithful' sung by an empty helmet that only knew half the words. (HP 4, 432)

---

263 See Neal 2002, 45, 82.
264 See Doughty 2004, 249.
265 See Jung 2004, 137; Neal 2002, 7, 127.
266 See Drexler, Wandinger 2004, 58.

Professor Flitwick, the Charms teacher, had already decorated his classroom with shimmering lights that turned out to be real, fluttering fairies.
(HP 3, 206)

The way magical world celebrates Christmas is not much different from
"Muggle" world,[267] but it is without any connection to Christian belief.[268] Obviously, Christmas is celebrated in the whole of Magical World. We hear about
Christmas in Beauxbatons (HP 4, 456) and Grimmauld Place where there is "a
great Christmas tree [...] decorated with live fairies [...] and even the stuffed elf-
heads on the hall wall wore Father Christmas hats and beards." (HP 5, 552) In
Deathly Hallows Hermione and Harry vist Godric's Hollow on Christmas Eve
(HP 7, 265). But how is it that wizards know about the "Muggle" Christmas cus-
toms, when they are completely ignorant of "Muggle" lifestyle in general?[269]
Apart from Christmas, we find references to Easter (HP 1, 248) and Halloween.
Halloween is of Celtic origin but has been transferred under Christian influence
to the day before All Saints' Day ("All Hallows Eve").[270] Just like Christmas
and Easter, Halloween is completely emptied of meaning.[271]

In *Deathly Hallows* we experience a wedding conducted by "the small,
tufty-haired wizard who had presided at Dumbledore's funeral" (HP 7, 121).
Rowling does not tell us what kind of office or position he has, but he seems to
be a representative of the Ministry. The ceremony very much resembles a Christian wedding. During the ceremony we hear familiar lines such as "'We are
gathered here today to celebrate the union of two faithful souls...' [...] and 'Do
you, William Arthur, take Fleur Isabelle [...]?'" (HP 7, 121) But what does the
term "faithful souls" refer to? In what moral authority do they have "faith"? This
is an obvious reference to transcendency without a clear definition as to whom
or what this is supposed to be. There is also mention of Lily and James' best
man which hints at a conventional Christian wedding ceremony.[272] We find yet
another parallel to Christian rites in the "Unbreakable Vow" which Snape has to
swear to Narcissa Malfoy. It reminds us of Christian weddings vows:

"Will you, Severus, watch over my son Draco as he attempts to fulfil the
Dark Lord's wishes?"
"I will," said Snape. [...]
"And will you, to the best of your ability, protect him from harm?"
"I will," said Snape.
[...]

267 Also HP 2, 230-232.
268 See Cornelius 2003, 24, 28.
269 See Cornelius 2003, 24.
270 See Cornelius 2003, 37-38.
271 See Cornelius 2003, 40.
272 See Cornelius 2003, 32.

"And should it prove necessary [...] will you carry out the deed [...]?"
[...]
"I will," said Snape. (HP 6, 41)

Magical World knows the concept of godparenthood: Sirius Black is Harry's godfather and Harry becomes godfather to Teddy Lupin. This usually means that the boys have been christened. But have they? What kind of ceremony is needed to make someone godfather? We do not find any mention of a baptism in Magical World.[273] So we do find references to Christian rites and ceremonies, but there is absolutely no examination of Christianity in *Harry Potter*.

V.5.D. Charity and Compassion

Charity is a fundamental concept of Jewish-Christian ethics and the basis of Jesus' teaching. We find the command of Charity in the Gospel of Matthew (Mt 22, 37-40), where the Old Testament is cited (3 Moses 18): "thou shalt love thy neighbour as thyself [...]." One of the most decisive characteristics of good characters is their ability to be compassionate and charitable. They can even feel for their enemies (see IV.2.B, 154). This is very obvious in Harry himself. When Filch's cat becomes petrified, he feels sympathy for him: "Much as he detested Filch, Harry couldn't help feeling a bit sorry for him [...]" (HP 2, 155). He also feels for Dobby, who has caused his "Quidditch" accident and a lot of trouble with his family: "[Dobby was] looking so pathetic that Harry felt his anger ebb away in spite of himself." (HP 2, 193).

A good person does not continue to fight when his enemy is defenceless. Harry, for example, refuses to kick Filch's cat, although he is hidden under his "Invisibility Cloak" and would not have to face any consequences: "'Oh, let's kick [Mrs Norris], just this once,' Ron whispered in Harry's ear, but Harry shook his head" (HP 1, 295). He obviously has a clear notion of what is right and what is wrong – this is something his adversaries do not have. Bothering others when they cannot defend themselves is everyday business in Voldemort's world. Voldemort tortures Pettigrew (HP 5, 703) and Draco Malfoy hits Harry who, just moments before, had spared hin (HP 2, 208).

Not helping a person in need seems to cast a shadow over Harry's activities: "But leaving Neville lying motionless on the floor didn't feel like a very good omen" (HP 1, 295). In *Prisoner of Azkaban* he prevents Lupin and Black from killing Pettigrew, something which Dumbledore points out to him: "'You did a very noble thing, in saving Pettigrew's life.'" (HP 3, 459) Renouncing revenge and showing mercy creates an emotional bond between people that is of paramount and unbreakable importance:

---

[273] See Blake 2002, 97; Cornelius 2003, 31.

"Pettigrew owes his life to you. You have sent Voldemort a deputy who is in your debt. When one wizard saves another wizard's life, it creates a certain bond between them ... and I'm much mistaken if Voldemort wants a servant in the debt of Harry Potter." (HP 3, 459)

Dumbledore is right. In *Deathly Hallows* we see that Pettigrew considers letting Harry go for a split second – and ends up "reaping his reward for his hesitation, his moment of pity" and "being strangled before their eyes" (HP 7, 380-381). Ron, on the other hand, cries out he wants to "kill Death Eaters" after they have murdered his brother Fred (HP 7, 514). This is a positive character vowing revenge instead of offering forgiveness.

Dumbledore declares compassion and protection to those in need to be a basic principle of Hogwarts ("'help will always be given at Hogwarts to those who ask for it.'", HP 2, 284). This includes non-human beings:

The [...] owls [...] had to be nursed back to health by Hagrid before they could fly off again. (HP 1, 210)
"That [Winky is not human] doesn't mean she hasn't got feelings, [...]." (HP 4, 156)
Harry learned quickly not to feel too sorry for the gnomes. (HP 2, 44)

In fact, Sirius' death is the immediate consequence of his treating Kreacher badly. Dumbledore explains to Harry: "'Kreacher is what he has been made by wizards, [...] he is to be pitied.'" (HP 5, 914) If Sirius had shown more sympathy to him, he would not have betrayed him to Voldemort and Sirius would have survived. It is his lack of compassion that kills Harry's godfather. This becomes all the more evident, when Harry begins to treat Kreacher nicely in *Deathly Hallows* (HP 7, 165) and sees the elf change dramatically (HP 7, 185). When Harry shows his respect for Kreacher and understands his tragic story, Kreacher becomes a loyal and faithful servant. In the end, he proudly leads the Hogwarts house-elves into battle against Voldemort – wearing Regulus Black's locket (HP 7, 588).

Sympathy and compassion are decisive principles in just about every situation. There is no excuse for not forgiving others as this dialogue between Draco and Dumbledore shows:

"Come over to the right side [...]. Draco ... you are not a killer ..."
Malfoy stared at Dumbledore. "But I got this far, didn't I?" he said slowly. "They thought I'd die in the attempt, but I'm here ... and you're in my power ... I'm the one with the wand ... you're at my mercy ..."
"No, Draco," said Dumbledore quietly. "It is my mercy, and not yours, that matters now." (HP 6, 551-553)

Defenceless and about to be killed, Dumbledore still trusts in the power of forgiveness. Although Draco is about to murder his headmaster, Dumbledore is
mightier. Compassion and sympathy are more powerful than violence. Harry,
losing his last remaining father figure when Dumbledore dies, shows true moral
greatness in his feelings for Draco:

> He despised Malfoy still for his infatuation with the Dark Arts, but now the
> tiniest drop of pity mingled with his dislike. Where, Harry wondered, was
> Malfoy now, and what was Voldemort making him do under threat of kill-
> ing him and his parents. (HP 6, 596)

Nevertheless, Harry is no do-gooder. When Lockhart and Snape are duelling,
he agrees with Ron: "'Wouldn't it be good if they finished each other off?'" (HP 2,
206) And gleefully he sees Draco suffer from a "Swelling Solution":

> [Malfoy's] head [was] drooping with the weight of a nose like a small melon.
> As half the class lumbered up to Snape's desk, some weighed down with arms
> like clubs, others unable to talk through gigantic puffed-up lips, [...].
> (HP 2, 204)

Negative characters never show any sympathy; they are cold and egoistic.
Voldemort "'does not forgive mistakes easily'" (HP 1, 313), and Wormtail has
to underline that he does not speak "'out of concern for the boy! [...] The boy is
nothing to me, nothing at all!'" (HP 4, 15) This is a perversion of Dumbledore's
values. Pointless torture is the proper thing to do in Voldemort's world –
"'[That's the Death Eaters'] idea of fun. Half the Muggle killings back when
You-Know-Who was in power were done for fun.'" (HP 4, 159)

So the *Harry Potter* novels promote compassion and forgiveness. The
Fifth Commandment "Thou shalt not kill" must be obeyed. Harry even spares
his adversaries, as we learn in *Deathly Hallows* (HP 7, 64). The novels conform
to Christian belief.

V.5.E. Falsehood and Truth

The Eighth Commandment is: "Thou shalt not bear false witness". Positive
characters tend to be honest in *Harry Potter*. Dumbledore explains Harry:

> "The truth [...] is a beautiful and terrible thing, and should therefore be
> treated with great caution. However, I shall answer your questions unless I
> have a very good reason not to, in which case I beg you'll forgive me.
> I shall not, of course, lie." (HP 1, 321)

And when the Ministry asks him to cover up Cedric Diggory's death Dumbledore says:

"[The] truth is generally preferable to lies, and that any attempt to pretend that Cedric died as a result of an accident, or some sort of blunder of his own, is an insult to his memory." (HP 4, 782-783)

But, very often, Harry does as he likes and deliberately breaks rules. He trusts in his own judgement to tell right from wrong – just like Christian martyrs.[274] Harry also resorts to white lies (for example when he tells McGonagall he and Ron wanted to visit Hermione in hospital: HP 2, 310-311), but feels bad about lying (HP 7, 411). He even lies to Dumbledore (HP 2, 227). But he never does so for egoistic reasons, which draws a distinction between him and Voldemort's followers.[275] Ethics in *Harry Potter* are more than just sticking to rules. Justice, mercy and loyalty are much more important than abiding by laws.[276] The plot shows that "truth-telling, submission to authority, and following the rules are not always the moral things to do, particularly when the stakes are high."[277] Harry challenges authorities, not for his own sake but because he feels they act against higher principles.[278] His apparent rebelliousness is a kind of civil disobedience.[279] And when Voldemort has seized power, parts of the magical community act heroically to protect the weak:

"However, we continue to hear truly inspirational stories of wizards and witches risking their own safety to protect Muggle friends and neighbours, often without the Muggles' knowledge. I'd like to appeal to all our listeners to emulate their example, perhaps by casting a protective charm over any Muggle dwellings in your street." (HP 7, 357)

This is the kind of rule-breaking Harry stands for. The most important criterion for making a decision is doing what you feel to be right. But truth is not subjective, either. Truth is unalterable and everyone can recognise it if he wants to.[280]

According to *Harry Potter* each citizen has not only the right, but the obligation to resist tyrants[281] – growing up means knowing how to prioritise.[282] But

274 See Cherrett 2003, 43-44.
275 See Smadja 2001, 127.
276 See David Baggett, "Magic, Muggles, and Moral Imagination," *Harry Potter and Philosophy: If Aristotle ran Hogwarts*, eds. David Baggett & Shawn Klein, Chicago, La Salle: Open Court, 2004, 158-171, here 166; Connie Neal, *What's a Christian to Do with Harry Potter?* Colorado Springs: Waterbrook Press, 2001, 17.
277 See Kern 2003, 72.
278 See Nel 2001, 29; Rebecca Skulnick & Jesse Goodman, "The Civic Leadership of *Harry Potter*: Agency, Ritual, and Schooling," *Harry Potter's World: Multidisciplinary Critical Perspectives*, ed. Elizabeth E. Heilman, New York, London: RoutledgeFalmer, 2003, 261-277, 262.
279 See Skulnick, Goodman 2003, 268.
280 See Deavel 2002, 54.
281 See Pinsent 2004, 37; Smadja 2001, 34-35.

it remains a fact that Harry continously breaks rules in the course of action[283] and thereby saves Wizarding World. Richard Abanes regards this as the antitheses to Christian values.[284] Connie Neal, on the other hand, says that lying and betraying are not *per se* opposed to Christian belief. Despite denying Christ three times, Peter is allowed to remain among the apostles.[285] It is important that the line between good and evil does not run between legal and illegal activities. A small-time ciminal like Mundungus Fletcher can be a member of the "Order of the Phoenix".[286]

Only negative characters ask unconditional obedience.[287] At the same time they play foul and betray others (non-members of their group) as the Slytherin "Quidditch" team does (HP 3, 333-336). The Dursleys are just as false, pretending that Harry's parents have died in a car crash for eleven years (HP 1, 27). Voldemort even violates the Eighth Commandment when he accuses Hagrid of setting loose the monster he himself has set on his fellow-students (HP 2, 268).

V.5.F. Love

Love is one of Rowling's[288] main issues and the whole series can be read as a hymn to (motherly) love.[289] "Nichts ist stärker in Rowlings Romanen als die Macht der Liebe, die über den Tod hinaus wirkt; [...]" writes Susanne Gaschke in her review of *Deathly Hallows*.[290] Harry has been saved because of Lily's love for her son:

> "[Love] as powerful as your mother's for you leaves its own mark. [... To] have been loved so deeply, even though the person who loved us is gone, will give us some protection for ever." (HP 1, 321)

The magic of motherly love protects Harry until he turns seventeen (HP 7, 33) and as long as he stays with the Dursleys. His aunt Petunia, knowing about the importance of her nephew staying with her, renews the charm each year by letting him return home (HP 5, 918-919). Love and family ties keep Harry alive and defeat Voldemort. Harry is able to love – a gift he disregards at first:

---

[282] Smadja 2001, 126; Pinsent 2004, 37; Walser 2004, 89.
[283] See Elster 2003, 218.
[284] See Abanes 2001, 70; 99-100.
[285] See Neal 2001, 172-174.
[286] See Kulik 2005, 309.
[287] See Smadja 2001, 126.
[288] von Lovenberg, "Ende gut", 2007.
[289] See Houghton 2001, 17.
[290] "There is nothing more powerful in Rowling's novels than love taking its effects even after death", Gaschke 2007 [my translation].

"You have a power that Voldemort has never had. You can –" "I know!" said Harry impatiently. "I can love!" It was only with difficulty that he stopped himself adding, "Big deal!" (HP 6, 476-477)

Only in *Deathly Hallows* do we see why this is so important. Only because he is able to love his friends so dearly is he ready to sacrifice his life for them. This is why he can finally protect them from Voldemort (HP 7, 591). Harry's death for saving the world mirrors the passion of Christ: both messiahs deliberately give their lives to fulfill their missions and to save mankind. Voldemort does not realise how powerful love is:

"But nothing I have seen in the world has supported your famous pronouncements that love is more powerful than my kind of magic, Dumbledore." (HP 6, 415)

Apart from his ability to love, it is Harry's purity of heart and his selflessness that help him defeat evil as Dumbledore points out to him:

"In spite of all the temptation you have endured, all the suffering, you remain pure of heart [... just] as pure as you were at the age of eleven, when you stared into a mirror that reflected your heart's desire, and it showed you only the way to thwart Lord Voldemort, and not immortality or riches. Harry, have you any idea how few wizards could have seen what you saw in that mirror?" (HP 6, 477-478)

Although Voldemort is unable to love, his followers are capable of feeling it. It is important that we see Narcissa Malfoy loving her son as ardently as Lily Potter loves Harry (HP 6, 38). When Narcissa pleads with Snape to save her son and betrays Voldemort in doing so she is just as willing to give her life for Draco as Lily was in giving hers for Harry. In the final battle for Hogwarts she pretends that Harry is dead just to be able to enter the castle and to look for her son (HP 7, 581-582). Molly Weasley is only able to defeat Bellatrix Lestrange because she does so to protect her children (HP 7, 589).

In contrast to these two mothers, Voldemort's mother Merope Gaunt dies because she loses hope. Being left by Tom's father she gives up on herself and in doing so her motherly love for her son. Tom grows up in an orphanage (HP 6, 245-258). Love is the initial point for all that happens in the *Potter* series. Merope's denial of love to her son is the basis for Tom's career as "Dark Lord". Lily Potter's self-sacrifice protects her son and marks him the messiah. It is no divine power that "chooses" Harry, but the love of his mother (see V.6.A, 369). So in the end it is love that defeats Voldemort's hatred and barbarity:

Es siegt die Macht der Liebe und Freundschaft. Der Topos, der alle sieben Romane von Beginn an durchzieht, uralt, unsterblich. Joanne K. Rowlings

Harry-Potter-Saga ist wohl die massenwirksamste Verarbeitung dieses Motivs in den vergangenen Jahren.[291]

V.5.G. Life and Death

The issue of death is one of the most important aspects of Rowling's novels. Harry is able to defeat Voldemort only because of love for his friends and because he renounces his fear of death. The question "wie man als Überlebender mit dem Verlust geliebter Menschen und mit der Gewissheit des eigenen Todes umgehen kann"[292] is pivotal to understanding *Harry Potter*. This is why the attitude characters have towards death is decisive. Because he fears death, Voldemort wants to become immortal and mutilates his soul. This is "the root of all evil".[293] Rowling has said in an interview[294] that the enormity and certainty of death is at the core of her novels. She herself tried to overcome the death of her mother by dealing with the little orphan boy Harry.

But what is Magical World's general conception of death? As there seems to be no religion, it is difficult to say what idea magical world has of paradise and life after death. Dumbledore explains to Harry that death is just the "next great adventure" for Flamel and his wife (HP 1, 320), but why? Luna Lovegood believes she will see her mother when she has died (HP 5, 769) – but we do not learn why she believes this.

When Severus Snape dies, a substance described as "Silver blue, neither gas nor liquid, [is gushing] from his mouth and his ears and his eyes, and Harry knew what it was, but did not know what to do –" (HP 7, 528). It is his thoughts, his memories and soul that are leaving his dying body. Harry pours it in a flask and is able to decipher it a little later, getting vital information about how to defeat Voldemort.

But where do these spirits usually go? Can they return? Nearly Headless Nick, the Gryffindor ghost, explains that each wizard can decide whether to return as a ghost or not (HP 5, 945-946). Rowling does not take up a thread she began in *Order of the Phoenix* where she describes a black arch in the "Department of Mysteries". When Sirius falls behind it he is dead, so this arch is a vital place for the wizards' idea of death. Obviously this is a kind of entrance to the

---

[291] "Love and friendship are victorious. This is the leitmotif of all the seven novels right from the start – ancient and immortal. Joanne K. Rowling's *Harry Potter* saga probably is the most popular version of this topos in recent times." Hugendick 2007 [my translation].

[292] "the question how as a survivor to deal with the loss of loved ones and the certainty of one's own death", von Lovenberg, "Ende gut", 2007 [my translation].

[293] See Wrigley 2005, 33.

[294] See Felicitas von Lovenberg, "Lebensspuren. Hüterin des Schatzes: Joanne K. Rowling gewährt seltene Einblicke," *F.A.Z.* 11 Jan 2006, 35.

realm of the dead (see III.5.E, 132). But Rowling never returns to this idea and does not give us further information. Instead, in *Deathly Hallows* she introduces another crossroads between life and death: King's Cross station. Having died, Harry first awakens here:

> He lay face down, listening to the silence. He was perfectly alone. Nobody as watching. Nobody else was there. He was not perfectly sure that he was there himself. [...] He lay in a bright mist, though it was not like mist he had ever experienced before. His surroundings were not hidden by cloudy vapour; rather the cloudy vapour had not yet formed into surroundings. The floor on which he lay seemed to be white, neither warm nor cold, but simply there, a flat, blank something on which to be. For the first time, he wished he were clothed. Barely had the wish formed in his head, than robes appeared [...]. (HP 7, 565-566)

The train station becomes a bizarre twilight zone between this world and the hereafter – just as it divides "Muggle" from Magical World. Harry meets Dumbledore who wonders about the place himself (HP 7, 570). A white nothingness forming into a train station is Rowling's idea of the hereafter. This is neither very innovative nor overly-stereotypical. It corresponds with the "technique of avoidance" Rowling usually applies when it comes to writing on an epic scale (see II.2.E, 46) and in a way the scene resembles the representation of Gandalf's death in the movie version of *The Two Towers* (2002).

Rowling has explained that death in Magical World is just as definite as in our world – the dead cannot return to life.[295] But in the course of the plot we see several of the dead return as visions or spirits. They can even interact with the living and influence the present, as the episode in the graveyard of Little Hangleton (*Goblet of Fire*) shows. It is only the interference of Voldemort's victims that can save Harry's life (HP 4, 721-724). Later, Hermione insists that "'they weren't really back from the dead'" (HP 7, 346) – but what else were they? Rowling leaves us in the dark.

In *Deathly Hallows* Voldemort's victims, i.e. those friends of Harry's who were murdered by the villain and his followers, accompany him to the final confrontation with Voldemort (HP 7, 560-561). Harry finally understands that although he has the "Resurrection Stone", a gem that is supposed to bring back the dead, things are not what he thought them to be:

> It did not matter about bringing them back for he was about to join them. He was not really fetching them: they were fetching him. [...] They were neither ghost nor truly flesh, he could see that. [...] Less substantial than living bodies, but much more than ghosts, they moved towards him, and on each face there was the same loving smile. [...] "Does it hurt?" [...] "Dying? Not

---

[295] See Hattenstone 2000.

at all," said Sirius. "Quicker and easier than falling asleep." [...] "Remus, I'm sorry –" "I'm sorry, too," said Lupin. "Sorry I will never know [my son] ... but he will know why I died and I hope he will understand. I was trying to make a world in which he could live a happier life." [...] "You'll stay with me?" "Until the very end," said James. "They won't be able to see you?" asked Harry. "We are part of you," said Sirius. "Invisible to anyone else." [...] they acted like Patronuses to him [... their] presence was his courage, and the reason he was able to keep putting one foot in front of the other. (HP 7, 559-561)

So the dead are within us: in our memories. They live with us and comfort us when we are desperate. Being reconciled to and losing the fear of death helps us on and frees us from fear itself. This is – together with the power of love – the main issue of the novels. Harry becomes

"the true master of death, because the true master does not seek to run away from Death. He accepts that he must die, and understands that there are far, far worse things in the living world than dying." (HP 7, 577)

Although he is the owner of the "Deathly Hallows" – the three magical objects that united make the bearer immortal – he only can defeat death because he looses his fear of it. So, as Dumbledore tells Harry, there are "far worse things" like living without love (HP 7, 578). So Harry finally fulfils what is written on his parents' tombstone:

The last enemy that shall be destroyed is death. (HP 7, 268)

He destroys this last enemy and sacrificing himself to Voldemort saves the world.

V.6 Why is Evil evil?

Harry against Voldemort: good against evil. But why is one of them good and the other bad? What makes Harry the hero and Tom Riddle the villain? Why does evil exist? Professor Quirrell, a follower of Voldemort's, explains that[296]

"There is no good and evil, there is only power, and those too weak to seek it." (HP 1, 313)

This is reminiscent of Nietzsche's "will to power". It is power and the wish to obtain it that differentiates people into good and bad. Speaking from the traitor's

---

[296] Baggett and Klein point to the obvious reference to Nietzsche's idea of "will to power" (Baggett & Klein 2004, 3).

perspective, the positive characters around Harry and Dumbledore are simply too weak to gain power. Morality is weakness, unscrupulousness is strength.

Jack Zipes has described two kinds of evil in the novels: "the vicious sadism of Voldemort and the cruel vindictiveness of the Dursleys."[297] For a long time, evil is not personified in the novels – but it is omnipresent nevertheless. It is possible that apparently good characters can turn out to be evil or vice versa. This makes *Harry Potter* different from many other fantasy texts.[298] Even the good characters are not entirely positive – they have their weaknesses.[299] Thus, Rowling's idea of good and bad is completely different from that of J.R.R. Tolkien or C.S. Lewis. Whereas predetermination and race are important criteria for a character's being good or evil in *The Lord of the Rings* and *The Chronicles of Narnia*, Rowling stresses the individual's freedom to decide what to do with his life (see V.6.A, 367). Edmund Kern is wrong when he places Rowling in the same category as Lewis or Tolkien.[300]

What is the nature of evil in *Harry Potter*? First, it is parasitic and only exits by exploiting others. This is symbolised in *Philosopher's Stone* with Voldemort surviving in Quirrell's body.[301] But evil does not only exist in Voldemort and his disciples. Dolores Umbridge is just as evil even if she is not a "Death Eater".[302] In contrast to many other fantasy novels, being ugly in Rowling's world does not automatically mark you as a bad character. Mundungus Fletcher is unkempt and dirty – but a (weak) member of the "Order of the Phoenix" (HP 5, 95).[303]

Where does evil come from? Why does it exist? First of all, everyone has freedom of choice. He can decide what he wants to become and what to make of his life (see V.6.A, 367).[304] Nevertheless, there are factors that influence people's decisions. Analysing the negative characters we see that they tend to come from the margins of society. They have experienced prejudice, oppression and neglect. There is Merope Gaunt who is looked down upon by her father and her brother – using magic she tricks Tom Riddle snr into marrying her (HP 6, 201). Her son Tom jnr experiences a lack of motherly love and grows up in an orphanage. From an early age he dreams of a distinguished position in society as Dumbledore tells Harry:

---

[297] Zipes 2001, 180-181.
[298] See Kulik 2005, 345; Misik 2005.
[299] See Alison Lurie, *Boys and Girls Forever: Children's Classics from Cinderella to Harry Potter*, London: Vintage, 2003, 117.
[300] See Kern 2003, 214.
[301] See Deavel 2002, 56.
[302] See Kulik 2005, 304.
[303] See Kulik 2005, 309.
[304] See Deavel 2002, 142.

"There he showed his contempt for anything that tied him to other people, anything that made him ordinary. Even then, he wished to be different, separate, notorious." (HP 6, 259)

Petunia Dursley must accept her sister as being something special – a witch her parents are proud of. Petunia feels inferior (see IV.4.G). This is why she hates magic and takes revenge on her nephew Harry after her sister's death. Barty Crouch only cares for his career and despises his son for risking his career – which makes Barty jnr an ardent admirer of Voldemort.[305] Kreacher is maltreated by Sirius and takes revenge by betraying him to the "Death Eaters" (HP 5, 911-914). Peter Pettigrew feels inferior to his friends James and Sirius. He feels that they do not really accept him. Only with Voldemort can he experience power and betrays the Potters to his new master. Likewise, Severus Snape and Draco Malfoy are attracted by evil because there they feel like part of a greater community. Thus, they can make up for the lack of love and warmth within their lives.[306] Because his father is a "Muggle" Snape feels ashamed and secretly names himself "Prince" after his mother. He calls himself "Half-Blood Prince". He is laughed at by James Potter and his friends (HP 5, 705-714). As a result, Snape takes revenge on James's son Harry. Draco on the other hand has to live up to his father's great expectations. This experience of "lack of love" is, as Nils Kulik has pointed out, a characteristic of many fantasy novels.[307] Evil characters are usually weak and marginalised grown-ups with an unhappy childhood.[308] Not all the bad characters conform to this pattern, but there is a general tendency to regard discrimination, neglect and marginalisation as the basis for a negative development. He who does not feel accepted by society will finally turn his back on its values and fight it. Society creates its enemies: terrorism emerges right in its middle. But not every abused child necessarily becomes a terrorist, as Harry or Sirius demonstrate.[309]

Memories and thoughts leave deep marks on a person's mind and can destroy. "According to Madam Pomfrey, thoughts could leave deeper scarring than almost anything else, [...]." (HP 5, 931) Desperation and the loss of hope make people vulnerable to moral corruption, a process perfectly symbolised by the "Dementors".[310] Only he who has seen happiness can successfully fight the soul eaters. This is why evil in *Harry Potter* always refers to the "monsters within [..]

---

[305] See Kulik 2005, 295.
[306] See Kulik 2005, 299.
[307] See Kulik 2005, 296.
[308] See Natov 2001, 322.
[309] See Doughty 2004, 248.
[310] See Natov 2001, 135.

367

the self."[311] The antidote for such haunting is happy memories: those that make children feel safe, loved, confident and good about themselves.

Once immersed in the "Dark Arts" people can no longer find personal freedom, but are enslaved by evil.[312] It is only when you become completely morally corrupted that you can use the "Unforgiveable Curses" correctly.[313] Evil finds it expression in a proto-fascist ideology of racism and unconditional subordination.[314]

It is decisive for understanding the ideological content of the novels that there is no clear distinction between good and bad: positive characters have negative character traits (see IV.3.B, 160) and bad characters can suddenly inspire sympathy (see IV.3.L, 196). Apparently good characters turn out to be traitors like Quirrell (representing the unity of good and evil physically)[315] or the impostor Moody. Evil pretends to be good,[316] good people can be untrustworthy[317] and even Lupin, a father figure for Harry, has his dark sides making him dangerous to everyone.[318] This feeling of uncertainty is constantly growing with every part of the series; the borderline between good and bad becomes increasingly unclear.[319] When Dumbledore dies we realise that Good does not always triumph in the end.[320] This mutation from good to evil is very common in fantasy literature, as Christina Tilmann points out in her review of the *Harry Potter and the Goblet of Fire* movie.[321] These conversions from good to bad and vice versa happen quite frequently in *Harry Potter*. It is therefore wrong to say that the demarcations between good and evil are too obvious and superficial.[322]

V.6.A. Inheritance vs. Self-determination – What is Man?

Summing up the "message" of *Harry Potter* there is one major point Rowling never ceases to stress: individual responsibility and the idea of "choice". "Wir sind diejenigen, die wir zu sein beschließen", as Felicitas von Lovenberg

[311] See Cockrell 2004, 18; Natov 2001, 321.
[312] See Hart Weed 2004, 152.
[313] See Benjamin J. Bruxvoort Lipscomb, W. Christopher Stewart, "Magic, Science and the ethics of Technology," *Harry Potter and Philosophy: If Aristotle ran Hogwarts*, eds. David Baggett & Shawn Klein, Chicago, La Salle: Open Court, 2004, 77-91, here 86.
[314] See Gupta 2003, 101-104.
[315] See Maar 2003, 65.
[316] See Deavel 2004, 139.
[317] See Blake 2002, 97-98; Bürvenich 2001, 110.
[318] See Natov 2001, 136.
[319] See Cockrell 2004, 24-25.
[320] See Cockrell 2004, 16.
[321] See Christina Tilmann, "Tote leben länger," *Tagesspiegel* 18 July 2005, 19.
[322] See Heidkamp 2001.

says in her review of *Deathly Hallows*.[323] In Dumbledore's words: "'It is our choices, Harry, that show, what we truly are, far more than our abilities'" (HP 2, 358). We are responsible for what we become and what we make of ourselves. We are not predestined by our families or abilities. Race, religion and heritage are irrelevant. It is our own behaviour and priorities which decide who we become. Therefore, good and bad characters are likewise to be found in every group and every race:

Group	Positive	Negative
Wizards	Dumbledore	Voldemort
Muggles	Grangers	Dursleys
Aristocracy	Sirius Black	Lucius Malfoy
Elves	Dobby	Kreacher
Giants	Grawp	Gurg, Golgomath
Pure-bloods	Weasleys	Malfoys
Mudbloods	Hermione	Snape
Rich	Harry Potter	Malfoys
Poor	Weasleys	House of Gaunt

Finally, through what is revealed in *Deathly Hallows*, we realise that

> [...] kindly Dumbledore, sinister Severus Snape and perhaps even the awful Muggle cousin Dudley Dursley may be more complicated than they initially seem, that all of them, like Harry, have hidden aspects to their personalities, and that choice — more than talent or predisposition — matters most of all.[324]

Being pure-blood neither makes someone racist nor does it guarantee magical excellence. The Weasleys are among the oldest wizarding families of the country, but all of them stand up for "Muggle" or "Muggle"-born rights. Harry and Hermione are highly talented wizards – but "Mudbloods" nevertheless. Whereas Draco and Neville seem to be less gifted, they come from pure-blood families. In contrast to, for example, Tolkien's *Lord of the Rings* there are no characters

---

[323] "We are who we choose to be", von Lovenberg, "Ende gut, alles gut?" 2007 [my translation].
[324] See Kakutani 2007. Unfortunately, this does not meet the level of characterisation: as pointed out in IV.7 (276) all the characters are rather flat. The last part of the novels only opens up the possibility of more complexity – which is never fulfilled by the author.

that are evil by definition.[325] Everyone has the chance to belong either to the good or the bad side as Dumbledore points out:

> "[It] matters not what someone is born, but what they grow to be! Your Dementor has just destroyed the last remaining member of a pure-blood family as old as any – and see what that man chose to make of his life!" (HP 4, 767-768)

Of this, we find many examples in the novels: the giant Grawp (Hagrid's half-brother) at first seems to be a hopeless case. We believe Hagrid's efforts to teach him speech and manners to be useless. But then we see Grawp saving Harry and Hermione from the centaurs (HP 5, 832-834). Although he is a giant and considered primitive, he can be socialised on a very basic level. Petunia Dursley saves Harry's life granting him asylum in her house. But she bullies him nevertheless and hates magic (see IV.4.G). When Harry saves Dudley from a "Dementor" in *Order of the Phoenix*, she suddenly admits to knowing much more about magical world than she has ever revealed before. She believes Harry and even explains things to her husband Vernon (HP 5, 47-49).

The most important factor in a person's biography is choice: one's own free decision what to become and which side to choose. There are, again, many examples of this to be found in the novels. "Choice" seems to be the keyword to the whole text.

Merope Gaunt gives up and dies, because she lacks the strength to continue her life. Doing so, she decides against her son Tom and gives his life into the hands of strangers. She is therefore contrasted with Harry's mother Lily who sacrifices her life to save Harry. Both mothers have the choice – but whereas Merope decides in favour of the easy way, Lily dies so that her child can live:

> "[Merope] had a choice, didn't she, not like my mother –" "Your mother had a choice, too," said Dumbledore gently. (HP 6, 246)

Just like this, Harry makes a fundamental decision when he first comes to Hogwarts (HP 1, 133-134). By asking the "Sorting Hat" not to place him in Slytherin house he associates with the values of Gryffindor right from the start. Tom Riddle refuses to accept a promising position in the ministry (HP 6, 403) and decides favours instead his own reckless way to immortality. He even chooses his own enemy: Sibyll's prophecy does not name a specific child (HP 5, 924-926). Voldemort singles out Harry by himself. But it is only in killing the Potters and making the Killing Curse backfire from the infant Harry that Voldemort marks them both as irreconcilable opponents:

---

[325] With Tolkien, it is clear that an orc is bad and an elf is destined to be good. There is no ambiguity. See Maar 2005.

"But Harry, never forget that what the prophecy says is only significant because Voldemort made it so. [...] Voldemort singled you out as the person who would be most dangerous to him – and in doing so, he *made* you the person who would be most dangerous to him!" (HP 6, 476)

If Harry did not believe in the prophecy, he could choose "'to turn your back on [it]'" as Dumbledore tells him (HP 6, 479). It is quite appropriate that people start calling him "The Chosen One" after the events of *Order of the Phoenix*. Because Magical World lacks religion (see V.5, 347) there is no transcendency. Who could have "chosen" Harry? In contrast to other fantasy novels,[326] there is no higher being, no transcendent force in *Harry Potter*. The hero is the product of his own decisions, Dumbledore's spiritual guidance and Voldemort's crime. If he has been chosen at all, then it is by the villain himself. If he finally is evenly matched with Voldemort, then it is because of his own deeds. If he is protected against the villain at all, then it is because his mother decided to give her life for her that of her son. So Harry is the end of a long chain of decisions made by individuals – not the messiah chosen by a higher being.[327] Everyone is responsible for his own history, which seems to be the basic message of the novels.[328]

The right decision very often means chosing the difficult and dangerous way: "[Evil] emerges from a failure to make the right choices rather than any inherent personal quality."[329] Man's freedom becomes manifest in his ability to make the right moral decisions: "It is in freedom that human dignity and human identity are found."[330] Choosing the easy way and the way leading to personal gain automatically leads to association with evil.[331] A person without the autonomy of decision, without "options" becomes the puppet of evil. It is a trademark of Voldemort's regime that he does not allow people the right to choose. His will is the law. The difference between having options and being caught in a seemingly hopeless situation is made clear in the following dialogue between Dumbledore and Draco Malfoy:

"So let us discuss your options, Draco."
"My options!" said Malfoy loudly. [...] "I haven't got any options! [...] I've got to do it! He'll kill me! He'll kill my whole family!" [...]

---

[326] In George Lucas' *Star Wars* Luke Skywalker is chosen by "the force"; in Tolkien the council of Elrond makes Frodo the "ringbearer" and in *Matrix* Neo is "The One" and chosen by an oracle.

[327] See Deavel 2002, 53.

[328] Florian Schuller, "Wie Harry Potter in die Katholische Akademie kam und warum er dorthin gehört," *Im Bann des Zauberlehrlings? Zur Faszination von Harry Potter*, ed. Kaspar H. Spinner, Regensburg: Friedrich Pustet, 2001, 60-71, here 65.

[329] Kern 2003, 213.

[330] See Deavel 2002, 53.

[331] See Kulik 2005, 324.

"I can help you, Draco."

"No, you can't," said Malfoy, his wand hand shaking very badly indeed. "Nobody can. He told me to do it or he'll kill me. I've got no choice." (HP 6, 551-553)

Draco has "no choice": if he does not kill Dumbledore he must fear for his family's life. Apparently, there is no way out. But in fact he does have the ability to choose – even in this rather hopeless situation. He could trust in Dumbledore: his family could be protected. But, panicking, the boy does not seriously consider this and evil makes him distrust his teacher.[332] Nevertheless, he lacks the determination to kill Dumbledore. Snape – in accordance with the headmaster – has to intervene.

Thus, in the *Harry Potter* series, man is the product of his own decisions in combination with the experiences he makes.[333] Even Remus Lupin, shunned by others, decides to support the same society that marginalises him. Harry, growing up an outcast from "Muggle" world, takes sides with Dumbledore – although he has not had the chance to experience parental love during his childhood. So, not even such bad experiences predetermine people. It is decisive what he (or she) chooses to make of his (or her) life. Self-determination is what gives man his dignity. Harry finally understands how important this is:

It was, [Harry] thought, the difference between being dragged into the arena to face a battle to the death and walking into the arena with your head held high. Some people, perhaps, would say that there was little to choose between the two ways, but Dumbledore knew – and so do I, thought Harry, with a rush of fierce pride, and so did my parents – that there was all the difference in the world. (HP 6, 479)

This is not about deciding between right or wrong, but between what the individual accepts as his grave responsibility and the easy way.[334]

"Remember, if the time should come when you have to make a choice between what is right, and what is easy, remember what happened to a boy who was good, and kind, and brave [...]." (HP 4, 784)[335]

This is a decision everyone must take. The excuse of social discrimination or a difficult childhood does not apply (unlike in modern legal practice). There

---

[332] See Deavel 2004, 142.
[333] See Deavel 2004, 144.
[334] See Cherrett 2003, 39-40; Granger 2004, 73.
[335] This corresponds with Matthew 7:13-14: "Enter through the narrow gate. For wide is the gate and broad is the road that leads to destruction, and many enter through it. But small is the gate and narrow the road that leads to life, and only a few find it."

are no extenuating circumstances: everyone is unconditionally and without exceptions responsible for what they do.[336] Victory over evil can only be achieved because Harry, again, in the end makes two fundamental decisions. Firstly, he decides against searching for the "Deathly Hallows" and looks for the "Horcruxes" instead.[337] Secondly, he not only gives his life to save his friends, but having died he is willing to return to battle. In the decisive King's Cross scene Dumbledore tells Harry that he has the choice either to return to the world of the living to face and possibly kill Voldemort or that he can "board a train" – probably to the realm of the dead.

> "By returning, you may ensure that fewer souls are maimed, fewer families are torn apart. If that seems a worthy goal, then we say goodbye for the present." (HP 7, 578)

Again, it is the choice between what is right and what is easy – and again, Harry decides in favour of the dangerous, difficult path and returns. It is only these deliberate choices which make victory possible.

In this idea of choice *Harry Potter* differs fundamentally from other fantasy literature. Neither Luke Skywalker (*Star Wars*) nor Frodo Baggins (*Lord of the Rings*) could decide differently – they have been chosen and must fulfill their mission. They are surrounded by people and creatures that *qua* race are either enemies or friends. There are simply no good "Orcs" in Tolkien and his "Elves" are (nearly) always basically good.[338]

This "ethos of responsibility" limits the use of magic: the "Unforgiveable Curses" cannot be used by positive characters.[339] Morality is more complex than simply obeying the rules: "[It's] about the kind of person one is and the sorts of moral good one cherishes, such as human dignity, freedom and life."[340] Magical World is ruled by the "ethos of responsibility" – magic can only be used for achieving something morally good.[341] But this poses yet another problem. The novels leave the decision as to what "good" means to a higher set of values to which the individual subdues himself automatically. This makes room for contradicting interpretations like Grindelwald's "For the Higher Good". The hero of the novels resorts to moral courage.[342] Being a hero in the world of Harry Potter

---

[336] See Kulik 2005, 312; Granger 2004, 70-72.
[337] See Kakutani 2007.
[338] See Maar 2003, 27.
[339] See Bachl 2002, 119.
[340] Baggett 2004, 166.
[341] Gottfried Bachl, "Gefährliche Magie? Religiöse Parabel? Gute Unterhaltung," *Im Bann des Zauberlehrlings? Zur Faszination von Harry Potter*, ed. Kaspar H. Spinner, Regensburg: Friedrich Pustet, 2001, 42-59, 50.
[342] See Skulnick, Goodman 2003, 264.

does not mean the ability to curse your opponents better than others do, but it consists of the ability to make the right decisions in moral terms.[343] With this emphasis on the responsibility of the individual and the longing for moral unambiguousness, Harry Potter is "the perfect hero for the late 1990s, a time when readers are looking for reassurance and a certain nannyish moral certainty."[344] In *Harry Potter* we see a murderous, fundamentalist terror network fighting the imperfect, but liberal system of Magical World.[345] Rowling presents a marvellously old-fashioned set of values of which the basis is: "Ziehe eigene Urteilskraft dem Konformismus vor! Respektiere, was dir anders und fremd erscheint! Duck dich nicht weg, wenn Ungerechtigkeiten geschehen!"[346] This makes *Harry Potter* fit very well into the overall spirit of the Western world after the breakdown of the Soviet Union, the rise of Islamist terrorism and 9/11. This chronological coincidence between real events and message might be one, if not *the* decisive factor behind the worldwide fascination *Harry Potter* has inspired.

V.6.B. Happy Ending: A Multi-ethnic Democracy?

Having dealt with the deficiency of the very last *Potter* chapter "Nineteen Years Later" (HP 7, 603-607) as far as plot-making is concerned, I now want to make a few remarks on the end of the series in the context of ideological content. Rowling obviously intends the last chapter to be a complete happy ending. Wounds have healed, conflicts have been solved and society seems to be reconciled after what must be deemed a civil war. Everything is back in order, the "Sorting Hat" – inspite of it having been burnt by Voldemort – again sorts the Hogwarts newcomers every year into their corresponding houses, lovers have been happily united and even Draco Malfoy cannot avoid having to greet Harry. A general atmosphere of harmony seems to be in the air when Harry tells his son that he does not care what house he is sorted into (HP 7, 607). But... is this down-the-line happy ending really convincing?

In fact, Rowling's happy ending is a rather disappointing delusion. The fact that children are already concerned about their house before entering Hogwarts makes clear that general reconciliation has not taken place. When Draco and his son Scorpio turn away from Harry and his family we realise they have not really come to terms with each other. When Hermione and Ron quarrel

---

[343] See Kern 2003, 86, 157.
[344] "Trust your own judgement! Respect strangers! Don't turn your back on injustice!" Terence Blacker "Why does everyone like Harry Potter? He is the perfect hero for readers looking for reassurance and a nannyish moral certainty," *Independent* 13 July 1999, 4 [my translation].
[345] See von Becker 2005.
[346] See Misik 2005.

about how to drive a "Muggle" car we are reminded of the stereotypical marriage cliché of the couple fighting over the right driving style.

Rowling does not tell us anything of the careers the four have chosen. Has Harry succeeded in becoming an "Auror"? What has happened to ingenious Hermione? Is she a stay-at-home-mother – like all the positive role models in Magical World she has had– or has she, with all her talent, become a successful working woman? By disposing of the only characters who might have raised questions (outcasts Tonks and Lupin) Rowling spares herself the answer to what might have become of them and their son. So at second glance we realise that Rowling has found a rather insipid ending to her saga. She bows to the banality of everyday life and to the conventional "happily ever after" of the fairy tale. It is the average middle-class bourgeois family that is the true victor over Voldemort.[347] As Thomas Steinfeld says: "Unglücklich ist, wer über ein solches Ende Glück verspürt."[348]

---

[347] See Steinfeld 2007.

[348] "Unhappy is he who considers such an ending happy", Steinfeld 2007 [my translation].

VI. "Harry Potter" in the Context of Fantasy Literature

VI.1 Defining the Fantastic

Until the '70s fantastic literature was often considered trivial and not worthy of scientific analysis.[1] Today, fantastic literature is a highly popular genre uniting a multitude of forms like the heroic epic (as in *Lord of the Rings*), science fiction (the "Dungeons and Dragons" series) or horror movies. I will concentrate on the sub-genres relevant for *Harry Potter* and on European variants of fantasy leaving aside phenomena such as South American *realismo mágico*.

So what is fantasy? Peter Hunt tries to define a basis for all further definition: "[Generally] fantasy is defined as text which portrays some obvious deviance from 'consensus reality'; whatever that could possibly be – usually a change in physical laws."[2] Usually, fantasy brings together two antagonistic levels of reality, or worlds: one corresponds with the readers' reality, the other is an anti-empiric world. These two worlds meet abruptly and the protagonist or reflector[3] cannot tell if what he experiences is real or an illusion. This uncertainty causes fear.[4]

In his *Introduction à la littérature fantastique* (1970), the Bulgarian philosopher Tzvetan Todorov produced a theory of the fantastic that no one has been able to convincingly refute to this day. For Todorov, the fantastic lies at the edges of the uncanny and the marvellous.[5] The most decisive criterion which classifies a text as fantastic is the "uncertainty" that suddenly breaks in on the real world and gives rise to the inexplicable.[6] At the end of most stories, the characters and the readers are in the position to sort out whether the events are rationally explicable or not. If a rational explanation can be found for the events, the story belongs to the uncanny. If the events remain inexplicable, however,

---

[1] See Harrison 2000, 1. See Renate Schmalenbach, *Topographie des Grauens: Zur Gestaltung literarischer Räume in unheimlich-phantastischen Erzählungen*, Essen: Die Blaue Eule, 2003, 27.

[2] See Hunt 2001, 271.

[3] See Stephan Berg. *Schlimme Zeiten, böse Räume: Zeit- und Raumstrukturen in der phanstastischen Literatur des 20. Jahrhunderts*, Stuttgart: Metzler, 1991, 5-8. See Louis Vax, "Die Phantastik," *Phaicon 1. Almanach der phantastischen Literatur, ed. Rein A. Zondergeld*, Frankfurt am Main: Insel, 1974, 11-43, 17.

[4] See Roger Caillois, "Das Bild des Phantastischen. Vom Märchen bis zur Science Fiction," *Phaicon 1. Almanach der phantastischen Literatur,* ed. Rein A. Zondergeld, Frankfurt am Main: Insel, 1974, 44-91, here 56; Vax 1974, 21.

[5] See Vax 1974, 40.

[6] See Tzvetan Todorov, *Einführung in die fantastische Literatur*, Munich: Carl Hanser, 1971, 26. In other places he formulates it explicitly: "The uncertainty of the reader is thus the first condition of the fantastic", Todorov 1972, 31.

then the text belongs to the marvellous.[7] Since almost all texts end by clarifying doubts, Todorov maintains that one seldom finds purely fantastic texts which carry doubt through to the end.[8] Stanislaw Lem, however, argues that Todorov's theory is too superficial and indeed harmful.[9] His core critical argument is that the Todorovian approach is too narrow – only a few texts of the genre actually meet the uncertainty criterion. Nevertheless, the interpretative tools Tzvetan Todorov provides remain unrivalled – despite the critiques – and that is why they will be the basis of the following analysis.

A text is fantastic when the events it relates contradict the common consensus of what is "real".[10] The illogical and inexplicable defy logic.[11] Nevertheless, fantasy does have laws of its own and usually is in itself logical. Fantasy worlds normally have their own rationality and not everything is possible.[12]

The genre itself is highly diverse, which is why Colin Manlove defines six variants:[13]

- secondary world fantasy
- metaphysical fantasy
- emotive fantasy
- comic fantasy
- subversive fantasy
- children's fantasy

Analysing *Harry Potter*, most of them are irrelevant, which is why I am going to concentrate on the forms related to Rowling's novels, i.e. secondary world, comic and children's fantasy. Secondary world fantasy introduces the reader to worlds not related to his own reality. These are "full of pain, tedium, confinements of spirit, or fear";[14] the protagonist has to commit heroic deeds. J.R.R. Tolkien said that the author of such texts was a "sub-creator" creating whole worlds with their own logic and rules.[15]

---

[7] See Todorov 1972, 31.
[8] See Todorov 1972, 42.
[9] See Stanislaw Lem, "Tzvetan Todorovs Theorie des Phantastischen," *Phaicon 1. Almanach der phantastischen Literatur*, ed. Rein A. Zondergeld, Frankfurt am Main: Insel, 1974, 92-120, here 120.
[10] See Hume 1984, 21; O'Keefe 2003, 22.
[11] See Schwarz 2001, 21, 24-25, 309.
[12] See O'Keefe 2003, 18.
[13] See Colin Manlove, *The Fantasy Literature of England*, London: Macmillan Press, 1999, 4.
[14] See Manlove 1999, 37.
[15] See Manlove 1999, 3-4; see John Ronald Reuel Tolkien, "On Fairy-Stories," [1939], John Ronald Reuel Tolkien, *The Monsters & the Critics and Other Essays*, ed. Christopher Tolkien, London: HarperCollins, 1997, 109-161, here 122.

What really happens is that the story-maker proves a successful "sub-creator". He makes a Secondary World which your mind can enter. Inside it, what he relates is "true": it accords with the laws of that world. You therefore believe it, while you are, as it were, inside.[16]

These secondary worlds are "projections of the Weltanschauung, of the particular authors' models of the world."[17] This kind of fantasy is very old. Medieval texts like *Beowulf* or *Sir Gawain and the Green Knight* and later classics like *A Midsummer Night's Dream*, *Gulliver's Travels* or Bunyan's *Pilgrim's Progress* belong to it. In Romantic literature secondary world fantasy reached its climax caused by "the desire, awakened often by repugnance at over-rapid industrialization, to create an alternative reality."[18] "Arts and Crafts" founder William Morris and his works *The Well at the World's End* and *The Water of the Wondrous Isles* highly influenced the genre.[19] Today this kind of fantasy produces huge international successes like *Star Wars*, *The Lord of the Rings* or *Matrix*.

Comic fantasy, as for example in the works of Douglas Adams and Terry Pratchett, parodies the readers' world.[20] It "deals with the extreme of fantasy, the impossible: it takes what we know cannot exist or hold together, and makes it do so – just."[21] Very often its comical aspects result from bringing together the conventions of secondary world fantasy with everyday life[22] or from making the fantastic world an exaggerated version of reality and, thus, making fun of it.[23] Puns, jokes and illogical logic are major means of entertaining the reader.[24]

Usually, one work unites various sub-genres.[25] In particular, fantasy written for children tends to combine elements of comic, emotive and secondary world fantasy. Being intended for children, these texts are often very successful

---

16 Tolkien [1939] 1997, 132.
17 Maria Nikolajeva, *The Magic Code: The use of magical patterns in fantasy for children*, Göteborg: Almqvist & Wiksell, 1988, 25. Nikolajeva distinguishes various forms of fantastic worlds according to a different system than Manlove's: the *closed world* is "a self-contained secondary world without any contact with the primary world (= high fantasy)", the "open world" is "a secondary world that has contact of some kind, and both primary and secondary worlds are present in the text, but intrudes on the primary world in some way (= low fantasy)" (Nikolajeva 1988, 36). According to this categorization, *Harry Potter* would be an "open world".
18 Tolkien [1939] 1997, 37.
19 Tolkien [1939] 1997, 43.
20 Tolkien [1939] 1997, 5.
21 Tolkien [1939] 1997, 114.
22 Tolkien [1939] 1997, 115.
23 Tolkien [1939] 1997, 118.
24 Tolkien [1939] 1997, 123.
25 Tolkien [1939] 1997, 6.

with adults, as well.[26] Other forms of fantasy are fairy tales and myth. Bruno Bettelheim says of myth:

> [The] dominant feeling a myth conveys is: this is absolutely unique; it could not have happened to any other person, or in any other setting; such events are grandiose, awe-inspiring, and could not possibly happen to an ordinary mortal like you or me.[27]

Whereas myth tells us about a very specific character struggling to fulfil a task given to him, fairy tales deal with everyday characters in a non-specified society or space.[28] They always have a happy ending and "both delight and instruct",[29] while myth normally has a tragic ending.[30] Fairy tales are "symbols of psychological happenings or problems"[31] and are written in a simple everyday style.[32] Myth likewise deals with its hero's inner conflicts, but it does so "in a majestic way; it carries spiritual force; and the divine is present and is experienced in the form of superhuman heroes who make constant demands on mere mortals."[33] In a fairy tale the reader simply accepts the supernatural elements, because the story is clearly set in another dimension of reality.[34] The fairy tale is populated by wondrous creatures and is defined by supernatural, magical events. Nothing is left unresolved, in Todorov's sense.[35]

Fantastic literature is always reproached with the claim that it serves the wish to flee from reality (escapism).[36] Yet this conception does not reach far enough: many texts comment on the reader's lived reality, precisely within the fantastic elements at work; many of them discuss philosophical questions, e.g. the works of the science fiction author Isaac Asimov.[37] A second type of criticism seeks to discredit the genre as a whole as unworthy of adult reading. Fantastic literature is, supposedly, only interesting for children and adolescents, while adults have outgrown the intellectual phase in which they still have a feel-

---

[26] Tolkien [1939] 1997, 6.
[27] See Bruno Bettelheim, *The Uses of Enchantment: The Meaning and Importance of Fairy Tales*, Middlesex: Penguin Books, 1978, 36-37.
[28] See Kulik 2005, 48.
[29] See Bettelheim 1978, 53.
[30] See Bettelheim 1978, 37, 40; Caillois 1974, 46.
[31] Caillois 1974, 155.
[32] See Clive Staples Lewis, "On three Ways of Writing for Children," [1966], *Essay Collection and Other Short Pieces,* ed. Lesley Walsmely, New York, London: Harper Collins, 2000, 505-514, here 508.
[33] Lewis [1966] 2000, 26.
[34] See Vax 1974, 12.
[35] See Kulik, 48.
[36] See Berg 1991, 28; Schwarz 2001, 20.
[37] See Berg 1991, 30.

ing for the unreal. When Antonia Byatt seeks to prove the growing infantilism of the adult world in light of the sky-rocketing popularity of *Harry Potter*,[38] she resorts to the common critical clichés which are used against the genre in general.[39] To counter these arguments, there are indeed many fantasy texts for children, but most of them have a subtext, an "adult code" (see VII.1.A, 419) which only the adult reader can decode and are therefore "addressed doubly". J.R.R. Tolkien also protests on behalf of his fellow authors and himself against the criticism to the utmost degree: he sees fantastic literature as a natural human need with rationality as its basis.[40] In the following section I will examine the sub-genres of fantastic literature to which *Harry Potter* belongs.

VI.1.A. Functions of the Fantastic

J.R.R. Tolkien was the first to offer an interpretation of fantastic elements in his ground-breaking and uncontested lecture, "The Monsters and the Critics":

> I would suggest, then, that the monsters are not an inexplicable blunder of taste; they are essential, fundamentally allied to the underlying ideas of the poem, which give it its lofty tone and high seriousness.[41]

The magical is for him always clearly related to the content of the texts and its meaning is never its own end. For Kathryn Hume on the other hand, magical elements replace e.g. familiar plots:

> [Magic and fantasy] replace common functions (killing, travelling, and learning a language) with a fantastic version of the same process, but the function remains the same. Such substitutions can be simple or complex, but they rarely present fundamental alterations in assumption or perspective.[42]

She calls this function "substitution". Fantastic elements can thus be used as caricatures of facts well known to the reader, as is the case in the novels of Douglas Adams or Terry Pratchett.[43]

---

38 See Byatt, 2003.
39 See Foote 1999, 204.
40 Tolkien [1939] 1997, 144.
41 John Ronald Reuel Tolkien, "Beowulf: The Monsters and the Critics," [1936], *The Monsters & the Critics and Other Essays,* ed. Christopher Tolkien, London: HarperCollins, 1997, 5-48, 19.
42 See Hume 1984, 165.
43 Peter Hunt explains Pratchett as a "vacuum-cleaner, hoovering up whole genres and sub-genres of fantasy and remaking them with a humour which is by terms scathing and ironic, but fundamentally optimistic", Hunt 2001, 110.

Yet what functions do fantastic texts have for the reader? Kathryn Hume sees them above all as expression of the reader's longing for escape. In his given reality, the reader feels like a "crippled horse", his wish for power and justice can only be satisfied in the pseudo-myth of fantastic literature.[44] For J.R.R. Tolkien, fantastic texts serve "certain primordial human desires."[45] Fantastic texts are primarily relevant for adults and not children:

> But fairy-stories offer also, in a peculiar degree or mode, these things: Fantasy, Recovery, Escape, Consolation, all things of which children have, as a rule, less need than older people.[46]

Recovery, escape and consolation – for Tolkien, these are the most important functions of fantastic literature. Kathryn Hume also insists that escapism is not a negative term to use.

> The desire evident at the literal level of many escapist stories may seem silly – success-and-conquest kingship, elite fellowship, or communication with ghosts – but those to whom they seem silly should ponder the reasons for the popularity of such fantasies. They point to the lack of fulfilling and satisfying values in everyday life. The democratic and bourgeois ideal leaves many desires unfulfilled, and [...] fantasy is [...] a form of subversion and protest.[47]

The heroism of the fantasy world constructs a contrast to dissatisfying, trivial reality.[48] Fantastic literature offers the reader a system of thinking that makes sense to him and which he lacks in the real world,[49] as Deborah O'Keefe emphasises:

> [Fantasy] today helps and delights readers not just by strengthening their poor small selves but by offering possible structures for the unstructurable stuff outside the self.[50]

In light of the conflicting value systems, terrorism and environmental destruction in contemporary life, transporting the action into a fantastic world pro-

---

[44] See Hume 1984, 66-68.
[45] See Tolkien [1939] 1997, 116.
[46] See Tolkien [1939] 1997, 138.
[47] See Hume 1984, 81. Callois depicts the same circumstance when he states: "[Fantastic texts] express the tension between what people can do and what they would like to do: flying in the skies or reaching the stars. The conflict between what he knows and what it is forbidden for him to know", see Callois 1974, 81.
[48] See Hume 1964, 92.
[49] See Hume 1984, 196.
[50] See O'Keefe 2003, 15-16.

vides readers with the opportunity to deal with topics that affect them in an imaginary yet nevertheless profound manner. O'Keefe sees the triumph of the genre here.[51] The use of fantastic elements can contribute to illustrating ethical, moral and religious questions, unhampered by any concrete context.[52] Less than offering a chance to escape, reading fantastic texts offers people a kind of freedom to interpret the world in an open and coherent way.[53] For this reason Tolkien claims such texts are a higher category of art:

> That the images are of things not in the primary world (if that indeed is possible) is a virtue not a vice. Fantasy (in this sense) is, I think, not a lower but a higher form of Art, indeed the most nearly pure form, and so (when achieved) the most potent.[54]

Like no other genre, fantastic material tends to have regular adept-meetings and fan club congregations. We can see this in the enormous number of fan clubs dedicated to *Harry Potter, Lord of the Rings, Star Wars* or *Star Trek*, as well as the numerous "conventions" at which members appear in appropriate costumed attire.[55]

Yet is the escapist function the reason for the huge success of the genre? In her work on *The Return of the Myth*, Karoline Furch identifies the factors which make the genre successful.[56] They are on one hand the "timeless good story", the stable value system, the representation of the eternal battle of good against evil; and on the other hand, the genre captures the human longing for love, heroism and hope. The myth contains political, religious and emotional themes. The acting figures are believable people confronted with real conflict situations. A central heroic character incarnates stability, wholeness and greatness – such a figure has timeless audience appeal. In the world depicted in myth, there is a clear division of Good and Evil, everyone has his place, his meaningful task and above all, a goal in life he can strive for. This absence of (moral) ambiguity satisfies the obvious need for security and a legitimate concept of values. Furthermore, the magical and the supernatural are an ever more attractive counter-model to a world qualified by science, reason and economic forces. It is certainly not to be dismissed that the large success of the genre, with *Harry Potter, Lord of the Rings,*

---

[51]   See O'Keefe 2003, 16.
[52]   See Hunt 2001, 270.
[53]   See O'Keefe 2003, 11.
[54]   See Tolkien [1939] 1997, 139.
[55]   See Hume 1984, 67.
[56]   See Karoline Furch, *Die Wiederkehr des Mythos: Zur Renaissance der Artus-Mythen in der modernen Fantasy-Literatur*, Wetzlar: Förderkreis Phantastik in Wetzlar, 1998, 102-111.

Star Wars and many others – extending to role-playing and computer games – is rooted in our Western society's need for order and clarity.

VI.1.B. Plot and Narrative Structure

The reader of fantasy literature is a "genre reader" and knows the genre thoroughly. This gives the author the opportunity to play with expectations – either by satisfying them or precisely the reverse.[57] The narrative style stretches from the experimental to the personal narrative situation to the authorial narrator.[58] The most common case, however, seems to be the personal or authorial narrative situation.[59] As follows, Deborah O'Keefe summarizes the basic plot of many fantasy texts:

> The hero as a child, often growing up in ignorance of his or her real power and identity. The hero being trained and tested, often, as a youth, making some bad choice out of impatience or pride. The hero on a quest, one of great importance to the community, often a war against evil, helpers appearing, to share the task – animals, wise mentors, comrades, magic objects. And the hero returning home, usually successful but at a cost – a sacrifice, a loss of normal life, a loss of special powers.[60]

The stages of the plot-outline are thereby always the same:[61]

1. hero in his normal everyday world
2. confrontation with a physically and spiritually challenging task, upon which depends the well-being of his community
3. hero hesitates and initially does not want to accept his role
4. preparation of the hero for his confrontation with the unknown
5. leaving the familiar environment and stepping over the threshold to the fantastic world
6. passing diverse tests, coming in contact with helpers, adversaries and antagonists
7. passing ever more arduous tests
8. confrontation with the most important enemies: battle of life and death
9. victory and reward of the hero in wisdom and life experience

---

[57] See Schwarz 2001, 333-334. I should here like to suggest why exactly *Harry Potter* seems so "original": the author keeps to the conventions of the genre yet combines the clichés of various genres together in an innovative way. The reader is constantly surprised by the developments because he does not know with which genre-background he ought to be reading the texts. See also Hume 1984, 83.
[58] See O'Keefe 2003, 40-43.
[59] See Schwarz 2001, 308.
[60] See O'Keefe 2003, 167.
[61] See Wallmann 2000, 96-97.

10. hero's planned return to the normal outside world
11. epiphany and transformation of the hero
12. hero's return to his outside world, where, equipped with his new strength and power, he can serve the good of the community

This narrative pattern is designated as a quest (search for meaning) and can be found in all heroic epics and sagas – in the Arthurian Saga as in *Lord of the Rings, Star Wars* and *Harry Potter*. An important aspect is that the fairy-tale texts mostly have a happy ending, while the myth tends to have a tragic ending. In fairy tales the dominant moral is: "the good are rewarded, the bad are punished [...]."[62]Indeed, for Tolkien, this is the most important quality of fantastic texts.[63]

Fantastic literature, moreover, makes use of continually recurring motifs. Below are the classic appearances:
– the hero's crossing over through a door or gate into a parallel world[64]
– the hero's initiation and coming of age in the course of the action[65]
– the appearance of a double[66]
– the appearance of ghosts or revenants, esp. the dead who come back to life[67]
– people in extreme states of consciousness, madness loss of reality[68]
– demonisation of woman as beautiful seductress[69]
– vampirism[70]
– children (often possessed or paranormal) in conflict with adults[71]

---

[62] See Lurie 2003, 176.
[63] "Far more important is the Consolation of the Happy Ending. Almost I would venture to assert that all complete fairy-stories must have it. [...] The consolation of fairy-stories, the joy of the happy ending: or more correctly of the good catastrophe, the sudden joyous 'turn' (for there is no true end to a fairytale): this joy, which is one of the things which fairy-stories can produce supremely well, is not essentially 'escapist', nor 'fugitive'." (Tolkien [1939] 1997, 153).
[64] See K. V. Bailey and Andy Sawyer "The Janus Perspective: Science Fiction and the Young Adult Reader in Britain," *Young Adult Science Fiction*, ed. C. W. III. Sullivan, Westport: Greenwood Press, 1999, 55-71, here 58.
[65] See Bailey, Sawyer 1999, 59.
[66] See Schwarz 2001, 316-317; Todorov 1972, 129.
[67] See Caillois 1974, 63-66; Schwarz 2001, 319.
[68] See Schwarz 2001, 321.
[69] See Schwarz 2001, 23-24.
[70] See Schwarz 2001, 325; Caillois 1974, 63-66; Vax 1974, 33-34.
[71] See George Slusser. "The Forever Child: 'Ender's Game' and the Mythic Universe of Science Fiction," *Nursery Realms: Chilrdren in the Worlds of Science Fiction, Fantasy*

- metamorphoses of humans into animals and vice-versa, as well as transformation of things, e.g., the werewolf motif[72]
- existence of supernatural entities and powers[73]
- imaginary causality – paranormal logic and change effects provide the foundation for rationally incomprehensible connections[74]
- sadism, death, cruelty, necrophilia[75]
- homosexuality[76]
- disembodied body-parts (usually eyes and brain) acting autonomously[77]
- disruption in identity[78]
- play of the visible and invisible[79]
- regression and return to the past, e.g. in deserted gardens, houses and antique shops[80]
- pact with the devil[81]
- ghost condemned to wild wandering ("wild hunt")[82]
- living statues, dolls, weapons or automatons[83]
- time stops or repeats itself[84]

The motif of the hidden origin plays a decisive role, especially in fantasy literature for children: at a certain stage of their development, children dream that they do not descend from their own parents, whom they perceive at this period as threatening authority-figures, but in reality from others. The real, i.e. fictional, origin is commonly one of higher prestige.[85]

In his successful fight against evil, the hero puts his trust in logic and moral integrity – while the villain represents the irrational and the corrupt. The

and Horror, eds. Gary Westfahl, George Slusser, Athens: University of Georgia Press, 1999, 73-90, here 74-75.

[72] See Todorov 1972, 98; Vax 1974, 31-32.
[73] See Todorov 1972, 99.
[74] See Todorov 1972, 99; Vax 1974, 38-40.
[75] See Todorov 1972, 121-122.
[76] See Todorov 1972, 115-119.
[77] See Vax 1974, 34.
[78] See Vax 1974, 35-36; Caillois 1974, 63-66.
[79] See Vax 1974, 37-38.
[80] See Vax 1974, 40-41. Vax writes of the antiquities dealer: "He does not only live in the present, but also, in a certain sense, in the decayed past of the old things he buys and sells. He is always old, his shop is deep, dark and dusty." It is noteworthy that in *Harry Potter* we can find, with Borgin's and Burke's, precisely this kind of antiques dealer.
[81] See Caillois 1974, 63-66.
[82] See Caillois 1974, 63-66.
[83] See Caillois 1974, 63-66.
[84] See Caillois 1974, 63-66.
[85] See Bettelheim 1978, 105.

fantasy-realms are not ideal worlds – the "ancient pattern of birth, life, and death" counts here too, death is unavoidable.[86]

Stefan Berg and Ellen Schwarz have analysed time structure for the Gothic Novel. The moment that sets the plot in motion is usually located in the long-ago past, i.e. clearly before the point of attack.[87] The main plot elucidates the events lying before the point of attack – in the sense of the detective novel, that is, the mystery plot (see II.1.B, 31).[88]

In the following, I am going to show that many elements of the narrative and plot structure termed here can be found in the *Harry Potter* novels. The texts belong to the categories characteristic of fantastic literature and demonstrate many similarities with the Gothic Novel.

VI.1.C. Character Constellation

Most of the studies pertaining to character constellations refer to the Gothic Novel and its fixed stock of characters. The constellation consists of the villain-hero, who is the actual catalyst of the plot, the innocent hero-couple und a few minor characters.[89] In her work *Untersuchung zu Parallelen zwischen "roman policier", "conte fantastique" und Gothic Novel*, Ellen Schwarz identifies four character types.

1. the often suffering hero, who goes out in order to seek or to find something
2. his antagonist, the evil-doer
3. his helper, who assists him in completing his tasks and liquidating the villains, and in particular, saves him when he is in dire straits
4. the false hero who also finds himself on a quest, but with unjust claims and who is in the end degenerate

The characters are often from the upper classes, are stereotyped and fall into a clearly positive-negative scheme, in which characters from humble social origins are usually positive figures.[90] Ellen Schwarz designates the evil-doer as the central figure of the Gothic Novel: his avarice, greed and a will to destruction incarnate the shadow side of human existence.[91]

The heroes represent the individualised battle of human beings for power and wisdom, recognition and introspection, honour and greatness.[92] The fate of

---

[86]   See Westfahl, Slusser 1999, 4.
[87]   See Berg 1991, 44-46; Schmalenbach 2003, 167.
[88]   See Schwarz 2001, 37.
[89]   See Berg 1991, 43-44; Schwarz 2001, 62.
[90]   See Schwarz 2001, 62-66.
[91]   See Schwarz 2001, 331.
[92]   See Pharr 2004, 54.

their world depends on them; they are the chosen ones and the bearers of hope for their society. It is noteworthy that in the successful fantasy film epics of the past 15 years, such as *Lord of the Rings*, the *Matrix*-trilogy and the *Star Wars* saga the "chosen ones" of the narrative do not only successfully complete their mission, they must also go through a painful growing process learning to accept their heroic role.[93] The heroes of pure fairy tale behave quite differently, for they are not confronted with inner conflicts or changes.[94] In fairy tales there are only the selflessly good or the selfishly evil,[95] who are respectively rewarded or punished at the end of the story for their good or bad deeds.[96] The classic fairy-tale hero is often the youngest child of the family or his origins are unknown; he is simple, naive and helpless.[97] Before he goes off on his adventure, he experiences a period of isolation or material hardship.[98]

Women play a rather secondary role in fantastic literature. Only since the '60s have women been given more and bigger roles.[99] Two types come across the most obviously: the "girl supergenius", who is clever and excellent in one particular area. The other is the "ordinary girl", who usually appears as the hero's younger sister or as a minor character, contributing healthy common sense to the group although she has no particular genius for the resolution of the action. In general, girls are frequently clever, but their true strengths lie in intuition and feeling.[100] Girls are moreover frequently represented as silly or giggling figures – as opposed to the male characters, they do not grasp the seriousness of their position and laugh insouciantly even in the most dramatic situations.[101]

The relationship between the sex of the author and the way the hero is characterised is interesting. As Maria Nikolajeva demonstrated, male authors often write about female villains, while female authors mostly choose weak men for their heroes.[102] Women authors often have their heroes express an idealised faith in the morally spotless natural mother yet must suffer at the hands of an evil, jealous step-mother. Bruno Bettelheim interprets this as a manifestation of the feminine Oedipus fantasty.[103]

---

[93] See Jan Distelmeyer, "Marke, Nachricht, Versprechen," *taz* 18 May 2005, 15.
[94] See Bettelheim 1978, 9.
[95] See Bettelheim 1978, 74.
[96] See Bettelheim 1978, 144.
[97] See Bettelheim 1978, 103; Nikolajeva 2002, 172.
[98] See Bettelheim 1978, 11.
[99] See Karen Sands and Marietta Frank, eds., *Back in the Spaceship Again: Juvenile Science Fiction Series Since 1945*, Westport: Greenwood Press, 1999, 38.
[100] See Sands, Frank 1999, 40-43.
[101] See Schwarz 2001, 53.
[102] See Nikolajeva 1996, 76.
[103] See Bettelheim 1978, 114.

Children in fantastic literature are often ambivalent characters: they are either mutants or heroic defenders of humankind. They possess paranormal qualities, are chosen or endowed with special abilities which distinguish them from other characters.[104] They are usually assisted by powerful wizards or magic objects.[105]

This mixture of danger and rescue, which child-figures in fantastic literature personify, gives expression to the ambivalent attitude towards children in Europe's intellectual history:[106] on one hand, in the Romantic tradition, children are innocent, natural and perfect creatures (e.g. William Blake or Jean-Jacques Rousseau), on the other hand, they are incomplete adults who require draconian measures to be redeemed from their sinful primitive condition.

VI.1.D. Structure of Space

Bipolarity is a principal element of the spatial structure of fantastic texts:[107] there are mostly two divisions of space set antagonistically against each other. Renate Schmalenbach elucidates the features of spatial representation in fantastic literature:[108]

- stark spatial contrasts or the collapse of spatial contrasts
- space's purpose incongruous with its function
- isolating details out of their actual contexts
- giving spatial reality a negative past
- anthropomorphism of the space
- preconceived expectations of spaces expressed in the form of rumours or warnings

The transformation of spaces into what is physically impossible is, according to Todorov,[109] typical of the depiction of space in fantastic texts: either the setting is far too large, far too magnificent or then far too small – they are not rationally possible. Throughout the action, the hero moves either circularly or linearly in the space represented.[110] One can find, moreover, a canon of spatial motifs. Ellen Schwarz identifies the following relevant themes: stormy

---

[104] See Gary Westfahl, "Return to Innocence," *Nursery Realms: Children in the Worlds of Science Fiction, Fantasy and Horror,* eds., Gary Westfahl & George Slusser, Athens: University of Georgia Press, 1999, IX-XIII, here XI.
[105] See Nikolajeva 2002, 221.
[106] See Westfahl 1999, X.
[107] See Berg 1991, 258.
[108] See Schmalenbach 2003, 298.
[109] See Todorov 1972, 108.
[110] Nikolajeva 1988, 42. As already shown, there is a circular journey in *Harry Potter.* (see III.6, 142).

weather, sudden unfamiliar noises, darkness, isolation, fog and illusions.[111] Renate Schmalenbach also adds: "anxiety", "awful silence", "subterranean regions", "cavern", "labyrinth", "darkness", "terror", "horror" and "suggestion".[112] There is, in addition, an underlying schema to the spatial structure that determines the spatial properties of good and evil respectively: while black and red, green and silver often indicate evil, gold and brightness usually stand for the good.[113] Landscapes associated with evil are frequently subject to the semantic field of [cold] and [empty] respectively.[114] In regard to the genre, the authors name several other typical spatial motifs:[115]

- trap door
- labyrinths
- living portraits or statues
- unidentified visual or acoustic phenomena
- contrasts (bright-dark, above-below, inner-outer, near-far)
- doors that open and close on their own
- winding stairs
- moonlight
- oppressive silence
- ruins
- "locked-room mystery" (something disappears from a hermetically sealed space)
- mysterious, impenetrable spaces
- closed, remote settings (castles, cloisters, ruins, manor-houses)

In the following I am going to examine which of these spatial motifs are also used in *Harry Potter* and what they say about the classification of the novels within fantastic literature.

VI.1.E. Value Systems

In light of the diversity of fantastic literature, it is very difficult to define an underlying value system within a multitude of texts. Fantasy literature generally is anti-modern, irrational, nostalgic and green.[116] The positive schema dominating fantastic literature in recent years "might well be called the Dream

---

[111] See Schwarz 2001, 312-314.
[112] See Schmalenbach 2003, 154.
[113] See Kulik 2005, 57, 339, 342.
[114] See Kulik 2005, 57.
[115] See Taubenböck 2002, 274-275; Schmalenbach 2003, 154-165; Schwarz 2001, 60, 327-328.
[116] See Jenny 2007.

of Democracy,"[117] and therefore represents a social system which orients itself towards Western society and its values of equality and freedom. In his *taz* review of *Star Wars – Episode III*, Jan Distelmeyer concludes: "[the] new [*Star Wars*] movies [try] to extend the question of good and evil to the scope of the subject of democracy".[118] Thus he identifies the change from the heroic team to the chosen single combatant.[119] The individual risks his life bravely and dauntlessly – much as in the Arthurian myth – to defend his values and the lives of his friends.[120] The world is unambiguously divided into good and evil powers, every human being has his place between the two poles and is thus given a clear orientation for his goals for his future life. Crossing sides from one set of values to the other – i.e. switching sides – is the exception, not the rule.[121]

Friendship and reason are often the secret to the success of positive powers; a hero who negotiates and thinks logically, and who can also rely on his friends, has more chances of succeeding than the enemy side. The good distinguishes itself by love, loyalty and courage, by morality, strength of will and intellectual superiority.[122] It overcomes selfishness and displays positive emotions such as joy, sympathy and devotion.[123] The positive characters are equipped with moral integrity and purity; they are brave and represent social warmth. The characters classified here tend towards immaterial values and often stand for feudal or only partly democratic systems whose representatives are legitimized by higher powers.[124] Texts of the "secondary fantasy world" (see VI.1, 376) are often lacking in a democratic point of view and moreover propagate misogynist and occasionally racist positions.[125] The good does not have to be infinitely good – it can also demonstrate negative behaviour. Positive figures can thus even feel hate and act brutally.[126] Finally, the forces of good usually triumph over evil – even though victory is often only temporary or is already threatened in the moment it is achieved. The good lives in harmony with nature and tries to resolve conflict through peaceful measures.[127]

Snobbery and prejudice are the pitfalls of evil and whoever judges from appearances runs the risk of making a fatal mistake.[128] Evil is proud, power-

---

[117] Wallmann 2000, 98. Wallmann observes this above all in science fiction.
[118] Distelmeyer 2005.
[119] Distelmeyer 2005.
[120] See Furch 1998, 107.
[121] See Kulik 2005, 345.
[122] See Kulik 2005, 59.
[123] See Kulik 2005, 335.
[124] See Kulik 2005, 335-337.
[125] See Hunt 2001, 271.
[126] See Kulik 2005, 334, 340.
[127] See Kulik 2005, 343-344.
[128] See Frank Sands, 1999, 2. The authors make their claims mostly in reference to the novels of Isaac Asimov.

hungry and uses unfair, mostly magical means to reach its goal.[129] It strives for illegitimate unilateral power and an absolute rule, a dependent justice system, non-transparent decisions and unfair legal methods. It is cruel, stupid and cowardly. The commensurate evil characters are proud, envious of other characters, lie, cheat and lead people astray. Negative characters strive for possessions and material goods as well as for ecological destruction; their actions are contrary to nature. It can either appear personified in a character or in the form of a bodiless cruel spirit.[130]

In the following section, I will demonstrate that many of these basic elements of fantastic texts are also taken up in *Harry Potter*.

VI.2 *"Harry Potter" as Fantastic Text*

At first glance, it seems perhaps surprising to consider at all whether the *Harry Potter* novels belong to the genre: magic, mythical creatures and supernatural events seem to classify the texts automatically in the category of fantastic literature. Based on Tzvetan Todorov's fundamental criterion of uncertainty, the texts belong to the "fantastic wonderful" or even "marvellous" and thus to the fairy tale (VI.1, 375). If we apply Todorov's definition consistently to *Harry Potter*, we can see the presence of the fantastic only in the first chapter of *Philosopher's Stone*, for when Harry enters the enchanted world, the story becomes a fairy tale, and raises the supernatural to the level of reality which none can doubt. If we look at the character structure, we come closer to identifying Propp's functions (see IV.1.A, 145) and can see them applied to the novels. Here too it has been demonstrated that the novels exhibit elements that are identical with or at least very similar to the fairy tale. In the following part of this work, I will examine the novels in light of further features of fantastic literature and demonstrate which commonalities it has with the genre.

As shown (see II.2.A, 34), a strong authorial drive is present in the personal narrative situations of the *Harry Potter* novels. In particular, intense moments strengthen the personal element, leading to a stream-of-consciousness narration. This is typical for the bulk of the genre. Numerous sub-plots are woven into the main plot, either in the form of reported experiences, overheard conversations and pieces of writing or newspaper reports, conveying both authenticity and additional content. (see II.3.E, 73). The incidents which set the plot in motion – the prophecy and murder of Harry's parents – are, as in the Gothic Novel, in the past. The main plot enlightens the events of the past. The narrative style is maintained with an economical and simple language (see

---

[129] See Sands, Frank 1999, 59.
[130] See Sands, Frank 1999, 335-339.

II.2.C, 42). All these elements give *Harry Potter* a strong affiliation to the Gothic Novel.

As in many other fantastic texts, the quest motif dominates in *Harry Potter*; the hero's search for recognition, his own role in his society and, after it has been saved, in the world. Living with the Dursleys, Harry suspects nothing of his identity and his future role. Only at eleven does he learn of his special destiny. Hesitating, wondering if he really is "the one", he leaves his familiar surroundings and travels to Hogwarts. Thus he becomes a part of the magical parallel world. Over the years at school he is repeatedly subject to tests – in class and in his confrontations with his enemies. Yet here he also makes friends for the first time in his life and thus acquires important helpers. He can also rely on helpful agents, such as his owl Hedwig, his magic wand or the spirit of his parents. The tasks and tests that Harry goes through become more and more difficult. Harry must repeatedly face the arch-villain long before the final confrontation. He finally learns (*Order of the Phoenix*) of his actual mission: only he can save magical world from Voldemort, he is "the chosen one". At the end of every school year, Harry returns to the Dursley's – i.e. his familiar surroundings – more mature with life-experience.   In *Deathly Hallows*, the author finally unites the happy ending of the fairy tale with the tragic ending of myth: Harry must die in order to prevail – but he rises from the dead and, as seen in the last chapter, "lives happily ever after". The following motifs typical of fantastic literature and the gothic novel in particular appear in *Harry Potter*:

- Harry grows up at the Dursley's and only later becomes part of the previously unknown parallel world. In the course of the plot, he matures.
- Doubles repeatedly come on the scene with the help of the "Polyjuice Potion" – thus Harry and Ron (*Chamber of Secrets*) appear as their counterparts Crabbe and Goyle and Barty Crouch as Mad-Eye Moody (*Goblet of Fire*).
- Ghosts as well as the living dead appear in the form of Nearly Headless Nick, Moaning Myrtle and Harry's parents in "Priori Incantatem" (*Goblet of Fire*).
- The motif of madness is represented first by Sirius Black (at first mistaken for being mad; *Prisoner of Azkaban*), Barty Crouch Jnr, whose fanaticism borders on insanity, and his father, who wanders aimlessly through the Forbidden Forest (*Goblet of Fire*)
- Women appear as demonic seductresses with the mythical creature "Veela", which is actually a hideous creature who takes on female human form and, siren-like, drives men to insanity (*Goblet of Fire*)
- Vampirism: the "Dementors" suck out the souls rather than the blood of their victims.

- Wizards transform into animals ("Animagi"), and in "Transfiguration"-class, students learn to transform animals into other animals or objects.
- Imaginary causality is created, e.g. in Harry's survival of Voldemort's attack when motherly love acts as a form of counter-magic, which protects him.
- Sadism and cruelty: repeatedly characters are killed (Sirius Black, Cedric Diggory, Albus Dumbledore and Severus Snape) or tortured (the Longbottom parents and Harry Potter himself). We can see a penchant for necrophilia and a black death-cult in the ceremony surrounding Voldemort's resurrection in *Goblet of Fire* (Black Mass).
- Time-travel: in *Prisoner of Azkaban*, time is turned back with the "Time-turner" and the past is changed.
- Visibility and invisibility: with his father's "Invisibility Cloak", Harry becomes invisible at decisive moments. Moody, in comparison, can see through everything with his magical eyes.
- Wild Hunt: in *Chamber of Secrets*, a wild hunt, known as the "Headless Hunt" participates in the anniversary-party of Nick's death.

The novels thus demonstrate all the relevant motifs of fantastic literature; both the quest as the central moment of the plot and the individual elements are typical of the genre.

As in the Gothic Novel, *Harry Potter*'s *dramatis personae* are also clearly delineated into good and evil (see IV.2.B, 152). The villain Voldemort who, as the plot's catalyst, represents avarice, greed and the urge to destroy and who tries to murder the innocent child Harry, represents the "hero-villain". Voldemort has inflicted so many magical changes on himself that he is no longer human – he has become a supernatural figure. Harry and Voldemort represent the individualised battle of human beings for power, glory and wisdom, of good against evil. As in the Gothic Novel, characters from humble social origins are positive figures (as the Weasley family; IV.3.J, 182).

Harry Potter, as the critics have repeatedly demonstrated, is an anti-hero; he is no superman or world-saviour.[131] He is the opposite of "today's wrestling 'heroes' who cross the line between good and evil with dull, misleading regularity."[132] Yet in having to undergo various tests, transgress taboos and transcend limits, he nevertheless exhibits all the qualities of a hero.[133] He accepts his destiny unwillingly and must earn his reputation and the support of his friends, precisely because he is not superhuman.[134] He has to learn that there are limits to

---

[131] See Hunt 2001, 122-123; Mayer 2003.
[132] Pharr 2004, 66.
[133] See Hiebert Alton 2003, 158; Natov 2001, 130.
[134] See Schafer 2000, 46.

his abilities and that a period of growing up lies ahead of him.[135] All in all, Harry is initially a rather passive hero, until he decides in *Half-Blood Prince* to face Voldemort. It is rather that things *happen to him* rather than that he seeks them out actively and directs them with a clear goal in mind.[136]

The *Harry Potter* novels make use of the classic spatial motifs particular to fantastic literature. It is not only the city of London, as a part of the moribund and uninviting "Muggle" world (see III.3.A, 107), that corresponds to the conventions of an ambivalent big city.

The *Harry Potter* texts present a bipolar structure made up of clear spatial contrasts. These oppositions arise from both levels in the locations, from "Muggle" and Magical World, and in the form of a semantic confrontation between the values relevant to the given schema. In the workings of the plot, the purpose of a room is often incongruent with its function. St Mungo's and Diagon Alley, for instance, are elaborately described, although for the plot they are no more than locations or settings. It is also contradictory that Grimmauld Place, as the representation of schematically negative values, should be the refuge of the resistance for the "Order of the Phoenix", i.e. a haven for the Good. Isolating particular details is also characteristic of the spatial structure in fantastic literature and is apparent in *Harry Potter*. In several cases individual objects bear symbolic meaning. In his visions in *Order of the Phoenix*, Harry repeatedly sees the corridor with the door to the Department of Mysteries – the small black door that eventually becomes symbolic of Voldemort's attempts to penetrate Harry's mind and discover the answer to the riddle.

Some of the settings spatialise past crimes; their characteristics represent the past, the negative. Grimmauld Place, for example, stands for the villainous Black family, every object in this house connotes evil, racism and arrogance. Individual rooms are likewise anthropomorphized, as when Grimmauld Place takes an active stand against the new inhabitants and exerts a baleful influence on them (see III.5.G, 135). There are clear pre-expectations associated with the spaces. From the very beginning, Azkaban and the "Shrieking Shack" are preceeded by negative expectations – even when the plot has nothing to do with the place, or unfolds there only considerably later in the narrative, the reader has a clear idea of the horror of the place. In the case of the "Shrieking Shack", the premonition is dissipated by a rational explanation.

Many of the spaces are physically impossible: both Hogwarts' and the Gringotts' dungeons are "miles under the school" or "hundreds of miles under London" (see 121), which is factually impossible. The means of transport, such

---

[135]   See Pharr 2004, 64; Schafer 2000, 219.
[136]   See Mendlesohn 2004, 165.

as "Floo Powder", "Knight Bus" or "Portkeys" are also physically unthinkable. These physical impossibilities are typical of spaces in fantastic literature.[137]

There are many motifs, associated foremost with the Gothic Novel, that also emerge in the texts, illustrated by the following few examples:

- Stormy weather: Harry sees Sirius in the form of a dog in a thunderstorm (HP 3, 193)
- Night and darkness: the decisive passages of the respective plots take place in darkness, for instance, the meeting between Harry and Voldemort in *Philosopher's Stone* and *Goblet of Fire*, as well as large parts of the duel in the Department of Mysteries and *Order of the Phoenix*.
- Underground spaces: the Chamber of Secrets, the dungeons at Hogwarts (see 121) as well as the Ministry of Magic (see III.5.E, 130) all lie deep under the earth.
- Labyrinths: in the final "Triwizard Tournament" in *Goblet of Fire*, the task is to get through a labyrinth, the path to the *Philosopher's Stone* of the self-same volume, which winds through a kind of obstacle course of varying tasks, and the Department of Mysteries (see III.5.E, 132) is a series of confusing corridors, doors and unfamiliar spaces
- "Gothic Castle" as well as "Big House": Hogwarts is a positive space, yet this palatial setting, where much of the plot unfolds, has all the qualities of a gothic castle – living armour and pictures, jails, dungeons, mazes, ghosts... Riddle House and Grimmauld Place, as negative spaces, correspond to this type (see III.3.C, 111 and III.5.G, 135).
- Living statues and pictures: one of the fundamental characteristics of the pictures in Harry Potter is that they are alive, the figures interact with each other and can make themselves understood to one another (e.g. Dumbledore sends the portrait of Hogwarts' former principle to Arthur Weasley's aid, HP 5, 516).
- Enclosed, out of the way settings: Hogwarts, Grimmauld Place, the Department of Mysteries, and also the Chamber of Secrets are not easy to access. They are either far away and/or can only be reached with the help of special mechanisms
- Inaccessible, mysterious spaces: Hogwarts dungeons with the Chamber of Secrets, the room with the Philosopher's Stone, the Forbidden Forest are inaccessible and / or mysterious.
- Extremes of temperature: cold spaces have negative associations, positive spaces are usually warm (see 101).
- Oppositions of brightness: positive spaces are bright, negative spaces dark (see 101).

---

[137] See Todorov 1972, 108.

- Colour scheme: silver and green in *Harry Potter* have negative connotations (see 103).

Harry Potter thus makes use of the classic spatial motifs of the Gothic Novel.

The expression of values in the *Harry Potter* novels correspond exactly to those made in fantastic literature, in particular in the "secondary world fantasy". Commensurate with the genre, the forces of good and evil are positioned antagonistically against one another and are easily distinguishable from each other. The concepts of freedom and equality found in Western democracies are the fundamental principles of the positive value-system. Even when the magical world in no way presents an ideal system – it nonetheless bases itself on the "dream of democracy". Yet the essence of the state that stands in contradistinction to Voldemort's dictatorship and provides a positive model for their world is not a pure democracy. It bears the traits of a feudal system, i.e. democratically illegitimate power structures (see V.1.B, 278).

The positive characters (see IV.2.A, 154) distinguish themselves by friendship and loyalty, e.g. amongst Harry, Hermione, Ron, Hagrid and the adult members of the "Order of the Phoenix". They stick together faithfully and take on personal risks to help their friends. In contrast to the evil henchmen such as Crabbe and Goyle, Harry and his friends stand for intellectual superiority and moral integrity. They represent reason, courage and mutual love. The positive characters do not value material goods and, mostly, do not have much money. In this way they exactly reflect the genre's established model.

Evil, on the other hand, stands for snobbery, superficiality and the striving for unilateral world-domination. Its representatives use unfair methods in their confrontations with their opponents, e.g. when Lucius Malfoy wrongly accuses little Ginny Weasley of having a diary possessed by black magic in order to discredit her father. The villains have racial prejudices, are hungry for power, stupid and cowardly (see IV.2.A, 154). They do not live in harmony with nature and have a negative rapport with animals. As opposed to most fantastic texts, in which evil is in either metaphysical or corporeal form, evil in *Harry Potter* undergoes a transformation: Voldemort, first completely weakened then almost physically annihilated, regains his body in *Goblet of Fire*. If we compare *Potter* with *Star Wars* (physical villain) or with *The Lord of the Rings* (incorporeal evil), we see that for the genre, this transforming act of evil is quite rare.[138] It is equally atypical for the genre to have characters change sides, which they do, both to and from the positive and the negative. The former "Death Eaters" Snape and Bagman are fully accepted by the powerful figures in Dumbledore's entourage. Finally, *Harry Potter*, like many fantastic texts, does not allow for an emancipatory reading (see V.4.D, 346).

---

[138] See Kulik 2005, 343.

Apart from the general similarities Rowling's text bears to the genre in general, we find – especially in *Deathly Hallows* – very obvious references to J.R.R. Tolkien: when Harry and Ron quarrel about who is going to carry the "Horcrux" locket we are reminded of the effect Sauron's ring has on the hobbit Frodo:

> Harry: "Take off the locket, Ron. [...] Please take it off. You wouldn't be talking like this if you hadn't been wearing it all day." (HP 7, 252)
> Ron: "Because that thing's bad for me! [...] I can't handle it! I'm not making excuses [...] but it affects me worse than it affected you and Hermione, it made me think stuff, stuff I was thinking anyway, but it made everything worse, I can't explain it, [...]." (HP 7, 305)

And when they are about to destroy the locket, it tries to deceive Ron – just like the ring and its corrupting influence deceive the characters in *Lord of the Rings*:

> "I have seen your heart, and it is mine. [...] I have seen your dreams, Ronald Weasley, and I have seen your fears. All you desire is possible, but all that you dread is also possible... [...] Least loved, always, by the mother who craved a daughter ... least loved, now by the girl who prefers your friend ... second best, always, eternally overshadowed..." (HP 7, 306)

In Tolkien's *The Return of the King* we find Frodo quarrelling with Sam about who is going to carry the "Ring" through Mordor:

> "No, you won't, you thief!" [Frodo] panted, staring at Sam [...]. The hideous vision had seemed so real to him [...]. Sam had changed before his very eyes into an orc again, leering and pawing at his treasure, a foul little creature with greedy ees and slobbering mouth. [...]. "O Sam!" cried Frodo. "What have I said? What have I done? Forgive me! [...] It is the horrible power of the Ring. [...] I must carry the burden to the end."[139]

In both scenes we find friends quarrelling about a cursed, evil piece of jewellery, which becomes a burden and brings out the worst in people. But there are more direct references to other works of fantasy. When Rowling describes how "Dementors" glide "amongst the Muggles who might not be able to see them, but would assuredly feel the despair they cast wherever they went," (HP 7, 235) we feel this to be highly reminiscent of Pullman's "Specters":

> "Well, when a Specter catch a grownup, that's bad to see. They eat the life out of them there and then, all right. [...] At first they know it's happening, and

---

[139] Tolkien, *The Return of the King*, 220-221.

they're afraid; they cry and cry. They try and look away and pretend it ain' happening, but it is. It's too late. [...] Then they get pale and they stop moving. They still alive, but it's like they been eaten from inside. You look in they eyes, you see the back of they heads. Ain' nothing there."[140]

This is exactly like Rowling describes the effect a "Dementor's Kiss" has on the victim:

> "[They] suck out his soul. [... It is] much worse than [being dead]. You can exist without your soul, you know, as long as your brain and heart are still working. But you'll have no sense of self any more, no memory, no ... anything. There's no chance at all of recovery. You'll just – exist. As an empty shell. And your soul is gone for ever ... lost." (HP 3, 268)

But more comparisons are possible in the context of J.K. Rowling. Peter Kemp even compares Rowling to Dickens. In his review for *Times Online* he writes:

> Dickens, the greatest exponent of this genre, is the greatest influence. Rowling shares his penchant for menaced orphans (Harry is far from the only one in her books). Like him, she loves intricate family ramifications, Christmas jollities, giveaway names (Crabbe, Goyle, Peeves) and surreal streetscapes (Diagon Alley, for instance, with stalls offering barrels of bat spleen and eels' eyes and shops such as Flourish and Blotts, purveyors of wizard stationery). All gaslights, cobwebby chandeliers, begrimed ancestral portraits and heaps of fascinating lumber, the old house that is the HQ of the Order of the Phoenix (a resistance movement against Voldemort) might have been air-lifted out of Dickens's pages.[141]

In my opinion Kemp is right so far, but does not mention another parallel between Rowling and Dickens: economic success – for both of them were best-selling authors of their time. Nevertheless, Dickens writes about contemporary society when he mentions "gaslights, cobwebby chandeliers" or "menaced orphans", i.e. child labour. Rowling, by contrast, creates a nostalgic world influenced, perhaps, by Dickens. This, I think, is quite an important difference. Furthermore, I disagree with Susanne Gaschke who says "doch ihre Anleihen sind nie Plagiate, sondern Weiterentwicklungen".[142] Rowling does use other texts

---

[140] Philipp Pullman, *The Subtle Knife* [1997], New York: Random House, 2003, 53-54. It is noteworthy to point out that Rowling's *Prisoner of Azkaban* was first published in 1999 – two years after *The Subtle Knife*.

[141] Kemp 2003.

[142] "but the things she borrows never are mere plagiarisms but further developments", Gaschke 2007 [my translation].

like *Lord of the Rings* or the *His Dark Materials* a.k.a. *Northern Lights Trilogy* as a foundation for her own creation.

Rowling does not describe an ideal dream world which can take the reader out of his consciousness. In this respect, *Harry Potter* is not an escapist text. Yet she satisfies the reader's longing for the possibility of justice, the wish for omnipotence and moral clarity. Harry appears as "everyman", as a simple, often insecure boy taking a stand against evil in his world. Good powers stand at his side and show him the morally right path to take. The novels have a clear message about good and evil, there is no moral relativism; nothing is arbitrary. True, the characters are not depicted as being black-and-white, but the division of values is unambiguous (see IV.2.A, 154). The texts stand for clarity, the battle against terrorist-like evil and the hope that a simple boy can change the situation forever. Like the heroes of myth, Harry is confronted with timeless decisions: should he kill Sirius or be merciful (*Prisoner of Azkaban*)? Can he have the girl he loves, or must he decide between her and his best-friend Ron (*Half-Blood Prince*)? Who was his father, really (*Order of the Phoenix*)? And not least of all, the novels, with their mistrust of technology and their nostalgic undertone, offer a congenial, apparently ideal counter-world to reason, science and the economic constraints of the reader's real world.

We can thus see that in their ideological messages, the *Harry Potter* novels are to the utmost degree typical of the genre.

VI.2.A. Fantastic Elements in "Harry Potter"

To assess the element of the fantastic in the *Harry Potter* novels more closely, I will examine below the forms in which it appears and then its function within the magical world and within the stages of narrative process.

VI.2.A.a The Use and Function of Magic

Magic defines the wizard's daily life. Everyone and everything works with magic. It provides not only help around the house, but also entertainment (e.g. in Wizard-chess, HP 1, 215-216), remedies and economic activities. For the people in *Harry Potter*, the field of magic is a source of income and presents various job profiles: apart from the activities in the Ministry of Magic, there are also professions such as "Curse Breaker" (HP 3, 15) or "Healer" (HP 5, 534).

It is strictly forbidden for under-age wizards to use magic in the "Muggle" world (HP 1, 91). This jinx is called "The Trace" and makes underage wizards using magic traceable. All wizards must respect the "Statute of Secrecy" which commits wizards to hide their magical abilities from the "Muggles" (HP 7, 261).

There are vastly different kinds of magic and various situations in which they can be used. Elf magic, for example, is different from human magic – which is why Dobby can "Apparate" inside Malfoy Manor and save Harry from Voldemort

(HP 7, 161). Likewise, Kreacher can escape from the cave, where Voldemort hides his "Horcrux" while Regulus Black dies (HP 7, 161).

We also find a whole series of magical objects which have very normal uses in the everyday world and there is a science of "curses", "jinxes" and "hexes", which the children have to learn. In "Potions"-class, lessons on the brewing of magical potions, the pupils are instructed on the various recipes and ingredients, like in chemistry class. Magic in *Harry Potter* is thus more than a certain kind of enchantment: everything in every kind of situation and for every kind of purpose is enchanted. I shall thus give an overview of the most important forms of magic that appear in *Harry Potter*.

In *Deathly Hallows*, the art of "wandlore" is of major importance. We are told that it is the wand that chooses the wizard – not vice versa. So the wizard must win the wand's allegiance, which is why, for example, Hermione cannot make proper use of Bellatrix Lestrange's wand (HP 7, 420) and why Voldemort feels obliged to kill Severus (HP 7, 527) to win the Elder Wand's support. And for the final victory over Voldemort it is of vital importance that the villain is deceived: it was not Snape who was master of the Elder Wand, but Draco, who in turn had been defeated by Harry (HP 7, 595). This means that Harry is the true owner of the wand and, thus, has possessed the three "Deathly Hallows" that united "make the possessor master of Death" (HP 7, 332-333). Therefore, Voldemort cannot kill Harry without his consent. As Harry, in the rather obscure King's Cross scene (HP 7, "King's Cross"), decides to return to life, Voldemort is defeated. Trying to kill the boy a second time, his "Killing Curse" backfires and destroys him once and for all.

Analysing the various types of magic presented in *Harry Potter*, one must first be able to differentiate between two different kinds of magic: the verbal magic formula, and the prepared potions and magical objects. The students at Hogwarts learn spells (subdivided into the categories "charms", "jinxes", "hexes" and "curses") in all their classes. Without exception, the relevant formulas affect every practical facet in a person's life. A glance at the selection of magic formulas confirms this:

Name	Characteristics	Source
Accio! (Summoning Charm)	Snatches objects away and turns them to the wizard's use	HP 4, 79; 325
Ageing Potion	Makes user older than he is	HP 4, 210, 285
Alohomora!	Opens door and windows	HP 1, 187; HP 3, 445

Name	Characteristics	Source
Apparition	Bodiless transfer between two places; in the magical world it has the same status as car driving in the real world	HP 3, 177; HP 4, 77
Avada Kedavra Curse	Curse of death	HP 4, 10, 237, 691
Avis!	Birds come out of the magic wand	HP 4, 339
Banishing Charm (Spell)	Wards off flying objects	HP 4, 522, 623
Bubble-Head Charm	Creates bubbles around the body and enables underwater breathing	HP 4, 551
Cheering Charm	Cheers up the sad	HP 3, 318
Cruciatus Curse	Torturing curse	HP 4, 233, 236
Enervate!	Deactivates "Stupefy!"	HP 4, 57; 608
Engorgement Charm	Enlarges objects and people	HP 4, 57-58, 236
Expelliarmus!	Disarms the opponent	HP 2, 209
Fidelius Charm	Transforms a human being into someone else's "Secret Keeper"	HP 3, 222
Finite Incantatem!	Puts an end to the effects of magic spells	HP 2, 209
Freezing Charm	Makes the opponent freeze	HP 2, 114
Imperius Curse	Robs the opponent of his will	HP 4, 233, 235, 255
Impervius	Keeps glass from fogging up in rain or mist	HP 4, 192
Incendio!	Sets objects on fire	HP 4, 55
Jelly-Legs Jinx	Makes legs as soft as jelly	HP 4, 661

Name	Characteristics	Source
Jiggery pokery, Hocus Pocus ... squiggly wiggly	Nonsense spell with which Harry terrifies his cousin	HP 2, 16
Locomoter Mortis!	Leg-Locker Curse	HP 1, 235
Love Potion	Makes people love-sick	HP 2, 256-257; HP 4, 557
Lumos!	Turns the magic wand into a desk-lamp	HP 2, 293
Memory Charm	Changes the other person's memory	HP 4, 18, 162
Mobiliarbus	Makes furniture move by itself	HP 3, 218
Mobilicorpus	Makes immovable people sway forwards	HP 3, 406
Morsmordre!	Conjures Voldemort's dark mark	HP 4, 144
Nox!	Puts an end to *Lumos!*	HP 3, 364
Obliviate!	Erases the opponent's memory	HP 2, 326; HP 4, 89
Orchideus!	Makes flowers grow out of the magic wand	HP 4, 338
Patronus Charm	Invokes a protective spirit	HP 3, 257-258
Peskipiksi Pesternomi	Lockhart's ineffective spell against Cornish Pixies	HP 2, 113
Petrificus Totalus	Makes the affected person totally motionless	HP 3, 294
Point me! (Four Point Spell)	Turns magic wand into compass	HP 4, 660-661, 665
Polyjuice Potion	Changes the person's appearance into another person	HP 2, 174-175, 180-181, 235

Name	Characteristics	Source
Potion for dreamless sleep		HP 4, 759
Prior Incantato	Shows the last spell the magic wand performed	HP 4, 152, 718-725
Quietus!	Ends the "Sonorus" magic	HP 4, 131
Reducio! (Reducing Charm / Reductor Curse)	Makes things smaller	HP 4, 236; 660
Relashio!	Releases people from chains	HP 4, 541
Reparo!	Brings shattered pieces of glass back together again	HP 4, 188
Rictusempra!	Magical punch to the opponent	HP 2, 208
Riddikulus!	Transforms a Boggart into a ridiculous form	HP 3, 147
Chocolate	Helps against evil magic	HP 3, 101, 259, 263, 418-420
Scouring Charm	Cleans fingernails	HP 4, 230
Serpensortia!	Conjures up a serpent	HP 2, 210
Severing Charm	Cuts materials	HP 4, 449
Shield Charm	Creates a shield around the user	HP 4, 661
Shrinking Solution	Makes objects shrink	HP 3, 136
Skele-Gro	Makes bones grow	HP 2, 190
Sleekeazy's Hair Potion	Straightens hair	HP 4, 473
Sleeping Draught	Sleeping drink	HP 2, 231

Name	Characteristics	Source
Sonorus!	Makes the speaker's voice loud, as if he were speaking into a microphone	HP 4, 116
Stupefy! (Stunning Spell)	Makes the opponent motionless	HP 4, 145; 358-359
Swelling Solution	Makes things swell up	HP 2, 203
Tarantalle-gra!	Makes the opponent dance the tarantella	HP 2, 209
Tickling Charm	Tickles the opponent	HP 2, 208
Transmog-rifian Tor-ture	Magical torture method	HP 2, 155
Unbreak-able Charm	Makes glass unbreakable	HP 4, 789
Veritase-rum	Truth drug	HP 4, 562-563
Wingar-dium Leviosa!	Makes things fly	HP 1, 187
Wit-Sharpening Potion	Helps people think	HP 4, 558
Wolfsbane Potion	Soothes werewolves' aggression	HP 3, 380

The second way in which magic appears is in the magical objects the wizards deal with and which lighten their everyday load or, at least, make it more pleasant. A selection should suffice here as well make the range clear:

Name	Characteristics	Source
Riddle's Diary	Conserves Voldemort's student persona	HP 2, 249-250, 260-268
Enchanted Ceiling	Imitates the weather outdoors in Hogwarts Great Hall	HP 2, 96

Name	Characteristics	Source
Flying Broom	Sports apparatus and status symbol; the labels are e.g. "Shooting Star", "Nimbus", "Comet", "Firebolt"	HP 2, 54
Flying Car	Manipulated by Mr Weasley	HP 2, 31, 75-80, 84-85, 295-302
Flying Carpet	A family vehicle forbidden in England	HP 4, 103
Foe Glass	Warns of the approach of enemies	HP 4, 376-377
Goblet of Fire	Goblet which controls the participants of the Triwizard Tournament	HP 4, 280-281, 286, 305
Gobstones	Magical murmuring which reacts insultingly to someone's defeat	HP 3, 58
Hand of Glory	Produces light only for the owner; work instrument for thieves	HP 2, 60
Howler	Letter which lets loose a loud tirade of swear words when it is opened	HP 2, 97-98
Invisibility Cloak	Makes the wearer invisible to most people	HP 1, 218; HP 2, 284
Lunascope	Shows the position of the moon and constellations	HP 3, 58
Magical Eye	Artificial eye which can see through everything	HP 4, 233
Magical Mess-Remover	Magical laundry detergent	HP 4, 336
Magical Books	Can have health-related consequences for the reader (speech impediment, blindness, etc.): e.g. *Monster Book of Monsters*	HP 1, 223; HP 2, 250; HP 3, 19-20, 60-61
Magical Box	Changes its contents with every turn of the key	HP 4, 737
Magical Practical Joke	Makes fun of the victim; can be bought at Zonko's or Weasley's Wizard Wheezes	HP 4, 203

Name	Characteristics	Source
Magic Wand	The wizard's most important magical instrument	HP 1, 93; 96
Marauder's Map	Boarding House blue-print; shows the movement of every person in Hogwarts in real time	HP 3, 208; HP 4, 499
Mirror of Erised	Rather than the reflection, shows the observer's most coveted wish	HP 1, 224-225, 231
Omniocu-lars	Binoculars which show things in slow motion or rewind	HP 4, 106
Opal neck-lace	Jewellery with curse of death on them	HP 2, 61
Pensieve	Bowl in which thoughts can be saved and later looked at	HP 4, 633, 648-649, 677
Philoso-pher's Sto-ne	Changes metal into gold; produces a elixir that promises eternal life	HP 1, 238
Photos (moving)	People in the pictures speak and move like living people	HP 2, 117, 154, 156; HP 3, 79, 250, 292
Delumina-tor ("Put-Outer")	Similar to a fire-extinguisher, it puts out street-lamps (and leads Ron to Harry and Hermione in *Deathly Hallows*)	HP 1, 15; HP 7, 312-313
Quick Quotes Quill	Magical stenographer's pen which can write and manipulate texts by itself	HP 4, 333
Remem-brall	Tells the owner if he has forgotten any-thing	HP 1, 159
Revealer	Opposite of an eraser – it makes things visible	HP 2, 252
Self-Shuffling playing cards	Cards that shuffle themselves	HP 2, 48
Shrinking Keys	"Muggles'" manipulated keys, which they can then no longer find because they have shrunk	HP 2, 45-46

Name	Characteristics	Source
Sneako-scope	Warns of impostors and traitors	HP 3, 16-17, 86; HP 4, 376
Sorting Hat	Sorts the students into houses; acts autonomously	HP 1, 130-131; HP 2, 343; HP 4, 196-197
Talking Mirror	Admonishes the house's inhabitants	HP 2, 50; HP 3, 63
Time-Turner	Turns back time	HP 3, 424
Weasley's Family Clock	Displays the activities and circum-stances of every family member	HP 2, 41; HP 4, 169

From this overview, we can see that magical objects have, above all practical functions. They:
- make the daily life of the wizard's society easier (e.g. "Lunascope", "Portkey", "Sneakoscope", "Quick-Quotes-Quill", "Deluminator")
- provide entertainment and fun (e.g. "Gobstones", party favours, sweets, chess)
- assist in the confrontation with other wizards ("Foe Glass", "Magical Eye", "Hand of Glory").

Higher functions are only attached to a few objects. These are, for instance, the "Timeturner", which turns back time and thus offers the possibility of changing the past, the *Goblet of Fire* and the "Sorting Hat", both of which – according to mysterious criteria – judge and select people. Transcendental meaning is also attached to the *Philosopher's Stone* and the Elixir of Life, for both intervene in the physical form of material objects, inexplicably transform metal into gold and change people's appearance. As with the use of magical spells and potions, we can see that in the magical world, magic is used to master everyday life.

This impression is confirmed when we look at the situations in which magic is used. It is often used for banal household chores: thus fires are magically lit in fireplaces and on candles (HP 2, 89; HP 3, 51, 256; HP 4, 295, 333), dishes are cleared as if by spectral hands (HP 2, 92-93; HP 3, 105; HP 4, 412, 455). Furniture need not be moved by hand: with the help of the right magical formula, they can fly by themselves (HP 3, 176, 247; HP 4, 457). Pumpkins are enlarged with an "Engorgement Charm" (HP 2, 129), broken glasses are magically repaired (HP 2, 64) and suitcases pack themselves (HP 1, 330).

Magic also plays an important role in the confrontation with other wizards. It can either be because wizards are using magic spells against each other (e.g. HP 1, 69; HP 2, 45, 124) or because they are protecting themselves and their possessions from attack (HP 1, 192; HP 3, 178, 292, 442-443; HP 4, 410). There is even pertinent magic reading for this extensive subject: *"Curses and Counter Curses (Bewitch your Friends and Befuddle your Enemies with the Latest Revenges: Hair Loss, Jelly Legs, Tongue-Tying and much, much more)* by Professor Vindictus Viridian" (HP 2, 134, 158). Magic can even conjure up the means with which to capture someone (HP 1, 311; HP 3, 378; HP 4, 637).

Magic is also used in medical practice, as we see with the existence of a wizard's hospital at St Mungo's (see III.5.F, 134). Madam Pomfrey, Hogwarts' nurse, is well-known for her magical healing practices. There is a remedy for every thinkable emergency (HP 2, 134, 158). With magic, even lost body parts can be replaced (HP 4, 703).

Magic suspends the laws of physics: only Dumbledore's intervention is responsible for saving Harry from death at the "Quidditch" match, by halting his fall into the abyss and having him float into the school's sick-ward on a stretcher (HP 3, 197). And finally, the wizards have means for travelling at their disposal, such as the trip with "Floo Powder" (HP 2, 56-57, the acceleration of a motor-boat (HP 1, 74), the bodiless "beaming" ("Apparition") and coaches that are drawn by invisible horses (HP 3, 98).

In summary, we can conclude that at various stages of the plot in *Harry Potter* the fantastic is used for:

- coping with everyday life and objects (making them accessible or fending them off)
- transforming an object (or animal) or its physical properties
- attacking or defending in a battle with other wizards
- treating wounds and illnesses
- overcoming distances and travelling in general

Magic thus appears more as a means of getting through everyday routine than as metaphysical power. There are rigidly defined formulas which bring about a clear result when used properly. Above all, wizardry in *Harry Potter*'s magical world supersedes the use of science and technology. Just as real children study mathematics, physics and chemistry at school, the children at Hogwarts are taught the equivalent sciences of their world. And just as a secondary school graduate is supposed to have acquired the necessary tools to find his way in the adult world, so can the wizard-apprentice of the magic boarding school subsequently decide for himself on his future career path. Magic in *Harry Potter* always has an explanation – in contradistinction to, e.g., *Lord of the Rings*, magic is clearly predictable and can be learned by anyone who is so gifted. With Tolkien, Gandalf's magic is inexplicable and defies generally comprehensible and rational rules. Wizardry in *Harry Potter*, on the other hand, is not a mystical secret science but a practically taught subject, open to all.

VI.2.A.b Magical Flora and Fauna

Apart from the magical formulas and enchanted objects, there are a multitude of magical animals and plants in the *Harry Potter* novels, of which I will list the following:

Name	Characteristics	Source
Basilisk	Parsle-speaking ancient giant snake whose look kills; King of Serpents	HP 2 132, 300, 303, 312, 326, 342-344
Blast-Ended Skrewt	Prickly, stinking giant lobster; dangerously strong; cannibal; moves with small explosion from the posterior	HP 4, 216-218, 290, 323-324, 403, 478, 678
Boggart	Lives in closed, dark rooms; transforms into the creature its opponent is the most afraid of; resistance is laughing	HP 3, 147
Centaur	Half man, half horse; its own society ("herd"); dislikes human beings; soothsayer; individual characters	HP 1, 273-275, 278-280
Dementor	Superhumanly large, corpse-like creature wrapped in a long cape; spreads spiritual chill and depression; destroys psyches; can be sensed by Muggles; does not know right or wrong	HP 3, 93-94, 96, 108, 203-204, 239, 260, 413-414; HP 4, 30, 238, 575, 637, 675-676
Dragon	Rare, dangerous and highly magical creature; various races are known, e.g. Hungarian Horntail, Common Welsh Green, Hebridean Blacks, Swedish Short Snout, Chinese Fireball, Norwegian Ridgeback; blood has magical power; there are books written about them; laws for their breeding	HP 1, 249-251; HP 4, 218, 358, 360, 367, 371

Name	Characteristics	Source
Dwarf	Ugly, not very intelligent inhabitant of gardens; considered "rodents"; own language	HP 2, 44-48, 256-257; HP 4, 69
Elf	Ugly magical creatures; have been living in slavery for centuries; great magical power	HP 2, 18-20, 25-26, 36, 192-193, 363-364; HP 4, 110, 112, 247, 292, 411
Giant	Immense, heavily-built, uncivilised creature; exterminated in Europe; greedy	HP 4, 268, 467, 470, 473, 479
Giant Octopus	Lives in Hogwart Lake; peaceful	HP 1, 339; HP 3, 454
Grindy-low	Green water-demon	HP 3, 168; HP 4, 540
Hinky-punk	One-legged smoke creature that leads wanderers away from the path	HP 3, 186, 202
Hippo-griff	Creature part horse part eagle; proud and headstrong	HP 3, 127-129; HP 4, 566
Kappa	Sea-creature that lure bathers into the deeps	HP 3, 154
Lepre-chaun	Small, bearded dwarf with lamp in his hand	HP 4, 118
Merpeo-ple	Ugly, powerful underwater creatures; aggressive; have their own language and administration	HP 4, 542, 547-548, 550-551
Niffler	Cute mouse-creature; can detect treasure	HP 4, 590-591
Phoe-nix	Magnificent red-gold bird which ends its life in a great conflagration and resurrects out of its ashes; tears have healing properties; loyal companion; bears great burdens; its song is supernaturally beautiful	HP 2, 225, 338-339, 343-350; HP 4, 632, 752, 757
Phantom	climbs up stone walls	HP 2, 150

Name	Characteristics	Source
Polter-geist	Plays rough with human beings; colourful clothing	HP 1, 141; HP 2, 139, 146; HP 3, 143; HP 4, 191
Sphinx	Makes rhymed riddles	HP 4, 682
Undead	Transparent, autonomous creature and undead human being; lives in hierarchical society with their own clubs like the "Headless Hunt"; their own music and rotten food; assorted characters	HP 1, 127, 136; HP 2, 135-136, 142-145, 148-149; HP 4, 192
Veela	Magical female figure who solicits men; in truth, however, is an ugly bird creature	HP 4, 116, 126, 141-142
Were-wolf	Person who mutates into a werewolf at the full moon; his bite turns other people into werewolves	HP 1, 380; HP 3, 382, 410
Troll	Threatening, aggressive giant	HP 1, 190; HP 3, 292
Unicorn	Extraordinarily beautiful creature; foals are made out of gold; will only allow itself to be touched by women; powerful magical creature; its blood keeps the critically ill alive	HP 1, 272, 277-279; HP 4, 476-477, 528

From this overview of only the most important magical creatures, we can see that *Harry Potter* makes use of a diverse, if by no means fundamentally new, inventory of magical creatures. J.K. Rowling draws on the traditional repertory of fantastic as well as fairy-tale literature when she has giants, dwarves, unicorns, werewolves or poltergeists appear. Centaurs and phoenixes are well known from ancient mythology, while trolls and goblins belong to the Nordic sagas.

Only a few of the spirits are independent individuals, such as the toilet spirit Moaning Myrtle. She lives in the girls' bathroom on the first floor and is known for her hysterical paroxysms during which she likes to flood the bathroom (HP 2, 145). The rather unattractive girl wears enormous glasses, weeps constantly (HP 2, 147, 248) and is occasionally flushed down with the water into the Hogwarts Lake. In life she was terrorised by her class-mate Olive Hornby, who eventually has her killed by a basilisk while running into the washroom. In revenge, Myrtle haunts her tormentor for years – until the Ministry of Magic forbids it (HP 4, 507).[143] She has a particular fondness for Harry Potter and generously offers to let him dwell in her toilet in the event of his death (HP 2, 350). Myrtle places a value on having feelings, despite her undead state, and takes it hard when someone ignores that (HP 2, 171; HP 4, 506).

Most of the undead are not individual characters; they are mostly just identified with their specific functions. None of the "Dementors" or "Boggarts" have names or personal qualities. Knowing about magical fauna is a far more important part of their education at Hogwarts and is taught in "Care of Magical Creatures" class.

Besides magical creatures, there are also magical plants that are important both for medical purposes as well as for producing magic potions. The object of the herbology department is to learn how to use them. Listed here are:

Name	Description	Source
Whomping Willow	Rare willow who hits whoever comes too near with its branches	HP 2, 84, 88, 99; HP 3, 197
Mandrake	The root is a stubborn creature whose cry is deathly; important magical healing plant	HP 2, 102-103, 105, 254, 271
Abyssinian Shrivelfig		HP 2, 289; HP 3, 136
Puffapod	Beans that bloom quite suddenly	HP 3, 161
Gillyweed	Seaweed like plant which can grow gills when it likes	HP 4, 535; 538-539
Devil's Snare	Plant that grows around everything and strangles	HP 1, 298-299

The author is much more innovative in this area than in her production of magical fauna. Except from the mandrake, which has been used as a mythical healing plant since the Middle Ages, she is purely creative with such plants as the "Abessinian Shrivelfig" or the "Whomping Willow", previously unknown.

VI.2.B. Function of the Fantastic in "Harry Potter"

As was shown, no metaphysical or transcendental meanings are associated with the fantastic element in *Harry Potter*. The fantastic makes use, rather, of what Kathryn Hume has called substitution of well-know activities (VI.1, 379). Furthermore, magic introduces new elements into the readers' reality, as when, for

---

[143] We can see here the Ministry's power; also that even ghosts submit to its administration.

example, he is revealed the magical parallel world that he never knew existed. This for Hume is another function of the fantastic. The reader's real world is uncomfortably alienating and a counter-world is established. The magical world of *Harry Potter* may not have its own languages, like the many diverse idioms found in *Lord of the Rings*, but the wizards have their own vocabulary which needs to be explained to non-wizards. When people talk about "Muggles", "Apparition", "Animagi" or "Patronus", only the initiated know what they mean. In *Harry Potter*, magic is used as a three-dimensional depiction of a counter-world – as a colourful formulation of a scenario and not as the metaphorical representation of psychological or ideological statements. But one of the most important functions of the fantastic in *Harry Potter* is to provide elements of caricature or satire: at many points in her magical world, J.K. Rowling sketches the reader's familiar reality exaggerated into the grotesque. (i.e. the description of St Mungo's; III.5.F, 134).

VI.2.B.a The Comic

Humour and comical effects have a fixed place in the fantastic literature written especially for children. On one hand they provide comic relief after dramatic situations, on the other hand, entertainment.[144] Karen Sands and Marietta Frank identify five kinds of humour typical of science fiction:[145]

- sarcasm/mockery
- gallows humour
- situation comedy
- word games
- facetious riddles

These forms of humour are also to be found in *Harry Potter*, extending to the comical alienation of the familiar (satire as well as the grotesque). The fantastic is always central to the humour in *Harry Potter*, as we will see below. Sarcasm and gallows humour appear above all in the dialogues between Harry and his aunt (HP 1, 49) or with Dolores Umbridge (HP 5, 271). The boy's cocky answers are always shrewd and therefore humorous.

There are many examples of situational comedy verging on the point of slapstick, a few of which are listed here:

- In Zonko's, a joke-article store, there are "Dungbombs, Hiccough Sweets, Frog Spawn Soap and a Nose-Biting Teacup" (HP 3, 302). Imagining how they work is what makes them comical.

---

[144] See Sands, Frank 1999, 49.
[145] See Sands, Frank 1999, 54

- The ghost Moaning Myrtle howls, "'My life was nothing but misery at this place and now people come along ruining my death! [...] I came in here and tried to kill myself. Then, of course, I remembered that I'm – that I'm –" (HP 2, 171). The funny thing here is that a ghost should want to commit suicide when she is already dead.
- An ugly, grouchy dwarf in an angel's costume distributes Valentine cards and assaults people to perform his task: "'Stay still' grunted the dwarf, grabbing hold of Harry's bag and pulling him back. [...] the dwarf seized him around the knees and brought him crashing to the floor. 'Right,' he said, sitting on Harry's ankles, 'here is your singing Valentine.'" (HP 2, 257). One would have imagined the delivery of a love-poem somewhat differently.
- The manager of the Flourish and Blotts bookstore complains, "'I thought we'd seen the worst when we bought two hundred books of The Invisible Books of Invisibility – cost a fortune, and we never found them...'" (HP 3, 61). Absurd problems only a magical world could have!
- Dumbledore explains to the retired teacher for "Care of Magical Creatures" that his goal is "[to] enjoy more time with his remaining limbs" (HP 3, 104). An original way to put a positive spin on serious injuries.
- Neville accidentally transfers his ears onto a cactus (HP 4, 260).
- The horses from Beauxbatons only drink single malt whiskey (HP 4, 270).
- Wizards regularly manipulate the "Muggle"-toilets, a result of which is the: "'Muggles are pulling the flush and instead of everything disappearing – well, you can imagine'" (HP 5, 152).
- Moody's magical eye stays stuck – he needs help (HP 5, 61).
- A tapestry at Hogwarts depicts "Barnabas the Barmy's foolish attempt to train trolls for the ballet" (HP 5, 43).
- The ghost Nick accounts for "'[t]he noble blood in my veins" (HP 5, 233) – while he does not have any blood at all.
- The magical janitorial troupe in the Ministry use the enchanted appearance of their office to protect their own interests "'We had two months of hurricanes last time they were angling for a pay raise...'" (HP 5, 149)
- Dumbledore hires "a troupe of dancing skeletons" to entertain the guests at the Halloween party (HP 2, 144).
- Dumbledore has a scar depicting "a perfect map of the London Underground" (HP 1, 22).
- Instead of giving a grave and solemn address at the beginning of the new school-year, Dumbledore says, "'I would like to say a few words. And here they are: Nitwit! Blubber! Oddment! Tweak!'" (HP 1, 135). The expression "a few words" is taken seriously and thus made ridiculous.

This kind of humour plays with the absurdities made possible in a magical world and thus with the element of the fantastic. The fantastic is clearly made instrumental for the purpose of entertainment and used to produce comical effects. The case is different when dealing with things familiar to the reader, which are comically alienated and objects of satire. A representative selection of scenes here should also suffice to clarify the character of this form of the comical:

- The constant search for keys which afflicts some people has a rational basis: "'Just Muggle-baiting [...]. Sell them a key that keeps shrinking to nothing so they can never find it'" (HP 2, 46).
- OWLs are the "Ordinary Wizarding Level" at Hogwarts and correspond to the former British secondary-school Ordinary Levels final exams (short form: O-levels) (HP 2, 54).
- Like qualification courses existing in the real world, Filch enrols in a correspondence school for magic called "KWIKSPELL A Correspondence Course in Beginners' Magic". As real correspondence courses, the school campaigns for student's enthusiastic, euphoric testimonials of its alumni (HP 2, 271).
- Mandrakes act like teenagers at puberty and get acne (HP 2, 254): "'The moment they start trying to move into each other's pots, we'll know they're fully mature'" (HP 2, 271).
- Protective measures against "Muggles" at the "Quidditch" World Cup are built on behaviour everyone is familiar with: "Every time Muggles have got anywhere near here all year, they've suddenly remembered urgent appointments and had to dash away again..." (HP 4, 108).
- The Dursleys are tempted out of the house with the promise that they are finalists at the "All-England Best Kept Suburban Lawn Competition" (HP 5, 59).
- At Christmas, Sirius sings "God Rest Ye, Merry Hippogriffs" (HP 5, 552) – and not "Gentlemen", as the Christmas carol actually goes.

In these passages things familiar to the reader are transferred and adapted to the magical world and thus made comical. The invention of new function names for pre-existing things falls under the same category. We can thus find for example, a "Chairwizard of the International Association of Quidditch" (HP 4, 120), "trained mediwizards" (HP 4, 123), a "spokeswizard" (HP 5, 602), "a watchwizard" (HP 5, 845) and the "spokesgoblin" (HP 1, 155). The familiar chess-game that wizards play distinguishes itself from the non-magical variant: the pieces scream wildly and give their opinions about the strategic positions into which they have been placed (HP 1, 215-216). And even Western society's pop-culture finds its reflection in the magical world when the punk-rock band

"Weird Sisters" are heard on the "CNN" or "BBC" of the magical world: "*WWN*" ("Wizarding Wireless Network") (HP 4, 428).

Changing normal idioms into the magical for usage in the enchanted world represents another form of adopting a familiar model. In the reversal of the meaningless preamble to a speech, the spirit Nick begins his birthday address with, "'My lamented lords, ladies and gentlemen, it is my great sorrow...'" (HP 2, 149), and Mrs Figg tries to comfort Harry with, "'It's no good crying over spilt potion, I suppose... but the cat's among the pixies now'" (HP 5, 32). The verbal expressions she corrupts are, "There's no use crying over spilt milk" (things cannot be changed) and "cat among the pidgeons" (to disturb the peace). Fred tells his brother Ron, "'Time is Galleons'" (HP 5, 81) meaning "time is money" according to the currency of the enchanted world. Such expressions are comical because the reader knows the actual idioms and sees how the conditions have been adjusted to the magical world.

The depiction of advertising in the magical world is another instance of comedic effect. Readers are familiar with sensational publicity slogans and notice with amusement that these forms of communication also function in the magical world, as, for example, the advertisements announced in the "Quidditch" Stadium:

> The Bluebottle: A Broom for All the Family – safe, reliable and with Inbuilt Anti-Burglary Buzzer ... Mrs Skower's All-Purpose Magical Mess-Remover: No Pain, No Stain! ... Gladrags Wizardwear – London, Paris, Hogsmeade ... (HP 4, 110).

When Argus Filch enrols in a correspondence class in magic, we can also read the typical kind of publicity found in this kind of advertising:

> Feel out of step in the world of modern magic? Find yourself making excuses not to perform simple spells? Ever been taunted for your woeful wandwork?
> There is an answer!
> Kwikspell is an all-new, fail-safe, quick-result, easy-learn course. Hundreds of witches and wizards benefited from the Kwikspell method!
> (HP 2, 139-140)

Even the book-titles of the fantasy world listed in the novels are funny versions more or less similar to those of actually existing books:

The Adventures of Martin Miggs, the Mad Muggle (HP 2, 48)
The Handbook of Hippogriff Psychology (HP 3, 324)
Fowl or Foul? A Study of Hippogriff Brutality (HP 3, 324)
Predicting the Unpredictable: Insulate Yourself against Shocks (HP 3, 61)

Broken Balls: When Fortunes Turn Foul (HP 3, 61)
Common Magical Ailments and Afflictions (HP 4, 28-29)
Magical Mediterranean Water-Plants and Their Properties (HP 4, 242)
Olde and Forgotten Bewitchments and Charmes (HP 4, 530-531)
Saucy Tricks for Tricky Sorts (HP 4, 530-531)
Weird Wizarding Dilemmas and Their Solutions (HP 4, 530-531)
Madcap Magic for Wacky Warlocks (HP 4, 530-531)
A Guide to Medieval Sorcery (HP 4, 532)
An Anthology of Eighteenth-Century Charms (HP 4, 532)
Dreadful Denizens of the Deep (HP 4, 532)
*Power You Never Knew You Had and What to Do With Them Now You've
    Wised Up* (HP 4, 532)
Where There's a Wand, There's a Way (HP 4, 534)

The handouts for magical-career guidance stand out above all. Gringotts bank advertises itself with this text:

> Are you seeking a challenging career involving travel, adventure and sub-
> stantial, danger-related treasure bonuses? Then consider a position with
> Gringotts Wizarding Bank, who are currently recruiting Curse-Breakers for
> thrilling opportunities abroad... (HP 5, 722).

A security company asks its potential applicants: "HAVE YOU GOT WHAT IT TAKES TO TRAIN SECURITY TROLLS?" (HP 5, 722), and a unit in the Ministry of Magic promises this entry into the profession: "MAKE A BANG AT THE DEPARTMENT OF MAGICAL ACCIDENTS AND CA-TASTROPHES" (HP 5, 722-723). Yet another joke lies in the fact that working together with "Muggles" does not require any special qualifications, only "en-thusiasm, patience and a good sense of fun" (HP 5, 722). Even the sale of sou-venirs by travelling salesmen at the "Quidditch" World Cup resembles the real-ity of the well-known mass-rally:

> Salesmen were Apparating every few feet, carrying trays and pushing carts
> full of extraordinary merchandise. There were luminous rosettes [...] which
> were squealing the names of the players, pointed green hats bedecked with
> dancing shamrocks, Bulgarian scarves adorned with lions that really roared,
> flags from both countries which played their national anthems as they were
> waved, [...] tiny models of Firebolts, which really flew, and collectible fig-
> ures of famous players, which strolled across the palm of your hand, preen-
> ing themselves. (HP 4, 106)

Whenever wizards and "Muggles" meet one another, there are causes for comical misunderstandings. Some examples are here representatively listed:

Mrs Weasley covers the whole envelope with stamps because she has no idea how the "Muggle" postal service works (HP 4, 39).

Mr Weasley tells the totally disconcerted Vernon, "'They run off eckeltricity [sic], don't they? [...] I collect plugs [...] and batteries'" (HP 4, 54).

A wizard dresses up as a woman at the "Quidditch World-Cup" because he cannot distinguish between the clothing of men and women (HP 4, 95-96).

Mr Weasley threatens Vernon: "'If you won't let Harry use the fellytone – 'Telephone,' whispered Hermione" (HP 5, 954-955).

St Mungo's Hospital is a particular example of fantasy's satirically inverted representations. Everything here recalls normal hospital bustle familiar to the reader – except that the illnesses, clinics and treatments are fundamentally different from those in reality. A sign hanging in the entrance hall reads:

> A CLEAN CAULDRON KEEPS POTIONS FROM BECOMING POISONS and ANTIDOTES ARE ANTI-DON'TS UNLESS APPROVED BY A QUALIFIED HEALER. (HP 5, 534).

A "welcomewitch" sits at the reception (HP 5, 535), who, like most public institution functionaries, has a distinct lack of charm when directing patients to the proper place:

> "It's these – ouch – shoes my brother gave me – ow – they're eating my – OUCH – feet – look at them, there must be some kind of - AARGH – jinx on them and I can't – AAAARGH – get them off." [...] "The shoes don't prevent you reading, do they?" said the blonde witch, irritably pointing at a large sign to the left of her desk. "You want Spell Damage, fourth floor. Just like it says on the floor guide. Next!" (HP 5, 534).

The situation will be recognisable to every reader. The comical effect lies in the fact that even in the magical world, where injuries and illnesses are treated completely differently, the familiar stereotypes are still present. In this case it is the unfriendly receptionist. At Christmas the hospital becomes the refuge for people who have been the victims of inter-family holiday disputes:

> [...] Harry found himself shunted aside by a witch with a satsuma jammed up her left nostril. "Family argument, eh?" smirked the blonde witch behind the desk. "You're the third I've seen today ... Spell Damage, fourth floor"(HP 5, 558-559),

The contrast between the real and the magical world is highlighted again (in caricature) when Arthur Weasley has been treated with "Muggle"-medicine and has had his wounds stitched. His wife reproaches him:

"You have been messing around with Muggle remedies? [...But] even you, Arthur, wouldn't be *that* stupid –" [...] "Typical Dad," said Ginny, shaking her head as they set off up the corridor. "Stitches... I ask you..." (HP 5, 558-559)

Humour in *Harry Potter* comes about first and foremost from the fantastic elements or the juxtaposition of the magical and real worlds. Aside from these there are also scenes of situation comedy, slapstick and the alienation and exaggeration of the reader's familiar world.

VII. "Harry Potter" in Context of Children's and Young Adult Literature

Fantastic literature presents a special quality of the genre: it frequently addresses children as well as adult. This is precisely the case with *Harry Potter*: originally conceived as a children's book, there are as many adult readers today as there are children and teenagers. The publishers have even produced an edition designed especially for adults, with an artistic cover and smaller print meant to target the adult reader.[1] In this part of the *Potter* analysis, I will look not at the genre itself, but rather define its characteristic features in order to provide a background with which to consider the *Harry Potter* novels themselves.

VII.1.A. The Basic Structures of Children's Literature

The narrative structure of children's literature has one special feature above all: it is adapted to the relevant age of the reader. The child's reading preferences change along with his or her growing cognitive, analytical and finally reading skill.

In contemporary criticism, one assumes that texts for children have two narrative levels: "one addressed to the child, another addressed, often unconsciously, to the adult beside or behind the child"; texts of this genre should therefore always be analysed according to these two levels.[2] The children's code stands against the adult code, and while the children's code cannot decrypt the adult code, the adult can read from both levels.[3] The technique of the hidden text is often associated with this, by which only the adult can decode the events lying behind the foreground of the actual story.[4] Modern texts for children no longer have an all-knowing, auctorial or I-narrator who reports from a later time period with perfect hindsight, but rather from a personal as well as focalised narrative situation, what Nikolajeva refers to as subjective realism: "[T]he events described are filtered through the mind of the character before they are presented to the reader."[5] The author frequently submerges him- or herself behind one of these perspectives.[6]

Plots especially aimed for children must have a simple structure and clear causality,[7] even though children have become more receptive to complicated,

---

[1] Mentioned here are the German Carlsen and the English Bloomsbury editions for adults – in which can be found the line "für Erwachsene" or "for adult readers".

[2] See Maria Nikolajeva, *Children's Literature Comes of Age: Toward a New Aesthetic*, New York, London: Garland Publishing, 1996, 57-58.

[3] See Nikolajeva 1996, 61.

[4] See Nikolajeva 1996, 106-107.

[5] See Nikolajeva 1996, 99-100.

[6] See Nikolajeva 1996, 99-100.

[7] See Nikolajeva 1996, 175.

confusing plots from television and computer games.[8] Texts for these age groups have usually only one plot, young adult literature on the other hand often combines several levels.[9] Plots for children must therefore have a clear beginning, middle and end (or at least, a happy exit) structure.[10] Conflicts are usually between individual characters that set the action.[11] If the texts are directed towards young children, the story is often narrated episodically, i.e. "single events or short episodes are linked together by common characters, settings, or themes. Within each episode, however, we can often distinguish the master plot."[12] The basic pattern of most of these texts is the circular journey: "That is, the plot follows the trajectory home – departure from home – adventure – return home."[13] The goal of the plot is that the hero grows up. The plot usually begins with the protagonist having to leave his ancestral surroundings. In the course of the plot, the hero must be able to withstand encounters with situations and creatures that are new to him.[14]

As opposed to the adult reader, children are not bothered by improbable storylines, simple plots and a simple character scheme[15] – they often want exactly that: children evince a "need for stories of wish fulfilment, stories which provide compensatory and escapist reading."[16] They thus identify themselves especially with children who are the same age or only slightly older[17] whom they can admire and see as role model. The child reader longs for authenticity and does not want to be disappointed by the narrator or author.[18] The story must have a tight tempo and offer a lot of action.

Typical motifs in texts for children are, for instance:[19]
- Arrival in a new home
- Birthdays and Christmas, Halloween
- First and last day of school
- Quest motif
- Journeys
- Surviving a threatening situation

---

[8]   See Nikolajeva 1996, 76.
[9]   See Nikolajeva 1996, 162.
[10] See Nikolajeva 1996, 166-167.
[11] See Nikolajeva 1996, 162.
[12] See Nikolajeva 1996, 160.
[13] See Nikolajeva 1996, 79.
[14] See Nikolajeva 1996, 167.
[15] See Nikolajeva 1996, 114.
[16] See Nikolajeva 1996, 114.
[17] See Nikolajeva 1996 115.
[18] See Nikolajeva 1996, 119.
[19] See Nikolajeva 1996, 163-164.

- Battle between good and evil
- The child protagonist is stigmatised and unjustly excluded from the group
- Old, remote house as setting[20]
- An old mentor introduces the protagonist to a magical world[21]
- Exile, death and experience of loss[22]
- Relationships to teachers, siblings and parents[23]
- Sleep, dream, unconsciousness[24]
- Search for identity in strange social surroundings[25]
- Conflict with and subsequent rejection of an adult representative of the value system[26]
- Motifs of the Arthurian Saga and medievalism[27]

Food plays a major role in children's literature: it serves to fulfil the physical needs of children and thus substitutes the function of the erotic in adult literature. At the same time, food signalises comfort and security.[28] Fear and terror are equally important elements for the young reader of children's literature: when they are overcome, the child feels reassured and courageous, accepted and competent.[29] The titles of books and chapters in children's literature are important signposts in the selection of reading material. Both must already foreshadow what is going to happen in the following pages, thus arousing the child's interest. The first chapter should already build an atmosphere of expectation, while promising excitement and adventure.[30]

Adventure and detective stories in which the child-characters help in a large part the adults in solving the crime or untangle the previous course of events are very popular among children. Successful children's books often appear as series, from which we can distinguish two kinds: the chronological back-to-back works in which the protagonists and settings underlie the shifts in action ("sequence"), texts in which characters and settings remain the same, and texts in which the characters stay the same, but the individual parts are not connected

---

[20] See Cogan Thacker, Webb 2002, 110-111.
[21] See Cogan Thacker, Webb 2002, 110-111.
[22] See Cogan Thacker, Webb 2002, 110-111; Maria Nikolajeva, *The Rhetoric of Character in Children's Literature*, Lanham, Maryland, London: The Scarecrow Press, 2002, 199.
[23] See Nikolajeva 2002, 111.
[24] See Nikolajeva 2002, 202.
[25] See Cogan Thacker, Webb 2002, 112.
[26] See Cogan Thacker, Webb 2002, 112.
[27] See Nikolajeva 1996, 158. This is especially relevant for English-speaking children's literature.
[28] See Nikolajeva 1996, 201; Lurie 2003, 176.
[29] Lurie 2003, 118-120.
[30] Lurie 2003, 112-123.

to each other ("cluster").[31] Branding is the central reason for the success of the sequel. When an author or more specifically a series is well established, the marketing expenditures are substantially less than for individual books. This is clearly in the interest of the publishers, who then encourage series. Both authors and titles receive their own branding, in order to build up fan-clubs around them, which for the publishers act as cost-free advertising and perpetuate the product.[32] This development began in the 1950s – Robert Druce identifies Enid Blyton as a trendsetter in self-marketing: the personality and private life of the author became increasingly important for the marketing of the text, in Enid Blyton's case her personal signature became her trade-mark.[33] Children in particular like to read books by familiar authors. Author names or identities of the title-character secure the confidence of children and move them and their parents to buy the books and the sequels.[34] Yet what makes a work so highly successful?

> To sell in very great numbers, sooner or later the book must "strike a nerve". If fiction, it must tell a story alluring enough for a great many readers to wish to participate in it in fantasy. It must in some way conform to or – more persuasively – give shape to a current ideology or group of ideologies.[35]

Among girls, boarding-school novels are particularly sought after.[36] Since most children wish for pets, animals as companions of the protagonist are a success guarantor.[37]

When it comes to temporal structure, we can see that, in children's literature, distinctly small periods of time are more common than in adult literature[38] and are based on a disjunctive pattern,[39] individual episodes are depicted elaborately and in detail. Ellipses divide the decisive scenes. The use of analepsis is an important means of creating a form, especially in characterisation (see II.1.A, 31).[40]

In terms of space, the plot in texts for children unfolds in usually close quarters – the hero rarely operates in an extended physical space.[41] Nature is

---

[31] See Robert Druce, *This Day Our Daily Fictions: An Enquiry into the Multi-Million Bestseller Status of Enid Blyton and Ian Fleming*, Atlanta: Rodopi, 1992.
[32] See Druce 1992, 111.
[33] See Druce 1992, 288.
[34] See Sheila G. Ray, *The Blyton Phenomenon: The controversy surrounding the world's most successful children's writer*, London: Andre Deutsch, 1982, 120.
[35] See Druce 1992, 290.
[36] See Ray 1982, 114. *Harry Potter* combines both genres very successfully.
[37] See Ray 1982, 114.
[38] See Nikolajeva 2002, 178.
[39] See Nikolajeva 2002, 178.
[40] See Nikolajeva 2002, 178.
[41] See Nikolajeva 2002, 127.

thus given greater meaning; it is haphazard, arbitrary and mysterious.[42] Maria Nikolajeva maintains that the space-time structure in novels for girls differs from that in novels for boys. Time and space in texts for boys are more precise, the plot takes place in the inner space at home or at school. The temporal structure is cyclical and is represented by constantly repeated remarks about the time. If the plot takes place over several years, certain spatial or temporal fixed-points will appear again and again. The spatial mobility in texts for girls consists mainly in the movement from one closed room to the next, e.g. from home to the boarding school. While boy-specific texts are rich in plot and display a linear time structure, literature for girls has less in the way of events and is defined by repeated return, the rhythm of the seasons or death and resurrection. The focus of the plot is more frequently the inner coming-of-age of the protagonist than the outer events.[43]

The language of texts for children can be both adapted to the supposed level of the child and creative in a childish sense. While, for instance, A.A. Milne plays with the correct use of language in *Winnie the Pooh* (1926)[44] and thus with childish "slang", many authors play with or change around normal language in order to better characterise their figures.[45] The linguistic possibilities in texts for children are necessarily limited to the fact that children cannot concentrate for long periods of time and love variety. This is why in texts for young children short sentences dominate, while long, detailed descriptions that do not contribute to the advancement of the plot are left out.[46] They also appreciate word games, situational comedy, characters transformed into the ridiculous and slapstick.[47]

VII.1.B. Character Structure in Children's Literature

Children's literature is traditionally plot-oriented, i.e. fixated on action and therefore often works with few characters, and these, furthermore, are often flat and static characters.[48] Texts for children generally have not one but several protagonists: in real life, children seldom bear sole responsibility for their actions, and the literature must represent this reality.[49] In literature for young children, protagonists are usually characterised by their external appearances; in young adult literature, on the other hand, characters are only indirectly portrayed. The

---

42 See Lurie 2003, 181.
43 See Lurie 2003, 125-126.
44 See Cogan Thacker, Webb 2002, 238.
45 See Nikolajeva 2002, 238.
46 See Nikolajeva 2002, 119.
47 See Nikolajeva 2002, 118.
48 See Nikolajeva 2002, 12, 111.
49 See Nikolajeva 2002, 110-111.

descriptions are often superficial and limited to a few selected qualities of the characters. Mentioned often are "figure, posture, face, eyes, and hair [...]. The characters' clothes are often included in descriptions to convey information about the characters' social status".[50] Female characters are often more elaborately described than their male counterparts.[51] While characters in the more elaborate children's literature go through changes appropriate for their ages, trivial literature demonstrates neither suitable behaviour for the figures' ages nor do they mature as character.[52]

Conspicuously, parents play either no or a negative role in texts for children: they either behave inappropriately or they want the protagonists to quit their adventure. Child characters often have parent substitutes, in fantastic children's literature often a wise old wizard (like Tolkien's Gandalf or Rowling's Dumbledore) or friend.[53]

A fixture of the character inventory in children's literature is, of course, the orphan[54] as well as the teacher: in texts for girls this type often appears as an idealised and admired (woman) teacher, while in literature for boys, the teacher is often a ridiculous figure.[55] Male characters have a whole peer group around them, all of whom are taken into account in the progress of the story. Girls on the other hand are often portrayed with a single best-friend.[56] In adventure stories there is the villainous opponent, who is usually the first to set the plot in motion with his actions.[57] Often, when the child figure faces a threat that is too great for him alone, an adult helper, frequently a powerful magician, appears, *deus ex machina*, and saves the child.[58] The trickster and the cheat or impostor who blow their cover in the course of the story and thus lose all their privileges are also typical of children's literature.[59] Maria Nikolajeva further states that male authors often turn active and independent girls into heroes, while female authors tend to show boys in battle against a villain.[60]

---

[50] See Nikolajeva 2002, 183-184.
[51] See Nikolajeva 2002, 189.
[52] See Nikolajeva 2002, 126-127.
[53] See Nikolajeva 2002, 172.
[54] See Nikolajeva 2002, 172.
[55] See Nikolajeva 2002, 121.
[56] See Nikolajeva 2002, 123.
[57] See Nikolajeva 2002, 111, 113.
[58] See Nikolajeva 2002, 124.
[59] See Nikolajeva 2002, 124.
[60] See Nikolajeva 2002, 77-78.

VII.1.C. Representation of Values in Children's Literature

More than any other genre, children's literature seeks to convey values and desirable modes of behaviour. The texts thus represent first and foremost adult concepts of morality.[61] Since parents pay particular attention to which children's literature is exciting and "good" – and which could have a bad influence on them – the genre is always subject to censorship. *Harry Potter* is attacked and banned from school libraries (see 347), particularly by the Christian Right in the US.[62] Behind all this is the adults' wish to control children's thoughts and mould the next generation after their image.[63] Above all, adults try to protect their children from harmful influences and keep them in a condition of ignorant innocence and purity. In the recent decades and especially since the 1970s, a different concept of children's literature has emerged: modern texts for children should now have the responsibility of providing children with a realistic view of the world in all its aspects – even the negative ones.[64] It is important for children that the texts they read formulate clear-cut, unambiguous moral statements, and thus one of Rowlings' particularly successful predecessors, Enid Blyton, provides her readers with "a consistent and powerful [...] system of ideologies".[65]

Children's literature is traditionally written by authors from the upper middle classes; until the 1960s at least, role models were thus derived from this milieu: fathers are often bankers, lawyers, doctors, pastors or military men, mothers, on the other hand, are predominantly house-wives.[66] Emancipation, equal rights or even just female autonomy remain issues of secondary importance.

Other value statements in texts for children refer to work and religion. Work in children's literature is something negative: it is punishment and a joyless burden, the goal of the protagonists is to free themselves of it. The hero is mostly successful in this and yet nevertheless lives up to all the demands made of him.[67] There is throughout a clear "right" and "wrong", but the authors refrain from any direct formulation of a conception of God or any religious commentary.

VII.1.D. The English School Story

The classic school story came out of the mid-nineteenth century and was a very successful genre for about a hundred years. With the end of the Second World

---

[61] See Musgrave 1985, 17.
[62] See Hunt 2001, 256.
[63] See Cogan Thacker, Webb 2002, 14.
[64] See Cogan Thacker, Webb 2002, 112.
[65] See Druce 1992, 300.
[66] See Nikolajeva 2002, 205.
[67] See Nikolajeva 2002, 216.

War and thus the ante-bellum societal value system, the genre sunk to the category of trivial literature.

Thomas Arnold (1795-1842), father of the poet Matthew Arnold (1822-1888), was a decisive figure in the development of the English public school and thus influential for the school story. The corner stone of Arnold's school organisation was to assign pupils to various so-called "houses," where the boys would construct or have constructed for them their long-lasting social networks. Every house had a housemaster from the teaching staff and a prefect from among the pupils.[68]

Most school stories correspond to a clear, all-embracing schema. The content is frequently quite trivial, the events limited. The Australian sociologist P. W. Musgrave quotes Canon Raven, theologian and Cambridge don, who summarised the "recipe" of the school story:

> Take a juvenile athlete as your chief ingredient; add a wit, a bully, a persecuted fag, an awkward scholar, a faithful friend, a dangerous rival, and a batch of distorted pedagogues; mix these up in an atmosphere of genial romanticism; insert a smoking scandal, a fight, a cribbing scene and sundry rags, and a house match or two; bring them all to the boil when the hero scores the winning try or does the hat trick; serve the whole hot, and with a title associating the desk with an establishment which the intimated can identify; and the suburbs will raid the libraries for the result.[69]

The plot serves as a pretext for making various groups and their values collide with one another and thus test their manliness.[70] Classic motifs of the school story are:

- Stolen exam questions
- Innocent pupils falsely suspected of wrong-doing, ostracised from the community, and in the end triumphantly rehabilitated
- Catastrophes of all kinds
- Students who have run away get into dangerous trouble and are then rescued and returned wounded to the school
- Rivalry between students and student groups
- Rebellion against and opposition to teachers
- A group leader establishes himself among the student body
- Sports competition in the school, final game for the school trophy
- Dangerous adventures that the students survive serve as basis for friendship
- Punishment (often absurd tasks or the cane)
- Meetings in the headmaster's office

---

[68] See Musgrave 1985, 60.
[69] See Nikolajeva 2002, 219.
[70] See Nikolajeva 2002, 244.

- Dignitaries from the world outside visit the school
- School reprimand or threat of same
- Special lessons for individual students
- Teatime with a teacher
- Death of school-mate
- Pets
- Unfair teachers
- Underground passages, secrets (found especially in *girls' school story*)

Lessons themselves are only seldom portrayed, descriptions of class-time or homework almost never. If these scenes are established, it is only as the setting for the students' actions and to clarify certain values.[71] The location of the school story is almost always in an old and venerable school building, in a remote place, if possible in a natural landscape near the coast.[72]
In terms of the cast of characters, the school story has a fixed stock of types who are hardly if at all individualised. The characters cluster around the hero and his adversary, usually an unkempt bully. The figure of the schoolmaster generally follows Matthew Arnold's model and values morality over intellect, cooperation over confrontation. Furthermore, honesty is rewarded and dishonesty is punished. Arnold was known for making students prefects based on how virtuous they were rather than on how well they did academically. The nineteenth-century boarding school knows nothing of the modern school's practices of democratic self-governing: the headmaster of the school story is a "benign dictator."[73]

Teachers are frequently wise, exact and pedantic, sometimes excessively bureaucratic and self-involved – "an image of a man obsessed with timetables and housematches and the peg for his gown, with habit and detail, the repeated joke and the dreary ritual."[74] The following characters are also found at the school:[75]

- The affectionate, good natured teacher
- The dry, old, humourless teacher
- The non-conformist games master
- The superficial, vain French teacher
- The pedant
- The sadistic teacher who enjoys flogging the pupils
- The friendly, doddering old man

---

[71] See Musgrave 1985, 59; Nikolajeva 2002, 217.
[72] See Ray 1982, 196.
[73] Ray 1982, 196.
[74] Quigly 1982, 28.
[75] Quigly 1982, 87-89.

- The vivacious housekeeper
- The comical maid
- The cheeky, impertinent pupil

Parents hardly ever make an appearance in the school story. Only in the girls' school story can we find a mostly revered mother or ersatz-mother, who is depicted as wise, warm-hearted and affectionate and who satisfies all the expectations of such a character.[76]

A particular type of the school story is the boarding-school story for girls. The classical elements of a school story for girls are:[77]

- Journey (often by train) to the school
- School with individual, almost human traits – which acts as a character in the plot
- Introduction of new students or teachers
- Internal school events such as selecting the hockey team, musical performances, or pupil-teacher relations direct the plot
- Call for tolerance in light of the differences and abilities of the pupils
- Considerate teachers
- Morally depraved French teacher
- Existence of a school-specific code of ethics that condemns meanness, sneakiness and snobbery
- The upper middle class dominates the school
- Friendship among small school-groups or cliques
- Process of growing up for the schoolgirls

With the rise of women's emancipation, these stories lost much of their moral foundation. Only Enid Blyton managed to weather this change in values – her novels are still sold successfully today, despite similar outdated normative values.

The school story has always been heavily ideological and is supposed to convey clear moral values. The personal development of the boys is of central importance,[78] and everything that happens in the text is directed towards "the achievement of a more worthy character."[79] The decisive component of the moral development is the internalisation of specific Christian values.[80] The school story portrays first and foremost a feeling of moral certainty, of the uniqueness of the English way of life, of the light-heartedness which in our pre-

---

[76] Quigly 1982, 215-216.
[77] See Pinsent 2005, 12-15.
[78] See Musgrave 1985, 28.
[79] See Musgrave 1985, 75.
[80] See Musgrave 1985, 132.

sent point in time is always harder to find: the school story always served nostalgic sentiments and expressed the longing for certainty and order.[81]

In the school story, the official value system is at odds with the schoolboy code. This code unites the students against the authority of the teachers and condemns a modern kind of Seven Deadly Sins according to their schoolboy code: "snobbery, self-seeking, dissipation, active sexuality, violence, sloth," as well as theft, deceit, treachery, sneakiness, cowardice, lying. Furthermore, pupils are supposed to solve their own conflicts without recourse to the teachers' interference.[82]

In the school story, it goes without saying that those in the upper rungs of the hierarchy – teachers as well as students – are moral role models for those younger or on the lower rungs of the hierarchy. The fulfilment of duties to the community of the school, to the family, to friends and to the authorities is central to the value code.[83] Courage and the backbone to fight for a position in the face of resistance are part of the school story's ideal of manliness.[84] Chivalry and the struggle against one's own negatively perceived emotions distinguish the gentleman.[85] In the school story, the individual has to learn obedience to those above and to accept his place in the society. Inner and outer discipline and behaviour are as important as keeping up team spirit.[86] It goes without saying that all the positive characters are English patriots. All these moral aspects are far more important for the characters' standing than the question of their academic performance.[87]

There are two value systems in the school story at loggerheads with each other. The positive one embodies leadership, friendliness and concern for others; the negative one dishonesty, tattling and snobbery.[88] Yet the negative characters can always hope for forgiveness, for the "good ones" are kindly and human, the bully is not taken seriously and the first-grader is allowed to make mistakes on his way to moral perfection.[89] The only unforgivable sin is social arrogance and snobbery which is seen as unmanly, superficial and unworthy of any cultured person.[90] Nevertheless, even when texts seem to criticise arrogance and snobbery, the classic school story sets stock in class differences and nationalistic arrogance. The school story does not demand any kind of change to existing social relations, rather their actual message runs: "kind hearts are more than coronets, but the gen-

---

[81] See Quigly 1982, 276.
[82] See Druce 1992, 207-209; Musgrave 1985, 133.
[83] See Musgrave 1985, 134, 244.
[84] See Musgrave 1985, 136.
[85] See Musgrave 1985, 155.
[86] See Musgrave 1985, 244-245.
[87] See Musgrave 1985, 155.
[88] See Pinsent 2005, 18.
[89] See Quigly 1982, 84.
[90] See Quigly 1982, 54.

eral attitude is, by present day standards, highly patronising even towards accept-able kind hearts."[91]

VII.1.E. Fantastic Texts for Children

Fantastic texts represent a special case in children's literature. In terms of the present work, it is particularly interesting, since it creates an interface between the fantastic genres relevant to *Harry Potter* and children's literature. With his 2003 monograph, *From Alice to Harry Potter: Children's Fantasy in England*, Colin Manlove has provided us with a comprehensive analysis particular to this variety of the genre. Manlove proves that contemporary texts of this genre fre-quently exhibit a very intense personal narrative situation. This communicates the same intimacy as a first-person narrator.[92] The most important value of these texts is the domestic, familial happiness of the protagonists.[93]

Characteristic of English children's fantasy is the love of contradictions and juxtapositions, rather than the play with metaphorical or symbolical mean-ing. English literature often deviates here from the quest motif and the plot-pattern of the fairy tale.[94] While there is still a clear division between real and magical worlds in early fantastic texts for children, this distinction dropped more and more in the late twentieth century: the Todorovian criterion of uncertainty extends also here and would classify these texts as "marvellous".[95] The fantastic elements of these stories can be traced back to extraordinary states of mind rather than to an actually supernatural event.[96] The fantastic seeks above all to satisfy children's impossible wishes, to do justice to their creativity and at the same time, to convey an explicit canon of values.[97]

What has become important for these texts since the twentieth century is the search for one's own individual identity and a general insecurity expressed in the concrete fear of being threatened by supernatural creatures, monstrous parents or the sadistic stepfamily.[98] Civilization is crumbling, there is no security – a general pessimism can be seen in many texts.[99] The confrontation with death as the last great threat to the child – either because his own life is in danger or because the loss of someone close to him is at hand – is equally prevalent in texts for children and tied up with the above mentioned themes. Children's lit-

---

[91] See Quigly 1982, 97.
[92] See Manlove 2003, 169.
[93] See Manlove 2003, 172.
[94] See Manlove 2003, 194-195.
[95] See Nikolajeva 1996, 71-72.
[96] See Manlove 2003, 172.
[97] See Manlove 2003, 201.
[98] See Manlove 2003, 195.
[99] See Cogan Thacker, Webb 2002, 111.

erature is more open to such taboo subjects as death, sexuality and violence. Since the 1990s, the prevalent motifs have been insecurity, fear (to the point of horror) and loss, and we will often find the fear of darkness, vampires or other fearsome ghosts. Many of the decisive elements of the plot are played out at night or in nightmares.[100] Evil lurks outside one's own fantasy and is a real threat rather than a figment of the imagination.[101]

VII.1.F. Enid Blyton: Between Criticism and Success

Enid Blyton (1897-1978) was the best known and at the same time most controversial author of children's books before J.K. Rowling. By the end of the 1980s, 700 titles had appeared under her name, she had sold 500 million books in 126 languages.[102] In 1970 alone, 128 Blyton books had been translated worldwide – to draw a comparison: in the same year, Shakespeare's dramas had "only" been translated 111 times, the Bible 273.[103] Her two best known boarding school series, *Malory Towers* and *St. Clare's* were the top-selling girls' book series of 1977. The former had a total print run of 2,300,000 copies; the latter reached almost 6 million.[104] For over thirty years, Enid Blyton was the most popular woman author among children between the ages of eight and twelve.[105]

There were several reasons for this success: on the one hand, in all her works, Blyton serves the particular needs of her target group of escaping from the everyday; a happy ending and a clear moral position.[106] Robert Druce terms this perspective the "congratulation system", in which the reader can import his own realistically unfeasible plot and wish-fulfilment into the novel and be rewarded at the end of the story in which he is the hero. In reality, on the other hand, he would never find himself in the situation in which these events could occur. But in the text, he can solve the riddles at the same time as the protagonist and conquer evil.[107] Enid Blyton consequently confirms the reader's expectations of her target group: the homogeneous structuring of the plot fulfils all the reader's wishes.[108] Blyton produces the illusion of the real, while at the same time excluding any kind of insecurity. She thus creates "textual comfort zones" for the reader and provides the child with retreat and escape in an adventure

---

[100] See Manlove 2003, 173-175; Cogan Thacker, Webb 2002, 111.
[101] See Manlove 2003, 178.
[102] See Bob Mullan, *The Enid Blyton Story*, London: Boxtree, 1987, 13.
[103] See Almut Prieger, *Das Werk Enid Blytons: eine Analyse ihrer Erfolgsserie in westdeutschen Ausgabe*, Frankfurt am Main: dipa, 1982, 40.
[104] See Prieger 1982, 43.
[105] See Ray 1982, 111.
[106] See Druce 1992, 298.
[107] See Druce 1992, 301.
[108] See Druce 1992, 296.

guaranteed to be completed without the least of risks.[109] In this way, she addresses above all a certain age-level in which children already have a certain reading ability but have not yet reached puberty – rebellion against authority and sexuality do not as yet come into play.[110] Blyton's works portray a "desirable experience rather than realistic experience."[111] Although the ambience of her works, with the boarding school and the coastal landscape, is typically English, Blyton avoids any clear spatial or temporal presentations in her texts – this way, she can be seamlessly consumed and understood in other cultural context.[112] Finally, the author skilfully meshes her works with one another. In all of her texts there are references to the events of past books, so that the reader begins to wish to know what happened in these stories. We could call this "surreptitious advertising" or, in marketing jargon, product placement.[113]

Enid Blyton met with a lot of criticism in her lifetime, this was especially hard in the 1970s. She was considered a "bad writer; her attitudes were suspect, her characterisation thought to be shallow and stereotyped, her plots unrealistic, her vocabulary repetitive and undemanding."[114] Her books were described of being of a

> [...] poor literary quality [... which may] lead to an unrewarding addiction, and may make it impossible for the child to move on to 'quality' literature. Moreover, the critics argue, her books pollute the cultural air we breathe with their middle-class values, their sexism and their racism.

Banality, unimaginativeness, lack of fantasy, limited vocabulary, racism, sexism, emphasis on middle-class values[115] – the critics did not accord Enid Blyton one redeeming feature. At the time, her books were even banned from public libraries.[116] She represents

> a lost world, of superior middle-class children against the background of a rosy England. She is disparaging about the working classes and foreigners. And even her most interesting "Five" character, George [...], is never fully emancipated – [...].[117]

---

[109] See Prieger 1982, 204.
[110] See Ray 1982, 111.
[111] See Ray 1982, 114.
[112] See Ray 1982, 117.
[113] See Druce 1992, 112.
[114] See Mullan 1987, 13-14.
[115] See Hunt 2001, 37.
[116] See Mullan 1987, 13-14.
[117] See Mullan 1987, 79.

She keeps children artificially dumb, ruins their vocabulary and does not take them seriously as readers.[118] The only positive effect Blyton's work is accorded is that it gets and keeps children reading at all.[119]

The literary quality of Enid Blyton's texts is not going to be discussed here. I merely want to stress that a simple language, clear moral values and an uncomplicated syntax correspond exactly to the needs of the young target-group. And finally, Enid Blyton moves, like her successor J.K. Rowling, on the thin ice between commercial success and literary demands, between addressing the reading needs of children and the aesthetic wishful thinking of adults. Bob Mullan sums it up for us this way: "Enid Blyton simply wrote too much and was too popular for many to accept."[120] A writer's fate that J.K. Rowling would share half a century later.

Blyton did not research much for her novels – she regularly "scribbled down" her texts at breakneck speed.[121] Her language code is correspondingly unelaborated: a small vocabulary, a lot of repetitions of the same expressions, no pictorial quality to her language and a lot of verbal speech with exclamation marks. There is never a narrator-character,[122] instead only a strong auctorial narrator with an irrefutable value system who describes things explicitly as "horrible", "exciting" or "marvellous".[123]

Blyton reduces all her material to a "cosy innocuousness", which she elaborates very little, and with which she presents constantly repeated patterns.[124] The author lacks any kind of narrative subtlety – her texts are defined by "telling" rather than by "showing". Every strand of plot is brought to a clear ending. Blyton's stories, set in the apparently real setting of the boarding school, are so far removed from the real world of her readers that her novels can almost count as fantastic literature.[125]

Enid Blyton made most use of two genres of children's literature: the adventure story and the boarding school novel, which I will discuss in further detail below. The 21 volume *Famous Five* series (1942 to 1963) or the *Adventure*-series with eight titles coming out between 1944 and 1955, to name only those best known in Germany, distinguish themselves by their always identical plot scheme:[126] "[The] characteristic Blyton adventure story features […] incredibly

---

[118]   See Mullan 1987, 148-150.
[119]   See Mullan 1987, 150. Blyton and J.K. Rowling have this criticism in common.
[120]   See Mullan 1987, 150.
[121]   See Ray 1982, 202.
[122]   See Ray 1982, 112.
[123]   See Ray 1982, 202.
[124]   See Hunt 2001, 37.
[125]   See Hunt 2001, 38-39.
[126]   See Druce 1992, 123.

clever children with a lot of time on their hands in the school holiday".[127] The children, who form a group with a clear hierarchical structure, solve a mystery or help in solving a crime. The main catalyst of the plot is always the confrontation between good and evil.[128] The adults, especially the stereotypically doltish village policeman, prove themselves to be incapable of solving the problem. The story comes to a climax in a scene which is particularly threatening to the children. They are rescued from great peril by official powers who come on the scene in the figure of the city chief inspector. All the heroes are celebrated at the end.[129] The clues towards solving the mystery are so obvious from the beginning, that the reader can hardly miss them.[130] The children do not go through any growing up process. They remain at the pre-pubescent stage, even when the time of the narrative takes place several years in the past.[131]

In the spatial structure of Blyton's texts there always appears a mysterious, locked room, ruins, remote settings, underground spaces such as caves or cellars in which the members of the children's group are imprisoned for a time by the villains.[132] Many scenes take place the outdoors, in a spectacular, heavily stylised natural stage.[133]

The second genre that Blyton represents is the girls' school story (see VII.2.A, 428). Enid Blyton wrote three school series between 1940 and 1951: *The Naughtiest Girl* (three parts from 1940 to 1945), *St Clare's* (six volumes from 1941 and 1945) and *Malory Towers* (six volumes from 1946 to 1951). The plot generally follows the same scheme:[134]

- The girls longingly look forward to returning to school after the vacation.
- New schoolgirls are the centre of attention.
- The heroines become prefects and are given special responsibilities.
- Portrayal of the New Girls – at least one "evil" character among them.
- Heroine makes a mistake which she regrets and which she has to learn from.

---

[127] See Mullan 1987, 87.

[128] See Druce 1992, 147.

[129] See Prieger 1982, 57.

[130] See Prieger 1982, 296.

[131] See Prieger 982, 58.

[132] See Druce 1992, 201.

[133] See Prieger 1982, 58; Hunt 2001, 39.

[134] See Prieger 1982, 96-97. *The Naughtiest Girl* is a particular exception: the young girl Elizabeth Allen is a spoiled and moody rich heiress whose parents send her to a boarding school (Whyteleafe School) after several varying attempts at bringing her up properly. She is reprimanded often for her wilful misconduct but learns in the end to value the boarding school, makes friends and integrates into the school community. We can see here a development in personality on one hand, on the other hand we do not see in the first volume the above-mentioned classic motifs of the Blyton stories, e.g. the identification with the school or the rejoicing at the beginning of the school year.

– The new girls make mistakes, learn from them or leave the school.
– Happy end.

The girls identify themselves strongly with the school.[135] Punishment – often cruel – is seen as a necessary evil,[136] athletic fitness is a part of their education as a matter of course.[137] The lessons themselves serve merely as a background for the girls' actions between each other. One of the strands of the plot focuses on the integration or conditioning of the new girl to the group's and the school's representative value[138] Next to the strict but just headmistress, the French teacher has a fixed place in the character stock: with her accent, her foreign ways and her occasionally ridiculous behaviour, she is the constant butt of jokes and a source of comic relief.[139]

The characters' external appearances are always, without fail, the reflection of inner values – ugliness is a sign of a moral taint.[140] All the characters are unambiguously good or evil – they are either adversaries or helpers. There are no ambivalent characters. Blyton economises on concrete description.[141]

The events of the adventure series centre most on "eine gemischtgeschlechtliche Gruppe, gebildet aus drei bis fünf Kindern im Alter der hauptsächlich angesprochenen Leserschaft."[142] The leader is "ein Junge, der sich durch Alter, Schlauheit, Vernunft oder auch Dominanzbedürfnis auszeichnet."[143] He often has two more boys in the group who give him advice from the side, while the girls are tag-alongs to the action.[144] The villains are often first fake friends or in Propp's sense fake heroes (see IV.1.A, 145), until the children expose them.[145]

The adults' behaviour is telling: in Enid Blyton's novels they provide comfort and warmth but also represent authority and fallibility (especially in the figures of the "dumb policemen"). By fighting against what in retrospect is a spurious pattern of behaviour and acting alone, they secure the victory of the good. They are successful in their transgression of the rules which the adult world really sanctions and for which their parents in the end praise them.[146] In

---

[135] See Prieger 1982, 59-60.
[136] See Prieger 1982, 105.
[137] See Prieger 1982, 103.
[138] See Prieger, 1982, 59-60.
[139] See Ray 1982, 199.
[140] See Prieger 1982, 94.
[141] See Ray 1982, 201.
[142] "a mixed group of boys and girls, made up of three to five children, mainly the same age as the intended reader", Prieger 1982, 56 [my translation].
[143] "a boy, who distinguishes himself by his age, cleverness, rationale or also his need to dominate", Prieger 1982, 56 [my translation].
[144] See Prieger 1982, 56.
[145] See Druce 1992, 296.
[146] See Ray 1982, 116.

Blyton's works animals have a special role in the cast's characterisation. In their reactions they point out a character's true nature and are never wrong.[147] Nature, fauna and flora are always to be found on the side of the positive characters in Blyton's work.

The headmistress is another stereotypical character in the boarding school story: depicted as grey-haired, dignified and usually with a "lovely smile", she has the power to see through her students in every kind of situation.[148] Her unassailable judgments fall, wise and just. She is the decisive moral instantiation in Enid Blyton's boarding school novels.

VII.2 "Harry Potter" as Novel for Children

The *Harry Potter* novels are first of all children's and young adult books, although they are also – and this is a decisive factor for the extensive success of the novels – read by a large amount of adults. We must therefore consider the texts above all from this angle. In the following chapter, I will explore the specific features of children's and boarding school literature in the *Harry Potter* novels. I will use Enid Blyton's novels, among others, as reference.

The *Harry Potter* series is part of the sequences where texts build up on each other and demonstrate character as well as plot development. They thus distinguish themselves from most of the Blyton series. The series character contributes to the creation of a label – *Harry Potter* has become its own brand which refers not just to the marketing of the books, but to toys and to food of all kind. The trust that children in particular build up around a brand contributes here as well to the continued purchase of further instalments in the series.

In terms of the narrative technique, the novels take up the schemata of children's literature: short interims of suspense in the sub-plots, episodic narration, a fast narrative tempo with a lot of action and the frequently scenic drama all speak to children. Harry Potter's story is predominantly told from the personal narrative situation, Harry himself is – according to Genette and Stanzel (see II.2.A, 34) the focaliser. Like many texts in children's literature *Harry Potter* also has two narrative levels. The children's code, which tells the events directly and without any reference to the reader's reality, is an adventure story; then there is the adult code, which, for example understands the scenes dealing with the political implications as well as the caricature of contemporary consumption orientation as a commentary on his own lived reality.

The plot and the sub-plots of the novels are certainly complex and multifaceted, yet we find a satisfactory resolution at the end of each book. When this

---

[147] See Druce 1992, 296.
[148] See Prieger 1982, 101.

is not the case, it is implicitly referred to in the next part of the series. We can expect that with the seventh instalment, all open questions will be answered and the remaining lose ends will be tied up. As is common with children's literature, all the elements are bound together in clear causality. And, in accordance with the dictates of the genre, every volume limits itself temporally to the period of the school year. The basic pattern of the plot at the level of each volume is circular and corresponds to the circular journey typical of children's literature and especially girls' texts: Harry leaves his familiar surroundings at the Dursleys' which he had known until the age of eleven and enters a new world and must prove himself there. At the end of every schoolyear, he returns home to his family.

In its motifs, *Harry Potter* takes up most of the standard elements of children's literature: Hogwarts is Harry's new home, in which he must find his own role in the interactions between students and with the teacher. The first schoolday with the trip to school is depicted exactly the same as the last day in which the students separate for the holiday. Halloween or Christmas holidays and birthdays play a distinct role (see II.4). With his quest, Harry intervenes in the battle between the good forces around Dumbledore and Voldemort's evil powers. In every volume he lands in extremely precarious situations and puts his life in danger. Harry is wrongly suspected of wrong-doing and excluded from the student society. In one instance, he is accused of having attacked a pupil (*Chamber of Secrets*), another time he is suspected of having smuggled his name into the drawing of the lottery at the school tournament (*Goblet of Fire*). Like many heroes of children's literature, Harry has a wise old mentor in Dumbledore who introduces him to the world of magic. Death and the experience of loss move like leitmotifs throughout the text – thus Harry's parents die before the point of attack, later Cedric Diggory is murdered by Voldemort (*Goblet of Fire*), Sirius Black by his cousin (*Order of the Phoenix*) and finally even Dumblebore by Snape (*Half-Blood Prince*). In *Order of the Phoenix*, where Harry again and again has visions of the Department of Mysteries, we find decisive scenes like Voldemort's attack on Mr Weasley taking place in dreams or even in trances. This is also typical of children's literature. In all these cases, Harry has to confront the value systems represented by the adults and find his own position: does he affiliate himself with the world of Dumbledore's values, with Voldemort's path of least resistance or to the pragmatic career opportunism of a Cornelius Fudge?

The spaces available to the protagonists are very limited: the plot plays out predominantly within Hogwarts or at places accessible from there. With Grimmauld Place (see III.5.G, 135), Riddle House (see III.3.C, 111) or the Shrieking Shack, we see the remote, old houses typical of children's literature. Nature in *Harry Potter* is mysterious and ambivalent: not only do dangerous creatures like the giant spider Aragog lurk in the Forbidden Forest – unicorns and centaurs and later the giant Grawp also live here (see 125).

The *Potter* texts also orient themselves thematically to the genre of children's literature: the relationship with pets who have their own personalities,[149] the conflict with step-parents and the preparation and consumption of food[150] belong to the inventory of classic themes within children's literature. Amy Billone sees an "equation between Harry's dreams and what he discovers to be true"[151] in the elaborate portrayal of food – an equation I can hardly fathom.

The *Harry Potter* novels have a place in the linguistic tradition of children's literature. Rowling avoids long descriptive passages of an epic breadth, but her use of comic elements and the plastic rendition of dialects and slang speak especially to the children's target group (see II.2.H, 55). Word games and funny distortion of words and comic elements make the texts even more attractive for children. J.K. Rowling uses chapter titles and titles for the construction of the reader's expectation in the very way which is customary of children's literature (see II.3.B, 64).

The content of the texts tries to appeal to the greatest consensus possible which the cross-section of children's varying reading needs. Harry Potter is a small eleven-year-old boy at the beginning of the plot. His foster-parents, the Dursley Family, treat him most unfairly and tyrannise him. He is actually too weak to stand first against them then later against the omnipotent and evil Voldemort. Yet, nevertheless, he is eventually able to strike back successfully, oppose the Dursleys and hold his own against the villains on the battlefield. The scheme corresponds exactly to children's favourite identification models of the small hero who – against all odds – can take up arms and win against the adult villains.

Harry Potter makes use of the reading preferences of boys and girls to the same extent, in that the adventure story series is here combined with the boarding school novel. The text's content speaks to lovers of fantasy as well as of non-fantasy literature, for the magical setting tends not to be metaphysical-esoteric. On the contrary, Rowling portrays wizards in entirely everyday situations and confronts them with often very banal problems. Cooking, housework,

---

[149] Harry's owl Hedwig has its own emotional life and interacts with the boy (e.g. HP 3, 13-14), Hermione's cat Crookshanks becomes friends with Sirius Black and is called "clever" (HP 3, 392), and the Weasleys' owl, Pigwidgeon, has the ambition to be the best carrier pigeon ever.

[150] Eating and consuming bizarre, magical sweets is a constant theme in the *Potter* novels: "The house-elves […] were outdoing themselves with a series of rich, warming stews and savoury puddings, […]" (HP 4, 441); regarding Christmas dinner at Hogwarts: "[…] at least a hundred turkeys and Christmas puddings, and large piles of Cribbages Wizardding Crackers" (HP 4, 448); the enumeration of Harry's favourite sweets: "Bertie Botts' Every Flavour Beans, Chocolate Frogs, Droobles Beast Blowing Gum and Fizzing Whizzbees" (HP 4, 448); "[…] food had appeared out of nowhere, so that the five long tables were groaning under joints and pies and dishes of vegetables, bread and sauces and flagons of pumpkin juice" (HP 5, 232).

[151] Billone 2004, 191.

travelling, fashion, sports – all these things have a given place in *Harry Potter*'s world. Even a master-wizard like Dumbledore may speak of his toiletries (HP 4, 456). To compare this with Tolkien, he would never portray his wizard, Gandalf – who in *The Lord of the Rings* has a comparable position to that of Dumbledore of *Harry Potter* – speaking about such base subjects. *Harry Potter* lacks the nobility, the ideological superstructure and the metaphysics which distinguish many fantasy texts. The Weasleys, apart from living in a hexed house and having a few magical objects which make their daily life easier, are a wholly normal, large family with a lot of children. Avoiding the esoteric typical of the genre and remaining down-to-earth and matter-of-fact has contributed a lot to children (and adults) with totally different reading preferences gobbling up these texts and making them equally attractive to boys and girl.

Children love heroes who have abilities that far exceed their actual ages, who point out to adults where they have failed and whom the reader can admire. *Harry Potter* thoroughly responds to this wish too: it is Harry and his friends who solve the respective mysteries and hinder Voldemort in his evil deeds. Harry demonstrates his magical and personal strengths, which constantly surprise Dumbledore (HP 5, 919-922). It is typical of the genre that the characters' psychological depths here recede behind the actual events; *Harry Potter* is plot-oriented, most of the characters are flat or at least static. As described above (see IV.2.A, 149), the portrayal of the characters is limited to a few select qualities. Parents play a very small role in *Harry Potter*, as is the general case in children's literature – Lily and James Potter only become relevant when the son's identity is discovered.[152] The Dursley foster-parents on the other hand tyrannise the orphan Harry and thus represent a common cliché in children's literature. When the boy learns that these people are not his real parents, the scene serves the wishful thinking of many children that they are in reality a princess or at least from a different origin to their real one.[153] Harry can on the other hand make a wise and just substitute father out of Dumbledore. The teachers in *Harry Potter* are either, as is common for children's literature, ridiculous (like Prof. Binns or Sybill Trelawney) or, as in the tradition of girls' texts, idealised, revered moral authorities (like Dumbledore or McGonagall). As is common in the adventure story so too in *Harry Potter*: it is the villainous opponent Voldemort who sets the action in motion. Dumbledore and his agents (*Philosopher's Stone, Chamber of Secrets, Prisoner of Azkaban* and *Goblet of Fire*) or the members of the "Order of the Phoenix" (*Order of the Phoenix*) appear always at the last second to rescue the children from dangerous situations – another frequent element in children's literature (see B. II, 7). And – another typical topos in children's literature – traitors like Mad-Eye Moody (*Goblet of Fire*), Voldemort's spy,

---

[152] See Jelinek 2006, 19.
[153] See Lurie 2003, 115.

Prof. Quirrell (*Philosopher's Stone*) or the impostor Lockhart are repeatedly un-covered. Here we can see that it is precisely the protector-figures the children should most distrust.[154]

The *Harry Potter* novels also prove to be typical of the genre of children's literature in terms of its ideological content: there is a clear orientation of values and an explicit division of "good" and "evil". This responds to the child's wish for moral clarity and certainty of values. That does not mean that the novels por-tray a prettified black-and-white world, rather – fully in the tradition of contem-porary children's literature – a multi-faceted world which has negative aspects even on the sides of the good. If we look at the social background of the children portrayed, it becomes clear that they all come from the middle classes. Mr Weasley and Mr Malfoy are ministry employees and high officials, Hermione's father is a dentist, Harry's parents obviously have no profession, but as former school speaker of Hogwarts clearly aspired to promising careers. Mrs Weasley and Mrs Dursley on the other hand are housewives through and through and have no other profession than to take care of the family. Only women who do not have children are rather independent (like e.g. McGonagall or Nymphadora Tonks). As in other children's literature, Rowling's world of values refers to the world of the upper middle classes. Harry and his friends defy the order of the adults – this too is a typical element of literature for children.[155] Work is some-thing negative, which also corresponds to the conventions of children's litera-ture. We do not come across any explicit statements about religious ideas; nature and the environment are important values.

If we look at *Harry Potter* in the special context of children's literature, we can see, with its personal narrative situation, the love of comparisons and the use of fantastic elements for the purpose of the reader's wish fulfilment, that it is typical of the genre. Like all the heroes of fantastic literature for children, Harry is searching for his identity and has to come to terms with his role as saviour of the world. In doing so, he realises that the apparently perfect environment is fragile, the feigned securities do not protect him and the official political system is corrupt (see V.1.C, 290). Evil, in the figure of Voldemort, really exists; in the battle against his power, Harry needs the help of, e.g. domestic, familial happi-ness which he finds in the Dumbledore foster-family and the Weasley family. He encounters terrifying creatures, like the spider Aragog or the three-headed dog Fluffy and realises that his world is fundamentally threatened, its future prospects rather bad. The reality that Voldemort will pursue Harry relentlessly for years has been a part of the tradition of children's fantasy since the 1990s,

---

[154] See David L. Russell. "From Alice to Harry Potter: Children's Fantasy in England (review)," *The Lion and the Unicorn* 28 (Jan 2004): 166-170, here 169.
[155] See Lexe 2003, 185-186; Lurie 2003, 120.

which has focused on scary situations, insecurity and horrific visions.[156] In this respect, Voldemort, in his abyssal diabolicalness, is one of the high points in children's literature of this century.[157] As opposed to other texts of the genre, the fantastic elements in *Harry Potter* are a part of reality and do not have any rational explanation which could organise the world of the reading. In Todorov's sense, the texts belong to the "marvellous".

Nevertheless, the *Potter* books are in various instances more realistic than the divisions of the genre might otherwise allow of fantastic literature. The representation of the incompetent bureaucracy, the political establishment or the characteristic brand-craze of the capitalist economic system point beyond the comical fantastic aspects of the texts to the satiric adult code of *Harry Potter*.[158] Even if we would like to criticise the author for not dealing with the material stock of fantastic literature her predecessors provided in any innovative, creative way, seeming to be "unaware that there is a history of children's fantasy literature",[159] *Harry Potter* does indeed follow in the tradition of *Alice in Wonderland* and *Peter Pan*. As Amy Billone maintains, *Harry Potter* unites the elements of both:

> He experiences Peter's ecstasy when he gracefully flies, Peter's superhuman aptness when he battles deadly foes, and Peter's effortless capacity to make dreams come alive. At the same time, like Alice, Harry struggles to understand the difference between what appears to be true and what is true.[160]

VII.2.A. "Harry Potter" as School Story

Reviewers like to describe *Harry Potter* as an exact replica of the classic "school story" – particularly the first three volumes. The only difference is that *Potter* deals with his own survival and that of his society, an issue that does not appear in the traditional school story.[161] The American author and literary critic and one of the sharpest critics of *Harry Potter* goes so far as to say, "Rowling has taken 'Tom Brown's School Days' and re-seen it in the magical mirror of Tolkien".[162] The similarities between *Harry Potter* and the school story are in-

---

[156] See Manlove 2003, 189.
[157] See Manlove 2003, 190.
[158] See Misik 2005.
[159] See John Pennington, "From Elfland to Hogwarts, or the Aesthetic Trouble with Harry Potter," *The Lion and the Unicorn* 26 (Jan 2002): 78-97, here 87.
[160] See Billone 2004, 178. We can also see that Peter Pan and Alice – as opposed to Harry – do not experience any character development: Peter is ageless and eternally young, Alice on the other hand episodic adventure, to which we cannot compare the dramaturgic structuring of the *Potter* text.
[161] See Pinsent 2005, 19-20.
[162] See Bloom 2000.

deed great: *Potter*, from all the possible classifications of the genre, is above all a school story.

As in the school story, in *Potter* the reader accompanies a group of schoolchildren on the road to growing up. From the motifs of the school story already mentioned, almost all of them appear in *Harry Potter*:

- Harry is falsely suspected of being behind the attack on the school-children, is then ostracised and in the end triumphantly rehabilitated (*Chamber of Secrets*).
- There are sports competitions within the school, as with the annual award-ing of the "Quidditch" trophy, but also with other wizard-schools such as at the Triwizard Tournament.
- Accidents happen in "Potions" class and at "Quidditch" again and again.
- Both Harry and Malfoy with their respective peer groups stand in compe-tition with one another.
- Harry rebels against Snape (HP 1, 151; HP 3, 389), Hermione against Umbridge (HP 5, 268-269) and Trelawney (HP 3, 119; HP 3, 322).
- Hermione first becomes friends with Harry and Ron when they go through the adventure with the troll in the washroom; danger here acts as the basis for friendship.
- Harry and Ron are often punished: e.g. with cleaning up the files at Argus Filch's (HP 2, 137), by being made to go through the Forbidden Forest (HP 1, 269), and later, Harry is punished by Umbridge (HP 5, 294-299).
- Foreign students and headmasters visit Hogwarts.
- Hagrid is expelled from school after being falsely suspected of murder.
- Harry is repeatedly called to Dumbledore's office and has appointments with teachers such as Umbridge or McGonagall.
- Cedric Diggory represents the death of a schoolmate.
- All the pupils have magical pets.
- Snape and Umbridge are highly unfair, biased teachers.
- The school is full of underground dungeons (*Philosopher's Stone, Chamber of Secrets*) and mysterious rooms such as, e.g. the Vanishing Room.

Also, in respect to the cast of characters, the novels remain true to the school story model: as a leader, Harry is not an especially good student, but he is an excellent "Quidditch" player – for which the younger students like Colin Creevey admire him (*Chamber of Secrets*). Headmaster Dumbledore corre-sponds to the "benign dictator" type, Hagrid is the unconventional teacher (not a sports teacher here but a biology teacher), and Argus Filch represents the sadis-tic flogger. The scatterbrained Prof. Binns provides us with the figure of the friendly doddery old man and Mme Pomfrey the nurse provides the figure of the vivacious housekeeper. Mme Maxime and her students provide the roles of the affected French who put a lot of stock in food and their outer appearances. As usual with school stories, parents play a minor part, while mothers like Mrs Weasley are portrayed positively in the role of housewife.

Other attributes specific to the girls' boarding school story also appear in the *Harry Potter* stories: team sports are highly valued, the stories always include the journey to the school and the boarding school itself has personal qualities. New teachers appear in every volume, school events such as sports competitions, tests or festive occasions play an important role. The teachers always call for tolerance on the part of the pupils and ensure that they adhere to the school code of honour. Meanness, sneakiness and above all snobbery are contemptible attitudes. *Potter* thus exhibits a whole series of elements specific to boarding school stories conceived for girls and can thus very much speak to female teenagers.

The value system of the school moulds the children, for, next to the teaching material, character development is prominent in time at the school. Hogwarts' ideological system resembles that of the public school in the classic school story. Thus students are expected to take part in the school competition for the House Cup, and moral as well as athletic strengths are highly valued. As hero of a school story, Harry is above all a moral rock and athletic success – not an academically outstanding model student. With the setting at Hogwarts and the world of the specifically English boarding school, the novels celebrate the very British way of life, just as the school stories have always done. The cohabitation of teachers and the taught models itself on a paternalistic system, in which power is conferred onto selected students or teachers. The students' own ethics is confronted with the official value codex: what counts among the youths is getting the schoolwork done with the least amount of effort, to undermine the teachers' authority and to do right by the peer group and the school. Active resistance to usurpers like Dolores Umbridge as well as to the mendacity of the political establishment of Fudge or Scrimgeour are part of these values just as much as the courage to take unpopular positions against the majority. We see this exact quality, for example, when Hermione rejects the "Divination" teacher Trelawney, in spite of the enthusiasm of all the other girls (e.g. HP 3, 322). The worst offence in the world of *Harry Potter* is (social) arrogance: all the figures around Voldemort are arrogant and patronise everyone around them into feeling their supposed superiority. And although such a demeanour is officially frowned upon, the text indirectly confirms class differences and nationalistic topoi.

Harry Potter thus exhibits all the qualities of the classic school story. It thereby demonstrates an especial closeness to the boarding school stories written specifically for girls and thus also to the works of Enid Blyton.

VII.2.B. Harry, Dolly and the Famous Five

If we compare the *Harry Potter* novels with school and adventure stories as well as with Enid Blyton, we can detect numerous similarities – but also some important divergence. The former shares something with the secret of success that both kinds of text share, while the latter, on the other hand, requires modernisation in light of the sixty years of difference between their creations. A fundamental difference between the two authors is the pace at which they write. While Enid Blyton was renowned for her mass-production, J. K Rowling has "only" written seven novels since the first *Potter* volume in 1997. Another difference is that a lot of adults also read Rowling's *Potter* and follow the series attentively, while Blyton's texts do not have any readers outside the children's target group.

Both text-types have a plot structure that is always the same or at least very similar in the individual serial parts. Thereby they both build up the reader's expectations as the series progresses. As opposed to Enid Blyton, J.K. Rowling disrupts these expectations repeatedly with mistake-inducing red herrings and false clues. Both authors use clues and cross-references in various serial parts.[163]

The main drive in both cases is the battle between good and evil, whereby the adults prove themselves to be unwilling or unable to stand-up to the confrontation. It is the children who, again and again, provide the needed and decisive clues and who surmount evil. Just as in Enid Blyton's *Adventure* stories in which a high-ranking representative of the governing powers appears and saves the children from terrible danger at the end of the story, in the *Harry Potter* novels, we can count on Albus Dumbore to come and save the title hero.[164] Like Enid Blyton, J.K. Rowling works with clear contrasts in character and values. There is no ambivalence when it comes to values or, at most, only two perspectives are presented that are equally in the right regarding a particular matter. Harry's perspective is the only one offered to the reader. At the same time, the

---

[163] This is especially evident in *Half-Blood Prince*. Events from past episodes are repeatedly mentioned: "[…] her friend Marietta, who was wearing a very thick layer of make-up that did not entirely obscure the odd formation of pimples still etched across her face" (HP 6, 136) refers to the *Order of the Phoenix*; Snape telling Harry, "'And with no flying car available you decide that bursting into the Great Hall […] ought to create a dramatic effect'" (HP 6, 154) points back to the beginning of *Chamber of Secrets*; "[…] the gigantic spider, Aragog, that dwelled deep in the Forbidden Forest and which he and Ron had only narrowly escaped four years previously" (HP 6, 217) comes from the same volume; and Harry remembers the third school-year (*Prisoner of Azkaban*), when Ron and Hermione "had not been talking to each other in the third year" (HP 6, 265).

[164] This is especially incisive in *Goblet of Fire* and *Order of the Phoenix*, but also Gryffindor's sword, which Phoenix Fawkes rescues and brings back (*Chamber of Secrets*) or the time-travel which averts catastrophe in *Prisoner of Azkaban* rely, in the end, on Dumbledore's intervention.

author of the *Potter*, just like Enid Blyton, passes judgment on events with value-laden adjectives.

There is a series of similarities that are particular to the Enid Blyton boarding school novels. Hogwarts is an old, venerable building built in the English style in a spectacular landscape. It has several magical features, secrets and surprising qualities. Within the school-groups there is a clear concept of the enemy – good and bad characters are set in rivalry against one another. The pupils identify themselves very strongly with the school[165] and especially with their Houses – whether someone is a Gryffindor, a Slytherin, a Hufflepuff or Ravenclaw contributes decisively to his (self-)perception and his socialisation. The rules of the school are regularly transgressed, an outright offence is, however – justly – punished with detention. The students accept and adhere to these measures, even when they seem highly unfair, as in the case with Dolores Umbridge in *Order of the Phoenix*. As in Blyton's books, punishment is part of the system. The plot scheme of the *Potter* novels also exhibits parallels to the Blyton stories. Harry's return to school is also salvation from his existence with the Dursleys. The boarding school is his real home (HP 2, 263-264). The assignment of official posts plays an important role in the school hierarchy. Whoever becomes a prefect sees this as a high distinction (HP 6, 104). The familial background of the children also plays a certain role with J.K. Rowling. The question of someone being "pure-blood" or "Muggle-born" contributes to his status. The family mindset influences the children's behaviour at school – whoever has "Death Eaters" for parents will also represent racist thinking at school.[166] Like in Blyton's novels, the hero repeatedly makes mistakes which he later regrets and learns from. Finally, the entire story ends with a "happy end".

Yet with all the similarities between J.K. Rowling's *Harry Potter* and the Blyton stories, there are also important differences: the way children deal with authority and the depiction of sexuality. As opposed to the child character in Enid Blyton's works, J.K. Rowling's protagonists repeatedly rebel against authority. Teachers are not untouchable; Snape is actually unjust and brutal and Lockhart is a vain charlatan. This kind of legitimate criticism of the academic body is unthinkable in Enid Blyton's works. Nonetheless, there is one (almost) unassailable entity at Hogwarts, just as there is at *Malory Towers* or *St Clare's*: Blyton's strict but fair headmistress is reincarnated in Rowling's world in the figures of the headmaster Albus Dumbledore and then the substitute headmistress Minerva McGonagall. Her just, morally certain judgement is without a doubt exalted beyond all contesting.

---

[165] This is especially clear in *Goblet of Fire,* when the story involves an international school competition, and at the annual "Quidditch"-Cup.

[166] The families Malfoy, Crabbe and Goyle should serve here for examples, their rivalry with the circle around the Potters continues through the generations.

Rowling depicts her heroes differently than Blyton in their age-apposite development – as of *Goblet of Fire*, the children enter puberty, in *Order of the Phoenix* we see their careful experiments with sexuality, and in *Half-Blood Prince* the author show the first long-term relationships between boys and girls. Blyton's heroes, on the other hand, are stuck in gender-stereotyped figures disinterested in sex. And in contrast to the world of Enid Blyton's boarding school, there are male as well as female teachers.

Finally, in *Harry Potter*, there is one stereotyped character who also has a fixed place in Blyton's novels: the Frenchwoman. With Blyton she is usually the language teacher, with Rowling this character appears in several variants. Both Mme Maxime and Fleur Delacour represent the qualities of the "Frenchwoman". They both distinguish themselves linguistically from the other characters with their dialects. Fleur, furthermore, embodies the characteristics considered typically French in Blyton's work: affectation, arrogance and a certain level of ridiculousnes.[167]

The novels of the *Harry Potter* series thus correspond – with the above-mentioned reservations – to the model which Enid Blyton already put to use in her work. How far these templates simply represent the core elements of children's and young adult literature in general or rather the carefully selected ingredients of a common recipe for success must, in the end, remain unanswered within the parameters of this work.

---

[167] This changes by the end of *Half-Blood Prince*, as she reconciles with her soon-to-be mother-in-law Mrs Weasley and – unexpectedly – takes sides with the deformed Bill Weasley (HP 6, 581).

VIII. Conclusion and Outlook

Harry Potter's global triumph is without precedent. But why is this so? What does the text offer its readers? Why especially is this book the most successful (children's) book of all time? What does this text have that others do not? A text which enjoys so much worldwide success must be read by adults and children alike. From the beginning, *Potter* spoke to adult readers, which various statistics will prove: a 2003 nationwide poll in the USA revealed that 60 percent of all children between the ages of six and seventeen – as well as 14 percent of of people over eighteen – had read at least one volume of the series.[1] It is estimated that 40 percent of copies of *Harry Potter* are (also) read by adults.[2] Adult enthusiasm for *Potter* can be seen from the user numbers of the at least 75,000 hits on internet sites[3]: at least a third is older than 18, and at websites dealing with the film adaptations the majority of the website visitors are over 24 years of age.[4] The most important element of "Pottermania" is that a very large amount of adults read the novels. The parents' generation consider *Harry Potter* either entertaining for themselves and purchase the books out of their own interests, or see in them pedagogical value and that they are good for their children to read.

Rowling has clearly managed – unlike other children's authors – to rouse interest in her novels in a high number of adults; no other young adult book has had so wide a reception among so many adult readers as the *Harry Potter* series. How many women over the age of 20 read Enid Blyton? How many adults discuss the contents of Pippi Longstockings? In this light, *Potter* is unique. *Potter's* popularity has as much to do with the stories about everyday events at Hogwarts which are suitable to children, as with the fundamental questions which deal with topics of ethics and psychology. The pains of learning, the petty meanness and pranks among the students are reported as elaborately as the decisive situations: How will Harry make up his mind? Will he take the easy path which will bring him closer to evil? Or will he adopt the positive values of bravery, sincerity and loyalty? These qualities make the texts attractive for adult readers. Next to these, the novels have a rich mine of psychologically credible characters. The adult reader enjoys, above all, recognising the character's motivations (which are probably concealed to young readers). The novel's characters are by no means black-or-white paper figures, determined auctorially by their good or bad behaviour. It is more often the case that good characters have bad qualities and bad characters good ones. This makes them more interesting.

---

[1] See Deborah O'Keefe, *Readers in Wonderland: The Liberating Worlds of Fantasy Fiction, from Dorothy to Harry Potter*, New York, London: Continuum: 2003, 13.
[2] See Bürnevich 2001, 28.
[3] See Jenny 2001.
[4] See Sutherland Borah 2004, 346-347.

Harry Potter has strong satirical elements (comic fantasy). The magical world is populated by curious characters who exhibit human behaviour, and bureaucratic institutions, which are common to comic fantasy. Like in the best-sellers by Douglas Adams, Terry Pratchett or Matt Groening (*Futurama*-series), Rowling uses fantastic elements to create satirical situations. The reader can laugh at the bureaucrats in the Ministry of Magic, about the overcrowding and inefficiency of St Mungo's Hospital, and be amused at the vain self-conceit of a Gilderoy Lockhart or the advertising world of wizard-capitalism. We can recognise the figure of the power-hungry, intriguing opportunist in Dolores Umbridge, we can see the figure of the crafty professional politician in Rufus Scrimgeour, and find an experienced and skilful networker in Horace Slughorn, just as we do in real life. This constitutes the special reading appeal for adults.

From a purely literary point of view, the success is not entirely comprehensible, since the *Harry Potter* novels are narrated very conventionally. The author tells her story with the usual means and dresses her story in a simple, unelaborate linguistic style. The texts exhibit a plot structure very similar to detective literature. The character constellation of the novels conforms in its representation to Vladimir Propp's categories relating the fairy tale. The author uses descriptive names, recurring, formulaic expressions, and employs comparisons with animals for the characterisation of her characters.

The unusual interconnection of a school story with (satirical) fantastic elements and detective story is, however, innovative from a literary perspective: *Potter* is a typical English school story. The setting in a remote boarding school, the rivalry of the teenage groups and the wide spectrum of highly varying teacher characters are all set fixtures of the school story. The school story has been a well loved young-adult genre among children and teenagers, and especially amongst girls, for decades. There are strong similarities between *Harry Potter* and Enid Blyton's texts. Moreover, *Potter* uses many of the elements of children's adventure and detective literature, both of which are traditionally very successful.

In many respects, and according to Tzvetan Todorov's definition, *Harry Potter* is a fairy tale. Also in respect to the character structures, the texts exhibit similarities with the fairy tale. The fantastic in *Harry Potter* does not have any metaphysical meaning, it serves above all to create a colourful, convincing and entertaining alternative to the reader's reality. There are no superior metaphysical statements. Magic and wizardry replace everyday performances like travelling or housework. Witchcraft here is a precise science which anyone gifted with magic powers can learn.

A wholly decisive factor in the rise of the world-success of *Potter* may, however, be the time of its appearance, for ideologically speaking, the novels hit the nerve of the world's security situation: the leader of a radical, terrorist (in the widest sense of the term) grouping seeks to dominate the world with any and all possible means. Since the end of the Cold War, the growing strength of Islamic fundamentalist and nationalistic terrorism worldwide has led to a worldwide sense of threat – there is no such thing anymore as true security from arbitrary violence and terror. People are made to feel insecure, just as in the world of *Harry Potter*. We are forced to doubt the basic values inherent to democratic freedom; the western democracies, with their protracted legal processes and state monopoly on the legitimate use of force seem to be overstrained with the situation and cannot effectively protect their citizens. A novel series like *Harry Potter*, which portrays a world with similar problems, but simultaneously presents a saviour – in the form of a normal Everyman – is especially attractive to this collective sentiment. While the officials are incompetent, corrupt and selfish, a small group of committed normal citizens is prepared to act.[5] Civic courage is the decisive opponent to Voldemort and his followers.

Furthermore, *Potter* is flexible and comprehensible in every cultural context: Rowling refrains from any explicit religious or political statement, making the series' statements "portable" – a compulsory prerequisite for the worldwide triumph of *Harry Potter*. That the text belongs to the genre it does comes in useful: fantastic literature for adolescents and young adults lends itself particularly well for large, well-invested merchandising, for the target group at this age is looking for role-models and tends towards group formations. Offered a hero with identification-potential, adolescents quickly become very emotional and make, among other things, purchasing decisions that are no longer based on rational criteria.[6]

Harry Potter is – seen ideologically – quite conservative in its values: straightforwardness, honesty, bravery, loyalty and family come before consumerism, individualistic self-fulfilment and hedonism. Corinna Cornelius explains:

> Harry Potter, from my point of view, has become such a "satisfying" literary work exactly because we can here find values that we look for in vain in daily life, because we are confronted with problems which we know all too well but which we often do not know how to solve.[7]

---

[5] With the exception of Dumbledore, the members of the "Order of the Phoenix" represent a very colourful mixture of the citizens of their society: the Weasley family as representatives of the dutiful administration, Mundungus as the ambivalent – but reliable at the core – nut, and the various teachers are in no way the social elite of their state.

[6] See Kristin Thompson, "Fantasy, Franchises, and Frodo Baggins: The Lord of the Rings and Modern Hollywood," *The Velvet Light Trap* 52 (Autumn 2003): 45-63.

[7] Corinna Cornelius, "Harry Potter und der Orden den Popanz," *Faszination "Harry Potter": Was steckt dahinter?* eds. Detlev Dormeyer and Friedhelm Munzel, Münster: LIT, 2005, 69-81, here 70.

Even while people's actual environment is getting ever more complicated, the characters in *Harry Potter* travel by steamtrain, heat their dwellings with their fireplaces, and communicate with the help of carrier pigeons. In the magical world, children have pets, play sports and live in the school community – in reality, computers, mobile phones, consumerism and television define the everyday of most adolescents. In a time when all one hears regarding schools is rising violence and racism or the meaning of achievement and learning, Hogwarts is an active school community in which no student is left behind and everyone has the right to individuality (which is still compatible with the group). These conservative and occasionally nostalgic elements constitute a very special reading for all those readers who are dissatisfied with the social developments in western societies. Andrzej Stasiuk maintains:

> I must confess that today's world rather bores and disappoints me. It compels us to study fairy-tales written for children, in the hope of figuring out how it all works. [...] And so the meaning of Harry Potter is more social-parareligious than literary. Potter guarantees us a quick and pleasant group therapy for relatively cheap money.[8]

The texts offer ideological clarity and orientation. A clear value system underlies the novels, which maintains above all love, compassion and civic courage as positive, whilst arrogance, opportunism and the gratuitous use of violence are negative. In times of moral subjectivity and unbounded individualism, they provide an attractive model around which those looking for direction can orient themselves. The texts propagate above all the freedom to make decisions and the personal responsibility of every human being: everyone has the freedom to shape his own path, there is no social determinism for good or evil.

Above all, the reader recognises his own lived reality, for *Harry Potter* does not portray any kind of spotlessly ideal world or simplified confrontation between the typically ideal good and abysmal evil. The world in *Harry Potter* reflects a much more pluralistic society with all its problems of discrimination, class differences, and personal rivalries. The magical world is also not a freely democratic system of Western character. The novels allow for an anti-emancipatory reading: many of the female figures fit the familiar clichés.

Moreover, *Potter* can take advantage of the popularity of fantastic dramas about saving the world. Material like the *Star Wars* saga, the various *Star Trek* treatments, television series like *Buffy the Vampire Slayer, Star Gate* or *The X-Files*, along with apocalypse movies like *The Matrix, Terminator* or *Mad Max* have all reached audiences of millions worldwide. Although these stories are diverse, they all belong to the category of Manlove's "secondary world fantasy", and their unifying core is the "quest" motif and the threat of supernatural powers

---

[8]   Stasiuk, 2001.

to humankind. This is the exact chief dramatic element of *Harry Potter*. Just as Luke Skywalker fights the evil Emperor in *Star Wars*, Neo, the messiah figure in the *Matrix* trilogy must lead humankind against the machines and Frodo Baggins must prevent Sauron's rule of terror in *The Lord of the Rings*, so is Harry Potter the chosen one, embodying the hope for humanity's rescue from Voldemort. Yet while the abovementioned reference-works are full of pathos and portray their heroes only occasionally as conflicted or in compromising everyday situations, *Potter* unfolds in a very ordinary world which the reader immediately recognises as the magical copy of his own. There is nothing lofty about *Potter*, he is a normal adolescent in every respect, with the same puberty-related dilemmas and school problems as any other youth his own age has.

Apart from these, there are other possible factors for the incredible success of *Potter*. What will remain of Harry and his friends after the hype subsides, after the publication of the long-awaited seventh volume? Reviewers constantly try to formulate a prognosis for the future status of the *Potter* series in the world of children's literature. *F.A.Z.* critic Wilfried von Bredow maintains,

> There must be a magic hanging over this book. Has the author bewitched us? Are we going to wake up from Muggle [...] one day, rub our eyes and ask ourselves if the whole literary adventure was just the success of advertising and refined marketing? Will, a serious concern, the making of the Harry Potter movies and the merchandising articles spring a leak in our imagination? Or will an entire generation remain defined by this experience, a kind of "Woodstock" for children?[9]

Most critics maintain the position that *Potter* is a literary one-day wonder, a phenomenon of global pop-culture that will disappear in a few years. The gauge is, supposedly, that no word from the *Potter*-specific lexicon has entered everyday speech. The *Potter* "all-ages phenomenon" is "hype, a short-term cult, not a myth that pervades our daily lives."[10] The German author and marketeer Peter Turi has used the sales numbers to demonstrate that the huge commercial success of *Potter* is already waning: while the release of the first volume in Germany amounted to 8,000 first editions, 5.1 million copies have been sold in the country since 1998. Sales of copies from the series since 1999 only reached 4.1 million (including 25,000 first editions). The actual sales-hype comes in between *Prisoner of Azkaban* and *Goblet of Fire*: both having sold 3.9 million copies to date in Germany – yet while sales of the third first-edition copy reached 30,000, Carlsen came out with 1 million copies of the fourth volume (2000). But

---

[9]   von Bredow 2000.
[10]   Horx 2005.

when the marketing campaign starts to ebb, *Potter* turns into a real shelf-warmer.[11]

It was part of the hype that rumours had it that the last chapter had been lying, completed, in a safe in a Scottish bank waiting to be published. The last word of the series was supposed to be "scar."[12] Probably, this was either part of the marketing strategy or Rowling changed her mind, for the last paragraph of the series is

> The scar had not pained Harry for nineteen years. All was well.

Potter and its author are always worth a headline, as we could see from the renewed media excitement which was following up on Rowling's hints that Harry might die in the final volume. Before the text had even come out, speculations about the contents were making headlines. And Rowling's most recent suggestions that she might be reconsidering her decision not to write another novel set in the world of Harry Potter has thrilled fans all over the world. So McGonagall's prophecy has thus become true:

> "He'll be famous – a legend – I wouldn't be surprised if today was known as Harry Potter Day in future – there will be books written about Harry – every child in our world will know his name!" (HP 1, 20).

---

[11]   See Turi 2005, 24.
[12]   See von Lovenberg 2006.

IX. Bibliography

IX.1.A. Sources

Pullman, Philip, *The Subtle Knife: His Dark Materials – Book II*, New York: Dell-Laurel Leaf, 1997.

Rowling, Joanne Kathleen, *Harry Potter and the Philosopher's Stone,* [1997] London: Bloomsbury, 2000.

Rowling, Joanne Kathleen, *Harry Potter and the Chamber of Secrets,* [1998] London: Bloomsbury, 2000.

Rowling, Joanne Kathleen, *Harry Potter and the Prisoner of Azkaban,* [1999] London: Bloomsbury, 1999.

Rowling, Joanne Kathleen, *Harry Potter and the Goblet of Fire*, London: Bloomsbury, 2000.

Rowling, Joanne Kathleen, *Harry Potter and the Order of the Phoenix,* London: Bloomsbury, 2003.

Rowling, Joanne Kathleen, *Harry Potter and the Half-Blood Prince*, London: Bloomsbury, 2005.

Rowling, Joanne Kathleen, *Harry Potter and the Deathly Hallows,* London: Bloomsbury, 2007.

Tolkien, John Ronald Reuel, *The Fellowship of the Ring: Being the first Part of The Lord of the Rings*, [1954] London: HarperCollins, 1999.

Tolkien, John Ronald Reuel, *The Return of the King: Being the third Part of The Lord of the Rings*, [1954] London: HarperCollins, 1999.

IX.1.B. Works Cited

Aaronovitch, David, "We've been muggled," *Observer* 22 June 2003. <http://books. guardian.co.uk./print/0,3858,4696309-108779,00.html> 29 Dec 2007.

Abanes, Richard, *Harry Potter and the Bible: The Menace behind the Magick*, Camp Hill, Pennsylvania: Horizon Books, 2001.

Abanes, Richard, *Harry Potter, Narnia, and The Lord of the Rings*, Eugene, Oregon: Harvest House, 2005.

Adams, Richard, "Quidditch quaintness," *Guardian* 18 June 2003. <http://books .guardian.co.uk/print/0,3858,4693385-108779,00.html> 29 Dec 2007.

Allison, Alida, "If Not Today, Then Tomorrow: Fact, Faith, and Fantasy in Isaac Bashevis Singer's Autobiographical Writings," *Nursery Realms: Children in the Worlds of Science Fiction, Fantasy and Horror*, eds., Gary Westfahl and George Slusser, Athens: University of Georgia Press, 1999, 142-149.

Althen, Michael, "Kinder, ist mir schlecht," *F.A.Z.* 13 Nov 2002, 35.

Aocella, Joan, "Under the spell," *New Yorker* 31 July 2000, 74-78.

Appelbaum, Peter, "Harry Potter's World: Magic, Technoculture, and Becoming Human," *Harry Potter's World: Multidisciplinary Critical Perspectives,* ed. Elizabeth E. Heilman, New York, London: RoutledgeFalmer, 2003, 25-51.

Bachl, Gottfried, "Gefährliche Magie? Religiöse Parabel? Gute Unterhaltung," *Im Bann des Zauberlehrlings? Zur Faszination von Harry Potter,* ed. Kaspar H. Spinner, Regensburg: Friedrich Pustet, 2001, 42-59.

Bachl, Gottfried, "Harry Potter theologisch gelesen," *"Alohomora!" Ergebnisse des Ersten Wiener Harry-Potter-Symposions,* ed. Heidi Lexe, Vienna: Edition Praesens, 2002, 109-123.

Baggett, David and Shawn Klein, eds., *Harry Potter and philosophy: If Aristotle ran Hogwarts*, Chicago, La Salle: Open Court, 2004.

Baggett, David, "Magic, Muggles, and Moral Imagination," *Harry Potter and philosophy: If Aristotle ran Hogwarts*, eds., David Baggett and Shawn Klein, Chicago, La Salle: Open Court, 2004, 158-171.

Bailey, K.V. and Andy Sawyer, "The Janus Perspective: Science Fiction and the Young Adult Reader in Britain," *Young Adult Science Fiction*, ed., C. W. Sullivan, III., Westport: Greenwood Press, 1999, 55-71.

Bak, Sandra, *Harry Potter: Auf den Spuren eines zauberhaften Bestsellers*, Frankfurt am Main: Peter Lang, 2004.

Beahm, George, *Fact, fiction, and folklore in Harry Potter's world: an unofficial guide*, Charlottesville, Virginia: Hampton Roads, 2005.

Berg, Stephan, *Schlimme Zeiten, böse Räume: Zeit- und Raumstrukturen in der phanstastischen Literatur des 20. Jahrhunderts*, Stuttgart: Metzler, 1991.

Berghahn, Daniela, *Raumdarstellung im englischen Roman der Moderne*, Frankfurt am Main: Peter Lang, 1989.

Bettelheim, Bruno, *The Uses of Enchantment: The Meaning and Importance of Fairy Tales*, Middlesex: Penguin Books, 1978.

Beyer, Susanne and Nikolaus von Festenberg, "Ein Volk von Zauberlehrlingen," *SPIEGEL* 20 Nov 2000. <http://www.spiegel.de/spiegel/0,1518,104665,00. html> 3 Jan 2008.

Billone, Amy Christine, "The Boy Who Lived: From Carroll's Alice and Barrie's Peter Pan to Rowling's Harry Potter," *Children's Literature* 32 (2004): 178-202.

Blacker, Terence, "Why does everyone like Harry Potter? He is the perfect hero for readers looking for reassurance and a nannyish moral certainty," *Independent* 13 July 1999, 4.

Blake, Andrew, *The Irresistible Rise of Harry Potter*, London, New York: Verso, 2002.

Bloom, Harold, "Can 35 million book buyers be wrong? Yes," *Wall Street Journal* 11 July 2000, A26.

Bröll, Claudia, "Besorgte Muggles," *F.A.Z.* 5 July 2007, 18.

Brown, Stephen, *Wizard!: Harry Potter's Brand Magic*, London: Cyan Books, 2005.

Bruxvoort Lipscomb, Benjamin J. and W. Christopher Stewart, "Magic, Science and the ethics of Technology," *Harry Potter and philosophy: If Aristotle ran Hogwarts*, eds., David Baggett and Shawn Klein, Chicago, La Salle: Open Court, 2004, 77-91.

Bürvenich, Paul, *Der Zauber des Harry Potter: Analyse eines literarischen Welterfolgs*, Frankfurt am Main: Peter Lang, 2001.

Byatt, Antonia S., "Harry Potter And The Childish Adult," *New York Times* 11 July 2003, n. pag.

Caillois, Roger, "Das Bild des Phantastischen. Vom Märchen bis zur Science Fiction," *Phaicon 1. Almanach der phantastischen Literatur,* ed., Rein A. Zondergeld, Frankfurt am Main: Insel, 1974, 44-91.

Carlyle, Thomas, "The Hero as King. Cromwell, Napoleon: Modern Revolutionism [Lecture VI, Friday, 22nd May, 1840]," *On Heroes, Hero-Worship, & the Heroic in History,* ed., Michael Goldberg, Berkeley, Los Angeles, Oxford: University of California Press, 1993.

Carlyle, Thomas, *On Heroes, Hero-Worship, & the Heroic in History*, ed., Michael Goldberg, Berkeley, Los Angeles, Oxford: University of California Press, 1993.

Cassirer, Ernst, "Mythischer, ästhetischer und theoretischer Raum," [1930] *Landschaft und Raum in der Erzählkunst,* ed., Alexander Ritter, Darmstadt: Wissenschaftliche Buchgesellschaft, 1975, 17-35.

Cherrett, Lisa, *The Triumph of Goodness: Biblical Themes in the Harry Potter Stories,* Oxford: The Bible Reading Fellowship, 2003.

Cockrell, Amanda, "Harry Potter and the Secret Password. Finding Our Way in the Magical Genre," *The Ivory Tower and Harry Potter: Perspectives on a Literary Phenomenon*, ed., Lana A. Whited, Columbia: University of Missouri Press, 2004, 15-26.

Cornelius, Corinna, "Harry Potter und der Orden den Popanz," *Faszination "Harry Potter": Was steckt dahinter?*, eds., Detlev Dormeyer and Friedhelm Munzel, Münster: LIT, 2005, 69-81.

Cornelius, Corinna, *Harry Potter – geretteter Retter im Kampf gegen dunkle Mächte? Religionspädagogischer Blick auf religiöse Implikationen, archaisch-mythologische Motive und supranaturale Elemente*, Münster: LIT, 2003.

Dallach, Christoph, "Verhexte Orte," *SPIEGEL* 41/2007, 220.

Deavel, Catherine, "Character, Choice, and Harry Potter," *Logos: A Journal of Catholic Thought and Culture* 4 (Autumn 2002): 49-64.

Deavel, David and Catherine, "A Skewed Reflection: The Nature of Evil," *Harry Potter and philosophy: If Aristotle ran Hogwarts*, eds., David Baggett and Shawn Klein, Chicago, La Salle: Open Court, 2004, 132-147.

Distelmeyer, Jan, "Marke, Nachricht, Versprechen," *taz* 18 May 2005, 15.

Dormeyer, Detlev and Friedhelm Munzel, eds., *Faszination "Harry Potter": Was steckt dahinter?*, Münster: LIT, 2005.

Dormeyer, Detlev, "Das apokryphe Kindheitsevangelium des Thomas und 'Harry Potter' von J.K. Rowling," *Faszination "Harry Potter": Was steckt dahinter?*, eds., Detlev Dormeyer and Friedhelm Munzel, Münster: LIT, 2005, 31-42.

Doughty, Terri, "Locating Harry Potter in the 'Boys' Book' Market," *The Ivory Tower and Harry Potter: Perspectives on a Literary Phenomenon*, ed., Lana A. Whited, Columbia: University of Missouri Press, 2004, 243-257.

Dresang, Eliza T. "Hermione Granger and the Heritage of Gender," *The Ivory Tower and Harry Potter: Perspectives on a Literary Phenomenon*, ed., Lana A. Whited, Columbia: University of Missouri Press, 2004, 211-242.

Drexler, Christoph and Nikolaus Wandinger, eds., *Leben, Tod und Zauberstab: Auf theologischer Spurensuche in Harry Potter*, Münster: LIT, 2004.

Druce, Robert, *This Day Our Daily Fictions: An Enquiry into the Multi-Million Bestseller Status of Enid Blyton and Ian Fleming*, Atlanta: Rodopi, 1992.

Eberls, Jason T., "Why Voldemort Won't Just Die Already: What Wizards Can Teach Us About Personal Identity," *Harry Potter and philosophy: If Aristotle ran Hogwarts*, eds., David Baggett and Shawn Klein, Chicago, La Salle: Open Court, 2004, 200-212.

Eco, Umberto, *Nachschrift zum "Namen der Rose"*, Munich: Carl Hanser, 1984.

Ehgartner, Reinhard, "J.K. Rowlings Harry-Potter-Romane in literarischen Koordinaten," *"Alohomora!" Ergebnisse des Ersten Wiener Harry-Potter-Symposions*, ed., Heidi Lexe, Vienna: Edition Praesens, 2002, 61-81.

Elster, Charles, "The Seeker of Secrets: Images of Learning, Knowing, and Schooling," *Harry Potter's World: Multidisciplinary Critical Perspectives*, ed., Elizabeth E. Heilman, New York, London: RoutledgeFalmer, 2003, 203-220.

Ernould, Roland, *Quatre approches de la magie: Du Rond des sorciers à Harry Potter*, Paris: Harmattan, 2003.

von Lovenberg, Felicitas, "Ende gut, alles gut?" *F.A.Z.* 23 July 2007. <http://www.F.A.Z..net/s/Rub1DA1FB848C1E44858CB87A0FE6AD1B68/Doc~ED1FD142EB4934D8D87BC67BE25ED7573~ATpl~Ecommon~Sspezial.html> 6 Aug 2007.

Fielitz, Sonja, *Roman: Text & Kontext*, Berlin: Cornelsen Verlag, 2001.

Finke, Beatrix, *Erzählsituationen und Figurenperspektiven im Detektivroman*, Amsterdam: Grüner, 1983.

Forster, Edward Morgan, *Aspects of the Novel*, [1927] Orlando: Harcourt, 1985.

Funke, Cornelia, "Kinder finden das Böse cool," *Tagesspiegel* 2 Jan 2005, S1.

Furch, Karoline, *Die Wiederkehr des Mythos. Zur Renaissance der Artus-Mythen in der modernen Fantasy-Literatur*, Wetzlar: Förderkreis Phantastik in Wetzlar, 1998.

Gehrmann, Wolfgang, "Mein Harry! Wie ein US-Medienkonzern sein Harry-Potter-Bild gegen den Rest der Welt durchsetzen will," *ZEIT* 11/2001. http://www.zeit.de/archiv/2001/11/200111_entscheiden_pott.xml 3 Jan 2008.

Genette, Gérard, *Die Erzählung*, Munich: Wilhelm Fink, 1998.

Gibbons, Fiachra, "JK Rowling is author of the year," *Guardian* 4 Feb 2000. <http://books.guardian.co.uk/print/0,3858,3958817-99819,00. html> 3 Jan 2008.

Gladstein, Mimi R., "Feminism and Equal Opportunity: Hermione and the Women of Hogwarts," *Harry Potter and philosophy: If Aristotle ran Hogwarts*, eds., David Baggett and Shawn Klein, Chicago, La Salle: Open Court, 2004, 49-59.

Gold, Tanja, "Spellbound," *Guardian* 2 Aug 2005. <http://books.guardian.co.uk/print/0,3858,5253251-108779,00.html> 3 Jan 2008.

Granger, John, *Looking for God in Harry Potter*, Wheaton, Illinois: Saltriver Tyndale House Publishers, 2004.

Grimes, Katharine M., "Harry Potter. Fairy Tale Prince, Real Boy and Archtypal Hero," *The Ivory Tower and Harry Potter: Perspectives on a Literary Phenomenon*, ed., Lana A. Whited, Columbia: University of Missouri Press, 2004, 89-122.

Gupta, Suman, *Re-reading Harry Potter*, Houndmills, New York: Palgrave Macmillan, 2003.

Hart Weed, Jennifer, "Voldemort, Boethius, and the Destructive Effects of Evil," *Harry Potter and philosophy: If Aristotle ran Hogwarts*, eds., David Baggett and Shawn Klein, Chicago, La Salle: Open Court, 2004, 148-157.

"Harry Potter is back!" *ZEIT* 29/2005. <http://www.zeit.de/2005/29/0pot ter_meldung> 29 Dec 2007.

"Harry Potter knocked off top spot," *Guardian* 8 July 2005. <http://blogs. guardian.co.uk/culturevulture/archives/2005/07/08/harry_potter-knocked_o ff> 28 Sept 2007.

"Harry Potter und das große Geld," *F.A.Z.* 7 Nov 2001, 32.

Hattenstone, Simon, "Harry, Jessie and me," *Guardian* 8 July 2000. <http://books.guardian.co.uk/print/0,3858,4037903-99943,00.html> 3 Jan 2008.

Hauser, Linus, "Harry Potter – einer der tausendgestaltigen Helden," *Faszination "Harry Potter": Was steckt dahinter?*, eds., Detlev Dormeyer and Friedhelm Munzel, Münster: LIT, 2005, 7-15.

Heidkamp, Konrad, "Harry, der Verlegertraum. Joanne K. Rowling verändert den Markt für Kinderbücher," *ZEIT* 27/2003. <http://www.zeit.de/ 2003/27/L-Glosse_27> 3 Jan 2008.

Heidkamp, Konrad, "Zauberhafte Abziehbilder," *ZEIT* 48/2001. <http://www.zeit. de/archiv/2001/48/200148_potterfilm.xml> 3 Jan 2008.

Heilman, Elizabeth E., "Blue Wizards and Pink Witches: Representations of Gender, Identity and Power," *Harry Potter's World: Multidisciplinary Critical Perspectives*, ed., Elizabeth E. Heilman, New York, London: RoutledgeFalmer, 2003, 221-239.

Heilman, Elizabeth E. and Anne E. Gregory, "Images of the Privileged Insider and Outcast Outsider," *Harry Potter's World: Multidisciplinary Critical Perspectives,* ed., Elizabeth E. Heilman, New York, London: Routledge-Falmer, 2003, 241-259.

Heilman, Elizabeth E., ed., *Harry Potter's World: Multidisciplinary Critical Perspectives*, New York, London: RoutledgeFalmer, 2003.

Hein, Rudolf, *Kennen Sie Severus Snape? – Auf den Spuren der sprechenden Namen bei Harry Potter*, Bamberg: Collibri & Erich Weiß, 2001.

Hiebert Alton, Anne, "Generic Fusion and the Mosaic of *Harry Potter*," *Harry Potter's World: Multidisciplinary Critical Perspective*, ed., Elizabeth E. Heilman, New York, London: RoutledgeFalmer, 2003, 141-162.

Hillebrand, Bruno, "Poetischer, philosophischer und mathematischer Raum," [1971] *Landschaft und Raum in der Erzählkunst*, ed., Alexander Ritter, Darmstadt: Wissenschaftliche Buchgesellschaft, 1975, 417-463.

Hoffmann, Gerhard, *Raum, Situation, erzählte Wirklichkeit: poetologische und historische Studien zum englischen und amerikanischen Roman*, Stuttgart: Metzler, 1978.

Holden, Anthony, "Why Harry Potter doesn't cast a spell over me," *Guardian* 25 June 2000. <http://books.guardian.co.uk/print/0,3858,4033193-99943, 00.html> 3 Jan 2008.

Houghton, John, *A Closer Look at Harry Potter: Bending and Shaping the Minds of Our Children*, Eastbourne: Kingsway Communications, 2001.

Hugendick, David, "Zelten und grübeln," *ZEIT* 29/2007. <http://images.zeit.de/ text/online/2007/30/harry-potter-rezension> 25 Aug 2007.

Hunt, Peter, *Children's Literature*, Oxford: Blackwell Publishers, 2001.

Iannone, Carol, "Lit critic struggles with muggles, wizards," *United Press International* 17 July 2000.

Jelinek, Linda, *Das Phänomen Harry Potter: Eine literaturwissenschaftliche Analyse des Welterfolgs*, Saarbrücken: VDM, 2006.

Jenny, Urs, "Crashkurs für Zauberlehrlinge," *SPIEGEL* 19 Nov 2001. <http:// www.spiegel.de/spiegel/0,1518,168282,00.html> 3 Jan 2008.

Jenny, Urs, "Muss Harry sterben?" *SPIEGEL Online* 20 July 2007. <http:// www.spiegel.de/kultur/literatur/0,1518,494949,00.html> 6 Aug 2007.

Jung, Mathias, *Der Zauber der Wandlung: Harry Potter oder das Abenteuer der Ichwerdung*, Lahnstein: emu, 2004.

Kakutani, Michiko, "An Epic Showdown as Harry Potter Is Initiated Into Adulthood," *New York Times* 19 July 2007. <http://www.nytimes.com/2007/07/ 19/books/19potter.html> 23 Nov 2007.

Kalka, Joachim, "Abfahrt am Gleis Neundreiviertel im Bahnhof King's Cross," *F.A.Z.* 6 July 2000, 56.

Kämpfe-Burghard, Klaus, "Vertriebszauber? Einblick ins Potter-Marketing," *Harry Potter oder Warum wir Zauberer brauchen*, ed., Olaf Kutzmutz, Wolfenbüttel: Bundesakademie für kulturelle Bildung, 2001, 44-59.

Kern, Edmund M., *The Wisdom of Harry Potter: What Our Favorite Hero Teaches Us about Moral Choices*, New York: Prometheus, 2003.

Killinger, John, *God, the Devil, and Harry Potter: A Christian Minister's Defense of the Beloved Novels*, New York: Thomas Dunne, 2004.

Kirk, Ann Connie, *J.K. Rowling: A Biography*, Westport, London: Greenwood Press, 2003.

Kornfeld, John and Laurie Prothro, "Comedy, Conflict, and Community: Home and Family in *Harry Potter,*" *Harry Potter's World: Multidisciplinary Critical Perspectives*, ed., Elizabeth E. Heilman, New York, London: RoutledgeFalmer, 2003, 187-202.

Kronsbein, Joachim, "Der Kuss des Magiers," *SPIEGEL* 30 June 2003. <http://www.spiegel.de/spiegel/0,1518,255899,00.html> 3 Jan 2008.

Kuby, Gabriele, *Harry Potter – der globale Schub in okkultes Heidentum*, Kisslegg: Fe-Medienverlag, 2002.

Kulik, Nils, *Das Gute und das Böse in der phantastischen Kinder-und Jugendliteratur. Eine Untersuchung bezogen auf Werke von Joanne K. Rowling, J.R.R. Tolkien, Michael Ende, Astrid Lindgren, Wolfgang und Heike Hohlbein, Otfried Preußler und Frederik Hertmann*, Oldenburg: Universitätsverlag, 2005.

Kutzmutz, Olaf, ed., *Harry Potter oder Warum wir Zauberer brauchen*, Wolfenbüttel: Bundesakademie für kulturelle Bildung, 2001.

Kutzmutz, Olaf, "Nachricht von Aschenputtel. Joanne K. Rowling in den Medien," *Harry Potter oder Warum wir Zauberer brauchen*, ed., Olaf Kutzmutz, Wolfenbüttel: Bundesakademie für kulturelle Bildung, 2001.

Lacoss, Jann, "Of Magicals and Muggles. Reversals and Revulsions at Hogwarts," *The Ivory Tower and Harry Potter: Perspectives on a Literary Phenomenon*, ed., Lana A. Whited, Columbia: University of Missouri Press, 2004, 67-88.

Langner, Michael, "Unheil aus Hogwart? Streiflichter zur Harry-Potter-Rezeption in Theologie und Kirche," *Faszination "Harry Potter": Was steckt dahinter?*, eds., Dormeyer, Detlev and Friedhelm Munzel, Münster: LIT, 2005, 17-29.

Lawson, Mark, "Rowling survives the hype," *Guardian* 8 July 2000. <http://books.guardian.co.uk/print/0,3858,4038362-99943,00.html> 3 Jan 2008.

Lehr, Susan, ed., *Beauty, Brains, and Brawn: The Construction of Gender in Children's Literature*, Portsmouth: Heinemann, 2001.

Lem, Stanislaw, "Tzvetan Todorovs Theorie des Phantastischen," *Phaicon 1. Almanach der phantastischen Literatur*, ed., Rein A. Zondergeld, Frankfurt am Main: Insel, 1974, 92-120.

Lembke, Judith, "Das magische Virus," *F.A.Z.* 21 July 2007, 18.

Lewis, Clive Staples, "On three Ways of Writing for Children," [1966] *Essay Collection and Other Short Pieces*, ed., Lesley Walsmely, New York, London: Harper Collins, 2000, 505-514.

Lewis, Clive Staples, *Clive Staples Lewis. Essay Collection and Other Short Pieces*, ed., Lesley Walsmely, New York, London: Harper Collins, 2000.

Lexe, Heidi, *"Alohomora!" Ergebnisse des Ersten Wiener Harry-Potter-Symposions*, Vienna: Edition Praesens, 2002.

Lexe, Heidi, *Pippi, Pan und Potter: Zur Motivkonstellation in den Klassikern der Kinderliteratur*, Vienna: Edition Praesens, 2003.

Lezard, Nicholas, "Under her spell," *Guardian* 28 June 2003. <http://books.guardian.co.uk/print/0,3858,4700210-99943,00.html> 3 Jan 2008.

Lotman, Jurij M., *Die Struktur literarischer Texte*, [1972] München: Wilhelm Fink, 1993.

Lurie, Alison, *Boys and Girls Forever: Children's Classics from Cinderella to Harry Potter*, London: Vintage, 2003.

Lütkehaus, Ludger, "Joseph Kardinal Ratzinger – Anti-Potter," *ZEIT* 48/2003. <http://www.zeit.de/2003/48/Lebenshilfe_2fEthikrat_48> 3 Jan 2008.

Maar, Michael, "Das Böse als junger Mann," *F.A.Z.net* 1 Oct 2005. <http://www.F.A.Z..net/s/Rub117C535CDF414415BB243B181B8B60AE/Doc~E7E1EDCDFCBF4021A3488CD43F2DDD64~ATpl~Ecommon~Scontent.html> 3 Jan 2008.

Maar, Michael, *Warum Nabokov Harry Potter gemocht hätte*, Berlin: Berliner Taschenbuch-Verlag, 2003.

Maatje, Frank C., "Versuch einer Poetik des Raumes. Der lyrische, epische und dramatische Raum," [1969] *Landschaft und Raum in der Erzählkunst*, ed., Alexander Ritter, Darmstadt: Wissenschaftliche Buchgesellschaft, 1975, 392-416.

Manlove, Colin, *From Alice to Harry Potter: Children's Fantasy in England*, Christchurch, New Zealand: Cybereditions, 2003.

Manlove, Colin, *The Fantasy Literature of England*, London: Macmillan Press, 1999.

Mattenklott, Gundel, "Text aus Texten. Phantastische Traditionen bei Harry Potter," *Harry Potter oder Warum wir Zauberer brauchen*, ed., Olaf Kutzmutz, Wolfenbüttel: Bundesakademie für kulturelle Bildung, 2001, 33-43.

Matthews, Gareth B., "Finding Platform 9 3/4: The Idea of a Different Reality," *Harry Potter and philosophy: If Aristotle ran Hogwarts*, eds., Baggett, David and Shawn Klein, Chicago, La Salle: Open Court, 2004, 175-185.

Mayer, Susanne, "In den Klauen der Pubertät," *ZEIT* 27/2003. <http://www.zeit.de/2003/27/SM-Potter> 3 Jan 2008.

McCrum, Robert, "My long, dark night with Harry," *Observer* 17 July 2005. <http://books.guardian.co.uk/print/0,3858,5241113-108779,00.html> 3 Jan 2008.

McCrum, Robert, "Plot, plot, plot that's worth the weight," *Observer* 9 July 2000. <http://books.guardian.co.uk/news/articles/0,6109,341394,00. html> 3 Jan 2008.

Mendlesohn, Farah, "Crowning the King. Harry Potter and the Construction of Authority," *The Ivory Tower and Harry Potter: Perspectives on a Literary Phenomenon*, ed., Lana A. Whited, Columbia: University of Missouri Press, 2004, 159-181.

Mertz Hsieh, Diana, "Dursley Duplicity. The Morality and Psychology of Self-Deception," *Harry Potter and philosophy: If Aristotle ran Hogwarts*, eds., David Baggett and Shawn Klein, Chicago, La Salle: Open Court, 2004, 22-37.

Meyer, Hermann, "Raumgestaltung und Raumsymbolik in der Erzählkunst," [1963] *Landschaft und Raum in der Erzählkunst*, ed., Alexander Ritter, Darmstadt: Wissenschaftliche Buchgesellschaft, 1975, 208-231.

Meyer-Gosau, Frauke, "Potterismus. Was der deutschen Gegenwartsliterateratur fehlt und Harry hat's," *Harry Potter oder Warum wir Zauberer brauchen*, ed., Olaf Kutzmutz, Wolfenbüttel: Bundesakademie für kulturelle Bildung, 2001, 7-19.

Misik, Robert, "Liebling der Muggel," *taz* 1/2/3 Oct 2005, 21.

Morris, Tom, "The Courageous Harry Potter," *Harry Potter and philosophy: If Aristotle ran Hogwarts*, eds., David Baggett and Shawn Klein. Chicago, La Salle: Open Court, 2004, 9-21.

Muir, Kate, "Explosive finales young hero enters his darkest chapter," *Times Online* 21 July 2007. <http://entertainment.timesonline.co.uk/tol/arts_and_entertainment/books/article2112815.ece> 6 Aug 2007.

Mullan, Bob, *The Enid Blyton Story*, London: Boxtree, 1987.

Mullan, John, "Into the gloom," *Observer* 23 July 2005. <http://books.guardian.co.uk/print/0,3858,5244854-108779,00.html> 3 Jan 2008.

Munzel, Friedhelm, "Harry Potter und die lebendigen Bücher. Aspekte zur Faszination des Lesens aus bibliotherapeutischer Sicht," *Faszination "Harry Potter": Was steckt dahinter?*, eds., Detlev Dormeyer and Friedhelm Munzel, Münster: LIT, 2005, 83-94.

Natov, Roni, "Harry Potter and the Extraordinariness of the Ordinary," *The Lion and the Unicorn* 25 (2001): 310-327.

Neal, Connie, *The Gospel According to Harry Potter: Spirituality in the Stories of the World's Most Famous Seeker*, Louisville, London: Westminster John Knox Press, 2002.

Neal, Connie, *What's a Christian to Do with Harry Potter?*, Colorado Springs: Waterbrook Press, 2001.

Nel, Philip, *J K Rowling's "Harry Potter" Novels: A Reader's Guide*, New York, London: Continuum, 2001.

Nikolajeva, Maria, "*Harry Potter* – A Return to the Romantic Hero," *Harry Potter's World: Multidisciplinary Critical Perspectives*, ed., Elizabeth E. Heilman, New York, London: RoutledgeFalmer, 2003, 125-140.

Nikolajeva, Maria, *Children's Literature Comes of Age: Toward a New Aesthetic*, New York, London: Garland Publishing, 1996.

Nikolajeva, Maria, *The Magic Code: The use of magical patterns in fantasy for children*, Göteborg: Almqvist & Wiksell, 1988.

Nikolajeva, Maria, *The Rhetoric of Character in Children's Literature*, Lanham, Maryland, London: The Scarecrow Press, 2002.

O'Keefe, Deborah, *Readers in Wonderland: The Liberating Worlds of Fantasy Fiction, from Dorothy to Harry Potter,* New York, London: Continuum, 2003.

O'Sullivan, Emer, "Der Zauberlehrling im Internat. Harry Potter im Kontext der britischen Literaturtradition," *"Alohomora!" Ergebnisse des Ersten Wiener Harry-Potter-Symposions*, ed., Heidi Lexe. Vienna: Edition Praesens, 2002, 15-39.

Osberghaus, Monika, "Keine Zeit für Muggle-Muffins," *F.A.Z.* 10 July 2000, 4.

Patterson, Steven W., "Is Ambition a Virtue? Why Slytherin Belongs at Hogwarts," *Harry Potter and philosophy: If Aristotle ran Hogwarts*, eds., David Baggett and Shawn Klein, Chicago, La Salle: Open Court, 2004, 121-131.

Pennington, John, "From Elfland to Hogwarts, or the Aesthetic Trouble with Harry Potter," *The Lion and the Unicorn* 26 (Jan 2002): 78-97.

Petsch, Robert, "Der Raum in der Erzählung," [1942] *Landschaft und Raum in der Erzählkunst*, ed., Alexander Ritter, Darmstadt: Wissenschaftliche Buchgesellschaft, 1975, 36-44.

Petzold, Dieter, "Die Harry Potter-Bücher: Märchen, *fantasy fiction, school stories* – und was noch?" *Im Bann des Zauberlehrlings? Zur Faszination von Harry Potter*, ed., Kaspar H. Spinner, Regensburg: Friedrich Pustet, 2001, 21-41.

Pfister, Manfred, *Das Drama: Theorie und Analyse*, [1977] Munich: Wilhelm Fink, 2001.

Pharr, Mary, "In Medias Res. Harry Potter as Hero-in-Progress," *The Ivory Tower and Harry Potter: Perspectives on a Literary Phenomenon*, ed., Lana A. Whited, Columbia: University of Missouri Press, 2004, 53-66.

Pinsent, Pat, "The Education of a Wizard. Harry Potter and His Predecessors," *The Ivory Tower and Harry Potter: Perspectives on a Literary Phenomenon*, ed., Lana A. Whited, Columbia: University of Missouri Press, 2004, 27-50.

Platthaus, Andreas, "Endstation Hogwarts," *F.A.Z.* 20 July 2002, 44.

Prieger, Almut, *Das Werk Enid Blytons: eine Anlayse ihrer Erfolgsserie in westdeutschen Ausgaben*, Frankfurt am Main: dipa, 1982.

Propp, Vladimir, *Morphology of the Folktale*, [1928] Austin: University of Texas Press, 2003.

Pullman, Philip, "Carnegie Medal Acceptance Speech." Chartered Institute of Library and Information Professionals (CILIP), 1996. <http://www.carnegie greenaway.org.uk/home/index.php> 30 Sep 2007.

Rathgeb, Eberhard, "Was meinst Du, Harry?" *F.A.Z.* 3 July 2000, 49.

"Ratzinger mag Potter nicht," *SPIEGEL Online* 14 July 2005. <http://www. spiegel.de/kultur/literatur/0,1518,365173,00.html> 2 Jan 2008.

Ray, Sheila G., *The Blyton Phenomenon. The controversy surrounding the world's most successful children's writer*, London: Andre Deutsch, 1982.

Rich, Motoko, "Long Lines and Wide Smiles Greet the Final Volume of 'Harry Potter'," *New York Times* 21 July 2007. <http://www.nytimes.com/2007 /07/21/books/21pott.html?pagewanted=print> 6 Aug 2007.

Ritter, Alexander, ed., *Landschaft und Raum in der Erzählkunst*, Darmstadt: Wissenschaftliche Buchgesellschaft, 1975.

Rowling, Joanne Kathleen, Live Interview on Scholastic.com, 16 Oct 2000. <http://www.scholastic.com/harrypotter/author/transcript2.htm> 3 Jan 2008.

Rowling, Joanne Kathleen, Live Interview on Scholastic.com, 3 Feb 2000. <http://www.scholastic.com/harrypotter/author/transcript1.htm> 3 Jan 2008.

Rowling, Joanne Kathleen, Transcript of J.K. Rowling's interview at the Edinburgh International Book Festival, 15 Aug 2004. <http://www.scholastic.com/harry potter/author/transcript4.htm> 3 Jan 2008.

Rushdie, Salman, "J.K. Rowling verändert die Welt," *F.A.Z.net* 15 July 2005. <http://www.f.A.Z..net/s/RubEBED639C476B40 7798B1CE808F1F6632/ Doc~EE23A2CF8C88F4E268855B6C1CE271894~ATpl~Ecommon~Scon tent.html> 6 Aug 2007.

Russell, David L., "From Alice to Harry Potter: Children's Fantasy in England (review)," *The Lion and the Unicorn* 28 (Jan 2004): 166-170.

Sadigh, Parvin, "Harry Potter in der Schule? Of course!" *ZEIT* 29/2005. <http://www.zeit.de/2005/29/harrypotter_pro> 3 Jan 2008.

Sands, Karen and Marietta Frank, eds., *Back in the Spaceship Again: Juvenile Science Fiction Series Since 1945*, Westport: Greenwood Press, 1999.

Schafer, Elizabeth D., *Exploring Harry Potter*, London: Ebury Press, 2000.

Schmalenbach, Renate, *Topographie des Grauens: Zur Gestaltung literarischer Räume in unheimlich-phantastischen Erzählungen*, Essen: Die Blaue Eule, 2003.

Schuller, Florian, "Wie Harry Potter in die Katholische Akademie kam und warum er dorthin gehört," *Im Bann des Zauberlehrlings? Zur Faszination von Harry Potter,* ed., Kaspar H. Spinner, Regensburg: Friedrich Pustet, 2001, 60-71.

Schwarz, Ellen, *Der phantastische Kriminalroman: Untersuchungen zu Parallelen zwischen "roman policier", "conte fantastique" und "Gothic Novel"*, Marburg: Tectum, 2001.

Seaton, Matt, "If I could talk to my mum again I'd tell her I had a daughter – and I wrote some books and guess what happened?" *Guardian* 18 April 2001. <http://books.guardian.co.uk/print/0,3858,4171517-99943,00.html> 3 Jan 2008.

Shapiro, Marc, *J.K. Rowling: The Wizard behind Harry Potter*, New York: St Martin's Griffin, 2004.

Silberstein, Michael, "Space, Time, and Magic," *Harry Potter and philosophy: If Aristotle ran Hogwarts*, eds., David Baggett and Shawn Klein, Chicago, La Salle: Open Court, 2004, 186-199.

Skulnick, Rebecca and Jesse Goodman, "The Civic Leadership of *Harry Potter*: Agency, Ritual, and Schooling," *Harry Potter's World: Multidisciplinary Critical Perspectives*, ed., Elizabeth E. Heilman, New York, London: RoutledgeFalmer, 2003, 261-277.

Slusser, George, "The Forever Child: 'Ender's Game' and the Mythic Universe of Science Fiction," *Nursery Realms: Chilrdren in the Worlds of Science*

Fiction, Fantasy and Horror, eds., Gary Westfahl and George Slusser, Athens: University of Georgia Press, 1999, 73-90.

Smadja, Isabelle, *Harry Potter: Les raisons d'un succès,* Paris: Presses Universitaires de France, 2001.

Smith, David, "Potter's magic spell turns boys into bookworms," *Observer* 10 July 2005. <http://books.guardian.co.uk/print/0,3858,5235620-108779,00. html> 3 Jan 2008.

Smith, Sean, *J.K. Rowling: A Biography,* London: Micheal O'Mara Books, 2001.

Spinner, Kaspar H., ed., *Im Bann des Zauberlehrlings? Zur Faszination von Harry Potter,* Regensburg: Friedrich Pustet, 2001.

Stanzel, Franz K., *Theorie des Erzählens,* [1979] Göttingen: Vandenhoeck & Ruprecht, 2001.

Stasiuk, Andrzej, "Nein, ich mag Harry Potter nicht," *F.A.Z.* 24 Feb 2001, 43.

Steege, David K., "Harry Potter, Tom Brown, and the British School Story. Lost in Transit?" *The Ivory Tower and Harry Potter: Perspectives on a Literary Phenomenon,* ed., Lana A. Whited, Columbia: University of Missouri Press, 2004, 140-156.

Steinfeld, Thomas, "Endlich wieder heile Welt," *Süddeutsche Zeitung* 23 July 2007. <http://www.sueddeutsche.de/kultur/artikel/930/124747> 6 Aug 2007.

Stöcker, Christian, "Blogs gesperrt wegen Potter-Sex," *SPIEGEL Online* 7 Aug 2007. <http://www.spiegel.de/netzwelt/web/0,1518,498677,00.html> 7 Aug 2007.

Sullivan, C. W., III, ed., *Young Adult Science Fiction,* Westport: Greenwood Press, 1999.

Sutherland Borah, Rebecca, "Apprentice Wizards Welcome. Fan Communities and the Culture of Harry Potter," *The Ivory Tower and Harry Potter: Perspectives on a Literary Phenomenon,* ed., Lana A. Whited, Columbia: University of Missouri Press, 2004, 343-364.

Taubenböck, Andrea, *Die binäre Raumstruktur in der Gothic novel: 18.-20. Jahrhundert,* München: Wilhelm Fink, 2002.

Teare, Elizabeth, "Harry Potter and the Technology of Magic," *The Ivory Tower and Harry Potter: Perspectives on a Literary Phenomenon,* ed., Lana A. Whited, Columbia: University of Missouri Press, 2004, 329-342.

Teather, David, "Harry Potter's adventures propel JK Rowling to billionares' row," *Guardian* 27 Feb 2004. <http://books.guardian.co.uk/print/ 0,3858,4868111-99943,00.html> 3 Jan 2008.

Thomas, Gina, "Unkorrumpiert vom Ruhm," *F.A.Z.* 10 Sep 2005, 37.

Thomas, Gina, "Konkurrenz für den Weihnachtsmann," *F.A.Z.* 16 Nov 2001, 53.

Thompson, Deborah L., "Deconstructing Harry: Casting a Critical Eye on the Witches and Wizards of Hogwarts," *Beauty, Brains, and Brawn. The Construction of Gender in Childre's Literature*, ed., Susan Lehr, Portsmouth: Heinemann, 2001, 42-50.

Thompson, Kristin, "Fantasy, Franchises, and Frodo Baggins: The Lord of the Rings and Modern Hollywood," *The Velvet Light Trap* 52 (Autumn 2003): 45-63.

Thorsrud, Harald, "Voldemort's Agents, Malfoy's Cronies, and Hagrid's Chums: Friendship in *Harry Potter*," *Harry Potter and philosophy: If Aristotle ran Hogwarts*, ed., David Baggett and Shawn Klein, Chicago, La Salle: Open Court, 2004, 38-48.

Tilmann, Christina, "Die größte Story der Welt," *Tagesspiegel* 14 March 2004, 25.

Tilmann, Christina, "Tote leben länger," *Tagesspiegel* 18 July 2005, 19.

Tilmann, Christina, "Wo der Werwolf heult," *Tagesspiegel* 3 June 2004, 25.

Todorov, Tzvetan, *Einführung in die fantastische Literatur*, Munich: Carl Hanser, 1971.

Tolkien, John Ronald Reuel, "Beowulf: The Monsters and the Critics," [1936], *The Monsters & the Critics and Other Essays*, ed., Christopher Tolkien, London: HarperCollins, 1997, 5-48.

Tolkien, John Ronald Reuel, "On Fairy-Stories," [1939], *The Monsters & the Critics and Other Essays*, ed., Christopher Tolkien, London: HarperCollins, 1997, 109-161.

Tolkien, John Ronald Reuel, *The Monsters & the Critics and Other Essays,* ed., Christopher Tolkien, London: HarperCollins, 1997.

Turi, Peter, "Probleme in Hogwart [sic!]" *Werben & Verkaufen* 14 July 2005, 24-28.

Turi, Peter, "Warum Harry Potter sterben muss," *SPIEGEL Online*, 16 July 2005. <http://www.spiegel.de/kultur/literatur/0,1518,365303,00.html> 3 Jan 2008.

Turner-Vorbeck, Tammy, "Pottermania: Good, Clean Fun or Cultural Hegemony?" *Harry Potter's World: Multidisciplinary Critical Perspectives*, ed., Elizabeth E. Heilman, New York, London: RoutledgeFalmer, 2003, 13-24.

Vax, Louis, "Die Phantastik," *Phaicon 1. Almanach der phantastischen Literatur*, ed., Rein A. Zondergeld, Frankfurt am Main: Insel, 1974, 11-43.

von Becker, Peter, "Das Geheimnis des Erfolges," *Tagesspiegel* 17 July 2005, S1.

von Bredow, Wilfried, "Lord Voldemort kommt immer näher," *F.A.Z.* 12 Aug 2000, SIV.

von Lovenberg, Felicitas, "Ein regelrechtes Blutbad," *F.A.Z.* 13 July 2007, 40.

von Lovenberg, Felicitas, "Im Bann des Guten. Auch im fünften ‚Harry Potter' macht J.K. Rowling alles richtig," *F.A.Z.* 24 June 2003, 34.

von Lovenberg, Felicitas, "Lebensspuren. Hüterin des Schatzes: Joanne K. Rowling gewährt seltene Einblicke," *F.A.Z.* 11 Jan 2006, 35.

von Lovenberg, Felicitas, "Rekordauflage, Rekordverkauf, Rekordrezensionen," *F.A.Z.* 25 July 2007, 38.

von Lovenberg, Felicitas, "Seele in sieben Portionen," *F.A.Z.net*, 18 July 2005. <http://www.F.A.Z..net/s/Rub117C535CDF414415BB243B181B8B60AE/Doc~EC7360A35FFF24830876ABF4420263694~ATpl~Ecommon~Sspezial.html> 3 Jan 2008.

Walser, Angelika, "Potter'sche Moralpädagogik," *Leben, Tod und Zauberstab. Auf theologischer Spurensuche in Harry Potter*, eds., Christoph Drexler and Nikolaus Wandinger, Münster: LIT, 2004, 79-102.

Walter, Natasha, "A hero of our time," *Guardian* 16 July 2005. <http://books.guardian.co.uk/departments/childrenandteens/story/0,6000,1529506,00.html> 3 Jan 2008.

Warner, Marina, "Did Harry have to grow up?" *Observer* 29 June 2003. <http://books.guardian.co.uk/print/0,3858,4701095-99943,00.html> 3 Jan 2008.

Westfahl, Gary and George Slusser, eds., *Nursery Realms: Children in the Worlds of Science Fiction, Fantasy and Horror*, Athens: University of Georgia Press, 1999.

Westfahl, Gary, ed., *Space and Beyond: The Frontier Theme in Science Fiction*, Westport: Greenwood Press, 2000.

Westfahl, Gary, "Return to Innocence," *Nursery Realms: Children in the Worlds of Science Fiction, Fantasy and Horror,* eds., Gary Westfahl and George Slusser, Athens: University of Georgia Press, 1999, IX-XIII.

Westman Karin E., "Specters of Thatcherism. Contemporary British Culture in J.K. Rowling's Harry Potter Series," *The Ivory Tower and Harry Potter: Perspectives on a Literary Phenomenon*, ed., Lana A. Whited, Columbia: University of Missouri Press, 2004, 305-328.

Whited, Lana A., "Harry Potter and the Order of the Phoenix Epilogue," *The Ivory Tower and Harry Potter: Perspectives on a Literary Phenomenon*, ed., Lana A. Whited, Columbia: University of Missouri Press, 2004, 365-373.

Whited, Lana A., "Harry Potter. From Craze to Classic?," *The Ivory Tower and Harry Potter: Perspectives on a Literary Phenomenon*, ed., Lana A. Whited, Columbia: University of Missouri Press, 2004, 1-12.

Whited, Lana A., ed., *The Ivory Tower and Harry Potter: Perspectives on a Literary Phenomenon*, Columbia: University of Missouri Press, 2004.

Whited, Lana A., "Mc Gonagall's Prophecy Fulfilled: The Harry Potter Critical Library," *The Lion and the Unicorn* 27 (2003): 416-447.

"Wie finden Sie den neuen 'Potter'?" *F.A.Z.net* 21 July 2007. <http://www.F.A.Z..net/d/common/umfrage.   aspx?rub={1DA1FB84-8C1E-4485-8CB8-7A0FE6AD1B68}&doc={083DFF6D-236B-4AF3-9507-E876C0233 A62}&set=true&go.x=6&go.y=11&votingbutton=%7bE46069AF-563C-4574-BC8B-B20448289E44%7d> 1 Aug 2007.

Williams, Hywel, "A whole new narrative," *Guardian* 7 Nov 2001. <http://books.guardian.co.uk/print/0,3858,4293510-99943,00.html> 3 Jan 2008.

Wolf, Martin, "Kassensturz im Zauberreich," *SPIEGEL-Jahreschronik 2001*. <http://www.spiegel.de/jahreschronik/0,1518,173852,00.html> 28 Aug 2008.

Wrigley, Christopher, *The return of the hero*, Lewes: Book Guild, 2005.

Wurst, Gottfried, "Harry Potter: eine heilsame Aufregung," *"Alohomora!" Ergebnisse des Ersten Wiener Harry-Potter-Symposions*, ed., Heidi Lexe, Vienna: Edition Praesens, 2002, 97-108.

"Zauberer-Outing: Dumbledore ist schwul," *SPIEGEL Online* 20 Oct 2007. <http://www.spiegel.de/kultur/literatur/0,1518,512613,00.html> 3 Jan 2008.

Zipes, Jack, *Sticks and Stones: The Troublesome Success of Children's Literature from Slovenly Peter to Harry Potter*, New York, London: Routledge, 2001.

Zondergeld, Rein A., ed., *Phaicon 1. Almanach der phantastischen Literatur*, Frankfurt am Main: Insel, 1974.

IX.1.C. Reference Works

"Alban," *Dictionary of First Names*, [1990] London: Bloomsbury 2000, 17.

"Biene," *Wörterbuch der Symbolik*, [1979] Stuttgart: Alfred Kröner, 1991, 91-92.

Biographisch-Bibliographisches Kirchenlexikon, <http://www.bautz.de/ bbkl> 3 Jan 2008.

"bona fide," *Oxford English Dictionary online*, Oxford: Oxford University Press, 2006. <http://erf.sbb.spk-berlin.de/han/356448509/dictionary.oed.

com/cgi/entry/50024829?single=1&query_type=word&queryword=bona+f
ide&first=1&max_ to_show=10> 5 Jan 2008.

"Brian," *Dictionary of First Names*, [1990] London: Bloomsbury, 2000, 42.

Der kleine Stowasser: *Lateinisch-Deutsches Schulwörterbuch*, Munich:
G. Freytag, 1980.

Dictionary of First Names, ed., Julia Cresswell, [1990] London: Bloomsbury, 2000.

"draco," *Der kleine Stowasser: Lateinisch-Deutsches Schulwörterbuch*. Munich:
G. Freytag, 1980, 148.

Encyclopædia Britannica: 2006, Encyclopædia Britannica Online. Accessed:
August 2006.

Enid Blyton Society, www.enidblytonsociety.co.uk, accessed June 2005.

"to fudge," *Oxford English Dictionary online*. Oxford: Oxford University Press,
2006.   <http://erf.sbb.spk-berlin.de/han/356448509/dictionary.oed.com/
cgi/entry/50090591?query_type=word&queryword=fudge&first=1&max_t
o_show=10&sort_type=alpha&result_place=1&search_id=mHwR-ClRQy
Y-3116&hilite=50090591> 5 Jan 2008.

"Genevieve," *Dictionary of First Names*, [1990] London: Bloomsbury, 2000, 103.

"Henry," *Dictionary of First Names*, [1990] London: Bloomsbury, 2000, 114.

"Hermione," *Dictionary of First Names*, [1990] London: Bloomsbury, 2000, 115.

"Hermióne," *Lexikon der Vornamen,* Mannheim: Dudenverlag, 1974, 110.

"Horace Slughorn," *Wikipedia, The Free Encyclopedia*, 22 Aug 2007. <http://
en.wikipedia.org/w/index.php?title=Horace_Slughorn&oldid=152871522>
22 Aug 2007.

"James," *Dictionary of First Names*, [1990] London: Bloomsbury, 2000, 128.

Lexikon der Vornamen, ed., Günther Drosdowski, Mannheim: Dudenverlag,
1974.

"Lilie," *Wörterbuch der Symbolik*, [1979] Stuttgart: Alfred Kröner, 1991, 435-436.

"Lily," *Dictionary of First Names*, [1990] London: Bloomsbury, 2000, 152.

"Maikäfer," *Wörterbuch der Symbolik,* [1979] Stuttgart: Alfred Kröner, 1991, 365.

"Narzisse," *Wörterbuch der Symbolik*, [1979] Stuttgart: Alfred Kröner, 1991, 517.

Oxford English Dictionary online, Oxford: University Press, 2006. <http://
erf.sbb.spk-berlin.de/han/356448509/dictionary.oed.com> 5 Jan 2008.

"Pendle witch trials," *Wikipedia, The Free Encyclopedia,* 17 Oct 2007. <http://en.wikipedia.org/w/index.php?title=Pendle_witch_trials&oldid=165 151189> 30 Oct 2007.

"Reginald," *Dictionary of First Names,* [1990] London: Bloomsbury 2000, 195.

"Reinhold," *Lexikon der Vornamen,* Mannheim: Dudenverlag, 1974, 175.

"rubēre", "ruber" and "rubeus," *Der kleine Stowasser: Lateinisch-Deutsches Schulwörterbuch,* Munich: G. Freytag, 1980.

"Rufus," *Dictionary of First Names,* [1990] London: Bloomsbury, 2000, 201.

"Salem witch trials," *Wikipedia, The Free Encyclopedia,* 12 Dec 2007. <http:// en.wikipedia.org/w/index.php?title=Salem_witch_trials&oldid=177493282 > 14 Dec 2007.

Salesianer, <http://www.salesianer.de> 3 Jan 2008.

Streetmap, <http://www.streetmap.co.uk> 3 Jan 2008.

"Sybil," *Dictionary of First Names,* [1990] London: Bloomsbury, 2000, 216.

"Sybille," *Wörterbuch der Symbolik,* [1979] Stuttgart: Alfred Kröner, 1991, 678-679.

"The House of Gaunt," *Wikipedia, The Free Encyclopedia,* 27 Aug 2007. <http://en.wikipedia.org/w/index.php?title=The_House_of_Gaunt&oldid=1 54008448> 28 Aug 2007.

"Thomas," *Dictionary of First Names,* [1990] London: Bloomsbury, 2000, 222.

"to umbrage," *Oxford English Dictionary online,* Oxford: Oxford University Press, 2006. <http://erf.sbb.spk-berlin.de/han/356448509/dictionary.oed. com/cgi/entry/50261688?query_type=word&queryword=umbrage&first=1 &max_to_show=10&sort_type=alpha&result_place=2&search_id=mHwR-bdiC5u-3128&hilite=50261688> 5 Jan 2008.

"umbrage," *Oxford English Dictionary online,* Oxford: University Press, 2006. <http://erf.sbb.spk-berlin.de/han/356448509/dictionary.oed.com/cgi/entry/5 0261687?query_type=word&queryword=umbrage&first=1&max_to_show =10&sort_type=alpha&search_id=mHwR-bdiC5u-3128&result_place=2.> 5 Jan 2008.

von Wilpert, Gero, *Sachwörterbuch der Literatur,* [1955] Stuttgart: Alfred Kröner, 1989.

"weiß," *Wörterbuch der Symbolik,* [1979] Stuttgart: Alfred Kröner, 1991, 824.

Wörterbuch der Symbolik, ed., Manfred Lurker, [1979] Stuttgart: Alfred Kröner, 1991.

Kulturelle Identitäten
Studien zur Entwicklung der europäischen Kulturen der Neuzeit

Herausgegeben von Sonja Fielitz

www.peterlang.de